Nāgārjuna's Treatise
On the Ten Bodhisattva Grounds

Volume One

To refrain from doing any manner of evil,
to respectfully perform all varieties of good,
and to purify one's own mind—
This is the teaching of all buddhas.

The Ekottara Āgama Sūtra
(T02 n.125 p.551a 13–14)

A Note on the Proper Care of Dharma Materials

Traditional Buddhist cultures treat books on Dharma as sacred. Hence it is considered disrespectful to place them in a low position, to read them when lying down, or to place them where they might be damaged by food or drink.

Kalavinka Press books are printed on acid-free paper.
Cover and interior designed by Bhikshu Dharmamitra.
Printed in the United States of America

Nāgārjuna's Treatise on the Ten Grounds

The Daśabhūmika Vibhāṣā

VOLUME ONE

As Translated into Chinese
By Tripiṭaka Master Kumārajīva
(c 410 CE)

Annotated Chinese-to-English Translation by Bhikshu Dharmamitra

Kalavinka Press
Seattle, Washington
www.kalavinkapress.org

KALAVINKA PRESS
8603 39TH AVE SW
SEATTLE, WA 98136 USA
(WWW.KALAVINKAPRESS.ORG)

Kalavinka Press is associated with the Kalavinka Dharma Association, a non-profit organized exclusively for religious educational purposes as allowed within the meaning of section 501(c)3 of the Internal RevenueCode. Kalavinka Dharma Association was founded in 1990 and gained formal approval in 2004 by the United States Internal Revenue Service as a 501(c)3 non-profit organization to which all donations are tax deductible.

Donations to KDA are accepted by mail and on the Kalavinka website where numerous free Dharma translations and excerpts from Kalavinka publications are available in digital format.

Edition: SZPPS-SA-ALL-1019-1.0-Bilingual
Kalavinka Buddhist Classics Book 13a
Copyright © 2019 by Bhikshu Dharmamitra / All Rights Reserved
Two-Volume Set ISBN: 978-1-935413-19-6 / LCCN: 2019032428
(Volume One ISBN: 978-1-935413-17-2)

Library of Congress Cataloging-in-Publication Data

Names: Kumārajīva, -412? translator. | Dharmamitra, Bhikshu, translator.
Title: Nāgārjuna's treatise on the ten Bodhisattva grounds : the Daśabhūmika vibhāṣā / as translated into Chinese by Tripiṭaka Master Kumārajīva (c 410 ce) ; annotated Chinese-to-English translation by Bhikshu Dharmamitra.
Other titles: Daśabhūmivibhāṣāśāstra. English
Description: Szpps-sa-all-1019-1.0-bilingual. | Seattle,Washington : Kalavinka Press, 2019. | Series: Kalavinka buddhist classics ; book 13a | Includes bibliographical references. | Summary: ""Nāgārjuna's Treatise on the Ten Bodhisattva Grounds" is Bhikshu Dharmamitra's extensively annotated original translation of Ārya Nāgārjuna's "Daśabhūmika Vibhāṣā" rendered from Tripiṭaka Master Kumārajīva's circa 410 ce Sanskrit-to-Chinese translation. It consists of 35 chapters that explain in great detail the cultivation of the ten highest levels of bodhisattva practice leading to buddhahood, focusing almost exclusively on the first two of the ten bodhisattva grounds. This is a work which has never been translated into English before. This special bilingual edition (English / Chinese) includes the facing-page simplified and traditional Chinese scripts to facilitate close study by academic buddhologists, students in Buddhist universities, and Buddhists in Taiwan, Hong Kong, Mainland China, and the West"-- Provided by publisher.
Identifiers: LCCN 2019032428 | ISBN 9781935413196 (paperback)
Subjects: LCSH: Tripiṭaka. Sūtrapiṭaka. Avataṃsakasūtra.
Daśabhūmikasūtra--Criticism, interpretation, etc. | Bodhisattva stages (Mahayana Buddhism) | Nāgārjuna, active 2nd century. Daśabhūmivibhāṣāśāstra.
Classification: LCC BQ1632.E5 D34 2019 | DDC 294.3/823--dc23
LC record available at https://lccn.loc.gov/2019032428

Dedication

Dedicated to the memory of the selfless and marvelous life of the Venerable Dhyāna Master Hsuan Hua, the Guiyang Ch'an Patriarch and the very personification of the bodhisattva's six perfections.

Dhyāna Master Hsuan Hua
宣化禪師
1918–1995

About the Chinese Text

This translation is supplemented by inclusion of Chinese source text on verso pages in both traditional (above) and simplified (below) scripts. For the traditional character version variant readings from other canonical editions are found as an appendix in the back of the book and, where I have incorporated those variants into the translation, they are usually signaled with an endnote along with my rationale for making the emendation. The traditional-character Chinese text and its variant readings are from the April, 2004 version of the Chinese Buddhist Electronic Text Association's digital edition of the Taisho Buddhist canon. The simplified-character Chinese text is as downloaded from the online Qianlong Chinese Buddhist Canon on July 23, 2018 (http://www.qldzj.com/).

Those following the translation in the traditional Chinese version should be aware that the original Taisho scripture punctuation contained in this 2004 edition is not traceable to original editions, is not reliable, and is probably best ignored altogether. (In any case, accurate reading of Classical Chinese should never depend on a previous editor's punctuation.)

Outlining in This Work

The thirty-five chapter titles in this work are from the Taisho Chinese text. All other outline headings originate with the translator. Buddhist canonical texts are often so structurally dense that they are best navigated with the aid of at least a simple outline structure such as I have supplied here.

Acknowledgments

The accuracy and readability of this translation have been greatly improved by many corrections, preview comments, and editorial suggestions generously contributed by Bhikkhu Bodhi, Bhikshu Jianhu, Feng Ling, Nicholas Weeks, and Jon Babcock.

Expenses incurred in bringing forth this publication were underwritten by generous donations from Craig and Karen Neyman, Madalena Lew, Shuyu Yang, Jiajing Li, Kam Chung Wong, Loritta Chan, David Fox, Nicholas Weeks, Yuen-Lin Tan, and the BDK English Tripiṭaka Project. Sponsorship of Adobe Indesign book layout was provided by Anagarika Mahendra.

Were it not for the ongoing material support provided by my late guru's Dharma Realm Buddhist Association and the serene translation studio provided by Seattle's Bodhi Dhamma Center, creation of this translation would have been much more difficult.

Additionally, it would have been impossible for me to produce this translation without the Dharma teachings and personal inspiration provided to me by my late guru, the awesomely wise and compassionate Dhyāna Master Hsuan Hua, the Guiyang Ch'an Patriarch, Dharma teacher, and exegete.

Finally, I owe an immense debt of gratitude to the members of the liver care and transplant teams at Seattle's University of Washington Medical Center who cured me of liver cancer in 2010 and then gave me a liver transplant several months later. In particular, if it weren't for over a decade of wonderfully attentive and compassionate care by Dr. Renuka Bhattacharya, now medical director of UW's liver transplant program, the kindness and skill in three major surgeries by my transplant surgeon, Dr. Jorge Reyes, and the marvelous generosity of an anonymous liver donor, I would have died years ago and thus never could have completed the scriptural translations I have produced in the last eight years.

List of Abbreviations

AN	Aṅguttara Nikāya
BB	Buddhabhadra (T278)
BCSD	Hirakawa's *Buddhist Chinese-Sanskrit Dictionary*
BDK	Bukkyo Dendo Kyokai English Tripiṭaka
BHSD	Edgerton's *Buddhist Hybrid Sanskrit Dictionary*
BR	Bodhiruci (T1522)
CBETA	Chinese Buddhist Electronic Text Association's edition of the Taisho edition of the Chinese Buddhist canon.
CDB	*The Connected Discourses of the Buddha*
DN	*Dīgha Nikāya*
DR	Dharmarakṣa (T278)
DSBC	Digital Sanskrit Buddhist Canon's digitized edition of *Daśabhūmikasūtram*, edited by P. L. Vaidya.
EA	*Ekottara Āgama*
KB	Kumārajīva and Buddhayaśas (T286)
KJ	Kumārajīva
MDPL	*Materials for a Dictionary of the Prajñāpāramitā Literature*
MLDB	*The Middle Length Discourses of the Buddha*
MN	*Majjhima nikāya*
Mppu	*Mahāprajñāpāramitā upadeśa*
MW	Monier Williams' *A Sanskrit-English Dictionary*
N	Nāgārjuna
NDB	*Numerical Discourses of the Buddha*
PTS	Pali Text Society
SA	Śikṣānanda (T279)
SD	Śīladharma (T287)
SN	Saṃyutta Nikāya
SYMG	The Song, Yuan, Ming, Gong editions of the Chinese Buddhist canon.
SZPPS	*Shizhu piposha lun*
T	Taisho Chinese Buddhist Canon via CBETA (Version 2004. ed. Taibei)
VB	Venerable Bhikkhu Bodhi

General Table of Contents
Volume One

Dedication	5
About the Chinese Text	6
Outlining in This Work	6
Acknowledgments	7
List of Abbreviations	8
General Table of Contents	9
Directory to Chapter Subsections	11
Translator's Introduction	31
Introduction Endnotes	39
Nāgārjuna's Treatise on the Ten Grounds	41
Ch. 1 - The Introduction	43
Ch. 2 - Entering the First Ground	77
Ch. 3 - The Characteristics of the Ground	117
Ch. 4 - Purification of the Ground	147
Ch. 5 - The Explanation of the Vows	167
Ch. 6 - On Producing the Bodhi Resolve	229
Ch. 7 - On Training the Mind	243
Ch. 8 - On the Avaivartika	265
Ch. 9 - On the Easy Practice	295
Ch. 10 - Getting Rid of Karma	333
Ch. 11 - Distinctions with Regard to Merit	357
Ch. 12 - Distinctions with Regard to Giving	381
Ch. 13 - Distinctions with Regard to the Giving of Dharma	425
Ch. 14 - The Characteristics of the Refuges	439
Ch. 15 - The Five Moral Precepts	459
Ch. 16 - On Realizing the Faults of the Householder's Life	477
Ch. 17 - On Entering the Temple	503
Ch. 18 - The Jointly Shared Practices	551
Ch. 19 - The Fourfold Dharmas	575
Ch. 20 - Mindfulness of the Buddhas	611
Volume One Endnotes	649

Volume Two

Volume Two Directory to Chapter Subsections	699
Ch. 21 - Forty Dharmas Exclusive to Buddhas (Part 1)	709
Ch. 22 - Forty Dharmas Exclusive to Buddhas (Part 2)	733
Ch. 23 - Forty Dharmas Exclusive to Buddhas (Part 3)	789
Ch. 24 - Verses Offered in Praise	847
Ch. 25 - Teachings to Aid Mindfulness-of-the-Buddha Samādhi	867
Ch. 26 - The Analogy Chapter	901
Ch. 27 - A Summarizing Discussion of the Bodhisattva Practices	933
Ch. 28 - Distinctions in the 2nd Ground's Courses of Karmic Action	961
Ch. 29 - Distinctions Pertaining to Śrāvakas and Pratyekabuddhas	1031
Ch. 30 - Distinctions Pertaining to the Great Vehicle	1057
Ch. 31 - Guarding the Moral Precepts	1121
Ch. 32 - An Explanation of the Dhūta Austerities	1167
Ch. 33 - Aids to Gaining the Fruits of Śīla	1223
Ch. 34 - In Praise of the Moral Precepts	1263
Ch. 35 - The Karmic Rewards of the Moral Precepts	1277
Volume Two Endnotes	1290
Variant Readings from Other Chinese Editions	1320
Bibliography	1352
Glossary	1354
About the Translator	1366
Kalavinka Buddhist Classics' Fall, 2019 Title List	1368

Directory to Chapter Subsections
Volume One

I. **Chapter One: The Introduction** — 43
  A. Verses Declaring the Three Refuges and the Treatise's Intent — 43
   1. Q: Why Explain the Ten Grounds? — 43
   2. A: The Plight of Beings and the Availability of Saviors — 43
   3. Q: Can Non-Bodhisattvas Also Transcend Saṃsāra? — 45
   4. A: Yes, But the Great Vehicle Requires the Ten Grounds — 45
   5. Q: How Long for Two Vehicles to Achieve Transcendence? — 45
   6. A: Two Vehicles are Rapid; Bodhisattvas Require Many Lives — 45
   7. Q: Is There Any Difference in the Quality of Liberation? — 47
   8. A: Nirvāṇa Does Not Differ; Levels of Awakening Are Very Different — 47
   9. Q: If Nirvāṇa Is Identical, Why Not Quickly Depart? — 47
   10. A: This is a Weak and Inferior Statement Devoid of Compassion — 47
     a. Without Bodhisattvas, How Could The Two Vehicles Exist? — 47
     b. This Would Put an End to the Three Vehicles and the Three Jewels — 49
       1) The Four Types of People — 49
       2) The Immense Superiority of One Who Perfects the Ten Grounds — 51
   11. Q: I Am Convinced, So Please Continue To Explain the Verses — 51
  B. Nāgārjuna Continues Explaining His Introductory Verses: — 51
   1. Q: Is Generating the Resolve Sufficient To Become a Bodhisattva? — 53
   2. A: Of Course Not, But Perhaps Yes. — 53
   3. Q: Why only praise the Bodhisattva's Solid Resolve? — 55
   4. A: It Is Essential For Success and Those Without It Would Turn Back — 55
     a. Why, Absent Solid Resolve, One Abandons the Bodhisattva Path — 55
       1) Fear of Continued Existence in Saṃsāra — 55
       2) Fear of the Hells — 55
       3) Fear of Rebirth in the Animal Realm — 59
       4) Fear of Rebirth in the Hungry Ghost Realm — 61
       5) Fear of Rebirth in the Human Realm — 61
       6) Fear of Rebirth in the Deva or Asura Realms — 63
     b. The Contrasting Response of One with Solid Resolve — 63
       1) The Bodhisattva's Vow — 63
       2) The Bodhisattvas Compassion, Vigor, and Success — 63
       3) Eight Bodhisattva Dharmas — 63
  C. Nāgārjuna Continues to Explain His Introductory Verses — 65
   1. Q: This Is Just as in Scripture. Why Be Redundant? For Fame, etc.? — 65
   2. A: This Treatise Is Not Composed for Self-Serving Reasons — 65
   3. Q: If Not, Then Why? — 65
   4. A: Out of Kindness and Compassion and for No Other Reason — 65
   5. Q: Why Just Repeat What Scripture Already Explains? — 67
   6. A: Some Beings Require or Delight in More Thorough Explanations — 67

	7.	Q: How Are Others' Unique Predilections Any of Your Business?	69
	8.	A: Because I Have Resolved Not To Abandon Anyone	69
	9.	Q: What Are the Qualities of Such a Good Person?	69
	10.	A: Immediate Dharma Understanding; Also, 10 Qualities, as Below:	69
	11.	A Vibhāṣā Helps Those Who Find Sutras Hard to Fathom	71
	12.	Such Explanation of Dharma Is an Offering to the Buddha	71
	13.	By Explaining Dharma One Lights the Dharma Lamp	73
	14.	This Leads To Accumulating the Four Bases of Meritorious Qualities	73
		a. Truth	73
		b. Relinquishment	73
		c. Quiescence	73
		d. Wisdom	75
	15.	Nāgārjuna's Final Statement of Intent	75
II.	Chapter Two: Entering the First Ground		77
	A. Q: What Are the Ten Grounds?		77
	B. A: The Ten Grounds Taught by All Buddhas Are as Follows:		77
	C. Q: How Does One Enter and Cultivate the First Ground?		81
	D. A: Five Stanzas on First Ground Cultivation		81
	1.	The Meaning of "Roots of Goodness"	81
		a. Abhidharma Categories of "Roots of Goodness"	81
		b. The Meaning of "Roots of Goodness" That Is Relevant Here	83
	2.	The Meaning of "Practicing the Practices"	83
		a. Seven Dharmas Essential to "Thorough Practice"	83
		b. The Importance of Dhyāna to Implementing the Practices	85
	3.	The Meaning of "Accumulating the Provisions"	85
		a. "Provisions" Includes the Topics Referenced Earlier	85
		b. "Provisions" Also Includes the Practice of 22 Good Dharmas	85
	4.	The Meaning of "Thoroughly Making Offerings to all Buddhas"	87
	5.	The Meaning of "Protected by the Good Spiritual Friend"	89
	6.	The Meaning of "Complete Development of Resolute Intentions"	89
		a. Q: Compared to Scripture, Isn't This a Deficient Explanation?	89
		b. Q: No. Each Ground Involves Specific Resolute Intentions	93
	7.	The Meaning of "Compassionate Mindfulness of Beings"	95
	8.	The Meaning of "Resolute Faith in the Unsurpassable Dharma"	95
	9.	The Meaning of "Bringing Forth the Vow"	95
		a. Q: Why Do You Say, "After I Have Achieved Liberation"?	95
		b. A: If One is Not Already Liberated, One Cannot Liberate Others	95
		c. Q: For What Sort of Benefit and with What Sort of Resolve?	97
		d. A: To Gain the Ten Powers and Enter the Stage of Certainty	97
		1) Q: What Are the Ten Powers?	97
		2) A: They Are as Follows	97
		3) To Gain The Powers, One Makes the Vow and Becomes Irreversible	99
		a) Q: Does Everyone Then Reach the Stage of Certainty?	99
		b) A: Some Do; Some Do Not	99
		4) Q: If Some Do Not, Why Claim Certainty Relies on Resolve?	99

5) A: Because This Is True of Some Bodhisattvas	101
a) Q: What is the Nature of This Initial Resolve?	101
b) A: The Initial Resolve Is Characterized by These 41 Aspects	101
(1) Q: Doesn't "Permanence" of Resolve Contradict Dharma?	105
(2) A: You Misunderstand the Concept	105
10. The Meaning of "Birth In the Family of the Tathāgatas"	105
a. The Meaning of "Tathāgata"	105
b. The Meaning of "the Family of the Tathāgatas"	109
c. The Meaning of "Having No Transgressions or Faults," etc.	111
d. Q: Why Is the First Ground Said To Be "Joyful"?	113
e. A: Because of the Immense Significance of the First Ground	113
III. Chapter Three: The Characteristics of the Ground	**117**
A. Q: What Are the Characteristics of the First Ground Bodhisattva?	117
B. A: He Immediately Acquires Seven Qualities (Verse)	117
1. Q: Why Only Say, "For the Most Part" He Has These Seven Traits?	121
2. A: Because He Still Hasn't Done Away with the Contaminants	121
3. Q: Is His Joyfulness Acquired by Him or Is It a Feature of This Ground?	121
4. A: It Is Due to Mindfulness of Buddhas & the Stage of Certainty	121
a. Q: What Is Unique about the First Ground Bodhisattva's Joyfulness?	123
b. A: He Realizes He Will Definitely Become a Buddha	123
c. From Which Types of Fear Has This Bodhisattva Been Freed?	127
d. Fear of Not Surviving, Death, the Wretched Destinies, etc. (Verse)	127
1) Fear of Not Surviving	127
a) Why Does This Bodhisattva Not Fear Failing to Survive?	127
b) Due to Great Merit, Endurance, Wisdom, and Easy Satisfaction	127
2) Fear of Death	131
3) Fear of the Wretched Destinies	137
4) Fear of Great Assemblies	139
5) Fear of Ill Repute and Fear of Being Disparaged	141
6) Fear of Imprisonment, shackles, manacles, or Beatings	141
e. Realizing Nonexistence of Self As the Basis of Fearlessness	141
1) Q: Why Does This Bodhisattva Have No Conception of a Self?	143
2) A: He Delights in Emptiness and Sees the Body as Not Self (Verse)	143
IV. Chapter Four: Purification of the Ground	**147**
A. Q: How Should the 1st Ground Bodhisattva Cultivate Its Purification?	147
B. A: One Cultivates 27 Dharmas (Verse)	147
1. "The Power of Faith Becomes Ever More Superior"	149
a. Q: Of the Two Types of Superiority, of Which Do You Speak?	149
b. A: Both "More" and "Better Quality"	149
2. "One Practices Deeply the Mind of Great Compassion"	149
3. "The Mind of Kindness"	149
4. "Tirelessly Cultivating the Mind of Goodness"	149
5. "One Finds Joyous Delight in Sublime Dharmas"	151
6. "Always Drawing Near to the Spiritual Guide"	151
7. "A Sense of Shame" and "a Dread of Blame"	151

8. "Reverence"	151
9. "Gentle and Harmonious"	151
10. "Delighting in Contemplating Dharmas"	151
11. "Staying Free of Attachment"	151
12. "Single-Mindedness"	151
13. "Striving to Acquire Abundant Learning"	153
14. "Refraining from Coveting Offerings of Benefits and Support"	153
15. "Staying Far from Cheating, Flattery, and Deception"	153
a. The Five Types of Wrong livelihood	153
1) Feigning Uniqueness	153
2) Taking Advantage of a Close Relationship	155
3) Inducement through Instigation	155
4) Manipulation through Praising and Blaming"	155
5) Seeking to Gain Benefits Based on One's Benefits	157
16. "One Does Not Defile the Family of the Buddhas"	157
17. "Not Damaging Moral Precepts" and "Not Cheating the Buddhas"	159
a. Might a Bodhisattva at the Stage of Certainty Break Precepts?	159
b. This Is Possible If He Has Not yet Cut off the Afflictions	159
18. "Deeply Delighting in All-Knowledge" and "Remaining Unmoving"	161
19. "Always Cultivating Ever More Superior Dharmas"	161
20. "Delighting in World-Transcending Dharmas," "Not Worldly Ones"	161
21. "Cultivating What Is Difficult to Cultivate"	163
22. Q: How Does One "Securely Abide" and Not Retreat?	165
23. A: By Always Practicing and Completely Developing These Dharmas	165
24. The Meaning of "Bodhisattva" and "Superior Dharmas"	165
V. Chapter Five: Explanation of the Vows	167
A. The First Bodhisattva Vow	167
B. The Second Bodhisattva Vow	167
C. The Third Bodhisattva Vow	169
D. The Fourth Bodhisattva Vow	171
E. The Fifth Bodhisattva Vow	171
F. The Sixth Bodhisattva Vow	173
G. The Seventh Bodhisattva Vow	181
1. An Exhaustive List of the Characteristics of Evil and Impurity	181
2. A Description of the Characteristics of Pure Lands	193
H. The Eighth Bodhisattva Vow	215
I. The Ninth Bodhisattva Vow	217
J. The Tenth Bodhisattva Vow	217
K. The Infinitely Vast Scope and Duration of the Ten Bodhisattva Vows	219
VI. Chapter Six: On Producing the Bodhi Resolve	229
A. The Seven Bases for Producing the Bodhi Resolve	229
1. The Influence of a Buddha	231
2. The Motivation to Protect the Dharma	231
3. Compassion for the Suffering of Beings	233
4. The Instructive Influence of a Bodhisattva	235

5.	The Aspiration to Emulate the Conduct of Bodhisattvas	235
6.	Inspiration Provoked by an Act of Giving	237
7.	Inspiration Arising from Observing a Buddha's Physical Marks	237
B.	The Relative Probability of Success in these Seven Bases	239

VII. **Chapter Seven: On Training the Mind** — 243
   A. A: Practicing Dharmas Resulting in Failure Entails Loss — 243
      1. Q: Which Dharmas Result in Loss — 243
      2. A: There Are Four Such Dharmas (Verse) — 243
      3. Q: Are There Only These Four or Are There More? — 249
      4. A: There Are Numerous Additional Cases (A Series of Verses) — 249
         a. Q: What Is Meant by "the Works of Māras"? — 251
         b. A: There Are Numerous Examples, As Follows: (List) — 253
   B. Q: Which Dharmas Cause One to Make the Vows Again in Each Life? — 261
   C. A: They Are as Follows: (Verse) — 261

VIII. **Chapter Eight: On the Avaivartika** — 265
   A. Q: What Are the Distinguishing Characteristics of an Avaivartika? — 265
   B. A: There are Five Defining Dharmas, as Follows: (Verse) — 265
      1. Maintaining a Mind of Equal Regard toward Beings — 265
      2. Not Envying Benefits and Support Obtained by Others — 267
      3. Not Speaking of a Dharma Master's Transgressions — 267
      4. Resolute Faith in the Profound and Sublime Dharma — 267
      5. Not Craving to Be the Object of Others' Reverence — 267
      6. One Does Not Retreat from Complete Enlightenment — 267
   C. Two Types of Reversible Bodhisattvas, Ruined Versus Progressing — 269
      1. Q: What Are the Signs of a "Ruined" Reversible Bodhisattva? — 269
      2. A: Seven Characteristics, as Follows: (Verse) — 269
         a. Absence of Determination and Ability — 269
         b. Delighting in Inferior Dharmas — 271
         c. Being Deeply Attached to Fame and Offerings — 271
         d. Having a Mind That Is Not Upright and Straight — 271
         e. Feeling a Miserly Cherishing toward Others' Households — 273
         f. Not Having a Resolute Belief in the Dharma of Emptiness — 273
         g. Only Esteeming All Manner of Verbal Discourse — 273
         h. These Are the Marks of One Fallen into Ruination — 273
      3. Q: What Are the Traits of the Reversible Bodhisattva Who Succeeds? — 273
      4. A: He Has Five Qualities, as Follows: (Verse) — 275
         a. Not Apprehending the Existence of any "Self" — 275
         b. Not Apprehending the Existence of Any "Being" — 277
         c. Not Engaging in Discriminations While Speaking on Dharma — 279
         d. Not Apprehending the Existence of Bodhi — 281
         e. Not Seeing a Buddha by His Signs — 283
   D. Q: What Are the Characteristic Signs of an Avaivartika? — 285
   E. A: The Avaivartika Has Numerous Characteristics, as Follows: — 287

IX. CHAPTER NINE: ON THE EASY PRACTICE	295
A. Q: How Difficult! Is There an Easier Path to the Avaivartika Ground?	295
B. A: How Weak & Inferior! But, If You Want That, I Will Explain	297
1. The Practice of Calling on Ten Buddhas, One in Each Direction	297
2. Q: Can One Instead Call on Other Buddhas and Bodhisattvas?	311
3. A: Yes, There is Amitābha as Well as Other Such Buddhas	311
a. Amitābha's Original Vows and a Praise Verse	315
4. Also, the Seven Buddhas of the Past as Well as Maitreya	321
5. Also, by Calling on Ten Other Buddhas	325
6. Also, by Calling on All Buddhas of the Three Times	327
7. Also, by Calling on the Great Bodhisattvas	329
X. CHAPTER 10: GETTING RID OF BAD KARMA	333
A. Q: Is Buddha Mindfulness All One Must Do to Become Irreversible?	333
B. A: One Should Also Repent, Entreat, Rejoice & Dedicate Merit	333
1. How Does One Perform These Endeavors?	333
2. "Repentance" Is Performed as Follows:	333
3. Q: How Does One Go about "Entreating"?	339
4. A: "Entreating" Is Performed as Follows:	339
5. Q: What is meant by "Rejoicing"?	343
6. A: "Rejoicing" Is Performed as Follows:	343
7. Q: What Is Meant by "Dedication"?	345
8. A: Dedication Is Performed as Follows:	347
9. Q: Which Ways of Performing These Accords with the Buddhas?	351
10. A: Whichever Ways Accord with This Passage from Scripture	351
XI. CHAPTER 11: DISTINCTIONS WITH REGARD TO MERIT	357
A. Q: How Should One Repent, Entreat, Rejoice, and Dedicate Merit?	357
B. A: With Reverence and Pressed Palms, Three Times Each Day & Night	357
C. Q: What Karmic Result Ensues from Doing This?	357
D. A: If One Did This but Once, the Merit Would Be Incalculably Great	357
E. Q: Why Have You Not Discussed the Merit Arising from Repentance?	367
F. A: The Merit Arising from Repentance Is the Greatest	367
G. Q: How Can You Say That Repentance Gets Rid of Karmic Offenses?	369
H. A: Although Not Eliminated Entirely, They Are Greatly Reduced	371
XII. CHAPTER 12: DISTINCTIONS WITH REGARD TO GIVING	381
A. With More Merit & Mental Pliancy, the Bodhisattva Develops Faith	381
B. The Bodhisattva's Sympathy for Beings Leads to Compassion for Them	381
C. The Bodhisattva Is Then Motivated to Rescue Beings from Suffering	381
D. Due to Kindness & Compassion, He Devotes Himself to Giving	383
1. The Bodhisattva Is Willing to Give Everything to Beings	383
2. Q: Is His Giving Done for Merit or Due to Kindness and Compassion?	387
3. A: He Knows, Has Faith, May Have the Heavenly Eye & So Gives All	387
a. Q: As You Said He Knows Them, Please Explain These Karmic Results	387
b. A: Akṣayamati Bodhisattva's Explanation Is As Follows:	387
c. The Karmic Results of Other Sorts of Giving	391
d. He Avoids Wrong Giving and Gives In Accordance with Emptiness	393

	1)	Q: Will You Please Discuss These Two Types of Giving?		393
	2)	Akṣayamati Bodhisattva Explains Them as Follows:		393
		a) The Types of Impure Giving		393
		b) Giving Conjoined with Emptiness, Signlessness, or Wishlessness		399
		c) Impure Giving Versus Pure Giving		401
			(1) The Bases for Presence or Absence of Purification	403
			(2) Q: Of These Four, Which Should Be Practiced?	405
			(3) A: Practice Two That Are Pure and Avoid Selfish Motives	405
			(4) Q: How Can One Possessed of Desires Practice Pure Giving?	407
			(5) A: Do Not Accumulate Things That Engender Miserliness	407
			(a) Q: How Can One Accomplish This with One's Own Body?	407
			(b) A: Consider One's Body to Be Like a Medicine Tree	407

- E. The Bodhisattva's Dedication of the Merit Arising from His Giving — 409
  1. Q: How Many Types of Right and Wrong Dedication Are There? — 409
  2. There Are 4 Pure Objectives of Dedication and 3 Not Practiced — 411
     a. The Three Types of Dedication One Does Not Practice — 411
     b. The Four Types of Dedication Done for the Sake of Pure Objectives — 411
        1) Q: Which Dharmas Diminish Its Benefit and Which Increase It? — 411
           a) A: There Are Four Causes of Diminishment, as Follows: — 413
           b) For Increase, Stop These Four and Adopt Three Types of Thought — 413
- F. One Gives for the Sake of Causing 3 Dharmas and Seeking 2 Dharmas — 415
  1. Q: You Said One Doesn't Seek Rewards. Isn't This Contradictory? — 421
  2. A: No, Because This Wealth Is Gained & Used Only to Benefit Beings — 421
- G. One Also Gives to Cut Off Two Dharmas and Gain Two Dharmas — 421
- H. One Also Gives to Increase Three Types of Wisdom — 423
- I. Others Say That Giving Is Practiced to Increase Two Dharmas — 423
- J. In Summary, the Bodhisattva Should Practice Four Kinds of Giving — 423

XIII. Chapter 13: Distinctions with Regard to the Giving of Dharma — 425
- A. Dharma Giving Is Supreme and the Wise Should Practice It — 425
- B. Q: Why Do You Say Only the Wise Should Practice Dharma Giving? — 425
- C. A: Erroneous Interpretations Do Not Benefit Anyone — 425
  1. Q: What Do You Mean by "Erroneous Interpretations"? — 425
  2. A: Wrong Ideas of Spurious Origin (Four Cases from Scripture) — 425
- D. Q: How Does One Know That Dharma Giving Is Supreme? — 429
- E. A: The Sutras Say So — 429
- F. A Sutra Explains Propriety in Speaking Dharma as Follows: — 429
  1. Four Qualities of a Qualified Dharma Speaker — 431
  2. Four Correct Behaviors When Ascending the High Seat to Teach — 431
  3. Four More Correct Behaviors for When One Sits on the High Seat — 431
  4. Another Four Correct Behaviors When Sitting on the High Seat — 433
  5. Eighteen More Qualifications For One Who Sits on the High Seat — 433
  6. Four More Dharmas To Be Observed When Sitting on the High Seat — 435
- G. A Scriptural Citation Regarding the Buddha's Teaching of Dharma — 435
- H. Conclusion: In Dharma Giving, One Should Practice Accordingly — 437

XIV. Chapter 14: The Characteristics of the [Three] Refuges	439
A. Distinctions Regarding Material Giving versus Dharma Giving	439
1. Laity Excel at Material Giving & Monastics Excel at Dharma Giving	439
2. Monastics Are Better Trained to Practice Dharma Giving	439
3. The Hazards to Monastics of Devotion to Material Giving	441
B. Taking Refuge in the Three Jewels	443
1. Q: What Is Meant by Taking Refuge in the Buddha?	443
2. A: The Primary Aspects of Taking Refuge in the Buddha	443
3. Q: What Is Meant by Taking Refuge in the Dharma?	445
4. A: The Primary Aspects of Taking Refuge in the Dharma	445
5. Q: What Is Meant by Taking Refuge in the Sangha?	445
6. A: The Primary Aspects of Taking Refuge in the Sangha	447
7. The Meaning of Mindfulness of the Buddha, Dharma, and Sangha	451
a. The Meaning of Mindfulness of the Buddha	451
1) Q: What Is Meant by "Mindfulness of the True Buddha"?	451
2) A: "Mindfulness of the True Buddha" as Set Forth in a Sutra	451
b. The Meaning of "Mindfulness of the Dharma"	455
c. The Meaning of Mindfulness of the Sangha	457
C. A Concluding Statement on the Three Refuges	457
XV. Chapter 15: The Five Moral Precepts	459
A. The Lay Bodhisattva Cultivates Goodness and Avoids Bad Actions	459
B. One Relinquishes Self Benefit, Benefits Others & Repays Kindness	459
C. Q: Relinquishing Self-Benefit to Benefit Others Is Wrong	461
D. A: No. This Is Good Even in Worldly Terms & Also Benefits Oneself	461
E. One Should Steadfastly Observe the Five Moral Precepts	465
1. Q: Does This Bodhisattva Only Observe These Precepts?	469
2. A: Uphold The 5 Precepts & Also Practice the Other Good Actions	469
a. He Should Explain Dharma for Beings & Proceed to Teach Them	469
b. One Should Provide Beings with Whatever They Are Deficient In	471
c. The Bodhisattva Teaches All Sorts of Evil Beings	471
d. When Evil Beings Disturb Him, He Must Not Think In These Ways:	471
e. He Should Redouble His Resolve & Act Like a Great Physician	473
f. Failing in This, He Would Be Worthy of the Buddhas' Censure	473
XVI. Chapter 16: On Realizing the Faults of the Householder's Life	477
A. The Bodhisattva Should Know the Faults of the Householder's Life	477
B. Q: What Are the Faults of the Householder's Life?	477
C. A: They Are Well Described in This Passage from a Sutra	477
D. Also Practice Giving, Uphold Precepts, and Contemplate Almsmen	481
1. Five Threefold Contemplations Whenever Seeing an Almsman	483
2. It Is Due to Almsmen That One Is Able to Perfect the Six Pāramitās	485
3. One Knows the Benefits of Giving and the Faults of Miserliness	487
a. Q: What Are the Merits of Giving and Faults of Keeping the Gift?	487
b. A: Using True Wisdom, the Bodhisattva Understands as Follows:	487
4. Contemplate Relatives and Possessions as Like Mere Illusions	489
5. One Should Reflect on Them All as the Results of Karma	491

Directory to Chapter Subsections 19

6. Use the Following Threefold Contemplations of One's Spouse	493
7. Use Wisdom to Reduce Bias Toward One's Own Children	497
8. Take up This Threefold Contemplation of One's Children	499
9. Use The Following Thoughts to Develop Equal Regard for All	499
XVII. Chapter 17: On Entering the Temple	**503**
A. One Should Be Able to Relinquish Whatever One Is Attached to	503
B. Q: If One Is Attached to Something, What if Someone Asks for It?	503
C. A: Exhort Oneself to Abandon Miserliness and Relinquish It	503
D. If One Is Still Unable to Relinquish It, One May Politely Decline	505
E. If a Divided Sangha Stops Functioning, One Should Try to Mediate	505
F. On Abstinence Days, the Lay Bodhisattva Takes the Eight Precepts	507
1. Q: How Should One Practice This Abstinence Dharma?	507
2. A: Solemnly Vow to Uphold the Eight Precepts as Follows:	507
3. Q: Should One Treat Bad Monks with Disdain and Anger?	511
4. A: Do Not Adopt a Disdainful or Angry Attitude toward Them	511
5. Q: If Hatred Is Wrong, What Attitude Is Most Appropriate?	513
6. A: Feel Pity for Him and Condemn His Afflictions Instead	513
G. On Entering a Temple, One Should Be Respectful and Make Offerings	525
H. One Should Reflect on the Merit of Becoming a Monastic	525
I. Ninety-Nine Reflections on the Advantages of Monastic Life	527
J. One Should Develop a Deep Yearning to Become a Monastic	537
K. Three Aspirational Thought When Bowing at a Stupa or Temple	539
L. On Meeting Any Monk, Serve, Follow Instructions, and Assist	539
M. Avoid Causing Afflictions in Those Not Receiving One's Gifts	543
N. Giving as an Opportunity to Encourage Highest Bodhi Resolve	545
O. Do Whatever Is Necessary to Preserve and Protect the Dharma	545
P. When Giving, Have No Regrets or Selfish Motives & Dedicate Merit	547
XVIII. Chapter 18: The Jointly Shared Practices	**551**
A. A: The Jointly Shared Practices Are as Follows: (List)	551
1. Patience, Dharma Giving, Dharmas Patience, and Contemplation:	551
a. Patience	553
b. Dharma Giving	553
c. Dharmas Patience	553
d. Contemplation	555
e. Not Distorting the Dharma	555
2. Esteem for Dharma, Nonobstruction, Offerings & Resolute Faith	555
a. Esteem for the Dharma	555
b. Offerings in Support of the Dharma	557
c. Resolute Faith	557
3. Emptiness, Non-Greed, Congruent Actions & Words, Lamp Light	557
a. Cultivation of Emptiness	557
b. Not Being Covetous or Envious	559
c. Acting in Accordance with One's Own Words	559
d. Giving Lamp Light	559
4. Music, Means of Transport, Right Vows, the Means of Attraction	559

			a. Giving Musical Performances	559
			b. Giving Means of Transport	561
			c. Right Vows	561
			d. Thought Imbued with the Means of Attraction	561
		5.	Benefiting and Comforting Beings and Equal Regard for All Beings	561
			a. Q: How Can One Differentiate a Buddha from Other People?	563
			b. A: A Buddha Possesses the Thirty-Two marks	563
			1) Q: How Can One Understand Such Matters?	563
			2) A: Each of the Thirty-Two marks Has Three Distinctions	563
			a) Q: What Is Meant by Each Mark Having Three Distinctions?	563
			b) A: This Refers to Each Mark's Substance, Fruition, and Karma	563
XIX.	Chapter 19: The Fourfold Dharmas			575
	A.	One Should Cultivate the Causes for Gaining the 32 Marks		575
		1.	Fourfold Dharmas Causing Either Loss or Gain of Wisdom	575
			a. Four Dharmas Causing Loss of Wisdom	575
			b. Four Dharmas Causing Attainment of Wisdom	575
		2.	Fourfold Dharmas Causing Decrease or Increase of Good Roots	577
			a. Four Dharmas That Decrease One's Roots of Goodness	577
			b. Four Dharmas That Increase One's Roots of Goodness	577
		3.	Fourfold Dharmas That Increase or Stop Flattery and Deviousness	579
			a. Four Dharmas Involving Flattery and Deviousness	579
			b. Four Dharmas Characteristic of a Straightforward Mind	579
		4.	Fourfold Dharmas of Ruined Bodhisattvas & Those Well-Trained	581
			a. Four Dharmas Practiced by a Bodhisattva Fallen into Ruin	581
			b. Four Dharmas Practiced by the Well-Trained Bodhisattva	583
		5.	Fourfold Bodhisattva Mistakes versus Good Paths of Conduct	583
			a. Four Kinds of Bodhisattva Mistakes	583
			b. Four Paths of Good Bodhisattva Conduct	585
		6.	Four Dharmas Indicative of an Imitation Bodhisattva	585
			a. Q: How Can One Abandon Imitation Bodhisattva Dharmas?	585
			b. A: Cultivate Four Qualities of the Initial Bodhisattva Practices	585
			1) The Four Qualities of the Initial Bodhisattva Practices	587
			2) To Develop The Qualities, Draw Near to a Good Spiritual Guide	587
			a) Fourfold Good and Bad Spiritual Friends	587
			i) The Four Kinds of Good Spiritual Friends	587
			ii) The Four Kinds of Bad Spiritual Friends	589
			3) Four Questions on the Good Effects of Good Spiritual Friends	589
			a) Answer #1: The Meaning of the Four Vast Treasuries	591
			b) Answer #2: The Meaning of Going Beyond the Works of Māra	591
			c) Answer #3: The Meaning of Producing Measureless Merit	591
			d) Answer #4: The Meaning of Accumulating All Good Dharmas	591
		7.	Eight Twofold Dharmas the Bodhisattva Must Completely Abandon	593
			a. The Two Hollow Attachments	593
			b. The Two Types of Bondage	593
			c. The Two Hindrance Dharmas	593

d. The Two Defiling Dharmas	595
e. The Two Ulcerous Sores	595
f. The Two Abyss-Like Dharmas	595
g. The Two Dharmas Leading to Being Burned	595
h. The Two Types of Illnesses	595
1) Q: Which Dharmas Lead to Bodhi & Which Earn Āryas' Praise?	595
2) A: The Four Truths' Practices and Four Additional Dharmas	595
a) The Four Dharmas Characteristic of Cultivating the Truths	597
b) The Four Dharmas Praised by the Three Classes of Āryas	597
8. The Bodhisattva's Relinquishing Mind & Freedom from Weariness	599
a. The Bodhisattva Doesn't Weary of Providing Two Kinds of Benefit	599
b. Q: Why Are Bodhisattvas Taught to Understand Worldly Dharmas?	601
c. A: Knowledge of the World Enables Dharma Teaching Expedients	601
9. One Must Have a Sense of Shame, Dread of Blame, and Respect	603
10. The Bodhisattva Must Never Retreat from Completing His Works	603
a. Q: How Can the Bodhisattva Succeed in Completing His Works?	605
b. A: He Has Patience, Makes Offerings, and Follows Teachings	605
11. Right Practice of Ten Dharmas Enabling 1st Ground Purification	605
a. Faith	605
b. Compassion	607
c. Kindness	607
d. Relinquishing	607
e. Tirelessly Patient Endurance	607
f. The Ability to Understand the Meaning of Teachings	607
g. Serving as Guide for Beings' Minds	609
h. A Sense of Shame and Dread of Blame	609
i. Making Offerings to the Buddha	609
j. Abiding in the Buddha's Teachings	609
XX. Chapter 20: Mindfulness of the Buddhas	**611**
A. On Finishing 1st Ground Practices, the Bodhisattva Sees Buddhas	611
1. Q: Is There Any Other Way to Be Able to See the Buddhas?	611
2. A: On Entering the Pratyutpanna Samādhi, One Sees the Buddhas	611
3. Q: How Can One Acquire This Samādhi?	611
4. A: Envision the Buddhas with the 32 Marks and 80 Characteristics	613
a. Recollection of the Buddhas' Qualities and Accomplishments	613
b. Recollection of the 32 Marks of the Buddhas	613
c. Recollection of Other Qualities of the Buddhas	617
d. Recollection of More Special Qualities & Abilities of Buddhas	621
e. Contemplative Recollection of the 80 Secondary Characteristics	625
f. Envisioning the Buddhas in an Assembly, Teaching, on the Lion Seat	633
1) Envisioning the Buddhas as They Sit on the Lion's Seat	633
2) Envisioning the Audience as the Buddhas Teach Dharma	633
3) Envisioning the Manner in Which They Teach Dharma	635
4) Envisioning the Effects of the Buddhas' Teaching of Dharma	637
5) Instruction on This Type of Contemplative Mindfulness	639

6) The Importance of Praising the Major Marks and Secondary Signs **639**
   a) Verses in Praise of the Buddhas' 32 Marks **639**
   b) Verses in Praise of the Buddhas Secondary Characteristics **643**
   c) Summation on Importance of Such Recollective Contemplation **647**

Directory to Chapter Subsections
Volume Two

XXI.	Chapter 21: Forty Dharmas Exclusive to Buddhas (Part 1)	709
A.	Introduction to the Forty Dharmas Exclusive to Buddhas	709
B.	1) Sovereign Mastery of the Ability to Fly	711
C.	2) [The Ability to Manifest] Countless Transformations	715
D.	3) Boundless Psychic Powers of the Sort Possessed by Āryas	717
E.	4) Sovereign Mastery of the Ability to Hear Sounds	721
F.	5) Immeasurable Power of Knowledge to Know Others' Thoughts	723
G.	6) Sovereign Mastery in [Training and Subduing] the Mind	723
H.	7) Constant Abiding in Stable Wisdom	725
I.	8) Never Forgetting	727
J.	9) Possession of the Powers of the Vajra Samādhi	727
XXII.	Chapter 22: Forty Dharmas Exclusive to Buddhas (Part 2)	733
A.	Q: Your Claim That Omniscience Exists Is False for these Reasons	733
B.	A: Wrong. As I Shall Now Explain, The Buddha Truly Is Omniscient	749
XXIII.	Chapter 23: Forty Dharmas Exclusive to Buddhas (Part 3)	789
A.	10) Thorough Knowing of Matters That Are Unfixed	789
B.	11) Thorough Knowing of Formless Absorption Phenomena	795
C.	12) The Knowledge of All Matters Related to Eternal Cessation	801
D.	13) Thorough Knowing of Non-Form Dharmas Unrelated to Mind	803
E.	14) The Great Powers Pāramitā	805
F.	15) The Four Unimpeded Knowledges Pāramitā	805
G.	16) The Pāramitā of Perfectly Complete Replies and Predictions	807
H.	17) Invulnerability to Harm by Anyone	813
I.	18) Their Words Are Never Spoken without a Purpose	815
J.	19) Their Speech Is Free of Error	819
K.	20) Complete Use of the Three Turnings in Speaking Dharma	821
L.	21) They Are the Great Generals among All Āryas	821
M.	22–25) They Are Able to Remain Unguarded in Four Ways	823
N.	26–29) They Possess the Four Types of Fearlessnesses	825
O.	30–39) They Possess the Ten Powers	829
	1. The First Power	829
	2. The Second Power	831
	3. The Third Power	833
	4. The Fourth Power	835
	5. The Fifth Power	835
	6. The Sixth Power	837
	7. The Seventh Power	837
	8. The Eighth Power	837
	9. The Ninth Power	839
	10. The Tenth Power	839

P.	40) They Have Achieved Unimpeded Liberation	839
Q.	Summary Discussion of the Dharmas Exclusive to the Buddha	841

XXIV. **Chapter 24: Verses Offered in Praise** — 847
- A. The Importance of Praises to Mindfulness-of-the-Buddha Practice — 847
- B. The Praise Verses — 847
  1. Verses in Praise of the Forty Dharmas Exclusive to the Buddhas — 847
  2. Verses Praising the Four Bases of Meritorious Qualities — 853
     a. Verses Praising the Truth Basis of Meritorious Qualities — 855
     b. Verses Praising the Relinquishment Basis of Meritorious Qualities — 855
     c. Verses Praising the Quiescence Basis of Meritorious Qualities — 859
     d. Verses Praising the Wisdom Basis of Meritorious Qualities — 861
  3. Concluding Praise Verses — 865

XXV. **Chapter 25: Teachings Aiding Mindfulness-of-the Buddha Samādhi** — 867
- A. Initial Instructions on the Mindfulness-of-the Buddha Samādhi — 867
- B. Four Dharmas Capable of Bringing Forth This Samādhi — 871
- C. Four More Dharmas Capable of Bringing Forth This Samādhi — 873
- D. Four More Dharmas Capable of Bringing Forth This Samādhi — 873
- E. Four More Dharmas Capable of Bringing Forth This Samādhi — 873
- F. Four More Dharmas Capable of Bringing Forth This Samādhi — 875
- G. Four More Dharmas Capable of Bringing Forth This Samādhi — 875
- H. Five More Dharmas Capable of Bringing Forth This Samādhi — 875
- I. Five More Dharmas Capable of Bringing Forth This Samādhi — 877
- J. The Guidelines for Lay and Monastic Cultivation of This Samādhi — 877
  1. Twenty Guidelines for Lay Cultivators of This Samādhi — 879
  2. Sixty Guidelines for Monastic Cultivators of This Samādhi — 879
  3. Fifty Dharmas Supporting Cultivation of This Samādhi — 885
- K. The Benefits of Cultivating This Pratyutpanna Samādhi — 889
- L. This Samādhi's Various Stations and Levels of Cultivation — 895
- M. Various Qualitative Variations in How This Samādhi Manifests — 895
- N. Various Abhidharmic Classifications of This Samādhi — 897
- O. The Practitioner's Offerings, Roots of Goodness, and Teaching — 897
- P. The Practitioner's Use of the Four Means of Attraction — 899
- Q. The Practitioner's Dedication of Roots of Goodness — 899

XXVI. **Chapter 26: The Analogy Chapter** — 901
- A. The Bodhisattva Should Study, Cultivate, and Reach the Grounds — 901
- B. Seven Practices Characteristic of the First Ground Bodhisattva — 901
- C. Eight Accomplishments Associated with Entering the First Ground — 903
- D. The Essential Aspects of the Bodhisattva's First Ground Cultivation — 905
- E. Additional Factors That the Bodhisattva Must Learn — 907
- F. The Benefit of Knowing These Dharmas and Their Skillful Means — 913
- G. An Analogy for a Bodhisattva's Knowledge of the 10 Grounds Path — 913

XXVII. **Chapter 27: A Summarizing Discussion of Bodhisattva Practices** — 933
- A. A Brief Presentation Intended to Finish the First Ground Discussion — 933
- B. Q: Before Finishing, Please Summarize the Bodhisattva Path — 935

Directory to Chapter Subsections

C. A: A Series of Statements Summarizing the Bodhisattva Practices	935
1. Practice All Bodhisattva Dharmas & Abandon All Transgressions	935
2. Be Single-Minded and Non-Neglectful in Practicing Good Dharmas	937
3. Two Dharmas That Subsume the Path to Buddhahood	937
4. Three Dharmas That Subsume the Path to Buddhahood	937
5. Four Dharmas That Subsume the Path to Buddhahood	939
6. Five Dharmas That Subsume the Path to Buddhahood	939
7. Six Dharmas That Subsume the Path to Buddhahood	939
8. Seven Dharmas That Subsume the Path to Buddhahood	941
9. Eight Dharmas That Subsume the Path to Buddhahood	941
10. Nine Dharmas That Subsume the Path to Buddhahood	943
11. Ten Dharmas That Subsume the Path to Buddhahood	943
12. Faults to Be Urgently Abandoned on the Path to Buddhahood	945
a. One Fault That Must Be Urgently Abandoned on the Buddha Path	945
b. Two Faults That Must Be Urgently Abandoned on the Buddha Path	945
c. Three Faults to Be Urgently Abandoned on the Buddha Path	947
d. Four Faults to Be Urgently Abandoned on the Buddha Path	947
e. Five Faults to Be Urgently Abandoned on the Buddha Path	949
f. Six Faults to Be Urgently Abandoned on the Buddha Path	949
g. Seven Faults to Be Urgently Abandoned on the Buddha Path	951
h. Eight Dharmas to Be Urgently Abandoned on the Buddha Path	951
i. Nine Dharmas to Be Urgently Abandoned on the Buddha Path	953
j. Ten Dharmas to Be Urgently Abandoned on the Buddha Path	953
13. The 32 Dharmas of Genuine Bodhisattvas	955
14. Seven Additional Dharmas of Genuine Bodhisattvas	959
XXVIII. Ch. 28: Distinctions in the 2nd Ground's Karmic Actions	961
A. The Ten Resolute Intentions Necessary for Entering the 2nd Ground	961
1. The Straight Mind and the Pliant Mind	963
2. The Capable Mind	963
3. The Restrained Mind	963
4. The Quiescent Mind	963
5. The Truly Sublime Mind	963
6. The Unmixed Mind	963
7. The Unattached Mind	965
a. Q: Doesn't an Unattached Mind Contradict the Bodhisattva Vow?	965
b. A: No, One Must Accord with the Mind of Equanimity	967
c. Q: Why Must the Bodhisattva Again Develop the Straight Mind, etc.?	969
d. A: Now, on the 2nd Ground, These Minds Become Solidly Established	969
e. Q: What Is the Result of Deep Delight and Solid Establishment?	969
f. A: These Types of Mind Will Forever After Be Effortlessly Invoked	969
g. Q: What Are the Fruits of Acquiring These Ten Types of Mind?	971
h. A: He Will Attain the Second Ground and a Threefold Stainlessness	971
B. The 2nd Ground Bodhisattva's Ten Courses of Good Karmic Action	971
1. Q: How Many Are Physical, How Many Verbal & How Many Mental?	971
2. A: Physical and Mental Are Threefold and Verbal Are Fourfold	973

	C.	Definitions of Each of the Ten Courses of Good & Bad Karmic Action	973
		1. Killing	973
		2. Stealing	973
		3. Sexual Misconduct	975
		4. False Speech	975
		5. Divisive Speech	977
		6. Harsh Speech	977
		7. Scattered or Inappropriate Speech	977
		8. Covetousness	977
		9. Ill Will	979
		10. Wrong Views	979
		11. Right View	979
	D.	Abhidharma Categories Analyzing the 10 Courses of Karmic Action	981
		1. Twenty Factors Used in Abhidharmic Analysis of Actions	981
		2. The Twelvefold Discussion of Origins and Such	1001
		3. The Seven Types of Bad Actions, Their Origins, and Four Distinctions	1007
		4. More Subsidiary Distinctions Related to the Good and Bad Actions	1011
		5. Distinguishing "Karmic Deeds" versus "Courses of Karmic Action"	1013
		6. Four Distinctions: "Karmic Deeds" and "Courses of Karmic Action"	1015
		7. Three Kinds of Purity Used to Move Beyond the First Ground	1017
		8. The 10 Courses of Good and Bad Karma As Arbiters of One's Destiny	1019
		9. Resolving to Abide in the 10 Good Actions & Teach This to Others	1021
		10. One Should Learn the Rebirth Results of the 10 Good & Bad Actions	1023
XXIX.	Chapter 29: Distinctions Pertaining to the Two Vehicles		1031
	1.	Q: Which Beings Can Use the 10 Courses to Fulfill the Śrāvaka Path?	1031
		a. Stanza #1 Commentary	1033
		b. Stanza #2 Commentary	1037
		c. Stanza #3 Commentary	1037
		d. Stanza #4 Commentary	1039
		e. Stanza #5–6 Commentary	1041
		f. Stanza #7 Commentary	1041
	2.	Q: Who Can Use the Ten Courses to Become a Pratyekabuddha?	1043
		a. Stanza#1 Commentary	1045
		b. Stanza#2 Commentary	1045
		c. Stanza #3 Commentary	1047
		d. Stanza #4 Commentary	1049
		e. Stanza #5 Commentary	1051
		f. Stanza #6–7 Commentary	1053
XXX.	Chapter 30: [Distinctions Pertaining to] the Great Vehicle		1057
	A.	Q: Which Beings Can Use the Ten Courses to Become Buddhas?	1057
	B.	A: The Ten Courses Enable Buddhahood for Beings of This Sort (Verse)	1057
	C.	An Extensive Line-by-Line Explanation of the Verse's Deep Meaning	1059
		1. "Superiority of the Bodhisattva's Cultivation of the Ten Courses"	1059
		a. Five Ways in Which the Bodhisattva's Practice is Superior	1061
		1) Superiority of Vows	1063

2) Superiority of Solid Resolve	1063
3) Superiority of Resolute Intentions	1065
4) Superiority of Thoroughgoing Purity	1065
5) Superiority in the Use of Skillful Means	1067
2. The Bodhisattva's "Measureless Cultivation"	1067
a. Immeasurability of Time	1067
b. Immeasurability of Roots of Goodness	1067
c. Immeasurability of Objective Conditions	1069
d. Immeasurability of Ultimate Ends	1069
e. Immeasurability of Dedication of Merit	1071
3. The Bodhisattva's "Extraordinary Cultivation"	1071
a. His Extraordinary Capacity to Endure	1071
b. His Extraordinary Vigor	1071
c. His Solidity of Resolve	1073
d. His Extraordinary Wisdom	1073
e. His Extraordinary Karmic Fruits	1073
4. The Bodhisattva's Vows	1075
a. The "Solidity" of His Vows	1075
b. The "Goodness" of His Vows	1075
5. The Bodhisattva's "Great Compassion"	1077
6. The "Unimpeded" Nature of the Bodhisattva's Compassion	1077
7. The Bodhisattva's "Thorough Practice of Skillful Means"	1079
a. His Knowledge of "the Correct Place and Time"	1079
b. His Knowledge of "What Delights the Minds of Others"	1081
c. His Knowledge of "What Causes Others to Turn & Enter the Path"	1081
d. His Knowledge of "What Constitutes the Correct Sequence"	1081
e. His Knowledge of "How to Lead and Guide Beings"	1087
8. The Bodhisattva's "Patient Endurance of Pain and Anguish"	1089
9. The Bodhisattva's "Never Abandoning Any Being"	1091
10. The Bodhisattva's "Deep Delight in the Buddhas' Wisdom"	1093
11. "Delight in Those Who Practice the Buddhas' Powers & Masteries"	1095
12. The Buddhas' "Practice of the Powers"	1095
13. The Buddhas' "Practice of the Sovereign Masteries"	1097
14. The Bodhisattva's "Ability to Refute All Wrong Views"	1099
15. The Bodhisattva's "Preservation and Protection of Right Dharma"	1099
16. The Bodhisattva's "Valor"	1103
17. The Bodhisattva's "Ability to Endure"	1105
18. The Bodhisattva's "Vigor"	1107
19. The Bodhisattva's "Solid Resolve in Teaching Beings"	1109
20. The Bodhisattva's "Not Coveting His Own Happiness"	1109
21. The Bodhisattva's "Not Coveting a Measurelessly Long Life"	1111
22. The Bodhisattva's "Supremacy in All Endeavors"	1113
23. The Bodhisattva's "Freedom from Fault in All the Works They Do"	1115
24. The Bodhisattva's "Complete Purity" & "Success in Supreme Bases"	1115
25. How the Ten Courses Enable the Attainment of Buddhahood	1117

XXXI. CHAPTER 31: GUARDING THE MORAL PRECEPTS	**1121**
A. GENERAL AND SPECIFIC RESULTS OF THE TEN COURSES OF KARMIC ACTION	1121
1. THE TEN COURSES OF GOOD KARMIC ACTION	1121
a. GENERAL KARMIC RESULTS OF THE TEN COURSES OF GOOD KARMIC ACTION	1121
b. SPECIFIC KARMIC RESULTS OF THE TEN COURSES OF GOOD KARMIC ACTION	1121
2. THE TEN COURSES OF BAD KARMIC ACTION	1123
a. GENERAL KARMIC RESULTS OF THE TEN COURSES OF BAD KARMIC ACTION	1123
b. SPECIFIC KARMIC RESULTS OF THE TEN COURSES OF BAD KARMIC ACTION	1123
B. THE BODHISATTVA'S IMPLEMENTATION OF MORAL VIRTUE ON THE PATH	1125
1. CHERISHING THE DHARMA AND INCREASING KINDNESS AND COMPASSION	1125
2. THE MOTIVATION TO TEACH BEINGS AND CAUSE THEM TO ENTER THE PATH	1127
3. THE GENESIS OF A BODHISATTVA'S WISH TO RESCUE BEINGS FROM SUFFERING	1127
4. THE VOW TO CAUSE 2 VEHICLES PRACTITIONERS TO ENTER THE MAHĀYĀNA	1131
5. THE POWER OF THE PRECEPTS AND DEEP ENTRY INTO THE SECOND GROUND	1135
6. REACHING THE 2ND GROUND, THE BODHISATTVA MAY SEE A 1000 BUDDHAS	1137
7. ONE MAKES OFFERINGS TO THE BUDDHAS & RECEIVES THE 10 COURSES AGAIN	1139
8. HAVING RECEIVED THEM AGAIN, ONE FOREVER UPHOLDS THE PRECEPTS	1139
9. ONE ABANDONS MISERLINESS, PRACTICES GIVING, & DELIGHTS IN PRECEPTS	1139
C. ŚĪLA PĀRAMITĀ'S ASPECTS, ARISING, POWERS, PURIFICATION & DISTINCTIONS	1141
1. THE SIXTY-FIVE ASPECTS OF THE PERFECTION OF MORAL VIRTUE	1141
2. THE ARISING OF THE MORAL PRECEPTS	1147
3. THE POWERS OF THE MORAL PRECEPTS	1151
4. THE PURIFICATION OF THE MORAL PRECEPTS	1151
5. DISTINCTIONS IN THE MORAL PRECEPTS	1153
D. THE ESSENTIAL CONSTITUENTS OF ŚĪLA (MORAL VIRTUE)	1155
1. Q: DOES MORAL VIRTUE CONSIST ONLY OF GOOD ACTIONS OF BODY & SPEECH?	1155
2. A: NO, THERE ARE OTHER FACTORS INTEGRAL TO MORAL VIRTUE	1155
3. THE SUPREME CULTIVATION OF MORAL VIRTUE	1157
a. Q: PLEASE EXPLAIN THE BASES OF SUPREME CULTIVATION OF MORAL VIRTUE	1157
b. A: NO "I," NO "MINE," NO ELABORATION, AND INAPPREHENSIBILITY	1157
c. SCRIPTURAL DESCRIPTIONS OF SUPREME CULTIVATION OF MORAL VIRTUE	1157
d. THE INEXHAUSTIBILITY OF THE BODHISATTVAS' MORAL VIRTUE	1161
4. A CLARIFICATION REGARDING ASPECTS VERSUS ESSENCE OF MORAL VIRTUE	1163
XXXII. CHAPTER 32: AN EXPLANATION OF THE DHŪTA AUSTERITIES	**1167**
A. HAVING SEEN 10 BENEFITS, WEAR CORRECT ROBES AND GO ON ALMS ROUND	1167
1. THE TEN BENEFITS OF THE APPROPRIATE ROBES	1167
2. THE TEN BENEFITS OF OBTAINING ONE'S FOOD FROM THE ALMS ROUND	1169
B. DWELLING IN A FOREST HERMITAGE	1169
1. TO DERIVE THE BENEFITS OF DHŪTA PRACTICE, DO NOT ACCEPT INVITATIONS	1169
2. HAVING OBSERVED TEN BENEFITS, REMAIN IN SOLITUDE WITH 3 EXCEPTIONS	1171
3. THE TEN BENEFITS OF DWELLING IN SOLITUDE IN FOREST HERMITAGE	1171
4. WHEN LEAVING, ONE SHOULD MAINTAIN THE PERCEPTION OF EMPTINESS	1171
5. TEN REASONS A FOREST DWELLER MIGHT COME TO A TEMPLE OR STUPA	1173
6. THE FOREST DWELLER'S VIGOROUS CULTIVATION OF RIGHT DHARMA	1173
7. SCRIPTURAL CITATION ON THE CORRECT PURPOSES OF A FOREST DWELLER	1175

8.	The Appropriate Dharmas of a Forest Dweller	1179
9.	The Means for Extinguishing Fear	1179
10.	Four Cases in Which a Forest Dweller May Gather with Others	1187
11.	The Aspects Defining Hermitage Dwelling Approved by the Buddhas	1189
12.	Hermitage Dwelling as a Means to Fulfill the Six Perfections	1193
13.	The Buddha's Four Prerequisite Dharmas for Hermitage Dwelling	1193
14.	Other Bodhisattvas for Whom Hermitage Dwelling Is Beneficial	1195
15.	Four Fourfold Dharmas for the Forest Dweller	1195
16.	The Bad Results of Forest Dwelling without Wisdom and Vigor	1197
C.	Additional Discussions of the Dhūta Austerities	1199
1.	A Listing and Brief Discussion of The Other Ten Dhūta Austerities	1201
2.	The Benefits of the Other Ten Dhūta Austerities	1203
a.	The Ten Benefits of Wearing Cast-Off Robes	1203
b.	The Ten Benefits of Taking One's Single Meal in a Single Sitting	1203
c.	The Ten Benefits of Always Sitting and Never Lying Down	1205
d.	The Ten Benefits of Not Accepting Food at the Wrong Time	1205
e.	The Ten Benefits of Possessing Only One Three-Part Set of Robes	1205
f.	The Ten Benefits of Accepting Robes Woven from Animal Hair	1207
g.	The Ten Benefits of Laying out One's Sitting Mat Wherever One Is	1207
h.	The Ten Benefits of Dwelling beneath a Tree	1207
i.	The Ten Benefits of Dwelling in a Charnel Field	1209
j.	The Ten Benefits of Dwelling out in the Open	1209
3.	Additional Discussion of Matters Related to Hermitage Dwelling	1211
a.	Five Types of Monks Who Dwell in a Forest Hermitage	1211
b.	Additional Discussion of When One May Leave a Hermitage	1211
1)	Proper Motivation When Leaving the Forest Hermitage	1213
2)	Generating the Motivation to Benefit Both Self and Others	1213
c.	On the Importance of Revering One's Spiritual Teacher	1215
1)	On the Difficulty of Repaying the Kindness of One's Teacher	1215
2)	On Maintaining the Proper Attitude toward One's Teacher	1217
3)	On Taking Direction from One's Teacher	1217
4)	On Not Seeking Praise or Benefit in Relating to a Teacher	1217
5)	On Making the Teacher's Good Qualities Well Known	1217
6)	On the Need to Become a Good Lineage-Preserving Disciple	1217
XXXIII.	Chapter 33: Aids to Gaining the Fruits of Śīla	1223
A.	On the Purification of Śīla, Moral Virtue	1223
1.	Four Dharmas Enabling Purification of Moral Virtue	1223
2.	Four More Dharmas Enabling Purification of Moral Virtue	1225
3.	Four More Dharmas Enabling Purification of Moral Virtue	1225
4.	Four More Dharmas Enabling Purification of Moral Virtue	1227
5.	Four More Dharmas Enabling Purification of Moral Virtue	1235
6.	Four More Dharmas Enabling Purification of Moral Virtue	1241
7.	Four Kinds of Monks Who Break the Moral Precepts	1247
8.	Four Kinds of Monks of Which One Should Become the Fourth	1247
a.	He Who Is a Monk Only in Form and Appearance	1249

b.	He Who Merely Feigns Extraordinary Deportment	1249
c.	He Who Is a Monk Only for Fame and Self-Benefit	1251
d.	The Monk Who Genuinely Carries on Right Practice	1251
9.	Wrong Motivations for Upholding the Practice of Moral Virtue	1253
10.	Right Motivations for Upholding the Practice of Moral Virtue	1255
11.	The Benefits of Perfecting the Practice of Moral Virtue	1257

XXXIV. Chapter 34: In Praise of the Moral Precepts — 1263

XXXV. Chapter 35: The Karmic Rewards of the Moral Precepts — 1277

- A. The Second Ground Bodhisattva as a Wheel-Turnining King — 1277
- B. The Wheel-Turning King's Treasures — 1277
  1. His Gold Wheel Treasure — 1277
  2. His Elephant Treasure — 1279
  3. His Horse Treasure — 1279
  4. His Prime Minister of Military Affairs Treasure — 1279
  5. His Treasury Minister Treasure — 1279
  6. His Jewel Treasure — 1281
  7. His Jade Maiden Treasure — 1281
- C. Four Qualities of the Wheel Turning King — 1285
- D. A Description of a Wheel-Turning King's Domain, Rule & Qualities — 1285

Translator's Introduction

As the latest in my series of translations of bodhisattva path texts important in the history of Classic Indian and Chinese Mahayana Buddhism, I present here my English translation of Tripiṭaka Master Kumārajīva's rendering from Sanskrit of Nāgārjuna's *Treatise on the Ten Grounds* (*Daśabhūmika-vibhāṣā*).[1] This is a text devoted to explaining in great detail the aspects of practice involved in ascending through the ten "grounds," "planes," or "levels" of bodhisattva path cultivation that are described in the *Ten Grounds Sutra* (*Daśabhūmika-sūtra*) and in the nearly identical "Ten Grounds" chapter of the *Flower Adornment Sutra* (*Avataṃsaka-sūtra*). (In order to encourage and facilitate deeper study of this topic, I have translated both of these closely related texts which are available under separate cover from Kalavinka Press.)

Although Dharmarakṣa was the first one to translate this text into Chinese, his 265 CE translation of this treatise has been lost.[2] The edition of Nāgārjuna's *Treatise on the Ten Grounds* that I have translated here is the only one that exists in any language, namely the 17-fascicle *Shizu piposha lun* (十住毘婆沙論) or *Daśabhūmika-vibhāṣā* that is preserved in the Taisho edition of the Buddhist canon (T no. 1521). It was translated from Sanskrit into English by Tripiṭaka Master Kumārajīva as dictated to him from memory by Tripiṭaka Master Buddhayaśas sometime between the latter's arrival in Chang'an in 408 and his return to Kashmir four years later.

Although, having studied it closely, I find this 35-chapter treatise to be beautifully and awesomely complete in itself as a close description of the principles and practices necessary for entering and mastering the first two of the ten bodhisattva grounds, it is probable that this text as translated by Kumārajīva was originally part of a much larger work. Fortunately, the edition that we have is, in and of itself, a wonderfully thorough training manual for moving from the life of a common unenlightened person to that of an irreversible bodhisattva well along on the path to buddhahood.

A Brief Description of the Treatise Contents

As noted above, this text consists of 35 chapters[3] in 17 fascicles that describe in great detail the principles and practices involved in entering the bodhisattva path and in perfecting in correct sequence the practices of the first and second grounds, "The Ground of Joyfulness" and "The Ground of Stainlessness."

Chapter 1, "The Introduction," discusses the author's motivations and aims in composing this treatise. Chapters 2 through 27 explain the first ground's practices. Chapters 28 through 35 explain the second ground's practices.

Chapter 2, "Entering the First Ground," through Chapter 17, "On Entering the Temple," focus on the practice methods of the lay bodhisattva. Chapter 18, "The Jointly Shared Practices," through Chapter 27, "Summarizing the Practice [of the First Ground]," focus more on the bodhisattva practices that are common to both the lay bodhisattva and the monastic bodhisattva. Chapter 28, "Distinctions in Courses of Karmic Action on the Second Ground," through Chapter 35, "The Karmic Rewards of the Moral Precepts," focus somewhat more strongly on the practices of the monastic bodhisattva or very advanced lay practitioner.

A Condensed Description of Each Chapter's Contents[4]

To give the reader a quick idea of the general content of each of the chapters, I present immediately below only the briefest of general descriptions. For a much more detailed outline of the contents of each chapter, I refer the reader to my 18-page "Directory to Chapter Subsections" which follows immediately after the "General Table of Contents.

1) The Introduction: This chapter consists of a general discussion of the whole treatise, a description of Nāgārjuna's motives in writing the treatise, and a close explanation of the "refuge" verse that opens the treatise.

2) Entering the First Ground: This chapter lists the names and meanings each of the ten grounds, explains how one enters the first ground, and discusses why this ground is called "The Ground of Joyfulness."

3) The Characteristics of the Ground: This chapter describes the character of the first-ground bodhisattva, focusing in particular on this bodhisattva's distinctive features. It also explains why his mind is for the most part joyful and explains the nature of his fearlessness.

4) Purification of the Ground: This chapter describes 27 dharmas involved in purifying the first ground.

5) The Explanation of the Vows: This chapter describes the bodhisattva's ten great vows in great detail.

6) On Producing the Bodhi Resolve: This chapter describes and explains the seven causes and conditions involved in generating the resolve to achieve the utmost, right, and perfect enlightenment.

7) On Training the Mind: This chapter describes the many different sorts of causes and conditions that might cause the bodhisattva to lose his resolve to reach the enlightenment of a buddha.

8) On the Avaivartika: This chapter describes the characteristics of the bodhisattva who has fallen into ruination and the characteristics of the bodhisattva who has become irreversible on the path to buddhahood.

9) On the Easy Practice: This chapter describes using the path of "the easy practice," mindfulness of the buddhas, to succeed in reaching the ground of the *avaivartika* or "irreversible" bodhisattva.

10) Getting Rid of Karma: This chapter describes the methods for purifying past bad karma, specifically referencing repentance, entreating, rejoicing in others' merit, and dedication of merit.

11) Distinctions with Regard to Merit: This chapter discusses the merit and karmic rewards of repentance, entreating, rejoicing, and transference of merit and also explains how repentance results in less severe retribution from grave karmic offenses.

12) Distinctions with Regard to Giving: This chapter discusses the karmic rewards of giving and also explains what constitutes pure giving and impure giving.

13) Distinctions with Regard to the Giving of Dharma: This chapter explains the superiority of Dharma giving over material giving and discusses the qualifications of someone who teaches the Dharma.

14) The Characteristics of the Refuges: This chapter discusses how one takes refuge in the Buddha, the Dharma, and the Sangha as well as how one practices mindfulness of the Buddha, mindfulness of the Dharma, and mindfulness of the Sangha.

15) The Five Moral Precepts: This chapter explains the practices beneficial to self and beneficial to others while also explaining the dharma of the five lay precepts.

16) On Realizing the Faults of the Householder's Life: This chapter details for the lay bodhisattva the faults of the household life, thereby encouraging the layperson to consider the advantages of becoming a monastic. It also describes the practice of the six perfections.

17) On Entering the Temple: This chapter describes the practices adopted by the layperson on entering the grounds of stupas and temples, explains how to take and maintain the eight abstinence precepts, and compares the lay practice with monastic practice.

18) The Jointly Shared Practices: This chapter describes the practices common to both lay and monastic bodhisattvas while also describing a buddha's 32 major marks and the karmic causes that bring them about.

19) The Fourfold Dharmas: This chapter explains how wisdom is the origin of the 32 marks while also setting forth many fourfold lists that explain how wisdom is acquired, how wisdom is lost, how one's roots of goodness are devoured, how one's roots of goodness increase, and so forth.

20) Mindfulness of the Buddhas: This chapter describes the method for acquiring the *pratyutpanna* samādhi wherein one is allowed to see the Buddhas. It explains that one should cultivate mindfulness and contemplation of the Buddhas' form bodies in reliance upon their 32 major marks and 80 subsidiary characteristics.

21) Forty Dharmas Exclusive to Buddhas (Part 1): This chapter lists 40 dharmas exclusive to buddhas and discusses the first nine of those 40 dharmas that serve as the basis for practicing mindfulness of all buddhas' Dharma body.

22) Forty Dharmas Exclusive to Buddhas (Part 2) – Challenges to the Reality of Omniscience: This entire chapter is devoted to refuting the various challenges to the claim that buddhas are omniscient.

23) Forty Dharmas Exclusive to Buddhas (Part 3): This chapter begins by explaining the tenth of the exclusive dharmas, that of "thorough knowing of matters that are unfixed," continues by explaining the rest of the 40 exclusive dharmas, and then ends by introducing an additional 44 exclusive dharmas.

24) Verses Offered in Praise: This chapter explains that one is to use the 40 dharmas exclusive to the Buddhas in one's practice of mindfulness of the Buddha and then presents praise verses to be used as a means for successfully entering the mindfulness-of-the-Buddha samādhi.

25) Teachings to Aid the Mindfulness-of-the-Buddha Samādhi: This chapter sets forth the method for acquiring the *pratyutpanna* samādhi while also describing the karmic rewards derived from this samādhi.

26) The Analogy Chapter: This chapter sets forth the analogy of the great guide leading fellow travelers across treacherous terrain to a great city while also describing in greater detail the knowledge essential to deeply understanding and practicing the bodhisattva path.

27) A Summarizing Discussion of the Bodhisattva Practices: This chapter presents a general explanation of all the dharmas practiced by the bodhisattva along with a discussion of the differences between the practitioner who is a bodhisattva in name only and the practitioner who truly is a genuine bodhisattva.

28) Distinctions in the Second Ground's Courses of Karmic Action: This chapter begins by introducing ten types of resolute intentions that should be adopted by the first-ground bodhisattva wishing to reach the second ground. It continues then with detailed explanations of each of the ten courses of good karmic action and the ten courses of bad karmic action.

29) Distinctions Pertaining to Śrāvakas and Pratyekabuddhas: This chapter begins by asserting that the ten courses of good karmic action enable the practitioner to access the ground of a *śrāvaka*-disciple, the ground of a *pratyekabuddha*, and the ground of a buddha. It then describes which sorts of beings may reach the grounds of *śrāvaka*-disciples and *pratyekabuddhas* by relying upon the practice of the ten courses of good karmic action.

30) Distinctions Pertaining to the Great Vehicle: This chapter describes which sorts of beings may reach the ground of a buddha through cultivation of the ten courses of good karmic action. It also asserts that a bodhisattva's cultivation of the ten courses of good karmic action is superior to such cultivation as undertaken by adherents of the *śrāvaka*-disciple and pratyekabuddha vehicles.

31) Guarding the Moral Precepts: This chapter describes the general and specific karmic rewards resulting from cultivating the ten courses of good karmic action. It then presents sixty-five aspects of the perfection of moral virtue in accordance with *The Jeweled Summit Sutra*.

32) An Explanation of the Dhūta Austerities: This chapter describes the correct practice of the twelve *dhūta* austerities, their benefits, and the conditions under which they may be set aside.

33) Aids to Gaining the Fruits of Śīla: This chapter describes the dharmas that enable purification of one's practice of moral virtue. It also describes four types of monks of which the first three are worthy of censure and the fourth is to be emulated.

34) In Praise of the Moral Precepts: This chapter begins by asserting that, "The bodhisattva who purifies his observance of the moral precepts in this manner is able to gather together all sorts of meritorious qualities and derive all manner of benefits." It then proceeds to quote Akṣayamati Bodhisattva's extensive praise of the moral precepts.

35) The Karmic Rewards of the Moral Precepts: This chapter describes the second-ground bodhisattva's manifestation as a wheel-turning king who instructs beings in the practice of the ten course of good karmic action.

On the Completeness and Ultimacy of This Treatise

Although this treatise primarily focuses its discussions on how to understand the principles, how to develop the qualities, and how to master the skills required to reach the first two of the bodhisattva grounds, its utility is not limited to accomplishing that already very amazing, beautiful, and daunting feat. In fact, the discussions in this text are so wide-ranging and deep that they apply to the entire path to buddhahood. Indeed, if one were to deeply study this text together with the Ten Grounds Sutra,[5] one would then already possess a very complete map of how to proceed all the way to the perfect enlightenment of a buddha.

So many other additional aspects of knowledge, wisdom, powers, skills, and qualities are mastered on these first two grounds that I think it would be fair to say that most of us would need to cultivate the bodhisattva path for many hundreds of lifetimes before we could move beyond the teachings presented in this wonderful treatise by Nāgārjuna.

As noted in Chapter 29, this treatise does indeed provide all of the teachings a practitioner would need to reach all the way to buddhahood: "These ten courses of good karmic action enable the practitioner to reach the grounds of the *śrāvaka* disciples, also enable him to reach the ground of the *pratyekabuddhas*, and also enable him to reach the ground of the Buddhas."

In the very next chapter, Chapter 30, Nāgārjuna answers the question, "Which sorts of beings can the ten courses of good karmic action also cause to reach the ground of buddhahood?", doing so by setting forth the following verse distinguishing these bodhisattvas from practitioners attracted to the individual-liberation paths idealizing arhats and *pratyekabuddhas*:

> The way they practice the ten courses of good karmic action
> is superior to that of the two other classes of practitioners,
> for they engage in measureless extraordinary cultivation
> superior to that of anyone else in the world.
>
> They bring forth vows that are both solid and good,
> perfect the great compassion that cannot be impeded,
> adeptly take on the practice of skillful means,
> and patiently endure every sort of pain and anguish.
>
> They do not abandon any being,
> deeply cherish the wisdom of the Buddhas,
> and delight in those who completely and thoroughly practice
> the Buddhas' powers and sovereign masteries.
>
> They are able to refute all ideas involving wrong views
> and accept and protect the Buddhas' right Dharma.
> They are valiant, able to endure, and vigorous,
> and are possessed of solid resolve in teaching beings.
>
> They do not covet or become attached to their own happiness
> or to living a measurelessly long life.
> They are supreme in all their endeavors
> and free of fault in all the works they do.
>
> They possess every kind of purity
> and come forth through the practice of all the supreme bases.[6]
> The courses of good karmic action enable these persons
> to reach the ground of the Bhagavats who possess the ten powers.

A close perusal of the above verses should bolster the practitioner's confidence in the completeness and ultimacy of the teachings presented in this treatise.

In Summation

I first happened on this text many years ago when searching the Buddhist canon for the most important bodhisattva path texts to translate into English. I immediately fell in love with it and started translating it back in 2004, but had to take a break from it for a few years due to health reasons and also because I was preoccupied with fourteen other bodhisattva path manuscripts I published as the first ten Kalavinka Press volumes in 2009.

I finally finished a first draft translation of this treatise in late spring of 2011 which I did not finish revising until early 2018, this because I was deeply involved in creating a translation of the Ten Grounds Sutra (now available) and the *Avataṃsaka Sutra* (which, though long since completed, is still being revised and edited).

I have always felt that Nāgārjuna's *Treatise on the Ten Grounds* is one of the most important and most inspiring bodhisattva path texts in the Buddhist canon and one that simply *must* be translated into English as soon as possible. Hence it gives me great pleasure to finally be able to bring forth this translation for the perusal of English-speaking Dharma students and practitioners devoted to the deep study of the bodhisattva path.

Although, aided by the critical comments of a group of Dharma friends and colleagues, I have given this translation my best effort and the greatest care to ensure accuracy, I am aware that there may still be room for refinements here and there. To that end, I invite constructive comments by email via the Kalavinka.org website. That said, I remain very confident that this book will suffice to advance the western reader's understanding of right practice of the bodhisattva path as taught by Ārya Nāgārjuna.

Bhikshu Dharmamitra
Seattle
April 23, 2019

Introduction Endnotes

1. Although it is common to see the Sanskrit title of this work reconstructed in English academic articles as *"Daśabhūmika-vibhāṣā-śāstra,"* this based on its Chinese title as *Shizhu piposha lun* (十住毘婆沙論), "Ten Grounds Vibhāṣā Treatise," Hirakawa reconstructs this title as simply *"Daśabhūmika-vibhāṣā,"* probably because he recognized that the *lun* (論) or "treatise" in the Chinese title was only ever intended by Kumārajīva and other translators to notify the Chinese reader that a *vibhāṣā* is a kind of treatise. That is to say, he most likely did *not* intend it as a translation of the Sanskrit word *śāstra*.

2. In an article on Nāgārjuna, Joseph Walser writes: "Of two things we can be fairly certain. First, according to two sixth-century catalogues of Buddhist texts translated into Chinese, Dharmarakṣa translated a work called the *Treatise Commentary on the Sūtra of Ten Stages* (the *Daśabhūmika-vibhāṣa-śāstra*) in 265 CE that he ascribes to Nāgārjuna." (Powers, p. 498)

3. Although the Taisho edition of this text restarts the chapter numbering after Chapter 27 by designating Chapter 28 as "Chapter One," I instead fol-low the chapter numbering of the SYMG editions, all of which number this treatise as consisting of a series of 35 continuously numbered chapters. The apparent rationale for the Taisho edition's restarting the numbering at Chapter 28 is to call the reader's attention to the fact that the first 27 chapters are at least nominally devoted to explaining the first ground whereas the final 8 chapters constitute a new section consisting of N's explanation of the second ground. In any case, the reader should be aware that headings of these sorts for the most part originate with the Chinese translation team, not with the Indian text.

4. This condensed description of each chapter borrows from and expands upon a very similar Chinese language narration found as part of "A Simplified Introduction to the Daśabhūmika Vibhāṣā" (十住毘婆沙論簡介) by the Chinese Buddhist monk Hou Guan of the Fuyan Buddhist Studies Institute (福嚴佛學院, 釋厚觀, 09/18/2001). As of this writing (July, 2018), the document can be found at this URL: http://www.fuyan.org.tw/main_edu/1521-00c.doc

5. My complete translation of the Ten Grounds Sutra is available from Kalavinka Press.

6. These "four bases of meritorious qualities" are truth, relinquishing, quiescence, and wisdom.

Nāgārjuna's Treatise on the Ten Bodhisattva Grounds

The Daśabhūmika Vibhāṣā

(T26.1521.20a02–122b13)

Composed by Ārya Nāgārjuna

Translated into Chinese in the Later Qin Era by
Tripiṭaka Master Kumārajīva from the State of Kuchā

Chinese to English Translation by Bhikshu Dharmamitra

正體字

```
020a04 ‖   No. 1521
020a05 ‖ 十住毘婆沙論卷第一   020a06 ‖
020a07 ‖     [4]聖者龍樹造
020a08 ‖     [5]後秦龜茲國三藏鳩摩羅什譯
020a09 ‖     [6]序品第一
020a10 ‖   敬禮一切佛    無上之大道
020a11 ‖   及諸菩薩眾    堅心住十地
020a12 ‖   聲聞辟支佛    無我我所者
020a13 ‖   今解十地義    隨順佛所說
020a14 ‖ 問曰汝欲解菩薩十地義。以何因緣故說。
020a15 ‖ 答曰。地獄畜生餓鬼人天阿修羅六趣險難
020a16 ‖ 恐怖大畏。是眾生生死大海旋流[7]洄澓。隨
020a17 ‖ 業往來是其濤波。涕淚乳汁流[8]汗膿血是
020a18 ‖ 惡水聚。瘡癩乾枯嘔血淋瀝。上氣熱病瘭疽
020a19 ‖ 癰漏吐逆脹滿。如是等種種惡病為惡羅剎。
020a20 ‖ 憂悲苦惱為水。嬈動啼哭悲號為波浪聲。苦
020a21 ‖ 惱諸受以為沃焦。死為崖岸無能越者。諸
020a22 ‖ 結煩惱有漏業風鼓扇不定。諸四顛倒以為
020a23 ‖ 欺誑。愚癡無明為大黑闇。
```

简体字

十住毗婆沙论卷第一
序品第一

　　敬礼一切佛　　无上之大道
　　及诸菩萨众　　坚心住十地
　　声闻辟支佛　　无我我所者
　　今解十地义　　随顺佛所说

　　问曰汝欲解菩萨

十地义。以何因缘故说。答曰。地狱畜生饿鬼人天阿修罗六趣险难恐怖大畏。是众生生死大海旋流洄澓。随业往来是其涛波。涕泪乳汁流汗脓血是恶水聚。疮癩干枯呕血淋沥。上气热病瘭疽痈漏吐逆胀满。如是等种种恶病为恶罗刹。忧悲苦恼为水。娆动啼哭悲号为波浪声。苦恼诸受以为沃焦。死为崖岸无能越者。诸结烦恼有漏业风鼓扇不定。诸四颠倒以为欺诳。愚痴无明为大黑闇。

CHAPTER 1
The Introduction

I. CHAPTER ONE: THE INTRODUCTION
   A. VERSES DECLARING THE THREE REFUGES AND THE TREATISE'S INTENT

I bow down in reverence to all buddhas,
to their unsurpassable great path,
to those in the bodhisattva sangha
who, equipped with solid resolve, abide on the ten grounds,

to the *śrāvaka* disciples, to the *pratyekabuddhas*,
and to those free of a self and anything belonging to a self.
I shall now explain the meaning of the ten grounds,
doing so in accordance with the utterances of the Buddha.

    1. Q: WHY EXPLAIN THE TEN GROUNDS?

Question: You are now about to explain the meaning of the bodhisattva's ten grounds. What are the reasons for this explanation?

    2. A: THE PLIGHT OF BEINGS AND THE AVAILABILITY OF SAVIORS

Response: The dangers and difficulties of the six rebirth destinies of the hells, animals, hungry ghosts, humans, devas, and *asuras* are terrifying and induce great fearfulness. In the churning whirlpool currents of the great sea of *saṃsāra*, the beings therein swirl about, going forth and coming back in accordance with their karma. This is what forms that sea's towering waves. Their tears, milk, flowing sweat, pus, and blood form its masses of noxious spume.

Their leprous sores, emaciation, regurgitated blood, and urinary disorders, their ascendant-energy febrile diseases, their carbuncles and flowing abscesses, their vomiting and bloating—all of these different sorts of diseases are that sea's *rākṣasas*.

Their worries, anguish, and bitter afflictions form its waters. Their being beset with troubles, weeping and wailing in grief—these are the sounds made by the churning of its waves. All of their feelings of bitterness and affliction—these are its "boiling and burning mountain."[1] Death is that cliff bank on the shore beyond which no one can climb.

The winds of their karma associated with the contaminants and connected to the fetters and afflictions pound and blow at them unpredictably. They are cheated and deceived by the four inverted views.[2] Their delusions and ignorance create a great black darkness.

正體字

随愛凡夫無始已
020a24 ‖ 來常行其中。如是往來生死大海。未曾有
020a25 ‖ 得到於彼岸。或有到者兼能濟渡無量眾
020a26 ‖ 生。以是因緣說菩薩十[9]地義。問曰。若人不
020a27 ‖ 能修行菩薩十地。不得度生死大海耶。
020a28 ‖ 答曰。[10]若有人行聲聞辟支佛乘者。是人得
020a29 ‖ 度生死大海。若人欲以無上大乘度生死
020b01 ‖ 大海者。是人必當具足修行十地。問曰。行
020b02 ‖ 聲聞辟支佛乘者。幾時得度生死大海。答
020b03 ‖ 曰。行聲聞乘者。或以一世得度。或以二
020b04 ‖ 世。或過是數。隨根利鈍。又以先世宿行因
020b05 ‖ 緣行辟支佛乘者。或以七世得度。或以
020b06 ‖ 八世。若行大乘者。或一恒河沙大劫。或二
020b07 ‖ 三四[11]至十百千萬[12]億。或過是數。

简体字

随爱凡夫无始已来常行其中。如是往来生死大海。未曾有得到于彼岸。或有到者兼能济渡无量众生。以是因缘说菩萨十地义。问曰。若人不能修行菩萨十地。不得度生死大海耶。答曰。若有人行声闻辟支佛乘者。是人得度生死大海。若人欲以无上大乘度生死大海者。是人必当具足修行十地。问曰。行声闻辟支佛乘者。几时得度生死大海。答曰。行声闻乘者。或以一世得度。或以二世。或过是数。随根利钝。又以先世宿行因缘行辟支佛乘者。或以七世得度。或以八世。若行大乘者。或一恒河沙大劫。或二三四至十百千万亿。或过是数。

Chapter 1 — *The Introduction* 45

Throughout the course of beginningless time, these common people, under the sway of their affections, have always moved along in the midst of this. So it is that they come and go in this fashion in the great sea of *saṃsāra* without ever reaching the far shore.

But there may be those who, having reached it, are also able to rescue and bring across an incalculable number of beings. It is due to these causes and conditions that we now set forth an explanation of the ten grounds of the bodhisattva.

3. Q: Can Non-Bodhisattvas Also Transcend Saṃsāra?

Question: Is it the case that, if a person is unable to cultivate the ten grounds of the bodhisattva, he will not succeed in crossing beyond the great sea of *saṃsāra*?

4. A: Yes, But the Great Vehicle Requires the Ten Grounds

Response: Someone cultivating the vehicles of the *śrāvaka* disciples or the *pratyekabuddha*s can cross beyond the great sea of *saṃsāra*. If, however, someone aspires to use the unsurpassable Great Vehicle to cross beyond the great sea of *saṃsāra*, this person certainly must perfect the cultivation of the ten grounds.

5. Q: How Long for Two Vehicles to Achieve Transcendence?

Question: In the case of those cultivating the vehicle of the *śrāvaka* disciples or the *pratyekabuddha*s, how long must they pursue their practice before they succeed in crossing beyond the great sea of *saṃsāra*?

6. A: Two Vehicles are Rapid; Bodhisattvas Require Many Lives

Response: In the case of those who cultivate the vehicle of the *śrāvaka* disciples, some may succeed in crossing beyond it in as little as a single lifetime. Some will require two lifetimes and yet others may require an even greater number of lifetimes. This is a matter dependent upon the relative sharpness or dullness of one's faculties. It is also a matter dependent upon the causes and conditions of one's cultivation in previous lives.

In the case of those cultivating the vehicle of the *pratyekabuddha*s, some will require seven lifetimes to succeed in crossing beyond whereas others will require eight lifetimes.

In the case of those who cultivate the Great Vehicle, some may require a number of great kalpas as numerous as the sands of a single Ganges River, and some may require a number of great kalpas as numerous as the sands in two, three, or four Ganges Rivers, and so forth until we come to those requiring kalpas as numerous as the sands contained in ten, one hundred, one thousand, ten thousand, or a *koṭi* of Ganges Rivers. They may require an even longer period of time than that.

正體字

　　　　　然後乃
020b08 ‖ 得具足修行菩薩十地而成佛道。亦隨根
020b09 ‖ 之利鈍。又以先世宿行因緣。問曰。聲聞辟支
020b10 ‖ 佛佛。俱到彼岸。於解脫中有差別不。答
020b11 ‖ 曰。是事應當分別。於諸煩惱得解脫是中
020b12 ‖ 無差別。因是解脫入無餘涅槃。是中亦無
020b13 ‖ 差別。無有相故。但諸佛甚深禪定障解脫。
020b14 ‖ 一切法障解脫。於諸聲聞辟支佛。[13]有差別
020b15 ‖ 非說所盡。亦不可以譬喻為比。問曰。三
020b16 ‖ 乘所學皆為無餘涅槃。若無餘涅槃中無差
020b17 ‖ 別者。我等何用於恒河沙等大劫。往來生
020b18 ‖ 死具足十地。不如以聲聞辟支佛乘速滅
020b19 ‖ 諸苦。答曰。是語弱劣。非是大悲有益之言。
020b20 ‖ 若諸菩薩効汝小心無慈[14]悲意。不能精勤
020b21 ‖ 修十地者。諸聲聞辟支佛何由得度。

简体字

然后乃得具足修行菩萨十地而成佛道。亦随根之利钝。又以先世宿行因缘。问曰。声闻辟支佛佛。俱到彼岸。于解脱中有差别不。答曰。是事应当分别。于诸烦恼得解脱是中无差别。因是解脱入无余涅槃。是中亦无差别。无有相故。但诸佛甚深禅定障解脱。一切法障解脱。于诸声闻辟支佛。有差别非说所尽。亦不可以譬喻为比。问曰。三乘所学皆为无余涅槃。若无余涅槃中无差别者。我等何用于恒河沙等大劫。往来生死具足十地。不如以声闻辟支佛乘速灭诸苦。答曰。是语弱劣。非是大悲有益之言。若诸菩萨効汝小心无慈悲意。不能精勤修十地者。诸声闻辟支佛何由得度。

Only after that may they completely fulfill the cultivation of the bodhisattva's ten grounds and then realize buddhahood. This too is a matter dependent on the relative sharpness or dullness of one's faculties. This too depends on the causes and conditions of one's previous-life cultivation.

7. Q: IS THERE ANY DIFFERENCE IN THE QUALITY OF LIBERATION?

Question: The *śrāvaka* disciples, the *pratyekabuddha*s, and the buddhas all succeed in reaching the far shore [of liberation from *saṃsāra*]. Are there or are there not any differences in the liberation they each achieve?

8. A: NIRVĀṆA DOES NOT DIFFER; LEVELS OF AWAKENING ARE VERY DIFFERENT

Response: This matter requires differentiation: As regards the achievement of liberation from the afflictions, there are no differences. It is on the basis of this achievement that one enters the nirvāṇa without residue. In this respect as well, there are no differences. This is because [nirvāṇa] has no distinguishing characteristics.

It is only with respect to the matters of a buddha's degree of liberation from the obstacles to extremely deep *dhyāna* absorption and his degree of liberation from the obstacles to [the knowledge of] all dharmas that there exist distinguishing factors relative to the *śrāvaka* disciples and the *pratyekabuddha*s. The degree of difference in these is so extensive that no amount of description could ever come to the end of it. No accurate comparison can be made even by resort to analogy.

9. Q: IF NIRVĀṆA IS IDENTICAL, WHY NOT QUICKLY DEPART?

Question: That which all Three Vehicles take as the goal of training is the nirvāṇa without residue. If there are no distinctions in the nirvāṇa without residue, what use could there be for us in going and coming in *saṃsāra* for great kalpas as numerous as the Ganges' sands, fulfilling the ten grounds' practices? That would not be nearly as good as using the vehicles of the *śrāvaka* disciples and the *pratyekabuddha*s to put a swift end to all suffering.

10. A: THIS IS A WEAK AND INFERIOR STATEMENT DEVOID OF COMPASSION

Response: This sort of statement is weak and inferior. It is not the beneficial discourse of someone possessed of the great compassion.

a. WITHOUT BODHISATTVAS, HOW COULD THE TWO VEHICLES EXIST?

Suppose all bodhisattvas emulated your small-mindedness so devoid of kindly or compassionate intent and thereby became unable to energetically and assiduously cultivate the ten grounds. In such a case, how could any *śrāvaka* disciple or *pratyekabuddha* aspirant ever attain liberation?

正體字	亦復 020b22 ‖ 無有[15]三乘差別。所以者何。一切聲聞辟支 020b23 ‖ 佛皆由佛出。若無諸佛。何由而出。若不修 020b24 ‖ 十地何有諸佛。若無諸佛亦無法僧。是故 020b25 ‖ 汝所說者則斷三寶種。非是大人有智之言。 020b26 ‖ 不可聽察。所以者何。世間有四種人。一者 020b27 ‖ 自利二者利[16]他三者共利四者不共利。是中 020b28 ‖ 共利者。能行慈悲饒益於他。名為上人。 020b29 ‖ 如說。 020c01 ‖ 　世間可愍傷　　常背於自利 020c02 ‖ 　一心求富樂　　墮於邪見網 020c03 ‖ 　常懷於[17]死畏　　流轉六道中 020c04 ‖ 　大悲諸菩薩　　能[18]極為希有 020c05 ‖ 　眾生死至時　　無能救護者 020c06 ‖ 　沒在深黑闇　　煩惱網所[19]纏 020c07 ‖ 　若有能發行　　大悲之心者 020c08 ‖ 　荷負眾生故　　為之作重任 020c09 ‖ 　若人決定心　　獨受諸勤苦 020c10 ‖ 　所獲安隱果　　而與一切共 020c11 ‖ 　諸佛所稱歎　　第一最上人 020c12 ‖ 　亦是希有者　　功德之大藏
简体字	亦复无有三乘差别。所以者何。一切声闻辟支佛皆由佛出。若无诸佛。何由而出。若不修十地何有诸佛。若无诸佛亦无法僧。是故汝所说者则断三宝种。非是大人有智之言。不可听察。所以者何。世间有四种人。一者自利二者利他三者共利四者不共利。是中共利者。能行慈悲饶益于他。名为上人。如说。 　　世间可愍伤　　常背于自利 　　一心求富乐　　堕于邪见网 　　常怀于死畏　　流转六道中 　　大悲诸菩萨　　能极为希有 　　众生死至时　　无能救护者 　　没在深黑闇　　烦恼网所缠 　　若有能发行　　大悲之心者 　　荷负众生故　　为之作重任 　　若人决定心　　独受诸勤苦 　　所获安隐果　　而与一切共 　　诸佛所称叹　　第一最上人 　　亦是希有者　　功德之大藏

Chapter 1 — *The Introduction*

b. This Would Put an End to the Three Vehicles and the Three Jewels

What's more, in such a case, there could not even be any differentiation into the Three Vehicles. How is this the case? All *śrāvaka* disciples and *pratyekabuddhas* come forth in direct reliance upon a buddha. If no buddhas existed, then, on what basis could they come forth? If there was no cultivation of the ten grounds, how could there be any buddhas? If there were no buddhas, there would also be no Dharma and no Sangha. Therefore your statement advocates complete severance of the lineage of the Three Jewels. These are not the wise words of a great man, and they are not such as could survive critical examination. Why [do I say this]?

1) The Four Types of People

There are four types of people in the world. The first benefits himself, the second benefits others, the third benefits both, and the fourth benefits no one. Among these, those who benefit both are able to cultivate kindness and compassion and benefit others. These are renowned as superior people.[3] As has been stated:

> People of the world are so deserving of pity:
> They always turn away from what otherwise benefits them,
> and, even as they single-mindedly seek wealth and happiness,
> they fall on down into the net of false views.
>
> Always haunted by the fear of death,
> they flow along, turning about in the six rebirth destinies.
> It is those greatly compassionate bodhisattvas
> who, by their ability to rescue them, are rare.[4]
>
> Beings, when confronted by the arrival of death,
> have no one able to rescue or protect them
> from their immersion in deep darkness
> wherein they are entangled in the net of afflictions.
>
> If there are those able to bring forth and implement
> the greatly compassionate resolve,
> because they shoulder the burden of beings' welfare,
> they undertake a heavy responsibility to act on their behalf.
>
> In a case where someone brings forth the resolute determination
> to undergo alone all manner of suffering through their diligence
> only to then take the fruits of peace and security gained
> and share them as a gift to be bestowed on everyone—
>
> These are the most supreme sorts of persons
> that are praised by all buddhas.
> They are also those who, rare indeed,
> are great treasuries of meritorious qualities.

正體字

020c13 ‖	世間有常言	家不生惡子
020c14 ‖	但能成己利	不能利於人
020c15 ‖	若生於善子	能利於人者
020c16 ‖	是則如滿月	照明於其家
020c17 ‖	有諸福德人	以種種因緣
020c18 ‖	饒益如大海	又亦如大地
020c19 ‖	無求於世間	以慈愍故住
020c20 ‖	此人生為貴	壽命第一最

020c21 ‖ 如是聲聞辟支佛佛煩惱解脫雖無差別。
020c22 ‖ 以度無量眾生久住生死多所利益具
020c23 ‖ 足菩薩十地故有大差別。問曰。佛有大悲。
020c24 ‖ 汝為弟子種種稱讚慈愍眾生誠如所說。
020c25 ‖ 汝以種種因緣明了分別開悟引導。行慈
020c26 ‖ 悲者聞則心淨我甚欣悅。汝先偈說十地之
020c27 ‖ 義。願為解釋。

简体字

世间有常言　　家不生恶子
但能成己利　　不能利于人
若生于善子　　能利于人者
是则如满月　　照明于其家
有诸福德人　　以种种因缘
饶益如大海　　又亦如大地
无求于世间　　以慈愍故住
此人生为贵　　寿命第一最

如是声闻辟支佛佛烦恼解脱虽无差别。以度无量众生久住生死多所利益具足菩萨十地故有大差别。问曰。佛有大悲。汝为弟子种种称赞慈愍众生诚如所说。汝以种种因缘明了分别开悟引导。行慈悲者闻则心净我甚欣悦。汝先偈说十地之义。愿为解释。

There is a saying commonly heard in the world:
"May this family never produce a bad son,"
one only able to benefit himself
while remaining unable to bestow benefit on others.

If, however, they produce a son who is good,
one well able to bring benefit to others—
This one is for them like the moon when full,
for he casts shining brightness upon his entire family.

There are people possessing all manner of merit
who avail themselves of all different sorts of causes and conditions
to then bestow on others benefit that is as vast as a great ocean
and that is also as expansive as the great earth itself.

There is nothing whatever that they seek from the world.
Rather they abide in it only out of kindness and pity.
The birth of such persons is precious indeed
and the lives that they lead are the most superior of all.

2) THE IMMENSE SUPERIORITY OF ONE WHO PERFECTS THE TEN GROUNDS

So it is that, although there are no distinctions as regards the liberation from afflictions achieved by *śrāvaka* disciples, by *pratyekabuddhas*, and by buddhas, there are nonetheless still huge distinctions associated with the buddhas' perfect fulfillment of the bodhisattva's ten grounds, with the liberation of countless beings, and with the bestowal of benefit on so many as they abide so long in *saṃsāra*.

11. Q: I AM CONVINCED, SO PLEASE CONTINUE TO EXPLAIN THE VERSES

Question: The Buddha does indeed possess the great compassion. For the sake of his disciples, you have set forth all manner of praises. This kindness and pity for beings is truly as you have described. You have used different sorts of reasons and considerations to make clear the distinctions, to invoke awakening, and to lead beings forth. When those aspiring to practice kindness and compassion hear this, their minds are purified. I have become deeply pleased by this. Please do explain those earlier verses set forth in preparing to explain the ten grounds' meaning.

B. NĀGĀRJUNA CONTINUES EXPLAINING HIS INTRODUCTORY VERSES:

Response:
[I bow down in reverence to all buddhas,
to their unsurpassable great path,
to those in the bodhisattva sangha
who, equipped with solid resolve, abide on the ten grounds, …][5]

正體字	
	答曰。敬名恭敬心。禮名曲身
020c28 ‖	接足。一切諸佛者。三世十方佛。無上大道者。
020c29 ‖	一切諸法如實知見通達無餘。更無勝者。故
021a01 ‖	曰無上。大人所行故曰大道。菩薩眾者。為
021a02 ‖	無上道發心名曰菩薩。問曰。但發心便是菩
021a03 ‖	薩耶。答曰。何有但發心而為菩薩。若人發
021a04 ‖	心必能成無上道乃名菩薩。或有但發心
021a05 ‖	亦名菩薩。何以故。若離初發心則不成無
021a06 ‖	上道。如大經說。新發意者名為菩薩。猶如
021a07 ‖	比丘雖未得道亦名道人。是名字菩薩。漸
021a08 ‖	漸修習轉成實法。後釋歡喜地中。當廣說
021a09 ‖	如實菩薩相。眾者從初發心。至金剛無[1]礙
021a10 ‖	解脫道。於其中間過去未來現在菩薩。名
021a11 ‖	之為眾。堅心者。心如須彌山王不可沮壞。
021a12 ‖	亦如大地不可傾動。

简体字

答曰。敬名恭敬心。礼名曲身接足。一切诸佛者。三世十方佛。无上大道者。一切诸法如实知见通达无余。更无胜者。故曰无上。大人所行故曰大道。菩萨众者。为无上道发心名曰菩萨。问曰。但发心便是菩萨耶。答曰。何有但发心而为菩萨。若人发心必能成无上道乃名菩萨。或有但发心亦名菩萨。何以故。若离初发心则不成无上道。如大经说。新发意者名为菩萨。犹如比丘虽未得道亦名道人。是名字菩萨。渐渐修习转成实法。后释欢喜地中。当广说如实菩萨相。众者从初发心。至金刚无碍解脱道。于其中间过去未来现在菩萨。名之为众。坚心者。心如须弥山王不可沮坏。亦如大地不可倾动。

"Reverence" refers here to the reverently respectful mind. "Bow down" refers to bending down the body and touching someone's feet. "All buddhas" refers to the buddhas of the ten directions and the three periods of time.

"Their unsurpassably great path" refers to the knowing, seeing, and penetrating comprehension in accordance with reality of all dharmas without exception. It is because there are none superior to it that it is said to be "unsurpassable." It is because it is cultivated by great men that it is said to be "the great path."

As for "the bodhisattva sangha," it is by virtue of generating the resolve to practice the unsurpassable path that one is described as a "bodhisattva."

1. Q: Is Generating the Resolve Sufficient To Become a Bodhisattva?

Question: Does one only need to bring forth this resolve to then become a bodhisattva?

2. A: Of Course Not, But Perhaps Yes.

Response: How could it be that, by merely generating this resolve, one thereby becomes a bodhisattva? If a person brings forth this resolve, he definitely must be able to accomplish the cultivation of the unsurpassable path. Only then might one qualify as a bodhisattva.

Then again, it may in fact be that the mere production of the resolve also qualifies one as a bodhisattva. How might that be? Apart from that initial generation of this resolve, there could be no realization of the unsurpassable path. This accords with the statement in the large edition of the *Sutra*[6] that declares that one who has but newly brought forth this resolve thereby qualifies as a bodhisattva.

This is comparable to the case of a bhikshu who, even though he has not yet realized the path, is nonetheless referred to as "a man of the path." This "nominal" bodhisattva then engages in a gradual cultivation whereby he transforms this into a genuinely realized dharma. Later on, in the explanation of the "Ground of Joyfulness," we shall set forth a comprehensive explanation of the characteristics of a bodhisattva who truly qualifies as such.

Now, as for "Sangha," all bodhisattvas of the past, future, and present from the stage of the initial generation of the resolve on through to the path of the vajra unimpeded liberation[7] all qualify as members of the "Sangha."

"Solid resolve" refers to having a resolve comparable to Sumeru, the king of mountains. As such, it cannot be hindered and cannot be destroyed. It is also comparable to the great earth which cannot be moved at all.

正體字

	住十地者。歡喜等十
021a13 ‖	地。後當廣說。問曰。若菩薩更有殊勝功德。
021a14 ‖	何故但稱堅心。答曰。菩薩有堅心功德能
021a15 ‖	成大業。不墮二乘。軟心者怖畏生死。自念
021a16 ‖	何為久在生死受諸苦惱。不如疾以聲聞
021a17 ‖	辟支佛乘速滅諸苦。又軟心者。於活地獄
021a18 ‖	黑繩地獄眾合地獄叫喚地獄大叫喚地獄燒
021a19 ‖	炙地獄大燒炙地獄無間大地獄。及眷屬炭
021a20 ‖	火地獄沸屎地獄燒林地獄劍樹地獄刀道地
021a21 ‖	獄銅[2]柱地獄刺棘地獄鹹河地獄。其中斧鉞
021a22 ‖	刀稍[3]矛戟弓箭鐵剗

简体字

住十地者。欢喜等十地。后当广说。问曰。若菩萨更有殊胜功德。何故但称坚心。答曰。菩萨有坚心功德能成大业。不堕二乘。软心者怖畏生死。自念何为久在生死受诸苦恼。不如疾以声闻辟支佛乘速灭诸苦。又软心者。于活地狱黑绳地狱众合地狱叫唤地狱大叫唤地狱烧炙地狱大烧炙地狱无间大地狱。及眷属炭火地狱沸屎地狱烧林地狱剑树地狱刀道地狱铜柱地狱刺棘地狱碱河地狱。其中斧钺刀槊矛戟弓箭铁划

Chapter 1 — The Introduction

"Abiding on the ten grounds" refers to "the Ground of Joyfulness" and the other grounds. These will be extensively discussed later on.

3. Q: Why only praise the Bodhisattva's Solid Resolve?

Question: If bodhisattvas possess additional especially superior meritorious qualities, why do you only praise "the solid resolve"?

4. A: It Is Essential For Success and Those Without It Would Turn Back

Response: It is due to the meritorious qualities of a solid resolve that the bodhisattva is able to accomplish his great works and refrain from falling down into the Two Vehicles' paths.

a. Why, Absent Solid Resolve, One Abandons the Bodhisattva Path
1) Fear of Continued Existence in Saṃsāra

As for one who possesses only a weak resolve, he becomes terrified of *saṃsāra* and then thinks to himself, "Why should I dwell for so long in the midst of *saṃsāra*, enduring all sorts of bitter affliction? That would not be nearly so good as to quickly avail myself of the vehicles of the *śrāvaka* disciples or the *pratyekabuddha*s whereby I might swiftly bring about the cessation of suffering."

2) Fear of the Hells

So, too, when one who possesses only a weak resolve sees or merely hears of:

The Living Hells (*saṃjīva naraka*);[8]
The Black Line Hells (*kālasūtra naraka*);
The Unification Hells (*saṃghāta naraka*);
The Screaming Hells (*raurava naraka*);
The Great Screaming Hells (*mahāraurava naraka*);
The Burning Hells (*tāpana naraka*);
The Great Burning Hells (*pratāpana naraka*);
Or the Great Non-intermittent Hells (*avici naraka*)—[9]

Or the subsidiary hells, including:

The Flaming Embers Hells (*kukūla naraka*);
The Boiling Excrement Hells (*kuṇapa naraka*);
The Burning Forest Hells (*ādīptavana naraka*);
The Sword Tree Hells (*asipattravana naraka*);
The Road of Knives Hells (*kṣuramārga naraka*);
The Copper Pillar Hells (*tāmrastambha naraka*);
The Piercing Thorns Hells (*ayaḥśalmalīvana*);
Or the Brine River Hells (*khārodakā nādi naraka*)—

Or the instruments of punishment therein, such as the hatchets, battle-axes, daggers, lances, spears, halberds, bows and arrows, iron

正體字	
	椎棒鐵[4]鏘[金*疾]鑠鐵[矛*贊]刀
021a23‖	鐵臼鐵杵鐵輪以如是等治罪器物斬斫割
021a24‖	刺打棒剝裂繫縛枷鎖燒煮[5]考掠。磨碎其
021a25‖	身擣令爛熟。狐狗虎狼師子惡獸競來[齒*(虎-儿+且)]掣
021a26‖	食噉其身。烏鵄鵰鷲鐵[6][口*(隹/乃)]所啄。惡鬼驅逼
021a27‖	令緣劍樹。上下火山以鐵火車加其頸領。
021a28‖	以熱鐵杖而隨搥之。千釘[7]鏒身剗刀刮削。
021a29‖	入黑闇中熻[8]勃臭處熱鐵鍱身臠割其肉
021b01‖	剝其身皮還繫手足。鑊湯涌沸炮煮其身。
021b02‖	鐵棒棒頭腦壞眼出。貫著鐵[9]弗擧[10]身火燃
021b03‖	血流澆地。或沒屎河。行於刀劍[11]鏘刺惡道。
021b04‖	自然刀劍從空而下。猶如駛雨割截支體。
021b05‖	辛[12]鹹苦臭穢惡之河浸漬其身。肌肉爛壞擧
021b06‖	身墮落唯有骨在。獄卒牽拽蹴蹋[13]搥撲。　　有
021b07‖	如是等無量苦毒。壽命極長求死不得。若
021b08‖	見若聞如是之事何得不怖求聲聞辟支
021b09‖	佛乘。又於寒冰地獄。

简体字

椎棒铁锵[金*疾]鑠铁[矛*赞]刀铁臼铁杵铁轮以如是等治罪器物斩斫割刺打棒剥裂系缚枷锁烧煮考掠。磨碎其身捣令烂熟。狐狗虎狼师子恶兽竞来[齿*(虎-儿+且)]掣食啖其身。乌鸱雕鹫铁嘴所啄。恶鬼驱逼令缘剑树。上下火山以铁火车加其颈领。以热铁杖而随搥之。千钉鏒身剗刀刮削。入黑闇中熻勃臭处热铁鍱身脔割其肉剥其身皮还系手足。镬汤涌沸炮煮其身。铁棒棒头脑坏眼出。贯着铁弗举身火燃血流浇地。或没屎河。行于刀剑锵刺恶道。自然刀剑从空而下。犹如驶雨割截支体。辛碱苦臭秽恶之河浸渍其身。肌肉烂坏举身堕落唯有骨在。狱卒牵拽蹴蹋搥扑。有如是等无量苦毒。寿命极长求死不得。若见若闻如是之事何得不怖求声闻辟支佛乘。又于寒冰地狱。

scrapers, hammers, cudgels, javelins, spikes, short swords, iron nets,[10] iron pestles, or iron wheels—

Or the use of such instruments of punishment to subject one's body to hacking, chopping, slicing, piercing, beating, striking, flaying, splitting open, tying up, shackling, roasting, boiling, interrogating with beatings, grinding up, pounding to a pulp—

Or the foxes, dogs, tigers, wolves, lions, and fearsome beasts struggling forth, gnashing at, pouncing on, and gulping down [the flesh of] one's body—

Or having one's flesh pecked at and devoured by the iron-beaked crows, owls, hawks, and vultures—

Or being hotly pursued by fearsome ghosts that force one to climb up sword trees and scramble up and run down flaming mountains, having one's neck run over by flaming iron carriages, being pursued and beaten with hot iron staves, being nailed down with a thousand nails, being cut apart and scraped out with knives, being plunged into darkness in a place with furiously dancing flames and stench, being placed onto a hot iron sheet that scorches the body as one is subjected to the slicing off of one's flesh, having one's skin completely peeled off and then used to tie up one's hands and feet, being thrown into a cauldron of water leaping in a raging boil, having one's body stewed as one is beaten with iron bats until one's head is broken and one's eyes pop out, being run through with an iron spit and plunged into flames where one's entire body is burned by flames as one's blood flows out and spills onto the ground—

Or being immersed in a flowing river of excrement or being driven along, running down a road of horrors where one is sliced and pierced by its knives, swords, and iron thorns, having daggers spontaneously rain down as if in a storm of flying blades that slice away the limbs of one's body, having a horrible flooding river of bitter salt, painful stench and filth swallow up one's body, having one's flesh entirely rot away and its flesh fall off, leaving only a skeleton that the hell minions drag along, kicking it, stamping it, beating it, and striking at it—

There are countless such intensely painful torments wherein one's life span is extremely long even as one seeks to die and yet remains unable to do so.

If one possessed of only a weak resolve were to see or merely hear of such experiences as these, how could he not be so stricken with terror that he would seek to be saved by the vehicles of the *śrāvaka* disciples or the *pratyekabuddha*s?

Also, one may fall into the Hells of Cold and Ice:

正體字	頞浮陀地獄。尼羅浮陀 021b10 ‖ 地獄。阿波波地獄。阿羅羅地獄阿睺睺地獄。 021b11 ‖ 青蓮華地獄。白蓮華地獄。雜色蓮華地獄。紅 021b12 ‖ 蓮華地獄。赤蓮華地獄。常在幽闇大怖畏處。 021b13 ‖ 謗毀賢聖生在其中。形如屋舍山陵[14]埠阜。 021b14 ‖ [15]麁惡冷風聲猛可畏。悲激吹身如轉枯草。 021b15 ‖ 肌肉墮落猶如冬葉。凍[16]剝創夷膿血流出。 021b16 ‖ 身體不淨臭處難忍。寒風切[17]裂苦毒辛酸。 021b17 ‖ 唯有憂悲啼哭更無餘心。號咷煢獨無所 021b18 ‖ 依恃。斯罪皆由誹謗賢聖。其軟心者見聞 021b19 ‖ 此事。何得不怖求聲聞辟支佛乘。又於畜 021b20 ‖ 生猪狗野干貓狸狐鼠獼猴[狂-王+加]獷虎狼師子兕 021b21 ‖ 豹熊羆象馬牛羊蜈蚣蚰蜒蚖蛇蝮[18]蠍鼉龜 021b22 ‖ 魚鼈蛟虬螺蜯[19]烏鵲鴟梟鷹[20]鴿之類。如是 021b23 ‖ 鳥獸共相殘害。又[21]弶網伺捕屠割不一。生 021b24 ‖ 則羈絆穿鼻絡首。負[22]乘捶杖鉤刺其身皮
简体字	頞浮陀地狱。尼罗浮陀地狱。阿波波地狱。阿罗罗地狱阿睺睺地狱。青莲华地狱。白莲华地狱。杂色莲华地狱。红莲华地狱。赤莲华地狱。常在幽闇大怖畏处。谤毁贤圣生在其中。形如屋舍山陵埠阜。粗恶冷风声猛可畏。悲激吹身如转枯草。肌肉堕落犹如冬叶。冻剥创夷脓血流出。身体不净臭处难忍。寒风切裂苦毒辛酸。唯有忧悲啼哭更无余心。号啕茕独无所依恃。斯罪皆由诽谤贤圣。其软心者见闻此事。何得不怖求声闻辟支佛乘。又于畜生猪狗野干猫狸狐鼠猕猴[狂-王+加]獷虎狼师子兕豹熊罴象马牛羊蜈蚣蚰蜒蚖蛇蝮蠍鼉龟鱼鳖蛟虬螺蜯乌鹊鸱枭鹰鸽之类。如是鸟兽共相残害。又弶网伺捕屠割不一。生则羁绊穿鼻络首。负乘捶杖钩刺其身

The Arbuda Hells;
The Nirarbuda Hells;
The Aṭaṭa Hells;
The Hahava Hells;
The Huhuva Hells;
The Blue Lotus Blossom Hells;
The White Lotus Blossom Hells;
The Hells of Varicolored Lotuses;
The Red Lotus Blossom Hells;
Or the Vermillion Lotus Blossom Hells.

One resides in these places of deep darkness and immense terror. One is born therein as retribution for slandering worthies and *āryas*.

These hells may take the form of a building, of a mountain peak, or of a river port hillside where one is blown by a harsh and horribly cold wind that makes a fierce, frightening, and mournful sound that blasts at the bodies [of the hell-dwellers] as if rolling through [fields of] dry grass. The flesh of the body then falls away like leaves dropping in the winter. The cold peels open one's wounds and both pus and blood come flowing forth. The filth and stench of the body are difficult to bear. The cold wind cuts one open as one experiences excruciating pain and bitter anguish. There is only one's lamentation, grief, weeping, and wailing. There are no other thoughts. Though one screams and wails, one is stranded alone without anyone to rely on. These punishments are all experienced because one has slandered worthies and *āryas*.

When one who possesses only a weak resolve sees or merely hears of these matters, how could he not become stricken with fear, seeking then to avail himself of the vehicles of the *śrāvaka* disciples or the *pratyekabuddhas*?

3) FEAR OF REBIRTH IN THE ANIMAL REALM

Also, among the animals, there are those such as boars, dogs, jackals, cats, foxes, gibbons, rats, monkeys, apes, tigers, wolves, lions, rhinoceroses, leopards, bears, elephants, horses, oxen, sheep, centipedes, venomous snakes, vipers, scorpions, tortoises, fish, turtles, dragons, snails, clams, crows, magpies, owls, hawks, and pigeons. All manner of birds and beasts such as these assail and kill each other.

Moreover, the snares, nets, predation, butchery, and slicing that are found there are not of a single sort. If born there, one is restrained with a halter, one has reins threaded through one's nose and strapped around one's head, one bears burdens, one is subjected to beating with cudgels and staves, and one is afflicted with hooks that pierce one's

| 正體字 | 021b25 ‖ 肉破裂痛不可忍。煙熏火燒苦毒萬端。死則
021b26 ‖ 剝皮食噉其肉。有如是等無量苦痛。其軟
021b27 ‖ 心者聞見此事。何得不怖求聲聞辟支佛
021b28 ‖ 乘。又於鍼頸餓鬼火口餓鬼[23]火癭餓鬼食
021b29 ‖ 吐餓鬼食盪滌餓鬼食膿餓鬼食[24]屎餓鬼浮
021c01 ‖ 陀鬼鳩槃茶鬼夜叉鬼羅刹鬼毘舍闍鬼富單
021c02 ‖ 那鬼迦羅富單那鬼等諸鬼。鬚髮蓬亂長爪
021c03 ‖ 大鼻。身中多虫臭穢可畏。眾惱所切常
021c04 ‖ 有慳嫉飢渴苦患。未曾得食得不能咽。
021c05 ‖ 常求膿血屎尿[25]涕唾盪滌不淨。有力者奪
021c06 ‖ 而不得食。裸形無衣寒熱倍甚。惡風吹
021c07 ‖ 身宛轉苦痛。蚊虻毒蟲唼食其體。腹中飢熱
021c08 ‖ 常如火然。　其軟心者見聞此事。何得不怖
021c09 ‖ 求聲聞辟支佛乘。又於人中恩愛別苦怨憎
021c10 ‖ 會苦老病死苦貧窮求苦。有如是等無量眾
021c11 ‖ 苦。 |

| 简体字 | 皮肉破裂痛不可忍。烟熏火烧苦毒万端。死则剥皮食啖其肉。有如是等无量苦痛。其软心者闻见此事。何得不怖求声闻辟支佛乘。又于针颈饿鬼火口饿鬼火瘿饿鬼食吐饿鬼食荡涤饿鬼食脓饿鬼食屎饿鬼浮陀鬼鸠槃茶鬼夜叉鬼罗刹鬼毗舍阇鬼富单那鬼迦罗富单那鬼等诸鬼。须发蓬乱长爪大鼻。身中多虫臭秽可畏。众恼所切常有悭嫉饥渴苦患。未曾得食得不能咽。常求脓血屎尿涕唾荡涤不净。有力者夺而不得食。裸形无衣寒热倍甚。恶风吹身宛转苦痛。蚊虻毒虫唼食其体。腹中饥热常如火然。其软心者见闻此事。何得不怖求声闻辟支佛乘。又于人中恩爱别苦怨憎会苦老病死苦贫穷求苦。有如是等无量众苦。 |

Chapter 1 — *The Introduction*

skin and flesh, causing it to split open and hurt unendurably. One is also immersed in smoke, burned by fire, and caused to endure agonizing pain of a myriad sorts. On dying, one's skin is peeled away, and one's flesh is devoured. One encounters therein countless such sorts of excruciating pain.

When one who possesses only a weak resolve hears of or sees these matters, how could he not become stricken with fear, seeking then to avail himself of the vehicles of the *śrāvaka* disciples or the *pratyekabuddhas*?

4) Fear of Rebirth in the Hungry Ghost Realm

Also, among the needle-throated hungry ghosts, there are those such as the fiery-mouthed hungry ghosts, the blazing-goiter hungry ghosts, the vomit-eating hungry ghosts, the rinsings-eating hungry ghosts, the pus-eating hungry ghosts, the excrement-eating hungry ghosts, the *bhūta* ghosts,[11] the *kumbhāṇḍa* ghosts, the *yakṣa* ghosts, the *rākṣasa* ghosts, the *piśaca* ghosts, the *pūtana* ghosts, the *kaṭa-pūtana* ghosts, and all other such ghosts. They have disheveled beards and hair, long nails, and large noses. Their bodies contain a multitude of insects, and are characterized by dreadful stench and filth. They are pierced by numerous sorts of torments and are constantly afflicted by the misery of miserliness, jealousy, hunger and thirst.

They are unable to acquire any food. Even when they do succeed in finding it, they are unable to even swallow it. They always seek after impurities such as pus, blood, excrement, urine, snot, spittle, and rinsings. Those that are strong attempt to steal these things by force, yet, even then, still cannot eat them. They are naked, have no clothes, and hence experience doubly intense cold and heat. A vicious wind blows on their bodies, spins them around, and afflicts them with bitter pain. Mosquitoes, horseflies, and poisonous insects bite them and feast upon their bodies. Their bellies are filled only with sensations of constantly burning hunger that roasts them like blazing flames.

When one who possesses only a weak resolve sees or merely hears of these matters, how could he not become stricken with fear, seeking then to avail himself of the vehicles of the *śrāvaka* disciples or the *pratyekabuddhas*?

5) Fear of Rebirth in the Human Realm

Moreover, among humans, there are the sufferings of separation from those one loves, encounters with those one detests, the sufferings of aging, sickness, and death, and the sufferings of the poverty-stricken in pursuit of whatever they seek, as well as the countlessly many other such sufferings.

正體字	及諸天阿修羅退沒時苦。其軟心者見此 021c12 ‖ 諸苦。何得不怖求聲聞辟支佛乘。若堅心 021c13 ‖ 者見地獄畜生餓鬼天人阿修羅中受諸苦 021c14 ‖ 惱。生大悲心無有怖畏。作是願言。是諸 021c15 ‖ 眾生深入衰惱。無有救[26]護無所歸依。我 021c16 ‖ 得滅度當度此等。以大悲心勤行精進。不 021c17 ‖ 久得成所願。是故我說。菩薩諸功德中堅 021c18 ‖ 心第一。復次菩薩有八法能集一切功德。 021c19 ‖ 一者大悲。二者堅心。三者智慧。　四者方便。五 021c20 ‖ 者不放逸。六者勤精進。七者常攝念。八者善 021c21 ‖ 知識。是故初發心者疾行八法如救頭然。 021c22 ‖ 然後當修諸餘功德。
简体字	及诸天阿修罗退没时苦。其软心者见此诸苦。何得不怖求声闻辟支佛乘。若坚心者见地狱畜生饿鬼天人阿修罗中受诸苦恼。生大悲心无有怖畏。作是愿言。是诸众生深入衰恼。无有救护无所归依。我得灭度当度此等。以大悲心勤行精进。不久得成所愿。是故我说。菩萨诸功德中坚心第一。复次菩萨有八法能集一切功德。一者大悲。二者坚心。三者智慧。四者方便。五者不放逸。六者勤精进。七者常摄念。八者善知识。是故初发心者疾行八法如救头然。然后当修诸余功德。

6) Fear of Rebirth in the Deva or Asura Realms

In addition, there are also the sufferings encountered by the devas and the *asuras* when they must fall back again [from their bliss-filled celestial existences].

When one who possesses only a weak resolve observes these sufferings, how then could he not become stricken with fear, seeking then to avail himself of the vehicles of the *śrāvaka* disciples or the *pratyekabuddhas*?

b. The Contrasting Response of One with Solid Resolve
1) The Bodhisattva's Vow

When a person with a solid resolve observes all the sufferings and afflictions endured by those in the hells, among animals, and among the hungry ghosts, devas, humans, and *asuras*, he brings forth the mind of great compassion and has no fear. He makes this vow, saying, "All of these beings have deeply entered into such a deteriorated and afflicted state. They have no one to rescue or protect them and have no place of refuge. If I myself am to realize nirvāṇa, I must also bring about the liberation of beings such as these."

2) The Bodhisattvas Compassion, Vigor, and Success

Relying on the mind of great compassion, he is assiduous in his practice of vigor and, before long, achieves what he has vowed to do. It is for this reason that I state that, among all the meritorious qualities of a bodhisattva, solid resolve is foremost.

3) Eight Bodhisattva Dharmas

Additionally, the bodhisattva possesses eight dharmas through which he is able to accumulate all meritorious qualities:

The first is the great compassion;
The second is the solid resolve;
The third is wisdom;
The fourth is skillful means;
The fifth is non-negligence;
The sixth is diligently applied vigor;
The seventh is constantly focused mindfulness;
And the eighth is the good spiritual guide.

Knowing this, one who has only initially generated the resolve therefore swiftly takes up these eight dharmas, doing so with the same urgency as felt by someone whose turban has caught fire. Having done so, he should then cultivate all the other types of meritorious qualities.

|正體字|

	又依此八法故。有一
021c23 ‖	切聲聞眾四雙八輩。所謂須陀洹向須陀洹
021c24 ‖	等。辟支佛無我我所者。世間無佛無佛法
021c25 ‖	時有得道者名辟支佛。諸賢聖離我我所
021c26 ‖	貪著故。名為無我我所者。今解[27]十地義
021c27 ‖	隨順佛所說者。十地經中次第說。今當隨
021c28 ‖	次具解。問曰。汝所說者不異於經。經義已
021c29 ‖	成何須更說。為欲自現所能求名利耶。
022a01 ‖	答曰。
022a02 ‖	我不為自現　　莊嚴於文辭
022a03 ‖	亦不貪利養　　而造於此論
022a04 ‖	問曰。若不爾者。何以造此論。答曰。
022a05 ‖	我為欲慈悲　　饒益於眾生
022a06 ‖	不以[1]餘因緣　　而造於此論

简体字

又依此八法故。有一切声闻众四双八辈。所谓须陀洹向须陀洹等。辟支佛无我我所者。世间无佛无佛法时有得道者名辟支佛。诸贤圣离我我所贪着故。名为无我我所者。今解十地义随顺佛所说者。十地经中次第说。今当随次具解。问曰。汝所说者不异于经。经义已成何须更说。为欲自现所能求名利耶。答曰。

　我不为自现　　庄严于文辞
　亦不贪利养　　而造于此论

问曰。若不尔者。何以造于此论。答曰。
　我为欲慈悲　　饶益于众生
　不以余因缘　　而造于此论

C. Nāgārjuna Continues to Explain His Introductory Verses

[I also bow down] to the *śrāvaka* disciples, to the *pratyekabuddhas*,
and to those free of a self and anything belonging to a self.
I shall now explain the meaning of the ten grounds,
doing so in accordance with the utterances of the Buddha.][12]

Additionally, it is in reliance on these same eight dharmas that there come to be the four pairs and eight classes of practitioners within the *śrāvaka*-disciple sangha, namely the practitioners on the verge of stream entry, those who have already become stream enterers, and so forth.[13]

As for "the *pratyekabuddhas*, and those free of a self and anything belonging to a self," even when there are neither buddhas nor the Dharma of a buddha currently extant in the world, there are still some who achieve enlightenment that are referred to as *"pratyekabuddhas."*[14] Because all worthies and *āryas* have transcended the covetous attachment to a self and anything belonging to a self, they are referred to as "those free of a self and anything belonging to a self."

As for "I shall now explain the meaning of the ten grounds in accordance with the utterances of the Buddha," the ten grounds are set forth in proper sequence in the scriptures. Now, we shall accord with that sequence in providing a complete explanation of them.

1. Q: This Is Just as in Scripture. Why Be Redundant? For Fame, etc.?

Question: Your explanations are no different from those contained in the scriptures. Since the meaning of the scriptures is already complete, what need do we have of your additional explanation? Is this not presented simply to display your own abilities and seek fame and benefit?

2. A: This Treatise Is Not Composed for Self-Serving Reasons

Response:
It is not for the sake of making a personal display
of literary adornments,
nor is it due to coveting profit or support
that I now compose this treatise.

3. Q: If Not, Then Why?

Question: If it is not for such reasons as these, why do you compose this treatise?

4. A: Out of Kindness and Compassion and for No Other Reason

Response:
It is because I wish, through kindness and compassion,
to liberally benefit beings.
It is not due to any other cause or condition
that I now compose this treatise.

正體字

022a07 ‖ 見眾生於六道受苦無有救護。為欲度
022a08 ‖ 此等故。以智慧力而造此論。不為自現
022a09 ‖ 智力求於名利。亦無嫉妬自高之心求於
022a10 ‖ 供養。問曰。慈愍饒益眾生事。經中已說。何
022a11 ‖ 須復解徒自疲苦。答曰。
022a12 ‖ 　　有但見佛經　　通達第一義
022a13 ‖ 　　有得善解釋　　而解實義者
022a14 ‖ 有利根深智之人。聞佛所說諸深經。即能
022a15 ‖ 通達第一義。所謂深經者。即是菩薩十地。第
022a16 ‖ 一義者即是十地如實義。有諸論師有慈悲
022a17 ‖ 心。隨佛所說造作論議莊[2]嚴辭句。有人
022a18 ‖ 因是而得通達十地義者。如說。
022a19 ‖ 　　有人好文飾　　莊嚴章句者
022a20 ‖ 　　有好於偈頌　　有好雜句者
022a21 ‖ 　　有好於譬喻　　因緣而得解
022a22 ‖ 　　所好各不同　　我隨而不捨
022a23 ‖ 章句名莊嚴句義。不為偈頌。

简体字

见众生于六道受苦无有救护。为欲度此等故。以智慧力而造此论。不为自现智力求于名利。亦无嫉妒自高之心求于供养。问曰。慈愍饶益众生事。经中已说。何须复解徒自疲苦。答曰。
　　有但见佛经　　通达第一义
　　有得善解释　　而解实义者
有利根深智之人。闻佛所说诸深经。即能通达第一义。所谓深经者。即是菩萨十地。第一义者即是十地如实义。有诸论师有慈悲心。随佛所说造作论议庄严辞句。有人因是而得通达十地义者。如说。
　　有人好文饰　　庄严章句者
　　有好于偈颂　　有好杂句者
　　有好于譬喻　　因缘而得解
　　所好各不同　　我随而不舍
章句名庄严句义。不为偈颂。

One observes that beings endure suffering in the six destinies of rebirth while having no one to rescue or protect them. It is from a wish to bring about the liberation of such beings that one summons the power of wisdom to compose a treatise such as this. It is not for the sake of displaying one's own wisdom power, nor is it due to coveting either fame or profit. Nor is there any sort of intention involving jealousy, arrogance, or the seeking of offerings.

5. Q: Why Just Repeat What Scripture Already Explains?

Question: This matter of kindly pity in benefiting beings has already been discussed in the scriptures. What need is there to explain it yet again, thus needlessly subjecting yourself to wearisome hardship?

6. A: Some Beings Require or Delight in More Thorough Explanations

Response:
> There are those who, on merely encountering a scripture of Buddha,
> reach a penetrating knowledge of the supreme meaning.
> There are others who, only on receiving a well-presented explanation,
> then gain a comprehension of its genuine meaning.

There are those persons possessed of sharp faculties and deep wisdom who, on hearing the profound scriptures spoken by the Buddha, are immediately able to reach a penetrating comprehension of the supreme meaning. The so-called "profound scriptures" refers to those describing the ten bodhisattva grounds. "The supreme meaning" is just the meaning of the ten grounds as understood in accordance with reality.

There are those treatise-authoring masters possessed of kind and compassionate minds who, in accordance with the utterances of the Buddha, compose treatises in explanation of them that are graced by well-adorned phrases and sentences. There are those persons who, because of these, are then able to gain a penetrating comprehension of the meaning of the ten grounds. This is as described here:

> There are people who are fond of literary finery
> in which there are adornments of passages and sentences.
> There are those who are fond of verses in praise,
> and there are those who are fond of the various sorts of sentences.
> There are those who are fond of analogies
> and others who understand through causes and conditions.
> In each case, their preferences differ.
> Hence I adapt explanations to each and thus do not forsake them.

The "passages and sentences" above refer to those in which there is adornment of the meaning contained in the sentences but in which there are no poetic verse lines.

正體字

[3]偈名義趣。
022a24 ‖ 言辭在諸句中。或四言五言七言等。偈有二
022a25 ‖ 種。一者四句偈名為[4]波蔗。二者六句偈名
022a26 ‖ 祇夜。雜句者名直說語言。譬喻者。以人不
022a27 ‖ 解深義故。假喻令解。喻有或實或假。因緣
022a28 ‖ 者。推尋所由隨其所好而不捨之。問曰。
022a29 ‖ 眾生自所樂不同。於汝何事。答曰。我發
022b01 ‖ 無上道心故。不捨一切隨力饒益。或以財
022b02 ‖ 或以法。如說。
022b03 ‖ 　若有大智人　　得聞如是經
022b04 ‖ 　不復須解釋　　則解十地義
022b05 ‖ 若有福德利根者。但直聞是十地經。即解
022b06 ‖ 其義不須解釋。不為是人而造此論。問
022b07 ‖ 曰。云何為善人。答曰。若聞佛語即能自解。
022b08 ‖ 如丈夫能服苦藥。小兒則以蜜和。

简体字

偈名义趣。言辞在诸句中。或四言五言七言等。偈有二种。一者四句偈名为波蔗。二者六句偈名祇夜。杂句者名直说语言。譬喻者。以人不解深义故。假喻令解。喻有或实或假。因缘者。推寻所由随其所好而不舍之。问曰。众生自所乐不同。于汝何事。答曰。我发无上道心故。不舍一切随力饶益。或以财或以法。如说。

　若有大智人　　得闻如是经
　不复须解释　　则解十地义

若有福德利根者。但直闻是十地经。即解其义不须解释。不为是人而造此论。问曰。云何为善人。答曰。若闻佛语即能自解。如丈夫能服苦药。小儿则以蜜和。

"Verses" refers to descriptive paraphrasing of the import of the sentence passage's meaning in which the lines are based on a fourfold, fivefold, or sevenfold word count, or on some other similar schema. The verse construction is basically of two types. In the case of the first, it is a verse-form comprised of four-line stanzas referred to as a *gāthā*. In the case of the second, it is a verse-form comprised of six-line stanzas referred to as a *geya*.

"The various sorts of sentences" refers to the phraseology used in making direct statements. As for "analogies," because people may not understand an especially profound concept, one uses comparative statements to cause them to comprehend. In some cases analogies are factually based, and in other cases they are artificially contrived. As for "causes and conditions," these involve tracing causal origins.

So it is that one adapts to individual preferences "and thereby does not forsake them."

7. Q: How Are Others' Unique Predilections Any of Your Business?

Question: Beings do delight in different things, but what business is that of yours?

8. A: Because I Have Resolved Not To Abandon Anyone

Response: Because I have brought forth the resolve determined to pursue the unsurpassable path, I avoid forsaking anyone at all. Thus I endeavor to benefit them by using whatever powers I may possess. In some cases, this is done by giving material things and in other cases, it is done with Dharma. This is as described here:

> If there be a person possessed of great wisdom
> who is able to hear a scripture like this,
> one need not explain it for him yet again,
> for he will then fathom the meaning of the ten grounds.

This is to say that, if there be a person possessed of merit and sharp faculties, then, simply by hearing the *Ten Grounds Sutra*, he will immediately comprehend its meaning and thus he will have no need of additional explanations. It is not for persons of this sort that I compose this treatise.

9. Q: What Are the Qualities of Such a Good Person?

Question: What is it that defines such a good person?

10. A: Immediate Dharma Understanding; Also, 10 Qualities, as Below:

Response: It is one who, on merely hearing the words of the Buddha, is immediately able to spontaneously comprehend them. He is like a grown man able to drink down even intensely bitter medicine when, for little children, one must mix it together with honey.

正體字

善人者
022b09 ‖ 略說有十法。何等為十。一者信。二者精進。
022b10 ‖ 三者念。四者定。五者善身業。六者善口業。七
022b11 ‖ 者善意業。八者無貪。九者無恚。十者無癡。如
022b12 ‖ 說。
022b13 ‖ 　若人以經文　　難可得讀誦
022b14 ‖ 　若作毘婆沙　　於此人大益
022b15 ‖ 若人鈍根懈慢。以經文難故。不能讀誦。難
022b16 ‖ 者文多難誦難說難[5]諳。若有好樂莊嚴語
022b17 ‖ 言雜飾譬喻諸偈頌等。為利益此等故造
022b18 ‖ 此論。是故汝先說但佛經便足利益眾生。何
022b19 ‖ 須解釋者。是語不然。如說。
022b20 ‖ 　思惟造此論　　深發於善心
022b21 ‖ 　以然此法故　　無比供養佛
022b22 ‖ 我造此論時思惟分別。多念三寶及菩薩
022b23 ‖ 眾。又念布施持戒忍辱精進禪定智慧故。

简体字

善人者略说有十法。何等为十。一者信。二者精进。三者念。四者定。五者善身业。六者善口业。七者善意业。八者无贪。九者无恚。十者无痴。如说。

　若人以经文　　难可得读诵
　若作毗婆沙　　于此人大益

若人钝根懈慢。以经文难故。不能读诵。难者文多难诵难说难谙。若有好乐庄严语言杂饰譬喻诸偈颂等。为利益此等故造此论。是故汝先说但佛经便足利益众生。何须解释者。是语不然。如说。

　思惟造此论　　深发于善心
　以然此法故　　无比供养佛

我造此论时思惟分别。多念三宝及菩萨众。又念布施持戒忍辱精进禅定智慧故。

As for the "good person," generally speaking, there are ten dharmas that qualify one as such. What are the ten? They are:

First, faith;
Second, vigor;
Third, mindfulness;
Fourth, concentration;
Fifth, good physical actions;
Sixth, good verbal actions;
Seventh, good mental actions;
Eighth, an absence of greed;
Ninth, an absence of hatred;
And tenth, an absence of delusion.

11. A Vibhāṣā Helps Those Who Find Sutras Hard to Fathom

As I was explaining:

When people take the text of the scriptures
to be difficult to study and recite,
if one but creates a *vibhāṣā*[15] for them,
this will provide great benefit to people such as these.

If a person with dull faculties is inclined toward indolence and arrogance, because he finds the text of the scriptures to be difficult, he may be unable to study and recite them. By "difficult," we refer to the texts being lengthy, difficult to recite, difficult to expound upon, and difficult to master.

Where there are those who are fond of such things as adorned phrases, refinement achieved through a variety of expressions, analogies, and verses—it is in order to benefit just such persons as these that I compose this treatise. Thus your earlier statement that the scriptures of the Buddha alone are sufficient to provide benefit to beings—this along with your questioning the need for additional explanations—such statements as those are incorrect. As I have stated:

12. Such Explanation of Dharma Is an Offering to the Buddha

The reflections made in composing this treatise
have involved the deep-seated generation of a mind of goodness.
Through illuminating these dharmas,
one makes an incomparably fine offering to the Buddha.

Because, when composing this treatise, the reflections and analyses have been accompanied by abundant mindfulness of the Three Jewels and the Bodhisattva Sangha while also bearing in mind giving, moral virtue, patience, vigor, *dhyāna* concentration, and wisdom, this

正體字	深 022b24 ‖ 發善心則是自利。又演說[6]照明此正法 022b25 ‖ 故。名為無比供養諸佛。則是利他。如說。 022b26 ‖ 　說法然法燈　　建立於法幢 022b27 ‖ 　此幢是賢聖　　妙法之印相 022b28 ‖ 　我今造此論　　諦捨及滅慧 022b29 ‖ 　是四功德處　　自然而修集 022c01 ‖ 今造此論。是四種功德自然修集。是故心無 022c02 ‖ 有倦。諦者一切真實名之為諦。一切實中 022c03 ‖ 佛語為真實。不變壞故。我解說此佛法即 022c04 ‖ 集諦處。捨名布施。施有二種。法施財施。二 022c05 ‖ 種施中法施為勝。如佛告諸比丘。一當法 022c06 ‖ 施二當財施。二施之中法施為勝。是故我 022c07 ‖ 法施時即集捨處。我若[7]義說十地時。無 022c08 ‖ 有身口意惡業。又亦不起欲恚癡念及諸 022c09 ‖ 餘結。障此罪故
简体字	深发善心则是自利。又演说照明此正法故。名为无比供养诸佛。则是利他。如说。 　　说法然法灯　　建立于法幢 　　此幢是贤圣　　妙法之印相 　　我今造此论　　谛舍及灭慧 　　是四功德处　　自然而修集 今造此论。是四种功德自然修集。是故心无有倦。谛者一切真实名之为谛。一切实中佛语为真实。不变坏故。我解说此佛法即集谛处。舍名布施。施有二种。法施财施。二种施中法施为胜。如佛告诸比丘。一当法施二当财施。二施之中法施为胜。是故我法施时即集舍处。我若义说十地时。无有身口意恶业。又亦不起欲恚痴念及诸余结。障此罪故

deep-seated generation of a mind of goodness then becomes a form of self-benefit.

Because I have expounded and elucidated this right Dharma, this also qualifies as an incomparably fine offering to the Buddhas. This is what constitutes the benefiting of others. As has been stated:

> 13. BY EXPLAINING DHARMA ONE LIGHTS THE DHARMA LAMP
>
> In explaining the Dharma, one lights the lamp of Dharma
> and erects the banner of the Dharma.
> This banner serves for worthies and *āryas*
> as the emblematic seal of the sublime Dharma.
>
> 14. THIS LEADS TO ACCUMULATING THE FOUR BASES OF MERITORIOUS QUALITIES
>
> As I now compose this treatise,
> truth and relinquishment as well as quiescence and wisdom,
> these four bases of meritorious qualities,
> are thereby naturally cultivated and accumulated.[16]

Now, in composing this treatise, these four kinds of meritorious qualities are naturally cultivated and accumulated. It is for this reason that the mind remains free of weariness in carrying out this endeavor.

a. TRUTH

As for "truth," everything that is true and genuine qualifies as "truth." Among all of those things that are genuine, the words of the Buddha are what are truly genuine. This is because they are not subject to change and ruination. As I present an explanation of this Dharma of the Buddha, this constitutes the accumulation of the "truth" basis.

b. RELINQUISHMENT

"Relinquishment," refers to giving. Giving is of two sorts, namely the giving of Dharma and the giving of material wealth. Among the two kinds of giving, it is the giving of Dharma that is supreme. This is illustrated by the statement of the Buddha to the bhikshus wherein he said, "First, one should engage in the giving of Dharma. Second, one should engage in the giving of material wealth. Of the two kinds of giving, it is the giving of Dharma that is supreme." So it is that, when I engage in the giving of Dharma, this constitutes the accumulation of the "relinquishment" basis.

c. QUIESCENCE

When I explain the meaning of the ten grounds,[17] there is no accumulation of evil karma by body, mouth, or mind. Additionally, there is no arising of thoughts characterized by covetousness, anger, delusion, or any of the other fetters. Because these sorts of karmic offenses

正體字	即名集滅處。為他解說 022c10 ‖ 法得大智報。以是說法故即集慧處。如是 022c11 ‖ 造此論。集此四功德處。復次。 022c12 ‖ 　　我說十地論　　其心得清淨 022c13 ‖ 　　深貪是心故　　精勤而不倦 022c14 ‖ 　　若人聞受持　　心[8]有清淨者 022c15 ‖ 　　我亦深樂此　　一心造此論 022c16 ‖ 此二偈其義已顯不須復說。但以自心他心 022c17 ‖ 清淨故。造此十地義。清淨心至所應至處 022c18 ‖ 得大果報。如佛語迦留陀夷。勿恨阿難。若 022c19 ‖ 我不記阿難。於我滅後作阿羅漢者。以 022c20 ‖ 是清淨心業因緣故。當於他化自在天七 022c21 ‖ 反為王。如經中廣說。
简体字	即名集灭处。为他解说法得大智报。以是说法故即集慧处。如是造此论。集此四功德处。复次。 　　我说十地论　　其心得清净 　　深贪是心故　　精勤而不倦 　　若人闻受持　　心有清净者 　　我亦深乐此　　一心造此论 此二偈其义已显不须复说。但以自心他心清净故。造此十地义。清净心至所应至处得大果报。如佛语迦留陀夷。勿恨阿难。若我不记阿难。于我灭后作阿罗汉者。以是清净心业因缘故。当于他化自在天七反为王。如经中广说。

are blocked off, this constitutes the accumulation of the "quiescence" basis.[18]

d. WISDOM

When one explains the Dharma for others, then one gains great wisdom as the karmic result. This act of explaining the Dharma constitutes the accumulation of the "wisdom" basis.

It is in this manner that, in composing such a treatise as this, one accumulates the bases for these four meritorious qualities. Additionally, as I have stated:

15. NĀGĀRJUNA'S FINAL STATEMENT OF INTENT

As I explain this treatise on the ten grounds,
one's mind becomes purified.
Due to a profound zeal to develop this sort of mind,
one remains intensely diligent and free of weariness.

If anyone hears, accepts, and upholds this
so that his mind becomes possessed of purity,
I, too, find deep delight in this,
and thus single-mindedly proceed with composing this treatise.

The meaning of these two stanzas has already been made clear. Hence it is unnecessary to discuss it again. It is solely for the sake of purifying one's own mind as well as the minds of others that this explanation of the meaning of the ten grounds is undertaken. When this pure mind reaches the point that it should reach, one gains a great karmic reward. This accords with the Buddha's words to Kālodāyin when he said, "Do not feel animosity toward Ānanda. In fact, if Ānanda had not received my prediction that he would attain arhatship after my nirvāṇa, because of this pure mind karma of his, he would have instead been bound for seven successive rebirths as the king of the Paranirmita Vaśavartin Heaven."[19] This is as extensively described in the scriptures.

The End of Chapter One

正體字

022c22 ‖　　　入初地品第二
022c23 ‖　問曰。汝說此語開悟我心甚以欣悅。今解
022c24 ‖　十地必多所利益。何等為十。答曰。
022c25 ‖　　此中十地法　　去來今諸佛
022c26 ‖　　為諸佛子故　　已說今當說
022c27 ‖　　初地名歡喜　　第二離垢地
022c28 ‖　　三名為明地　　第四名焰地
022c29 ‖　　五名難勝地　　六名現前地
023a01 ‖　　第七深遠地　　第八不動地
023a02 ‖　　九名善慧地　　十名法雲地
023a03 ‖　　分別十地相　　次後當廣說
023a04 ‖　此中者大乘義中。十者數法。地者菩薩善根
023a05 ‖　階級住處。諸佛者。十方三世諸如來。說者。開
023a06 ‖　示解釋。諸佛子者。諸佛真實子諸菩薩是。是
023a07 ‖　故菩薩名為佛子。

简体字

入初地品第二

问曰。汝说此语开悟我心甚以欣悦。今解十地必多所利益。何等为十。答曰。

　　此中十地法　　去来今诸佛
　　为诸佛子故　　已说今当说
　　初地名欢喜　　第二离垢地
　　三名为明地　　第四名焰地
　　五名难胜地　　六名现前地
　　第七深远地　　第八不动地
　　九名善慧地　　十名法云地
　　分别十地相　　次后当广说

此中者大乘义中。十者数法。地者菩萨善根阶级住处。诸佛者。十方三世诸如来。说者。开示解释。诸佛子者。诸佛真实子诸菩萨是。是故菩萨名为佛子。

Chapter 2
Entering the First Ground

II. Chapter Two: Entering the First Ground
    A. Q: What Are the Ten Grounds?

Question: These words you have spoken have awakened my mind and I have been extremely pleased by them. If you were to now explain the ten grounds, there would certainly be many who would benefit. What are the ten grounds?

    B. A: The Ten Grounds Taught by All Buddhas Are as Follows:

Response:

> The dharma of the ten grounds contained herein
> has been, is now, and shall continue to be explained
> by the buddhas of the past, the future, and the present
> for the sake of all buddhas' sons,

> The first ground is known as the Ground of Joyfulness.
> The second is known as the Ground of Stainlessness.
> The third is known as the Ground of Shining Light.
> The fourth is known as the Ground of Blazing Brilliance.

> The fifth is known as the Difficult-to-Conquer Ground.
> The sixth is known as the Ground of Direct Presence.
> The seventh is known as the Far-Reaching Ground.
> The eighth is known as the Ground of Immovability.

> The ninth is known as the Ground of Excellent Intelligence.
> The tenth is known as the Ground of the Dharma Cloud.
> In analyzing the aspects of the ten grounds,
> we shall next present extensive explanations. [20]

"Herein" refers to the sphere of the meaning set forth in the Great Vehicle. "Ten" is simply a term of enumeration. "Grounds" refers to the various stations on which a bodhisattva resides in accordance with his roots of goodness.

"Buddhas" refers to all *tathāgatas* of the ten directions and three periods of time. "Explaining" refers to instruction and explication. As for "buddhas' sons," the true sons of all buddhas are the bodhisattvas. It is for this reason that the bodhisattvas are referred to as "buddhas' sons."

| 正體字 | 過去未來現在諸佛。皆說
023a08 ‖ 此十地。是故言已說今說當說。菩薩在初
023a09 ‖ 地始得善法味心多歡喜[1]故名歡喜地。
023a10 ‖ 第二地中行十善道離諸垢故名離垢地。
023a11 ‖ 第三地中廣博多學為眾說法能作照明故
023a12 ‖ 名為明地。第四地中布施持戒多聞轉增。威
023a13 ‖ 德熾盛故名為炎地。第五地中功德力盛。一
023a14 ‖ 切諸魔不能壞故名難勝地。第六地中[2]障
023a15 ‖ 魔事已。諸菩薩道法皆現在前故名現前地。
023a16 ‖ 第七地中去三界遠近法王位故名深遠
023a17 ‖ 地。第八地中若天魔梵沙門婆羅門無能動
023a18 ‖ 其願故名不動地。第九地中其慧轉明調柔
023a19 ‖ 增上故名善慧地。第十地中菩薩於十方無
023a20 ‖ 量世界。能一時雨法雨如劫燒已普澍[3]大
023a21 ‖ 雨名法雲地。

简体字 | 过去未来现在诸佛。皆说此十地。是故言已说今说当说。菩萨在初地始得善法味心多欢喜故名欢喜地。第二地中行十善道离诸垢故名离垢地。第三地中广博多学为众说法能作照明故名为明地。第四地中布施持戒多闻转增。威德炽盛故名为炎地。第五地中功德力盛。一切诸魔不能坏故名难胜地。第六地中障魔事已。诸菩萨道法皆现在前故名现前地。第七地中去三界远近法王位故名深远地。第八地中若天魔梵沙门婆罗门无能动其愿故名不动地。第九地中其慧转明调柔增上故名善慧地。第十地中菩萨于十方无量世界。能一时雨法雨如劫烧已普澍大雨名法云地。

It is because all buddhas of the past, the future and the present explain these ten grounds that the text says, "has been, is now, and shall continue to be explained."

As the bodhisattva on the first ground begins to gain the flavor of good dharmas, his mind abounds in joyfulness. It is for this reason that it is referred to as "the Ground of Joyfulness" (*pramudita*).

On the second ground, as one cultivates the path of the ten good karmic deeds, one leaves behind all stains. It is for this reason that it is referred to as "the Ground of Stainlessness" (*vimala*).

On the third ground, as one engages in vastly comprehensive learning and speaks Dharma for beings, one becomes able to provide radiant illumination. It is for this reason that it is referred to as "the Ground of Shining Light" (*prabhākara*).

On the fourth ground, one's giving, moral virtue, and extensive learning so increase that one's awe-inspiring qualities blaze forth abundantly. It is for this reason that it is referred to as "the Ground of Blazing Brilliance" (*arciṣmati*).

On the fifth ground, the power of one's meritorious qualities becomes so completely full that none of the *māras* are able to bring about one's ruin. It is for this reason that it is referred to as "the Difficult-to-Conquer Ground" (*sudurjaya*).

On the sixth ground, the issue of obstruction by *māras* has come to an end and all path dharmas of the bodhisattva have manifest directly before him. It is for this reason that it is referred to as "the Ground of Direct Presence" (*abhimukha*).

On the seventh ground, one has gone far beyond the three realms and has gained close proximity to the station in which one becomes a Dharma king. It is for this reason that it is referred to as "the Far-Reaching Ground" (*dūraṃgama*).

On the eighth ground, one's vows cannot be moved even by devas, by Māra, by Brahmā, by any *śramaṇa*, or by any brahman. It is for this reason that it is referred to as "the Ground of Immovability" (*acala*).

On the ninth ground, one's wisdom becomes ever more radiant, supple, and superior. It is for this reason that it is referred to as "the Ground of Excellent Intelligence" (*sādhumati*).

On the tenth ground, the bodhisattva becomes able to simultaneously rain down the Dharma rain in countless worlds throughout the ten directions just as when, after the kalpa-ending blaze, there then falls a great universally drenching rain. It is for this reason that it is referred to as "the Dharma Cloud Ground" (*dharmamegha*).

正體字	問曰。已聞十地名。今云何入 023a22 ‖ 初地。得地相貌及修習地。答曰。 023a23 ‖ 　若厚種善根　善行於諸行 023a24 ‖ 　善集諸資用　善供養諸佛 023a25 ‖ 　善知識所護　具足於深心 023a26 ‖ 　悲心念眾生　信解無上法 023a27 ‖ 　具此八法已　當自發願言 023a28 ‖ 　我得自度已　當復度眾生 023a29 ‖ 　為得十力故　入於必定聚 023b01 ‖ 　則生如來家　無有諸過咎 023b02 ‖ 　即轉世間道　入出世上道 023b03 ‖ 　是以得初地　此地名歡喜 023b04 ‖ 厚種善根者。如法修集諸功德。名為厚種 023b05 ‖ 善根。善根者不貪不恚不癡。一切善法從此 023b06 ‖ 三生故名為善根。如一切惡法皆從貪恚 023b07 ‖ 癡生。是故此三名不善根。阿毘曇中種種分 023b08 ‖ 別。欲界繫
简体字	问曰。已闻十地名。今云何入初地。得地相貌及修习地。答曰。 　若厚种善根　善行于诸行 　善集诸资用　善供养诸佛 　善知识所护　具足于深心 　悲心念众生　信解无上法 　具此八法已　当自发愿言 　我得自度已　当复度众生 　为得十力故　入于必定聚 　则生如来家　无有诸过咎 　即转世间道　入出世上道 　是以得初地　此地名欢喜 　厚种善根者。如法修集诸功德。名为厚种善根。善根者不贪不恚不痴。一切善法从此三生故名为善根。如一切恶法皆从贪恚痴生。是故此三名不善根。阿毗昙中种种分别。欲界系

Chapter 2 — Entering the First Ground

C. Q: How Does One Enter and Cultivate the First Ground?

Question: Now that we have heard the names of the ten grounds, how does one enter the first ground, gain the characteristic features of that ground, and carry forth cultivation of that ground?

D. A: Five Stanzas on First Ground Cultivation

Response:[21]

Having densely planted one's roots of goodness,
having thoroughly practiced the practices,
having well accumulated all the provisions,
having thoroughly made offerings to all buddhas,

having become protected by the good spiritual friend,
having completely developed the resolute intentions,
having become compassionately mindful of beings,
and having resolute faith in the unsurpassable Dharma—

Once one has become completely equipped with these eight dharmas,
at one's own behest, one should bring forth the vow, saying,
"After I have achieved my own liberation,
I shall return and liberate other beings."

For the sake of gaining the ten powers,
one enters the congregation of those at the stage of certainty.[22]
Then one is born into the family of the Tathāgatas
that is free of any transgressions or faults.

One immediately turns away from the worldly path
and enters the supreme path that goes beyond the world.
It is because of this that one gains the first ground.
This ground is referred to as "the Ground of Joyfulness."

1. The Meaning of "Roots of Goodness"

"Plants one's roots of goodness densely" refers to cultivating and accumulating all forms of meritorious qualities, doing so in a manner that accords with Dharma. This is what is meant by "dense planting of roots of goodness."

"Roots of goodness" refers to not being influenced by greed, not being influenced by hatred, and not being influenced by delusion. It is because all good dharmas are born from these three factors that one is then able to speak of "roots of goodness." So too, all forms of bad dharmas are born from greed, hatred, and delusion. It is because of this that these three are known as "roots of evil."

a. Abhidharma Categories of "Roots of Goodness"

In the Abhidharma, these are distinguished in various ways whereby they are categorized as connected with the desire realm, as connected

正體字	色界繫無色界繫不繫合為十二。 023b09 ‖ 有心相應有心不相應合二十四。此中無漏善 023b10 ‖ 根得阿耨多羅三藐三菩提時修集。餘九菩 023b11 ‖ 薩地中修集。又未發心時[4]久修集。或一心中 023b12 ‖ 有三。或一心中有六。或一心中有九。或一 023b13 ‖ 心中有十二。或但集心相應不集心不相 023b14 ‖ 應。或集心不相應不集心相應。或集心相 023b15 ‖ 應亦心不相應。或不集心相應心不相應。是 023b16 ‖ 諸善根分別。如阿毘曇中廣說。此中善根為 023b17 ‖ 眾生求無上道故。所行諸善法皆名善根。 023b18 ‖ 能生薩婆若智故名為善根。行於諸行者。 023b19 ‖ 善行名清淨。諸行名持戒。清淨持戒次第 023b20 ‖ 而行。是持戒與七法和合故[5]名為善行。何 023b21 ‖ 等為[6]七。
简体字	色界系无色界系不系合为十二。有心相应有心不相应合二十四。此中无漏善根得阿耨多罗三藐三菩提时修集。余九菩萨地中修集。又未发心时久修集。或一心中有三。或一心中有六。或一心中有九。或一心中有十二。或但集心相应不集心不相应。或集心不相应不集心相应。或集心相应亦心不相应。或不集心相应心不相应。是诸善根分别。如阿毗昙中广说。此中善根为众生求无上道故。所行诸善法皆名善根。能生萨婆若智故名为善根。行于诸行者。善行名清净。诸行名持戒。清净持戒次第而行。是持戒与七法和合故名为善行。何等为七。

with the form realm, as connected with the formless realm, or as having no specific connection, the result being that, taken together, there are twelve such categories. Additionally, they are categorized as being "associated with the mind," or as "not associated with the mind," thus yielding a total of twenty-four categories. Of these [twelve roots of goodness], the roots of goodness free of the contaminants are cultivated and attained in the acquisition of *anuttarasamyaksaṃbodhi*, whereas the other nine [roots of goodness] are cultivated and accumulated on the bodhisattva grounds.

Additionally, when one has not yet brought forth the resolve, one engages in cultivating and accumulating them over a long period of time. In some cases, three of these categories may be present in a single thought. In some cases, six of these categories may be present in a single thought. In some cases, nine of these categories may be present in a single thought. And in some cases, twelve of these categories may be present in a single thought.

In some cases, one collects only those associated with the mind while not collecting those unassociated with the mind. In some cases, one collects those unassociated with the mind while not accumulating those associated with the mind. In some cases, one collects those associated with the mind as well as those unassociated with the mind. In some cases, one accumulates neither those associated with the mind nor those unassociated with the mind. All such analytic distinctions regarding roots of goodness are such as one will find extensively discussed in the Abhidharma.

b. The Meaning of "Roots of Goodness" That Is Relevant Here

The roots of goodness that are relevant here are those that are planted as one strives to realize the unsurpassable path, doing so for the sake of beings. All good dharmas that one cultivates may be referred to as "roots of goodness." It is because they are able to produce the wisdom of all-knowledge that they are referred to as "roots of goodness."

2. The Meaning of "Practicing the Practices"

In "practicing the practices," "thorough practice" refers to that which is characterized by purity. "The practices" refers to the upholding of the moral precepts. One remains pure in upholding the moral precepts while practicing in accordance with the correct sequence. It is when this upholding of the moral precepts is combined with seven dharmas that it qualifies as "thorough practice."

a. Seven Dharmas Essential to "Thorough Practice"

Which factors constitute these seven? They are as follows:

正體字	
	一慚二愧三多聞四精進五念六慧
023b22 ‖	七淨命淨身口業。行此七法具持諸戒。是
023b23 ‖	名善行諸行。又經說諸禪為行處。是故得
023b24 ‖	禪者名為善行諸行。此論中不必以禪乃
023b25 ‖	得發心。所以者何。佛在世時無量眾生皆亦
023b26 ‖	發心不必有禪。又白衣在家亦名為[7]行。善
023b27 ‖	集資用者。上偈中所說。厚種善根善行諸
023b28 ‖	行多供養佛善知識護具足深心悲念眾
023b29 ‖	生信解上法。是名資用。又本行善法必應
023c01 ‖	修行[8]亦名資用。所謂布施忍辱

简体字

一惭二愧三多闻四精进五念六慧七净命净身口业。行此七法具持诸戒。是名善行诸行。又经说诸禅为行处。是故得禅者名为善行诸行。此论中不必以禅乃得发心。所以者何。佛在世时无量众生皆亦发心不必有禅。又白衣在家亦名为行。善集资用者。上偈中所说。厚种善根善行诸行多供养佛善知识护具足深心悲念众生信解上法。是名资用。又本行善法必应修行亦名资用。所谓布施忍辱

First, a sense of shame;
Second, a dread of blame;
Third, extensive learning;
Fourth, vigor;
Fifth, mindfulness;
Sixth, wisdom;
And seventh, pure livelihood characterized by pure physical and verbal actions.

As one implements these seven dharmas, one remains perfect in upholding all of the moral precepts. It is this that qualifies as "thorough practice of the practices."

    b. THE IMPORTANCE OF DHYĀNA TO IMPLEMENTING THE PRACTICES

Additionally, it is explained in the scriptures that the *dhyānas* constitute the stations in which one implements the practices. Hence it is the realization of the *dhyānas* that constitutes the thorough practice of the practices. In this treatise, we do not assert that it is definitely required that one use the *dhyānas* in the generation of the resolve. Why is this? When the Buddha was abiding in the world, countless beings brought forth the resolve but did not necessarily possess the *dhyānas* when they did so. Moreover, the practice of the laity's householders also qualifies as thorough practice."[23]

   3. THE MEANING OF "ACCUMULATING THE PROVISIONS"

As for "having well accumulated all the provisions," this refers to the [other] factors mentioned in the above verse, namely:

    a. "PROVISIONS" INCLUDES THE TOPICS REFERENCED EARLIER

Densely planting roots of goodness;
Thoroughly practicing the practices;
Making many offerings to the Buddhas;
Being protected by the good spiritual friend;
Completely developing the resolute intentions;[24]
Being compassionately mindful of beings;
And having resolute faith in the supreme Dharma.

These are what constitute the "provisions."

    b. "PROVISIONS" ALSO INCLUDES THE PRACTICE OF 22 GOOD DHARMAS

Also, the fundamental practice of the good dharmas—these must certainly have been cultivated. These also constitute "provisions." Specifically, these include:

Giving;
Patience;

正體字	質直不諂心 023c02 ‖ 柔和同止。樂無慍恨性殫盡不隱過。不偏 023c03 ‖ 執不[9]佷戾。不諍訟不自恃不放逸。捨憍 023c04 ‖ 慢。離矯異。不讚身堪忍事。決定心能果敢 023c05 ‖ 受。不捨易教授。少欲知足樂於獨處。如是 023c06 ‖ 等諸法隨行已。漸能具足殊勝功德。是法 023c07 ‖ [10]味堅牢故名為本行。若離是法不能進 023c08 ‖ 得勝妙功德。是故此本行法與八法和合 023c09 ‖ 故。為初地資用。善[11]供養諸佛者。若菩薩世 023c10 ‖ 世。如法常多供養諸佛。供養有二種。一者 023c11 ‖ 善聽大乘正法若廣若略。二者四事供養恭 023c12 ‖ 敬禮侍等。具此二法供養諸佛。名為善供 023c13 ‖ 養諸佛。
简体字	质直不谄心柔和同止。乐无愠恨性殚尽不隐过。不偏执不佷戾。不诤讼不自恃不放逸。舍憍慢。离矫异。不赞身堪忍事。决定心能果敢受。不舍易教授。少欲知足乐于独处。如是等诸法随行已。渐能具足殊胜功德。是法味坚牢故名为本行。若离是法不能进得胜妙功德。是故此本行法与八法和合故。为初地资用。善供养诸佛者。若菩萨世世。如法常多供养诸佛。供养有二种。一者善听大乘正法若广若略。二者四事供养恭敬礼侍等。具此二法供养诸佛。名为善供养诸佛。

A straightforward character;
A mind that refrains from flattery;
Dwelling harmoniously with others;
Happiness free of resentment;
Being, by nature, utterly committed [to the practice];
Not concealing one's faults;
Not cherishing one-sided attachments;
Not being perversely cruel;
Not being contentious;
Not being presumptuous;
Not being negligent;
Doing away with arrogance;
Remaining free of affectation;
Not praising oneself;
Being able to endure things as they are;
Possessing a decisive mind;
Being able to courageously accept whatever comes;
Not abandoning or changing teachers;
Finding satisfaction with but few desires;
And being fond of solitude.

Once one's practice accords with all such dharmas, one can then gradually perfect the especially supreme meritorious qualities. It is because these dharmas have not yet become solidly established that they are referred to as "fundamental" practices.²⁵ If one departs from these dharmas, one cannot advance to realization of the superior and sublime qualities. It is because of this that the combination of these fundamental practices and the above eight dharmas constitute the first ground's "provisions."

4. The Meaning of "Thoroughly Making Offerings to all Buddhas"

Now, as for "thoroughly making offerings to all buddhas," this is just like the practice of those bodhisattvas who, in life after life, always make many offerings to all buddhas, doing so in accordance with the Dharma.

Offerings are of two types. The first involves listening well to the Great Vehicle's right Dharma, no matter whether that presentation is extensive or abridged. The second involves such matters as making offerings of the four requisites while providing respectful and reverential service. It is the complete implementation of these two dharmas in making offerings to the Buddhas that qualifies as "thoroughly making offerings to all buddhas."

正體字

023c14 ‖	善知識者。菩薩雖有四種善知識。此中所說能教入大乘。具諸波羅蜜。能令
023c15 ‖	住十地者。所謂諸佛菩薩及諸聲聞。能示
023c16 ‖	教利喜大乘之法令不退轉。守護者。常能
023c17 ‖	慈愍教誨。令得增長善根。是名守護。具足
023c18 ‖	深心者。深樂佛乘無上大乘一切智乘。名
023c19 ‖	為具足深心。問曰。無盡意菩薩。於和合品
023c20 ‖	中。告舍利弗。諸菩薩所有發心皆名深心。
023c21 ‖	從一地至一地故名為趣心。增益功德故
023c22 ‖	名為過心。得無上事故名為[12]頂心。攝取
023c23 ‖	上法故名為上心。現前得諸佛法故名為
023c24 ‖	現前心。集利益法故名為緣心。[13]通達一切
023c25 ‖	法故名為度心。所願不倦故名為決定心。
023c26 ‖	滿所願故名為喜心。身自成辦故名無侶
023c27 ‖	心。離敗壞相故名調和心。無諸惡故名為
023c28 ‖	善心。遠離惡人故名不雜心。以頭施故名
023c29 ‖	難捨心。

简体字

善知识者。菩萨虽有四种善知识。此中所说能教入大乘。具诸波罗蜜。能令住十地者。所谓诸佛菩萨及诸声闻。能示教利喜大乘之法令不退转。守护者。常能慈愍教诲。令得增长善根。是名守护。具足深心者。深乐佛乘无上大乘一切智乘。名为具足深心。问曰。无尽意菩萨。于和合品中。告舍利弗。诸菩萨所有发心皆名深心。从一地至一地故名为趣心。增益功德故名为过心。得无上事故名为顶心。摄取上法故名为上心。现前得诸佛法故名为现前心。集利益法故名为缘心。通达一切法故名为度心。所愿不倦故名为决定心。满所愿故名为喜心。身自成办故名无侣心。离败坏相故名调和心。无诸恶故名为善心。远离恶人故名不杂心。以头施故名难舍心。

5. The Meaning of "Protected by the Good Spiritual Friend"

As for "good spiritual friend," although the bodhisattva has four different types of good spiritual friends, the type that is being referred to here is the one who is able to teach him to enter into the Great Vehicle and to perfect the *pāramitās* while also being able to cause him to dwell on the ten grounds. This refers then specifically to those buddhas, bodhisattvas, and even *śrāvaka* disciples who are able to instruct, benefit, and inspire him with joy in the Great Vehicle Dharma while also preventing him from retreating from it.

"Protecting" refers to [the good spiritual friend's] ability to always maintain kindness and sympathy as he instructs and influences one to increase one's roots of goodness. It is precisely this that is meant by "protection."

6. The Meaning of "Complete Development of Resolute Intentions"

"Complete development of resolute intentions" refers to being deeply delighted in the Buddha Vehicle, the unsurpassable Great Vehicle, the vehicle of all-knowledge. This is what is meant by "completely developing the resolute intentions."

a. Q: Compared to Scripture, Isn't This a Deficient Explanation?

Question: In the "Unity Chapter,"[26] Akṣayamati Bodhisattva tells Śāriputra:

> Every instance of a bodhisattva's production of an intention is a "resolute intention." In proceeding from one ground to another ground, it is known as "the advancing mind." In the increasing of meritorious qualities, it is known as "the excelling mind." In the realization of unsurpassable endeavors, it is known as "the mind of utmost supremacy." In its assimilation of superior dharmas, it is known as "the superior mind."
>
> In its direct manifestation of the acquisition of dharmas of the buddhas, it is known as "the mind of direct manifestation." In its accumulation of beneficial dharmas, it is known as "the mind that engages with conditions." In its penetrating understanding of all dharmas, it is known as "the mind that achieves liberation." In its tireless fulfillment of vows, it is known as "the resolute mind." In its fulfillment of vows, it is known as "the joyful mind."
>
> In its independent achievement of endeavors, it is known as "the unaccompanied mind." In its abandonment of any signs of corruption, it is known as "the well-trained mind." In its freedom from all forms of evil, it is known as "the mind of goodness." In its separating far from evil people, it is known as "the unmixed mind."
>
> In its making a gift even of one's head, it is known as "the mind that relinquishes what is difficult to relinquish." In its rescuing of

正體字

024a01 ‖ 救破戒人故名持難戒心。能[14]受下
024a02 ‖ 劣加惡故名難忍心。得涅槃能捨故名難
024a03 ‖ 精進心。不貪禪故名難禪定心。助道善根
024a04 ‖ 無厭足故名難慧心。能成一切事故。名度
024a05 ‖ 諸行心。智慧善思惟故名離慢大慢我慢心。
024a06 ‖ 不望報故是一切眾生福田心。觀諸佛深
024a07 ‖ 法故名無畏心。不障[1]閡故名增功德心。
024a08 ‖ 常發精進故名無盡心。能荷受重擔故名
024a09 ‖ 不悶心。又深心義者。等念眾生普慈一切。
024a10 ‖ 供養賢善悲念惡人尊敬師長。救無救
024a11 ‖ 者無歸作歸無洲作洲。無究竟者為作
024a12 ‖ 究竟。無有侶者能為作侶。[2]曲人中行[3]於
024a13 ‖ 直心。敗壞人中[4]真正心。諛諂人中行
024a14 ‖ 無諂心。不知恩中行於知恩。不知作中而
024a15 ‖ 行知作。無利益中能行利益。邪眾生中行
024a16 ‖ 於正行。憍慢人中

简体字

救破戒人故名持难戒心。能受下劣加恶故名难忍心。得涅槃能舍故名难精进心。不贪禅故名难禅定心。助道善根无厌足故名难慧心。能成一切事故。名度诸行心。智慧善思惟故名离慢大慢我慢心。不望报故是一切众生福田心。观诸佛深法故名无畏心。不障阂故名增功德心。常发精进故名无尽心。能荷受重担故名不闷心。又深心义者。等念众生普慈一切。供养贤善悲念恶人尊敬师长。救无救者无归作归无洲作洲。无究竟者为作究竟。无有侣者能为作侣。曲人中行于直心。败坏人中行真正心。谀谄人中行无谄心。不知恩中行于知恩。不知作中而行知作。无利益中能行利益。邪众生中行于正行。憍慢人中

persons who have broken precepts, it is known as "the mind that supports those who find difficulty in the precepts." In its enduring of evil inflicted by inferior beings, it is known as "the mind that is patient with what is difficult." In its ability to forgo the realization of nirvāṇa, it is known as "the mind that remains vigorous even when difficult." In its refraining from coveting [states encountered in] *dhyāna*, it is known as "the mind that cultivates *dhyāna* concentration even when it is difficult."

In its insatiable development of the roots of goodness that aid acquisition of the path, it is known as "the mind that maintains wisdom even when it is difficult." In its ability to bring all endeavors to completion, it is known as "the mind that completes all practices." In its skillfulness in carrying on wisdom-based reflection, it is known as "the mind that abandons pride, extreme pride, and pride in oneself."

In its not cherishing any sort of reward, it is known as "the mind that serves as a field of merit for all beings." In its contemplation of the profound dharmas of the Buddhas, it is known as "the fearless mind." In its refraining from obstructionism, it is known as "the mind that increases meritorious qualities." In its constant production of vigor, it is known as "the inexhaustible mind." In its ability to shoulder even heavy burdens, it is known as "the undiscouraged mind."

Moreover, as for the meaning of "the resolute intentions," this refers to [the mind of] one who remains equally mindful of beings and brings forth an all-encompassing kindness for all of them. He makes offerings to those who are worthy and good, is compassionately mindful of evil people, and esteems and reveres teachers and elders.

He rescues those who have no one to rescue them. He serves as a refuge for those who have no refuge. He serves as an island for those who have no island. He serves as the ultimate resort for those who have no last resort. He is able to serve as a companion for those who have no companions.

Even in the midst of those who are devious, he practices the straight mind. Even when among those people who have become corrupted, he practices genuine and correct thought. Even when among those who engage in flattery, his mind is free of flattery.

Among those who are ungrateful, he practices gratitude. Among those who are unaware of how to act, he practices the correct way of acting. Among those who are unbeneficial, he is able to act in a beneficial manner.

正體字

	行無慢行。不隨教中而
024a16 ‖	不慍恚罪眾生中常作守護。眾生所有過不
024a17 ‖	見其失。供養福田隨順教誨受化不難。
024a18 ‖	阿練若處一心精進。不求利養不惜身命。
024a19 ‖	復次內心清淨故無有諂惑。善口業故不自
024a20 ‖	稱歎。知止足故不行威迫。心無垢故行於
024a21 ‖	柔和。集善根故能入生死。為眾生故忍一
024a22 ‖	切苦。菩薩有如是等深心相。[5]故不可窮
024a23 ‖	盡。汝今但說深心相何得不少。答曰。不少
024a24 ‖	也。無盡意。總一切深心相在一處說。而此
024a25 ‖	中分布諸地。此十住經。地地別說深心相。
024a26 ‖	是故菩薩隨諸地中皆得深心深心之義即
024a27 ‖	在其地。今初地中說二深心。一者發大願。
024a28 ‖	二者在必定地。是故當知隨在十地善說
024a29 ‖	深心。汝說何得不少。是事不然。

简体字

行无慢行。不随教中而不慍恚罪众生中常作守护。众生所有过不见其失。供养福田随顺教诲受化不难。阿练若处一心精进。不求利养不惜身命。复次内心清净故无有谄惑。善口业故不自称叹。知止足故不行威迫。心无垢故行于柔和。集善根故能入生死。为众生故忍一切苦。菩萨有如是等深心相。故不可穷尽。汝今但说深心相何得不少。答曰。不少也。无尽意。总一切深心相在一处说。而此中分布诸地。此十住经。地地别说深心相。是故菩萨随诸地中皆得深心深心之义即在其地。今初地中说二深心。一者发大愿。二者在必定地。是故当知随在十地善说深心。汝说何得不少。是事不然。

Among those beings inclined toward deviance, he practices right action. Among arrogant people, he remains free of arrogant behavior. Among those who do not accord with instructions, he does not become resentful or angry. Even among beings who have committed offenses, he always strives to protect them. Even amidst all of the transgressions committed by beings, he refrains from focusing on their faults.

He makes offerings to those who serve as fields of merit, accords with their instructions, and finds no difficulty in accepting their transformative teaching. When dwelling in a forest hermitage,[27] he is single-mindedly vigorous. He does not seek benefits or offerings and does not indulge any stinting attachment to his own body or life.

Moreover, because his mind is inwardly pure, he is free of deceptiveness. Because he practices good verbal karma, he does not praise himself. Because he is readily satisfied, he does not act in an intimidating fashion. Because his mind is free of defilement, he behaves gently and harmoniously. Because he accumulates roots of goodness, he is able to enter the realm of *saṃsāra*. Because he acts for the sake of all beings, he patiently endures all forms of suffering.

The bodhisattva possesses an inexhaustible number of such characteristics associated with resolute intentions.[28]

Now, however, you only present a simple explanation of the characteristics of resolute intentions. How is this not a deficient explanation?

    b. Q: No. Each Ground Involves Specific Resolute Intentions

Response: No, this is not a deficient presentation. Akṣayamati provides in a single place a comprehensive description of all of the characteristics of the resolute intentions. However, here, we are concerned with their distribution as they occur on the various grounds.

This *Ten Grounds Sutra* provides specific explanations of the characteristics of the resolute intentions as they occur on each succeeding ground. Thus the bodhisattva in every case gains realizations of aspects of the resolute intentions in accordance with the particular ground upon which he abides. The meaning of the resolute intentions is defined according to each particular ground.

Now, on the first ground, we describe two types of resolute intention: The first is the one involved in bringing forth great vows. The second is the one involved in dwelling at the stage of certainty.

Therefore one should realize that it is by according with their respective locations on each of the ten grounds that one presents a thorough explanation of [these various aspects of what constitutes] "the resolute intentions." Thus the circumstantial basis of your challenge, "How is this not a deficient presentation?" is incorrect.

正體字

```
             悲心於眾
024b01 ‖ 生者。成就悲故名為悲者。何謂為悲。悼愍
024b02 ‖ 眾生救濟苦難。信解諸上法者。於諸佛法
024b03 ‖ 信力通達。發願我得自度已當度眾生者。
024b04 ‖ 一切[6]諸法願為其本。離願則不成。是故
024b05 ‖ 發願。問曰。何故不言我當度眾生。而言
024b06 ‖ 自得度已當度眾生。答曰。自未得度不
024b07 ‖ 能度彼。如人自沒[7]淤泥。何能拯拔餘人。
024b08 ‖ 又如為水所[8][漂＊寸]不能濟溺。是故說我度
024b09 ‖ 已當度彼。如說。
024b10 ‖   若人自度畏    能度歸依者
024b11 ‖   自未度疑悔    何能度所歸
024b12 ‖   若人自不善    不能令人善
024b13 ‖   若不自寂滅    安能令人寂
```

简体字

悲心于众生者。成就悲故名为悲者。何谓为悲。悼愍众生救济苦难。信解诸上法者。于诸佛法信力通达。发愿我得自度已当度众生者。一切诸法愿为其本。离愿则不成。是故发愿。问曰。何故不言我当度众生。而言自得度已当度众生。答曰。自未得度不能度彼。如人自没淤泥。何能拯拔余人。又如为水所[漂＊寸]不能济溺。是故说我度已当度彼。如说。

　　若人自度畏　　能度归依者
　　自未度疑悔　　何能度所归
　　若人自不善　　不能令人善
　　若不自寂灭　　安能令人寂

7. The Meaning of "Compassionate Mindfulness of Beings"

Now, as for "having become compassionately mindful of beings," it is on the basis of having completely developed compassion that one is referred to as "compassionate." What then is meant by "compassion"? This refers to a feeling of commiseration and pity for beings that also seeks to rescue them from the sufferings associated with their difficulties.

8. The Meaning of "Resolute Faith in the Unsurpassable Dharma"

When it states that "one has resolute faith in supreme dharmas," this means that, with respect to the dharmas of the Buddha, one's power of faith has become completely penetrating.

9. The Meaning of "Bringing Forth the Vow"

As for making the vow in which one resolves, "After I have achieved my own liberation, I shall [return and] liberate beings," this vow is the very origin of all buddhas' Dharma.[29] If one abandons this vow, then one cannot succeed in achieving the realization [of buddhahood]. It is for this reason that one brings forth this vow.

a. Q: Why Do You Say, "After I Have Achieved Liberation"?

Question: Why do you not say, "I shall bring about the liberation of beings," but rather say instead, "After I have achieved my own liberation, I shall then [return and] bring about the liberation of beings"?

b. A: If One is Not Already Liberated, One Cannot Liberate Others

Response: If one has as not yet achieved one's own liberation, one cannot liberate others. This is just as when one has oneself sunken down into the mud. How could one then be able to rescue and extricate anyone else? This is also just as when one has been carried away by floodwaters and is thus incapable of rescuing others from drowning. It is for this reason that it says, "After I have achieved my own liberation, I shall then [return and] liberate others." This is as described in the following verse:

> If a person liberates himself from what is fearsome,
> he can then liberate those who take refuge in him.
> If one has not become liberated from doubt and regret,
> how could he liberate those taking refuge in him?
>
> If a person has not yet become good himself,
> he remains unable to influence others to become good.
> If one has not reached quiescent cessation himself,
> how then could he cause others to reach that quiescence?[30]

正體字

024b14 ‖ 是故先自善寂而後化人。又如法句偈說。
024b15 ‖ 　若能自安身　　在於善處者
024b16 ‖ 　然後安餘人　　自同於所利
024b17 ‖ 凡物皆先自利後能利人。何以故。如說。
024b18 ‖ 　若自成己利　　乃能利於彼
024b19 ‖ 　自捨欲利他　　失利後憂悔
024b20 ‖ 是故說自度已當度眾生。問曰。得何利故
024b21 ‖ 能成此事入必定地。又以何心能發是願。
024b22 ‖ 答曰。得佛十力能成此事。入必定地能發
024b23 ‖ 是願。問曰。何等是佛十力。答曰。佛悉了達
024b24 ‖ 一切法因果名為初力。如實知去來今所
024b25 ‖ 起業果報處名為二力。如實知諸禪定三
024b26 ‖ 昧分別垢淨入出相名為三力。

简体字

是故先自善寂而后化人。又如法句偈说。
　若能自安身　　在于善处者
　然后安余人　　自同于所利
凡物皆先自利后能利人。何以故。如说。
　若自成己利　　乃能利于彼
　自舍欲利他　　失利后忧悔
是故说自度已当度众生。问曰。得何利故能成此事入必定地。又以何心能发是愿。答曰。得佛十力能成此事。入必定地能发是愿。问曰。何等是佛十力。答曰。佛悉了达一切法因果名为初力。如实知去来今所起业果报处名为二力。如实知诸禅定三昧分别垢净入出相名为三力。

Chapter 2 — *Entering the First Ground*

Therefore one first becomes thoroughly quiescent oneself and then later takes up the transformative teaching of others. This is also just as described in a verse from the *Dharmapada*:

> If one is able to establish himself
> in the station of what is good,
> afterward, one is able to establish other people
> in that same benefit that one has gained himself.³¹

It is commonly the case that beings first benefit themselves and only afterward are able to benefit others. And why is this? This is as described in the following verse:

> If one accomplishes one's own self-benefit,
> only then is one able to benefit others.
> If one forsakes oneself wishing to benefit others,
> one fails to be beneficial and later feels distress and regret.

It is for this reason that [the preceding verse] reads, "After I have achieved my own liberation, I shall [return and] liberate beings."

  c. Q: For What Sort of Benefit and with What Sort of Resolve?

Question: It is in order to acquire what sort of benefit is it that one becomes able to accomplish this endeavor and enter the stage of certainty? Also, with what sort of resolve does one become able to bring forth this vow?

  d. A: To Gain the Ten Powers and Enter the Stage of Certainty

Response: It is in order to acquire a buddha's ten powers that one becomes able to accomplishes this endeavor and it is in order to enter the stage of certainty that one becomes able to bring forth this vow.

  1) Q: What Are the Ten Powers?

Question: What then are the ten powers of a buddha?

  2) A: They Are as Follows

Response: [As for the ten powers, they are as follows]:³²

> The Buddha possesses a completely penetrating comprehension of the causes and effects involved in all dharmas. This is the first power.
> He knows in accordance with reality the past, future, and present stations wherein one creates karma and undergoes retribution as the effect. This is the second power.
> He knows in accordance with reality the characteristic aspects of all *dhyāna* absorptions and samādhis, their distinctions, their defilement and purity, and their entry and emergence. This is the third power.

正體字

如實知眾
024b27 ‖ 生諸根利鈍名為四力。如實知眾生所樂
024b28 ‖ 不同名為五力。如實知世間種種異性名
024b29 ‖ 為六力。如實知至一切處道名為七力。如
024c01 ‖ 實知宿命事名為八力。如實知生死事名
024c02 ‖ 為九力。如實知漏盡事。名為十力。為得
024c03 ‖ [9]如是佛十力故。大心發願即入必定聚。問
024c04 ‖ 曰。凡初發心皆有如是相耶。答曰。或有人
024c05 ‖ 說。初發心便有如是相。而實不爾。何以故。
024c06 ‖ 是事應分別不應定答。所以者何。一切菩
024c07 ‖ 薩初發心時。不應悉入於必定。或有初發
024c08 ‖ 心時即入必定。或有漸修功德。如釋迦牟
024c09 ‖ 尼佛。初發心時不入必定。後修集功德值
024c10 ‖ 燃燈佛得入必定。是故汝說一切菩薩初
024c11 ‖ 發心便入必定是為邪論。問曰。若是邪論
024c12 ‖ 者。何故汝說以是心入必定。

简体字

如实知众生诸根利钝名为四力。如实知众生所乐不同名为五力。如实知世间种种异性名为六力。如实知至一切处道名为七力。如实知宿命事名为八力。如实知生死事名为九力。如实知漏尽事。名为十力。为得如是佛十力故。大心发愿即入必定聚。问曰。凡初发心皆有如是相耶。答曰。或有人说。初发心便有如是相。而实不尔。何以故。是事应分别不应定答。所以者何。一切菩萨初发心时。不应悉入于必定。或有初发心时即入必定。或有渐修功德。如释迦牟尼佛。初发心时不入必定。后修集功德值燃灯佛得入必定。是故汝说一切菩萨初发心便入必定是为邪论。问曰。若是邪论者。何故汝说以是心入必定。

He knows in accordance with reality the relative sharpness or dullness of all faculties possessed by beings. This is the fourth power.

He knows in accordance with reality the differences among beings' inclinations. This is the fifth power.

He knows in accordance with reality all of the world's many different sorts of realms.³³ This is the sixth power.

He knows in accordance with reality the paths that lead to all destinations. This is the seventh power.

He knows in accordance with reality all the circumstances of previous lives. This is the eighth power.

He knows in accordance with reality all circumstances involved in all births and deaths. This is the ninth power.

He knows in accordance with reality the matter of the cessation of the contaminants. This is the tenth power.

3) To Gain The Powers, One Makes the Vow and Becomes Irreversible

For the sake of acquiring ten powers of the buddha such as these, one brings forth the vow with great resolve and then directly enters the group of those who have reached the stage of certainty.

a) Q: Does Everyone Then Reach the Stage of Certainty?

Question: Is it generally so of everyone that, once they first bring forth the resolve, they then possess such a characteristic?

b) A: Some Do; Some Do Not

Response: There may be some people who claim that, when one first brings forth the resolve, one then possesses such a characteristic. However, this is not actually the case. And why is this? This is a situation in which one should make distinctions. One should not set forth a fixed answer to this. Why? It should not be the case that, when all bodhisattvas first bring forth the resolve, they all then enter the stage of certainty.

In some cases, on first bringing forth the resolve, one *does* immediately enter the stage of certainty. In some cases, however, one gradually cultivates meritorious qualities. Take for example Śākyamuni Buddha. When he first brought forth the resolve, he did not immediately enter the stage of certainty. Rather, it was only after he had accumulated meritorious qualities and encountered Burning Lamp Buddha that he then entered the stage of certainty. Therefore, if you were to assert that all bodhisattvas directly enter the stage of certainty upon first generating the resolve, that would be an erroneous theory.

4) Q: If Some Do Not, Why Claim Certainty Relies on Resolve?

Question: If it is an erroneous theory, why do you claim that it is in reliance upon this resolve that one enters the stage of certainty?

正體字	答曰。有菩 024c13 ‖ 薩初發心即入必定。以是心能得初地。因 024c14 ‖ 是人故說初發心入必定中。問曰。是菩薩 024c15 ‖ 初心。釋迦牟尼佛初發心。是心云何。答曰。是 024c16 ‖ 心不雜一切煩惱。是心相續不貪異乘。是 024c17 ‖ 心堅牢一切外道無能勝者。是心一切眾魔 024c18 ‖ 不能破壞。是心為常能集善根。是心能知 024c19 ‖ 有為無[10]常。是心無動能攝佛法。是心無覆 024c20 ‖ 離諸邪行。是心安住不可動故。是心無比 024c21 ‖ 無相違故。是心如金剛通達諸法故。是心 024c22 ‖ 不盡集無[11]盡福德故。是心平等等一切眾 024c23 ‖ 生故。是心無高下無差別故。是心清淨性 024c24 ‖ 無垢故。是心離垢慧炤明故。是心無[12]垢不 024c25 ‖ 捨深心故。是心為廣慈如虛空故。是心為 024c26 ‖ 大受一切眾生故。是心無閡至無障智故。
简体字	答曰。有菩萨初发心即入必定。以是心能得初地。因是人故说初发心入必定中。问曰。是菩萨初心。释迦牟尼佛初发心。是心云何。答曰。是心不杂一切烦恼。是心相续不贪异乘。是心坚牢一切外道无能胜者。是心一切众魔不能破坏。是心为常能集善根。是心能知有为无常。是心无动能摄佛法。是心无覆离诸邪行。是心安住不可动故。是心无比无相违故。是心如金刚通达诸法故。是心不尽集无尽福德故。是心平等等一切众生故。是心无高下无差别故。是心清净性无垢故。是心离垢慧昭明故。是心无垢不舍深心故。是心为广慈如虚空故。是心为大受一切众生故。是心无阂至无障智故。

Chapter 2 — *Entering the First Ground*

5) A: Because This Is True of Some Bodhisattvas

Response: There are in fact bodhisattvas who, on first generating the resolve, then immediately gain entry into the stage of certainty. In such a case, it *is* in reliance upon this resolve that they become able to gain the first ground. It is on account of this particular category of persons that it is said that, on first generating the resolve, one may then immediately enter the stage of certainty.

a) Q: What is the Nature of This Initial Resolve?

Question: What is the nature of these bodhisattvas' initial resolve and Śākyamuni Buddha's initial generation of the resolve?

b) A: The Initial Resolve Is Characterized by These 41 Aspects

Response:
This resolve is not admixed with any of the afflictions;
This resolve is continuous and does not wish for any other vehicle;
This resolve is solid and cannot be overcome by any non-Buddhist;
This resolve cannot be destroyed by any of the many sorts of *māras*;
This resolve is always able to accumulate roots of goodness;
This resolve is able to know the impermanence of all conditioned things;
This resolve, even while remaining unmoving, is able to accumulate the dharmas of a buddha;
This resolve is free of hindrances and abandons all wrong actions;
This resolve is established in stability because it is unshakable;
This resolve is peerless because it remains free of contradictions;
This resolve is like vajra because it possesses a penetrating comprehension of all dharmas;
This resolve is inexhaustible because it accumulates an inexhaustible amount of merit;
This resolve regards others equally because it sees all beings as equal;
This resolve remains free of "high" or "low" due to making no discriminations;
This resolve is pure because, by nature, it is free of defilement;
This resolve is stainless because its intelligence is characterized by radiant illumination;
This resolve remains free of defilement because it never relinquishes its resolute intentions;
This resolve is vast because its kindness is as expansive as empty space;
This resolve is magnanimous because it takes in all beings;
This resolve is unobstructed because it has arrived at unimpeded wisdom;

正體字	024c27 ‖ 是心遍到不斷大悲故。是心不斷能正迴 024c28 ‖ [13]向故。是心眾所趣向。智者所讚故。是心可 024c29 ‖ 觀小乘瞻仰故。是心難見。一切眾生不能 025a01 ‖ 覩故。是心難破能善入佛法故。是心為住 025a02 ‖ 一切樂具所住處故。是心莊嚴福德資用故。 025a03 ‖ 是心選擇智慧資用故。是心淳厚以布施為 025a04 ‖ 資用故。是心大願持戒資用故。是心難沮忍 025a05 ‖ 辱資用故。是心難勝精進資用故。是心寂滅 025a06 ‖ 禪定資用故。是心無惱害[1]慧資用故。是心 025a07 ‖ 無瞋閡慈心深故。是心根深悲心厚故。是心 025a08 ‖ 悅樂喜心厚故。是心苦樂不動捨心厚故。是 025a09 ‖ 心護念諸佛神力故。是心相續三寶不斷故。
简体字	是心遍到不断大悲故。是心不断能正回向故。是心众所趣向。智者所赞故。是心可观小乘瞻仰故。是心难见。一切众生不能睹故。是心难破能善入佛法故。是心为住一切乐具所住处故。是心庄严福德资用故。是心选择智慧资用故。是心淳厚以布施为资用故。是心大愿持戒资用故。是心难沮忍辱资用故。是心难胜精进资用故。是心寂灭禅定资用故。是心无恼害慧资用故。是心无瞋阂慈心深故。是心根深悲心厚故。是心悦乐喜心厚故。是心苦乐不动舍心厚故。是心护念诸佛神力故。是心相续三宝不断故。

Chapter 2 — *Entering the First Ground*

This resolve is universal in its reach because it never cuts off its great compassion;

This resolve is never cut off because it is able to practice correct dedication of merit;

This resolve is that toward which the multitude proceeds because it is praised by the wise;

This resolve is a fit object of admiring regard because even adherents of the Small Vehicle look up to it;

This resolve is difficult to observe, because no being is able to see it;

This resolve is difficult to destroy because it has been able to skillfully enter the Dharma of the Buddha;

This resolve serves as a dwelling because it is the place in which all sources of happiness abide;

This resolve is adorned because it possesses the provision of merit;

This resolve is skillfully selective because it possesses the provision of wisdom;

This resolve is completely generous because it takes giving as one of the provisions;[34]

This resolve is attended by great vows because it possesses the provision of moral virtue;

This resolve is difficult to hinder because it possesses the provision of patience;

This resolve is difficult to overcome because it possesses the provision of vigor;

This resolve is quiescent because it possesses the provision of *dhyāna* absorption;

This resolve is harmless because it possesses the provision of wisdom;

This resolve remains unimpeded by hatred because its mind of kindness is deeply seated;[35]

This resolve is deeply rooted because its mind of compassion is fully established;

This resolve abides in happiness because its mind of sympathetic joy is fully established;

This resolve is unmoved by either pain or pleasure because its mind of equanimity is fully established;

This resolve is the object of protective mindfulness because of the spiritual power of the Buddhas;

This resolve remains continuous because the lineage of the Three Jewels remains unsevered.

正體字

025a10 ‖	如是等無量功德莊嚴初必定心。如無盡意
025a11 ‖	品中廣說。是心不雜一切煩惱者。見諦思
025a12 ‖	惟所斷二百九十四煩惱不與心和合故名
025a13 ‖	為不雜。是心相續不貪異乘者。從初心相
025a14 ‖	續來。不貪聲聞辟支佛乘。但為阿耨多羅
025a15 ‖	三藐三菩提故。名為相續不貪異乘。如是
025a16 ‖	等四十句論。應如是知。問曰。汝說是心常。
025a17 ‖	一切有為法皆無常。如法印經中說。行者觀
025a18 ‖	世間空無有常而不變壞。是事何得不相
025a19 ‖	違耶。答曰。汝於是義不得正理故作此
025a20 ‖	難。是中不說心為常。此中雖口說常。常義
025a21 ‖	名必定初心生必能常集諸善根不休不
025a22 ‖	息故名為常。生如來家者。如來家則是佛
025a23 ‖	家。如來者。

简体字

如是等无量功德庄严初必定心。如无尽意品中广说。是心不杂一切烦恼者。见谛思惟所断二百九十四烦恼不与心和合故名为不杂。是心相续不贪异乘者。从初心相续来。不贪声闻辟支佛乘。但为阿耨多罗三藐三菩提故。名为相续不贪异乘。如是等四十句论。应如是知。问曰。汝说是心常。一切有为法皆无常。如法印经中说。行者观世间空无有常而不变坏。是事何得不相违耶。答曰。汝于是义不得正理故作此难。是中不说心为常。此中虽口说常。常义名必定初心生必能常集诸善根不休不息故名为常。生如来家者。如来家则是佛家。如来者。

Countless meritorious qualities such as these adorn the initial resolve of those who abide in the stage of certainty. This is as extensively described in the Akṣayamati Chapter.³⁶

    i) THE MEANING OF "NOT ADMIXED WITH AFFLICTIONS"

"This resolve is not admixed with any of the afflictions" refers to the resolve not being conjoined with any of the two hundred and ninety-four afflictions cut off on the path of seeing the truths (*darśana-mārga*) and on the path of meditation (*bhāvana-mārga*). Hence it is said that "it is not admixed."

    ii) THE MEANING OF "CONTINUOUS, NOT WISHING FOR OTHER VEHICLES"

As for "this resolve is continuous and does not wish for any other vehicle," as it continues forth from the initial production of the resolve, it does not wish for the vehicles of the *śrāvaka* disciples or the *pratyeka-buddha*s. It is because one remains motivated solely by the goal of reaching *anuttarasamyaksaṃbodhi* that it is referred to as "continuous" and as "not wishing for any other vehicle."

One should understand this forty-statement discussion in this manner.

    (1) Q: DOESN'T "PERMANENCE" OF RESOLVE CONTRADICT DHARMA?

Question: You are asserting that this resolve is permanently enduring. However, all conditioned dharmas are impermanent. This is as explained in the *Seals of the Dharma Sutra* wherein it states that the practitioner is to contemplate the world as empty, as devoid of anything that is permanent, and as containing nothing not subject to destruction. How then does this matter not involve a contradiction?

    (2) A: YOU MISUNDERSTAND THE CONCEPT

Response: You pose this challenge because you fail to grasp the correct principle of this concept. It is not the case that any claim is being made herein for "permanency" of resolve. Although we spoke of constancy here, this was merely a reference to the fact that one who has initially generated the resolve and reached the stage of certainty is definitely "always able to accumulate roots of goodness." It is because one does not rest and does not desist from doing this that we refer here to such constancy.

    10. THE MEANING OF "BIRTH IN THE FAMILY OF THE TATHĀGATAS"
      a. THE MEANING OF "TATHĀGATA"

[Returning again to the verses],³⁷ as for "being born into the family of the Tathāgatas," "the family of the Tathāgatas" is the family of the Buddhas. In "the Tathāgatas," (lit. "the Thus Come Ones"), the "thus"

正體字

025a24 ‖ 如名為實。來名為至。至真實中
025a24 ‖ 故名為如來。何等[2]為真實所謂涅槃。不虛
025a25 ‖ 誑故是名如實。如經中說。佛告比丘。第一
025a26 ‖ 聖諦無有虛誑涅槃是也。復次如名不壞
025a27 ‖ 相。所謂諸法實相是。來名智慧。到實相中
025a28 ‖ 通達其義故名為如來。復次空無相無作名
025a29 ‖ 為如。諸佛來至三解脫門。亦令眾生到此
025b01 ‖ 門故。名為如來。復次如名四諦。以一切種
025b02 ‖ 見四諦故名為如來。復次如名六波羅蜜
025b03 ‖ 所謂布施持戒忍辱精進禪定智慧。以是六
025b04 ‖ 法來至佛地故名為如來。復次諦捨滅慧四
025b05 ‖ 功德處。名為如[3]來。以是四法來至佛地
025b06 ‖ 故名為如來。復次一切佛法名為如。[4]是如
025b07 ‖ 來至諸佛故。名為如來。復次一切菩薩地
025b08 ‖ 喜淨明炎難勝現前深遠不動善慧法雲名為
025b09 ‖ 如。諸菩薩以

简体字

如名为实。来名为至。至真实中故名为如来。何等为真实所谓涅槃。不虚誑故是名如实。如经中说。佛告比丘。第一圣谛无有虚誑涅槃是也。复次如名不坏相。所谓诸法实相是。来名智慧。到实相中通达其义故名为如来。复次空无相无作名为如。诸佛来至三解脱门。亦令众生到此门故。名为如来。复次如名四谛。以一切种见四谛故名为如来。复次如名六波罗蜜所谓布施持戒忍辱精进禅定智慧。以是六法来至佛地故名为如来。复次谛舍灭慧四功德处。名为如来。以是四法来至佛地故名为如来。复次一切佛法名为如。是如来至诸佛故。名为如来。复次一切菩萨地喜净明炎难胜现前深远不动善慧法云名为如。诸菩萨以

(*tathatā*) is a reference to reality whereas the "come" (*āgata*) is a reference to the ultimate point that is reached. It is because they have arrived at genuine reality that they are referred to as "Thus Come Ones."

What then is it that constitutes "genuine reality"? It is what is referred to as "nirvāṇa." It is because it involves no falseness or deceptiveness that this is referred to as "according with reality." This is as explained in the sutra where the Buddha tells a bhikshu, "The foremost among the truths of the Āryas is free of deceptiveness. This is nirvāṇa."[38]

Additionally, "thus" is a reference to being characterized by indestructibility. It is a reference to the so-called "true character of dharmas." "Come" is a reference to wisdom. One is referred to as a "Thus Come One" because, having arrived in the realm of the true character of dharmas, one possesses a penetrating comprehension of its meaning.

Also, it is emptiness, signlessness, and wishlessness that qualify as being "thus." When the Buddhas "come," they have arrived at these three gates of liberation while also then being able to cause beings to reach these gates. They are therefore referred to as "the Thus Come Ones."

Furthermore, "thus" is a reference to the four truths. It is because they see the four truths in all their modes that they are referred to as "the Thus Come Ones."

Moreover, "thus" refers to the six *pāramitās*, namely: giving, moral virtue, patience, vigor, *dhyāna* concentration, and wisdom. It is because they utilize these six dharmas to "come" and arrive at the ground of buddhahood that they are referred to as "the Thus Come Ones."

Additionally, it is in reference to their possession of the four bases of meritorious qualities consisting of truth, relinquishment, quiescence, and wisdom that they are referred to as "the Thus Come Ones." It is because they utilize these four dharmas to "come" and arrive at the ground of buddhahood that they are referred to as "the Thus Come Ones."

Also, all of the dharmas of a buddha are synonymous with "suchness" [and hence are "thus"]. It is because this suchness "comes forth" and extends to all buddhas that they are referred to as "the Thus Come Ones."

Then again, all of the bodhisattva grounds including the grounds of "Joyfulness," "Stainlessness," "Shining Light," "Blazing Brilliance," "Difficult-to-Conquer," "Direct Presence," "Far-Reaching," "Immovability," "Excellent Intelligence," and "Dharma Cloud" are synonymous with "suchness" (*tathatā*). It is because the bodhisattvas

正體字

```
         是十地來至阿耨多羅三藐
025b10 ‖ 三菩提故名為如來。又以如實八聖道分
025b11 ‖ 來故名為如來。復次權智二足來至佛故名
025b12 ‖ 為如來。如去不還故名為如來。如來者。所
025b13 ‖ 謂十方三世諸佛是。是諸佛家名為如來家。
025b14 ‖ 今是菩薩行如來道。相續不斷故名為生
025b15 ‖ 如來家。又是菩薩必成如來故。名為生如
025b16 ‖ 來家。譬如生轉輪聖王家有轉輪聖王相。
025b17 ‖ 是人必作轉輪聖王。是菩薩亦如是生如來
025b18 ‖ 家。發是心故必成如來。是名生如來家。如
025b19 ‖ 來家者。有人言。是四功德處所謂諦捨滅慧。
025b20 ‖ 諸如來從此中生故。名為如來家。有人言。
025b21 ‖ 般若波羅蜜及方便。是如來家。如助道經中
025b22 ‖ 說。
025b23 ‖    智度無極母    善權方便父
025b24 ‖    生故名為父    養育故名母
```

简体字

是十地来至阿耨多罗三藐三菩提故名为如来。又以如实八圣道分来故名为如来。复次权智二足来至佛故名为如来。如去不还故名为如来。如来者。所谓十方三世诸佛是。是诸佛家名为如来家。今是菩萨行如来道。相续不断故名为生如来家。又是菩萨必成如来故。名为生如来家。譬如生转轮圣王家有转轮圣王相。是人必作转轮圣王。是菩萨亦如是生如来家。发是心故必成如来。是名生如来家。如来家者。有人言。是四功德处所谓谛舍灭慧。诸如来从此中生故。名为如来家。有人言。般若波罗蜜及方便。是如来家。如助道经中说。

　　智度无极母　　善权方便父
　　生故名为父　　养育故名母

"come" and arrive at *anuttarasamyaksaṃbodhi* by way of these ten grounds that they are therefore known as "*Thus* Come Ones" (*tathāgata*).

Additionally, it is because they "come forth" by the eightfold path of the Āryas that accords with reality that they are referred to as "Thus Come Ones."

Also, it is because they "come forth" and arrive at buddhahood on the two "feet" of provisional means and wisdom that they are referred to as the "Thus Come Ones."

And it is because they went forth in "suchness," never to return again that they are referred to as "the Thus Gone Ones."

b. The Meaning of "the Family of the Tathāgatas"

"Tathāgatas" is a reference to all buddhas throughout the ten directions and the three periods of time. It is the family consisting of all of these buddhas that is referred to as the "the family of the Tathāgatas." It is because these bodhisattvas now travel along the path of the Tathāgatas and do so continuously and unceasingly that one speaks of their "birth into the family of the Tathāgatas."

Furthermore, it is because these bodhisattvas are certainly bound to become *tathāgatas* that one refers to their "birth into the family of the Tathāgatas." This is just as when someone possessed of the marks of a wheel-turning king is born into the family of a wheel-turning king. This person will certainly become a wheel-turning king. So too it is in the case of these bodhisattvas who, in this same way, are born into the family of the Tathāgatas. It is because they have brought forth this resolve that they will certainly become *tathāgatas*. This is what is meant by "birth into the family of the Tathāgatas."

Now, as for "the family of the Tathāgatas," there are those who assert that this is a reference to the four bases of meritorious qualities, namely truth, relinquishment, quiescence, and wisdom. It is because all of *tathāgatas* are born from these factors that they are collectively referred to as "the family of the Tathāgatas."

Then again, there are those who assert that it is based on *prajñāpāramitā* and skillful means that this is known as "the family of the Tathāgatas." This accords with the *Sutra on the Factors Assisting the Path* wherein it states:

> The perfection of wisdom is the peerless mother
> and it is skillful means that serves as the father.
> It is due to the act of begetting that one is known as a father,
> and due to raising and nourishing that one is known as a mother.

正體字

025b25 ‖ 一切世間以父母為家。是二似父母故名
025b26 ‖ 之為家。有人言。善慧名諸佛家。從是二法
025b27 ‖ 出生諸佛。是二則是一切善法之根本。如經
025b28 ‖ 中說。是二法俱行能成正法。善是父慧是母。
025b29 ‖ 是二和合名為諸佛家。如說。
025c01 ‖ 　　菩薩善法父　　智慧以為母
025c02 ‖ 　　一切諸如來　　皆從是二生
025c03 ‖ 有人言。般舟三昧及大悲名諸佛家。從此二
025c04 ‖ 法生諸如來。此中般舟三昧為父。大悲為
025c05 ‖ 母。復次般舟三昧是父。無生法忍是母。如
025c06 ‖ 助菩提中說。
025c07 ‖ 　　般舟三昧父　　大悲無生母
025c08 ‖ 　　一切諸如來　　從是二法生
025c09 ‖ 家無過咎者。家清淨故。清淨者。六波羅蜜
025c10 ‖ 四功德處方便般若波羅蜜善慧般舟三昧大
025c11 ‖ 悲諸忍。是諸法清淨無有過故名家清淨。
025c12 ‖ 是菩薩以此諸法為家故無有過咎。

简体字

一切世间以父母为家。是二似父母故名之为家。有人言。善慧名诸佛家。从是二法出生诸佛。是二则是一切善法之根本。如经中说。是二法俱行能成正法。善是父慧是母。是二和合名为诸佛家。如说。

　　菩萨善法父　　智慧以为母
　　一切诸如来　　皆从是二生

有人言。般舟三昧及大悲名诸佛家。从此二法生诸如来。此中般舟三昧为父。大悲为母。复次般舟三昧是父。无生法忍是母。如助菩提中说。

　　般舟三昧父　　大悲无生母
　　一切诸如来　　从是二法生

家无过咎者。家清净故。清净者。六波罗蜜四功德处方便般若波罗蜜善慧般舟三昧大悲诸忍。是诸法清净无有过故名家清净。是菩萨以此诸法为家故无有过咎。

Chapter 2 — *Entering the First Ground*

Throughout the world, it is the father and mother that are taken as the basis of the family. It is because these two factors are analogous to a father and mother that they are referred to as the "family."

There are also those persons who claim that goodness and wisdom are what constitute the family of the Buddhas. It is from these two dharmas that the Buddhas are born. This being the case, these two then constitute the very root of all good dharmas.

This accords with a statement in the scriptures that states, "When these two are practiced to completion, one becomes able to realize right Dharma. Goodness is the father and wisdom is the mother. It is with the coming together of these two that one then refers to 'the family of the Buddhas.'" This is as explained in the following verse:

> A bodhisattva takes the dharma of goodness as his father
> and takes wisdom as his mother.
> Every single one of the Tathāgatas
> is in every case born from these two.

There are yet others who claim that the *pratyutpanna* samādhi[39] and the great compassion constitute the family of the Buddhas and that it is from these two dharmas that all *tathāgatas* are born. Of these two, it is the *pratyutpanna* samādhi that serves as the father and the great compassion that serves as the mother.

Then again, one may say that the *pratyutpanna* samādhi serves as the father whereas it is the unproduced-dharmas patience that serves as the mother. This accords with a verse from the *Bodhisaṃbhāra [Śāstra]* that states:

> It is the *pratyutpanna* samādhi that serves as father.
> Great compassion and the unproduced [patience] serve as mother.
> Every single one of the Tathāgatas
> is born from these two dharmas.[40]

c. The Meaning of "Having No Transgressions or Faults," etc.

[Returning to the "grounds-entry" verse], as for "the family [of the Tathāgatas] having no transgressions or faults,"[41] this is because that family is pure. "Purity" here refers to the six *pāramitās*, the four bases of meritorious qualities,[42] skillful means, *prajñāpāramitā*, goodness, wisdom, the *pratyutpanna* samādhi, the great compassion, and all of the forms of patient acquiescence. It is because all of these dharmas are themselves pure and "free of any transgressions or faults" that one then refers to the "family" itself as "pure." It is because these bodhisattvas take these dharmas as the basis of their "family" that they qualify as being "free of any transgressions or faults."

正體字

轉於
025c13 ‖ 過咎轉於世間道入出世上道者。世間道
025c14 ‖ 名即是凡夫所行道轉名休息。凡夫道者不
025c15 ‖ 能究竟至涅槃常往來生死。是名凡夫道。
025c16 ‖ 出世間者。因是道得出三界故名[5]世間
025c17 ‖ 道。上者妙故名為上。入者正行道故名為
025c18 ‖ 入。以是心入初地名歡喜地。問曰。初地
025c19 ‖ 何故名為歡喜。答曰。
025c20 ‖ 　　如得於初果　　究竟至涅槃
025c21 ‖ 　　菩薩得是地　　心常多歡喜
025c22 ‖ 　　自然得增長　　諸佛如來種
025c23 ‖ 　　是故如此人　　得名賢善者
025c24 ‖ [6]如得初果者。如人得須陀洹[7]道。善閉三
025c25 ‖ 惡道門。見法入法得法。住堅牢法不可
025c26 ‖ 傾動。究竟至涅槃。斷見諦所斷法故心大
025c27 ‖ 歡喜。設使睡眠嬾[8]惰不至二十九有。

简体字

转于过咎转于世间道入出世上道者。世间道名即是凡夫所行道转名休息。凡夫道者不能究竟至涅槃常往来生死。是名凡夫道。出世间者。因是道得出三界故名世间道。上者妙故名为上。入者正行道故名为入。以是心入初地名欢喜地。问曰。初地何故名为欢喜。答曰。

　　如得于初果　　究竟至涅槃
　　菩萨得是地　　心常多欢喜
　　自然得增长　　诸佛如来种
　　是故如此人　　得名贤善者

如得初果者。如人得须陀洹道。善闭三恶道门。见法入法得法。住坚牢法不可倾动。究竟至涅槃。断见谛所断法故心大欢喜。设使睡眠懒惰不至二十九有。

They turn away from transgressions and faults. As for their "turning away from the worldly path and entering the supreme world-transcending path," this reference to "the worldly path" is just a reference to that very path in which common people course. "Turning away" refers to "desisting." As for the path of the common person, it is unable to ultimately take one to nirvāṇa, for one is bound therein to always come and go in *saṃsāra*. This is what is meant by "the path of the common person."

As for "world-transcendence," it is by virtue of the fact that, in reliance upon this path, one then succeeds in escaping from the three realms that it is therefore referred to as "the supreme world-transcending path."[43]

As for [that path being described in the verse as] "supreme," it is because it is sublime that one refers to it as supreme. As for "entering" [the supreme path], it is because one engages in right practice of the path that reference is made to "entering." It is in reliance upon this resolve that one enters the first ground, the ground referred to as "the Ground of Joyfulness."

  d. Q: WHY IS THE FIRST GROUND SAID TO BE "JOYFUL"?

Question: Why is it that the first ground is said to be characterized by "joyfulness"?

  e. A: BECAUSE OF THE IMMENSE SIGNIFICANCE OF THE FIRST GROUND

Response:

> It is just as with one who gains the first fruit
> and who is then ultimately bound to reach nirvāṇa.
> When the bodhisattva gains this ground,
> his mind is always abundantly joyful.
>
> He then naturally succeeds in extending
> the lineage of all the Buddhas, the Tathāgatas.
> It is for this reason that a person such as this
> acquires the designation as "one who is worthy and good."

As for its being "just as with one who gains the first fruit," this means that it is just as when someone gains the path of a stream enterer.[44] He succeeds thereby in completely shutting the gates leading to the three wretched destinies.[45] He has seen the Dharma, entered the Dharma, and gained the Dharma. He abides unshakably in the dharma of stability and is ultimately bound to reach nirvāṇa. Because he has severed the dharmas that are severed at the point of seeing the truths, his mind is filled with immense joyfulness, [for he realizes then that], even if he were to fall asleep or become indolent, he could not stray into some twenty-ninth realm of existence.[46]

正體字

025c28 ‖ 如以一毛為百分。以一分毛分取大海水若二
025c29 ‖ 三[9]渧。苦已滅者如大海水。餘未滅者如二
026a01 ‖ 三渧。心大歡喜。菩薩如是得初地已。名生
026a02 ‖ 如來家。一切天龍夜叉乾闥婆阿修羅迦樓
026a03 ‖ 羅緊那羅摩睺羅伽天王梵王沙門婆羅門一
026a04 ‖ 切聲聞辟支佛等所共供養恭敬。何以故。是
026a05 ‖ 家無有過咎故。轉世間道入出世間道。
026a06 ‖ 但樂敬佛得四功德處得六波羅蜜果報滋
026a07 ‖ 味。不斷諸佛種故心大歡喜。是菩薩所有
026a08 ‖ 餘苦如二三水渧。雖百千億劫得阿耨多羅
026a09 ‖ 三藐三菩提。於無始生死苦。如二三水渧。
026a10 ‖ 所可滅苦如大海水。是故此地名為歡喜。
026a11 ‖ 十住毘婆沙論卷第一

简体字

如以一毛为百分。以一分毛分取大海水若二三渧。苦已灭者如大海水。余未灭者如二三渧。心大欢喜。菩萨如是得初地已。名生如来家。一切天龙夜叉乾闼婆阿修罗迦楼罗紧那罗摩睺罗伽天王梵王沙门婆罗门一切声闻辟支佛等所共供养恭敬。何以故。是家无有过咎故。转世间道入出世间道。但乐敬佛得四功德处得六波罗蜜果报滋味。不断诸佛种故心大欢喜。是菩萨所有余苦如二三水渧。虽百千亿劫得阿耨多罗三藐三菩提。于无始生死苦。如二三水渧。所可灭苦如大海水。是故此地名为欢喜。

[This first ground bodhisattva's circumstance] is also analogous to that of someone who has sliced a single hair into a hundred parts and then used but a single one of those hair segments to draw forth two or three drops from the great ocean's waters. [He realizes that] the suffering already brought to an end at this point is comparable to all of the waters of the great ocean, whereas what has not yet been brought to an end is comparable only to those two or three drops. [Because he realizes this], his mind is filled with great joyfulness.

After the bodhisattva has thus gained the first ground, he is then known as one who has been "born into the family of the Tathāgatas." At this point, he becomes one worthy of offerings and reverence from all devas, dragons, *yakṣas, gandharvas, asuras, garuḍas, kinnaras, mahorāgas*, deva kings, Brahmā, kings, *śramaṇas*, the brahmans, all *śrāvaka* disciples, *pratyekabuddhas*, and others. Why? It is because his family is one that is free of any transgressions or faults.

He then "turns away from the worldly path and enters the world-transcending path." He then only delights in revering the Buddhas, in establishing himself in the four bases of meritorious qualities, and in gaining the flavor of the six *pāramitās*. Because he has prevented the severance of the lineage of all buddhas, his mind is filled with great joyfulness.

The entire quantity of this bodhisattva's remaining suffering is comparable to but two or three drops of water. Then, although there might remain a hundred thousand *koṭis* of kalpas before he gains *anuttarasamyaksaṃbodhi*, still, his remaining suffering is only like two or three drops of water when compared to that great ocean of suffering that he has already successfully brought to an end, namely that suffering that he has endured throughout beginningless lifetimes in *saṃsāra*. It is for these reasons that this ground is known as "the Ground of Joyfulness."

The End of Chapter Two

正體字

026a13 ‖ 十住毘婆沙論卷第二　026a14 ‖
026a15 ‖ [*]聖者龍樹造　026a16 ‖[*]後秦龜茲國三藏鳩摩羅什譯
026a17 ‖ 　　地相品第三
026a18 ‖ 問曰。得初地菩薩有何相貌。答曰。
026a19 ‖ 　菩薩在初地　　多所能堪受
026a20 ‖ 　不好於諍訟　　其心多喜悅
026a21 ‖ 　常樂於清淨　　悲心愍眾生
026a22 ‖ 　無有瞋恚心　　多行是七事
026a23 ‖ 菩薩若得初地。即有是七相。能堪受者。能
026a24 ‖ 為難事修集無量福德善根。於無量恒河
026a25 ‖ 沙劫往來生死。教堅心難化惡眾生。心不
026a26 ‖ 退沒。能堪受如是等事故名為堪忍。無諍
026a27 ‖ 訟者。雖能成大事而不與人諍競。共相違
026a28 ‖ 返。喜者。能令身得柔軟心得安隱。悅者於
026a29 ‖ 轉上法中心得踊悅。清淨者。離諸煩惱垢
026b01 ‖ 濁。有人言。信解名為清淨。有人言。堅固信
026b02 ‖ 名為清淨。

简体字

十住毗婆沙论卷第二
地相品第三

　　问曰。得初地菩萨有何相貌。答曰。
　菩萨在初地　　多所能堪受
　不好于诤讼　　其心多喜悦
　常乐于清净　　悲心愍众生
　无有嗔恚心　　多行是七事
菩萨若得初地。即有是七相。能堪受者。能为难事修集无量福德善根。于无量恒河沙劫往来生死。教坚心难化恶众生。心不退没。能堪受如是等事故名为堪忍。无诤讼者。虽能成大事而不与人诤竞。共相违返。喜者。能令身得柔软心得安隐。悦者于转上法中心得踊悦。清净者。离诸烦恼垢浊。有人言。信解名为清净。

Chapter 3
The Characteristics of the Ground

III. Chapter Three: The Characteristics of the Ground
   A. Q: What Are the Characteristics of the First Ground Bodhisattva?

Question: What are the characteristics of the bodhisattva who has gained the first ground?

   B. A: He Immediately Acquires Seven Qualities (Verse)

Response:

> The bodhisattva who abides on the first ground
> has much that he is able to endure,
> He is not fond of struggle or disputation,
> and, for the most part, his mind is joyous and pleased.
>
> He always delights in purity.
> He has a compassionate mind and feels pity for beings.
> He has no thoughts of hatred or anger,
> and, for the most part, practices these seven things.

If a bodhisattva reaches the first ground, he immediately acquires these seven characteristics. "Having much that he is able to endure," refers to his ability to cultivate and accumulate measureless merit and roots of goodness in order to accomplish a difficult endeavor. He comes and goes in *saṃsāra* for countless kalpas as numerous as the sands of the Ganges as he instructs evil beings who are obdurate-minded and difficult to transform. Still, his mind does not retreat or withdraw. It is because he is able to bear taking on such endeavors as these that he is said to be "able to endure."

As for his being "free of struggle and disputation," although he is able to achieve great works, he still refrains from struggling with or opposing others as he does so.

As for his being "joyous," this is a function of his ability to bring about both physical pliancy and a peaceful, stable of mind. As for his being "pleased," his mind becomes buoyantly exultant when encountering ever more superior dharmas.

As for his "purity," he abandons all forms of defilement associated with the afflictions. There are those who explain that it is his resolute conviction that qualifies him as "pure." There are others who explain that it is solid faith that makes him pure.

正體字

```
                是清淨心於佛法僧寶。於苦集
026b03 ||  滅道諦。於六波羅蜜。於菩薩十地。於空無
026b04 ||  相無作法。略而言之。一切深經諸菩薩及其
026b05 ||  所行一切佛法。悉皆心信清淨。悲者。於眾
026b06 ||  生憐愍救護。是悲漸漸增長而成大悲。有人
026b07 ||  言。在菩薩心名為悲。悲及眾生名為大
026b08 ||  悲。大悲以十因緣生。如第三地中廣說。不
026b09 ||  瞋者[1]是菩薩結未斷故[2]名為行善心少於
026b10 ||  瞋恨。如是菩薩在於初地。心不畏沒故名
026b11 ||  為能有堪忍。樂寂滅故名為不好諍訟。
026b12 ||  得順阿耨多羅三藐三菩提大悲故名為心
026b13 ||  多喜。離諸煩惱垢濁故於佛法僧寶諸
026b14 ||  菩薩所心常清淨。心安隱無患故名為心
026b15 ||  悅。深愍眾生故名為悲。心常樂慈行故名
026b16 ||  為不瞋。是[3]名菩薩在初地相貌。
```

简体字

有人言。坚固信名为清净。是清净心于佛法僧宝。于苦集灭道谛。于六波罗蜜。于菩萨十地。于空无相无作法。略而言之。一切深经诸菩萨及其所行一切佛法。悉皆心信清净。悲者。于众生怜愍救护。是悲渐渐增长而成大悲。有人言。在菩萨心名为悲。悲及众生名为大悲。大悲以十因缘生。如第三地中广说。不嗔者是菩萨结未断故名为行善心少于嗔恨。如是菩萨在于初地。心不畏没故名为能有堪忍。乐寂灭故名为不好诤讼。得顺阿耨多罗三藐三菩提大悲故名为心多喜。离诸烦恼垢浊故于佛法僧宝诸菩萨所心常清净。心安隐无患故名为心悦。深愍众生故名为悲。心常乐慈行故名为不嗔。是名菩萨在初地相貌。

Chapter 3 — *The Characteristics of the Ground*

This pure mind is in regard to the Buddha, Dharma, and Sangha Jewels, is in regard to the truths of suffering, origination, cessation, and the path, is in regard to the six *pāramitās*, is in regard to the ten grounds of the bodhisattva, and is in regard to the dharmas of emptiness, signlessness, and wishlessness. In short, in every case, his mind abides in pure faith with regard to all of the profound scriptures, with regard to the bodhisattvas, and with regard to all buddha dharmas that they practice.

As for "compassion" with regard to beings, he feels pity for them and strives to rescue and protect them. This compassion gradually increases and develops, thus transforming into the great compassion. There are those who explain that, in its presence within the mind of the bodhisattva, it may be referred to simply as "compassion," whereas, when this compassion actually reaches to other beings, it then qualifies as "the great compassion."

The great compassion is born in reliance upon ten types of causes and conditions. This is as extensively discussed in relation to the third ground.

As for "not hating," because this bodhisattva has not yet completely severed the fetters, it is said of him that, for the most part,[47] he practices goodness and his mind is seldom beset by animosity.

When a bodhisattva such as this abides on the first ground, because his mind is not prone to fearfulness or discouragement, he is therefore said to be able to have patience. It is because he is fond of quiescence that he is said "to not be fond of struggle or disputation."

It is because he is able to accord with [the path to] *anuttara-samyak-saṃbodhi* and the great compassion that it states "for the most part, his mind is joyous."

It is because he has abandoned the turbidity of all affliction-caused defilements that his mind is always pure in its relationship with the Buddha, Dharma, and Sangha Jewels, as well as with bodhisattvas.

Because his mind abides in peace and security and remains untroubled, it states here that "his mind is pleased."

It is because he feels profound pity for beings that he is said to be "compassionate."

It is because his mind always delights in practicing kindness that it is said to be "free of hatred."

These are the characteristics of the bodhisattva who dwells on the first ground.

正體字

問曰。何 026b17 ‖ 故不說菩薩於初地中有此[4]七事而言
026b18 ‖ 多。答曰。是菩薩漏未盡故。或時懈怠於[5]此
026b19 ‖ 事中暫有廢退。以其多行故說為多。於初
026b20 ‖ 地中已得是法。後諸地中轉轉增益。問曰。
026b21 ‖ 初歡喜地菩薩在此地中名多歡喜。為得
026b22 ‖ 諸功德故歡喜為地。法應歡喜。以何而歡
026b23 ‖ 喜。答曰。
026b24 ‖ 　　常念於諸佛　　及諸佛大法
026b25 ‖ 　　必定希有行　　是故多歡喜
026b26 ‖ 如是等歡喜因緣故。菩薩在初地中心多
026b27 ‖ 歡喜。念諸佛者。念然燈等過去諸佛阿彌
026b28 ‖ 陀等現在諸佛彌勒等將來諸佛。常念如是
026b29 ‖ 諸佛世尊如現在前。三界第一無能勝者。
026c01 ‖ 是故多歡喜。念諸佛大法者。略說諸佛四
026c02 ‖ 十不共法。一自在飛行隨意。二自在變化無
026c03 ‖ 邊。三自在所[6]聞無礙。四自在以無量種門
026c04 ‖ 知一切眾生心。如是等法後當廣說。

简体字

问曰。何故不说菩萨于初地中有此七事而言多。答曰。是菩萨漏未尽故。或时懈怠于此事中暂有废退。以其多行故说为多。于初地中已得是法。后诸地中转转增益。问曰。初欢喜地菩萨在此地中名多欢喜。为得诸功德故欢喜为地。法应欢喜。以何而欢喜。答曰。

　　常念于诸佛　　及诸佛大法
　　必定希有行　　是故多欢喜

如是等欢喜因缘故。菩萨在初地中心多欢喜。念诸佛者。念然灯等过去诸佛阿弥陀等现在诸佛弥勒等将来诸佛。常念如是诸佛世尊如现在前。三界第一无能胜者。是故多欢喜。念诸佛大法者。略说诸佛四十不共法。一自在飞行随意。二自在变化无边。三自在所闻无碍。四自在以无量种门知一切众生心。如是等法后当广说。

Chapter 3 — *The Characteristics of the Ground*

1. Q: Why Only Say, "For the Most Part" He Has These Seven Traits?

Question: Why not say of the bodhisattva on the first ground that he "possesses" these seven traits rather than say of him that he has them "for the most part"?

2. A: Because He Still Hasn't Done Away with the Contaminants

Response: Because this bodhisattva has not yet completely done away with the contaminants,[48] there are times when he may be somewhat indolent and thus have temporary lapses in demonstrating these traits. It is because, for the most part, he *does* implement them that the text states "for the most part." On the first ground, he has already acquired these dharmas. On the subsequent grounds, they develop and increase.

3. Q: Is His Joyfulness Acquired by Him or Is It a Feature of This Ground?

Question: On the first ground, the Ground of Joyfulness, this bodhisattva for the most part experiences joyfulness. Is it because he has acquired meritorious qualities that he experiences joyfulness or is it rather because of it simply being an inherent dharma of this ground that one should experience joyfulness? Why is it that he experiences joyfulness here?

4. A: It Is Due to Mindfulness of Buddhas & the Stage of Certainty

Response:

He is always mindful of the Buddhas,
of the great dharmas of the Buddhas,
of those at the station of certain success, and of their rare practices.
It is because of this that he is for the most part joyful.

It is due to reasons for joyfulness such as these that, on the first ground, the bodhisattva's mind is mostly joyful.

As for his "being mindful of the Buddhas," he is mindful of Burning Lamp and the other buddhas of the past, is mindful of Amitābha and the other buddhas of the present, and is mindful of Maitreya and the other buddhas of the future. He "is always mindful" of them just as if they were appearing directly in front of him and realizes that, throughout the three realms of existence, there is no one able to be superior to them. It is for this reason that he is mostly joyful.

As for his being mindful of "the great dharmas of the Buddhas," to state it briefly, this refers to the forty dharmas exclusive to the Buddha.[49] The first is sovereign mastery in the ability to fly wherever one wishes. The second is sovereign mastery in the ability to perform boundless transformations. The third is sovereign mastery of the unimpeded faculty of hearing. The fourth is sovereign mastery in knowing in countless ways the minds of all beings. Dharmas of these sorts will be extensively discussed later in this work.

正體字

```
             念必
026c05 ‖ 定諸菩薩者。若菩薩得阿耨多羅三藐三菩
026c06 ‖ 提記入法位得無生法忍。千萬億數魔之
026c07 ‖ 軍眾不能壞亂。得大悲心成大人法。不
026c08 ‖ 惜身命為得菩提勤行精進。[7]是念必定
026c09 ‖ 菩薩。念希有行者。念必定菩薩第一希有行
026c10 ‖ 令心歡喜。一切凡夫所不能及。一切聲聞
026c11 ‖ 辟支佛所不能行。開示佛法無礙解脫及
026c12 ‖ 薩婆若智。又念十地諸所行法。名為心多
026c13 ‖ 歡喜。是故菩薩得入初地名為歡喜。問曰。
026c14 ‖ 有凡夫人未發無上道心。或有發心者未
026c15 ‖ 得歡喜地。是人念諸佛及諸佛大法。念必
026c16 ‖ 定菩薩及希有行亦得歡喜。得初地菩薩
026c17 ‖ 歡喜。與此人有何差別。答曰。
026c18 ‖    菩薩得初地    其心多歡喜
026c19 ‖    諸佛無量德    我亦定當得
026c20 ‖ 得初地必定菩薩念諸佛有無量功德。
```

简体字

念必定诸菩萨者。若菩萨得阿耨多罗三藐三菩提记入法位得无生法忍。千万亿数魔之军众不能坏乱。得大悲心成大人法。不惜身命为得菩提勤行精进。是念必定菩萨。念希有行者。念必定菩萨第一希有行令心欢喜。一切凡夫所不能及。一切声闻辟支佛所不能行。开示佛法无碍解脱及萨婆若智。又念十地诸所行法。名为心多欢喜。是故菩萨得入初地名为欢喜。问曰。有凡夫人未发无上道心。或有发心者未得欢喜地。是人念诸佛及诸佛大法。念必定菩萨及希有行亦得欢喜。得初地菩萨欢喜。与此人有何差别。答曰。

　　菩萨得初地　　其心多欢喜
　　诸佛无量德　　我亦定当得

　　得初地必定菩萨念诸佛有无量功德。

Chapter 3 — The Characteristics of the Ground

In his mindfulness of those bodhisattvas on "the station of certainty," he is aware that, once the bodhisattva receives his prediction of eventual realization of *anuttarasamyaksaṃbodhi*, he enters "the Dharma position" and acquires the unproduced-dharmas patience whereupon not even armies of thousands of myriads of *koṭis* of *māras* would be able to destroy or interfere with him. When one acquires the mind of great compassion and develops the dharmas of a great man, one does not stint even in sacrificing one's own body and life for, in order to realize bodhi, one is persistently diligent in practicing vigor. It is in this way that he is mindful of the bodhisattvas who have gained the stage of certainty.

As for his being mindful of "their rare practices," when he brings to mind the supremely rare practices of the bodhisattvas who have gained the stage of certainty, this causes his mind to be filled with joy. They are of a sort that no common person can match them and no *śrāvaka* disciple or *pratyekabuddhas* can practice them. They open forth and demonstrate the Buddha Dharma's unimpeded liberation and wisdom of all-knowledge. He is also mindful of all dharmas practiced on the ten grounds.

This is what is meant when it is said that, "for the most part, his mind is joyful." It is for these reasons that the bodhisattva who has succeeded in entering the first ground is said to be "joyful."

    a. Q: What Is Unique about the First Ground Bodhisattva's Joyfulness?

Question: There are common persons not yet resolved on realizing the unsurpassable path and there may also be those who have already brought forth the resolve but have not yet reached the Ground of Joyfulness. When these persons are mindful of the Buddhas and the great dharmas of the Buddhas and also when they are mindful of the bodhisattvas who have gained the stage of certainty and their rare practices—these persons, too, experience joyfulness. What differences are there between the joyfulness of the bodhisattva who has reached the first ground and the joyfulness experienced by these other persons?

    b. A: He Realizes He Will Definitely Become a Buddha

Response:

    When the bodhisattva reaches the first ground
    His mind is, for the most part, joyful.
    Regarding the countless qualities of the Buddhas,
    he realizes, "I too shall definitely attain them."

When the first-ground bodhisattva at the stage of certainty brings to mind the countless meritorious qualities of the Buddhas, he thinks,

正體字

我 026c21 ‖當必得如是之事。何以故。我[8]以得此初
026c22 ‖ 地入必定中。餘者無有是心。是故初地菩
026c23 ‖ 薩多生歡喜。餘者不爾。何以故。餘者雖念
026c24 ‖ 諸佛。不能作是念。我必當作佛。譬如轉輪
026c25 ‖ 聖子生[*]是轉輪王家。成就轉輪王相。念過
026c26 ‖ 去轉輪王功德尊貴。作是念。我今亦有是
026c27 ‖ 相。亦當得是豪富尊貴。心大歡喜。若無轉
026c28 ‖ 輪王相者無如是喜。必定菩薩若念諸佛
026c29 ‖ 及諸佛大功德威儀尊貴。我有是相必當作
027a01 ‖ 佛。即大歡喜。餘者無有是事。定心者深入
027a02 ‖ 佛法心不可動。復次菩薩在初地念諸佛
027a03 ‖ 時。作是思惟。我亦不久當作利益諸世間
027a04 ‖ 者及念佛法。我亦當得相好嚴身成[1]就
027a05 ‖ [2]佛不共法。隨諸眾生所種善根心力大小
027a06 ‖ 而為說法。又我已得善法滋味。不久當如
027a07 ‖ 必定菩薩遊諸神通。又念必定菩薩所行之
027a08 ‖ 道。一切世間所不能信。我亦當行。如是念
027a09 ‖ 已心多歡喜。餘者不爾。何以故。是菩薩入
027a10 ‖ 初地故。其心決定願不移動求所應求。

简体字

我当必得如是之事。何以故。我以得此初地入必定中。余者无有是心。是故初地菩萨多生欢喜。余者不尔。何以故。余者虽念诸佛。不能作是念。我必当作佛。譬如转轮圣子生是转轮王家。成就转轮王相。念过去转轮王功德尊贵。作是念。我今亦有是相。亦当得是豪富尊贵。心大欢喜。若无转轮王相者无如是喜。必定菩萨若念诸佛及诸佛大功德威仪尊贵。我有是相必当作佛。即大欢喜。余者无有是事。定心者深入佛法心不可动。复次菩萨在初地念诸佛时。作是思惟。我亦不久当作利益诸世间者及念佛法。我亦当得相好严身成就佛不共法。随诸众生所种善根心力大小而为说法。又我已得善法滋味。不久当如必定菩萨游诸神通。又念必定菩萨所行之道。一切世间所不能信。我亦当行。如是念已心多欢喜。余者不尔。何以故。是菩萨入初地故。其心决定愿不移动求所应求。

"I shall definitely gain qualities such as these. Why? Because I have already[50] reached this first ground and have entered the stage of certainty."

Those others do not have this thought. It is for this reason that the bodhisattva on the first ground for the most part experiences joyfulness whereas this is not the case for the others. Why? Although the others are mindful of the Buddhas, they cannot think, "I will definitely become a buddha."

This circumstance is analogous to that of a wheel-turning prince born into the family of a wheel-turning king who completely manifests the signs of a wheel-turning king. When he brings to mind the meritorious qualities and venerable nobility of the wheel-turning kings of the past, he thinks, "Now I too have these signs and I too shall acquire just such power, wealth, and venerable nobility as theirs." His mind is then filled with great joy. If one does not have these signs of a wheel-turning king, he does not experience such joyfulness as this.

When the bodhisattva at the stage of certainty brings to mind the Buddhas and the great meritorious qualities, awesome deportment, and venerable nobility of the Buddhas, he thinks, "I have these qualities. I shall certainly become a buddha." He is then immediately filled with great joyfulness. The others have no such experience as this.

One whose mind has reached the stage of certainty has so deeply entered the Dharma of the Buddha that his resolve is unshakable. Additionally, when the bodhisattva on the first ground brings to mind the Buddhas, he reflects, "Before long, I too shall become one who benefits the entire world."

When he brings to mind the Dharma of the Buddha, he thinks, "I too shall acquire the body adorned with the major marks and minor characteristics, shall perfect the dharmas exclusive to the Buddha, and shall teach the Dharma in a manner adapted to the roots of goodness planted by beings and to the relative strength of their minds. Moreover, I have already acquired the flavor of good dharmas. Before long, just like the bodhisattva at the stage of certainty, I shall be able to roam about with the power of the spiritual superknowledges."

He also brings to mind the path practiced by the bodhisattva at the stage of certainty that is of a sort that no ordinary worldly being could believe. He then thinks, "I too shall practice it." Having reflected in this way, his mind is then filled with abundant joyfulness. This is not the case with those others. Why? Because this bodhisattva has entered the first ground, his resolve has become definitely fixed, his vows remain unshakable, and he seeks what should be sought.

正體字

譬
027a11 ‖ 如香象所作唯有香象能作。餘獸不能。是
027a12 ‖ 故汝所說者。是事不然。復次菩薩得初地
027a13 ‖ 無諸怖畏故心多歡喜。若怖畏者心則不
027a14 ‖ 喜。問曰。菩薩無何等怖畏。答曰。
027a15 ‖ 　無有不活畏　　死畏惡道畏
027a16 ‖ 　大眾威德畏　　惡名毀訾畏
027a17 ‖ 　繫閉桎梏畏　　拷掠刑戮畏
027a18 ‖ 　無我我所[3]故　　何有是諸畏
027a19 ‖ 問曰。菩薩何故住初地無不活畏。答曰。有
027a20 ‖ 大威德故。能堪受故。大智慧故。知止足故。
027a21 ‖ 作是念。我多修福德。有福之人衣服飲食。
027a22 ‖ 所須之物自然即至。如昔劫初大人群臣士
027a23 ‖ 民請以為王。若薄福德者。雖生王家以
027a24 ‖ 身力自營。衣食尚不充足。何況國土。菩薩
027a25 ‖ 作是念。我多修福德。如劫初王

简体字

譬如香象所作唯有香象能作。余兽不能。是故汝所说者。是事不然。复次菩萨得初地无诸怖畏故心多欢喜。若怖畏者心则不喜。问曰。菩萨无何等怖畏。答曰。

　无有不活畏　　死畏恶道畏
　大众威德畏　　恶名毁訾畏
　系闭桎梏畏　　拷掠刑戮畏
　无我我所故　　何有是诸畏

问曰。菩萨何故住初地无不活畏。答曰。有大威德故。能堪受故。大智慧故。知止足故。作是念。我多修福德。有福之人衣服饮食。所须之物自然即至。如昔劫初大人群臣士民请以为王。若薄福德者。虽生王家以身力自营。衣食尚不充足。何况国土。菩萨作是念。我多修福德。如劫初王

Chapter 3 — The Characteristics of the Ground

This is analogous to the case of an elephant in musth which does what only an elephant in musth is able to do and other beasts are unable to do.[51] Therefore the idea that you implied [in the above question] is incorrect.

Additionally, it is because the bodhisattva who has reached the first ground has no fear that his mind experiences abundant joyfulness. If one is beset by fear, one is not joyful.

    c. FROM WHICH TYPES OF FEAR HAS THIS BODHISATTVA BEEN FREED?

Question: From which types of fear has this bodhisattva been freed?

    d. FEAR OF NOT SURVIVING, DEATH, THE WRETCHED DESTINIES, ETC. (VERSE)

Response:

> He is free of the fear of not surviving,
> the fear of death, the fear of the wretched destinies,
> the fear of the Great Assembly's awesome virtue,
> the fear of ill repute, and the fear of being disparaged.[52]
>
> As for fear of imprisonment, shackles, and manacles,
> and the fear of beatings or capital punishment,
> given that he is free of a self or any possessions of self,
> how then could he have any such fears as these?

    1) FEAR OF NOT SURVIVING

        a) WHY DOES THIS BODHISATTVA NOT FEAR FAILING TO SURVIVE?

Question: Why is it that a bodhisattva dwelling on the first ground is free of the fear of not surviving?

        b) DUE TO GREAT MERIT, ENDURANCE, WISDOM, AND EASY SATISFACTION

Response: It is because he possesses great awesome virtue, because he has the ability to endure whatever comes, because he possesses great wisdom, and because he is easily satisfied.

He thinks to himself, "I have engaged in much cultivation of merit. The clothes, food and drink, and other requisites of a person possessed of merit naturally and immediately come to him."

This is comparable to the circumstance at the beginning of previous kalpas when great men were requested to serve as kings by the government officials and the people. In the case of those who possessed only scant merit, even though they might have been born into the household of a king, they had to rely on their own personal strengths to sustain themselves. If they could not even provide sufficient clothing and food for themselves, how much the less might they be able to provide for the country?

The bodhisattva thinks to himself, "I have engaged in much cultivation of merit. Just as in the beginning of the kalpa when the king

正體字

自然登位。　027a26 ‖　我亦如是。亦當復得如是事故。不應有
027a27 ‖ 不活畏。復次人雖薄福有堪受力。勤修方
027a28 ‖ 便能生衣食。如經說。以三因緣得有財
027a29 ‖ 物。一者現世自作方便。二者他力作與。三者
027b01 ‖ 福德因緣。我能堪受難成之事。現世亦有
027b02 ‖ 方便力故。不應有不活畏。有智之人少設
027b03 ‖ 方便能得自活。能求佛道[4]智慧分今已有
027b04 ‖ 之。是智慧利能得自活也。不應有不活
027b05 ‖ 畏。復次菩薩作是念。我住世間。世間有利
027b06 ‖ 衰毀譽稱譏苦樂。如是八事何得無也。不
027b07 ‖ 應以不得故有不活畏。復次是菩薩以知
027b08 ‖ 足故好醜美惡隨得而安。不應有不活畏。
027b09 ‖ 若不知足者。設得滿世間財物。意猶不足。
027b10 ‖ 如說。
027b11 ‖ 　若有貧窮者　　但求於衣食
027b12 ‖ 　既得衣食已　　復求美好者
027b13 ‖ 　既得美好者　　復求於尊貴
027b14 ‖ 　既得尊貴已　　求王一切地

简体字

自然登位。我亦如是。亦当复得如是事故。不应有不活畏。复次人虽薄福有堪受力。勤修方便能生衣食。如经说。以三因缘得有财物。一者现世自作方便。二者他力作与。三者福德因缘。我能堪受难成之事。现世亦有方便力故。不应有不活畏。有智之人少设方便能得自活。能求佛道智慧分今已有之。是智慧利能得自活也。不应有不活畏。复次菩萨作是念。我住世间。世间有利衰毁誉称讥苦乐。如是八事何得无也。不应以不得故有不活畏。复次是菩萨以知足故好丑美恶随得而安。不应有不活畏。若不知足者。设得满世间财物。意犹不足。如说。

　若有贫穷者　　但求于衣食
　既得衣食已　　复求美好者
　既得美好者　　复求于尊贵
　既得尊贵已　　求王一切地

Chapter 3 — The Characteristics of the Ground

was able to naturally ascend to his position, so too shall it be with me, for I too shall be bound to once again acquire such circumstances. Hence I should not have any fear of not surviving."

Additionally, even though a person might have only scant merit, still, if he possesses the power to endure whatever comes, then he will diligently cultivate the means to be able to produce clothing and food for himself.

This is as set forth in the scriptures where it states, "There are three causes for acquiring material wealth. The first consists of the skillful means one has utilized in the present lifetime. The second consists of the power that others possess to bestow such things. The third consists of the causes and conditions relating to one's own merit."

He thinks: "I am able to endure difficult circumstances. Because I also have the power of skillful means in this present life, I should not have any fear of not surviving."

He thinks: "A wise person is able to ensure his own survival merely through instituting a few skillful means. I already possess a measure of wisdom adequate to enable pursuit of the Buddha path. Through the benefits arising from this wisdom I shall be able to survive. Therefore I should not have any fear of not surviving."

Moreover, the bodhisattva has this thought: "I dwell within the world. The world is characterized by the presence of gain and loss, slander and prestige, praise and blame, suffering and happiness. How could it be that these eight circumstances might ever not exist? I should not fear failing to survive simply because I do not acquire something."

Furthermore, it is because the bodhisattva is easily satisfied that he adapts to whatever comes his way, remaining at peace whether the circumstances be fine or foul, excellent or deplorable. Thus he realizes that he should not have any fear of not surviving. If one is not easily satisfied, even if he were to acquire enough material possessions to fill up the entire world, his mind would still be unsatisfied. This is as described here:

> When a person is poverty-stricken,
> he only seeks clothing and food.
> Once he has obtained clothing and food,
> he then also seeks to obtain what is fine.
>
> Having gotten what is fine,
> he then also seeks honor and nobility.
> Once he has acquired honor and nobility,
> he then strives to rule all lands.

正體字

027b15 ‖　　設得盡王地　　復求為天王
027b16 ‖　　世間貪欲者　　不可以財滿
027b17 ‖ 若知足之人。得少財物。今世後世能成其
027b18 ‖ 利。是菩薩樂布施故。具足智慧故。多能發
027b19 ‖ 起不貪善根。若不樂施[5]若多作眾惡。以慳
027b20 ‖ 貪愚癡因緣故。增益慳貪不善根。無厭足法
027b21 ‖ 屬於慳貪。是故菩薩多發不貪善根故知
027b22 ‖ 足。知足故無不活畏。復次無死畏者。多
027b23 ‖ 作福德故。念念死故。不得免故。無始世界
027b24 ‖ 習受死法故。多修習空故。菩薩作是念。若
027b25 ‖ 人不修福德則畏於死。自恐後世墮惡道
027b26 ‖ 故。我多集諸福德。死便生於勝處。是故不
027b27 ‖ 應畏死。如說。
027b28 ‖　　待死如愛客　　去如至大會
027b29 ‖　　多集福德故　　捨命時無畏
027c01 ‖ 復作是念。死名隨所受身。末後心滅為死。
027c02 ‖ [6]若心滅為死者。心念念滅故皆應是死。

简体字

　　设得尽王地　　复求为天王
　　世间贪欲者　　不可以财满
若知足之人。得少财物。今世后世能成其利。是菩萨乐布施故。具足智慧故。多能发起不贪善根。若不乐施若多作众恶。以悭贪愚痴因缘故。增益悭贪不善根。无厌足法属于悭贪。是故菩萨多发不贪善根故知足。知足故无不活畏。复次无死畏者。多作福德故。念念死故。不得免故。无始世界习受死法故。多修习空故。菩萨作是念。若人不修福德则畏于死。自恐后世堕恶道故。我多集诸福德。死便生于胜处。是故不应畏死。如说。
　　待死如爱客　　去如至大会
　　多集福德故　　舍命时无畏
　　复作是念。死名随所受身。末后心灭为死。若心灭为死者。心念念灭故皆应是死。

If he gains complete dominion over all lands,
he then also seeks to become king of the devas.
The desires of those in the world
cannot be satisfied by wealth.

In the case of someone who is easily satisfied, if he obtains a little in the way of wealth or possessions, then he is able to provide for his own benefit in both the present and future lives. Because this bodhisattva delights in giving and because he is fully possessed of wisdom, he is abundantly able to generate the roots of goodness arising from non-covetousness.

If one does not delight in giving or if one engages in a multitude of evil actions, due to the causes and conditions of miserliness and delusion, one increases the roots of non-goodness produced by miserliness. The dharma of insatiability exists because of covetousness. Hence, because the bodhisattva has extensively developed roots of goodness associated with not being covetous, he is therefore easily satisfied. Because he is easily satisfied, he has no fear of not surviving.

2) Fear of Death

Also, as for "having no fear of dying," this comes from extensive creation of merit, from realizing one dies in each successive mind-moment,[53] from realizing it is unavoidable, from realizing that, throughout beginningless time, one has already practiced experiencing dying in the world, and from extensive cultivation of emptiness.

The bodhisattva reflects in this manner: "If a person has failed to cultivate merit, then he will fear death due to personally dreading descent into the wretched destinies in future lives. However, I have extensively cultivated all manner of merit. Hence, when I die, I will be reborn in a superior place. Therefore I should not fear death." This is as described here:

> One awaits his death as if it were a dearly beloved guest
> and then takes his leave as if going to a grand assembly.
> Having accumulated an abundance of merit,
> when one relinquishes this life, one has no fear.

He also has this thought:

> Death refers to that circumstance where, in whichever body one has taken on, one's very last thought is extinguished. That is what defines death. Since this extinguishing of thought is what constitutes death, then, because thoughts are ceasing in every successive mind-moment, every one of these circumstances should itself qualify as "death."

若畏死者心念念滅皆應有畏。非但畏末後心滅。亦應當畏前心盡滅。何以故。前後心滅無有差別故。若謂畏墮惡道故畏末後心滅者。福德之人不應畏墮惡道。如先說。我當受念念滅故。於末後心滅。不應有死畏。復作是念。我於無始世界往來生死受無量無邊阿僧祇死法。無有處所能免死者。佛說生死無始。若人於一劫中死已積骨高於雪山。如是諸死不為自利不為利他。我今發無上道願。為欲自利亦為利他故。勤心行道有大利故。云何驚畏。如是菩薩即捨死畏。復次作是念。今此死法必當應受無有免者。何以故。劫初諸大王。頂生喜見照明王等有三十二大人相莊嚴其身。七寶導從天人敬愛。王四天下常行十善道。是諸大王皆歸於死。復有蛇提羅諸小轉輪王。自以威力王閻浮提。

若畏死者心念念灭皆应有畏。非但畏末后心灭。亦应当畏前心尽灭。何以故。前后心灭无有差别故。若谓畏堕恶道故畏末后心灭者。福德之人不应畏堕恶道。如先说。我当受念念灭故。于末后心灭。不应有死畏。复作是念。我于无始世界往来生死受无量无边阿僧祇死法。无有处所能免死者。佛说生死无始。若人于一劫中死已积骨高于雪山。如是诸死不为自利不为利他。我今发无上道愿。为欲自利亦为利他故。勤心行道有大利故。云何惊畏。如是菩萨即舍死畏。复次作是念。今此死法必当应受无有免者。何以故。劫初诸大王。顶生喜见照明王等有三十二大人相庄严其身。七宝导从天人敬爱。王四天下常行十善道。是诸大王皆归于死。复有蛇提罗诸小转轮王。自以威力王阎浮提。

Chapter 3 — *The Characteristics of the Ground*

If one fears death, then one should fear every single instance of this moment-after-moment extinguishing of thought. It is not the case that one should only fear the extinction of that very last thought.

One should then also experience fearfulness with respect to the complete cessation of the immediately previous thought. Why? This is because there is no distinction between the immediately previous thought and one's very last thought as regards their vulnerability to being extinguished.

If one were to say that it is because he fears falling into the wretched destinies that he dreads the perishing of the very last thought—a person possessed of merit should not fear falling into the wretched destinies. This is as mentioned earlier. I should simply accept this process of perishing that occurs with each successive mind-moment and hence should not have any fear of the death that is just the perishing of the very last thought.

He also has this additional thought:

Throughout the course of beginningless existences in the world, I have come and gone in *saṃsāra*, undergoing death in measurelessly and boundlessly many *asaṃkhyeyas*[54] of ways. There is no place in which one is able to avoid dying.

The Buddha declared that *saṃsāra* is beginningless. If a person were to stack up all of his bones left in death from but a single kalpa of his existences, they would exceed the height of the Himalaya Mountains. All of the deaths of this sort have not brought about any benefit for oneself, nor have they benefited others.

Now, however, I have made the vow to follow the unsurpassable path. I have done this wishing to benefit myself while also benefiting others and also because practicing the path with a diligent mind brings immense benefits. Why then should I be frightened?

It is in this fashion that the bodhisattva is able to immediately relinquish the fear of death. Additionally, the bodhisattva has this thought:

This dharma of death is one which I must now definitely accept. There is no one who is able to avoid it. How is this so? Even though all the great kings at the beginning of the kalpa such as King "Crown-Born," King "Joy-to-Behold," and King "Radiant Brilliance" all had the thirty-two marks of a great man as physical adornments, were led and followed by their "seven treasures,"[55] were revered and loved by both devas and men, were ruling over the four continents, and were practicing the ten good courses of karmic action, still, in each and every case, all of these great kings finally succumbed to death.

Furthermore, the lesser *kṣatriya*[56] wheel-turning kings who use their own awesome power to rule over Jambudvīpa, whose physical

正體字

```
         身色端正猶如天人。於色聲香味觸
027c21   自恣無乏。所向皆伏無有退却善通射術。
027c22   是諸王等霸王天下人民眷屬皆不免死。
027c23   又諸仙聖迦葉憍瞿摩等行諸苦行得五神
027c24   通。造作經書皆不免死。又諸佛辟支佛阿
027c25   羅漢。心得自在離垢得道。皆為死法之所
027c26   磨滅。一切眾生無能過者。我發無上道心
027c27   不應畏死。又為破死畏故。發心精進自除
027c28   死畏亦除於他。是故發心行道。云何於死
027c29   而生驚畏。菩薩如是思惟無常即除死畏。
028a01   復次菩薩常修習空法故。不應畏死。如說。
028a02   離死者無死    離死無死者
028a03   因死有死者    因死者有死
028a04   死成成死者    死先未成時
028a05   無有決定相    無死無成者
028a06   離死有死者    死者應自成
028a07   而實離於死    無有死者成
```

简体字

身色端正犹如天人。于色声香味触自恣无乏。所向皆伏无有退却善通射术。是诸王等霸王天下人民眷属皆不免死。又诸仙圣迦叶憍瞿摩等行诸苦行得五神通。造作经书皆不免死。又诸佛辟支佛阿罗汉。心得自在离垢得道。皆为死法之所磨灭。一切众生无能过者。我发无上道心不应畏死。又为破死畏故。发心精进自除死畏亦除于他。是故发心行道。云何于死而生惊畏。菩萨如是思惟无常即除死畏。复次菩萨常修习空法故。不应畏死。如说。

离死者无死　　离死无死者
因死有死者　　因死者有死
死成成死者　　死先未成时
无有决定相　　无死无成者
离死有死者　　死者应自成
而实离于死　　无有死者成

Chapter 3 — The Characteristics of the Ground

bodies are so handsome as to be comparable to devas, who enjoy unrestrained and unlimited enjoyment of sights, sounds, fragrances, flavors, and touchables, who cause everyone everywhere to submit to them, who do not retreat from anything, and who are so consummately skilled in archery—even all such kings as these who rule as kings over an entire continent—even they as well as all their citizens and retainers—none of them are able to avoid death.

Additionally, all of the rishis, *āryas*, Kāśyapa, *jiaojumo*,[57] and all of the others who have practiced the ascetic practices and gained the five types of spiritual superknowledges—these as well as those who created all of the classic scriptures—none of them are able to avoid death.

Additionally, all buddhas, *pratyekabuddhas*, and arhats, those whose minds have achieved sovereign mastery, who have abandoned the defilements, and who have realized [the fruits of] the path—all of them have been destroyed by the dharma of death. There are no beings at all who have been able to get past it.

Having brought forth the resolve to succeed in following the unsurpassable path, I should not fear death.

Then again, in order to destroy the fear of death, one brings forth the resolve and proceeds vigorously to dispel the fear of death in oneself while also assisting others in dispelling it. One therefore brings forth the resolve to cultivate the path. How then could one feel alarm and fearfulness regarding death?

The bodhisattva reflects upon impermanence in this way and thus immediately dispels the fear of death.

Additionally, the bodhisattva always cultivates the practice of the dharma of emptiness. Thus he should not fear death. This is as described in the following verse:

> Apart from one who dies, there is no death.
> Apart from death, there is no one who dies.[58]
> It is because of death that one who dies is held to exist.
> It is because of one who dies that death is held to exist.

> As for it being death's occurrence that establishes "one who dies,"
> prior to death, before it has occurred,
> they have no fixed characteristics.
> Hence there is neither any death nor anyone in whom it occurs.

> If there were someone who dies apart from death itself,
> then "the one who dies" ought to be self-established.
> However, in truth, apart from the dying itself,
> there is no "one who dies" [whose existence] is established.

正體字

028a08 ‖ 　而世間分別　　是死是死者
028a09 ‖ 　不知死去來　　是故終不免
028a10 ‖ 　以是等因緣　　觀於諸法相
028a11 ‖ 　其心無有異　　終不畏於死
028a12 ‖ 無惡道畏者。菩薩常修福德故。不畏墮
028a13 ‖ 惡道。作是念。罪人墮惡道。非是福德者。我
028a14 ‖ 乃至一念中。不令諸惡得入。而於身口意
028a15 ‖ 常起清淨業。是故我得無量無邊功德成
028a16 ‖ 就。如是大功德聚。云何畏墮惡道。復次菩
028a17 ‖ 薩一發心為利安一切眾生故。大慈悲所護
028a18 ‖ 故。住四功德處。得無量功德。度一切惡道。
028a19 ‖ 何以故。是心勝一切聲聞辟支佛。如淨毘尼
028a20 ‖ 經中。迦葉白佛言。希有世尊。善說[1]菩薩以
028a21 ‖ 是薩婆若[2]多心能勝一切聲聞辟支佛。我
028a22 ‖ 成就如是大功德。住如是大法。云何當畏
028a23 ‖ 墮[3]於惡道。復作是念。我無始已來。往來
028a24 ‖ 生死墮諸惡道受無量苦。不為自利亦不
028a25 ‖ 利他。我今發無上大願。

简体字

　而世间分别　　是死是死者
　不知死去来　　是故终不免
　以是等因缘　　观于诸法相
　其心无有异　　终不畏于死

无恶道畏者。菩萨常修福德故。不畏堕恶道。作是念。罪人堕恶道。非是福德者。我乃至一念中。不令诸恶得入。而于身口意常起清净业。是故我得无量无边功德成就。如是大功德聚。云何畏堕恶道。复次菩萨一发心为利安一切众生故。大慈悲所护故。住四功德处。得无量功德。度一切恶道。何以故。是心胜一切声闻辟支佛。如净毗尼经中。迦葉白佛言。希有世尊。善说菩萨以是萨婆若多心能胜一切声闻辟支佛。我成就如是大功德。住如是大法。云何当畏堕于恶道。复作是念。我无始已来。往来生死堕诸恶道受无量苦。不为自利亦不利他。我今发无上大愿。

Chapter 3 — The Characteristics of the Ground

Nonetheless, those in the world engage in discriminations, saying: "This is death and this is the one who dies."
Hence they do not understand death or how one comes or goes.
Consequently, they can never avoid undergoing it.

For reasons such as these,
one who contemplates the [true] character of dharmas
is one whose mind remains unvarying
and who is never fearful of death.

3) Fear of the Wretched Destinies

As for "having no fear of the wretched destinies," because the bodhisattva always cultivates merit, he does not fear falling into the wretched destinies. He reflects to himself, "It is those persons who engage in karmic offenses who fall into the wretched destinies. This does not happen to those who cultivate merit. I do not allow any evil influences to enter even for the space of a single mind-moment and thus I am always bringing forth pure actions of body, speech, and mind. Therefore I have acquired a measureless and boundless number of meritorious qualities. Having developed such a great accumulation of meritorious qualities as this, how could I fear falling into the wretched destinies?"

Additionally, from the very time when the bodhisattva brings forth the resolve, because he does so for the sake of benefiting and bringing peace to all beings and because he is protected by his great kindness and compassion, he abides in the four foundations of meritorious qualities, gains a measureless number of meritorious qualities, and crosses beyond all the wretched destinies.

How is it that this is so? This resolve of his is superior to that of any *śrāvaka* disciple or *pratyekabuddha*. This is as stated in the *Pure Vinaya Sutra* in which Kāśyapa addressed the Buddha, saying, "It is rare indeed, O Bhagavat. You have so well explained how it is that, because of his resolve to realize all-knowledge, the bodhisattva is able to surpass all *śrāvaka* disciples and *pratyekabuddhas*."

One reflects, "Given that I have produced such a great amount of merit and have come to abide in such great dharmas as these, why should I have any fear of falling into the wretched destinies?"

One also thinks:

> Throughout the course of beginningless time on up to the very present, I have been going and coming in *saṃsāra*, have fallen into all the wretched destinies, and have undergone measureless suffering and in doing so, it has not been to benefit myself or to benefit others. I now bring forth the unsurpassable great vow in order to fulfill the

正體字	為欲自利亦為利 028a26 ‖ 他。先來墮惡道無所利益。今為利益眾 028a27 ‖ 生故。設墮惡道不應有畏。復次實行菩薩 028a28 ‖ 發如是心。假令我於阿鼻地獄一劫受苦 028a29 ‖ 然後得出。能令一人生一善心。積集如是 028b01 ‖ 無量善心。堪任受化令發三乘。如是教恒 028b02 ‖ [4]河沙等眾生聲聞乘。恒河沙等眾生辟支佛 028b03 ‖ 乘。恒河沙等眾生發大乘。然後我當得阿 028b04 ‖ 耨多羅三藐三菩提心。尚不應退沒。何況我 028b05 ‖ 今修集無量無邊功德遠離惡道。菩薩如 028b06 ‖ 是思惟。何得有惡道畏。復次如叫喚地獄 028b07 ‖ 經中說。菩薩答魔言。 028b08 ‖ 　我以布施故　　墮在叫喚獄 028b09 ‖ 　所受我施者　　皆生於天上 028b10 ‖ 　若爾猶尚應　　常行於布施 028b11 ‖ 　眾生在天上　　我受叫喚苦 028b12 ‖ 菩薩如是等種種因緣。能遮惡道畏。　無有 028b13 ‖ 大眾畏者。成就聞慧
简体字	为欲自利亦为利他。先来堕恶道无所利益。今为利益众生故。设堕恶道不应有畏。复次实行菩萨发如是心。假令我于阿鼻地狱一劫受苦然后得出。能令一人生一善心。积集如是无量善心。堪任受化令发三乘。如是教恒河沙等众生声闻乘。恒河沙等众生辟支佛乘。恒河沙等众生发大乘。然后我当得阿耨多罗三藐三菩提心。尚不应退没。何况我今修集无量无边功德远离恶道。菩萨如是思惟。何得有恶道畏。复次如叫唤地狱经中说。菩萨答魔言。 　我以布施故　　墮在叫唤狱 　所受我施者　　皆生于天上 　若尔犹尚应　　常行于布施 　众生在天上　　我受叫唤苦 　菩萨如是等种种因缘。能遮恶道畏。无有大众畏者。成就闻慧

wish to benefit myself while also benefiting others. Throughout the past on forward to the very present, I have fallen into the wretched destinies without deriving any benefit from it. Now, even if I were to fall into the wretched destinies while striving to benefit other beings, that should not cause me to be fearful.

Moreover, the bodhisattva whose practice is genuine has this thought:

> Even if I was caused to fall into the Avīci Hells and undergo suffering for an entire kalpa after which I only then succeeded in getting out again, yet, by doing this, I was thus able to cause but a single person to produce a single good thought [and even if I had to continue in this way to cause him] to accumulate an immeasurable number of such good thoughts so that he eventually developed the capacity to undergo teaching influencing him to set forth in the Three Vehicles—and if in this same way, I was thereby able to instruct beings as numerous as the Ganges' sands to set forth in the Śrāvaka Disciple Vehicle, beings as numerous as the Ganges' sands to set forth in the Pratyekabuddha Vehicle, and beings as numerous as the Ganges' sands to set forth in the Great Vehicle, after which I only then was able to realize *anuttarasamyaksaṃbodhi*—even if this had to be the case, I should still not retreat and fall away from pursuing this course of action. How much the less should I [retreat from this] in the present circumstance wherein, by accumulating a measureless and boundless number of meritorious qualities, I am thereby able to leave the wretched destinies far behind?

When the bodhisattva ponders the matter in this way, how could he have any fear of falling into the wretched destinies?

Then again, this is as illustrated in the *Sutra on the Screaming Hells* wherein a bodhisattva replies to Māra, saying:

> If on account of giving,
> I were to fall into the Screaming Hells,
> yet all who received my gifts
> were thereby able to be reborn in the heavens—
>
> Even if this were to be the case, I should still
> always practice such giving
> if it results in beings dwelling in the heavens
> and in my enduring the sufferings of the Screaming Hells.

Through many different rationales such as these, the bodhisattva is able to deflect the fear of the wretched destinies.

    4) FEAR OF GREAT ASSEMBLIES

As for "not having any fear in great assemblies," because he perfects the wisdom gained through learning, the wisdom gained through

正體字

028b14 ‖ 思慧修慧故。又離諸
028b14 ‖ 論過咎故。是菩薩建立語端所說無失。能
028b15 ‖ 以因緣譬喻結句不多不少無有疑惑。言
028b16 ‖ 無非義無有諂誑。質直柔和種種莊嚴。易
028b17 ‖ 解易持義趣次序。能顯己事能破他論離
028b18 ‖ 四邪因具四大因。如是等莊嚴言辭。大眾
028b19 ‖ 中說無有所畏。無惡名畏呵罵畏者。不貪
028b20 ‖ 利養故。身口意行清淨故。無有繫閉桎梏
028b21 ‖ [5]考掠畏者。無有罪故。慈愍一切眾生故。
028b22 ‖ 忍受一切眾苦惱故。依止業果報故。我先
028b23 ‖ 自作今還受報。是菩薩以如是等因緣故。
028b24 ‖ 無有不活等畏。復次樂觀一切法無我。是
028b25 ‖ 故無一切怖畏。一切怖畏皆從[6]我見生。我
028b26 ‖ 見皆是諸衰憂苦之[7]根本。是菩薩利智慧故。
028b27 ‖ 如實深入

简体字

思慧修慧故。又离诸论过咎故。是菩萨建立语端所说无失。能以因缘譬喻结句不多不少无有疑惑。言无非义无有谄诳。质直柔和种种庄严。易解易持义趣次序。能显己事能破他论离四邪因具四大因。如是等庄严言辞。大众中说无有所畏。无恶名畏呵骂畏者。不贪利养故。身口意行清净故。无有系闭桎梏考掠畏者。无有罪故。慈愍一切众生故。忍受一切众苦恼故。依止业果报故。我先自作今还受报。是菩萨以如是等因缘故。无有不活等畏。复次乐观一切法无我。是故无一切怖畏。一切怖畏皆从我见生。我见皆是诸衰忧苦之根本。是菩萨利智慧故。如实深入

contemplative thought, and the wisdom gained through cultivation, and also because he abandons the faults involved in mere theorizing, when this bodhisattva establishes points of discourse, whatever he says is free of error. He is able to use reasoning, analogies, and conclusions that are neither excessive nor deficient, and that leave no room for doubt.

His words have nothing in them that contradicts what is meaningful and nothing in them that tends toward flattery or deception. They are direct, suffused with pliancy, and graced with all manner of adorning phrases. They are easy to understand, conducive to ease in retaining their meaning, and orderly in the sequence of their exposition. They are able to reveal the contents of his own case while refuting the theories of others. His speech is free of the four erroneous types of reasoning and is equipped with the four major types of correct reasoning. Using well-adorned types of discourse such as these, he is fearless when speaking before a great assembly.

    5) Fear of Ill Repute and Fear of Being Disparaged

As for "having no fear of ill repute" and "having no fear of cursing and scolding," these are a consequence of having no craving for gain and offerings and due to maintaining pure physical, verbal, and mental conduct.

    6) Fear of Imprisonment, shackles, manacles, or Beatings

As for "freedom from fear of imprisonment, shackles, manacles, or beatings," this is because one remains free of karmic offenses, because one feels kindness and sympathy for all beings, because one is able to endure all the many different sorts of sufferings and afflictions, and because one relies on karmic actions entailing their results and retributions. [Hence one reflects], "Because it is I who previously performed this act, I am now bound to undergo such retribution in return."

It is for reasons such as these that this bodhisattva has no fear of not surviving, nor does he have any of the other such sorts of fear.

    e. Realizing Nonexistence of Self As the Basis of Fearlessness

Then again, he delights in contemplating all dharmas as having nothing constituting a self. Therefore he remains free of all fear, for all types of fear are born from the view that assumes the existence of a self. The view that assumes the existence of a self is in every case the root of all sufferings associated with worry about loss. Because this bodhisattva possesses sharp wisdom and because he penetrates deeply into the true character of all dharmas doing so in a manner that accords with

正體字

028b28 ‖ 　　　　諸法實相故則無有我。我無故
028b29 ‖ 何從有怖畏。問曰。是菩薩云何無有我心。
028c01 ‖ 答曰。樂空法故。菩薩觀身離我我所故。如
　　　　說。
028c02 ‖ 　　我心因我所　　我所因我生
028c03 ‖ 　　是故我我所　　二性俱是空
028c04 ‖ 　　我則是主義　　我所是主物
028c05 ‖ 　　若無有主者　　主所物亦無
028c06 ‖ 　　若無主所物　　則亦無有主
028c07 ‖ 　　我即是我見　　我物我所見
028c08 ‖ 　　實觀故無我　　我無無非我
028c09 ‖ 　　因受生受者　　無受無受者
028c10 ‖ 　　離受者無受　　云何因受成
028c11 ‖ 　　若受者成受　　受則為不成
028c12 ‖ 　　以受不成故　　不能成受者
028c13 ‖ 　　以受者空故　　不得言是我
028c14 ‖ 　　以受是空故　　不得言我所
028c15 ‖ 　　是故我非我　　亦我亦非我
028c16 ‖ 　　非我非無我　　是皆為邪論

简体字

诸法实相故则无有我。我无故何从有怖畏。问曰。是菩萨云何无有我心。答曰。乐空法故。菩萨观身离我我所故。如说。

　　我心因我所　　我所因我生
　　是故我我所　　二性俱是空
　　我则是主义　　我所是主物
　　若无有主者　　主所物亦无
　　若无主所物　　则亦无有主
　　我即是我见　　我物我所见
　　实观故无我　　我无无非我
　　因受生受者　　无受无受者
　　离受者无受　　云何因受成
　　若受者成受　　受则为不成
　　以受不成故　　不能成受者
　　以受者空故　　不得言是我
　　以受是空故　　不得言我所
　　是故我非我　　亦我亦非我
　　非我非无我　　是皆为邪论

Chapter 3 — *The Characteristics of the Ground*

reality, he remains free of any concept of a self. Since he has no self, how could he continue to be fearful?

1) Q: W*HY* D*OES* T*HIS* B*ODHISATTVA* H*AVE* N*O* C*ONCEPTION OF A* S*ELF*?

Question: How is it that this bodhisattva has no thoughts of a self?

2) A: H*E* D*ELIGHTS IN* E*MPTINESS AND* S*EES THE* B*ODY AS* N*OT* S*ELF* (V*ERSE*)

Response: This is because he delights in the dharma of emptiness and because the bodhisattva contemplates the body as apart from any "self" or anything belonging to a self. This is as explained here:

> The thought of "self" is caused by that of "mine."
> That of "mine" is produced from that of "self."
> Therefore, as for "self" and "mine,"
> the nature of both of these is complete emptiness.
>
> As for "self," it has the meaning of "subject."
> As for "mine," this refers to whatever belongs to that subject.
> If no "subject" exists,
> whatever belongs to a subject is also nonexistent [as such].
>
> If there is nothing that belongs to a subject,
> then there is no subject, either.
> As for "self," it is just the view imputing existence of a "self."
> As for "a self's possessions," it is just the view imputing "mine."
> Contemplating in accordance with reality, there is no "self."
> In the absence of a self, there is no "nonself."
>
> Because of "experiencing," "one who experiences" is produced.
> In the absence of experiencing, there is no "one who experiences."
> Apart from "one who experiences," there is no experiencing.
> How then could it be established based on "experiencing"?
>
> If it were so that "one who experiences" established "experiencing,"
> then experiencing could not be established.
> Because experiencing is thus not established,
> then one cannot establish "one who experiences."
>
> Because an "one who experiences" is empty [of inherent existence],
> one cannot speak of it as constituting a self.
> Because "experiencing" is empty [of inherent existence],
> One cannot speak of it as something belonging to a self.
>
> Therefore "self," "nonself,"
> "both self and nonself,"
> and "neither self nor nonself"—
> These are all fallacious concepts.

正體字

028c17 ‖ 　　我所非我所　　亦我非我所
028c18 ‖ 　　非我非我所　　是亦為邪論
028c19 ‖ 菩薩如是常樂修空無我故。離諸怖畏。所
028c20 ‖ 以者何。空無我法能離諸怖畏。[8]故菩薩在
028c21 ‖ 歡喜地。有如是等相貌。

简体字

　　我所非我所　　亦我非我所
　　非我非我所　　是亦为邪论
　菩萨如是常乐修空无我故。离诸怖畏。所以者何。空无我法能离诸怖畏。故菩萨在欢喜地。有如是等相貌。

"Mine," "not mine,"
"both mine and not mine,"
and "neither mine nor not mine"—
These too are fallacious concepts.

It is because the bodhisattva always delights in this way in the cultivation of emptiness and nonexistence of self that he abandons all types of fear. And why is this so? This is because the dharmas of emptiness and nonexistence of self are able to cause one to abandon all types of fear.

The bodhisattva who dwells on the Ground of Joyfulness is possessed of characteristics such as these.

The End of Chapter Three

正體字

028c22 ‖	**[9]淨地品第四**
028c23 ‖	問曰。菩薩已得初地。應云何修治。答曰。
028c24 ‖	信力轉增上　深行大悲心
028c25 ‖	慈愍眾生類　修善心無倦
028c26 ‖	喜樂諸妙法　常近善知識
028c27 ‖	慚愧及恭敬　柔軟和其心
028c28 ‖	樂觀法無著　一心求多聞
028c29 ‖	不貪於利養　離姦欺諂誑
029a01 ‖	不污諸佛家　不毀戒欺佛
029a02 ‖	深樂薩婆若　不動如大山
029a03 ‖	常樂修習行　轉上之妙法
029a04 ‖	樂出世間法　不樂世間法
029a05 ‖	即治歡喜地　難治而能治
029a06 ‖	是故常一心　勤行此諸法
029a07 ‖	菩薩能成就　如是上妙法
029a08 ‖	是則為安住　菩薩初地中

简体字

净地品第四

问曰。菩萨已得初地。应云何修治。答曰。
信力转增上　深行大悲心
慈愍众生类　修善心无倦
喜乐诸妙法　常近善知识
惭愧及恭敬　柔软和其心
乐观法无著　一心求多闻
不贪于利养　离奸欺谄诳
不污诸佛家　不毁戒欺佛
深乐萨婆若　不动如大山
常乐修习行　转上之妙法
乐出世间法　不乐世间法
即治欢喜地　难治而能治
是故常一心　勤行此诸法
菩萨能成就　如是上妙法
是则为安住　菩萨初地中

Chapter 4
Purification of the Ground

IV. Chapter Four: Purification of the Ground
  A. Q: How Should the 1st Ground Bodhisattva Cultivate Its Purification?

Question: In the case of the bodhisattva who has already gotten to the first ground, how should he go about cultivating its purification?

  B. A: One Cultivates 27 Dharmas (Verse)

Response:

> The power of faith becomes ever more superior
> as one practices deeply the mind of great compassion.
> One acts with kindness toward all types of beings
> and tirelessly cultivates the mind of goodness.
>
> One finds joyous delight in sublime dharmas,
> always draws close to the good spiritual guide,
> maintains a sense of shame, dread of blame, and reverence,
> and makes one's mind gentle and harmonious.
>
> One delights in contemplating dharmas and stays free of attachment,
> single-mindedly strives to acquire abundant learning,
> refrains from coveting offerings of benefits and support,
> while staying far from treacherous cheating, flattery, and deception.
>
> One does not defile the family of the Buddhas
> and does not damage moral precepts or cheat the Buddhas.
> One deeply delights in all-knowledge,[59]
> and remains as unmoving as an immense mountain.
>
> One always delights in cultivating and practicing
> ever more superior sublime dharmas.
> One delights in the world-transcending dharmas
> and does not delight in worldly dharmas.
>
> Even as one cultivates the Ground of Joyfulness,
> one is able to cultivate what is difficult to cultivate.
> Therefore one is always single-minded
> in the diligent practice of these dharmas.
>
> The bodhisattva is able to perfect
> such supremely sublime dharmas as these.
> It is this then that constitutes secure abiding
> in the bodhisattva's first ground.

正體字	029a09 ‖ 菩薩以是二十七法淨治初地。信力[1]增上 029a10 ‖ 者。信名有所聞見必受無疑。增上名殊 029a11 ‖ 勝。問曰。有二種增上。一者多二者勝。今說 029a12 ‖ 何者。答曰。此中二事俱說。菩薩入初地。得 029a13 ‖ 諸功德味故信力轉增。以是信力籌量諸 029a14 ‖ 佛功德無量深妙能信受。是故此心亦多亦 029a15 ‖ 勝。深行大悲者。愍念眾生徹入骨髓故名 029a16 ‖ 為深。為一切眾生求佛道故名為大。慈心 029a17 ‖ 者。常求利事安隱眾生。慈有三種。後當廣 029a18 ‖ 說。修善心無倦者。善法名可親近修習能 029a19 ‖ 與愛果。修如是法時心不懈墮。善法因緣 029a20 ‖ 名四攝法十善道六波羅蜜菩薩十地等及 029a21 ‖ 諸功德。
简体字	菩萨以是二十七法净治初地。信力增上者。信名有所闻见必受无疑。增上名殊胜。问曰。有二种增上。一者多二者胜。今说何者。答曰。此中二事俱说。菩萨入初地。得诸功德味故信力转增。以是信力筹量诸佛功德无量深妙能信受。是故此心亦多亦胜。深行大悲者。愍念众生彻入骨髓故名为深。为一切众生求佛道故名为大。慈心者。常求利事安隐众生。慈有三种。后当广说。修善心无倦者。善法名可亲近修习能与爱果。修如是法时心不懈堕。善法因缘名四摄法十善道六波罗蜜菩萨十地等及诸功德。

Chapter 4 — *Purification of the Ground*

The bodhisattva relies on these twenty-seven dharmas in the purifying cultivation of the first ground.

1. "The Power of Faith Becomes Ever More Superior"

As for "the power of faith becomes ever more superior," "faith" refers here to definitely accepting, without doubts, what one learns and perceives. "Superiority" refers here to "exceptional supremacy."

    a. Q: Of the Two Types of Superiority, of Which Do You Speak?

Question: There are two sorts of "superiority." In the case of the first, it refers to having a greater amount of something. In the case of the second, it refers to being of superior quality. Which is it that you now discuss?

    b. A: Both "More" and "Better Quality"

Response: We speak here of both definitions. When the bodhisattva enters the first ground, because he experiences the flavor of the meritorious qualities, his power of faith becomes ever greater. Because of this power of faith, having assessed all buddhas' meritorious qualities and their measurelessly many extremely sublime aspects, he is able then to have faith in and accept them. Hence this mind [of faith] becomes both greater in its extensiveness and more superior in its quality.

2. "One Practices Deeply the Mind of Great Compassion"

As for "one practices deeply the mind of great compassion," it is because one's sympathetic mindfulness of beings penetrates to one's very marrow that its practice is described as "deep." It is because one seeks to realize the Buddha path for the sake of all beings that [the practice of compassion as] is described as "great."

3. "The Mind of Kindness"

As for "the mind of kindness," one always strives to benefit beings and promote their peace and security. There are three kinds of kindness. This should be more extensively discussed later on.

4. "Tirelessly Cultivating the Mind of Goodness"

As for "tirelessly cultivating the mind of goodness," the dharma of goodness is what one draws near to and cultivates, and it is what yields desirable results. As one cultivates dharmas such as these, one's mind does not fall into indolence. As for the causes and conditions comprising good dharmas, this refers to the dharmas comprising the four means of attraction, the ten courses of good karmic action, the six *pāramitās*, the ten bodhisattva grounds, and all of the meritorious qualities.

正體字	喜樂妙法者。常思惟修習深得法 029a22 ‖ 味久則生樂。如人在花林與愛色相娛樂。 029a23 ‖ 常近善知識者。菩薩有四種善知識。後當 029a24 ‖ 廣說。此中善知識者。諸佛菩薩是。常以正心 029a25 ‖ 親近能令歡悅。慚愧名為喜羞恥。恭敬名 029a26 ‖ 念其功德尊重其人。柔軟名其心和悅同止 029a27 ‖ 安樂樂觀法者。法名五陰十二入十八界空 029a28 ‖ 無相無作等。以正憶念常觀此法。無著者。 029a29 ‖ 著名心歸趣三有。是眾生所歸。有人言。五 029b01 ‖ 欲諸邪見是所歸趣。何以故。眾生心常繫著 029b02 ‖ 故。菩薩利智心無貪著。一心名貴重佛法 029b03 ‖ 心無餘[2]想。
简体字	喜乐妙法者。常思惟修习深得法味久则生乐。如人在花林与爱色相娱乐。常近善知识者。菩萨有四种善知识。后当广说。此中善知识者。诸佛菩萨是。常以正心亲近能令欢悦。惭愧名为喜羞耻。恭敬名念其功德尊重其人。柔软名其心和悦同止安乐乐观法者。法名五阴十二入十八界空无相无作等。以正忆念常观此法。无著者。著名心归趣三有。是众生所归。有人言。五欲诸邪见是所归趣。何以故。众生心常系着故。菩萨利智心无贪着。一心名贵重佛法心无余想。

5. "One Finds Joyous Delight in Sublime Dharmas"

As for "one finds joyous delight in sublime dharmas," this means that, if one always reflects on them, cultivates them, and deeply experiences the flavor of these dharmas, after a long while, this produces happiness. This is just as when someone amidst flowers and forest groves takes pleasure in sights he finds lovely.

6. "Always Drawing Near to the Spiritual Guide"

As for "always drawing near to the good spiritual guide," the bodhisattva has four different types of good spiritual guides, a matter that shall be discussed extensively later on. As for the "good spiritual guides" that are intended here, it refers to buddhas and bodhisattvas. One always draws close to them with a mind that is correct and with which one is able to please them.

7. "A Sense of Shame" and "a Dread of Blame"

"A sense of shame and a dread of blame" refers to that mind that happily subjects itself to feeling self-consciously abashed.

8. "Reverence"

"Reverence" refers to bearing in mind someone else's meritorious qualities and revering him for that reason.

9. "Gentle and Harmonious"

"Gentle and harmonious" refers to having a mind that is congenially pleased in dwelling together with others.

10. "Delighting in Contemplating Dharmas"

In "delighting in contemplating dharmas," "dharmas" refers to the five aggregates, the twelve sense bases, the eighteen sense realms, emptiness, signlessness, wishlessness, and so forth. One always contemplates these dharmas with right mindfulness.

11. "Staying Free of Attachment"

In "staying free of attachment," "attachment" refers to the tendency of the mind to take refuge in the three realms of existence. This is where beings take refuge. There are those who explain that it is the five desires and all manner of erroneous views that constitute the places in which beings take refuge. Why is this? This is because the minds of beings always become bound up in attachment to them. The sharp wisdom of the bodhisattva is such that his mind has no such desire-based attachments.

12. "Single-Mindedness"

As for "single-mindedness," this means that one so esteems the Buddha's Dharma that one does not think of anything else.

正體字	求多[3]名聞者。佛說九部經。能 029b04 ‖ 盡推尋修學明了若少不盡。不貪利養者。 029b05 ‖ 利名得飲食財物等。養名恭敬禮拜施設床 029b06 ‖ 座迎來送去。菩薩應以是事施與眾生不 029b07 ‖ 自貪著。姦欺名斗秤邪偽衣物不真。諂名心 029b08 ‖ 不端直。誑名五邪命法。一名矯異。二名自 029b09 ‖ 親。三名激動。四名抑揚。五名因利求利。 029b10 ‖ 矯異者。有人貪求利養故。若作阿練若著 029b11 ‖ 納衣。若常乞食若一坐食。若常坐。若中後不 029b12 ‖ 飲漿。受如是等頭陀行。作是念。他作是 029b13 ‖ 行。得供養恭敬。我作是行或亦得之。為 029b14 ‖ 利養故改易威儀名為矯異。
简体字	求多名闻者。佛说九部经。能尽推寻修学明了若少不尽。不贪利养者。利名得饮食财物等。养名恭敬礼拜施设床座迎来送去。菩萨应以是事施与众生不自贪着。奸欺名斗秤邪伪衣物不真。谄名心不端直。诳名五邪命法。一名矫异。二名自亲。三名激动。四名抑扬。五名因利求利。矫异者。有人贪求利养故。若作阿练若着纳衣。若常乞食若一坐食。若常坐。若中后不饮浆。受如是等头陀行。作是念。他作是行。得供养恭敬。我作是行或亦得之。为利养故改易威仪名为矫异。

Chapter 4 — *Purification of the Ground*

13. "Striving to Acquire Abundant Learning"

"Striving to acquire abundant learning"[60] refers to the ability to exhaustively investigate, cultivate, study, and entirely comprehend the nine categories of scripture set forth by the Buddha, [realizing that] if one learns but little, one will never completely fathom them.

14. "Refraining from Coveting Offerings of Benefits and Support"

In "refraining from coveting offerings of benefits and support," "benefits" refers to the acquisition of food and drink, wealth, material possessions, and so forth. "Support" refers to others' reverential respect, ceremonial obeisance, arrangement of a place for one to rest and sit, welcoming one upon one's arrival, and escorting one off when one departs. The bodhisattva should be inclined to provide such assistance to other beings and should not covet and become attached to such things for himself.

15. "Staying Far from Cheating, Flattery, and Deception"

"Cheating" refers to deception in weights and measures and to dealing in clothing and other goods that are not genuine.

"Flattery" means one's mind is not upstanding and direct.

"Deception" refers to taking up dharmas associated with the five sorts of wrong livelihood:

a. The Five Types of Wrong Livelihood

The first is feigning uniqueness;
The second is taking advantage of a close relationship;
The third is inducement through instigation;
The fourth is [manipulation] through praising and blaming;
And the fifth is seeking to gain benefits based on one's benefits.

1) Feigning Uniqueness

As for "feigning uniqueness," there are those persons who, because they covet benefit and support, may wear the patched robes of the forest hermitage dweller, may take up the practice of only accepting food obtained on the alms round, may take up the practice of limiting all food intake to that consumed in but a single sitting, may take up the practice of always sitting [and never lying down,] or may take up the practice of not taking any sort of beverage other than water after midday. They take on the practice of such *dhūta* austerities as these, thinking, "Others who have adopted these practices have been able to come by offerings and reverence. If I take up these practices, perhaps I too shall be able to obtain them." This alteration of one's outward appearance and demeanor for the sake of acquiring benefit and support is what is meant by "feigning uniqueness."

正體字

```
           自親者。有人
029b15 || 貪利養故。詣檀越家語言。如我父母兄弟
029b16 || 姊妹親戚無異。若有所須我能相與。欲有
029b17 || 所作我能為作。我不計遠近能來問訊。我
029b18 || 住此者正相為耳。為求供養貪著檀越。能
029b19 || 以口辭牽引人心。如是等名為自親。激動
029b20 || 者。有人不計貪罪欲得財物。作得物相
029b21 || 如是言。是鉢好若衣好若戶鉤好若尼師[4]檀
029b22 || 好。若我得者則能受用。又言。隨意能施此
029b23 || 人難得。又至檀越家作是言。汝家羹飯餅
029b24 || 肉香美。衣服復好。常供養我。[5]我以親舊必
029b25 || 當見與。如是示現貪相。是名激動抑揚者。
029b26 || 有人貪利養故語檀越言。汝極慳惜。尚不
029b27 || 能與父母兄弟姊妹妻子親戚。誰能得汝
029b28 || 物者。檀越愧恥俛仰施與。又至餘家作是
029b29 || 言。汝有福德受人身不空。阿羅漢常入出
029c01 || 汝家。
```

简体字

自亲者。有人贪利养故。诣檀越家语言。如我父母兄弟姊妹亲戚无异。若有所须我能相与。欲有所作我能为作。我不计远近能来问讯。我住此者正相为耳。为求供养贪着檀越。能以口辞牵引人心。如是等名为自亲。激动者。有人不计贪罪欲得财物。作得物相如是言。是钵好若衣好若户钩好若尼师檀好。若我得者则能受用。又言。随意能施此人难得。又至檀越家作是言。汝家羹饭饼肉香美。衣服复好。常供养我。我以亲旧必当见与。如是示现贪相。是名激动抑扬者。有人贪利养故语檀越言。汝极悭惜。尚不能与父母兄弟姊妹妻子亲戚。谁能得汝物者。檀越愧耻俯仰施与。又至余家作是言。汝有福德受人身不空。阿罗汉常入出汝家。

Chapter 4 — *Purification of the Ground*

2) Taking Advantage of a Close Relationship

As for "taking advantage of a close relationship," there are those persons who, because they covet benefit and support, therefore visit the households of benefactors[61] and say to them, "You are to me just like and no different from my father, mother, brother, sister, or other close relative. If there is anything at all that you need, I will be able to assist you with it. If there's anything you need done, I will be able to see that it is done. No matter how far away I might be, I will be able to come and greet you. Actually, if I were to live right here, then that would really be the right course of action for us." Thus, because he seeks offerings, and because he has a covetous attachment to a benefactor, he resorts to particular phrasings that manipulate the minds of other people. Such behaviors as these exemplify what is meant by "taking advantage of a close relationship."

3) Inducement through Instigation

As for "inducement through instigation," there are those who pay no heed to incurring the karmic offense of covetousness, desire to obtain valuable possessions, and so indicate an interest in obtaining material possessions by saying such things as, "This bowl is a fine one," or "This robe is a fine one," or "This house is a fine one," or "This sitting mat[62] is a fine one," or "If I were to somehow obtain such a thing, I would be able to put it to use." They may then add the statement, "It is a rare person who is able to give spontaneously."

He may also go to some benefactor's home and speak in this fashion: "Your household's stew, rice, cakes, and meats are so fragrant and exquisite and your clothes are finer yet. If you were to make a regular practice of making offerings to me, based on the long-standing nature of our close relationship, I would certainly accept your gifts."

And so, in just this sort of fashion, he makes his desires apparent to others. This is what is meant by "inducement through instigation."

4) Manipulation through Praising and Blaming"

As for "manipulation through praising and blaming," there are those who, because they covet benefit and support, speak to a benefactor, saying, "You are the most extremely miserly person. You don't even make gifts to your father or mother, your brothers, your sisters, your wife, your children, or your relatives. Just who is it that might ever be able to receive anything at all from you?" Thereupon the benefactor, feeling ashamed and embarrassed, immediately gives him gifts.

He may then go to yet another household and speak in this fashion: "You have such merit that, indeed, you have not taken on this human rebirth in vain. Even arhats always come and go from your home so

正體字

```
           汝與坐起語言作是念想檀越或生
029c02 ||  是心。更無餘人入出我家必謂我。是名為
029c03 ||  抑揚。因利求利者。有人以衣若鉢[6]僧伽梨
029c04 ||  若尼師[*]檀等資生之物。持示人言。若王王
029c05 ||  等及餘貴人與我是物。作是念。檀越或能生
029c06 ||  心。彼諸王貴人尚能供養。況我不與是人。
029c07 ||  因以此利更求餘利故名因利求利。是故
029c08 ||  應當[7]遠離如此諂偽。不污諸佛家者。何
029c09 ||  等為污諸佛家。有人言。若人發求無上道
029c10 ||  心已。後迴向聲聞辟支佛道。不能住世繼
029c11 ||  三寶種。是名污諸佛家。是義不然。何以故。
029c12 ||  是人能度生死。又得諸無漏根力覺道。亦是
029c13 ||  佛子。云何言污諸佛家。如經說。佛告比丘。
029c14 ||  汝是我子。從我心生口生得法分者。又聲
029c15 ||  聞人言諦捨滅慧處。
```

简体字

汝与坐起语言作是念想檀越或生是心。更无余人入出我家必谓我。是名为抑扬。因利求利者。有人以衣若鉢僧伽梨若尼师檀等资生之物。持示人言。若王王等及余贵人与我是物。作是念。檀越或能生心。彼诸王贵人尚能供养。况我不与是人。因以此利更求余利故名因利求利。是故应当远离如此谄伪。不污诸佛家者。何等为污诸佛家。有人言。若人发求无上道心已。后回向声闻辟支佛道。不能住世继三宝种。是名污诸佛家。是义不然。何以故。是人能度生死。又得诸无漏根力觉道。亦是佛子。云何言污诸佛家。如经说。佛告比丘。汝是我子。从我心生口生得法分者。又声闻人言谛舍灭慧处。

that you are able to sit down and converse with them." He does this thinking, "Perhaps the benefactor shall now reflect on this and think: 'Nobody else comes and goes from my home,' thereby concluding that this must certainly be referring to me."

These are examples of what is meant by "manipulation through praising and blaming."

5) SEEKING TO GAIN BENEFITS BASED ON ONE'S BENEFITS

As for "seeking to gain benefits based on one's benefits," there are those who take up some item of clothing, a bowl, a *saṃghāṭī* robe, a sitting mat, or other such requisite, hold them in hand, and then say to someone, "This item was given to me by the king," or "by the equal of a king," or "by others among the nobility." He speaks in this fashion, thinking, "Perhaps the benefactor will now be able to conclude, 'If he is one to whom even the king and members of the nobility make offerings, how much the less could someone like me fail to present gifts to this man?'"

It is because he seeks by means of this previously acquired benefit to gain additional benefits that this practice is referred to as "seeking to gain benefits based on one's benefits."

One should therefore leave these sorts of obsequious and fraudulent behaviors far behind.

16. "ONE DOES NOT DEFILE THE FAMILY OF THE BUDDHAS"

In "One does not defile the family of the Buddhas," just what sorts of things constitute "defilement of the family of the Buddhas"?

There are those who say that if someone who has brought forth the resolve to seek the unsurpassable path then later reverts to the *śrāvaka*-disciple or *pratyekabuddha* paths so that he is unable to remain in the world to see to the continuance of the lineage of the Three Jewels, this is what constitutes "defiling the family of the Buddhas." However, this is a wrong explanation of its meaning. How is this so? The person referenced herein is one who is still able to achieve liberation from *saṃsāra*. Moreover, he is able to achieve a state of realization of the [five] root faculties, [five] powers, [seven] limbs of enlightenment, and [eightfold] path that is free of the contaminants. Moreover, he is still "a son of the Buddha." How then can one assert that this amounts to "defiling the family of the Buddhas"?

As stated in a sutra: "The Buddha told the bhikshus, 'You are my sons who are born from my mind, are born from my mouth, and who are heirs to the Dharma.[63'''']"

Furthermore, *śrāvaka* disciples claim that it is the [four] bases [of meritorious qualities] consisting of truth, relinquishment, quiescence,

正體字

029c16 ‖ 名諸佛家。何以故。從
029c16 ‖ 是四事出生諸佛故。若污此四法名污諸
029c17 ‖ 佛家。是故若人虛妄慳貪狂亂愚癡。是污佛
029c18 ‖ 家。若正行此四。則不污諸佛家。有人言。六
029c19 ‖ 波羅蜜是諸佛家。從此生諸佛故。若違此
029c20 ‖ 六事。是污佛家。有人言。般若波羅蜜是諸佛
029c21 ‖ 母。方便為父。是名諸佛家。以此二法出生
029c22 ‖ 諸佛。若違此法是污佛家。復次偈中自說
029c23 ‖ 污不污相。所謂不毀戒不欺佛。若受佛戒
029c24 ‖ 不能護持則欺諸佛。是污佛家。何以故。受
029c25 ‖ 戒時生佛家中。破戒則欺諸佛。名污佛家。
029c26 ‖ 問曰。必定菩薩有破戒耶。答曰。不斷煩惱
029c27 ‖ 是事可畏未久入必定菩薩或有破戒。如
029c28 ‖ 大勝佛法中[8]說。難陀故破戒。我說

简体字

名诸佛家。何以故。从是四事出生诸佛故。若污此四法名污诸佛家。是故若人虚妄悭贪狂乱愚痴。是污佛家。若正行此四。则不污诸佛家。有人言。六波罗蜜是诸佛家。从此生诸佛故。若违此六事。是污佛家。有人言。般若波罗蜜是诸佛母。方便为父。是名诸佛家。以此二法出生诸佛。若违此法是污佛家。复次偈中自说污不污相。所谓不毁戒不欺佛。若受佛戒不能护持则欺诸佛。是污佛家。何以故。受戒时生佛家中。破戒则欺诸佛。名污佛家。问曰。必定菩萨有破戒耶。答曰。不断烦恼是事可畏未久入必定菩萨或有破戒。如大胜佛法中说。难陀故破戒。我说

and wisdom that constitute the basis for abiding within the family of the Buddhas. How so? It is because all buddhas are born from these four factors. If one defiles these four dharmas, then this is what constitutes "defiling the family of the Buddhas."

Therefore, if a person acts in a false, miserly, covetous, manically deranged or foolish fashion, this is what constitutes "defiling the family of the Buddhas." If one is correct in his implementation of these four bases, then one does not "defile the family of the Buddhas."

There are others who claim that the six *pāramitās* constitute the bases for belonging to the family of the Buddhas, doing so because these are the dharmas that give birth to the Buddhas. Consequently they infer that, if one acts in a manner that contradicts these six sorts of endeavors, this is what constitutes "defiling the family of the Buddhas."

Then again, there are yet others who state that *prajñāpāramitā* serves as the mother of the Buddhas whereas skillful means serve as the father of the Buddhas. They hold that these are the factors that serve as the basis for belonging to the family of the Buddhas. They claim that, because these two dharmas give birth to all buddhas, if one transgresses against these dharmas, this constitutes "defilement of the family of the Buddhas."

17. "Not Damaging Moral Precepts" and "Not Cheating the Buddhas"

Then again, the verse itself explains what constitutes the marks of defilement and non-defilement, in particular referring to "not damaging the moral precepts" and "not cheating the Buddhas."

If one takes on the Buddha's moral precepts yet remains unable to guard and uphold them, it is this that constitutes "cheating the Buddhas" and "defiling the family of the Buddhas." How is this the case? It is because, when one takes on the moral precepts, one is born into the family of the Buddhas. If one then breaks the precepts, it is this, then, that constitutes "cheating the Buddhas" and it is this, then, that constitutes "defiling the family of the Buddhas."

a. Might a Bodhisattva at the Stage of Certainty Break Precepts?

Question: Is it possible that the bodhisattva who has reached the stage of certainty may have instances in which he breaks the moral precepts?

b. This Is Possible If He Has Not yet Cut off the Afflictions

Response: So long as one has not yet cut off the afflictions, this remains as a circumstance to be feared. Thus, when it has still not been long since he achieved entry into the stage of certainty, the bodhisattva may still have instances in which he breaks the precepts. This is as described in "the Dharma of Greatly Supreme Buddha"[64] wherein it states, "Nanda deliberately broke precepts. I declare that

正體字

	此事猶
029c29 ‖	以為畏。但以經有此說。信佛語故心則信
030a01 ‖	受。若受戒不破不欺諸佛。名為不污佛
030a02 ‖	家。復次戒名三學。戒學心學慧學。破此學
030a03 ‖	名污佛家。如法受戒而後毀破名為欺佛。
030a04 ‖	如是二句各有義趣。欺佛者。空自發願不
030a05 ‖	如說行。欺誑眾生是名欺佛。復次一切法
030a06 ‖	中不如說行。名為欺佛。堅住薩婆若不
030a07 ‖	動如[1]大山者。是菩薩一切發願求薩婆若
030a08 ‖	種種因緣。乃至大地獄苦心不移動。如須彌
030a09 ‖	山王吹不可動。常修轉上法者。從初發心
030a10 ‖	常求索勝法。入初地中更修上法。如是展
030a11 ‖	轉心無厭足。樂出世間法不樂世間[2]者。
030a12 ‖	世間法名隨順世[3]間事增長生死。六趣三
030a13 ‖	有五陰十二入

简体字

此事犹以为畏。但以经有此说。信佛语故心则信受。若受戒不破不欺诸佛。名为不污佛家。复次戒名三学。戒学心学慧学。破此学名污佛家。如法受戒而后毁破名为欺佛。如是二句各有义趣。欺佛者。空自发愿不如说行。欺诳众生是名欺佛。复次一切法中不如说行。名为欺佛。坚住萨婆若不动如大山者。是菩萨一切发愿求萨婆若种种因缘。乃至大地狱苦心不移动。如须弥山王吹不可动。常修转上法者。从初发心常求索胜法。入初地中更修上法。如是展转心无厌足。乐出世间法不乐世间者。世间法名随顺世间事增长生死。六趣三有五阴十二入

Chapter 4 — Purification of the Ground

this possibility still remains as something to be feared." It is only on the basis of the sutras that there is this claim. Because one has faith in the words of the Buddha, one's mind believes and accepts this.

If, having taken on the moral precepts, one does not break them and does not cheat the Buddhas, it is this that qualifies as "not defiling the family of the Buddhas."

Then again, the moral precepts are synonymous with the three trainings, namely: the training in the moral precepts, the training of the mind [in *dhyāna* meditation], and the training in wisdom. If one breaks with these trainings, then this is "defiling the family of the Buddhas." If one takes on the precepts in a context that accords with the Dharma and yet later damages or breaks them, this is "cheating the Buddhas."

Thus, when one explains the matter in this fashion, each of these two phrases possesses a particular meaning and implication. As for "cheating the Buddhas," if one's making of vows has been merely an empty exercise and thus one does not carry them out in practice in a manner according to one's declarations, one thereby cheats and deceives beings. It is this, then, that constitutes "cheating the Buddhas."

Then again, if one fails to practice any of the dharmas in accordance with the way it was taught, this is "cheating the Buddhas."

18. "Deeply Delighting in All-Knowledge" and "Remaining Unmoving"

As for "deeply delighting in all-knowledge" and "remaining unmoving like a great mountain," in every vow that he makes, this bodhisattva seeks the goal of all-knowledge so that, no matter what causes and conditions he encounters, even if it entails having to undergo the sufferings of the Great Hells, his resolve is still never shaken. In this, he is just like Sumeru, the king of the mountains, that cannot be moved by the blowing of the winds.

19. "Always Cultivating Ever More Superior Dharmas"

As for "always cultivating ever more superior dharmas," from that very time when one first brings forth the resolve, one always strives to acquire supreme dharmas. Upon entering the first ground, one is even more involved in cultivating superior dharmas. One's resolve then continues insatiably onward in this manner.

20. "Delighting in World-Transcending Dharmas," "Not Worldly Ones"

As for "delighting in world-transcending dharmas" and "not delighting in worldly dharmas," "worldly dharmas" refers to endeavors that follow along and accord with worldly affairs and prolong one's involvement in *saṃsāra*. These include the six rebirth destinies, the three realms of existence, the five aggregates, the twelve sense bases,

正體字	十八界十二因緣諸煩惱有漏 030a14 ‖ 業等出世間法名隨所用法能出三界。所 030a15 ‖ 謂五根五力七覺八道四念處四正勤四如意 030a16 ‖ 足空無相無作解脫門戒律儀多聞無貪恚癡 030a17 ‖ [4]善根厭離心不放逸等。是菩薩利根故。不 030a18 ‖ 樂世間虛妄法。但樂出世間真實法。即治 030a19 ‖ 歡喜地。難治而能治者。治名通達無礙。如 030a20 ‖ 人破竹初節為難餘者皆易。初地難治治已 030a21 ‖ 餘皆自易。何以故。菩薩在初地。勢力未足 030a22 ‖ 善根未厚。修習善法未久故。眼等諸根猶 030a23 ‖ 隨諸塵心未調伏。是故諸煩惱猶能為患。 030a24 ‖ 如人勢力未足逆水則難。又此地中魔及魔 030a25 ‖ 民多為障礙故。以方便力勤行精進。是故 030a26 ‖ 此地名為難治。如是信力轉增上為首。不 030a27 ‖ 樂世間法為後。修此二十七法。治菩薩初 030a28 ‖ 歡喜地。是故說菩薩應常修行此法。修行 030a29 ‖ 名一心
简体字	十八界十二因缘诸烦恼有漏业等出世间法名随所用法能出三界。所谓五根五力七觉八道四念处四正勤四如意足空无相无作解脱门戒律仪多闻无贪恚痴善根厌离心不放逸等。是菩萨利根故。不乐世间虚妄法。但乐出世间真实法。即治欢喜地。难治而能治者。治名通达无碍。如人破竹初节为难余者皆易。初地难治治已余皆自易。何以故。菩萨在初地。势力未足善根未厚。修习善法未久故。眼等诸根犹随诸尘心未调伏。是故诸烦恼犹能为患。如人势力未足逆水则难。又此地中魔及魔民多为障碍故。以方便力勤行精进。是故此地名为难治。如是信力转增上为首。不乐世间法为后。修此二十七法。治菩萨初欢喜地。是故说菩萨应常修行此法。修行名一心

the eighteen sense realms, the twelvefold chain of causes and conditions, the afflictions, contaminated karmic actions, and so forth.

As for "world-transcending dharmas," this means that, whatever dharmas one puts to use are able to bring about transcendence of the three realms of existence. These include the five root faculties, the five powers, the seven limbs of enlightenment, the eightfold path, the four stations of mindfulness, the four right efforts, the four bases of psychic power, the gates of liberation consisting of emptiness, signlessness, and wishlessness, the moral precept codes, extensive learning, the roots of goodness consisting of non-greed, non-aversion, and non-delusion, the mind of renunciation, non-neglectfulness, and so forth.

Because this bodhisattva possesses sharp faculties, he does not delight in the false dharmas of the world. Rather, he delights only in true world-transcending dharmas.

21. "Cultivating What Is Difficult to Cultivate"

As for "Even as one cultivates the Ground of Joyfulness, one is able to cultivate what is difficult to cultivate," this "cultivation" is a reference to reaching an utterly penetrating unimpeded understanding. Just as when someone splits bamboo, the first section is difficult, but the rest are easy, so too, the first ground is difficult to cultivate, but after one has cultivated it, the rest are naturally easy to cultivate.

How is this the case? This is because, when the bodhisattva abides on the first ground, his strength has not yet become completely developed and his roots of goodness have not yet grown thick, for he has not yet cultivated the dharmas of goodness over a long time. Hence the eye sense faculty and the other sense faculties are all still prone to follow their respective sense objects and the mind has not yet become well controlled. Therefore the afflictions are still able to cause trouble for him. This is just as when someone's strength has not yet become fully developed, one finds it difficult to swim upstream, against the current.

Moreover, because Māra and Māra's minions create more of an obstacle on this ground, one is therefore compelled to use the power of skillful means and be diligent in the practice of vigor. It is for these reasons that this ground is said to be "difficult to cultivate."

So it is that, beginning with "the power of faith becomes ever more superior" as the foremost factor and "does not delight in worldly dharmas" as the last, one proceeds with the practice of these twenty-seven dharmas, carrying out one's cultivation of the bodhisattva's first ground, the Ground of Joyfulness.

It is therefore stated that the bodhisattva ought to always cultivate these dharmas. "Cultivation" refers here to single-mindedness and

正體字

030b01 ‖ 不放逸。常行常觀除諸過惡。故名
030b01 ‖ 為治。如人所行道路治令清淨。是諸法不
030b02 ‖ 但修治初地。一切諸地皆以此法。問曰。汝
030b03 ‖ 已說[5]得初地方便及淨治法。菩薩云何安
030b04 ‖ 住而不退失。答曰。常行成就。如是信力轉
030b05 ‖ 增上等法。名為安住初地。菩提名上道。薩
030b06 ‖ 埵名深心。深樂菩提故名為菩提薩埵。復
030b07 ‖ 次眾生名薩埵。為眾生修集菩提故名菩
030b08 ‖ 提薩埵。上法者。信等法能令人成佛[6]道故
030b09 ‖ 名為上法。

简体字

不放逸。常行常观除诸过恶。故名为治。如人所行道路治令清净。是诸法不但修治初地。一切诸地皆以此法。问曰。汝已说得初地方便及净治法。菩萨云何安住而不退失。答曰。常行成就。如是信力转增上等法。名为安住初地。菩提名上道。萨埵名深心。深乐菩提故名为菩提萨埵。复次众生名萨埵。为众生修集菩提故名菩提萨埵。上法者。信等法能令人成佛道故名为上法。

non-neglectfulness in always practicing them, in always contemplating them, and in getting rid of all transgressions and evils. It is for this reason that it refers here to "cultivation." This is just as when one maintains a walking path and thereby causes it to remain clean.

As for all of these dharmas, they are not cultivated solely on the first ground. Rather, one uses these dharmas on all the grounds.

22. Q: How Does One "Securely Abide" and Not Retreat?

Question: You have now completed the discussion of the skillful means and purification dharmas used to attain the first ground. How then does the bodhisattva "securely abide" in it so that he does not retreat from it and lose it?

23. A: By Always Practicing and Completely Developing These Dharmas

Response: This is a matter of always practicing and completely developing dharmas such as these consisting of "the power of faith becomes ever more superior," and so forth. This is what constitutes the basis for "secure abiding" in the first ground.

24. The Meaning of "Bodhisattva" and "Superior Dharmas"

Now, as for the "*bodhi*" of bodhisattva, this is a reference to the superior path. "*Sattva*" refers to [a being] that is possessed of resolute intentions. Hence it is because someone deeply delights in bodhi that he is referred to as a "bodhisattva." Then again, one may explain that "*sattva*" refers to "beings." Hence it is on the basis of a person's cultivating and accumulating [the bases for realization of] bodhi, doing so for the sake of other beings, that one is referred to as a "bodhisattva." "Superior dharmas," refers to dharmas such as "faith" and the others. It is because they enable a person to realize buddhahood that they are referred to as "superior dharmas."

The End of Chapter Four

正體字

030b10 ||　　釋願品第五
030b11 || 已說入初地方便及淨治法。菩薩因願故得
030b12 || 入諸地。又成就信力增上等功德故安住
030b13 || 其地。今當分別此願。
030b14 || 　願供養奉給　　恭敬一切佛
030b15 || 　願皆守護持　　一切諸佛法
030b16 || 此是諸菩薩初願。從初發心乃至得阿耨多
030b17 || 羅三藐三菩提。於其中間所有諸佛。盡當
030b18 || 供養奉給恭敬。供養名花香瓔珞幡蓋燈明
030b19 || 起塔廟等。奉給名衣服臥具所須之物。恭敬
030b20 || [7]名尊重禮拜迎來送去合掌[8]親侍。復次以
030b21 || 小乘法教化眾生名為供養。以辟支佛法
030b22 || 教化眾生名為奉給。以大乘法教化眾生
030b23 || 名為恭敬。是第一願。護持一切諸佛法者。
030b24 || 菩薩作是念。

简体字

释愿品第五

　　已说入初地方便及净治法。菩萨因愿故得入诸地。又成就信力增上等功德故安住其地。今当分别此愿。

　　愿供养奉给　　恭敬一切佛
　　愿皆守护持　　一切诸佛法

　　此是诸菩萨初愿。从初发心乃至得阿耨多罗三藐三菩提。于其中间所有诸佛。尽当供养奉给恭敬。供养名花香璎珞幡盖灯明起塔庙等。奉给名衣服卧具所须之物。恭敬名尊重礼拜迎来送去合掌亲侍。复次以小乘法教化众生名为供养。以辟支佛法教化众生名为奉给。以大乘法教化众生名为恭敬。是第一愿。护持一切诸佛法者。菩萨作是念。

CHAPTER 5
The Explanation of the Vows

V. CHAPTER FIVE: EXPLANATION OF THE VOWS

We have now finished explaining the skillful means that are used in entering the first ground and the dharmas that are used in its purification. It is because of his vows that the bodhisattva gains entry into all of the grounds. It is also due to completely developing the meritorious qualities associated with the [above-discussed dharmas beginning with] "the power of faith becoming ever more superior" that one is able to securely abide on one's ground. We shall now proceed with a differentiating discussion of these vows:

A. THE FIRST BODHISATTVA VOW

I vow to make offerings to, supply the needs of,
and extend reverence to all buddhas.
I vow that in every case I shall protect and uphold
the Dharma of all buddhas.

This ["making of offerings"] is what constitutes the bodhisattva's first vow.[65] During the interim period between the time when one first brings forth the resolve up until the time one gains *anuttarasamyaksaṃbodhi*, one should make offerings to, supply the needs of, and extend reverence to all buddhas.

"Making offerings" refers to offerings of flowers, incense, strings of jewels, banners, canopies, lamplight, the erecting of stupas with shrines, and so forth. "Supplying needs" refers to providing them with robes, bedding, and necessities. "Reverence" refers to honoring them, treating them as important, making full reverential bows to them, welcoming them on arrival, seeing them off when leaving, placing the palms together, and serving them personally.

Then again, [it may be explained that] "making offerings" refers to using the dharmas of the Small Vehicle to teach beings, "supplying needs" refers to using the dharmas of the Pratyekabuddha Vehicle to teach beings, and "extending reverence" refers to using the dharmas of the Great Vehicle to teach beings.

These constitute the bases of the first vow.

B. THE SECOND BODHISATTVA VOW

As for [the second vow], "protecting and upholding the Dharma of all buddhas," the bodhisattva has this thought, "I should guard and

正體字	一切過去未來現在十方三世 030b25 ‖ 諸佛法我應守護。問曰。過去諸佛已滅法亦 030b26 ‖ 隨滅。未來諸佛未出法亦未有。尚無初轉 030b27 ‖ 法輪。何況餘法。云何當得守護。正可守護 030b28 ‖ 現在諸佛法。以諸佛現在故。答曰。過去未 030b29 ‖ 來現在諸佛法。皆是一體一相。是故若守護 030c01 ‖ 一佛法。則為守護三世諸佛法。如經說。佛 030c02 ‖ 告諸比丘。毘婆尸佛法出家受戒著衣持鉢 030c03 ‖ 禪定智慧說法教化亦如我也。是故汝難不 030c04 ‖ 然。是第二願也。復次。 030c05 ‖ 　諸佛從兜[9]術　　退來在世間 030c06 ‖ 　乃至教化訖　　永入無餘界 030c07 ‖ 　處胎及生時　　出家趣道場 030c08 ‖ 　降魔成佛道　　初轉妙法輪 030c09 ‖ 　奉迎諸如來　　[10]及於餘時中 030c10 ‖ 　願我悉當得　　盡心而供養 030c11 ‖ 諸佛始從兜[11]術天上退下世間。終至無餘 030c12 ‖ 涅槃。於其中間入[12]胎時大設供養。[13]及生 030c13 ‖ 時出家趣道場。降魔王
简体字	一切过去未来现在十方三世诸佛法我应守护。问曰。过去诸佛已灭法亦随灭。未来诸佛未出法亦未有。尚无初转法轮。何况余法。云何当得守护。正可守护现在诸佛法。以诸佛现在故。答曰。过去未来现在诸佛法。皆是一体一相。是故若守护一佛法。则为守护三世诸佛法。如经说。佛告诸比丘。毗婆尸佛法出家受戒着衣持钵禅定智慧说法教化亦如我也。是故汝难不然。是第二愿也。复次。 　　诸佛从兜术　　退来在世间 　　乃至教化讫　　永入无余界 　　处胎及生时　　出家趣道场 　　降魔成佛道　　初转妙法轮 　　奉迎诸如来　　及于余时中 　　愿我悉当得　　尽心而供养 　诸佛始从兜术天上退下世间。终至无余涅槃。于其中间入胎时大设供养。及生时出家趣道场。降魔王

Chapter 5 — *The Explanation of the Vows* 169

protect the Dharma of all past, future, and present buddhas of the ten directions."⁶⁶

Question: All buddhas of the past have already entered nirvāṇa and their Dharma has subsequently also become extinct. The buddhas of the future have not yet come forth and their Dharma does not yet even exist. They have not yet even initiated their turning of the wheel of Dharma, how much the less have they brought forth any other dharmas. How then could one succeed in protecting it? That which one might rightly be able to protect is the Dharma of the buddhas of the present, this because all of those buddhas are still present.

Response: The Dharma of all buddhas of the past, future and present is in every case of a single substance and of a single character. Hence, if one protects the Dharma of a single buddha, then this constitutes protection of the Dharma of all buddhas of the three periods of time. This is as stated in a sutra that reads, "The Buddha informed the bhikshus: 'The Dharma of Vipaśyin Buddha—the leaving of the home life, the taking on of the moral precepts, the wearing of the robes, the holding of the bowl, the *dhyāna* absorptions, the wisdom, the proclamation of Dharma, and their transformative teaching—it is all the same as mine.'" Thus the challenge you have posed is invalid. This [protection of the Dharma] is what constitutes the second of the vows.

Next, we have the following:

C. THE THIRD BODHISATTVA VOW

> From that time when all buddhas depart from the Tuṣita Heaven
> and come back to abide in the world,
> on forward to the conclusion of their teaching
> and their eternal entry into the realm [of nirvāṇa] without residue,
>
> including when they abide in the womb, take birth,
> leave the home life, proceed to the *bodhimaṇḍa*,
> conquer Māra, achieve buddhahood,
> and begin turning the wheel of the sublime Dharma—
>
> From the time when I respectfully welcome them
> and on through to the other occasions throughout their lives,
> I vow that in all cases I shall completely
> devote my mind to making offerings to them.⁶⁷

This refers to that entire time beginning with the buddhas' withdrawal from the Tuṣita Heaven and descent into the world on up to their entry into the nirvāṇa without residue. During that entire interval, commencing with their entry into the womb, I shall arrange grand presentations of offerings to them, including as well those times when they are born, leave the home life, proceed to the *bodhimaṇḍa*, conquer Māra,

正體字

```
              成佛道轉法輪
030c14 ‖ 奉迎如來。餘時者。現大神通人天大會廣
030c15 ‖ 度眾生。爾時當以華香幡蓋伎[14]樂歌頌稱
030c16 ‖ 讚。出家受法如說修行。以第一供養之具
030c17 ‖ 供養諸佛。是第三願。復次。
030c18 ‖   願教化眾生    令悉入諸道
030c19 ‖ 教名[15]教他以善法。化名遠離惡法。我當
030c20 ‖ 以此二法令無量阿僧祇眾生。住聲聞辟
030c21 ‖ 支佛道。是第四願。復次。
030c22 ‖   願一切眾生    成就佛菩提
030c23 ‖   有人向聲聞    辟支佛道者
030c24 ‖ 是人修集聲聞辟支佛法未入法位。我當
030c25 ‖ 教化令趣佛道。有人不向聲聞辟支佛道。
030c26 ‖ 我當教化令向無上佛道。有人向無上佛
030c27 ‖ 道者。我當示教利喜令其功德轉更增益。如
030c28 ‖ 是教化一切眾生。是第五願。
```

简体字

成佛道转法轮奉迎如来。余时者。现大神通人天大会广度众生。尔时当以华香幡盖伎乐歌颂称赞。出家受法如说修行。以第一供养之具供养诸佛。是第三愿。复次。

　　愿教化众生　　令悉入诸道

教名教他以善法。化名远离恶法。我当以此二法令无量阿僧祇众生。住声闻辟支佛道。是第四愿。复次。

　　愿一切众生　　成就佛菩提
　　有人向声闻　　辟支佛道者

是人修集声闻辟支佛法未入法位。我当教化令趣佛道。有人不向声闻辟支佛道。我当教化令向无上佛道。有人向无上佛道者。我当示教利喜令其功德转更增益。如是教化一切众生。是第五愿。

Chapter 5 — *The Explanation of the Vows* 171

the king of the demons, realize buddhahood, and turn the wheel of Dharma. I shall respectfully serve the Tathāgatas at these times.

As for "and on through to the other occasions throughout their lives," this refers to when they manifest great spiritual powers, abide in great assemblies of humans and devas, and engage in the extensive liberation of beings. [He vows]: "On such occasions, I shall make offerings to them of flowers, incense, banners, canopies, music, songs, verses, and praises. I shall leave behind the home life, take on the Dharma, and cultivate its practice in accordance with the way it has been taught. And I shall make offerings to the Buddhas of the foremost sorts of offering gifts." This is what constitutes the third vow.

D. The Fourth Bodhisattva Vow

Next, we have the following:

> I vow to engage in the transformative teaching of beings,
> causing them all to enter the paths.[68]

"Teaching" refers here to the teaching of good dharmas. "Transformation" refers to influencing them to abandon evil dharmas. [One resolves]: "Using these two types of dharmas I shall cause an incalculable number of *asaṃkhyeyas* of beings to abide in the paths of *śrāvaka* disciples and *pratyekabuddhas*." This is what constitutes the fourth of the vows.

E. The Fifth Bodhisattva Vow

Next, we have the following:

> I vow to enable all beings'
> complete realization of the Buddha's bodhi
> even where there are those tending toward *śrāvaka*-disciple
> or *pratyekabuddha* paths—[69]

In instances where these persons cultivating the paths of the *śrāvaka* disciples and the *pratyekabuddhas* have not yet entered the [right and fixed] Dharma position,[70] I shall teach and transform them, inducing them to instead proceed toward the path to buddhahood. Where there are those who have not taken up the paths of *śrāvaka* disciples or *pratyekabuddhas*, I shall teach and transform them in a manner that influences them to proceed toward the unsurpassable path to buddhahood. In instances where others have already begun to proceed toward the unsurpassable path to buddhahood, I shall reveal [aspects of Dharma], instruct, benefit, and delight them,[71] thereby causing their meritorious qualities to progressively increase. The fifth vow consists of adopting these means in the teaching and transforming of all beings.

正體字	復次。 030c29 ‖　　願使一切法　　信解入平等 031a01 ‖ 一切法者。凡所有法。度法非度法。攝覺意法。 031a02 ‖ 非攝覺意法。助道法非助道法。聖道所攝法 031a03 ‖ 非聖道所攝法。應修法不應修法。應近法不 031a04 ‖ 應近法。應生法不應生法。生法不生法。現在 031a05 ‖ 法非現在法。因緣生法非因緣生法。因緣法 031a06 ‖ 非因緣法。從思惟生法不從思惟生法。麁法 031a07 ‖ 細法。受法不受法。內法外法。內入所攝法非 031a08 ‖ 內入所攝法。外入所攝法非外入所攝法。五 031a09 ‖ 陰所攝法非五陰所攝法。五受陰所攝法非 031a10 ‖ 五受陰所攝法。
简体字	复次。 　　愿使一切法　　信解入平等 　一切法者。凡所有法。度法非度法。摄觉意法。非摄觉意法。助道法非助道法。圣道所摄法非圣道所摄法。应修法不应修法。应近法不应近法。应生法不应生法。生法不生法。现在法非现在法。因缘生法非因缘生法。因缘法非因缘法。从思惟生法不从思惟生法。粗法细法。受法不受法。内法外法。内入所摄法非内入所摄法。外入所摄法非外入所摄法。五阴所摄法非五阴所摄法。五受阴所摄法非五受阴所摄法。

F. The Sixth Bodhisattva Vow

Next, we have the following:

> Through resolute faith, I vow
> to cause all dharmas to enter [a state of] uniform equality.[72]

"All dharmas" is a general reference to all dharmas whatsoever, including:

- Dharmas conducing to liberation and dharmas not conducing to liberation;
- Dharmas subsumed within the limbs of enlightenment and dharmas not subsumed within the limbs of enlightenment;
- Dharmas constituting provisions assisting the path and dharmas not constituting provisions assisting the path;
- Dharmas subsumed within the paths of the Āryas and dharmas not subsumed within the paths of the Āryas;
- Dharmas that should be cultivated and dharmas that should not be cultivated;
- Dharmas to which one should draw near and dharmas to which one should not draw near;
- Dharmas one should bring forth and dharmas one should not bring forth;
- Dharmas that are produced and dharmas that are unproduced;
- Dharmas of the present and dharmas not of the present;
- Dharmas that are the product of causes and conditions and dharmas that are not the product of causes and conditions;
- Dharmas constituting causes and conditions and dharmas not constituting causes and conditions;
- Dharmas produced through meditative contemplation and dharmas not produced through meditative contemplation;
- Dharmas that are coarse and dharmas that are subtle;
- Dharmas associated with feeling and dharmas not associated with feeling;
- Inward dharmas and outward dharmas;
- Dharmas belonging to the inward sense bases and dharmas not belonging to inward sense bases;
- Dharmas belonging to outward sense bases and dharmas not belonging to outward sense bases;
- Dharmas subsumed within the five aggregates and dharmas not subsumed within the five aggregates;
- Dharmas subsumed within the five appropriated aggregates and dharmas not subsumed within the five appropriated aggregates;

正體字

四諦所攝法非四諦所攝法。
031a11 ‖ 助世法非助世法。依貪法依出法。顛倒法非
031a12 ‖ 顛倒法。變法非變法。悔法非悔法。大法小法。
031a13 ‖ 受處法非受處法。可斷法不可斷法。知見法
031a14 ‖ [1]不知見法。有漏法無漏法。有繫法無繫法。
031a15 ‖ 有淨法無淨法。有上法無上法。有覺法無覺
031a16 ‖ 法。有觀法無觀法。可喜法[*]不可喜法。相應
031a17 ‖ 法不相應法。有分別法無分別法。行法無行
031a18 ‖ 法。有緣法無緣法。有次第法無次第法。可見
031a19 ‖ 法不可見法。有對法無對法。可見有對法不
031a20 ‖ 可見無對法。

简体字

四谛所摄法非四谛所摄法。助世法非助世法。依贪法依出法。颠倒法非颠倒法。变法非变法。悔法非悔法。大法小法。受处法非受处法。可断法不可断法。知见法不知见法。有漏法无漏法。有系法无系法。有净法无净法。有上法无上法。有觉法无觉法。有观法无观法。可喜法不可喜法。相应法不相应法。有分别法无分别法。行法无行法。有缘法无缘法。有次第法无次第法。可见法不可见法。有对法无对法。可见有对法不可见无对法。

Dharmas subsumed by the four truths and dharmas not subsumed by the four truths;

Dharmas assisting the world and dharmas not assisting the world;

Dharmas dependent on covetousness and dharmas dependent on transcendence;

Dharmas associated with inverted views and dharmas not associated with inverted views;

Dharmas associated with transformations and dharmas not associated with transformations;

Dharmas associated with regret and dharmas not associated with regret;

Dharmas that are great and dharmas that are small;

Dharmas based in the feeling aggregate and dharmas not based in the feeling aggregate;

Dharmas subject to severance and dharmas not subject to severance;

Dharmas associated with knowledge and vision and dharmas not associated with knowledge and vision;

Dharmas associated with the contaminants and dharmas not associated with the contaminants;

Dharmas involving the bonds and dharmas free of the bonds;

Dharmas characterized by purity and dharmas devoid of purity;

Dharmas that are surpassable and dharmas that are unsurpassable;

Dharmas involving initial ideation (*vitarka*) and dharmas not involving initial ideation;

Dharmas involving mental discursion (*vicāra*) and dharmas not involving mental discursion;

Dharmas in which one can delight and dharmas in which one cannot delight;

Dharmas that are associated [with the mind] and dharmas not associated [with the mind];

Dharmas involving the making of discriminations and dharmas not involving the making of discriminations;

Dharmas associated with formative factors (*saṃskāra*) and dharmas not associated with formative factors;

Dharmas involving conditions and dharmas not involving conditions;

Dharmas involving sequence and dharmas devoid of sequence;

Dharmas that are visible and dharmas that are not visible;

Dharmas that may be opposed [as objective conditions] and dharmas that cannot be opposed [as objective conditions];

Dharmas that are visible and opposable [as objective conditions] and dharmas that are invisible and not opposable;

正體字	有相法無相法。可行法不可行 031a21 ‖ 法有為法無為法。險法非險法。有本法無本 031a22 ‖ 法。有出法無出法。眾生法非眾生法。苦者法 031a23 ‖ 非苦者法。惱法非惱法。有法非有法。逆法非 031a24 ‖ 逆法。樂報法非樂報法。苦報法非苦報法。憶 031a25 ‖ 生法非憶生法。智首行法非智首行法。信首 031a26 ‖ 行法非信首行法。思惟首行法非思惟首行 031a27 ‖ 法。願首行法非願首行法。色法非色法。教法 031a28 ‖ 非教法。變化法非變化法。如意遊行法非如 031a29 ‖ 意遊行法。欲本法非欲本法。
简体字	有相法无相法。可行法不可行法有为法无为法。险法非险法。有本法无本法。有出法无出法。众生法非众生法。苦者法非苦者法。恼法非恼法。有法非有法。逆法非逆法。乐报法非乐报法。苦报法非苦报法。忆生法非忆生法。智首行法非智首行法。信首行法非信首行法。思惟首行法非思惟首行法。愿首行法非愿首行法。色法非色法。教法非教法。变化法非变化法。如意游行法非如意游行法。欲本法非欲本法。

Dharmas possessing characteristic signs and dharmas that are signless;

Dharmas that can be implemented in practice and dharmas that cannot be implemented in practice;

Dharmas that are conditioned and dharmas that are unconditioned;

Dharmas that are dangerous and dharmas that are not dangerous;

Dharmas possessed of a foundation and dharmas not possessed of any foundation;

Dharmas conducive to transcendence and dharmas not conducive to transcendence;

Dharmas associated with beings and dharmas not associated with beings;

Dharmas of one who is suffering and dharmas of one who is not suffering;

Dharmas associated with the afflictions and dharmas not associated with the afflictions;

Dharmas associated with existence and dharmas not associated with existence;

Dharmas that are contrary and dharmas that are not contrary;

Dharmas associated with the karmic result of happiness and dharmas not associated with the karmic result of happiness;

Dharmas associated with the karmic result of suffering and dharmas not associated with the karmic result of suffering;

Dharmas produced through recollection and dharmas not produced through recollection;

Practice dharmas in which knowledge is foremost and practice dharmas in which knowledge is not foremost;

Practice dharmas in which faith is foremost and practice dharmas in which faith is not foremost;

Practice dharmas in which meditative contemplation is foremost and practice dharmas in which meditative contemplation is not foremost;

Practice dharmas in which vows are foremost and practice dharmas in which vows are not foremost;

Form dharmas and dharmas not associated with form;

Teaching dharmas and non-teaching dharmas;

Dharmas associated with transformationally created phenomena and dharmas unassociated with transformationally created phenomena;

Dharmas associated with roaming wherever one wishes and dharmas unassociated with roaming wherever one wishes;

Dharmas rooted in zeal and dharmas not rooted in zeal;

正體字	因善法非因善 031b01 ‖ 法。因善根法非因善根法。定法非定法。身法 031b02 ‖ 非身法。口法非口法。意法非意法。有對觸生 031b03 ‖ 法非有對觸生法。意觸生法非意觸生法。惡 031b04 ‖ 法非惡法。善法非善法。能生法非能生法。念 031b05 ‖ 念滅法非念念滅法。攝聚法非攝聚法。明分 031b06 ‖ 法非明分法。因法非因法。緣法非緣法。因 031b07 ‖ 緣法非因緣法。因生法非因生法。有因法非 031b08 ‖ 有因法。一法異法。滅法非滅法。攝根法非攝 031b09 ‖ 根法。共心法非共心法。
简体字	因善法非因善法。因善根法非因善根法。定法非定法。身法非身法。口法非口法。意法非意法。有对触生法非有对触生法。意触生法非意触生法。恶法非恶法。善法非善法。能生法非能生法。念念灭法非念念灭法。摄聚法非摄聚法。明分法非明分法。因法非因法。缘法非缘法。因缘法非因缘法。因生法非因生法。有因法非有因法。一法异法。灭法非灭法。摄根法非摄根法。共心法非共心法。

Chapter 5 — *The Explanation of the Vows*   179

Dharmas in which the cause is goodness and dharmas in which the cause is not goodness;

Dharmas in which the cause is roots of goodness and dharmas in which the cause is not roots of goodness;

Dharmas that are fixed and dharmas that are unfixed;

Dharmas associated with the physical body and dharmas not associated with the physical body;

Dharmas associated with speech and dharmas not associated with speech;

Dharmas associated with the mind faculty and dharmas not associated with the mind faculty;

Dharmas arising through contact with opposable objects and dharmas not arising through contact with opposable objects;

Dharmas arising through mind faculty contact and dharmas not arising through mind faculty contact;

Evil dharmas and dharmas that are not evil;

Good dharmas and dharmas that are not good;

Dharmas that are able to initiate production and dharmas that are not able to initiate production;

Dharmas destroyed in each successive mind-moment and dharmas not destroyed in each successive mind-moment;

Dharmas that are accumulated and dharmas that are not accumulated;

Dharmas associated with the factors conducing to clear understanding[73] and dharmas not associated with the factors conducing to clear understanding;

Dharmas that are causal and dharmas that are not causal;

Dharmas associated with conditions and dharmas not associated with conditions;

Dharmas associated with causes and conditions and dharmas not associated with causes and conditions;

Dharmas produced through causes and dharmas not produced through causes;

Dharmas that are caused and dharmas that are not caused;

Dharmas associated with singular identity and dharmas associated with difference;

Dharmas associated with cessation and dharmas unassociated with cessation;

Dharmas associated with restraint of the sense faculties and dharmas not associated with restraint of the sense faculties;

Dharmas occurring in conjunction with the mind and dharmas not occurring in conjunction with the mind;

正體字	心法非心法。心數法 031b10 ‖ 非心數法。共觸五法非共觸五法。共得十六 031b11 ‖ 法非共得十六法。細法麁法。迴向法非迴向 031b12 ‖ 法。善法不善法。無記法見諦所斷法思惟所 031b13 ‖ 斷法不斷法。學法無學法。非學非無學法等。 031b14 ‖ 無量千萬種諸法。皆令入空無相無作門平 031b15 ‖ 等無二。以信解力故。是第六願。[2]復次。 031b16 ‖ 十住毘婆沙論卷第二 031b19 ‖ 十住毘婆沙論卷第三　031b20 ‖ 031b21 ‖　　[*]聖者龍樹造 031b22 ‖　　[*]後秦龜茲國三藏鳩摩羅什譯 031b23 ‖　　**[3]釋願[4]品之[5]餘** 031b24 ‖　願淨佛土故　　滅除諸雜惡 031b25 ‖ 殺生偷盜邪婬妄語兩舌惡口綺語。貪恚邪 031b26 ‖ 命飲酒等。有如是惡名為不淨。復次國土 031b27 ‖ 中有地獄畜生餓鬼等諸惡道名為不淨。復 031b28 ‖ 次眾生
简体字	心法非心法。心数法非心数法。共触五法非共触五法。共得十六法非共得十六法。细法粗法。回向法非回向法。善法不善法。无记法见谛所断法思惟所断法不断法。学法无学法。非学非无学法等。无量千万种诸法。皆令入空无相无作门平等无二。以信解力故。是第六愿。 十住毗婆沙论卷第三 释愿品第五之余 　　复次。 　　愿净佛土故　　灭除诸杂恶 　　杀生偷盗邪淫妄语两舌恶口绮语。贪恚邪命饮酒等。有如是恶名为不净。复次国土中有地狱畜生饿鬼等诸恶道名为不净。复次众生

Mind dharmas and dharmas that are not mind;
Dharmas associated with the mind and dharmas unassociated with the mind;
The five dharmas associated with contact and dharmas that are not the five dharmas associated with contact;
Sixteen dharmas the acquisition of which is held in common and dharmas unassociated with the sixteen dharmas the acquisition of which is held in common;
Subtle dharmas and coarse dharmas;
Dharmas associated with dedication of merit and dharmas not associated with dedication of merit;
Good dharmas and dharmas that are not good;
Neutral dharmas;
Dharmas severed on the path of seeing the truths;
Dharmas severed on the path of meditation;
Dharmas that are not severed;
Dharmas of those still in training;
Dharmas of those already beyond training;
Dharmas neither of those still in training nor of those beyond training;
And all of the other incalculably many thousands of myriads of types of dharmas.

In every case one causes all of these dharmas to enter into the gates of emptiness, signlessness, and wishlessness so that they are realized to be uniformly equal and beyond duality. This is accomplished through the power of resolute faith. This is the sixth of the vows.

G. The Seventh Bodhisattva Vow

Next, we have the following:

Having vowed to purify the buddhalands,
I shall therefore extinguish all the various forms of evil.[74]

1. An Exhaustive List of the Characteristics of Evil and Impurity

"[The various forms of evil]" refers to killing beings, stealing, sexual misconduct, false speech, divisive speech, harsh speech, frivolous or lewd speech, greed, anger, wrong livelihood, consumption of intoxicants, and so forth. Wherever evils of these sorts are present, it is these places that are referred to as "impure."

Additionally, where a land includes the wretched destinies of the hells, animals, hungry ghosts, and such, these too are deemed to be "impure." Then again, it is also the case that "impurity" refers to circumstances in which beings have become covered over by such qualities as the following:

| 正體字 | 　　　無信懈怠亂心愚癡諂曲慳嫉忿恨重
031b29 ‖ 邪見慢憍慢大慢我慢邪慢。矯異自親激動
031c01 ‖ 抑揚。因利求利貴於世樂。放逸自恣多欲
031c02 ‖ 惡欲邪貪邪婬。不識父母沙門婆羅門。不
031c03 ‖ 忍辱破威儀難與語。邪覺觀貪欲瞋恚睡眠
031c04 ‖ 調戲[6]疑所覆蔽名為不淨。 |

| 简体字 | 无信懈怠乱心愚痴谄曲悭嫉忿恨重邪见慢憍慢大慢我慢邪慢。矫异自亲激动抑扬。因利求利贵于世乐。放逸自恣多欲恶欲邪贪邪淫。不识父母沙门婆罗门。不忍辱破威仪难与语。邪觉观贪欲嗔恚睡眠调戏疑所覆蔽名为不净。 |

Chapter 5 — *The Explanation of the Vows*

Absence of faith;
Indolence;
Mental scatteredness;
Stupidity;
Flattery;
Deviousness;
Miserliness;
Jealousy;
Rage;
Enmity;
Gravely erroneous views;
Pride;
Arrogance;
Pride based on estimations of greatness;
Pride based on the view of a self;
Deviancy-based pride;
Feigning uniqueness;
Manipulation of feelings of close relationship;
Inducement through instigation;
Manipulation through praising and blaming;
Seeking to gain benefits based on one's benefits;[75]
Esteeming worldly pleasures;
Negligence;
Absence of self-restraint;
Abundant desires;
Evil desires;
Deviant types of desire;
Sexual misconduct;
Failing to acknowledge [indebtedness to] one's father or mother, *śramaṇas*, or brahmans;
Failing to practice patience;
Breaking with the awesome deportment [required by the monastic moral code];
Making oneself difficult to remonstrate with;
Indulging in erroneous forms of initial ideation and secondary mental discursion;
Sensual desire;
Ill will;
[Lethargy and] sleepiness;
Agitated excitedness;
Or doubtfulness.[76]

正體字	復次惡鳥獸多 031c05 ‖ 怨賊。無水漿飢饉災疫人畏非人畏。內反 031c06 ‖ 逆[7]外賊寇。若多雨若亢旱諸衰惱小劫盡諸 031c07 ‖ 苦惱等名為不淨。復次眾生短命惡色無力 031c08 ‖ 多諸憂苦。少膽幹多疾病少威力。少眷屬 031c09 ‖ 惡眷屬易壞眷屬。小居家儜劣邪出家名為 031c10 ‖ 不淨。復次僧佉榆伽[8]憂樓迦王那波羅他毘 031c11 ‖ 佉那[9]洴莎王。那吉略仙人象仙人
简体字	复次恶鸟兽多怨贼。无水浆饥馑灾疫人畏非人畏。内反逆外贼寇。若多雨若亢旱诸衰恼小劫尽诸苦恼等名为不净。复次众生短命恶色无力多诸忧苦。少胆干多疾病少威力。少眷属恶眷属易坏眷属。小居家儜劣邪出家名为不净。复次僧佉榆伽忧楼迦王那波罗他毗佉那洴莎王。那吉略仙人象仙人

Chapter 5 — The Explanation of the Vows

Yet again, "impurity" is present in circumstances where there are manifestations such as the following:

Vicious birds and beasts;
An abundance of hostile bandits;
An absence of water or other things to drink;
Hunger;
Famine;
Disasters;
Pestilence;
Terror wrought by humans;
Terror wrought by nonhumans;
Rebellion from within [the state];
Pillaging invaders from beyond [the borders];
Excessive rains;
Drought;
Distress associated with [societal] decline;
Or all of the various sorts of suffering and affliction typical of the ending of minor kalpas.

Then again, "impurity" is also present in circumstances where beings are beset by manifestations such as:

A short life span;
A horribly ugly physical body;
Weakness;
An abundance of every sort of worry and suffering;
Insufficient courage or ability;
An abundance of sickness;
Inferior charismatic power;
A small retinue;
An evil retinue;
A retinue that is easily brought to ruin;
Small residences;
Or weak-willed, base, and deviant mendicants.

Also, "impurity" is present wherever there manifest among the householders or renunciates any of the wrong views and wrong practices exemplified by the following:

Seng-qu-yu-jia-you-lou-jia kings;
Na-bo-luo-ta-pi-qu-na-ping-sha kings;
Na-ji-liao rishis;[77]
Elephant rishis;

正體字	斷婬人上 031c12 ‖ 弟子行者。放羊者。大心者。忍辱者。喬曇摩鳩 031c13 ‖ 蘭陀磨活人者。度人者。[10]緣水者。婆羅沙伽 031c14 ‖ 那頗羅墮闍。著衣者。無衣者。韋索衣者。皮衣 031c15 ‖ 者。草衣者。著下衣者。角鶚毛衣者。木皮衣 031c16 ‖ 者。三洗者。隨順者。事梵王者。事究摩羅 031c17 ‖ 者。事毘舍闍者。事金翅鳥者。事乾闥婆 031c18 ‖ 者。事閻羅王者。事毘沙門王者。事密迹 031c19 ‖ 神者。事浮陀神者。事龍者。裸形沙門。白衣 031c20 ‖ 沙門。染衣沙門。末迦梨沙門。毘羅哆子者。迦 031c21 ‖ 旃延[11]尼子者。薩耆遮子者。持牛戒者。鹿戒 031c22 ‖ 者。狗戒者。馬戒者。
简体字	断淫人上弟子行者。放羊者。大心者。忍辱者。乔昙摩鸠兰陀磨活人者。度人者。缘水者。婆罗沙伽那颇罗堕阇。着衣者。无衣者。韦索衣者。皮衣者。草衣者。着下衣者。角鸥毛衣者。木皮衣者。三洗者。随顺者。事梵王者。事究摩罗者。事毗舍闍者。事金翅鸟者。事乾闼婆者。事阎罗王者。事毗沙门王者。事密迹神者。事浮陀神者。事龙者。裸形沙门。白衣沙门。染衣沙门。末迦梨沙门。毗罗哆子者。迦旃延尼子者。萨耆遮子者。持牛戒者。鹿戒者。狗戒者。马戒者。

Chapter 5 — *The Explanation of the Vows*   187

Those [whose path is merely] celibacy;
Those whose practice is that of "the superior disciple";
The sheep herders;
The "great-mind" practitioners;
The "patient ones";
The *qiao-tan-mo-jiu-lan-to-mo* "live ones";
The "deliverers";
The "swimmers";
The *po-luo-sha-jia-na-po-luo-duo-she* practitioners;
The "robe-wearers";
The "robeless ones";
Those wearing leather robes;
Those who dress in skins;
Those who dress in grass;
Those who dress in the lower robe;
Those who dress in horned-owl feathers;
Those who dress in tree bark;
Those who wash three times;
The "adapters";
Those who serve the king of the Brahma Heaven;
Those who serve the *kumāra* virgins;
Those who serve the *piśācī* ghosts;
Those who serve the golden-winged *garuḍa* bird;
Those who serve the *gandharvas*;
Those who serve King Yāma;
Those who serve Vaiśravana;
Those who serve the *guhyapāda* vajra spirits;
Those who serve the *bhūta* spirits;
Those who serve the dragons;
The naked *śramaṇas*;[78]
The white-robed *śramaṇas*;[79]
The dyed-robe *śramaṇas*;
The Maskarī Gośālīputra *śramaṇas*;[80]
The followers of Piluochizi;[81]
The followers of Jiazhanyannizi;[82]
The followers of Saqizhezi;[83]
Those practicing cow morality;
Those practicing deer morality;
Those practicing dog morality;
Those practicing horse morality;

正體字	象戒者。乞戒者。究摩羅 031c23 ‖ 戒者。諸天戒者。上戒者。婬欲戒者。淨潔戒 031c24 ‖ 者。[12]火戒者。說色滅涅槃者。說聲滅涅槃 031c25 ‖ 者。說香滅涅槃者。說味滅涅槃者。說觸滅 031c26 ‖ 涅槃者。說覺觀滅涅槃者。說[13]喜滅涅槃 031c27 ‖ 者。說苦樂滅涅槃者。水衣為鬘者。水淨者。 031c28 ‖ 食淨者。生淨者。執杵臼者。打石者。喜洗者。 031c29 ‖ 浮沒者。空地住者。臥刺蕀者。世性者。大者 032a01 ‖ 我者。色等者。聲等者。香等者。味等者。觸等 032a02 ‖ 者。地知者。水知者。火知者。
简体字	象戒者。乞戒者。究摩罗戒者。诸天戒者。上戒者。淫欲戒者。净洁戒者。火戒者。说色灭涅槃者。说声灭涅槃者。说香灭涅槃者。说味灭涅槃者。说触灭涅槃者。说觉观灭涅槃者。说喜灭涅槃者。说苦乐灭涅槃者。水衣为鬘者。水净者。食净者。生净者。执杵臼者。打石者。喜洗者。浮没者。空地住者。卧刺蕀者。世性者。大者我者。色等者。声等者。香等者。味等者。触等者。地知者。水知者。火知者。

Chapter 5 — The Explanation of the Vows

Those practicing elephant morality;
Those whose morality consists in begging;
Those whose morality is that of the *kumāra* virgins;
Those whose morality is that of devas;
Those whose practice is the "superior" precepts;
Those whose moral code is defined by indulgence of sexual desire;
Those whose moral code is remaining pristinely immaculate;
Those who practice the "fire" morality;
Those who declare nirvāṇa to derive from the extinction of visually-perceived forms;
Those who declare nirvāṇa to derive from the extinction of sounds;
Those who declare nirvāṇa to derive from the extinction of smells;
Those who declare nirvāṇa to derive from the extinction of tastes;
Those who declare nirvāṇa to derive from the extinction of touchables;
Those who declare nirvāṇa to derive from the extinction of initial ideation and mental discursion;
Those who declare nirvāṇa to derive from the extinction of joy;
Those who declare nirvāṇa to derive from the extinction of pain and pleasure;[84]
Those who wear the water-robe headdress;
Those whose practice is rooted in purity of water;
Those whose practice is rooted in purity of food;
Those whose practice is rooted in purity of caste;
Those who carry about the mortar and pestle;
Those who are breakers of rocks;
Those who delight in bathing;
Those who float and then sink;
Those who abide out on the open ground;
Those who lie down on sharp thorns;
Those of a worldly nature;
Those who are "the Great Ones";
Those whose practice is rooted in the self;
Those who posit identity with forms;
Those who posit identity with sounds;
Those who posit identity with smells;
Those who posit identity with tastes;
Those who posit identity with touchables;
The earth-realizers;
The water-realizers;
The fire-realizers;

正體字	風知者。虛空知 032a03 ‖ 者。和合知者。變知者。眼知者。耳知者。鼻知 032a04 ‖ 者。舌知者。身知者。意知者。神知者。如是等 032a05 ‖ 在家出家種種邪見邪行名為不淨。復次其 032a06 ‖ 地高下坑坎[1]埠阜榛叢刺棘多所妨[2]閡。塵 032a07 ‖ 土坌穢泥潦臼陷。惡山巉巖屈曲限障。重嶺 032a08 ‖ 隔塞峻峭難上。鹹鹵乾燥沙礫瓦石。眾果少 032a09 ‖ 味色香不具。藥草不良。勢力薄少[3]少有妙 032a10 ‖ 色聲香味觸。
简体字	风知者。虚空知者。和合知者。变知者。眼知者。耳知者。鼻知者。舌知者。身知者。意知者。神知者。如是等在家出家种种邪见邪行名为不净。复次其地高下坑坎埠阜榛丛刺棘多所妨阂。尘土坌秽泥潦臼陷。恶山巉岩屈曲限障。重岭隔塞峻峭难上。碱卤干燥沙砾瓦石。众果少味色香不具。药草不良。势力薄少少有妙色声香味触。

Chapter 5 — *The Explanation of the Vows*

The wind realizers;
The space realizers;
The unity realizers;
The transformation realizers;
The eye-faculty realizers;
The ear-faculty realizers;
The nose-faculty realizers;
The tongue-faculty realizers;
The physical-body realizers;
The mind faculty realizers;
The spirit realizers.

All such instances of the many different sorts of wrong views and wrong practices on the part of householders and renunciates qualify as "impure."

Then again, "impurity" is involved wherever the lands are characterized by the following:

Precipitous terrain;
Abysses;
Steep coastlines;
Dense thickets;
Brambles and thorns;
Many sorts of obstacles;
Lands characterized by dustiness, dirtiness, muddiness, flooding, or quicksand pits;
Fearsome mountains with precipitous terrain and peaks;
Twisting defiles;
Deep obstructing inlets;
Rows of mountain peaks obstructing travel;
Towering cliffs;
Places that are difficult to ascend;
Saline waters;
Parched sands;
Terrains marked by stones, rubble, and rocks;
The various fruits characterized by merely weak flavor and deficient appearance and fragrance;
Unbeneficial herbs and plants possessing only scant and feeble potency;
A relative rarity of marvelous forms, sounds, smells, tastes, and touchables;

正體字

園林樓閣流水浴池小山土嶺。
032a11 ‖ 登緣遠望娛樂之處皆悉尠少。郡縣聚落不
032a12 ‖ 相接近。地多丘荒人民希少。多[4]見無福貧
032a13 ‖ 窮下劣諸城。宰牧大官貴人諸賈客主。巧匠
032a14 ‖ 工師學讀之人。亦復甚[5]少。衣服臥具醫藥便
032a15 ‖ 身之具甚為難得。雖得非妙名為不淨。不
032a16 ‖ 淨略說有二種。一以眾生因緣。二以行業因
032a17 ‖ 緣。眾生因緣者。眾生過惡故。行業因緣者。諸
032a18 ‖ 行過惡故。此二事上已說。轉此二事則有
032a19 ‖ 眾生功德行業功德。此二功德名為淨土。是
032a20 ‖ 淨國土當知隨諸菩薩本願因緣。諸菩薩能
032a21 ‖ 行種種大精進故。所願無量不可說盡。是
032a22 ‖ 故今但略說開示事端。其餘諸事應如是
032a23 ‖ 知。略說淨土相。所謂

简体字

园林楼阁流水浴池小山土岭。登缘远望娱乐之处皆悉鲜少。郡县聚落不相接近。地多丘荒人民希少。多见无福贫穷下劣诸城。宰牧大官贵人诸贾客主。巧匠工师学读之人。亦复甚少。衣服卧具医药便身之具甚为难得。虽得非妙名为不净。不净略说有二种。一以众生因缘。二以行业因缘。众生因缘者。众生过恶故。行业因缘者。诸行过恶故。此二事上已说。转此二事则有众生功德行业功德。此二功德名为净土。是净国土当知随诸菩萨本愿因缘。诸菩萨能行种种大精进故。所愿无量不可说尽。是故今但略说开示事端。其余诸事应如是知。略说净土相。所谓

Only rare encounters with parks and groves, viewing towers, freely running streams, bathing ponds, small mountains and buttes to ascend for distant views, or other enjoyable places;

Provinces, counties, and villages that are not in favorable proximity to each other;

Lands full of desolate hills;

Scant populations;

Cities of inferior character where one frequently encounters poverty-stricken people bereft of merit;

Cities of inferior character;

Very few representatives of governing officialdom, magistrates, high ministers, members of the nobility, leaders among the merchant and professional classes, artists, craftsmen, and scholars;

Or extreme difficulties in coming by clothing, bedding, medicines, and conveniences providing enhancement of one's physical existence, and, in instances where they are obtainable, they are not particularly fine.

Places such as these qualify as impure. As a general statement, "impurity" is of two types. Those of the first type arise due to the beings' own causes and conditions. Those of the second type arise due to the causes and conditions of the karma of their actions.

In the case of those that arise due to beings' own causes and conditions, this is because of beings' faults and evils.

As regards that type of impurity that arises due to the causes and conditions of the karma of their karmic actions, these originate with the transgressions and evils of karmic actions. These two matters were already discussed earlier on.

Where one transforms these two types of circumstances, then there are beings with meritorious qualities and karmic actions that are meritorious. These two types of meritorious qualities constitute the bases for lands being referred to as "pure."

One should realize that this purifying of the lands is associated with the causes and conditions of bodhisattvas' original vows. Because the bodhisattvas are able to implement immense vigor many ways, what they vow to bring about is itself so measurelessly vast as to be impossible to fully describe. Consequently we shall now only provide a summary description explaining the main points of the matter. As for the remaining aspects, one should be able to understand them as of essentially the same sort.

2. A Description of the Characteristics of Pure Lands

As for a general description of the characteristics of pure lands, they include:

正體字	[6]菩薩善得阿耨多羅 032a24 ‖ 三藐三菩提。佛功德力法具足。聲聞具足。菩 032a25 ‖ 提樹具足。世界莊嚴眾生善利。可度者多大 032a26 ‖ 眾集會佛力具足。善得菩提者以十事莊 032a27 ‖ 嚴。一離諸苦行。二無厭劣心。三速疾得。四 032a28 ‖ 無求外道師。五菩薩具足。六無有魔怨。七 032a29 ‖ 無諸留難。八諸天大會。九希有事具足。十時 032b01 ‖ 具足。離諸苦行者。若菩薩為阿耨多羅三 032b02 ‖ 藐三菩提出家。不行諸苦行。所謂若四日 032b03 ‖ 若六日若八日。若半月若一月。乃至食一麻 032b04 ‖ 一米一果。或但飲水或但服氣。不以如是 032b05 ‖ 苦行求道。安坐道場。而成佛道。無厭劣 032b06 ‖ 心者。若菩薩少得厭離心即時出家。速疾 032b07 ‖ 得者。若菩薩出家已即得阿耨多羅三藐三 032b08 ‖ 菩提。不求外道師者。若菩薩出家已時。有 032b09 ‖ 外道大師。有名稱者。
简体字	菩萨善得阿耨多罗三藐三菩提。佛功德力法具足。声闻具足。菩提树具足。世界庄严众生善利。可度者多大众集会佛力具足。善得菩提者以十事庄严。一离诸苦行。二无厌劣心。三速疾得。四无求外道师。五菩萨具足。六无有魔怨。七无诸留难。八诸天大会。九希有事具足。十时具足。离诸苦行者。若菩萨为阿耨多罗三藐三菩提出家。不行诸苦行。所谓若四日若六日若八日。若半月若一月。乃至食一麻一米一果。或但饮水或但服气。不以如是苦行求道。安坐道场。而成佛道。无厌劣心者。若菩萨少得厌离心即时出家。速疾得者。若菩萨出家已即得阿耨多罗三藐三菩提。不求外道师者。若菩萨出家已时。有外道大师。有名称者。

A bodhisattva who has thoroughly realized *anuttarasamyaksaṃbodhi*;
The complete presence of the dharmas associated with a buddha's meritorious qualities and powers;
The complete presence of the Dharma;
The complete presence of *śrāvaka* disciples;
The completeness of the bodhi tree;
A world that is adorned;
Beings that are well-endowed with good fortune;
The abundant presence of beings capable of achieving liberation;
The gathering of an immense congregation;
And completeness in the powers of a buddha.

"Thorough realization of bodhi" refers to the presence of ten enhancing factors:

First, the abandonment of asceticism.
Second, the absence of weak thoughts of renunciation.
Third, the rapid achievement of realization.
Fourth, the absence of anything sought from non-Buddhist gurus.
Fifth, the complete presence of bodhisattvas.
Sixth, the absence of demon adversaries.
Seventh, the absence of any of the entangling difficulties.
Eighth, the presence of immense deva congregations.
Ninth, the complete presence of rarely encountered phenomena.
And tenth, its occurrence at the perfect time.

"Abandonment of ascetic practices" means that, when the bodhisattva leaves the home life for the sake of realizing *anuttarasamyaksaṃbodhi*, he does not undertake ascetic practices.[85] In particular, this refers to practices such as going four days, six days, eight days, a half month, or even a month during which one eats as little as a single sesame seed, a single rice grain, or a single piece of fruit, drinks only water, or only ingests subtle energy. He does not resort to ascetic practices of this sort in striving to reach enlightenment. He sits peacefully in the *bodhimaṇḍa* and thereby realizes buddhahood.

"Absence of weak thoughts of renunciation" means that, when a bodhisattva is able to bring forth even a minor thought of renunciation, he immediately abandons the home life.

"Rapid achievement of realization" means that, once the bodhisattva has left the home life, he soon reaches *anuttarasamyaksaṃbodhi*.

"Refraining from seeking anything from non-Buddhist gurus" means that, once the bodhisattva has left behind the home life, even if there is a great non-Buddhist guru, one who has become very famous,

正體字

```
           不往諮求。汝等說何
032b10 ||  法論何事以何為利。亦不於四方求索。菩
032b11 ||  薩具足者。菩薩欲成佛道時。三千大千世
032b12 ||  界中諸菩薩及他方諸菩薩。各持供養具來
032b13 ||  圍繞已。待佛成道放大光明各共供養。從
032b14 ||  佛聞法皆是不退轉一生補處。無魔怨者。
032b15 ||  若菩薩垂成佛時。無有魔軍能來破者。無
032b16 ||  諸留難者。菩薩垂成佛時。乃至無有毫釐
032b17 ||  煩惱來入其心。[7]諸大眾集會者。若菩薩垂
032b18 ||  成佛時。四天王諸天忉利諸天夜摩天兜率
032b19 ||  陀天化樂天他化自在天梵天乃至阿迦膩吒
032b20 ||  天。諸龍神夜叉乾闥婆阿修羅迦樓羅緊那
032b21 ||  羅摩睺羅伽等一切諸神。十方無量世界。各
032b22 ||  持第一上妙供養之具來供養菩薩。名為
032b23 ||  大眾集會。又聲聞人言。十世界諸天盡來。名
032b24 ||  為諸天大會。希有行具足者。若菩薩得佛
032b25 ||  時。地六種震動。十方無量三千大千世界諸
032b26 ||  魔王宮殿。皆變壞無色光不復現。無量須彌
032b27 ||  山皆悉動搖。
```

简体字

不往咨求。汝等说何法论何事以何为利。亦不于四方求索。菩萨具足者。菩萨欲成佛道时。三千大千世界中诸菩萨及他方诸菩萨。各持供养具来围绕已。待佛成道放大光明各共供养。从佛闻法皆是不退转一生补处。无魔怨者。若菩萨垂成佛时。无有魔军能来破者。无诸留难者。菩萨垂成佛时。乃至无有毫厘烦恼来入其心。诸大众集会者。若菩萨垂成佛时。四天王诸天忉利诸天夜摩天兜率陀天化乐天他化自在天梵天乃至阿迦腻吒天。诸龙神夜叉乾闼婆阿修罗迦楼罗紧那罗摩睺罗伽等一切诸神。十方无量世界。各持第一上妙供养之具来供养菩萨。名为大众集会。又声闻人言。十世界诸天尽来。名为诸天大会。希有行具足者。若菩萨得佛时。地六种震动。十方无量三千大千世界诸魔王宫殿。皆变坏无色光不复现。无量须弥山皆悉动摇。

Chapter 5 — The Explanation of the Vows

still, he does not go to consult him, inquiring, "What dharma is it that you proclaim? What topics do you discuss? What is it that you set forth as beneficial?" Nor does he wander off in any of the four directions searching out [such gurus].

"The complete presence of bodhisattvas" means that, when the bodhisattva is on the verge of realizing buddhahood, all of the bodhisattvas throughout the great trichiliocosm as well as the bodhisattvas from other regions—they each take up offerings and they all come and surround him. Then, having waited until that buddha has realized buddhahood and emanated great radiance, they each present their offerings. They have heard the Dharma from the buddhas, have all become irreversible on the path, and have reached the stage of having but one life remaining prior to realizing buddhahood.

"Absence of demon adversaries" means that, when that bodhisattva is about to achieve buddhahood, there are no armies of Māra able to come forth and destroy him.

As for there being "the absence of any entangling difficulties," when the bodhisattva is about to attain the realization of buddhahood, there is not even the most infinitesimally minor degree of affliction that enters his mind.[86]

As for there being "immense congregations that convene," when the bodhisattva is about to gain buddhahood, the devas from the Heaven of the Four Heavenly Kings, the devas from the Trāyastriṃśa Heaven, and the devas from the Yāma Heaven, the Tuṣita Heaven, the Nirmāṇarati Heaven, the Paranirmita Vaśavartin Heaven, the Brahma Heaven, and the others up to and including the Akaniṣṭha Heaven—these, together with the dragons, the spirits, the *yakṣas*, the *gandharvas*, the *asuras*, the *garuḍas*, the *kinnaras*, the *mahoragas*, and all of the other sorts of spirits from all of the immeasurably many worlds throughout the ten directions—each of them takes up the most superior and marvelous of offerings and comes forth to make offerings to the bodhisattva. It is this that constitutes the convening of an immense congregation.

Then again, the *śrāvaka* disciples explain that, when all the devas abiding in ten world systems come forth, it is this that constitutes an immense congregation of devas.

As for there being "the complete presence of rarely encountered phenomena,"[87] when the Bodhisattva realizes buddhahood, rarely encountered phenomena occur: The earth moves and shakes in six ways; throughout the worlds of the ten directions' countless great trichiliocosms, all of the Māras' palaces deteriorate and no longer shine forth with radiance; the countless Sumeru mountains shake; the

正體字	
	無量大海皆悉振蕩。一切世界
032b28 ‖	出非時華。雨栴檀末香及諸天名[8]華諸希
032b29 ‖	有事。時具足者。時無疾疫飢饉刀兵流離逃
032c01 ‖	迸。雨澤隨時無諸災[9]橫。諸國王等如法治
032c02 ‖	化。人民安樂壽命延長。無有怨賊諸惡鳥獸
032c03 ‖	毒虫鬼神惱害眾生。佛功德力者。一切去來
032c04 ‖	今佛威力。功德智慧無量深法。等無差別。但
032c05 ‖	隨諸佛本願因緣。或有壽命無量。或有見
032c06 ‖	者即得必定。聞名者亦得必定。女人見者
032c07 ‖	即成男子身。若聞名者亦轉女身。或有聞
032c08 ‖	名者即得往生。或有無量光明眾生遇者
032c09 ‖	離諸障蓋。或以光明即入必定。或以光明
032c10 ‖	滅一切苦惱。無量壽命者。壽命無量劫過諸
032c11 ‖	算數。一劫百劫千劫萬劫億劫百千萬億那
032c12 ‖	由他阿僧祇劫。如是久住為利益憐愍眾
032c13 ‖	生故。一切諸佛雖力能無量壽。以本願故。
032c14 ‖	有久住世者。有不久住者。

简体字

无量大海皆悉振荡。一切世界出非时华。雨栴檀末香及诸天名华诸希有事。时具足者。时无疾疫饥馑刀兵流离逃迸。雨泽随时无诸灾横。诸国王等如法治化。人民安乐寿命延长。无有怨贼诸恶鸟兽毒虫鬼神恼害众生。佛功德力者。一切去来今佛威力。功德智慧无量深法。等无差别。但随诸佛本愿因缘。或有寿命无量。或有见者即得必定。闻名者亦得必定。女人见者即成男子身。若闻名者亦转女身。或有闻名者即得往生。或有无量光明众生遇者离诸障盖。或以光明即入必定。或以光明灭一切苦恼。无量寿命者。寿命无量劫过诸算数。一劫百劫千劫万劫亿劫百千万亿那由他阿僧祇劫。如是久住为利益怜愍众生故。一切诸佛虽力能无量寿。以本愿故。有久住世者。有不久住者。

Chapter 5 — The Explanation of the Vows

measurelessly vast seas are all roiled; throughout all worlds, the blossoms bloom out of season; a rain of powdered sandalwood incense descends; and there is a rain of the most renowned celestial flower blossoms.

As for "it occurs at a perfect time," this refers to a time when there is no pestilence, famine, war, or fleeing refugees. It is free of torrential rains and flooding. There are never any disasters. All the kings and other [authorities] govern in accordance with the Dharma. The people are at peace and their lives are long. There are no enemy insurgents, terrible birds and beasts, poisonous insects, or ghosts and spirits that harass and harm beings.

As for [complete presence of the dharmas associated with] "a buddha's meritorious qualities and powers," the awesome powers, meritorious qualities, wisdom, and immeasurably many profound dharmas of the buddhas of the past, the future, and the present are the same and no different. There are only [distinctions] in accordance with the causes and conditions of each buddha's original vows. Thus, in some cases, he may possess an immeasurably long life span. In other cases, if one but sees him, one immediately gains the stage of certainty. Or it may be that, upon hearing his name, one also becomes able in that way to gain the stage of certainty. Or it may be that when women see him, they are able to immediately gain the body of a man. Or it may be that on hearing his name, they are immediately able to transform that woman's body. It may be as well that, upon hearing his name, they are immediately able to go off to rebirth [in accordance with their wishes].

In some cases, he has measureless radiance that, when beings encounter it, they leave behind all impeding hindrances. In some cases, due to encountering such light, beings immediately enter the stage of certainty. It may also happen that, on encountering such light, they extinguish all suffering and afflictions.

As for the possession of "an immeasurably long life span," it may be that his life span extends in its duration to immeasurably many kalpas beyond counting, extending for a kalpa, a hundred kalpas, a thousand kalpas, a myriad kalpas, a *koṭi* of kalpas, or even a hundred thousand myriads of *koṭis* of *nayutas* of *asaṃkhyeyas* of kalpas. He may abide for such a long time in order to benefit beings and because of his pity for beings.

Although all buddhas possess the power to extend their life spans for an immeasurably long time, due to differences in their original vows, there are those who do dwell in the world for a long time and those who do not dwell in the world for a long time.

正體字	見時得入必 032c15 ‖ 定者。有眾生見佛即住阿耨多羅三藐三 032c16 ‖ 菩提阿惟越致地。何以故。是諸眾生見佛身 032c17 ‖ 者。心大歡喜清淨悅樂。其心即攝得如是菩 032c18 ‖ 薩三昧。以是三昧力通達諸法實相。能直 032c19 ‖ 入阿耨多羅三藐三菩提必定地。是諸眾生 032c20 ‖ 長夜深心種見佛入必定善根。以大悲心為 032c21 ‖ 首。善妙清淨。為通達一切佛法故。為度 032c22 ‖ 一切眾生故。是善根成就時至。是故得值 032c23 ‖ 此佛。又以諸佛本願因緣二事和合故此事 032c24 ‖ 得成。聞佛名入必定者。佛有本願。若聞 032c25 ‖ 我名者即入必定。如見佛聞亦如是。女人 032c26 ‖ [10]見得轉女形者。若有一心求轉女形。深 032c27 ‖ 自厭患。有信解力誓願男身。如是女人得 032c28 ‖ 見佛者即轉女形。若女人無有如是業因 032c29 ‖ 緣。又女身業未盡。不得值如是佛。女人 033a01 ‖ 聞佛名轉女形者。
简体字	见时得入必定者。有众生见佛即住阿耨多罗三藐三菩提阿惟越致地。何以故。是诸众生见佛身者。心大欢喜清净悦乐。其心即摄得如是菩萨三昧。以是三昧力通达诸法实相。能直入阿耨多罗三藐三菩提必定地。是诸众生长夜深心种见佛入必定善根。以大悲心为首。善妙清净。为通达一切佛法故。为度一切众生故。是善根成就时至。是故得值此佛。又以诸佛本愿因缘二事和合故此事得成。闻佛名入必定者。佛有本愿。若闻我名者即入必定。如见佛闻亦如是。女人见得转女形者。有一心求转女形。深自厌患。有信解力誓愿男身。如是女人得见佛者即转女形。若女人无有如是业因缘。又女身业未尽。不得值如是佛。女人闻佛名转女形者。

Chapter 5 — The Explanation of the Vows

As for "being able to gain the stage of certainty on seeing [a buddha]," there are beings who, upon seeing a buddha, become immediately able to dwell on the ground of the *avaivartika's* [irreversibility] with respect to the attainment of *anuttarasamyaksaṃbodhi*. How is this the case? It is because, when these beings see the body of a buddha, their minds are filled with great delight, joy, and pure happiness. Their minds immediately become focused and acquire a bodhisattva samādhi of this sort. Due to the power of this samādhi, they achieve a penetrating understanding of the true character of all dharmas. They then become able to immediately enter the ground of certainty with respect to the attainment of *anuttarasamyaksaṃbodhi*. Due to their resolute intentions that have persisted during the long night [of previous lifetimes], beings of this sort have planted those roots of goodness whereby, upon seeing a buddha, they enter the stage of certainty.

This is because they have taken the mind of great compassion as foremost, because their goodness is sublime and pure, because they have sought to achieve a penetrating understanding of all the dharmas of a buddha, because they have sought to liberate all beings, and because the time has arrived for the perfection of these roots of goodness that they therefore succeed in meeting this buddha. Additionally, it is due to the particular causes and conditions of that buddha's original vows. It is because of the coming together of these two factors that this circumstance is then able to occur.

As for "entering the stage of certainty upon hearing the name of a buddha," a buddha may have made an original vow, declaring, "If there be anyone who so much as hears my name, then he shall immediately enter the stage of certainty." Hence, just as with the case of seeing a buddha, so too it is in this case of hearing a buddha's name.

As for a woman "being able to transform the woman's body as a result of having seen a buddha," if there be someone who single-mindedly wishes to change away from her female form and who has herself developed a profound renunciation for the troubles it involves, and who, based on the power of resolute faith has vowed to seek instead the physical form of a male—when a woman of this sort succeeds in seeing such a buddha, she immediately transforms and leaves behind the female body.

In the event that a woman does not have karmic causal conditions of this sort and also has not yet exhausted the karma that brings about birth in a female body, she will remain unable to encounter a buddha of this sort.

As for a woman "being able to transform and leave behind the female form upon hearing the name" of a given buddha, the causal

正體字

此事因緣如見[1]佛中
033a02 ‖ 說。聞佛名得往生者。若人信解力多。諸善
033a03 ‖ 根成就。業障礙已盡。如是之人得聞佛名。
033a04 ‖ 又是諸佛本願因緣便得往生。無量光明者。
033a05 ‖ 一切佛光明所炤。隨意遠近。此說無量者
033a06 ‖ 是其常光。常光明不[2]可由旬里數以為限
033a07 ‖ 量。遍滿東方若干百千萬億由旬。不可得
033a08 ‖ 量。南西北方四維上下亦復如是。但知其
033a09 ‖ 無量而莫知邊際。遇光明得除諸蓋者。
033a10 ‖ 是諸佛本願力所致。貪欲瞋恚睡眠調悔[3]疑
033a11 ‖ 除此障蓋。眾生遇光即能念佛。念佛因緣
033a12 ‖ 故念法。念法故諸蓋得除。光明觸身苦惱
033a13 ‖ 皆滅者。若眾生墮地獄畜生餓鬼非人[4]之
033a14 ‖ 中。多諸苦惱。以佛本願神通之力光觸其
033a15 ‖ 身即得離苦。法具足者。一切諸佛法悉皆
033a16 ‖ 具足。無有具足不具足者。諸佛

简体字

此事因缘如见佛中说。闻佛名得往生者。若人信解力多。诸善根成就。业障碍已尽。如是之人得闻佛名。又是诸佛本愿因缘便得往生。无量光明者。一切佛光明所昭。随意远近。此说无量者是其常光。常光明不可由旬里数以为限量。遍满东方若干百千万亿由旬。不可得量。南西北方四维上下亦复如是。但知其无量而莫知边际。遇光明得除诸盖者。是诸佛本愿力所致。贪欲瞋恚睡眠调悔疑除此障盖。众生遇光即能念佛。念佛因缘故念法。念法故诸盖得除。光明触身苦恼皆灭者。若众生堕地狱畜生饿鬼非人之中。多诸苦恼。以佛本愿神通之力光触其身即得离苦。法具足者。一切诸佛法悉皆具足。无有具足不具足者。诸佛

conditions for this are just as explained with regard to achieving this by seeing a buddha.

As for "being enabled to go forth to rebirth" upon hearing the name of a buddha, if a person is possessed of much power arising from his resolute faith, if his roots of goodness have become completely developed, and if his karmic obstacles have already become exhausted, where this corresponds to the causes and conditions of the original vows of buddhas, when such a person hears the name of one of these buddhas, he will then be able to go forth to rebirth [in accordance with his wishes].

As for "measureless light," the illumination from the light of all buddhas is such that the distance it reaches accords with their wishes. The "measureless light" we speak of here is the illumination that they always emanate. Their always-emanated illumination is not limited to any given number of *yojanas* of distance whereby one might say of it that it extends universally in the eastern direction a given number of hundreds of thousands of myriads of *koṭis* of *yojanas*. It is not even amenable to calculation. This applies as well to its reach to the south, west, north, the four midpoints, the zenith, and the nadir. One may only know of it that it is measureless and no one knows its bounds.

As for "becoming able to get rid of all hindrances due to encountering this light," this is an effect brought about by the power of the original vows made by buddhas. Sensual desire, ill will, lethargy-and-sleepiness, excitedness-and-regretfulness, and doubtfulness—one gets rid of these hindrances.

When beings encounter such light, they immediately become able to abide in mindfulness of the Buddha. Due to this mindfulness of the Buddha, they then become mindful of the Dharma. Due to becoming mindful of the Dharma, they then become able to rid themselves of these hindrances.

When it is said that the contact of such illumination with the body brings about "the extinguishing of suffering and affliction," this refers to instances in which beings who have descended into the hell realms, animal realms, hungry ghost realms, and other nonhuman realms undergo the manifold sufferings and afflictions characteristic of these realms. Due to the power produced by a buddha's original vows and spiritual superknowledges, when that buddha's light touches their bodies, they immediately become able to abandon such sufferings.

As for there being "the complete presence of the Dharma," there is the complete presence of the Dharma of all buddhas. There is no such thing as [there being buddhas who] completely possess it as opposed to those who do not completely possess it. Because all buddhas are

正體字	說法同故法 033a17 ‖ 俱具足。但以本願因緣故差別不同。或有 033a18 ‖ 久住不久住耳。何謂法具足。法有略說有 033a19 ‖ 廣說。有略廣說。有具足聲聞乘。有具足辟 033a20 ‖ 支佛乘。有具足大乘。以諸神通力守護。令 033a21 ‖ 不為外道所壞。不為諸魔所破。久住於 033a22 ‖ 世。略說者。以少言辭包含多義。利根之人 033a23 ‖ 聞則開悟。廣說者。於一事一義種種因緣 033a24 ‖ 為諸鈍根樂分別者敷演解說。若略廣說 033a25 ‖ 者。亦以一言包舉廣義。又亦種種演散一 033a26 ‖ 義。有具足聲聞乘具足辟支佛乘具足大乘 033a27 ‖ 者。此義後當說。神力護法者。以佛神力護 033a28 ‖ 念是法。以諸佛印印之。諸佛印者。所謂四 033a29 ‖ 大因離四黑因。不為外道所壞者。一切沙 033b01 ‖ 門婆羅門外道
简体字	说法同故法俱具足。但以本愿因缘故差别不同。或有久住不久住耳。何谓法具足。法有略说有广说。有略广说。有具足声闻乘。有具足辟支佛乘。有具足大乘。以诸神通力守护。令不为外道所坏。不为诸魔所破。久住于世。略说者。以少言辞包含多义。利根之人闻则开悟。广说者。于一事一义种种因缘。为诸钝根乐分别者敷演解说。若略广说者。亦以一言包举广义。又亦种种演散一义。有具足声闻乘具足辟支佛乘具足大乘者。此义后当说。神力护法者。以佛神力护念是法。以诸佛印印之。诸佛印者。所谓四大因离四黑因。不为外道所坏者。一切沙门婆罗门外道

identical as regards the Dharma that they proclaim, the Dharma of each of them is therefore perfectly complete. It is solely a function of the causal conditions specific to their original vows that there are differences whereby their Dharma may remain for a long time or not remain for a long time. That's all.

What is meant by "the complete presence of the Dharma"? [When it is completely present], the Dharma includes:

Concise explanations;
Extensive explanations;
Explanations that are both concise and extensive;
Complete presence of the Śrāvaka Disciple Vehicle;
Complete presence of the Pratyekabuddha Vehicle;
Complete presence of the Great Vehicle;
Protection by the power of the spiritual superknowledges;
Prevention of ruination by non-Buddhist traditions;
Invulnerability to destruction by *māras*;
And long endurance in the world.

In "concise explanations" one uses but a few words and phrases that embrace an abundance of meanings. When those with sharp faculties hear it, they immediately become awakened.

In "extensive explanations," for the sake of those with dull faculties or those who delight in making distinctions, one presents a lengthy explanation of all of the causes and conditions associated with a single matter or single meaning.

In "explanations that are both concise and extensive," one both uses single statements to comprehensively include a wide range of meanings and also uses many different explanations to spread forth [the nuances of] a single meaning.

As for "complete presence of the Śrāvaka Disciple Vehicle, complete presence of the Pratyekabuddha Vehicle, and complete presence of the Great Vehicle," these are matters that shall be extensively discussed later on.

"Protection by the power of the spiritual superknowledges" refers to the use of the Buddha's spiritual powers in providing his protective mindfulness of this Dharma and it also refers to its being sealed with the seal of the Buddhas.

"The seal of the Buddhas" refers to [the Dharma's] association with the four great causal factors and its abandonment of the four black causes.

"Prevention of ruination by non-Buddhist traditions" refers to [the Dharma's countering of] all the deviant views of non-Buddhist

|正體字|

論師。所有邪見。說生滅味患
033b02 ‖ 出。又覺一切善。說破壞因緣。不為一切魔
033b03 ‖ 所壞者。諸佛有無量無邊功德智慧方便神
033b04 ‖ 通力故。魔雖有力而不能壞。又諸菩薩力
033b05 ‖ 故魔不能壞。法久住者。若一劫若減一劫。
033b06 ‖ 若[5]過數百劫千劫萬劫十萬劫百萬劫千萬
033b07 ‖ 劫萬萬劫無量千萬億那由他阿僧祇劫乃至
033b08 ‖ 無量無邊劫。聲聞具足者。一切諸佛悉皆具
033b09 ‖ 足聲聞僧。但諸佛本願因緣故。有少多差別。
033b10 ‖ 何謂具足。所謂如來聲聞眾。具足持戒禪定
033b11 ‖ 智慧解脫解脫知見。同等清淨悉是利根。[6]益
033b12 ‖ 諸菩薩形色嚴淨。具足持戒者。遠離殺生
033b13 ‖ 偷盜邪婬妄語兩舌惡口綺語飲酒邪命等諸
033b14 ‖ 惡法。又毘尼所制皆悉遠離。又能成就無漏
033b15 ‖ 戒故。具足禪定者。四禪

|简体字|

论师。所有邪见。说生灭味患出。又觉一切善。说破坏因缘。不为一切魔所坏者。诸佛有无量无边功德智慧方便神通力故。魔虽有力而不能坏。又诸菩萨力故魔不能坏。法久住者。若一劫若减一劫。若过数百劫千劫万劫十万劫百万劫千万劫万万劫无量千万亿那由他阿僧祇劫乃至无量无边劫。声闻具足者。一切诸佛悉皆具足声闻僧。但诸佛本愿因缘故。有少多差别。何谓具足。所谓如来声闻众。具足持戒禅定智慧解脱解脱知见。同等清净悉是利根。益诸菩萨形色严净。具足持戒者。远离杀生偷盗邪淫妄语两舌恶口绮语饮酒邪命等诸恶法。又毗尼所制皆悉远离。又能成就无漏戒故。具足禅定者。四禅

Chapter 5 — *The Explanation of the Vows* 207

śramaṇas, brahmans, and treatise masters by presenting [correct] teachings on arising, passing away, enjoyment, danger, and escape.[88]

Additionally, it refers to instigating awareness of all forms of goodness and explaining the causes and conditions that could bring about their ruination.

As for "invulnerability to destruction by *māras*," because the Buddhas possess a measureless and boundless number of meritorious qualities, wisdom, skillful means, and the powers of the spiritual superknowledges, even though *māras* are themselves possessed of powers, they still cannot destroy [the Dharma].

It is also because of the powers possessed by the bodhisattvas that the *māras* cannot destroy [the Dharma].

As for the Dharma's "long endurance," it may even be for so long as an entire kalpa or somewhat less than an entire kalpa, and in fact it may even extend for even longer to a hundred kalpas, a thousand kalpas, a myriad kalpas, ten myriads of kalpas, a hundred myriads of kalpas, a thousand myriads of kalpas, a myriad myriads of kalpas, for an immeasurable number of thousands of myriads of *koṭis* of *nayutas* of *asaṃkhyeyas* of kalpas, and so forth on up to a measureless and boundless number of kalpas during which it continues to endure.

As for "the complete presence of the Śrāvaka Disciple [Vehicle]," all buddhas are attended by a perfectly complete *śrāvaka*-disciple sangha. The fact that there are a lesser or greater number of distinctions between one instance and another instance is solely a reflection of the original vows of each respective buddha.

What then is it that is meant here by "complete presence"? This is to say that the Tathāgata's *śrāvaka*-disciple congregation is perfectly complete as regards observance of the moral prohibitions and accomplishment in the *dhyāna* absorptions, wisdom, liberation, and the knowledge and vision of liberation. They are identical in their equality, are pure, and are all possessed of sharp faculties. They benefit the bodhisattvas and are possessed of physical forms that are dignified and pure.

"Completeness in the observance of the moral prohibitions" means that they have abandoned any killing of beings, stealing, sexual misconduct, false speech, divisive speech, harsh speech, frivolous or lewd speech, consumption of intoxicants, wrong livelihood, and all of the other sorts of evil dharmas. Moreover, they have abandoned whatever is restricted by the *vinaya* and they are also able to completely develop their observance of the moral precepts so that is free of the contaminants.

As for "completeness in the *dhyāna* absorptions," this refers to such accomplishments as acquisition of the four *dhyānas*, the four

正體字

四無量心四無色
033b16 ‖ 定八解脫八背捨八勝處十一切入等。及得
033b17 ‖ 無漏諸禪定故。具足智慧者。成就四種智
033b18 ‖ 慧。從多聞生從思惟生。從修集生從先
033b19 ‖ 世業因緣果報生。具足解脫者。於一切煩
033b20 ‖ 惱得解脫。又於一切障[7]閡得解脫。具足
033b21 ‖ 解脫知見者。知名識其事。見名明了其事。
033b22 ‖ 於解脫中了了知見無疑。又知名盡智。見
033b23 ‖ 名見四諦。同等者。諸入須陀洹果。悉皆同
033b24 ‖ 等。乃至阿羅漢亦如是。清淨者成就三種清
033b25 ‖ 淨。身清淨口清淨意清淨。利智者。但聞少
033b26 ‖ 語能廣解了通達義趣。略能作廣廣能作
033b27 ‖ 略。義理微隱能令易解。利益菩薩者。念諸
033b28 ‖ 菩薩乃至初發心者亦不輕慢。深愛敬故。常
033b29 ‖ 開示善惡為說佛道方便因緣。形色嚴淨
033c01 ‖ 者。身體姝美姿容具足兼有相好。

简体字

四无量心四无色定八解脱八背舍八胜处十一切入等。及得无漏诸禅定故。具足智慧者。成就四种智慧。从多闻生从思惟生。从修集生从先世业因缘果报生。具足解脱者。于一切烦恼得解脱。又于一切障阂得解脱。具足解脱知见者。知名识其事。见名明了其事。于解脱中了了知见无疑。又知名尽智。见名见四谛。同等者。诸入须陀洹果。悉皆同等。乃至阿罗汉亦如是。清净者成就三种清净。身清净口清净意清净。利智者。但闻少语能广解了通达义趣。略能作广广能作略。义理微隐能令易解。利益菩萨者。念诸菩萨乃至初发心者亦不轻慢。深爱敬故。常开示善恶为说佛道方便因缘。形色严净者。身体姝美姿容具足兼有相好。

immeasurable minds, the four formless absorptions, the eight liberations (aṣṭā vimokṣa),[89] [otherwise known as] the eight abandonments, the eight bases of mastery (abhibhvāyatana), and the ten universal meditation bases (daśa kṛtsnāyatana)[90] as well as the acquisition of the *dhyāna* absorptions free of the contaminants.

"Completeness in wisdom" refers to bringing the four types of wisdom to completion: that which arises through extensive learning; that which arises through meditative reflection; that which arises through cultivation and accumulation; and that which arises as the result of the karmic causes and conditions of previous lives.

"Completeness in liberation" refers to having gained liberation from all afflictions. Additionally, it refers to becoming liberated from all the hindrances.

In "completeness in the knowledge and vision of liberation," "knowledge" refers to the cognitive awareness of phenomena whereas "vision" refers to a complete understanding of those matters. Thus, in one's liberation, one gains a complete and utter knowledge and vision that is entirely free of doubts. Then again, one may also explain that "knowledge" refers to the knowledge of the destruction [of the contaminants], whereas "vision" refers to the seeing of the four truths.

As for "identical in their equality," all those who attain the fruit of a stream enterer are entirely equal. So too, all those [who attain the higher fruits of the path] on up to arhatship are just the same.

"Purity" refers to having completely developed the three types of purity, namely purity in physical actions, purity in verbal actions, and purity in mental actions.

"Sharp wisdom"[91] means that, when one merely hears a few words, one is able to gain a vast understanding through which one penetrates a meaning's import. Thus one is able to provide extensive presentations of concise [teachings], is able to provide concise presentations of extensive [teachings], and in an instance where the principle is subtle and obscure, one is able to render it easily understandable.

As for "benefiting the bodhisattvas," they remain mindful of the bodhisattvas, including even those who have only initially produced the resolve, and have no slighting arrogance toward them, this because they have a deep affection and respect for them. They always provide instruction in [the distinctions] between good and bad and explain for them the causes and conditions of the Buddha path's skillful means.

As for their having "physical forms that are dignified and pure," this means their bodies have an especially fine presence and their appearance is complete with the major marks and secondary characteristic signs. Consequently, those who observe them are filled with

正體字	見者歡 033c02 ‖ [8]喜如辟支佛。行來進止坐臥[9]寐寤。飲食澡 033c03 ‖ 浴著衣持鉢。威儀庠序無所闕少。若人見者 033c04 ‖ 心則清淨。菩提樹具足者。所有大樹娑羅樹 033c05 ‖ 多羅樹提羅迦樹多摩羅樹婆求羅樹瞻蔔樹 033c06 ‖ 阿輸迦樹娑呵迦羅樹分那摩樹[10]那摩樹那 033c07 ‖ 迦樹尸[11]利沙樹涅劬陀樹阿輸陀樹波勒叉 033c08 ‖ 樹[*]憂曇鉢羅樹等。於此諸大樹中隨取一 033c09 ‖ 樹。在平地者高廣具足根莖枝葉滋潤茂盛。 033c10 ‖ 華色鮮明無有傷缺。其樹舉高五十由旬。端 033c11 ‖ 直平澤無有[12]盤節。皮膚細軟色白鮮淨。無 033c12 ‖ 有刺閡內不朽腐。又不空中[13]虫蝎傷齧。 033c13 ‖ 其根深固連編相次。其華嚴飾如鬘瓔珞。枝 033c14 ‖ 葉[14]蔚茂猶如圓蓋。次第分布功殊人造。其 033c15 ‖ 葉青鮮猶如寶色。枝無絞戾萎黃枯葉。無 033c16 ‖ 有虫[15]蟻蚊蚋虻蟻。其下清淨布諸金沙。種 033c17 ‖ 種光明周匝炤燿。栴檀香水以灑其地。平坦 033c18 ‖ 柔軟清涼快樂。牛頭栴檀細末布上。諸天常 033c19 ‖ 雨曼陀羅華。燒黑沈香芬馨流溢。五色天 033c20 ‖ 繒參羅垂列。清風微動猗靡隨順。鳥獸遊側 033c21 ‖ 寂然無聲。
简体字	见者欢喜如辟支佛。行来进止坐卧寐寤。饮食澡浴着衣持钵。威仪庠序无所阙少。若人见者心则清净。菩提树具足者。所有大树娑罗树多罗树提罗迦树多摩罗树婆求罗树瞻卜树阿输迦树娑呵迦罗树分那摩树那摩树那迦树尸利沙树涅劬陀树阿输陀树波勒叉树忧昙钵罗树等。于此诸大树中随取一树。在平地者高广具足根茎枝叶滋润茂盛。华色鲜明无有伤缺。其树举高五十由旬。端直平泽无有盘节。皮肤细软色白鲜净。无有刺阂内不朽腐。又不空中虫蝎伤啮。其根深固连编相次。其华严饰如鬘瓔珞。枝叶蔚茂犹如圆盖。次第分布功殊人造。其叶青鲜犹如宝色。枝无绞戾萎黄枯叶。无有虫蚁蚊蚋虻蚁。其下清净布诸金沙。种种光明周匝昭耀。栴檀香水以洒其地。平坦柔软清凉快乐。牛头栴檀细末布上。诸天常雨曼陀罗华。烧黑沉香芬馨流溢。五色天缯参罗垂列。清风微动猗靡随顺。鸟兽游侧寂然无声。

Chapter 5 — *The Explanation of the Vows*

delight in the same way as when they behold a *pratyekabuddha*. Thus, in their walking forth, their advancing, stopping, sitting, lying down, sleeping, awakening, partaking of food and drink, bathing, donning the robe, and holding the bowl, their awesome deportment accords with the correct sequence and remains free of any defects or omissions. Thus, when a person observes this, his mind is then purified.

As for "completeness of the bodhi tree," the rest of all the great trees there such as the *sala* tree, the *tāla* tree, the *tiluojia* tree, the *duomoluo* tree, the *poqiuluo* tree, the *campaka* tree, the *aśoka* tree, the *suohejialuo* tree, the *fennamo* tree, the *namo* tree, the *nāga* tree, the *śirīṣa* tree, the *niequtuo* tree, the *āśvattha*, the *bolecha* tree, the *udumbara* tree, and so forth—no matter which of these great trees we speak of, when growing out on level land, they are tall, broad, perfect in the growth of their roots, trunk, branches, and leaves, and are perfect in their luster and luxuriant fullness. The coloration of their blossoms is fresh, bright, and free of any defects from damage.

His [bodhi] tree rises to a height of fifty *yojanas*. It is perfectly erect and level. It is lustrously smooth and free of any contorted branches. Its bark is fine and soft and its coloration is white, fresh, and clean. It has no thorns and is free of any internal decay. Additionally, it is not hollow and is free of any injury or gnawing by insects. Its roots are deep in their penetration, solid, and orderly in their interwoven plaiting. Its flowers gracefully adorn it, just as when one is graced by a floral garland and gemstone necklace.

Its branches and leaves are luxuriant and full in their growth and are comparable to a circular pavilion in their shape. It is orderly and sequential in the way that it spreads out and, in its gracefulness, it is more distinctive than anything made by man. Its leaves are green and fresh and comparable in color to jewels. Its branches are free of any distorting crisscrossing, yellowness caused by withering, or dried-out leaves, and it has no insects such as moths,[92] mosquitoes, midges, horseflies, or ants.

The ground below is pure and spread with golden sands. It emanates all manner of illumination and sends forth shining brightness all around. Sandalwood-scented waters are sprinkled over its grounds that are themselves level, soft, cool, and pleasing. Fine powders of ox-head sandalwood are spread over it. The devas always rain down *mandārava* flowers. The fragrance of burning aloe wood incense wafts all about. Five-colored celestial banners are suspended at intermittent intervals. A subtle breeze gently moves them, causing them to ripple and flutter in response to it. Birds and animals quietly roam about off to the sides, making no sounds.

正體字	其樹左右天常雨華。眾妙雜色自 033c22 ‖ 然間錯垂以為[16]瓔猶如龍身身上往往懸 033c23 ‖ 以金色華貫。四面大枝垂寶羅網。眾寶莊嚴 033c24 ‖ 猶紫金山。[17]巍巍姝妙如帝釋幢。斯由菩薩 033c25 ‖ 百千萬億阿僧祇劫修集善行功德所致。種 033c26 ‖ 種妙寶化為師子王。四師子頂上有廣大寶 033c27 ‖ 床敷諸天繒。四天王天忉利諸天夜摩天兜 033c28 ‖ 率陀天化樂天他化自在天梵天乃至阿迦膩 033c29 ‖ 吒天。乘琉璃[18]車璖馬瑙大青寶帝青寶金剛 034a01 ‖ [1]頗梨眾寶宮殿。其色無比光明遠炤。俱集 034a02 ‖ 寶樹圍繞供養。又十方無量世界諸菩薩 034a03 ‖ [2]眾隨本所願備諸供具。雨眾寶物花香幡 034a04 ‖ 蓋種種伎樂等。是名具足菩提樹。世間莊嚴 034a05 ‖ 者。菩薩觀察十方清淨國土最上妙者而發 034a06 ‖ 大願。[3]我修集功德所得國土。復勝於此 034a07 ‖ 第一無比。眾生善利者。眾生端正無諸疾患 034a08 ‖ 無有老病。[4]壽無量阿僧祇劫悉皆化生。身 034a09 ‖ 無眾穢具足三十二相。光明無量。煩惱
简体字	其树左右天常雨华。众妙杂色自然间错垂以为璎犹如龙身身上往往悬以金色华贯。四面大枝垂宝罗网。众宝庄严犹紫金山。巍巍姝妙如帝释幢。斯由菩萨百千万亿阿僧祇劫修集善行功德所致。种种妙宝化为师子王。四师子顶上有广大宝床敷诸天缯。四天王天忉利诸天夜摩天兜率陀天化乐天他化自在天梵天乃至阿迦腻吒天。乘琉璃车碟马瑙大青宝帝青宝金刚颇梨众宝宫殿。其色无比光明远昭。俱集宝树围绕供养。又十方无量世界诸菩萨众随本所愿备诸供具。雨众宝物花香幡盖种种伎乐等。是名具足菩提树。世间庄严者。菩萨观察十方清净国土最上妙者而发大愿。我修集功德所得国土。复胜于此第一无比。众生善利者。众生端正无诸疾患无有老病。寿无量阿僧祇劫悉皆化生。身无众秽具足三十二相。光明无量。烦恼

Chapter 5 — *The Explanation of the Vows*

To its left and right, devas are always sprinkling down flowers of the many marvelous and varied colors that naturally intersperse as they descend like strands of jewels like the golden flower garlands worn on the bodies of the dragons. A jeweled net hangs down from the larger branches on all four sides. The many sorts of jewels adorn it, making it appear like a purple-golden mountain. It stands there in awe-inspiring grandeur, distinctive and sublime, like Indra's canopy.

This is an effect brought about as a result of the Bodhisattva's hundreds of thousands of myriads of *koṭis* of *asaṃkhyeyas* of kalpas of cultivating and accumulating meritorious qualities deriving from the practice of goodness. The many different sorts of marvelous jewels have been used to create the appearance of the king of lions. On the crowns of four lions, there rests a broad and grand jeweled platform cushioned with celestial tapestries. The devas from the Heaven of the Four Heavenly Kings, the Trāyastriṃśa heaven, the Yāma Heaven, the Tuṣita Heaven, the Nirmāṇarati Heaven, the Paranirmita Vaśavartin Heaven, the Brahma Heaven, and so forth all the way up to the Akaniṣṭha Heaven—all of them appear riding along in their palaces composed of the many sorts of precious jewels consisting of such jewels as lapis lazuli, *musāra-galva*, carnelian, *mahānīla* sapphires, *indranīla* sapphires, vajra, and *sphaṭika*. They emanate an incomparable colored light that illuminates even to a great distance. They all assemble at the bejeweled tree, circumambulating it and presenting offerings.

Additionally, in accordance with their original vows, all of the congregations of bodhisattvas from the countless worlds throughout the ten directions, having prepared in abundance all of the various sorts of offerings, rain down the many sorts of precious gifts, including flowers, incense, banners, canopies, the many different sorts of music, and other such offerings. This is what is meant by "completeness of the bodhi tree."

As for "a world that is adorned," the bodhisattvas contemplate the most marvelous among all the pure lands throughout the ten directions and then make a great vow, "The land that I acquire through the cultivation of meritorious qualities shall even be superior to these. It shall be foremost and incomparable."

As for "the beings being well-endowed with good fortune,"[93] the beings there are fine in appearance, free of any sort of physical afflictions or calamities, and are not troubled by aging and sickness. Their life spans extend for a measureless number of *asaṃkhyeyas* of kalpas. In all cases, they are born there transformationally. Their bodies are free of the many sorts of defilement. They are possessed of the thirty-two major marks. They radiate measureless light. Their afflictions are

正體字

```
            微
034a10 ||  薄易可化度。可度具足者。一坐說法恒河
034a11 ||  沙眾生同時得度自有餘佛演說法時度
034a12 ||  一人二人。是諸眾生宿種善根。結使微薄聞
034a13 ||  說即悟。大眾集會者。有佛大會滿一由旬。
034a14 ||  或十由旬。有百千萬億由旬。有滿三千大千
034a15 ||  世界。此中大集會者。十方恒河沙世界以為
034a16 ||  大會。又其會中但是福德之人。及諸天八部。
034a17 ||  初地菩薩乃至十住悉共[5]來會。唯除諸佛。
034a18 ||  佛力具足者。諸佛所行四十不共法。是一一
034a19 ||  法所行處。一切無量無邊。是第七願。復次。
034a20 ||    俱行於一事    願無有怨競
034a21 ||  若菩薩所作福德。若布施持戒忍辱精進禪
034a22 ||  定智慧。若諦捨滅慧四功德處。若因諸大願。
034a23 ||  求佛道時應作是願。若有餘人同我行
034a24 ||  此六波羅蜜四功德處
```

简体字

微薄易可化度。可度具足者。一坐说法恒河沙众生同时得度自有余佛演说法时度一人二人。是诸众生宿种善根。结使微薄闻说即悟。大众集会者。有佛大会满一由旬。或十由旬。有百千万亿由旬。有满三千大千世界。此中大集会者。十方恒河沙世界以为大会。又其会中但是福德之人。及诸天八部。初地菩萨乃至十住悉共来会。唯除诸佛。佛力具足者。诸佛所行四十不共法。是一一法所行处。一切无量无边。是第七愿。复次。

　　俱行于一事　　愿无有怨竞

若菩萨所作福德。若布施持戒忍辱精进禅定智慧。若谛舍灭慧四功德处。若因诸大愿。求佛道时应作是愿。若有余人同我行此六波罗蜜四功德处

Chapter 5 — The Explanation of the Vows

merely subtle and slight and they are easily taught and led across to liberation.

As for being "complete in those capable of achieving liberation," during but a single sitting in which he teaches the Dharma, beings as numerous as the sands of the Ganges all simultaneously attain liberation. [This may be contrasted with the circumstance of] other buddhas for whom, in a single instance of proclaiming Dharma, they bring one or two people across to liberation. These beings have all planted roots of goodness in previous lives. Their fetters are but slight and scant, so much so that, when hearing an explanation, they awaken immediately.

As for "the gathering of an immense congregation," there are buddhas whose great assemblies fill up an area one *yojana* across, or in some cases, ten *yojanas*, or in some cases a hundred thousand myriads of *koṭis* of *yojanas*, or in some cases, they fill the worlds of an entire great trichiliocosm.

As for the "immense congregation" referred to here, it is one equal in scope to world systems as numerous as the sands in all the Ganges Rivers throughout the ten directions. This is what constitutes "an immense congregation." Moreover, the people in his assembly are only those who have accumulated merit. Also included in the congregations are all the devas, the beings in the eight divisions [of ghosts and spirits], and the bodhisattvas from the first through the tenth grounds. They have all come together there, with the sole exception of the buddhas themselves.

"Completeness in the powers of a buddha" refers to the forty dharmas exclusive to the buddhas that all buddhas practice. For each and every one of these dharmas, the places in which they have been practiced are all measurelessly and boundlessly many. This is the seventh vow.

H. The Eighth Bodhisattva Vow

Next, we have:

> When joining together with others in doing any single endeavor,
> I vow that there will be no enmity or contentiousness.[94]

In all merit-generating deeds a bodhisattva does, whether it be through the practice of giving, upholding moral precepts, patience, vigor, *dhyāna* meditation, or wisdom, whether it be through the four bases of meritorious qualities consisting of truth, relinquishment, quiescence, and wisdom, or whether it be through other endeavors in which, due to one's great vows, one pursues the attainment of buddhahood, one should make this vow: "In circumstances where others join with me in practicing the six *pāramitās* or the four bases of meritorious qualities,

正體字

　　　　　　　求佛道者。願我以
034a25 ‖ 此福德因緣。不於餘人而生怨競。何以故。
034a26 ‖ 同行一事。諸有智者說有怨相。世間亦復
034a27 ‖ 現有此事。除此過故發是大願。是第八願。
034a28 ‖ 復次。
034a29 ‖ 　願行菩薩道　　轉不退轉輪
034b01 ‖ 　令除諸煩惱　　得入信清淨
034b02 ‖ 輪者法輪。不退轉者無人能壞。菩薩應如
034b03 ‖ 是發願。我當如說行道。必轉不退法輪。轉
034b04 ‖ 此法輪除諸眾生三毒煩惱。轉捨生死入
034b05 ‖ 佛法眾。苦集滅道中使得清淨。是第九願。
034b06 ‖ 復次。
034b07 ‖ 　願一切世界　　皆示成菩提
034b08 ‖ 隨諸世界應有佛事處。盡於其中示得
034b09 ‖ 阿耨多羅三藐三菩提。安樂一切眾生故。
034b10 ‖ 滅度一切眾生故。以阿耨多羅三藐三菩提
034b11 ‖ 大故[6]獨說。其餘入胎出胎生長在家出家受
034b12 ‖ 戒苦行。降伏魔眾梵王勸請及轉法輪。大
034b13 ‖ 眾集會廣度眾生。現大神力示大滅度。如
034b14 ‖ 此諸事悉皆如是應作。

简体字

求佛道者。愿我以此福德因缘。不于余人而生怨竞。何以故。同行一事。诸有智者说有怨相。世间亦复现有此事。除此过故发是大愿。是第八愿。复次。

　　愿行菩萨道　　转不退转轮
　　令除诸烦恼　　得入信清净

轮者法轮。不退转者无人能坏。菩萨应如是发愿。我当如说行道。必转不退法轮。转此法轮除诸众生三毒烦恼。转舍生死入佛法众。苦集灭道中使得清净。是第九愿。复次。

　　愿一切世界　　皆示成菩提

随诸世界应有佛事处。尽于其中示得阿耨多罗三藐三菩提。安乐一切众生故。灭度一切众生故。以阿耨多罗三藐三菩提大故独说。其余入胎出胎生长在家出家受戒苦行。降伏魔众梵王劝请及转法轮。大众集会广度众生。现大神力示大灭度。如此诸事悉皆如是应作。

doing so with the aim of attaining buddhahood, I vow that I shall not create enmity or contention with others over the causes and conditions involved in such creation of merit." Why? The wise say that, among those jointly carrying out a single endeavor, the signs of enmity may develop. So, too, these sorts of circumstances appear in the world even now. It is in order to do away with such transgressions as these that one brings forth this great vow. This is the eighth vow.

I. THE NINTH BODHISATTVA VOW

Next, we have:

> I vow to practice the bodhisattva path
> and set turning the irreversible wheel,
> thereby enabling the dispelling of all afflictions
> and the entry into faith that is pure.[95]

"The wheel" is a reference to the wheel of Dharma. That it is "irreversible" signifies that there is no one who is able to interfere [with its continuing to turn]. The bodhisattva should bring forth a vow such as this: "I shall practice the path just as it has been taught and will certainly set turning the irreversible wheel of Dharma. I shall turn this wheel of Dharma to dispel beings' afflictions born of the three poisons, to cause them to turn away from *saṃsāra* and enter the domain of the Buddha, the Dharma, and the Sangha, and to cause them to accomplish their own purification through [the teaching of] suffering, origination, cessation, and the path." This is the ninth vow.

J. THE TENTH BODHISATTVA VOW

Next, we have:

> I vow that, in all worlds,
> I shall manifest the realization of bodhi.[96]

In whichever worlds that are appropriate as places for the appearance of the works of a buddha, one manifests the realization of *anuttarasamyaksaṃbodhi* in all of them, doing so for the sake of bringing peace and happiness to all beings and for the sake of leading all beings to nirvāṇa. It is due to the greatness of *anuttarasamyaksaṃbodhi* that its attainment is the only one [of a buddha's deeds] that is mentioned here. As for all the other deeds including entering the womb, taking birth, growing up in the home, leaving behind the home life, taking on the moral precepts, taking up the practice of austerities, conquering Māra's demon hordes, accepting the entreaties of the Brahma Heaven King, turning the wheel of Dharma, assembling an immense congregation, liberating beings on a vast scale, displaying great spiritual powers, and manifesting the great passing into final nirvāṇa, one should accomplish all such deeds as these in this same way.

正體字

| 034b15 ‖ | 是知有如是無量
力。能利無量無邊眾生。不應但於一國示 |
034b16 ‖	成佛道。有人言。於一佛國所有四天下。諸
034b17 ‖	閻浮提是一佛土。過此[7]已外唯佛能知。而
034b18 ‖	實不爾。是第十願。復次。
034b19 ‖	如是諸菩薩　　十大願為首
034b20 ‖	廣大如虛空　　盡於未來際
034b21 ‖	及餘無量願　　亦各分別說
034b22 ‖	願名心所貪樂求欲。必成十者有十種門。
034b23 ‖	廣大如虛空者。願所緣方如所有虛空處
034b24 ‖	願亦如是。盡未來際者。願時所住盡一切眾
034b25 ‖	生未來生死際。有人言。阿耨多羅三藐三菩
034b26 ‖	提。是未來世生死際。若諸佛入無餘涅槃。是
034b27 ‖	生死後際。菩薩志願無盡而實成佛則止。一
034b28 ‖	切十方世界諸大菩薩。皆有是願。餘無量願
034b29 ‖	者。諸菩薩成就無量希有功德故。諸所有願
034c01 ‖	不可盡說。復次。
034c02 ‖	菩薩發如是　　十大願究竟

简体字

是知有如是无量力。能利无量无边众生。不应但于一国示成佛道。有人言。于一佛国所有四天下。诸阎浮提是一佛土。过此已外唯佛能知。而实不尔。是第十愿。复次。

　如是诸菩萨　　十大愿为首
　广大如虚空　　尽于未来际
　及余无量愿　　亦各分别说

愿名心所贪乐求欲。必成十者有十种门。广大如虚空者。愿所缘方如所有虚空处愿亦如是。尽未来际者。愿时所住尽一切众生未来生死际。有人言。阿耨多罗三藐三菩提。是未来世生死际。若诸佛入无余涅槃。是生死后际。菩萨志愿无尽而实成佛则止。一切十方世界诸大菩萨。皆有是愿。余无量愿者。诸菩萨成就无量希有功德故。诸所有愿不可尽说。复次。

　菩萨发如是　　十大愿究竟

Chapter 5 — *The Explanation of the Vows*

One knows from this that, where one possesses immeasurable powers such as these whereby one is capable of benefiting an incalculable and boundless number of beings, one should not merely manifest the realization of buddhahood in but a single land. There are those who state that, within a single buddha's domain consisting of the four continents, it is the entirety of the continent of Jambudvīpa that constitutes that single buddha's buddha land and anything beyond that is a matter comprehensible only to a buddha. However, this is not actually the case. This is the tenth vow.

K. The Infinitely Vast Scope and Duration of the Ten Bodhisattva Vows

Next, we have:

> For all such bodhisattvas as these,
> it is the ten great vows that are foremost.
> They are as vast as empty space
> and exhaust even the bounds of the future.
> This extends to all of their other measurelessly many vows
> as well as to their distinguishing and explanation of each of them.

"Vows" is a reference to what the mind wishes for and what it is determined to definitely achieve. "Ten" is a reference to the existence of ten such gateways.

"They are as vast as empty space" refers to the fact that the regions taken as the objective focus of the vows are equal in their extensiveness to all of empty space. The scope of the vows is so very vast as this.

"Exhausting even the bounds of the future" means that the length of time during which these vows shall abide will exhaust the bounds of the future births and deaths of all beings.

There are others who claim that *anuttarasamyaksaṃbodhi* itself is what sets the bounds of future births and deaths. Or they may assert that, when buddhas enter the nirvāṇa without residue, it is this that constitutes the bounds of future births and death. Or they may say that, although the bodhisattva's vows may be endless, in fact, they end with the realization of buddhahood.

All of the great bodhisattvas throughout the worlds of the ten directions have made these vows. "All of their other measurelessly many vows" refers to the fact that, because all bodhisattvas perfect measurelessly many rare meritorious qualities, one could never exhaustively describe all the vows that they have made.

Next, we have:

> As the bodhisattva makes ten great vows such as these,
> [he does so in ways by which] they are ultimately enduring.

正體字

```
034c03 ‖ 是十大願。有十究竟事。何等為十。答曰。
034c04 ‖   眾生性世性    虛空性法性
034c05 ‖   涅槃佛生性    諸佛智性竟
034c06 ‖   一切心所緣    諸佛行處智
034c07 ‖   世間法智轉    是名十究竟
034c08 ‖ 初眾生性竟。二世間性竟。三虛空性竟。四法
034c09 ‖ 性[8]性竟。五涅槃性竟。六佛生性竟。七諸佛
034c10 ‖ 智性竟。八一切心所緣竟。九諸佛行處智竟。
034c11 ‖ 十世間法智轉竟。是名十究竟。問曰。汝言
034c12 ‖ 竟何者為竟。此義應分別。答曰。
034c13 ‖   眾生性若竟    我願亦復竟
034c14 ‖   如眾生等竟    如是諸願竟
034c15 ‖   竟義名無竟    我善根無竟
034c16 ‖ 眾生性竟者。若眾生都盡滅。我願便應息。隨
034c17 ‖ 世間性盡。
```

简体字

是十大愿。有十究竟事。何等为十。答曰。

　　众生性世性　　虚空性法性
　　涅槃佛生性　　诸佛智性竟
　　一切心所缘　　诸佛行处智
　　世间法智转　　是名十究竟

初众生性竟。二世间性竟。三虚空性竟。四法性性竟。五涅槃性竟。六佛生性竟。七诸佛智性竟。八一切心所缘竟。九诸佛行处智竟。十世间法智转竟。是名十究竟。问曰。汝言竟何者为竟。此义应分别。答曰。

　　众生性若竟　　我愿亦复竟
　　如众生等竟　　如是诸愿竟
　　竟义名无竟　　我善根无竟

众生性竟者。若众生都尽灭。我愿便应息。随世间性尽。

Chapter 5 — The Explanation of the Vows

These ten great vows have ten ways in which they are caused to be ultimately enduring.

Question: What then are those ten ways?

Response:

> They are made until the end of realms of beings, of realms of worlds,
> of realms of empty space, of the Dharma realm,
> of the realm of nirvāṇa, of the realms in which buddhas are born,
> of the realms of all buddhas' knowledge—[97]
> Until the end of anything taken as an object of mind,
> the end of the knowledge associated with buddhas' range of actions,
> and of the permutations of their knowledge of worldly dharmas.

These are the ten ways they are ultimately enduring. [Hence these vows are made]:

> First, until the end of the realms of beings;
> Second, until the end of the realms of worlds;
> Third, until the end of the realms of empty space;
> Fourth, until the end of the Dharma realm;
> Fifth, until the end of the realm of nirvāṇa;
> Sixth, until the end of the realms in which buddhas are born;
> Seventh, until the end of the realms of all buddhas' knowledge;
> Eighth, until the end of everything that can be taken as an object of mind;
> Ninth, until the end of the knowledge associated with all buddhas' range of actions;[98]
> And tenth, until the end of the permutations of their knowledge of worldly dharmas.

These are the ten ways they are ultimately enduring.

Question: You speak of an ultimate "end." What is it that constitutes an ultimate "end"? You should distinguish what is meant by this.

Response:

> If the realms of beings were to come to an end,
> only then would my vows also come to an end.
> Just as it is with the ending of beings and the other things,
> so too it is with the ending of these vows.
> The meaning of "end" then is that there is no end,
> hence my roots of goodness are endless.

As for "if the realms of beings were to come to an end," this is to say: "If all beings became entirely extinct, my vows should then also cease." Thus, if even the realms of the world were to come to an end,

正體字

034c18 ||　　　　虛空性盡。諸法性盡。涅槃性盡。諸
034c18 || 佛生性盡。[9]諸智性盡。一切眾生心所緣性
034c19 || 盡。入佛法智性盡。世間轉法轉智轉盡。我此
034c20 || 十願爾乃盡息。但是眾生性等十事實不盡。
034c21 || 我是福德善根亦不盡不息。不息義者。無量
034c22 || 無邊不可思議。過諸算數名為不息。如此
034c23 || 三千大千世界。十方無量無邊過諸算數故
034c24 || 名為世間無邊。是諸世界中三界六趣眾生
034c25 || 無邊故名為眾生性無邊。是一切世界中內
034c26 || 外二種虛空性無邊故名為虛空性無邊。是
034c27 || 諸世界中。欲色無色無漏性所攝有為法無
034c28 || 邊故名為法性無邊。若一切眾生滅度涅槃
034c29 || 性不增不減。是故涅槃性無邊。若過去十
035a01 || 方諸佛無量無邊。今現在十方諸佛亦無量
035a02 || 無邊。未來十方世界諸佛亦無量無邊。是故
035a03 || 佛[1]生性無邊。　　　　諸佛智無量。不可稱不可量無
035a04 || 等無等等無對無比故。諸佛智性亦無量無
035a05 || 邊。如佛告阿難。

简体字

虚空性尽。诸法性尽。涅槃性尽。诸佛生性尽。诸智性尽。一切众生心所缘性尽。入佛法智性尽。世间转法转智转尽。我此十愿尔乃尽息。但是众生性等十事实不尽。我是福德善根亦不尽不息。不息义者。无量无边不可思议。过诸算数名为不息。如此三千大千世界。十方无量无边过诸算数故名为世间无边。是诸世界中三界六趣众生无边故名为众生性无边。是一切世界中内外二种虚空性无边故名为虚空性无边。是诸世界中。欲色无色无漏性所摄有为法无边故名为法性无边。若一切众生灭度涅槃性不增不减。是故涅槃性无边。若过去十方诸佛无量无边。今现在十方诸佛亦无量无边。未来十方世界诸佛亦无量无边。是故佛生性无边。诸佛智无量。不可称不可量无等无等等无对无比故。诸佛智性亦无量无边。如佛告阿难。

if even the realms of empty space were to come to an end, if even the Dharma realm were to come to an end, if even the realm of nirvāṇa were to come to an end, if even the realms in which buddhas are born were to come to an end, if even the realms of all buddhas'[99] knowledge were to come to an end, if even the realms of conditions taken by all beings as objects of mind were to come to an end, if even the realms of the knowledge that fathoms the Buddha's Dharma were to come to an end, and if even the permutations of worlds, permutations of dharmas, and permutations of knowledge were to come to an end, then and only then would my ten vows finally come to an end.

However, as a matter of fact, these ten phenomena consisting of "the realms of beings" and so forth will never come to an end. Hence my merit and roots of goodness will never come to an end and will never cease.

As for the meaning of "will not cease," it refers to never ceasing even after a period of time that is immeasurable, boundless, inconceivable, and beyond calculation. It is because, throughout the ten directions, worlds of the sort that exist in this great trichiliocosm are measurelessly, boundlessly, and incalculably numerous that worlds are said to be boundless. It is because the beings within all of these worlds' three realms of existence and six rebirth destinies are boundlessly numerous that the realms of beings are said to be boundlessly many.

It is because the realms of the two types of empty space both within and beyond all these worlds are boundless that we refer here to the boundlessness of the realms of empty space.

It is because of the boundlessness of the conditioned dharmas contained within all these worlds' desire realms, form realms, formless realms, and uncontaminated realms that we refer here to the boundlessness of the Dharma realm.

Even if all beings attained nirvāṇa, still the realm of nirvāṇa would neither increase nor decrease. Therefore the realm of nirvāṇa is boundless.

Because the buddhas of the past throughout the ten directions were immeasurably and boundlessly many, because the buddhas of the present throughout the ten directions are immeasurably and boundlessly many, and because the buddhas of the future throughout the ten directions will be immeasurably and boundlessly many, the realms into which buddhas are born are therefore boundlessly many.

Because the buddhas' knowledge is measurelessly vast, indescribable, immeasurable, unequaled, equal to the unequaled, unrivaled, and incomparable, therefore the realms of all buddhas' knowledge are also measureless and boundless. This is just as stated by the Buddha

正體字

是聲聞人諸佛智無量。是
035a06 ‖ 故諸佛智性無量無邊。於過去世一一眾生
035a07 ‖ 無量無邊心。是諸心皆有緣生。未來世亦如
035a08 ‖ 是。現在世一切眾生心。亦無量無邊皆有緣
035a09 ‖ 生。是故心所緣亦無量無邊。諸佛力略說有
035a10 ‖ 四十不共法。是四十不共法。一一法行處無
035a11 ‖ 量無邊。行處無量無邊故智亦無量無邊。是
035a12 ‖ 故說佛行處智無量無邊。世間轉法轉智轉
035a13 ‖ 者。轉名以此法有所轉。世間者。世間有二
035a14 ‖ 種。國土世間眾生世間。此中說眾生世間。諸
035a15 ‖ 佛及諸菩薩。以無量無邊方便力引導眾
035a16 ‖ 生。法轉者。以無量無邊善根福德攝取諸
035a17 ‖ 佛法。智轉者。無量諸善法六波羅蜜十地等
035a18 ‖ 攝取佛智。是故智[2]轉無邊。此三同轉故合
035a19 ‖ 為一願。是菩薩一一願牢堅故。成是十無盡
035a20 ‖ 願。

简体字

是声闻人诸佛智无量。是故诸佛智性无量无边。于过去世一一众生无量无边心。是诸心皆有缘生。未来世亦如是。现在世一切众生心。亦无量无边皆有缘生。是故心所缘亦无量无边。诸佛力略说有四十不共法。是四十不共法。一一法行处无量无边。行处无量无边故智亦无量无边。是故说佛行处智无量无边。世间转法转智转者。转名以此法有所转。世间者。世间有二种。国土世间众生世间。此中说众生世间。诸佛及诸菩萨。以无量无边方便力引导众生。法转者。以无量无边善根福德摄取诸佛法。智转者。无量诸善法六波罗蜜十地等摄取佛智。是故智转无边。此三同转故合为一愿。是菩萨一一愿牢坚故。成是十无尽愿。

when he told Ānanda, "The knowledge possessed by these *śrāvaka* disciples and by all buddhas is measureless." Therefore the realms of the knowledge possessed by the Buddhas are measureless and boundless.

The mind states produced by each and every one of all beings throughout the past were measurelessly and boundlessly many. All of these mind states had corresponding objective conditions serving as the bases of their arising. So too shall this be so of the mind states produced by the beings of the future. So too, the mind states produced by all the beings of the present era are measurelessly and boundlessly many. In every case, they have corresponding objective conditions that serve as the bases of their arising. Therefore the objective conditions taken as the object of those mind states are themselves also measurelessly and boundlessly many.

As for the powers of all buddhas, briefly speaking, they are manifested in the forty dharmas exclusive [to buddhas]. As for these forty exclusive dharmas, the range of implementation of each and every one of these dharmas is measureless and boundless. Because their range of implementation is measureless and boundless, so too then, their corresponding knowledge is also measureless and boundless. It is for this reason that it is stated here that the knowledge associated with the range of all buddhas' actions is itself measureless and boundless.

As for the permutations of worlds, the permutations of dharmas, and the permutations of wisdom, this "permutation" is a designation used to refer to the fact that each of these dharmas has transformational permutations.

As for the reference here to "worlds," worlds are of two types, namely the world that consists of lands and the world that consists of beings themselves. We speak here of the world of beings wherein all buddhas as well as all bodhisattvas guide beings by using the power of a measureless and boundless number of skillful means.

"Permutations of dharmas" refers to the use of measurelessly and boundlessly voluminous roots of goodness and merit in gathering together and acquiring all dharmas of a buddha.

As for "permutations of knowledge," one uses an incalculable number of good dharmas associated with the six *pāramitās* and ten grounds to gather together and acquire the knowledge of a buddha. Hence the permutations of knowledge are boundless. Because these three factors [of worlds, dharmas, and knowledge] are the same in their involvement of transformational permutations, they are therefore gathered together in a single pledge.

Because each and every [one of the ten great] vows of this bodhisattva is firm and solid, he establishes [for each of them] these ten pledges

正體字

035a21 ‖ 方如虛空時如未來際。如是以略說廣
說。解是十願究竟。

简体字

方如虚空时如未来际。如是以略说广说。解是十愿究竟。

of endless duration, declaring those vows to be as spatially vast as empty space and as long-enduring as the bounds of future time. It is in this way that, using these condensed discussions and extensive discussions, we come to the end of this explanation of these ten vows' ultimately enduring duration.

The End of Chapter Five

正體字	035a22 ‖　　發菩提心品第六 035a23 ‖ 問曰。初發心是諸願根本。云何為初發心。答 035a24 ‖ 曰。 035a25 ‖　　初發菩提心　　或三四因緣 035a26 ‖ 眾生初發菩提心。或以三因緣。或以四因 035a27 ‖ 緣。如是和合有七因緣。發阿耨多羅三藐 035a28 ‖ 三菩提心。問曰。何等為七。答曰。 035a29 ‖　　一者諸如來　　令發菩提心 035b01 ‖　　二見法欲壞　　守護故發心 035b02 ‖　　三於眾生中　　大悲而發心 035b03 ‖　　四或有菩薩　　教發菩提心 035b04 ‖　　五見菩薩行　　亦隨而發心 035b05 ‖　　或因布施已　　而發菩提心 035b06 ‖　　或見佛身相　　歡喜而發心 035b07 ‖　　以是七因緣　　而發菩提心
简体字	发菩提心品第六 　问曰。初发心是诸愿根本。云何为初发心。答曰。 　　初发菩提心　　或三四因缘 　众生初发菩提心。或以三因缘。或以四因缘。如是和合有七因缘。发阿耨多罗三藐三菩提心。问曰。何等为七。答曰。 　　一者诸如来　　令发菩提心 　　二见法欲坏　　守护故发心 　　三于众生中　　大悲而发心 　　四或有菩萨　　教发菩提心 　　五见菩萨行　　亦随而发心 　　或因布施已　　而发菩提心 　　或见佛身相　　欢喜而发心 　　以是七因缘　　而发菩提心

Chapter 6
On Producing the Bodhi Resolve

VI. CHAPTER SIX: ON PRODUCING THE BODHI RESOLVE
  A. THE SEVEN BASES FOR PRODUCING THE BODHI RESOLVE

Question: The initial production of the resolve [to attain buddhahood] is the root of all vows. What then is meant by this "initial production of resolve"?

Response:
> The initial resolve to attain bodhi
> May involve three reasons or four reasons.

When beings initially produce the resolve to attain bodhi, this may find its origin in [one of] three reasons or else in [one of] four reasons.[100] Thus, when one combines them, there are a total of seven causes and conditions associated with producing the resolve to attain *anuttarasamyaksaṃbodhi*.

Question: What then are those seven?

Response:
> In the case of the first, a Tathāgata
> may influence one to bring forth the resolve to attain bodhi.
> As for the second, seeing that the Dharma is about to be destroyed,
> one produces the resolve in order to guard and protect it.

> In the case of the third, with respect to beings,
> one feels great compassion for them and thus produces the resolve.
> As for the fourth, there may be a bodhisattva
> who instructs one in the production of the resolve to attain bodhi.

> In the case of the fifth, one may observe the conduct of a bodhisattva
> and also then consequently produce the resolve.
> Or, alternatively, following upon an act of giving,
> one may produce the resolve to attain bodhi [based on that].

> Or else, having observed the marks of a buddha's body,
> one may feel delight and then proceed to produce the resolve.
> Thus it may be due to [any one of] these seven causes and conditions
> that one produces the resolve to attain bodhi.

正體字	035b08 ‖ 佛令發心者。佛以佛眼觀眾生。知其善根 035b09 ‖ 淳熟堪任能得阿耨多羅三藐三菩提。如是 035b10 ‖ 人者。佛教令發心作是言。善男子來。今可 035b11 ‖ 發心當度苦惱眾生。或復有人生在惡世。 035b12 ‖ 見法欲壞。為守護故。發心作是念。咄哉 035b13 ‖ 從無量無邊百千萬億阿僧祇劫來。唯有一 035b14 ‖ 人二處行出三界。四聖諦大導師。知五種法 035b15 ‖ 藏脫於六道。有七種正法大寶。深行八解 035b16 ‖ 脫。以九部經教化。有十大力說十一種功 035b17 ‖ 德。善轉十二因緣相續。說十三助聖道法。 035b18 ‖ 有十四覺意大寶。除十五種貪欲。并得十 035b19 ‖ 六心無礙解脫。出十六地獄眾生。
简体字	佛令发心者。佛以佛眼观众生。知其善根淳熟堪任能得阿耨多罗三藐三菩提。如是人者。佛教令发心作是言。善男子来。今可发心当度苦恼众生。或复有人生在恶世。见法欲坏。为守护故。发心作是念。咄哉从无量无边百千万亿阿僧祇劫来。唯有一人二处行出三界。四圣谛大导师。知五种法藏脱于六道。有七种正法大宝。深行八解脱。以九部经教化。有十大力说十一种功德。善转十二因缘相续。说十三助圣道法。有十四觉意大宝。除十五种贪欲。并得十六心无碍解脱。出十六地狱众生。

1. THE INFLUENCE OF A BUDDHA

In the case where a buddha "influences one to bring forth the resolve," a buddha uses the buddha eye to observe beings. He may then realize that a person's roots of goodness have become so completely ripe that he is capable of taking on this endeavor and that he will be able to realize *anuttarasamyaksaṃbodhi*. For a person such as this, the Buddha instructs him and enjoins him to bring forth the resolve, saying to him, "Son of good family, come forth. You may now bring forth that resolve by which you should bring suffering and afflicted beings across to liberation."

2. THE MOTIVATION TO PROTECT THE DHARMA

Or then again there may be a person born into a dreadful era who, on observing that the Dharma is on the verge of destruction, then, for the sake of protecting it, brings forth the resolve, reflecting as follows:

Alas! From a time in the past an immeasurable and boundless number of hundreds of thousands of myriads of *koṭīs* of *asaṃkhyeyas* of kalpas ago on forth to the very present, there has only been:

A single person;
On two bases;
Whose practice has transcended the three realms;
Who has served as the great guide to the four truths of the Āryas;
Who is that one who has known the fivefold treasury of Dharma;
Who has gained liberation from the six destinies of rebirth;
Who has taken possession of the great jewel of the seven kinds of right Dharma;[101]
Who has deeply practiced the eight liberations;
Who uses the nine categories of sutra text in teaching;
Who has taken possession of the ten great powers;
Who has described the eleven kinds of meritorious qualities;[102]
Who has skillfully set forth the continuous cycle of the twelve causes and conditions;
Who has explained the thirteen dharmas assisting realization of the path of the Āryas;
Who has taken possession of the great jewel of the fourteen factors fundamental to awakening;
Who has dispelled the fifteen kinds of craving;
Who has both attained the realization of the sixteen mind states involved in unimpeded liberation and has also extricated beings from the sixteen kinds of hells;

正體字

及身十七
035b20 ‖ 具足十八不共法。善分別十九住果人。善知
035b21 ‖ 分別學人阿羅漢辟支佛諸佛二十根是。大
035b22 ‖ 悲心者。是大將主大眾主大醫王大導師大
035b23 ‖ 船師。久乃得是法。行難行苦行。乃得是法。
035b24 ‖ 而今欲壞。我當發阿耨多羅三藐三菩提心。
035b25 ‖ 厚種善根得成佛道。令法久住無數阿僧
035b26 ‖ 祇劫。又行菩薩道時。護持無量諸佛法故
035b27 ‖ 勤行精進。或復有人見眾生苦惱。可愍無
035b28 ‖ 救無歸無所依止。流轉生死險難惡道。有
035b29 ‖ 大怨賊諸惡虫獸生死恐怖諸惡鬼等。常有
035c01 ‖ 憂悲苦惱刺蕀。恩愛別離怨會深坑。喜樂之
035c02 ‖ 水甚為難得。大寒大熱獨行其中。曠絕無
035c03 ‖ 蔭難得度脫。眾生於中多諸怖畏。

简体字

及身十七具足十八不共法。善分别十九住果人。善知分别学人阿罗汉辟支佛诸佛二十根是。大悲心者。是大将主大众主大医王大导师大船师。久乃得是法。行难行苦行。乃得是法。而今欲坏。我当发阿耨多罗三藐三菩提心。厚种善根得成佛道。令法久住无数阿僧祇劫。又行菩萨道时。护持无量诸佛法故勤行精进。或复有人见众生苦恼。可愍无救无归无所依止。流转生死险难恶道。有大怨贼诸恶虫兽生死恐怖诸恶鬼等。常有忧悲苦恼刺蕀。恩爱别离怨会深坑。喜乐之水甚为难得。大寒大热独行其中。旷绝无荫难得度脱。众生于中多诸怖畏。

Who has also mastered the seventeen physical dharmas;[103]
Who has completely perfected the eighteen dharmas exclusive [to the buddhas];
Who has skillfully distinguished the nineteen stations of persons who have gained the fruits [of the path];
And who has well known and distinguished the twenty kinds of faculties [consisting of five each] for those still in training, the arhats, the *pratyekabuddhas*, and all buddhas.[104]

This greatly compassionate one, this great lord of generals, this great lord of assemblies, this great king of physicians, this great guide, this great captain of the ship—only after a very long time then acquired this Dharma, and only after cultivating those ascetic practices so difficult to practice then acquired this Dharma. But now, it is on the verge of destruction. I should bring forth the resolve to attain *anuttarasamyaksaṃbodhi*, should plant thick roots of goodness, should thus attain buddhahood, and thus should cause the Dharma to abide for a long time, enduring even for countless *asaṃkhyeyas* of kalpas.

[Of this same sort are those who], while cultivating the bodhisattva path, strive with diligence and vigor to guard and uphold the Dharma of the incalculably many buddhas.

3. COMPASSION FOR THE SUFFERING OF BEINGS

Or, alternatively, there may be those who observe:

That beings, beset as they are by bitter afflictions, are pitiful;
That they have no one to rescue them, no refuge, and no one on whom they can rely;
That they flow along in *saṃsāra*'s dangerous and difficult wretched destinies;
That they are afflicted by great enemies, by all manner of fearsome insects and animals, by the terrors involved in births and deaths, by all manner of fearsome ghosts, and so forth;
That they are always beset by the piercing thorns of worry, sadness, pain, and distress;
That they fall into the deep pit of [sufferings associated with] separation from those they love and encounters with those they detest;
That the waters of joy and happiness are only very rarely encountered;
That they travel alone in the midst of intense cold and intense heat;
That they are stranded without shade in the vast wilderness and find it difficult to make their way across to liberation;
That beings in the midst of all this are possessed by every sort of terror and fear;

正體字	無有救 035c04 ‖ 護將導之者。見如是眾生。入此生死險惡 035c05 ‖ 道中受諸苦惱。以大悲故發阿耨多羅三 035c06 ‖ 藐三菩提心。作是言。我當為無救作救無 035c07 ‖ 歸作歸無依作依。我得度已當度眾生。 035c08 ‖ 我得脫已當脫眾生。我得安已當安眾生。 035c09 ‖ 復有人但從人聞以信樂心等。發無上道 035c10 ‖ 心。作是念。我[3]當修善法不斷絕故。或墮 035c11 ‖ 必定得無生法忍。集諸[4]福德善根淳熟故。 035c12 ‖ 或值諸佛或值大菩薩。能知眾生諸根利 035c13 ‖ 鈍深心本末性欲差別。善知方便為般若 035c14 ‖ 波羅蜜所護。能作佛事者知我發願。善根 035c15 ‖ 成熟故令住必定。若無生[5]法忍。是諸菩薩。 035c16 ‖ 在第七第八第九第十地。如佛善知眾生心 035c17 ‖ 力教令發心。不以但有信樂力等教令發 035c18 ‖ 心。復有人
简体字	无有救护将导之者。见如是众生。入此生死险恶道中受诸苦恼。以大悲故发阿耨多罗三藐三菩提心。作是言。我当为无救作救无归作归无依作依。我得度已当度众生。我得脱已当脱众生。我得安已当安众生。复有人但从人闻以信乐心等。发无上道心。作是念。我当修善法不断绝故。或堕必定得无生法忍。集诸福德善根淳熟故。或值诸佛或值大菩萨。能知众生诸根利钝深心本末性欲差别。善知方便为般若波罗蜜所护。能作佛事者知我发愿。善根成熟故令住必定。若无生法忍。是诸菩萨。在第七第八第九第十地。如佛善知众生心力教令发心。不以但有信乐力等教令发心。复有人

And that they have no one to rescue them, protect them, or serve as guides for them.

Having observed that beings have entered in this manner into the dangerous and wretched destinies involved in *saṃsāra*, that they undergo all manner of suffering and affliction, such a person, because of the great compassion, may then bring forth the resolve to attain *anuttarasamyaksaṃbodhi* and may then proclaim, "I shall become a rescuer for those who have no one to rescue them. I shall become a refuge for those who have no refuge. I will become a support for those with no one to rely on.

Once I have gained liberation, I shall strive to liberate other beings as well. Once I have gained liberation, I shall then also liberate these beings. Once I have gained peace, I shall also bring peace to other beings."

4. THE INSTRUCTIVE INFLUENCE OF A BODHISATTVA

Then again, there are also those persons who need only hear of this matter from others and then, due to thoughts of resolute belief[105] and other such factors, they produce the resolve to achieve the unsurpassed enlightenment and reflect:

By always[106] and ceaselessly cultivating wholesome dharmas, I may reach the stage of certainty and realize the unproduced-dharmas patience.[107] Due to accumulating all manner of merit and due to the ripening of roots of goodness, I may then encounter buddhas or may encounter great bodhisattvas who are able to know the relative acuity or dullness of beings' faculties, are able to know from root to branch their deep-seated inclinations and the differences in their individual natures and aspirations, who thoroughly understand the use of skillful means, and who are under the protection of the *prajñāpāramitā*.

Those [beings such as these] who are able to carry on the works of a buddha will realize that I have brought forth the vow. Then, because of the ripening of my roots of goodness, they may influence me to abide in the stage of certainty or the unproduced-dharmas patience.[108]

These bodhisattvas [to which he refers] are those who abide on the seventh, eighth, ninth, or tenth bodhisattva grounds. They are those who, like a buddha, thoroughly know the strengths of beings' minds and thereby teach them to produce the resolve.

5. THE ASPIRATION TO EMULATE THE CONDUCT OF BODHISATTVAS

But it is not solely through their possession of the power of resolute belief and other such factors that they are taught to bring forth the resolve. In addition, there are those persons who [bring forth the

|正體字|

　　　　見餘菩薩行道修諸善根大悲
035c19 ‖ 所護。具足方便教化眾生。不惜身命多
035c20 ‖ 所利益。廣博多聞世間奇特人中標勝。疲苦
035c21 ‖ 眾生為作蔭覆。安住布施持戒忍辱精進禪
035c22 ‖ 定智慧慚愧質直柔軟調和。其心清淨深樂
035c23 ‖ 善法。見如是人而作是念。是人所行我亦
035c24 ‖ 應行所修願行我亦應修。我為得是法故
035c25 ‖ 當發是願。作是念已發無上道心。復有人
035c26 ‖ 行大布施。施佛及僧或但施佛以飲食衣
035c27 ‖ 服等。是人因是布施。念過去諸菩薩能行
035c28 ‖ 施者。韋藍摩韋首多羅薩婆檀尸毘王等。即
035c29 ‖ 發菩提心。以此施福迴向阿耨多羅三藐
036a01 ‖ 三菩提。復有人若見若聞佛三十二相。足
036a02 ‖ 下平。手足輪。指網縵。手足柔軟。七處滿。

|简体字|

见余菩萨行道修诸善根大悲所护。具足方便教化众生。不惜身命多所利益。广博多闻世间奇特人中标胜。疲苦众生为作荫覆。安住布施持戒忍辱精进禅定智慧惭愧质直柔软调和。其心清净深乐善法。见如是人而作是念。是人所行我亦应行所修愿行我亦应修。我为得是法故当发是愿。作是念已发无上道心。复有人行大布施。施佛及僧或但施佛以饮食衣服等。是人因是布施。念过去诸菩萨能行施者。韦蓝摩韦首多罗萨婆檀尸毗王等。即发菩提心。以此施福回向阿耨多罗三藐三菩提。复有人若见若闻佛三十二相。足下平手足轮指网缦手足柔软七处满

Chapter 6 — On Producing the Bodhi Resolve

resolve] by observing other bodhisattvas practicing the path, cultivating all manner of roots of goodness, proceeding under the protection of the great compassion, and perfecting skillful means as they teach and transform beings. [They observe that]:

> They accomplish an abundance of beneficial deeds without indulging any cherishing regard for their own bodies or lives;
> They develop vastly extensive learning;
> They become especially distinctive people in the world;
> They become the most emblematically superior people;
> They serve as a source of shade for weary and suffering beings;
> They become securely established in the practices of giving, moral virtue, patience, vigor, *dhyāna* concentration, wisdom, a sense of shame, a dread of blame, straightforwardness in character, mental pliancy, and congeniality;
> Their minds are pure;
> And they deeply delight in good dharmas.

By observing persons such as these, they are inspired to reflect, "I too should practice what these people practice. I too should cultivate the vows and conduct that they cultivate. I should bring forth this vow for the sake of acquiring this Dharma." Having had this thought, they then bring forth the resolve to attain the unsurpassable enlightenment.

6. INSPIRATION PROVOKED BY AN ACT OF GIVING

Yet again, there are those persons who engage in acts of great giving, acts whereby they present gifts to a buddha or to his sangha, or acts whereby they simply offer food, drink, or robes to a buddha. Due to such acts of giving, these persons may then call to mind those bodhisattvas of the past who were able to practice giving, bodhisattvas such as Velāma,[109] Viśvantara,[110] Sarvadā, and King Śibi. [Having called them to mind], they may then immediately bring forth the resolve to attain bodhi and then dedicate the merit from their act of giving to [their future attainment of] *anuttarasamyaksaṃbodhi*.

7. INSPIRATION ARISING FROM OBSERVING A BUDDHA'S PHYSICAL MARKS

Yet again, there may be those persons who directly observe or merely hear about the thirty-two marks of the Buddhas, namely such marks as:

> The evenness of their soles;
> The wheel-marks on the hands and feet;
> The webbing at the roots of their fingers;
> The softness of their hands and feet;
> The fullness in seven places;

正體字

036a03 ‖ 纖長指。足跟廣。身傭直。足趺高平。毛上旋。伊泥[[跳-兆+專]>[跳-兆+專]]。臂長
036a04 ‖ 過膝。陰馬藏。身金色。皮軟薄。一一孔一毛生。眉
036a05 ‖ 間白毫。上身如師子。肩圓大。腋下滿。得知妙味。
036a06 ‖ 身方如尼拘樓陀樹。頂有肉髻。廣長舌。梵音
036a07 ‖ 聲。師子頰。四十齒。齊白密緻。眼睛紺青色。睫如
036a08 ‖ 牛王等相。心則歡喜作是念。我亦當得如
036a09 ‖ 是相。如是相人所得諸法我亦當得。即發
036a10 ‖ 阿耨多羅三藐三菩提心。以是七因緣發菩
036a11 ‖ 提心。問曰。汝說七因緣發菩薩心。為皆當
036a12 ‖ 成有成有不成。答曰。是不必盡成。或有成
036a13 ‖ 有不成。問曰。若爾者應解說。

简体字

纤长指足跟广身佣直足趺高平毛上旋伊泥[跳-兆+專]臂长过膝阴马藏身金色皮软薄一一孔一毛生眉间白毫上身如师子肩圆大腋下满得知妙味身方如尼拘楼陀树顶有肉髻广长舌梵音声师子颊四十齿齐白密致眼睛绀青色睫如牛王等相。心则欢喜作是念。我亦当得如是相。如是相人所得诸法我亦当得。即发阿耨多罗三藐三菩提心。以是七因缘发菩提心。问曰。汝说七因缘发菩萨心。为皆当成有成有不成。答曰。是不必尽成。或有成有不成。问曰。若尔者应解说。

Chapter 6 — On Producing the Bodhi Resolve

The slenderness and length of their fingers;
The breadth of their heels;
The straightness of their bodies;
Their high and even ankles;
The vertical swirling shape of their bodily hairs;
Their thighs resembling those of the *aiṇeya* antelope;
Their arms whereby the fingers reach even below the knees;
Their genital ensheathment like that of a stallion;
The gold color of their bodies;
The softness and thinness of their skin;
The placement of but a single hair in each and every pore;
Their white "hair mark" between their brows;
Their lion-like bodies;
Their round and large shoulders;
The fullness of the axillary region;
Their ability to distinctly know sublime flavors;
Their physical girth like that of the *nyagrodha* tree;
Their fleshy prominence atop the crown of their heads;
Their vast and long tongues;
Their voices possessed of the sound like Brahmā;
Their lion-like jaws;
Their forty teeth which are straight, white, and closely set;
Their blue eyes;
And their eyelashes like those of the king of the bulls.

[Having observed or heard of these marks of a buddha's body], they may then become delighted and think, "I too should strive to gain these physical marks and I too should strive to gain those dharmas gained by those who possess such physical marks." They may then immediately produce the resolve to attain *anuttarasamyaksaṃbodhi*.

Thus it may be because of any of these seven causes and conditions that one then brings forth the resolve to attain bodhi.

B. The Relative Probability of Success in these Seven Bases

Question: You stated that there are these seven reasons for a person's generation of the bodhisattva's resolve. Will they all result in success or is it instead the case that some will result in success but others will not?

Response: It is not necessarily the case that they will all result in success. They may result in success or they may not result in success.

Question: If that is so, you should explain this.

正體字

答曰。
036a14 ||　　於七發心中　　佛教令發心
036a15 ||　　護法故發心　　憐愍故發心
036a16 ||　　如是三心者　　必定得成就
036a17 ||　　其餘四心者　　不必皆成就
036a18 || 是七心中佛觀其根本。教令發心必得成。
036a19 || 以不空言故。若為尊重佛法為欲守護。
036a20 || 若於眾生有大悲心。如是三心必得成就。
036a21 || 根本深故。餘菩薩教令發心。見菩薩所行
036a22 || 發心。因大布施發心。若見若聞佛相發心。
036a23 || 是四心多不成。或有成者。根本微弱故。[1]
036a24 || 十住毘婆沙論卷第三

简体字

答曰。
　　于七发心中　　佛教令发心
　　护法故发心　　怜愍故发心
　　如是三心者　　必定得成就
　　其余四心者　　不必皆成就
是七心中佛观其根本。教令发心必得成。以不空言故。若为尊重佛法为欲守护。若于众生有大悲心。如是三心必得成就。根本深故。余菩萨教令发心。见菩萨所行发心。因大布施发心。若见若闻佛相发心。是四心多不成。或有成者。根本微弱故。

Response:

> Of the seven reasons for generating the resolve,
> where the Buddha has instructed one to produce the resolve,
> where one produces the resolve in order to protect the Dharma,
> and where one produces the resolve out of pity for others—
>
> those who have the three motivations such as these
> will certainly find success in this.
> As for the other four types of motivation,
> It is not certain that they will all be successful in this.

Among these seven reasons for generating the resolve, in a circumstance where a buddha has contemplated one's origins and then instructed one in a way that one is caused to produce the resolve, that will certainly result in success. This is because [buddhas] do not speak in vain.

So too is this true of those instances where [one's production of the resolve occurs] because one reveres and esteems the Dharma of the buddhas and one is motivated by the determination to protect it.

So too is this true of those instances where [one's production of the resolve occurs] because one has the mind of great compassion for beings. These three reasons for generating the resolve will definitely result in success, for the roots [of such resolve] are deeply anchored.

In instances where other bodhisattvas have provided instruction which has influenced one to produce the resolve, in instances where one has observed the practices of bodhisattvas and therefore produced the resolve, in instances where one has produced the resolve due to an act of great giving, and in instances where one has produced the resolve because of seeing or hearing about the physical marks of a buddha—for the most part, these four instances of generating the resolve do not result in success, though it may be that there are still those that do succeed. [When these do not result in success], it is due to the relative weakness of the foundations [of their practice].

The End of Chapter Six

正體字

```
036b02 ‖ 十住毘婆沙論卷第四  036b03 ‖
036b04 ‖     聖者龍樹造
036b05 ‖     後秦龜茲國三藏鳩摩羅什譯
036b06 ‖   [2]調伏心品第七
036b07 ‖ 問曰。如上品說。三發心必成。餘四不必成。
036b08 ‖ 云何為成。云何不成。答曰。若菩薩發菩提
036b09 ‖ 心行。失菩提心法。是則不成。若行不失菩
036b10 ‖ 提心法。是則必成。是故偈說。
036b11 ‖   菩薩應遠離    失菩提心法
036b12 ‖   應一心修行    不失菩提法
036b13 ‖ 遠離名除滅惡法不令入心。若入疾滅。失
036b14 ‖ 名若今世若後世忘菩提心。不復隨順修
036b15 ‖ 行。應遠離如是法。若不失菩提法。不忘
036b16 ‖ 菩提心。應常一心勤行。問曰。何等法失菩
036b17 ‖ 提心。答曰。
036b18 ‖   一不敬重法    二有憍慢心
036b19 ‖   三妄語無實    四不敬知識
```

简体字

调伏心品第七

问曰。如上品说。三发心必成。余四不必成。云何为成。云何不成。答曰。若菩萨发菩提心行。失菩提心法。是则不成。若行不失菩提心法。是则必成。是故偈说。

　　菩萨应远离　　失菩提心法
　　应一心修行　　不失菩提法

远离名除灭恶法不令入心。若入疾灭。失名若今世若后世忘菩提心。不复随顺修行。应远离如是法。若不失菩提法。不忘菩提心。应常一心勤行。问曰。何等法失菩提心。答曰。

　　一不敬重法　　二有憍慢心
　　三妄语无实　　四不敬知识

CHAPTER 7
On Training the Mind

VII. CHAPTER SEVEN: ON TRAINING THE MIND
   A. Q: WHAT ARE THE BASES OF SUCCESS OR FAILURE OF ONE'S BODHI RESOLVE?

Question: According to the explanation in the previous chapter, there are three cases where production of the resolve [to attain buddhahood] will definitely result in success whereas, in the remaining four cases, it is not necessarily the case that they will result in success. Why is it that some of these result in success and why is it that some of these do not result in success?

   B. A: PRACTICING DHARMAS RESULTING IN FAILURE ENTAILS LOSS

Response: If a bodhisattva has brought forth the bodhi resolve yet practices dharmas conducing to loss of the bodhi resolve, this will not meet with success. If he practices the dharmas not conducing to losing bodhi resolve, this will certainly bring success. Hence this verse says:

> The bodhisattva should abandon
> any dharmas conducing to loss of the bodhi resolve
> and should single-mindedly cultivate
> those dharmas that prevent loss of bodhi.

By "abandonment," it is meant that one entirely extinguishes those dharmas that are bad and thus prevents them from entering one's mind. If they do enter, one swiftly extinguishes them. "Loss" refers to the forgetting, either in the present life or the future life, of one's resolve to realize bodhi whereupon one would no longer pursue it through cultivation of the practices. One must leave such dharmas far behind. If one is to succeed in avoiding losing those dharmas facilitating the realization of bodhi, and if one is to avoid forgetting the resolve to realize bodhi, then one should always pursue single-minded and diligent practice.

     1. Q: WHICH DHARMAS RESULT IN LOSS

Question: Which sorts of dharmas result in loss of the bodhi resolve?

     2. A: THERE ARE FOUR SUCH DHARMAS (VERSE)

Response:
> The first is failing to revere and esteem the Dharma.
> The second is possessing an arrogant mind.
> The third is false speech or being untruthful.
> The fourth is failing to revere spiritual guides.

正體字

036b20 ‖ 有是四法者。若於今世死時。若次後世。則
036b21 ‖ 忘失菩提心。不能自知我是菩薩。不復
036b22 ‖ [3]發願。菩薩行法不復在前。不恭敬法者。法
036b23 ‖ 名諸佛所說上中下乘。取要言之。是諸佛
036b24 ‖ 如來所用教法。於此法中不恭敬供養尊重
036b25 ‖ 讚歎。不生希有想難得想寶物想滿願想。是
036b26 ‖ 法能失菩提心。慢心者。自高其心。未得謂
036b27 ‖ 得未證謂證。空無相無願。若無生忍法。若
036b28 ‖ 六波羅蜜。若菩薩十地。如是等及諸餘從修
036b29 ‖ 生者。於此法中未得謂得。妄語者。有屬
036c01 ‖ 突吉羅。有屬波夜提。有屬偷蘭遮。有屬
036c02 ‖ 僧伽婆尸沙。有屬波羅夷。或有人言。有第
036c03 ‖ 六妄語。是妄語心生懺悔。上五妄語初輕後
036c04 ‖ 重。第六者最輕。屬波羅夷者。自無過人法。
036c05 ‖ 若口言若形示。趣以方便現有此德。

简体字

有是四法者。若于今世死时。若次后世。则忘失菩提心。不能自知我是菩萨。不复发愿。菩萨行法不复在前。不恭敬法者。法名诸佛所说上中下乘。取要言之。是诸佛如来所用教法。于此法中不恭敬供养尊重赞叹。不生希有想难得想宝物想满愿想。是法能失菩提心。慢心者。自高其心。未得谓得未证谓证。空无相无愿。若无生忍法。若六波罗蜜。若菩萨十地。如是等及诸余从修生者。于此法中未得谓得。妄语者。有属突吉罗。有属波夜提。有属偷兰遮。有属僧伽婆尸沙。有属波罗夷。或有人言。有第六妄语。是妄语心生忏悔。上五妄语初轻后重。第六者最轻。属波罗夷者。自无过人法。若口言若形示。趣以方便现有此德。

Those possessed of any of these four dharmas—whether it be at the time of death in this present lifetime or whether it be in a subsequent lifetime—they will forget and lose their bodhi resolve. Thus they will become unable to realize, "I am a bodhisattva," and so they will no longer bring forth the vow. Thus the dharmas of bodhisattva practice will no longer manifest before them.

As for "failing to revere and esteem the Dharma," "Dharma" refers to the superior, middling, and lesser vehicles set forth by all buddhas. To take up what is essential here, it refers to all of those dharmas that all buddhas, all *tathāgatas*, have used in providing instruction. If, with respect to these dharmas, one does not revere them, does not make offerings to them, does not honor and esteem them, does not praise them, does not produce thoughts regarding them as rare, does not think of them as difficult to encounter, does not think of them as precious objects, or does not think of them as the means for the fulfillment of one's aspirations, these very dharmas [of disesteem] can bring about the loss of one's bodhi resolve.

As for an "arrogant mind," this refers to elevating the status of one's own mind and then claiming to have gained what one has not yet gained and claiming to have realized what one has not yet realized, claiming for instance that one has realized emptiness, signlessness, or wishlessness or the unproduced-dharmas patience, the six *pāramitās*, the ten bodhisattva grounds or any of the other dharmas that arise through cultivation. With regard to these dharmas, even though one has not yet attained them, one nonetheless claims to have attained them.

As for "false speech," there are instances that constitute *duṣkṛta* offenses, those that constitute *pāyantika* offenses, those that constitute *sthūlātyaya* offenses, those that constitute *saṃghāvaśeṣa* offenses, and those that constitute *pārājika* offenses.[111] There may be others who claim that there exists a sixth category of false speech. This refers to when one brings forth repentance with a mind that itself involves an instance of false speech.

Among the above five categories of false speech, the first is the lightest form of offense whereas the last is the most severe form of offense. The sixth category is the lightest of them all.

In the case of the *pārājika* offense, this is an instance where one does not in fact possess any of the superhuman dharmas but nonetheless tends to use various means to create the impression that he possesses such qualities, whether this impression be created through what is spoken by the mouth or what is signaled by the body.

正體字

```
                屬僧
036c06 ‖ 伽婆尸沙者。若口言若形示。於彼比丘四事
036c07 ‖ 中。以一一有根無根事謗。屬偷蘭遮者。欲
036c08 ‖ 以有根無根事謗而說不成。屬波夜提者。
036c09 ‖ 以無根僧伽婆尸沙事謗。屬突吉羅者。除
036c10 ‖ 入四種罪餘妄語是。自心除滅者。若說戒
036c11 ‖ 時自知有小罪。不得[4]向他說。即自心悔。
036c12 ‖ 問曰。是妄語者。但在比丘不在白衣。而此
036c13 ‖ 論通在家出家。答曰。凡知事實爾。而異知
036c14 ‖ 說者。此論中說是總相妄語。以有眾生分別
036c15 ‖ 故。事分別故。時分別故。五眾罪分別故。住處
036c16 ‖ 分別故。則有輕重。雖輕妄語習久則[5]重。能
036c17 ‖ 失[6]菩提心。眾生分別者。斷善根邪見者。及
036c18 ‖ 餘深煩惱者。是則為重。事分別者。若說過
036c19 ‖ 人法破僧是。
```

简体字

属僧伽婆尸沙者。若口言若形示。于彼比丘四事中。以一一有根无根事谤。属偷兰遮者。欲以有根无根事谤而说不成。属波夜提者。以无根僧伽婆尸沙事谤。属突吉罗者。除入四种罪余妄语是。自心除灭者。若说戒时自知有小罪。不得向他说。即自心悔。问曰。是妄语者。但在比丘不在白衣。而此论通在家出家。答曰。凡知事实尔。而异知说者。此论中说是总相妄语。以有众生分别故。事分别故。时分别故。五众罪分别故。住处分别故。则有轻重。虽轻妄语习久则重。能失菩提心。众生分别者。断善根邪见者。及余深烦恼者。是则为重。事分别者。若说过人法破僧是。

As for the *saṃghāvaśeṣa* offense, this refers to an instance where, with respect to any one of those four circumstances [constituting *pārājika* offenses] for a bhikshu, whether through spoken words or physical signs, [a fully-ordained bhikshu or bhikshuni] commits a slander [of another bhikshu or bhikshuni by [testifying to the existence of] any one of the bases [for a *pārājika* offense] when in fact there was no such basis [for such an accusation].

As for the *sthūlātyaya* offense, this refers to an instance where, wishing to slander someone, one brings forth either a plausible or baseless allegation, but that allegation is then not established [as truthful].[112]

As for the *pāyantika* offense, this refers to when one commits a slander in a circumstance involving a baseless *saṃghāvaśeṣa* allegation.

As for the *duṣkṛta* offense, this refers to any instance of false speech not subsumed among the other four categories of false speech.

As for those instances [of abandonment] where one is able to extinguish [bad dharmas] from one's own mind,[113] this refers to when, at the time when the precepts are being recited [each half month], one realizes that one has committed a minor offense but cannot bring oneself to declare it to anyone else, yet one nonetheless immediately repents of it in one's own mind.

Question: These types of "false speech" are exclusive to bhikshus and irrelevant to laity and yet this treatise is ostensibly intended to address both laity and monastics.

Response: Whenever anyone knows that some circumstance is actually this particular way and yet speaks of it in a manner that differs from what one knows to be the case, that is what we refer to in this treatise as generally constituting a lie. Due to distinctions in types of beings, distinctions in circumstances, distinctions in the time of commission, distinctions in five classes of transgressions, and distinctions in dwelling place, the transgression may be either minor or grave.

Also, although a given transgression may be relatively minor, when it is repeated for a long time, then it qualifies as grave and may cause one to lose the resolve to attain bodhi.

"Distinctions in types of beings" refers to instances involving lying transgressions committed by those with wrong views who have severed their roots of goodness or lying transgressions committed by others who are beset with heavy afflictions. These are grave transgressions.

"Distinctions in circumstances" refers for instance to untruthful claims to possess superhuman attainments and to those that create a schism in the monastic sangha.

正體字	036c20 ‖ 時分別者。出家人妄語則重。 036c20 ‖ 五眾罪分別者。如波羅夷僧伽婆尸沙罪則 036c21 ‖ 重。住處分別者。僧中妄語若證時則重。不 036c22 ‖ 恭敬善知識者。不生恭敬畏難想。多行此 036c23 ‖ 四法。則失菩提心。問曰。但是四法能失菩 036c24 ‖ 提心。更有餘法。答曰。 036c25 ‖ 　悋惜最要法　　貪樂於小乘 036c26 ‖ 　謗毀諸菩薩　　輕賤坐禪者 036c27 ‖ 悋惜要法者。師所知甚深難得之義。多所 036c28 ‖ 利者。貪著利養恐與己等故。祕惜不說。 036c29 ‖ 貪樂小乘者。不得大乘滋味故。貪樂二 037a01 ‖ 乘。謗諸菩薩者。無罪而言有罪名為謗。 037a02 ‖ 菩薩義先已說。此人無過而妄加其罪。若實 037a03 ‖ 有罪而論說者。此雖有罪比前為輕。何以 037a04 ‖ 故。經說。
简体字	时分别者。出家人妄语则重。五众罪分别者。如波罗夷僧伽婆尸沙罪则重。住处分别者。僧中妄语若证时则重。不恭敬善知识者。不生恭敬畏难想。多行此四法。则失菩提心。问曰。但是四法能失菩提心。更有余法。答曰。 　　悋惜最要法　　贪乐于小乘 　　谤毁诸菩萨　　轻贱坐禅者 　悋惜要法者。师所知甚深难得之义。多所利者。贪着利养恐与己等故。秘惜不说。贪乐小乘者。不得大乘滋味故。贪乐二乘。谤诸菩萨者。无罪而言有罪名为谤。菩萨义先已说。此人无过而妄加其罪。若实有罪而论说者。此虽有罪比前为轻。何以故。经说。

As for "distinctions in the time of commission" if someone tells a lie when they are monastic, this is a grave transgression.

"Distinctions in five classes of transgressions," if one commits either a *pārājika* or a *saṃghāvaśeṣa* offense, these are grave transgressions.[114]

Distinctions according to the location: Lies committed by monastics at times of certification are grave transgressions.[115]

"Failing to revere good spiritual guides" refers to failing to have thoughts of reverence and awe toward them.

If one often engages in these four [behavioral] dharmas, then one is bound to lose the resolve to attain bodhi.

3. Q: ARE THERE ONLY THESE FOUR OR ARE THERE MORE?

Question: Are there only these four dharmas by which one is able to lose the bodhi resolve or are there additional dharmas leading to the same outcome?

4. A: THERE ARE NUMEROUS ADDITIONAL CASES (A SERIES OF VERSES)

Response:
If one is stingy with the most essential dharmas,
if one covets and delights in the Small Vehicle,
if one slanders bodhisattvas,
or if one slights those who practice *dhyāna* meditation—

"If one is stingy with the most essential dharmas," refers to circumstances where a teacher [of Dharma] understands an extremely profound and rare principle beneficial to many, yet, because he covets offerings and fears others might equal him [in his understanding of Dharma], he keeps that teaching secret, cherishes it as his own, and refrains from explaining it to others.

"If one covets and delights in the Small Vehicle" refers to circumstances in which, because one fails to realize and appreciate the flavor of the Great Vehicle, one instead covets and delights in [the paths taught by followers of] the Two Vehicles.[116]

In "if one slanders bodhisattvas," "slander" refers to [maliciously] ascribing an offense to one who has not committed an offense. The meaning of "bodhisattva" has already been explained. This refers to an instance where there has been no offense at all and yet this person falsely claims [that a particular bodhisattva] has committed an offense.

If [some bodhisattva practitioner] truly *has* committed a transgression and one then discusses the matter with others, although this itself constitutes a transgression, it is relatively light compared to the former case. What is the basis for this? The scriptures state that, whether or

正體字

諸菩薩若實有罪若無有罪。皆不
應說。輕賤坐禪者。若在家出家為斷諸煩
惱故勤行精進。[1]為遮一切煩惱集助佛
道法。此人或不善論議。或無才辯。或無重
威德。無[2]智之人而輕賤之。則得重罪。復次
[3]若於善知識其心懷結恨。亦有諂曲心。貪
諸利養等。善知識義先已說。於此教化說法
者生嫌恨心。如嫌父母得重罪。諂者心佞
媚。曲者身口業現有所作。貪利養等者。貪著
利樂稱譽。以此法壞質直心故。不能深
起善根。如惡色染衣更不受好色。復次。

　　不覺諸魔事　　菩提心劣弱
　　業障及法障　　亦失菩提心

不覺魔事者。若不知諸魔事。則不能制
伏。若不制伏則失菩提心。問曰。何等是諸
魔事。

简体字

诸菩萨若实有罪若无有罪。皆不应说。轻贱坐禅者。若在家出家为断诸烦恼故勤行精进。为遮一切烦恼集助佛道法。此人或不善论议。或无才辩。或无重威德。无智之人而轻贱之。则得重罪。复次若于善知识其心怀结恨。亦有谄曲心。贪诸利养等。善知识义先已说。于此教化说法者生嫌恨心。如嫌父母得重罪。谄者心佞媚。曲者身口业现有所作。贪利养等者。贪着利乐称誉。以此法坏质直心故。不能深起善根。如恶色染衣更不受好色。复次。

　　不觉诸魔事　　菩提心劣弱
　　业障及法障　　亦失菩提心

不觉魔事者。若不知诸魔事。则不能制伏。若不制伏则失菩提心。问曰。何等是诸魔事。

not any bodhisattva has committed a karmic offense, one should not discuss the matter in any case.

As for "if one slights those who practice *dhyāna* meditation," this refers to a case where, for the sake of cutting off afflictions, someone, either a layperson or a monastic, practices [*dhyāna* meditation] with diligence and vigor in order to block off the arising of any of the afflictions and in order to assemble dharmas supporting progress on the path to buddhahood. Such persons may not be skillful in doctrinal discourse, may be lacking in eloquence, or may have no esteem for the awe-inspiring deportment. Still, if some unwise person therefore slights or disparages them, he thereby commits a grave offense.

Next we have the following:

> If one harbors enmity
> toward a good spiritual guide
> and also if one is possessed of flattering, devious thoughts
> covetous of obtaining offerings and such,[117]

The meaning of "good spiritual guide" has already been explained. If one has thoughts of enmity toward this person when he is engaged in teaching and speaking on the Dharma, one thereby commits a grave karmic offense comparable to that of cherishing enmity toward one's own father or mother.

"Flattering" refers to the intention to ingratiate oneself with others. "Devious" refers to instances where one displays physical and verbal actions that create the [false] impression of having accomplished something. "Covetous of obtaining offerings and such" refers to seeking for and being attached to gaining benefit, pleasures, praise, or a fine reputation. It is because such dharmas damage one's straightforwardness of character, one becomes unable to develop deeply anchored roots of goodness. This is just as when a robe that has been dyed an ugly color cannot then be dyed a fine color.

Next, we have the following:

> If one fails to become aware of the works of *māras*,
> if one's bodhi resolve is inferior and weak,
> or if one encounters karmic obstacles or Dharma obstacles,
> then, too, one is bound to lose the resolve to attain bodhi.

As for "if one fails to become aware of the works of *māras*," if one remains unaware of the various works of *māras*, then one cannot control and overcome them. If one fails to control and overcome them, then one is bound to lose the resolve to attain bodhi.

    a. Q: What Is Meant by "the Works of Māras"?

Question: What all is meant by "the works of *māras*"?

正體字	答曰。說應布施持戒忍辱精進禪定智 037a20 ‖ 慧波羅蜜時。及說大乘所攝深義時。不疾 037a21 ‖ 樂說。若樂說於其中間餘緣散亂。若書讀解 037a22 ‖ 說論議聽受等。憍慢自大其心散亂。緣想餘 037a23 ‖ 事妄念戲笑。互相譏論兩不和合。不能通 037a24 ‖ 達實義。從座而去作是念。我於此中無有 037a25 ‖ 受記心不清淨。亦不說我城邑聚落居家 037a26 ‖ 生處。是故不欲聞法不得滋味從座而 037a27 ‖ 去。捨大乘所說諸波羅蜜。及於聲聞辟支佛 037a28 ‖ 自調度經中求薩婆若。若書讀解說聽受等 037a29 ‖ 時。欲樂說餘種種事。破散般若波羅蜜。所 037b01 ‖ 謂說方國聚落城邑園林[4]帥事賊事。兵甲器 037b02 ‖ 仗憎愛苦樂父母兄弟男女妻子衣服飲食臥 037b03 ‖ 具醫藥資生之物。心則散亂失般若波羅蜜。 037b04 ‖ 又說貪恚癡怨家親屬好時惡時歌舞伎樂
简体字	答曰。说应布施持戒忍辱精进禅定智慧波罗蜜时。及说大乘所摄深义时。不疾乐说。若乐说于其中间余缘散乱。若书读解说论议听受等。骄慢自大其心散乱。缘想余事妄念戏笑。互相讥论两不和合。不能通达实义。从座而去作是念。我于此中无有受记心不清净。亦不说我城邑聚落居家生处。是故不欲闻法不得滋味从座而去。舍大乘所说诸波罗蜜。及于声闻辟支佛自调度经中求萨婆若。若书读解说听受等时。欲乐说余种种事。破散般若波罗蜜。所谓说方国聚落城邑园林帅事贼事。兵甲器仗憎爱苦乐父母兄弟男女妻子衣服饮食卧具医药资生之物。心则散乱失般若波罗蜜。又说贪恚痴怨家亲属好时恶时歌舞伎乐

b. A: THERE ARE NUMEROUS EXAMPLES, AS FOLLOWS: (LIST)

Response: [These are illustrated by the following examples]:

When, in explaining how one ought to take up the *pāramitās* of giving, moral virtue, patience, vigor, *dhyāna*, and wisdom or when explaining profound ideas included within the Great Vehicle, one does not readily delight in speaking about them or delights in speaking of them, but then becomes scattered and confused in discussing peripheral topics.

Whether one is involved in writing out, studying, setting forth explanations, discussing points of doctrine, or listening to and absorbing teachings, one becomes haughty, full of oneself, and one's mind becomes so scattered and disordered that one focuses one's thoughts on peripheral topics.

One mistakenly brings to mind frivolous or joking topics or becomes involved in mutually ridiculing dialogue resulting in the two people involved become disharmonious and unable to penetrate through to the actual meaning of the topic at issue.

One gets up from his seat and departs, thinking to himself, "There is no way that my capacities would be acknowledged here. Their minds are not pure and, what's more, they will not deign to engage in any discussion concerning my city, village, clan, or birthplace." Consequently one does not wish to listen to the Dharma, fails to realize its flavor, gets up from his seat, and then leaves.

One may relinquish the *pāramitās* discussed in the Great Vehicle and may even then seek all-knowledge through the scriptures of *śrāvaka* disciples and *pratyekabuddhas* that promote individual training and liberation.

When one is involved in writing out, studying, setting forth explanations, listening to absorbing teachings, and so forth, one may wish instead to delight in speaking of various other sorts of topics, thereby demolishing and scattering [discussions focused on] *prajñāpāramitā*, doing so through turning the discussion toward topics related to the country, one's village or city, parks and forests, matters to do with military commanders, matters to do with bandits, military armor or weaponry, hate and love, pain and pleasure, parents, siblings, men and women, wives and children, apparel, food and drink, bedding and cushions, medicines, or other things serving as supplementary aspects of one's life. Thus one's mind then becomes so scattered and disordered that one loses [the focus on] *prajñāpāramitā*.

It might also be that one speaks of matters involving greed, hatred, stupidity, adversaries, close relationships, when times were good, when times were bad, singing, dancing, performances, music,

正體字
憂 037b05 ‖ 愁戲笑經書文頌往世古事國[5]主帝王地水 037b06 ‖ 火風五欲富貴及利養等世間諸事。令心喜 037b07 ‖ 悅。若魔化作比丘比丘尼形。以聲聞辟支佛 037b08 ‖ 經因緣令得而作是言。汝應習學是經捨 037b09 ‖ 本所習。聽法之人不樂聽受。說法者其心懈 037b10 ‖ 怠各有餘緣。聽者須法而說者欲至餘方。 037b11 ‖ 說者樂說而聽者欲至餘方。說者多欲貪諸 037b12 ‖ 利養。聽者無有與心。聽者信心樂欲聞法。 037b13 ‖ 而說者不樂為說。說者樂說聽者不樂。或 037b14 ‖ 時有說地獄諸苦。不如此身盡苦早取涅 037b15 ‖ 槃是最為利。說畜生無量苦惱餓鬼阿修羅 037b16 ‖ 種種過惡。說諸生死多有憂患汝於此身 037b17 ‖ 早取涅槃是最為利。又稱讚世間尊貴富 037b18 ‖ 樂。

简体字
忧愁戏笑经书文颂往世古事国主帝王地水火风五欲富贵及利养等世间诸事。令心喜悦。若魔化作比丘比丘尼形。以声闻辟支佛经因缘令得而作是言。汝应习学是经舍本所习。听法之人不乐听受。说法者其心懈怠各有余缘。听者须法而说者欲至余方。说者乐说而听者欲至余方。说者多欲贪诸利养。听者无有与心。听者信心乐欲闻法。而说者不乐为说。说者乐说听者不乐。或时有说地狱诸苦。不如此身尽苦早取涅槃是最为利。说畜生无量苦恼饿鬼阿修罗种种过恶。说诸生死多有忧患汝于此身早取涅槃是最为利。又称赞世间尊贵富乐。

worrisome topics, playful joking and laughter, the classics, literature, poetry, ancient times, traditional stories, rulers of the state, emperors and kings, earth, water, fire, and wind, the five objects of desire, wealth and aristocratic birth, and also offerings and other such worldly matters that tend to delight one's mind.

Or it could be that a *māra* transforms himself into the appearance of a bhikshu or bhikshuni, causes one to encounter scriptures of the *śrāvaka* disciples or the *pratyekabuddha*s, and says, "You should study these scriptures and set aside what you were originally practicing."

Or it may be that those listening to explanations of Dharma do not delight in listening to or accepting the teachings. Alternatively, the Dharma teacher's mind may fall prey to indolence, or then again, each of the parties may have other conditions [to which they are drawn].

It may be that, although those who come to listen have a need to hear the Dharma, the teacher explaining it prefers instead to move on to some other place.

It might also be that, although the teacher delights in providing explanations, those listening desire to go somewhere else instead.

It may happen that someone explaining Dharma has an inordinate desire to receive offerings or that those listening do not feel any motivation to give.

Then again, it may be that those listening have faith-filled minds, delight in the Dharma, and wish to hear teachings on Dharma whereas the one who explains it does not enjoy speaking it for them. Alternatively, it may be that someone explaining Dharma delights in discussing it but those listening do not wish to hear it.

There may be times when discussions turn to the sufferings in the hells, whereupon [the Dharma teacher] may claim that nothing would be quite so fine as putting an utter end to suffering in this very life. He may then recommend that the most beneficial option would be to choose an early entry into nirvāṇa.

Or else, when the discussion turns to the measureless suffering and torments of the animal realm or turns to the many different sorts of faults associated with [rebirth in the realms of] the hungry ghosts and *asuras*, [the Dharma teacher] may explain that all realms of *saṃsāra* are beset by misery. He may then recommend, "It would be most beneficial for you to choose, in this very life, an early entry into nirvāṇa."

Or else he may praise the wealth and happiness of the world's aristocrats.

正體字

```
037b19 ||   稱讚色無色界功德快善。生此中者是
037b19 ||   為大利。稱讚須陀洹乃至阿羅漢果功德之
037b20 ||   利。汝於此身證此諸果。是汝大利。[6]又說
037b21 ||   法者樂於眷屬。聽法者不欲隨從。說法者
037b22 ||   欲至飢亂不安隱國土。語聽者言。汝今何
037b23 ||   用隨我至此諸國。即生厭懈而不隨逐。說
037b24 ||   法者貴敬檀越數行問訊。使聽法者不得
037b25 ||   聽受。於深法中令生疑惑。此非諸佛所說
037b26 ||   經法。我所說者是佛經法。若菩薩能行是
037b27 ||   法得證實際。如是等種種因緣兩不和合。
037b28 ||   當知是等悉是魔事。取要言之於一切善
037b29 ||   法有障[7]閡者皆是魔事。菩提心劣弱者。諸
037c01 ||   煩惱有力故。道心劣弱無有勢力。於阿耨
037c02 ||   多羅三藐三菩提志願永絕。業障者[8]誰有
037c03 ||   種種業障。此中說能令求大乘人退轉者。
037c04 ||   是法障者樂行不善法。惡空無相無願及諸
037c05 ||   波羅蜜等諸深妙法。
```

简体字

称赞色无色界功德快善。生此中者是为大利。称赞须陀洹乃至阿罗汉果功德之利。汝于此身证此诸果。是汝大利。又说法者乐于眷属。听法者不欲随从。说法者欲至饥乱不安隐国土。语听者言。汝今何用随我至此诸国。即生厌懈而不随逐。说法者贵敬檀越数行问讯。使听法者不得听受。于深法中令生疑惑。此非诸佛所说经法。我所说者是佛经法。若菩萨能行是法得证实际。如是等种种因缘两不和合。当知是等悉是魔事。取要言之于一切善法有障阂者皆是魔事。菩提心劣弱者。诸烦恼有力故。道心劣弱无有势力。于阿耨多罗三藐三菩提志愿永绝。业障者谁有种种业障。此中说能令求大乘人退转者。是法障者乐行不善法。恶空无相无愿及诸波罗蜜等诸深妙法。

Or he may instead praise the meritorious qualities, bliss, and excellence of life in the form realm and formless realm [heavens], claiming then that great benefit can be realized by pursuing rebirth in those places.

Then again, he may praise the benefits associated with the qualities of the fruits of the path acquired by stream enterers and the others up to and including the arhats. He may then claim, "It would be most beneficial for you to gain these realizations in this very life."

It might be that the teacher delights in having a retinue of followers, but those who listen to Dharma do not wish to follow him. It might also be that the speaker of Dharma decides he wishes to go to some unsafe country afflicted with famine and civil disorder, telling those who listen to his teachings, "What use would there be in your following me to such countries?" Consequently they become disenchanted with the idea and decline to follow along with him.

It could also be that the speaker of Dharma esteems benefactors and repeatedly goes off to pay his respects to them, thereby causing those who listen to Dharma teachings to no longer be able to hear and absorb them.

Then again, he may cause listeners to produce doubts regarding the most profound Dharma, saying such things as, "That is not the Dharma proclaimed by the Buddhas in the sutras. However, the Dharma as I explain it corresponds to the Dharma set forth by the Buddha in the sutras. If a bodhisattva is able to practice this version of the Dharma, he will attain the realization of ultimate reality."

For all sorts of reasons such as these, the two parties may fail to abide in harmony. One should realize that any circumstances such as these are the work of *māras*. To sum it up, all situations in which obstacles arise to the prevalence of good dharmas—these are all the work of *māras*.

As for "if one's bodhi resolve is inferior and weak," this refers to circumstances wherein, due to the power of the afflictions, one's resolve to pursue the path becomes so weak and devoid of strength that the vow to attain *anuttarasamyaksaṃbodhi* becomes cut off forever.

As for "karmic obstacles," although[118] there are many different types of karmic obstacles, this refers to those capable of causing a person in quest of the Great Vehicle to turn back from that resolve.

"Dharma obstacles" here refers to delight in the practice of unwholesome dharmas and to dislike of emptiness, signlessness, wishlessness, and the other profound and sublime dharmas associated with the *pāramitās* and other such teachings.

正體字

　　　　如是四法能失菩提心。　037c06 ‖ 復次。
037c07 ‖　　許施師而誑　　其罪甚深重
037c08 ‖　　人無有疑悔　　強令生疑悔
037c09 ‖　　信樂大乘者　　[9]深加重瞋恚
037c10 ‖　　呵罵說惡名　　處處廣流布
037c11 ‖　　於諸共事中　　心多行諂曲
037c12 ‖　　如此四黑法　　則失菩提心
037c13 ‖ 施師不與者。應施師物若許若未許而後
037c14 ‖ 不與。若與非時與非處與不如法與。此是
037c15 ‖ 世間外道法。佛法中從師得經法。若有財
037c16 ‖ 物供養法故則以與師。若無無咎無有疑
037c17 ‖ 悔。令生疑悔者。此人實不破戒。有少罪
037c18 ‖ 相而言大罪。若破正命威儀若破正見皆
037c19 ‖ 令生疑悔。瞋大乘人者。有人乘大乘無
037c20 ‖ 上乘如來乘大人乘一切智人乘。乃至初發心
037c21 ‖ 者於此人中深生瞋恚呵罵譏[10]論。

简体字

如是四法能失菩提心。复次。
　　许施师而诳　　其罪甚深重
　　人无有疑悔　　强令生疑悔
　　信乐大乘者　　深加重嗔恚
　　呵骂说恶名　　处处广流布
　　于诸共事中　　心多行谄曲
　　如此四黑法　　则失菩提心
　施师不与者。应施师物若许若未许而后不与。若与非时与非处与不如法与。此是世间外道法。佛法中从师得经法。若有财物供养法故则以与师。若无无咎无有疑悔。令生疑悔者。此人实不破戒。有少罪相而言大罪。若破正命威仪若破正见皆令生疑悔。嗔大乘人者。有人乘大乘无上乘如来乘大人乘一切智人乘。乃至初发心者于此人中深生嗔恚呵骂讥论。

Dharmas of the same sort as the above four[119] are able to bring about loss of the resolve to attain bodhi.

Next, we have the following:

> If one pledges a gift to a teacher, but deceives him,
> the karmic offense incurred is extremely grave.
> If someone is free of doubts
> but one then forcefully causes him to develop doubts and regrets—
>
> If one directs an extreme degree of intense hatred and anger
> toward someone who has resolute faith in the Great Vehicle,
> vilifying him and speaking in a way that gives him a bad reputation,
> spreading such talk broadly about in place after place—
>
> Or if, when participating in joint endeavors,
> one's mind is much given to flattery and deviousness—
> If one's actions resemble any of these four black dharmas,
> then one is bound to lose the resolve to attain bodhi.

As for "pledging a gift to a teacher" but then not giving it, this refers to something that, whether or not one has already pledged it, one should nonetheless bestow it on one's teacher and yet, even so, one ends up not giving it. Also, if in giving, one gives at the wrong time, gives at the wrong place, or gives in a manner not according with the Dharma, these are methods typical of the world's non-Buddhist traditions.

Within the Buddha's Dharma, it is from one's teacher that one obtains the Dharma of the sutras. If one is possessed of some measure of wealth, then, in order to make offerings to the Dharma, one gives to one's teacher. If one has nothing to give, then there is no fault in that.

As for "if someone is free of doubts, but one then forcefully causes him to develop doubts and regrets—," this refers to an instance where someone has not actually broken any precept but merely appears to have committed some minor transgression and yet one claims he has committed a major offense against the moral code. Whether someone has departed from standard deportment in regard to right livelihood or has committed some infraction with regard to right doctrinal views, one then causes him to give birth to doubts and regrets.

"Hatred toward someone [with firm belief] in the Great Vehicle" refers to directing hatred toward those who have taken up the practice of the Great Vehicle, the unsurpassable vehicle, the vehicle of the Tathāgata, the vehicle of the great men, the vehicle of those possessed of omniscience, doing so even with regard to those who have only just brought forth the initial resolve to pursue that path. One feels intense hatred toward these people, rebuking and ridiculing them,

正體字

說其惡
037c22 ‖ 名令廣流布。共事諂曲心者。於和[11]上阿闍
037c23 ‖ 梨諸善知識所。不以直心親近。習行曲心
037c24 ‖ 故。乃至未曾所識亦行諂曲。四黑法者。黑
037c25 ‖ 名垢穢不淨。能失菩提心。如說。
037c26 ‖ 　轉此五四法　　世世[12]修善行
037c27 ‖ 　如是則不失　　無上菩提心
037c28 ‖ 五四合為二十法。是失菩提心。轉此法修
037c29 ‖ 習行。世世不忘阿耨多羅三藐三菩提心。轉
038a01 ‖ 者轉上五四法。所謂恭敬法破慢心遠離
038a02 ‖ 妄語。深尊重善知識。餘應如是知。問曰。以
038a03 ‖ 何等法世世增長菩提願。又後復能更發大
038a04 ‖ 願。答曰。
038a05 ‖ 　乃至失身命　　轉輪聖王位
038a06 ‖ 　於此尚不應　　妄語行諂曲

简体字

说其恶名令广流布。共事谄曲心者。于和上阿阇梨诸善知识所。不以直心亲近。习行曲心故。乃至未曾所识亦行谄曲。四黑法者。黑名垢秽不净。能失菩提心。如说。
　转此五四法　　世世修善行
　如是则不失　　无上菩提心
五四合为二十法。是失菩提心。转此法修习行。世世不忘阿耨多罗三藐三菩提心。转者转上五四法。所谓恭敬法破慢心远离妄语。深尊重善知识。余应如是知。问曰。以何等法世世增长菩提愿。又后复能更发大愿。答曰。
　乃至失身命　　转轮圣王位
　于此尚不应　　妄语行谄曲

and spreading claims about them that give them a bad reputation that is then caused to circulate widely.

"Flattery and deviousness in the midst of joint endeavors" refers to failing to use a straightforward mind, resorting instead to devious means to establish close relations with monastic preceptors, monastic Dharma teachers,[120] and good spiritual guides, even going so far as to use flattery and deviousness to curry favor with those one has never met.

In "the four black dharmas," "black" refers here to something dirty and impure that is capable of causing one to lose one's resolve to attain bodhi. This is as described here:

> If one turns away from these five sets of four dharmas
> and cultivates wholesome actions in life after life,
> one will thereby prevent the loss
> of one's resolve to attain the unsurpassable bodhi.

Five sets of four dharmas make twenty dharmas. It is because of these that one loses one's bodhi resolve. If one turns away from these dharmas in one's cultivation of the practices, then, even across the course of lifetimes, one will not forget one's resolve to attain *anuttarasamyaksaṃbodhi*.

"Turning away from" refers to turning away from the above five sets of four dharmas, doing so as follows:

> By revering and esteeming the Dharma,
> by doing away with arrogance,
> by abandoning false speech,
> and by deeply revering and esteeming good spiritual guides.

As for the rest, one should understand them in this same manner.

C. Q: Which Dharmas Cause One to Make the Vows Again in Each Life?

Question: Through which dharmas might one cause increase and growth in one's vow to attain bodhi, doing so across the course of lifetimes while also additionally causing one later on to be able to bring forth the great vows yet again?

D. A: They Are as Follows: (Verse)

Response:

> Even at the cost of losing one's life
> or of losing the throne of a wheel-turning king—
> even in such instances as these—one still should not
> commit false speech or engage in flattery or deviousness.

正體字

038a07 ‖ 　　能令諸世間　　一切眾生類
038a08 ‖ 　　於諸菩薩眾　　而生恭敬心
038a09 ‖ 　　若有人能行　　如是之善法
038a10 ‖ 　　世世得增長　　無上菩提願
038a11 ‖ 菩薩以是法世世增長菩提願。[1]又[2]復能
038a12 ‖ 生清淨大願。若以實語故。死失轉輪王位。
038a13 ‖ 及失天王位。猶應實說不應妄語。況小因
038a14 ‖ 緣而不實語。又於眷屬及諸外人離於諂
038a15 ‖ 曲。又從初發心已來。一切菩薩生恭敬心。
038a16 ‖ 尊重稱讚如佛無異。又當隨力令[3]住大
038a17 ‖ 乘。[4]

简体字

　　能令诸世间　　一切众生类
　　于诸菩萨众　　而生恭敬心
　　若有人能行　　如是之善法
　　世世得增长　　无上菩提愿

菩萨以是法世世增长菩提愿。又复能生清净大愿。若以实语故。死失转轮王位。及失天王位。犹应实说不应妄语。况小因缘而不实语。又于眷属及诸外人离于谄曲。又从初发心已来。一切菩萨生恭敬心。尊重称赞如佛无异。又当随力令住大乘。

One is able through this to cause the entire world,
including all the beings within it,
to develop thoughts of reverence
toward the community of bodhisattvas.

If there is anyone able to practice
such good dharmas as these,
in each successive lifetime, he will succeed in increasing
[the strength of] his vows to realize the unsurpassable bodhi.

Employing these dharmas, the bodhisattva increases [the strength of] his vows to attain bodhi and also becomes able yet again to bring forth these pure and great vows. If, due to telling the truth, one thereby dies or loses the position of the wheel-turning king or even loses a position as one of the deva kings, even then, he should speak the truth and should not engage in false speech. How much the less might one fail to tell the truth in matters of only minor consequence.

In addition, one abandons flattery and deviousness in interactions with one's own retinue and with outsiders as well.

Furthermore, one brings forth thoughts of reverence toward all bodhisattvas from the very moment they bring forth their initial resolve, honoring, esteeming, and praising them no differently than if they were buddhas.

One should also do whatever is in one's powers to influence others to abide in the Great Vehicle.

The End of Chapter Seven

正體字

038a18 ||　　　[5]阿惟越致相品第八
038a19 || 問曰。是諸菩薩有二種。一惟越致。二阿惟越
038a20 || 致應說其相。是惟越致是阿惟越致。答曰。
038a21 ||　　等心於眾生　　不嫉他利養
038a22 ||　　乃至失身命　　不說法師過
038a23 ||　　信樂深妙法　　不貪於恭敬
038a24 ||　　具足此五法　　是阿惟越致
038a25 || 等心眾生者。眾生六道所攝。於上中下心
038a26 || 無差別。是名阿惟越致。問曰。如說於諸佛
038a27 || 菩薩應生第一敬心。餘則不爾。又言親近
038a28 || 諸佛菩薩恭敬供養。餘亦不爾。云何言
038a29 || 於一切眾生等心無二。答曰。說各有義不
038b01 || 應疑難。於眾生等心者。若有眾生視菩
038b02 || 薩如怨賊。有視如父母。

简体字

十住毗婆沙论卷第四
阿惟越致相品第八

　　问曰。是诸菩萨有二种。一惟越致。二阿惟越致应说其相。是惟越致是阿惟越致。答曰。
　　　等心于众生　　不嫉他利养
　　　乃至失身命　　不说法师过
　　　信乐深妙法　　不贪于恭敬
　　　具足此五法　　是阿惟越致
　　等心众生者。众生六道所摄。于上中下心无差别。是名阿惟越致。问曰。如说于诸佛菩萨应生第一敬心。余则不尔。又言亲近诸佛菩萨恭敬供养。余亦不尔。云何言于一切众生等心无二。答曰。说各有义不应疑难。于众生等心者。若有众生视菩萨如怨贼。有视如父母。

Chapter 8
On the Avaivartika

VIII. Chapter Eight: On the Avaivartika
  A. Q: What Are the Distinguishing Characteristics of an Avaivartika?

Question: These bodhisattvas are of two kinds: First, those who are *vaivartika* (reversible), and second, those who are *avaivartika* (irreversible). One should explain the characteristics that determine whether one is a *vaivartika* or an *avaivartika*.

  B. A: There are Five Defining Dharmas, as Follows: (Verse)

Response:

> He maintains a mind of equal regard toward beings,
> does not envy the benefits and support obtained by others,
> and, even at the cost of his own body and life,
> does not speak of a Dharma master's transgressions.
>
> He has resolute faith in the profound and sublime Dharma
> and does not crave to be the object of others' reverence.
> One who embodies these five dharmas
> Is an *avaivartika*.

    1. Maintaining a Mind of Equal Regard toward Beings

As for "maintaining a mind of equal regard toward beings," beings are those within the six rebirth destinies. One's mind remains free of discriminating judgments by which one might regard them as either superior, middling, or inferior. This is a defining quality of an *avaivartika*.

Question: As has been explained, one should bring forth a mind of supreme reverence for buddhas and bodhisattvas. As for the other beings, this is not the case. Moreover, it has been stated that one should draw near to buddhas and bodhisattvas, revere them, and making offerings to them. As for the other beings, they are not to be treated in this way. Why then do you claim here that one maintains a mind of equal regard toward all beings and refrains from any duality in this?

Response: Each of these statements is principled and such as one should neither doubt nor challenge.

As for "maintaining a mind of equal regard toward beings," there are beings who look upon the bodhisattva as if he were an enemy, those who look upon him as if he were a father or mother, and those

正體字

038b03 ‖ 有視如中人。於
038b03 ‖ 此三種眾生中。等心利益欲度脫故無有
038b04 ‖ 差別。是故汝不應致難。不嫉他利養者。
038b05 ‖ 若他得衣服飲食臥具醫藥房舍產業金銀
038b06 ‖ 珍寶[6]村邑聚落國城男女等。於此施中不
038b07 ‖ 生嫉妬。又不懷恨而心欣悅。不說法師
038b08 ‖ 過[7]者。若有人說應大乘空無相無作法若
038b09 ‖ 六波羅蜜若四功德處若菩薩十地等諸大乘
038b10 ‖ 法。乃至失命因緣。尚不出其過惡。何況加
038b11 ‖ 諸惡事。信樂深妙法者。深法[8]名空無相無
038b12 ‖ 願及諸深經。如般若波羅蜜菩薩藏等。於此
038b13 ‖ 法一心信樂無所疑惑。於餘事中無如是
038b14 ‖ 樂。於深經中得滋味故。不貪恭敬者。通
038b15 ‖ 達諸法實相故。於名譽毀辱利與不利等無
038b16 ‖ 有異。具此五法者。如上所說。於阿耨多
038b17 ‖ 羅三藐三菩提不退轉不懈廢。是名阿惟
038b18 ‖ 越致。與此相違名惟越致。

简体字

有视如中人。于此三种众生中。等心利益欲度脱故无有差别。是故汝不应致难。不嫉他利养者。若他得衣服饮食卧具医药房舍产业金银珍宝村邑聚落国城男女等。于此施中不生嫉妒。又不怀恨而心欣悦。不说法师过者。若有人说应大乘空无相无作法若六波罗蜜若四功德处若菩萨十地等诸大乘法。乃至失命因缘。尚不出其过恶。何况加诸恶事。信乐深妙法者。深法名空无相无愿及诸深经。如般若波罗蜜菩萨藏等。于此法一心信乐无所疑惑。于余事中无如是乐。于深经中得滋味故。不贪恭敬者。通达诸法实相故。于名誉毁辱利与不利等无有异。具此五法者。如上所说。于阿耨多罗三藐三菩提不退转不懈废。是名阿惟越致。与此相违名惟越致。

who look upon him as a neutral person. It is because he maintains a mind of equal regard toward these three categories of beings as he benefits and strives to liberate them that he does not indulge any notions of differences among them. Hence you should not pose any challenge on this account.

2. NOT ENVYING BENEFITS AND SUPPORT OBTAINED BY OTHERS

As for "not envying the benefits and support obtained by others," in a case where someone else obtains robes, food and drink, bedding, medicines, dwellings, property, gold, silver, precious gems, villages, towns, states, cities, male and female attendants, and so forth, one does not feel envy toward them. Not only does one refrain from harboring any hostility toward them, one's mind is instead pleased by this.

3. NOT SPEAKING OF A DHARMA MASTER'S TRANSGRESSIONS

As for "He does not speak of a Dharma master's transgressions," in a case where someone is teaching the Great Vehicle dharmas of emptiness, signlessness, and wishlessness, the six *pāramitās*, the four bases of meritorious qualities, the bodhisattva's ten grounds, or any other such Great Vehicle dharmas, even if it would cost one his own life to do this, one still refrains from exposing any of that person's transgressions or negative aspects. How much the less might one create a bad situation for him.

4. RESOLUTE FAITH IN THE PROFOUND AND SUBLIME DHARMA

As for "he has a resolute faith in the profound and sublime Dharma," "profound Dharma" refers to emptiness, signlessness, wishlessness, and all of the abstruse scriptures such as the *Prajñāpāraamitā*, the *Bodhisattvapiṭaka*, and other such scriptures. One maintains a single-minded resolute faith in this Dharma and has no doubts about it. Because one has obtained the flavor of the profound scriptures, one does not find this sort of delight in anything else.

5. NOT CRAVING TO BE THE OBJECT OF OTHERS' REVERENCE

As for "not craving to be the object of others' reverence," because one has reached a penetrating understanding of the true character of dharmas,[121] one sees no difference between esteem and disgrace, gain and absence of gain, and so forth.[122]

As for "embodying these five dharmas," they are those just listed above.

6. ONE DOES NOT RETREAT FROM COMPLETE ENLIGHTENMENT

One does not retreat from *anuttarasamyaksaṃbodhi*, nor does one allow one's efforts in pursuit of it to deteriorate through indolence. These are the factors that characterize one who is an *avaivartika* (irreversible). The opposite qualities characterize one who is *vaivartika* (reversible).

正體字

　　　　是惟越致菩薩
038b19 ‖ 有二種。或敗壞者。或漸漸轉進得阿惟越
038b20 ‖ 致。問曰。所說敗壞者其相云何。答曰。
038b21 ‖ 　若無有志幹　　好樂下劣法
038b22 ‖ 　深[9]著名利養　　其心不端直
038b23 ‖ 　悋護於他家　　不信樂空法
038b24 ‖ 　但貴諸言說　　是名敗壞相
038b25 ‖ 無有志幹者。顏貌無色威德淺薄。問曰。非
038b26 ‖ 以身相[10]威德是阿惟越致相。而作[11]此說
038b27 ‖ 是何謂耶。答曰。斯言有謂不應致疑。我說
038b28 ‖ 內有功德故身有威德。不但說身色顏貌
038b29 ‖ 端正而已。志幹者所謂威德勢力。若有人能
038c01 ‖ 修集善法除滅惡法。於此事中有力名為
038c02 ‖ 志幹。雖復身若天王光如日月。若不能
038c03 ‖ 修集善法除滅惡法者。名為無志幹也。

简体字

是惟越致菩萨有二种。或败坏者。或渐渐转进得阿惟越致。问曰。所说败坏者其相云何。答曰。
　若无有志干　　好乐下劣法
　深著名利养　　其心不端直
　吝护于他家　　不信乐空法
　但贵诸言说　　是名败坏相
　无有志干者。颜貌无色威德浅薄。问曰。非以身相威德是阿惟越致相。而作此说是何谓耶。答曰。斯言有谓不应致疑。我说内有功德故身有威德。不但说身色颜貌端正而已。志干者所谓威德势力。若有人能修集善法除灭恶法。于此事中有力名为志干。虽复身若天王光如日月。若不能修集善法除灭恶法者。名为无志干也。

C. Two Types of Reversible Bodhisattvas, Ruined Versus Progressing

Among those who are *vaivartika* (reversible) bodhisattvas, there are two types, those who fall into ruination and those who gradually develop and advance until they become *avaivartikas* (irreversible).

1. Q: What Are the Signs of a "Ruined" Reversible Bodhisattva?

Question: As for those described as having fallen into ruination, what are their characteristic qualities?

2. A: Seven Characteristics, as Follows: (Verse)

Response:

> In a case where one has no determination and ability,
> delights in inferior dharmas,
> is deeply attached to fame and offerings,
> or has a mind that is not upright and straight—
>
> Where one feels a miserly cherishing toward others' households, [123]
> does not have a resolute belief in the dharma of emptiness,
> and only esteems all manner of verbal discourse—
> These are the marks of one fallen into ruination.

a. Absence of Determination and Ability

In the case of "one who has no determination and ability," his countenance is lackluster in appearance and whatever awe-inspiring personal qualities he might have are only shallow and scant.

Question: It is not on the basis of a dignified physical appearance that one is an *avaivartika*. That being the case, what meaning is there in making such a statement?

Response: This is a meaningful statement and should not be a cause for doubt. I am saying that, because, inwardly, one possesses meritorious qualities, the body manifests a correspondingly awe-inspiring personal presence. This is not simply a case of claiming that, [independent of these causes], he has a handsome physical appearance and countenance.

As for "determination and ability," this is what may be referred to as the power of one with an awe-inspiring personal presence.

If a person is able to cultivate and accumulate good dharmas while ridding himself of bad dharmas and then develops strength in accomplishing this endeavor, he then becomes one who possesses this "determination and ability." Even though one might possess a body like that of a king of the devas and radiance comparable to the sun and moon, so long as one is unable to cultivate and accumulate good dharmas and entirely rid oneself of bad dharmas, one is still a person who is devoid of "determination and ability."

正體字

038c04 ‖ 雖復身色醜陋形如餓鬼。能修善除惡乃
038c05 ‖ 名[12]為志幹耳。是故汝難非也。好樂下劣法
038c06 ‖ 者。除佛乘已餘乘比於佛乘。小劣不如故
038c07 ‖ 名為下。非以惡也。其餘惡事亦名為下。二
038c08 ‖ 乘所得於佛為下耳。[13]俱出世間入無餘涅
038c09 ‖ 槃故不名為惡。是故若人遠離佛乘信樂
038c10 ‖ 二乘。是為樂下法。是人雖樂上事。以信
038c11 ‖ 樂二乘遠離大乘故亦名樂下法。復次下
038c12 ‖ 名惡事。所謂五欲又斷常等六十二見一切
038c13 ‖ 外道論議。一切增長生死。是為下法。行此
038c14 ‖ 法故名為樂下法。深著名利者。於布施財
038c15 ‖ 利供養稱讚事中。深心繫念善為方便。不
038c16 ‖ 得清淨法味故貪樂此事。心不端直者。其
038c17 ‖ 性諂曲喜行欺誑。

简体字

虽复身色丑陋形如饿鬼。能修善除恶乃名为志干耳。是故汝难非也。好乐下劣法者。除佛乘已余乘比于佛乘。小劣不如故名为下。非以恶也。其余恶事亦名为下。二乘所得于佛为下耳。俱出世间入无余涅槃故不名为恶。是故若人远离佛乘信乐二乘。是为乐下法。是人虽乐上事。以信乐二乘远离大乘故亦名乐下法。复次下名恶事。所谓五欲又断常等六十二见一切外道论议。一切增长生死。是为下法。行此法故名为乐下法。深著名利者。于布施财利供养称赞事中。深心系念善为方便。不得清净法味故贪乐此事。心不端直者。其性谄曲喜行欺诳。

[On the other hand], even though one's physical appearance might be ugly and one might have the physique of a hungry ghost, if he is able to cultivate the good and get rid of the bad, he then becomes one who possesses "determination and ability."

It is for these reasons that the challenge you have posed here has no merit.

b. DELIGHTING IN INFERIOR DHARMAS

As for "delighting in inferior dharmas," when compared to the Buddha Vehicle, with the exception of the Buddha Vehicle, all other vehicles are small in scope, inferior, and incapable of measuring up to it. It is for these reasons that they are referred to as "inferior," not because they are "bad" *per se*. Still, any other peripheral unwholesome factors would indeed also qualify as "inferior."

Whatever has been achieved by adherents of the Two Vehicles is relatively inferior when compared with the Buddha, that's all. Still, because they have entirely escaped the world and have entered the nirvāṇa without residue, this cannot be said to be "bad."

It is for reasons such as these that, if someone distances himself from the Buddha Vehicle and instead has a resolute belief in the Two Vehicles, this amounts to delighting in inferior dharmas. Although such people do delight in superior endeavors, because they have anchored their resolute faith in the teachings of the Two Vehicles and have abandoned the Great Vehicle, they are still referred to as "delighting in inferior dharmas."

Then again, "inferior" refers as well to matters that are themselves "bad," namely the five objects of desire,[124] annihilationism, eternalism, and the rest of the sixty-two wrong views, all of the doctrinal tenets typical of non-Buddhist traditions, and any preoccupations that would increase one's entanglement in *saṃsāra*. These are "inferior dharmas." It is due to practicing these sorts of dharmas that one is said to delight in inferior dharmas.

c. BEING DEEPLY ATTACHED TO FAME AND OFFERINGS

Being "deeply attached to fame and offerings" refers to having deep-seated inclinations to focus one's thoughts on skillfully arranging ways to receive gifts of material wealth and other sorts of offerings and praises. It is due to failing to experience the flavor of the pure Dharma that one may then covet and delight in such matters.

d. HAVING A MIND THAT IS NOT UPRIGHT AND STRAIGHT

As for "the mind not being upright and straight," this refers to someone whose nature is given over to flattery and deviousness and who delights in being deceptive.

正體字

```
         恪護他家者。是人隨所
038c18 ‖ 入家。見有餘人得利養恭敬讚歎。即生嫉
038c19 ‖ 妒憂愁不悅。心不清淨計我深故。貪著利
038c20 ‖ 養生嫉妒心嫌恨檀越。不信樂空法者。
038c21 ‖ 諸佛三種說空法。所謂三解脫門。於此空
038c22 ‖ 法不信不樂不以為貴。心不通達故。但
038c23 ‖ 貴言說者。但樂言辭不能如說修行。但
038c24 ‖ 有口說不能信解諸法得其趣味。是名
038c25 ‖ 敗壞相。若人發菩提心。有如是相者。當知
038c26 ‖ 是敗壞菩薩。敗壞名不調順。譬如最弊惡馬
038c27 ‖ 名為敗壞。但有馬名無有馬用。敗壞菩薩
038c28 ‖ 亦如是。但有空名無有實行。若人不欲
038c29 ‖ 作敗壞菩薩者。當除惡法隨法受名。問
039a01 ‖ 曰。汝說在惟越致地中。有二種菩薩。一者
039a02 ‖ 敗壞菩薩。二者
```

简体字

恡护他家者。是人随所入家。见有余人得利养恭敬赞叹。即生嫉妒忧愁不悦。心不清净计我深故。贪着利养生嫉妒心嫌恨檀越。不信乐空法者。诸佛三种说空法。所谓三解脱门。于此空法不信不乐不以为贵。心不通达故。但贵言说者。但乐言辞不能如说修行。但有口说不能信解诸法得其趣味。是名败坏相。若人发菩提心。有如是相者。当知是败坏菩萨。败坏名不调顺。譬如最弊恶马名为败坏。但有马名无有马用。败坏菩萨亦如是。但有空名无有实行。若人不欲作败坏菩萨者。当除恶法随法受名。问曰。汝说在惟越致地中。有二种菩萨。一者败坏菩萨。二者

e. FEELING A MISERLY CHERISHING TOWARD OTHERS' HOUSEHOLDS

In the case of one who "feels a miserly cherishing toward others' households," this person, no matter which household he enters, whenever he witnesses others receiving offerings, reverence, or praise, he immediately becomes envious, saddened, and displeased. Because his mind is impure and because he is deeply habituated to conceiving of the existence of a self, he is covetous of and attached to offerings, has thoughts of jealousy, and harbors resentment toward others' benefactors.

f. NOT HAVING A RESOLUTE BELIEF IN THE DHARMA OF EMPTINESS

As for "not having a resolute belief in the dharma of emptiness," the buddhas have three ways in which they discuss the dharma of emptiness, namely the three gates to liberation. As for these dharmas associated with emptiness, this person does not believe in them, does not delight in them, and does not esteem them as precious. This is because his mind has not achieved a penetrating comprehension of them.

g. ONLY ESTEEMING ALL MANNER OF VERBAL DISCOURSE

As for "only esteeming all manner of verbal discourse," this means that one only delights in words and phrases, but cannot practice in accordance with them. One is only able in such a case to carry on verbal discourse, but still cannot develop a resolute belief in these dharmas to the degree that one realizes their true import and flavor.

h. THESE ARE THE MARKS OF ONE FALLEN INTO RUINATION

As for "these are the marks of one fallen into ruination," if someone has formerly brought forth the bodhi resolve but then displays signs such as these, one should realize that this is a bodhisattva who has fallen into ruination.

"Fallen into ruination" designates the quality of not being well trained or compliant. For instance, a poorly-bred, ill-tempered horse might appropriately be thought of as "ruined." It merely bears the name "horse" without having any of a horse's uses.

A bodhisattva fallen into ruination is just like this, bearing only an empty designation while not carrying on any genuine practice. If one wishes to avoid becoming a bodhisattva fallen into ruination, one should rid himself of bad dharmas and accord with the Dharma in a manner worthy of one's name.

3. Q: WHAT ARE THE TRAITS OF THE REVERSIBLE BODHISATTVA WHO SUCCEEDS?

Question: You stated that there are two kinds of bodhisattvas still on the grounds of the *vaivartika* (reversible) bodhisattva: First, the bodhisattva fallen into ruination and, second, someone who, after

正體字

```
039a03 ||      漸漸精進後得阿惟越致。敗
039a03 || 壞菩薩已解說。漸漸精進後得阿惟越致者。
039a04 || 今可解說。答曰。
039a05 ||   菩薩不得我    亦不得眾生
039a06 ||   不分別說法    亦不得菩提
039a07 ||   不以相見佛    以此五功德
039a08 ||   得名大菩薩    成阿惟越致
039a09 || 菩薩行此五功德。直至阿惟越致。不得我
039a10 || 者。離我著故。是菩薩於內外五陰十二入
039a11 || 十八界中求我不可得。作是念。
039a12 ||   若陰是我者    我即生滅相
039a13 ||   云何當以受    而即作受者
039a14 ||   若離陰有我    陰外應可得
039a15 ||   云何當以受    而異於受者
039a16 ||   若我有五陰    我即離五陰
039a17 ||   如世間常言    牛異於牛主
039a18 ||   異物共合故    此事名為有
039a19 ||   是故我有陰    我即異於陰
```

简体字

渐渐精进后得阿惟越致。败坏菩萨已解说。渐渐精进后得阿惟越致者。今可解说。答曰。

　　菩萨不得我　　亦不得众生
　　不分别说法　　亦不得菩提
　　不以相见佛　　以此五功德
　　得名大菩萨　　成阿惟越致

菩萨行此五功德。直至阿惟越致。不得我者。离我着故。是菩萨于内外五阴十二入十八界中求我不可得。作是念。

　　若阴是我者　　我即生灭相
　　云何当以受　　而即作受者
　　若离阴有我　　阴外应可得
　　云何当以受　　而异于受者
　　若我有五阴　　我即离五阴
　　如世间常言　　牛异于牛主
　　异物共合故　　此事名为有
　　是故我有阴　　我即异于阴

Chapter 8 — On the Avaivartika

the consistent application of vigor, gradually becomes an *avaivartika* (irreversible) bodhisattva. Having already explained what is meant by "the bodhisattva fallen into ruination," you could now explain what is meant by the one who, after consistent application of vigor, gradually becomes *avaivartika* (irreversible).

4. A: He Has Five Qualities, as Follows: (Verse)

Response:

> The bodhisattva does not apprehend the existence of any self
> and also does not apprehend the existence of any being.
> He does not engage in discriminations as he discourses on Dharma,
> nor does he apprehend the existence of bodhi.

> He does not see a buddha by his signs.
> It is because of these five meritorious qualities
> that he can be referred to as a great bodhisattva
> who is bound to become an *avaivartika*.

If a bodhisattva implements these five meritorious qualities, he thereby proceeds directly to the stage of the *avaivartika*.

a. Not Apprehending the Existence of any "Self"

As for "not apprehending the existence of any self," this is due to having abandoned attachment to the existence of any self. When this bodhisattva searches among the inwardly related and outwardly related five aggregates, twelve sense bases, and eighteen sense realms, he cannot apprehend the existence of a self anywhere among them. He contemplates thus:[125]

> If it were the case that the aggregates constituted a self,
> then that "self" would be characterized by birth and destruction.
> How could one, merely on the basis of feelings,
> immediately create some entity that experiences feelings?

> If a self were to exist apart from the aggregates,
> one should be able to apprehend it apart from the aggregates.
> But how could one take it that feelings
> are something separate from what experiences feelings?

> If it were the case that the self possessed the five aggregates,
> that self would be something apart from the five aggregates
> in the same way that it is commonly said in worldly parlance
> that an ox is different from the ox-herder.

> It is on the basis of the conjunction of different things
> that this phenomenon is said to exist.
> Therefore, if it were the case that some self possessed the aggregates,
> that self would be something different from the aggregates.

正體字	039a20 ‖ 　若陰中有我　　如房中有人 039a21 ‖ 　如床上聽者　　我應異於陰 039a22 ‖ 　若[1]我中有陰　　如器中有果 039a23 ‖ 　如乳中有蠅　　陰則異於我 039a24 ‖ 　如可然非然　　不離可然然 039a25 ‖ 　然無有可然　　然可然中無 039a26 ‖ 　我非陰離陰　　我亦無有陰 039a27 ‖ 　五陰中無我　　我中無五陰 039a28 ‖ 　如是染染者　　煩惱煩惱者 039a29 ‖ 　一切瓶衣等　　皆當如是知 039b01 ‖ 　若說我有定　　及諸法異相 039b02 ‖ 　當知如是人　　不得佛法味 039b03 ‖ 菩薩如是思惟即離我見。遠離我見故則 039b04 ‖ 不得我。不得眾生者。眾生名異於菩薩 039b05 ‖ 者。離貪我見故作是念。若他人實有我者。 039b06 ‖ 彼可為他因有我故以彼為他。而實求我 039b07 ‖ 不可得。彼亦不可得故無彼亦無我。是故菩 039b08 ‖ 薩亦不得彼。	
簡體字	若阴中有我　　如房中有人 　如床上听者　　我应异于阴 　若我中有阴　　如器中有果 　如乳中有蝇　　阴则异于我 　如可然非然　　不离可然然 　然无有可然　　然可然中无 　我非阴离阴　　我亦无有阴 　五阴中无我　　我中无五阴 　如是染染者　　烦恼烦恼者 　一切瓶衣等　　皆当如是知 　若说我有定　　及诸法异相 　当知如是人　　不得佛法味 菩萨如是思惟即离我见。远离我见故则不得我。不得众生者。众生名异于菩萨者。离贪我见故作是念。若他人实有我者。彼可为他因有我故以彼为他。而实求我不可得。彼亦不可得故无彼亦无我。是故菩萨亦不得彼。	

> If it were the case that the self existed within the aggregates,
> then this is just like there being a person inside of a room
> or like there being someone there on a couch, listening.
> The self then should be something different from the aggregates.
>
> If it were the case that the aggregates existed within a self,
> this would be analogous to fruit being contained in a bowl
> or like milk in which there are flies.
> The aggregates then would be different from the self.
>
> This is just as with a combustible not being the burning itself
> even as burning cannot occur apart from a combustible.
> Combustion does not possess its combustible
> nor does combustion itself abide within what is combustible.
>
> A self isn't identical with nor separate from the aggregates,
> nor does a self possess the aggregates.
> There is no self within the five aggregates
> and there are no five aggregates within a self.
>
> Similarly analogous are dye and that which is dyed,
> the afflictions and whoever is affected by the afflictions,
> a vase [and its clay], cloth [and its threads], and so forth.
> All of these phenomena should be understood in this same way.
>
> If someone asserts that the self exists as a fixed entity
> or that dharmas are possessed of differentiating characteristics,
> one should realize that such a person
> has not realized the flavor of the Buddha's Dharma.

When the bodhisattva carries out such contemplations, he immediately abandons any view imputing the existence of a self. Because he abandons any view conceiving of the existence of a self, he becomes unable to apprehend the existence of any self at all.

 b. NOT APPREHENDING THE EXISTENCE OF ANY "BEING"

As for his being unable "to apprehend the existence of any being," the term "being" here refers to any entity other than this bodhisattva. Because he has abandoned any view clinging to the existence of a self, he contemplates thus: "If others truly had a self, then they would constitute an 'other.' It is based on the existence of a self that one is able to regard someone else as constituting an 'other.' However, in reality, when one seeks to find some 'self,' it cannot be apprehended. Because an 'other' cannot be apprehended, either, then there is neither any 'other' nor any 'self.'" It is in this manner that the bodhisattva remains unable to apprehend any [being that is] "other," either.

正體字	不分別說法者。是菩薩信解 039b09 ‖ 一切法不二故無差別故作是念。 039b10 ‖ 一切法皆從邪憶想分別生虛妄欺誑。是菩 039b11 ‖ 薩滅諸分別無諸衰惱。即入無上第一義 039b12 ‖ 因緣法不隨他慧。 039b13 ‖ 　實性則非有　　亦復非是無 039b14 ‖ 　非亦有亦無　　非非有非無 039b15 ‖ 　亦非有文字　　亦不離文字 039b16 ‖ 　如是實義者　　終不可得說 039b17 ‖ 　言者可言言　　是皆寂滅相 039b18 ‖ 　若性寂滅者　　非有亦非無 039b19 ‖ 　為欲說何事　　為以何言說 039b20 ‖ 　云何有智[2]人　　而與言者言 039b21 ‖ 　若諸法性空　　諸法即無性 039b22 ‖ 　隨以何法空　　是法不可說 039b23 ‖ 　不得不有言　　假言以說空 039b24 ‖ 　實義亦非空　　亦復非不空 039b25 ‖ 　亦非空不空　　非非空不空 039b26 ‖ 　非虛亦[3]非實　　非說非不說
简体字	不分别说法者。是菩萨信解一切法不二故无差别故一相故作是念。一切法皆从邪忆想分别生虚妄欺诳。是菩萨灭诸分别无诸衰恼。即入无上第一义因缘法不随他慧。 　实性则非有　　亦复非是无 　非亦有亦无　　非非有非无 　亦非有文字　　亦不离文字 　如是实义者　　终不可得说 　言者可言言　　是皆寂灭相 　若性寂灭者　　非有亦非无 　为欲说何事　　为以何言说 　云何有智人　　而与言者言 　若诸法性空　　诸法即无性 　随以何法空　　是法不可说 　不得不有言　　假言以说空 　实义亦非空　　亦复非不空 　亦非空不空　　非非空不空 　非虚亦非实　　非说非不说

c. Not Engaging in Discriminations While Speaking on Dharma

As for, "he does not engage in discriminations as he discourses on Dharma," because this bodhisattva has a resolute belief in the nonduality of all dharmas, in the nonexistence of any distinctions among them, and in their being characterized by a singular character, he contemplates thus, "All dharmas arise from erroneous perceptions and discriminations. They are false and deceptive." This bodhisattva extinguishes all discriminations, becomes free of all distress, immediately enters into the unsurpassable supreme meaning's dharma of conditioned origination, and then no longer needs to rely upon the wisdom imparted by others.

> The nature of reality is not something that exists,
> nor is it the case that it does not exist,
> nor does it both exist and not exist,
> nor does it neither exist nor not exist.[126]

> Nor does it abide in verbal expressions,
> nor is it something apart from verbal expressions.
> So it is that the meaning of ultimate reality
> can never be expressed by resort to speech.

> The speaker and the words that can be spoken—
> —these are all characterized by quiescent cessation.
> Whatsoever has the nature of quiescent cessation
> is neither existent nor nonexistent.

> No matter what one might wish to speak about
> and no matter which means one might choose to speak,
> how could there be someone who is wise and yet [still conceives]
> of there being any "speaking" that takes place with some "speaker."

> If the nature of all dharmas is emptiness,
> then dharmas are devoid of any [inherently existent] nature.
> Consequently whatever dharmas are empty [of inherent existence],
> those very dharmas are ineffable.

> One cannot fail to have words that one speaks,
> hence we borrow words to speak about emptiness.
> The true meaning is neither empty
> nor non-empty,

> nor both empty and not empty,
> nor neither empty nor not empty.
> It is not false nor is it true,
> nor is it spoken, nor is it not spoken.

正體字		
039b27 ‖	而實無所有	亦非無所有
039b28 ‖	是為悉捨離	諸所有分別
039b29 ‖	因及從因生	如是一切法
039c01 ‖	皆是寂滅相	無取亦無捨
039c02 ‖	無灰衣不淨	灰亦還污衣
039c03 ‖	非言不宣實	言說則有過
039c04 ‖	菩薩如是觀信解通達於說法中。無所分	
039c05 ‖	別。不得菩提者。是菩薩信解空法故。如	
039c06 ‖	凡夫所得菩提。不如是得作是念。	
039c07 ‖	佛不得菩提	非佛亦不得
039c08 ‖	諸果及餘法	皆亦復如是
039c09 ‖	有佛有菩提	佛得即為常
039c10 ‖	無佛無菩提	不得即斷滅
039c11 ‖	離佛無菩提	離菩提無佛
039c12 ‖	若[4]一異不成	云何有和[5]合
039c13 ‖	凡諸一切法	以異故有合
039c14 ‖	菩提不異佛	是故二無合
039c15 ‖	佛及與菩提	異共俱不成
039c16 ‖	離二更無三	云何而得成

简体字

　　而实无所有　　亦非无所有
　　是为悉舍离　　诸所有分别
　　因及从因生　　如是一切法
　　皆是寂灭相　　无取亦无舍
　　无灰衣不净　　灰亦还污衣
　　非言不宣实　　言说则有过
　菩萨如是观信解通达于说法中。无所分别。不得菩提者。是菩萨信解空法故。如凡夫所得菩提。不如是得作是念。
　　佛不得菩提　　非佛亦不得
　　诸果及余法　　皆亦复如是
　　有佛有菩提　　佛得即为常
　　无佛无菩提　　不得即断灭
　　离佛无菩提　　离菩提无佛
　　若一异不成　　云何有和合
　　凡诸一切法　　以异故有合
　　菩提不异佛　　是故二无合
　　佛及与菩提　　异共俱不成
　　离二更无三　　云何而得成

And yet, in truth, there is nothing that exists,
and yet it is not the case that nothing exists at all.
This constitutes the complete relinquishment
of the discrimination of anything at all as existent.

Causes as well as whatever arises from causes—
All such dharmas as these
are in every case characterized by quiescent cessation.
There is neither any seizing on them nor any relinquishing of them.

Without ash-soap, a robe cannot be made clean,
But still, ashes may have the contrary effect of staining a robe.
[So too], were it not for words, one could not proclaim the truth.
Still, if one uses words and speech, that too may have its faults.[127]

It is in this manner that the bodhisattva contemplates, develops resolute belief in, and then achieves a penetrating understanding whereby, in his discoursing on the Dharma, "he does not engage in discriminations."

d. Not Apprehending the Existence of Bodhi

As for being "unable to apprehend the existence of bodhi," because this bodhisattva possesses a resolute belief in the dharma of emptiness, his "apprehension" here is not of the same sort as the common person's apprehension of bodhi. He contemplates in this manner:

The buddhas have not apprehended bodhi
and those who are not buddhas do not apprehend it, either.
As for the fruits of the path and the other related dharmas,
in every case, this also applies in the same way to them.

Where there is a buddha, there is bodhi.
but to hold that a buddha has "apprehended" it is just eternalism.
Without a buddha, there is no bodhi,
but to hold that it cannot be apprehended is just annihilationism.

Apart from a buddha, there is no bodhi
and apart from bodhi, there is no buddha.
If they are singular, their difference cannot be established.
So how could there be any sort of conjoining of them?

In general, as regards all dharmas,
it is because they are different that they may be conjoined.
But bodhi is not something distinctly different from a buddha.
Therefore, in the case of these two, there is no conjoining.

In the case of a buddha and bodhi,
neither their difference nor their conjoining can be established.
There is no third alternative apart from these two.
How then could [such concepts] be validly established?

正體字	039c17 ‖ 　是故佛寂滅　　菩提亦寂滅	
	039c18 ‖ 　是二寂滅故　　一切皆寂滅	
	039c19 ‖ 不以相見佛者。是菩薩信解通達無相法。	
	039c20 ‖ 作是念。	
	039c21 ‖ 　一切若無相　　一切即有相	
	039c22 ‖ 　寂滅是無相　　即為是有相	
	039c23 ‖ 　若觀無相法　　無相即為相	
	039c24 ‖ 　若言修無相　　即非修無相	
	039c25 ‖ 　若捨諸貪著　　名之為無相	
	039c26 ‖ 　取是捨貪相　　則為無解脫	
	039c27 ‖ 　凡以有取故　　因取而有捨	
	039c28 ‖ 　誰取取何事　　名之以為捨	
	039c29 ‖ 　取者所用取　　及以可取法	
	040a01 ‖ 　共離俱不有　　是皆名寂滅	
	040a02 ‖ 　若法相因成　　是即為無性	
	040a03 ‖ 　若無有性者　　此即無有相	
	040a04 ‖ 　若法無有性　　此即無相者	
	040a05 ‖ 　云何言無性　　即為是無相	
	040a06 ‖ 　若用有與無　　亦遮亦應聽	
	040a07 ‖ 　雖言心不著　　是則無有過	
简体字	是故佛寂灭　　菩提亦寂灭	
	是二寂灭故　　一切皆寂灭	
	不以相见佛者。是菩萨信解通达无相法。作是念。	
	一切若无相　　一切即有相	
	寂灭是无相　　即为是有相	
	若观无相法　　无相即为相	
	若言修无相　　即非修无相	
	若舍诸贪着　　名之为无相	
	取是舍贪相　　则为无解脱	
	凡以有取故　　因取而有舍	
	谁取取何事　　名之以为舍	
	取者所用取　　及以可取法	
	共离俱不有　　是皆名寂灭	
	若法相因成　　是即为无性	
	若无有性者　　此即无有相	
	若法无有性　　此即无相者	
	云何言无性　　即为是无相	
	若用有与无　　亦遮亦应听	
	虽言心不着　　是则无有过	

Therefore buddhas are characterized by quiescent cessation.
So too is bodhi characterized by quiescent cessation.
Because these two are characterized by quiescent cessation,
everything is characterized by quiescent cessation.

e. Not Seeing a Buddha by His Signs

As for "he does not see a buddha by his signs," this bodhisattva has a resolute belief in and an utterly penetrating understanding of the dharma of signlessness. He reflects thus:[128]

If everything is signless,
then everything is identical with whatever possesses signs.
Quiescent cessation is signless
and is identical with whatever is possessed of signs.[129]

If one contemplates the dharma of signlessness,
whatever is signless is [seen to be] the same as what possesses signs.
If one says that one is cultivating signlessness,
that is just a non-cultivation of signlessness.

Were one to relinquish all covetousness[130]
and designate that as constituting signlessness,
such seizing on this sign of having relinquished covetousness[131]
then becomes the very absence of liberation.

In general, it is because of the existence of grasping
that then, because of that grasping, there then is relinquishing.
There is someone who grasps and something that is grasped[132]—
It is on this basis that one then refers to "relinquishing."

As for the one who grasps, the grasping to which he resorts,
and also that dharma that is subject to being grasped—
whether as conjoined or separate, they all do not exist,[133]
for these are all synonymous with quiescent cessation.

If a dharma's signs are established on the basis of causes,
this is just something devoid of any [inherently existent] nature.
Whatever is devoid of any [inherently existent] nature—
this is just something devoid of any [inherently existent] signs.

If a dharma has no [inherently existent] nature—
this is just something that is signless.
How can one assert that it has no [inherently existent] nature?
It is precisely because it is signless.[134]

If one uses [such terms as] "existence" and "nonexistence,"
"both" and "neither" should be permissible as well,[135] for,
although one may speak thus, so long as one's mind is not attached,
one thereby remains free of any fault in doing so.

正體字

040a08 ‖	何處先有法	而後不滅者
040a09 ‖	何處先有然	而後有滅者
040a10 ‖	是有相寂滅	同無相寂滅
040a11 ‖	是故寂滅語	及寂滅語者
040a12 ‖	先亦非寂滅	亦非不寂滅
040a13 ‖	亦非寂不寂	非非寂不寂

040a14 ‖ 是菩薩如是通達無相慧故無有疑悔。不
040a15 ‖ 以色相見佛。不以受想行識相見佛。問
040a16 ‖ 曰。云何不以色相見佛。不以受想行識
040a17 ‖ 相見佛。答曰。非色是佛。非受想行識是佛。
040a18 ‖ 非離色有佛。非離受想行識有佛。非佛
040a19 ‖ 有色。非佛有受想行識。非色中有佛。非
040a20 ‖ 受想行識中有佛。非佛中有色。非佛中有
040a21 ‖ 受想行識。菩薩於此五種中不取相。得至
040a22 ‖ 阿惟越致地。問曰。已知得此法是阿惟越
040a23 ‖ 致。阿惟越致有何相貌。

简体字

何处先有法　　而后不灭者
何处先有然　　而后有灭者
是有相寂灭　　同无相寂灭
是故寂灭语　　及寂灭语者
先亦非寂灭　　亦非不寂灭
亦非寂不寂　　非非寂不寂

是菩萨如是通达无相慧故无有疑悔。不以色相见佛。不以受想行识相见佛。问曰。云何不以色相见佛。不以受想行识相见佛。答曰。非色是佛。非受想行识是佛。非离色有佛。非离受想行识有佛。非佛有色。非佛有受想行识。非色中有佛。非受想行识中有佛。非佛中有色。非佛中有受想行识。菩萨于此五种中不取相。得至阿惟越致地。问曰。已知得此法是阿惟越致。阿惟越致有何相貌。

> Where has there ever first existed some dharma
> that, afterward, was not destroyed?
> Wherever there has first existed some fire
> that, afterward, was then extinguished,
> the quiescent cessation of these existent signs
> is identical to the quiescent cessation of whatsoever is signless.
>
> Therefore, as for these words about quiescent cessation
> as well as the one who speaks about quiescent cessation,
> from the beginning, too, they have not been quiescent[136]
> nor have they been non-quiescent,
> nor have they been both quiescent and non-quiescent,
> nor have they been neither quiescent nor non-quiescent.

Because this bodhisattva has such a penetrating comprehension of the wisdom of signlessness, he is free of any doubts or regrets. He does not see a buddha in terms of the signs of his physical form, nor does he see a buddha in terms of feelings, perceptions, formative factors, or consciousness.

Question: How is it that he does not see a buddha by the signs of his physical form? And how is it that he does not see a buddha in terms of feelings, perceptions, formative factors, or consciousness?

Response: It is not the case that physical form is a buddha, nor is it the case that feelings, perceptions, formative factors, or consciousness are what constitute a buddha.[137]

Nor is it the case that a buddha exists apart from physical form, nor is it the case that he exists apart from feelings, perceptions, formative factors, or consciousness.

Nor is it the case that a buddha possesses physical forms, nor is it the case that a buddha possesses feelings, perceptions, formative factors, or consciousness.

Nor is it the case that a buddha exists within physical form. Nor is it the case that a buddha exists within feelings, perceptions, formative factors, or consciousness.

Nor is it the case that physical form resides within a buddha. Nor is it the case that feelings, perceptions, formative factors, or consciousness reside within a buddha.

The bodhisattva who does not seize on any signs of these five aggregates succeeds in reaching the ground of the *avaivartika*.

D. Q: WHAT ARE THE CHARACTERISTIC SIGNS OF AN AVAIVARTIKA?

Question: Now that we already know that one who acquires these dharmas is an *avaivartika*, what characteristic signs does the *avaivartika* possess?

正體字

答曰。
040a24 ‖ 　　般若已廣說　　阿惟越致相
040a25 ‖ 若菩薩觀凡夫地聲聞地辟支佛地佛地。不
040a26 ‖ 二不分別無有疑悔。當知是阿惟越致。阿
040a27 ‖ 惟越致。有所言說皆有利益。不觀他人長
040a28 ‖ 短好醜。不悕望外道沙門有所言說。應知
040a29 ‖ 即知應見便見。不禮事餘天。不以華香幡
040b01 ‖ 蓋供養。不宗事餘師。不墮惡道不受女
040b02 ‖ 身。常自修十善道。亦教他令行。常以善法
040b03 ‖ 示教利喜。乃至夢中不捨十善道。不行十
040b04 ‖ 不善道。身口意業所種善根。皆為安樂度
040b05 ‖ 脫眾生。所得果報與眾生共。若聞深法不
040b06 ‖ 生疑悔。少於語言利安語和悅語柔軟語。
040b07 ‖ 少於眠睡行來進止心不散亂。威儀[1]庠雅
040b08 ‖ 憶念堅固。身無諸虫。衣服臥具淨潔無垢。
040b09 ‖ 身心清淨閑靜少事。

简体字

答曰。
　　般若已广说　　阿惟越致相
　　若菩萨观凡夫地声闻地辟支佛地佛地。不二不分别无有疑悔。当知是阿惟越致。阿惟越致。有所言说皆有利益。不观他人长短好丑。不悕望外道沙门有所言说。应知即知应见便见。不礼事余天。不以华香幡盖供养。不宗事余师。不堕恶道不受女身。常自修十善道。亦教他令行。常以善法示教利喜。乃至梦中不舍十善道。不行十不善道。身口意业所种善根。皆为安乐度脱众生。所得果报与众生共。若闻深法不生疑悔。少于语言利安语和悦语柔软语。少于眠睡行来进止心不散乱。威仪庠雅忆念坚固。身无诸虫。衣服卧具净洁无垢。身心清净闲静少事。

Chapter 8 — On the Avaivartika

E. A: The Avaivartika Has Numerous Characteristics, as Follows:

Response:

The *Prajñāpāramitā* has already extensively explained the characteristic signs of the *avaivartika*.

If, in contemplating the ground of the common person, the grounds of the *śrāvaka* disciple, the ground of the *pratyekabuddha*, and the ground of a buddha, a bodhisattva does not engage in duality-based perceptions, does not engage in discriminating thoughts, and has no doubts or regrets, one should realize that this is an *avaivartika*.

Whenever an *avaivartika* speaks, it is beneficial in some way.

He does not contemplate others' relative strengths and shortcomings or good and bad aspects.

He does not long to hear the discourses of non-Buddhist *śramaṇas*.

What should be known, he immediately learns. Whatever should be seen, he then sees.

He does not revere or serve others' deities, nor does he make offerings to them of flowers, incense, banners, or canopies. Nor does he venerate or serve the gurus of those other traditions.

He does not fall into the wretched destinies nor, when reborn, does he take on a female body.

He always cultivates the ten courses of good karmic action himself while also teaching them to others, thereby causing them to practice them.

He always uses good dharmas in revealing [truths], instructing, benefiting, and delighting others. Even in his dreams, he never relinquishes the ten courses of good karmic action and never engages in any of the ten courses of bad karmic action.

The roots of goodness that he plants through physical, verbal, and mental actions are all done in order to facilitate beings' peace and happiness and their liberation [from *saṃsāra*]. He shares with other beings the karmic rewards that result from his endeavors.

Whenever he hears discussions of profound dharmas, he does not develop either doubts or regrets.

He tends to be one of relatively few words. His discourse is beneficial and peaceful, agreeable and pleasing, soft and pliant.

He sleeps but little and, whether going or coming, moving along or stopping, his mind is not scattered. He is refined in his deportment and his thoughts are stable and resolute.

His body is free of parasites. His robes and mat are clean and unstained. He is pure in both body and mind and he is serene and uninvolved in extraneous matters.

正體字

心不諂曲不懷慳嫉。
040b10 ‖ 不貴利養衣服飲食臥具醫藥資生之物。於
040b11 ‖ 深法中無所諍競。一心聽法常欲在前。
040b12 ‖ 以此福德具足諸波羅蜜。於世技術與眾
040b13 ‖ 殊絕。觀一切法皆順法性。乃至惡魔變現
040b14 ‖ 八大地獄化作菩薩而語之言。汝若不捨
040b15 ‖ 菩提心者當生此中。見是怖畏而心不捨。
040b16 ‖ 惡魔復言。摩訶衍經非佛所說。聞是語時
040b17 ‖ 心無有異。常依法相不隨於他。於生死
040b18 ‖ 苦惱而無驚畏。[2]聞菩薩於阿僧祇劫修集
040b19 ‖ 善根而退轉者。其心不沒。又聞菩薩退為
040b20 ‖ 阿羅漢得諸禪定說法度人心亦不退。常
040b21 ‖ [3]能覺知一切魔事。若聞薩[4]波若空大乘十
040b22 ‖ 地亦空[5]可度眾生亦空諸法無所有亦如
040b23 ‖ 虛空。若聞如是惑亂其心欲令退轉疲厭
040b24 ‖ 懈廢。而[6]是菩薩倍加精進深行慈悲。

简体字

心不谄曲不怀悭嫉。不贵利养衣服饮食卧具医药资生之物。于深法中无所诤竞。一心听法常欲在前。以此福德具足诸波罗蜜。于世技术与众殊绝。观一切法皆顺法性。乃至恶魔变现八大地狱化作菩萨而语之言。汝若不舍菩提心者当生此中。见是怖畏而心不舍。恶魔复言。摩诃衍经非佛所说。闻是语时心无有异。常依法相不随于他。于生死苦恼而无惊畏。闻菩萨于阿僧祇劫修集善根而退转者。其心不没。又闻菩萨退为阿罗汉得诸禅定说法度人心亦不退。常能觉知一切魔事。若闻萨波若空大乘十地亦空可度众生亦空诸法无所有亦如虚空。若闻如是惑乱其心欲令退转疲厌懈废。而是菩萨倍加精进深行慈悲。

His mind is free of flattery and deviousness nor does it tend toward miserliness or jealousy.

He does not prize offerings, robes, food and drink, mats, medicines, or other physical necessities.

He has no tendency to engage in disputation over profound dharmas. He listens single-mindedly to explanations of the Dharma and always wishes to be in front [wherever it is taught].

Through the merit gained in these various ways, he succeeds in perfecting his practice of the *pāramitās*.

He excels over others in mastery of the world's cultural skills and arts.

He contemplates all dharmas in accordance with the nature of dharmas.

Even if Māra, the Evil One, were to manifest an apparition of the eight great hells while transformationally appearing before him as a bodhisattva, saying, "If you do not relinquish the resolve to attain bodhi, you will be reborn here"—even when witnessing such a terrifying circumstance as this, his mind would still refuse to relinquish its resolve.

Should Māra, the Evil One, then also say, "The sutras of the Mahāyāna were not spoken by the Buddha"—even when hearing this declaration, his resolve would remain unchanged. He continues to rely on the characteristic aspects of the Dharma and does not follow others.

He is not terrorized by the sufferings of *saṃsāra*. Even were he to hear of bodhisattvas who finally fell back and retreated [from the bodhi resolve] after *asaṃkhyeyas* of kalpas of cultivating and accumulating roots of goodness, his resolve would still not sink away as a result.

Also, were he to hear of a bodhisattva that had retreated to become an arhat, even then, he would still not retreat from his resolve to acquire the *dhyāna* absorptions, proclaim the Dharma, and liberate others [from *saṃsāra*].

He is always able to become aware of and recognize all actions of *māras*. Even if he were to be informed that omniscience is empty, that the Great Vehicle's ten grounds are empty, that the beings amenable to liberation [from *saṃsāra*] are empty, and that all dharmas are nonexistent and like empty space—were he to be told such things by someone attempting to throw his mind into confusion, someone wishing thereby to influence him to turn back due to weariness and diminishing intensity of effort—this bodhisattva would still respond by redoubling his practice of vigor and his deep practice of kindness and compassion.

正體字	意若 040b25 ‖欲入初禪第二第三第四禪而不隨禪生 040b26 ‖還起欲界法。除破憍慢不貴稱讚心無瞋 040b27 ‖ [7]礙。若在居家不染著五欲。以厭離心受 040b28 ‖如病服藥。不以邪命自活。不以自活因 040b29 ‖緣惱亂於他。但為眾生得安樂故處在居 040c01 ‖家。密迹金剛常隨侍衛人及非人不能壞亂。 040c02 ‖諸根具足無所缺少。不為呪術惡藥伏人 040c03 ‖害物。不好鬪諍不自高身[8]不卑他人。不 040c04 ‖占相吉凶不樂說眾事。所謂帝王臣民國 040c05 ‖土[9]疆界。戰鬪器仗衣物酒食。女人事古昔事 040c06 ‖大海中事。如是等事悉不樂說。不[10]往觀聽 040c07 ‖歌舞伎樂。但樂說應諸波羅蜜義。樂說應諸 040c08 ‖波羅蜜法令得增益。離諸鬪訟常願見 040c09 ‖佛。聞他方現在有佛願欲往生。常生中國 040c10 ‖終不自疑我是阿惟越致非阿惟越致。決定 040c11 ‖自知是阿惟越致。種種魔事覺而不隨。乃至 040c12 ‖轉身不生聲聞
简体字	意若欲入初禅第二第三第四禅而不随禅生还起欲界法。除破憍慢不贵称赞心无嗔碍。若在居家不染着五欲。以厌离心受如病服药。不以邪命自活。不以自活因缘恼乱于他。但为众生得安乐故处在居家。密迹金刚常随侍卫人及非人不能坏乱。诸根具足无所缺少。不为咒术恶药伏人害物。不好斗诤不自高身不卑他人。不占相吉凶不乐说众事。所谓帝王臣民国土疆界。战斗器仗衣物酒食。女人事古昔事大海中事。如是等事悉不乐说。不往观听歌舞伎乐。但乐说应诸波罗蜜义。乐说应诸波罗蜜法令得增益。离诸斗讼常愿见佛。闻他方现在有佛愿欲往生。常生中国终不自疑我是阿惟越致非阿惟越致。决定自知是阿惟越致。种种魔事觉而不随。乃至转身不生声闻

Whenever he wishes to enter the first *dhyāna*, second *dhyāna*, third *dhyāna*, or fourth *dhyāna* meditation states, though he may do so, he nonetheless refrains from taking rebirth in those corresponding *dhyāna* [heavens], but rather returns and takes up dharmas suitable for practice within the desire realm.

He crushes and expels any potential arrogance, does not prize the praise of others, and keeps his mind free of the hindrance of hatred.

In lives spent as a householder, he remains unstained by the five objects of desire, merely taking them on with a mind of renunciation just as one would take medicine when beset with disease.

He does not live by wrong livelihoods and does not live in a manner that disrupts others' lives.

It is only for the sake of bringing peace and happiness to beings that he might abide in the role of a householder.

Traceless vajra-wielding dharma protectors[138] always follow him, serving and protecting him and ensuring that he cannot be harmed or interfered with by any human or nonhuman being.

All of his faculties are normally intact and free of defect. He does not use magical spells or noxious elixirs to subdue people or harm beings.

He is not fond of disputation and does not elevate himself or degrade others.

He does not perform divinations to determine auspiciousness or misfortune.

He is not fond of discussing manifold topics, topics such as: kings, ministers and the people, the state and its frontier lands, wars and battles, weaponry, clothing, possessions, alcoholic beverages and cuisine, matters associated with women, historical happenings, or maritime matters. He does not delight in discussing any matters such as these.

He does not attend, watch, or listen to singing, dancing, or music.

He only wishes to discuss the meaning of the *pāramitās* and only wishes to discuss dharmas related to the *pāramitās*, seeking thereby to cause those listening to gain increased benefit from this.

He abandons all disputation and always wishes to see the Buddha. If he hears of there now being a buddha in some other region, he wishes to take rebirth there. He is always reborn in a country central [to the presence of Dharma]. He never entertains doubts in himself whereby he wonders, "Am I or am I not an *avaivartika*?" He knows with complete certainty that he is an *avaivartika*.

He recognizes the various works of the *māras*, but does not accord with them. [His resolve is so solid that], even after he has taken rebirth, he does not then generate any aspiration to follow the paths of *śrāvaka*

正體字

```
           辟支佛心。乃至惡魔現作
040c13 ||  佛身。語言汝應證阿羅漢。我今為汝說法。
040c14 ||  即於此中成阿羅漢。亦不信受。為護法故
040c15 ||  不惜身命常行精進。若說法時無有疑
040c16 ||  難。無有闕失。如是等事名阿惟越致相。能
040c17 ||  成就此相者。當知是阿惟越致。或有未具
040c18 ||  足者。何者是未久入阿惟越致地者。隨後
040c19 ||  諸地修集善根。隨善根轉深故。得是阿惟
040c20 ||  越致相。[11]
040c21 ||  十住毘婆沙論卷第四
```

简体字

辟支佛心。乃至恶魔现作佛身。语言汝应证阿罗汉。我今为汝说法。即于此中成阿罗汉。亦不信受。为护法故不惜身命常行精进。若说法时无有疑难。无有阙失。如是等事名阿惟越致相。能成就此相者。当知是阿惟越致。或有未具足者。何者是未久入阿惟越致地者。随后诸地修集善根。随善根转深故。得是阿惟越致相。

disciples or *pratyekabuddha*s. Even if Māra, the Evil One, were to manifest before him in the body of a buddha, telling him, "You must attain arhatship. I shall now speak the Dharma for you so that you may immediately achieve arhatship right here," even then, he would refuse to believe or accept this.

He does not spare even his own body or life in his efforts to preserve the Dharma and always practices vigor.

When explaining the Dharma, he is free of doubt or uncertainty and does so in a manner that is free of any deficiencies or errors.

It is factors such as these that constitute the characteristic signs of an *avaivartika*. One should realize that whoever is able to perfect these signs is an *avaivartika*. It might also happen that one encounters those who have not yet completely developed these signs. What sort of individual is this? This individual will, before long, ascend to the ground of the *avaivartika*. He is one who, after having cultivated and accumulated roots of goodness on later grounds and after having developed ever deeper roots of goodness, shall then acquire these characteristic signs of the *avaivartika*.

The End of Chapter Eight

正體字

```
040c24 ‖ 十住毘婆沙論卷第五  040c25 ‖
040c26 ‖     聖者龍樹造
040c27 ‖     後秦龜茲國三藏鳩摩羅什譯
040c28 ‖   [12]易行品第九
040c29 ‖ 問曰。是阿惟越致菩薩初事如先說。至阿惟
041a01 ‖ 越致地者。行諸難行久乃可得。或墮聲聞
041a02 ‖ 辟支佛地。若爾者是大衰患。如助道法中說。
041a03 ‖   若墮聲聞地    及辟支佛地
041a04 ‖   是名菩薩死    則失一切利
041a05 ‖   若墮於地獄    不生如是畏
041a06 ‖   若墮二乘地    則為大怖畏
041a07 ‖   墮於地獄中    畢竟得至佛
041a08 ‖   若墮二乘地    畢竟遮佛道
041a09 ‖   佛自於經中    解說如是事
041a10 ‖   如人貪壽者    斬首則大畏
041a11 ‖   菩薩亦如是    若於聲聞地
041a12 ‖   及辟支佛地    應生大怖畏
041a13 ‖ 是故若諸佛所說有易行道疾得至阿惟越
041a14 ‖ 致地方便者。願為說之。
```

簡體字

易行品第九

问曰。是阿惟越致菩萨初事如先说。至阿惟越致地者。行诸难行久乃可得。或堕声闻辟支佛地。若尔者是大衰患。如助道法中说。

　　若堕声闻地　　及辟支佛地
　　是名菩萨死　　则失一切利
　　若堕于地狱　　不生如是畏
　　若堕二乘地　　则为大怖畏
　　堕于地狱中　　毕竟得至佛
　　若堕二乘地　　毕竟遮佛道
　　佛自于经中　　解说如是事
　　如人贪寿者　　斩首则大畏
　　菩萨亦如是　　若于声闻地
　　及辟支佛地　　应生大怖畏

是故若诸佛所说有易行道疾得至阿惟越致地方便者。愿为说之。

Chapter 9
On the Easy Practice

IX. Chapter Nine: On the Easy Practice
   A. Q: How Difficult! Is There an Easier Path to the Avaivartika Ground?

Question: Given that this *avaivartika* bodhisattva's initial endeavors are such as previously discussed, one aspiring to reach the ground of the *avaivartika* would have to practice all manner of difficult practices for a long time and only then be able to reach it. [This being the case], he might become prone then to fall down onto the grounds of the *śrāvaka* disciples or *pratyekabuddhas*. If that were the case, this would be for him an immensely ruinous calamity. As stated in the Dharma of *The Provisions Essential for Bodhi* (*Bodhisambhāra Śāstra*):[139]

> If one were to fall onto the ground of the *śrāvaka* disciples
> or onto the ground of the *pratyekabuddhas*,
> this amounts to "death" for a bodhisattva,
> for he then loses all beneficial effects [of his bodhisattva practice].

> If one faced the prospect of falling into the hells,
> he would not become filled with such fear as this.
> If one were to [contemplate] falling onto the Two Vehicles' ground,
> then this would bring about great terror.

> If one were to fall into the hells,
> he could still ultimately succeed in reaching buddhahood.
> If one were to fall onto the grounds of the Two Vehicles, however,
> this would ultimately block the realization of buddhahood.

> In the scriptures, the Buddha himself
> explained matters such as these, stating that
> this is just as with a person who covets a long life span:
> If he is faced with decapitation, he is then filled with great fear.

> The bodhisattva is also just like this.
> If [confronted with the prospect of] the *śrāvaka* disciples' ground
> or the *pratyekabuddhas*' ground,
> he should react with great terror.

Therefore, if, as a skillful means, the Buddhas have mentioned the existence of an easily-practiced path by which one might rapidly succeed in arriving at the ground of the *avaivartika*, then please explain it for me.

正體字

```
          答曰。如汝所說是
041a15 ‖ 懦弱怯劣無有大心。非是丈夫志幹之言
041a16 ‖ 也。何以故。若人發願欲求阿耨多羅三藐三
041a17 ‖ 菩提。未得阿惟越致。於其中間應不惜
041a18 ‖ 身命。晝夜精進如救頭燃。如助道中說。
041a19 ‖   菩薩未得至    阿惟越致地
041a20 ‖   應常勤精進    猶如救頭燃
041a21 ‖   荷負於重擔    為求菩提故
041a22 ‖   常應勤精進    不生懈怠心
041a23 ‖   若求聲聞乘    辟支佛乘者
041a24 ‖   但為成己利    常應勤精進
041a25 ‖   何況於菩薩    自度亦度彼
041a26 ‖   於此二乘人    億倍應精進
041a27 ‖ 行大乘者佛如是說。發願求佛道。重於
041a28 ‖ 舉三千大千世界。汝言阿惟越致地是法甚
041a29 ‖ 難久乃可得。若有易行道疾得至阿惟越
041b01 ‖ 致地者。是乃怯弱下劣之言。非是大人志幹
041b02 ‖ 之說。汝若必欲聞此方便今當說之。佛法
041b03 ‖ 有無量門。如世間道
```

简体字

答曰。如汝所说是懦弱怯劣无有大心。非是丈夫志干之言也。何以故。若人发愿欲求阿耨多罗三藐三菩提。未得阿惟越致。于其中间应不惜身命。昼夜精进如救头燃。如助道中说。

　　菩萨未得至　　阿惟越致地
　　应常勤精进　　犹如救头燃
　　荷负于重担　　为求菩提故
　　常应勤精进　　不生懈怠心
　　若求声闻乘　　辟支佛乘者
　　但为成己利　　常应勤精进
　　何况于菩萨　　自度亦度彼
　　于此二乘人　　亿倍应精进

行大乘者佛如是说。发愿求佛道。重于举三千大千世界。汝言阿惟越致地是法甚难久乃可得。若有易行道疾得至阿惟越致地者。是乃怯弱下劣之言。非是大人志干之说。汝若必欲闻此方便今当说之。佛法有无量门。如世间道

Chapter 9 — On the Easy Practice

B. A: How Weak & Inferior! But, If You Want That, I Will Explain

Response: Statements such as you have just made are symptomatic of a weak, pusillanimous, and inferior mind devoid of the great resolve. These are not the words of a heroic man possessed of determination and ability.

How is this so? If a person has brought forth the vow to strive for the realization of *anuttarasamyaksaṃbodhi*, during that interim period in which he has not yet gained the *avaivartika* stage, he must not be sparing of even his own body or life. Rather he should strive with vigor both day and night, acting with the same urgency to save himself as someone whose turban has just caught fire. This is as stated in the *Bodhisambhara Śāstra*:

> So long as the bodhisattva has not yet succeeded in reaching
> the ground of the *avaivartika*,
> he should always diligently practice vigor,
> acting with the urgency of one whose turban has caught fire.
>
> Taking up the heavy burden
> for the sake of striving to attain bodhi,
> he should always act with diligent vigor,
> refraining from developing an indolent mind.[140]
>
> Even were one to seek the *śrāvaka* disciples' vehicle
> or the *pratyekabuddha*'s vehicle,
> thus seeking only to perfect one's own benefit,
> even then, one should always diligently practice vigor.
>
> How much the more should this be so in the case of the bodhisattva,
> one who strives to liberate both himself and others.
> Compared to these men of the Two Vehicles,
> he should be a *koṭi's* number of times more vigorous than they are.[141]

In speaking of the practice of the Great Vehicle, the Buddha described it thus: "As for generating the vow to attain buddhahood, it is a challenge heavier than lifting all of the worlds in a great trichiliocosm."

As for your saying, "This dharma of the *avaivartika* ground is so extremely difficult to accomplish that one can only reach it after a long time" and "If there were only some easily-traveled path by which one could swiftly reach the *avaivartika* ground," these are the words of those who are weak and inferior. These are not statements of a great man possessed of determination and ability. Still, if you definitely do wish to hear of this skillful means, then I shall now explain it for you.

1. The Practice of Calling on Ten Buddhas, One in Each Direction

The Dharma of the Buddha has measurelessly many gateways. This is just as with the world's various routes among which there are those

正體字

```
            有難有易。陸道步行
041b04 ||  則苦。水道乘船則樂。菩薩道亦如是。或有
041b05 ||  勤行精進。或有以信方便易行疾至阿惟
041b06 ||  越致者。如偈說。
041b07 ||    東方善德佛    南栴檀德佛
041b08 ||    西無量明佛    北方相德佛
041b09 ||    東南無憂德    西南寶施佛
041b10 ||    西北華德佛    東北三[1]行佛
041b11 ||    下方明德佛    上方廣眾德
041b12 ||    如是諸世尊    今現在十方
041b13 ||    若人疾欲至    不退轉地者
041b14 ||    應以恭敬心    執持稱名號
041b15 || 若菩薩欲於此身得至阿惟越致地成
041b16 || [2]就阿耨多羅三藐三菩提者。應當念是十
041b17 || 方諸佛稱其名號。如寶月童子所問經阿惟
041b18 || 越致品中說。佛告寶月。東方去此過無量
041b19 || 無邊不可思議恒河沙等佛土有世界名無
041b20 || 憂。其地平坦七寶合成。紫磨金縷交絡[3]其
041b21 || 界。寶樹羅列以為莊嚴。無有地獄畜生餓
041b22 || 鬼阿修羅道及諸難處。清淨無穢無有沙礫
041b23 || 瓦石山陵[4]堆阜深坑幽壑。天常雨華以布  041b24 ||其地。
```

簡體字

有难有易。陆道步行则苦。水道乘船则乐。菩萨道亦如是。或有勤行精进。或有以信方便易行疾至阿惟越致者。如偈说。

　　东方善德佛　　南栴檀德佛
　　西无量明佛　　北方相德佛
　　东南无忧德　　西南宝施佛
　　西北华德佛　　东北三行佛
　　下方明德佛　　上方广众德
　　如是诸世尊　　今现在十方
　　若人疾欲至　　不退转地者
　　应以恭敬心　　执持称名号

若菩萨欲于此身得至阿惟越致地成就阿耨多罗三藐三菩提者。应当念是十方诸佛称其名号。如宝月童子所问经阿惟越致品中说。佛告宝月。东方去此过无量无边不可思议恒河沙等佛土有世界名无忧。其地平坦七宝合成。紫磨金缕交络其界。宝树罗列以为庄严。无有地狱畜生饿鬼阿修罗道及诸难处。清净无秽无有沙砾瓦石山陵堆阜深坑幽壑。天常雨华以布其地。

that are difficult and those that are easy. When taking overland routes, the traveling may involve suffering, whereas in the case of water routes where one boards a boat, it may instead be pleasurable.

So too it is in the case of the bodhisattva path. In some instances, one is diligently devoted to the practice of vigor, whereas in others that involve faith and skillful means, one adopts an easy practice by which one swiftly arrives at the station of the *avaivartika*. This is as described in the following verse:

> In the East, there is Meritorious Qualities Buddha.
> In the South, there is Candana Qualities Buddha.
> In the West, there is Measureless Light Buddha.
> In the North, there is Emblematic Qualities Buddha.

> In the Southeast, there is Sorrowless Qualities Buddha.
> In the Southwest, there is Giver of Jewels Buddha.
> In the Northwest, there is Floral Qualities Buddha.
> In the Northeast, there is Three Vehicles' Practices Buddha.[142]

> Toward the Nadir, there is Brilliant Qualities Buddha.
> Toward the Zenith, there is Vast Multitude of Qualities Buddha.
> *Bhagavats* such as these
> now abide throughout the ten directions.

> If a person wishes to swiftly reach
> the ground of irreversibility,
> he should, with a reverential mind,
> take up and maintain the practice of invoking these buddhas' names.

If a bodhisattva wishes in this very body to succeed in reaching the ground of the *avaivartika* and then attain *anuttarasamyaksaṃbodhi*, then he should bear in mind these buddhas of the ten directions and invoke their names. This is just as explained in the "Avaivartika Chapter" of the *Sutra Spoken in Response to the Questions of the Youth Precious Moon*,[143] in which the Buddha told Precious Moon:

> Off in the East, going beyond a number of buddha lands equal to the sands in a measureless, boundless, and inconceivable number of Ganges Rivers, there is a world system named Sorrowless. Its ground is level and composed of the seven precious things. Strands of purple powdered gold are woven throughout that realm and rows of jeweled trees serve as adornments there.
>
> There are no destinies of the hells, animals, hungry ghosts, or *asuras*, nor are there any places beset by difficulties. It is pure, free of any filth, and also free of gravel, ceramic shards, stones, mountains, hillocks, deep pits, and dark ravines. The devas always rain down flowers that cover its ground.

正體字

```
           時世有佛號曰善德如來應[5]供正遍
041b25 ||  知明行足善逝世間解無上士調御丈夫天人
041b26 ||  師佛世尊。大菩薩眾恭敬圍繞。身相光色如
041b27 ||  燃大金山如大珍寶聚。為諸大眾[6]廣說
041b28 ||  正法。初中後善有辭有義。所說不雜具足
041b29 ||  清淨如實不失。何謂不失不失地水火風。
041c01 ||  不失欲界色界無色界。不失色受想行識。
041c02 ||  寶月。是佛成道已來過六十億劫。又其佛國
041c03 ||  晝夜無異。但以此間閻浮提日月歲數說
041c04 ||  彼劫壽。其佛光明常照世界。於一說法令
041c05 ||  無量無邊千萬億阿僧祇眾生住無生法忍。
041c06 ||  倍此人數得住初忍第二第三忍。寶月。其
041c07 ||  佛本願力故。若有他方眾生。於先佛所種
041c08 ||  諸善根。是佛但以光明觸身。即得無生法
041c09 ||  忍。寶月。若善男子善女人聞是佛名能信受
041c10 ||  者。即不退阿耨多羅三藐三菩提。餘九佛事
041c11 ||  皆亦如是。今當解說諸佛名號及國土名 041c12 ||號。
```

简体字

时世有佛号曰善德如来应供正遍知明行足善逝世间解无上士调御丈夫天人师佛世尊。大菩萨众恭敬围绕。身相光色如燃大金山如大珍宝聚。为诸大众广说正法。初中后善有辞有义。所说不杂具足清净如实不失。何谓不失不失地水火风。不失欲界色界无色界。不失色受想行识。宝月。是佛成道已来过六十亿劫。又其佛国昼夜无异。但以此间阎浮提日月岁数说彼劫寿。其佛光明常照世界。于一说法令无量无边千万亿阿僧祇众生住无生法忍。倍此人数得住初忍第二第三忍。宝月。其佛本愿力故。若有他方众生。于先佛所种诸善根。是佛但以光明触身。即得无生法忍。宝月。若善男子善女人闻是佛名能信受者。即不退阿耨多罗三藐三菩提。余九佛事皆亦如是。今当解说诸佛名号及国土名号。

That world now has a buddha named Meritorious Qualities Tathāgata, Worthy of Offerings, of Right and Universal Enlightenment, Perfect in Knowledge and Conduct, Well Gone One, Knower of the Worlds, Unsurpassable One, Tamer of Those to Be Tamed, Teacher of Devas and Humans, Buddha, Bhagavat. He is respectfully surrounded by an assembly of great bodhisattvas. His body's characteristic radiance and appearance are like a great flaming gold mountain and like a great aggregation of precious jewels.

For the sake of everyone in that great assembly, he extensively proclaims the right Dharma that is good in the beginning, middle, and end, that is eloquently presented and meaningful. Whatever he proclaims is free of admixture, perfect in its purity, accordant with reality, and free of error.

What is meant by "free of error"? It is free of any error with respect to the [four great elements of] earth, water, fire, and wind, is free of any error with respect to the desire realm, the form realm, and the formless realm and is free of error with respect to [the five aggregates of] form, feelings, perceptions, formative factors, and consciousness.

Precious Moon, from the time this buddha achieved buddhahood until the present, sixty *koṭis* of kalpas have passed. Moreover, in that buddha's country, there is no difference between the day and the night. It is only by reference to the enumeration of days, months and years of Jambudvīpa that one describes his lifetime in terms of a particular number of kalpas.

The light from that buddha always illuminates that world. In the course of a single discourse on Dharma, he causes a measureless and boundless number of thousands of myriads of *koṭis* of *asaṃkhyeyas* of beings to abide in the unproduced-dharmas patience. Twice this number of people are thereby caused to abide in the first, second, and third type of patience.

Precious Moon, the power of that buddha's original vows is such that, if there are any beings in other regions who have planted roots of goodness under a previous buddha, he need only be touched by this buddha's light in order to immediately attain the unproduced-dharmas patience.

Precious Moon, if there is a son or daughter of good family who but hears this buddha's name and is then able to have faith and accept him, such a person will immediately achieve irreversibility with respect to the attainment of *anuttarasamyaksaṃbodhi*.

The circumstances related to the other nine buddhas are just like this. Now we shall explain the names of those Buddhas as well as the names of their lands.

正體字

041c13 ‖ 善德者。其德淳善但有安樂。非如諸天
041c13 ‖ 龍神福德[7]惑惱眾生。栴檀德者。南方去此
041c14 ‖ 無量無邊恒河沙等佛土有世界名歡喜。
041c15 ‖ 佛號栴檀德。今現在說法。譬如栴檀香而
041c16 ‖ 清涼。彼佛名稱遠聞如香流布。滅除眾生三
041c17 ‖ 毒火熱令得清涼。無量明佛者。西方去此
041c18 ‖ 無量無邊恒河沙等佛土有世界名[8]善。佛
041c19 ‖ 號無量明。今現在說法。其佛身光及智慧明
041c20 ‖ 炤無量無邊。相德佛者。北方去此無量無邊
041c21 ‖ 恒河沙等佛土有世界名不可動。佛名相
041c22 ‖ 德。今現在說法。其佛福德高顯猶如幢相。
041c23 ‖ 無憂德者。東南方去此無量無邊恒河沙等
041c24 ‖ 佛土有世界名月明。佛號無憂德。今現在
041c25 ‖ 說法。其佛神德令諸天人無有憂愁。寶施
041c26 ‖ 佛者。西南方去此無量無邊恒河沙等佛土
041c27 ‖ 有世界名眾相。佛號寶施。今現在說法。其
041c28 ‖ 佛以諸無漏根力覺道等寶常施眾生。華德
041c29 ‖ 佛者。西北方去此無量無邊恒河沙等佛土

简体字

善德者。其德淳善但有安乐。非如诸天龙神福德惑恼众生。栴檀德者。南方去此无量无边恒河沙等佛土有世界名欢喜。佛号栴檀德。今现在说法。譬如栴檀香而清凉。彼佛名称远闻如香流布。灭除众生三毒火热令得清凉。无量明佛者。西方去此无量无边恒河沙等佛土有世界名善。佛号无量明。今现在说法。其佛身光及智慧明昭无量无边。相德佛者。北方去此无量无边恒河沙等佛土有世界名不可动。佛名相德。今现在说法。其佛福德高显犹如幢相。无忧德者。东南方去此无量无边恒河沙等佛土有世界名月明。佛号无忧德。今现在说法。其佛神德令诸天人无有忧愁。宝施佛者。西南方去此无量无边恒河沙等佛土有世界名众相。佛号宝施。今现在说法。其佛以诸无漏根力觉道等宝常施众生。华德佛者。西北方去此无量无边恒河沙等佛土

Chapter 9 — On the Easy Practice

As for "Meritorious Qualities Buddha," his qualities are associated with pure goodness and the possession of peace and happiness. They are unlike the meritorious qualities of devas, dragons, and spirits which delude and trouble beings.

As for "Candana Qualities Buddha," in the South, off at a distance from here of buddha lands as numerous as the sands in incalculably and boundlessly many Ganges Rivers, there is a world named Delightful. The name of the buddha there is Candana Qualities. He is right now proclaiming the Dharma that is as fragrant and cooling as *candana*.[144] The fame of that buddha's name is heard afar, circulating and spreading about like the fragrance of incense. It extinguishes the heat from the fire of beings' three poisons and thereby causes them to experience refreshing coolness.

As for "Measureless Light Buddha," off in the West, at a distance from here of buddha lands as numerous as the sands in incalculably and boundlessly many Ganges Rivers, there is a world named "Excellence." That buddha is named Measureless Light. He is at this very time proclaiming the Dharma. The light from that buddha's body and the brilliant illumination from his wisdom reach an incalculable and boundless distance.

As for "Emblematic Qualities Buddha," off in the North, at a distance from here of buddha lands as numerous as the sands in incalculably and boundlessly many Ganges Rivers, there is a world known as "Immovable." Its buddha is known as Emblematic Qualities. He is right now proclaiming the Dharma. That buddha's meritorious qualities are lofty and prominently displayed, appearing like a banner.

As for "Sorrowless Qualities Buddha," in the Southeast, off at a distance from here of buddha lands as numerous as the sands in incalculably and boundlessly many Ganges Rivers, there is a world named "Lunar Brilliance." The buddha who abides there is named Sorrowless Qualities. He is even now proclaiming the Dharma. That buddha's spiritual qualities are such that they cause all of the devas and men there to be free of any sort of sorrow.

As for "Giver of Jewels Buddha," in the Southwest, off at a distance from here of buddha lands as numerous as the sands in incalculably and boundlessly many Ganges Rivers, there is a world named "Multitude of Signs." The buddha who abides there is known as Giver of Jewels. Even now he is proclaiming the Dharma. That buddha always bestows on beings the jewels of the uncontaminated root faculties, powers, limbs of enlightenment, the path, and so forth.

As for "Floral Qualities Buddha," in the Northwest, off at a distance from here of buddha lands as numerous as the sands in incalculably

正體字

042a01 ‖ 有世界名眾音。佛號華德。今現在說法。其
042a02 ‖ 佛色身猶如妙華其德無量。三乘行佛者。東
042a03 ‖ 北方去此無量無邊恒河沙等佛土有世界
042a04 ‖ 名安隱。佛號三乘行。今現在說法。其佛常
042a05 ‖ 說聲聞行辟支佛行諸菩薩行。有人言。說上
042a06 ‖ 中下精進故。號為三乘行。明德佛者。下方
042a07 ‖ 去此無量無邊恒河沙等佛土有世界名
042a08 ‖ 廣大。佛號明德。今現在說法。明名身明智
042a09 ‖ 慧明寶樹光明。是三種明常照世間。廣眾德
042a10 ‖ 者。上方去此無量無邊恒河沙等佛土有世
042a11 ‖ 界名眾月。佛號廣眾德。[1]今現在說法。其
042a12 ‖ 佛[2]弟子福德廣大故號廣眾德。[3]今是十方
042a13 ‖ 佛善德為初。廣眾德為後。若人一心稱其
042a14 ‖ 名號。即得不退於阿耨多羅三藐三菩提。
042a15 ‖ 如[4]偈說。
042a16 ‖ 若有人得聞   說是諸佛名
042a17 ‖ 即得無量德   如為寶月說

简体字

有世界名众音。佛号华德。今现在说法。其佛色身犹如妙华其德无量。三乘行佛者。东北方去此无量无边恒河沙等佛土有世界名安隐。佛号三乘行。今现在说法。其佛常说声闻行辟支佛行诸菩萨行。有人言。说上中下精进故。号为三乘行。明德佛者。下方去此无量无边恒河沙等佛土有世界名广大。佛号明德。今现在说法。明名身明智慧明宝树光明。是三种明常照世间。广众德者。上方去此无量无边恒河沙等佛土有世界名众月。佛号广众德。今现在说法。其佛弟子福德广大故号广众德。今是十方佛善德为初。广众德为后。若人一心称其名号。即得不退于阿耨多罗三藐三菩提。如偈说。

　　若有人得闻　　说是诸佛名
　　即得无量德　　如为宝月说

Chapter 9 — On the Easy Practice

and boundlessly many Ganges Rivers, there is a world known as "Multitude of Sounds." The Buddha who abides there is known as Floral Qualities. Even now, he is proclaiming the Dharma. That buddha's physical body is like a marvelous flower and his meritorious qualities are incalculably numerous.

As for "Three Vehicles Practices Buddha," in the Northeast, off at a distance from here of buddha lands as numerous as the sands in incalculably and boundlessly many Ganges Rivers, there is a world known as "Peaceful and Secure." The buddha who abides there is known as Three Vehicles' Practices Buddha. Even now, he is proclaiming the Dharma. That buddha always explains the practices of the *śrāvaka* disciples, the practices of the *pratyekabuddhas*, and the practices of the bodhisattvas. There are those who state that it is because he explains the superior, the middling, and the lesser levels of vigor that he is named Three Vehicles' Practices.

As for "Brilliant Qualities Buddha," in the Nadir, off at a distance from here of buddha lands as numerous as the sands in incalculably and boundlessly many Ganges Rivers, there is a world known as "Expansive." The buddha who abides there is known as Brilliant Qualities. Even now he is proclaiming the Dharma. "Brilliant" refers to the light that shines from his body, the light of his wisdom, and the light that shines from his jeweled tree. These three kinds of brilliance always illuminate that world.

As for "Vast Multitude of Qualities Buddha," in the Zenith, off at a distance from here of buddha lands as numerous as the sands in incalculably and boundlessly many Ganges Rivers, there is a world known as "Many Moons." The buddha who abides there is known as Vast Multitude of Qualities. Even now he is proclaiming the Dharma. It is because the meritorious qualities of that buddha's disciples are vast that he is known as Vast Multitude of Qualities.

Now, as for these buddhas of the ten directions, beginning with Meritorious Qualities Buddha and concluding with Vast Multitude of Qualities Buddha, if a person single-mindedly invokes their names, he will thereby immediately succeed in gaining irreversibility with respect to the attainment of *anuttarasamyaksaṃbodhi*. This is as described in a verse:

> If there is a person who is able to hear
> the utterance of all these buddhas' names,
> he will immediately acquire countless meritorious qualities,
> just as was explained for Precious Moon.

正體字	042a18 ‖ 我禮是諸佛 今現在十方 042a19 ‖ 其有稱名者 即得不退轉 042a20 ‖ 東方無憂界 其佛號善德 042a21 ‖ 色相如金山 名聞無邊際 042a22 ‖ 若人聞名者 即得不退轉 042a23 ‖ 我今合掌禮 願悉除憂惱 042a24 ‖ 南方歡喜界 佛號栴檀德 042a25 ‖ 面淨如滿月 光明無有量 042a26 ‖ 能滅諸眾生 三毒之熱惱 042a27 ‖ 聞名得不退 是故稽首禮 042a28 ‖ 西方善世界 佛號無量明 042a29 ‖ 身光智慧明 所照無邊際 042b01 ‖ 其有聞名者 即得不退轉 042b02 ‖ 我今稽首禮 願盡生死際 042b03 ‖ 北方無動界 佛號為相德 042b04 ‖ 身具眾相好 而以自莊嚴 042b05 ‖ 摧破魔怨眾 善化諸[5]人天 042b06 ‖ 聞名得不退 是故稽首禮 042b07 ‖ 東南月明界 有佛號無憂 042b08 ‖ 光明踰日月 遇者滅[6]煩惱	
简体字	我礼是诸佛 今现在十方 其有称名者 即得不退转 东方无忧界 其佛号善德 色相如金山 名闻无边际 若人闻名者 即得不退转 我今合掌礼 愿悉除忧恼 南方欢喜界 佛号栴檀德 面净如满月 光明无有量 能灭诸众生 三毒之热恼 闻名得不退 是故稽首礼 西方善世界 佛号无量明 身光智慧明 所照无边际 其有闻名者 即得不退转 我今稽首礼 愿尽生死际 北方无动界 佛号为相德 身具众相好 而以自庄严 摧破魔怨众 善化诸人天 闻名得不退 是故稽首礼 东南月明界 有佛号无忧 光明踰日月 遇者灭烦恼	

I bow in reverence to these buddhas
presently abiding throughout the ten directions.
Whosoever invokes their names
immediately attains irreversibility.

Off in the East, in the realm known as Sorrowless,
that buddha named Meritorious Qualities
has a form resembling a mountain of gold.
The reach of his fame is boundless.

If a person so much as hears his name,
he immediately attains irreversibility.
With palms pressed together, I now bow in reverence to him
and pray that worries and afflictions may be entirely dispelled.

Off in the South, in the realm known as Delightful,
there is a buddha named Candana Qualities.
His countenance is as pristine as the full moon
and the radiance of his light is measureless.

He is able to bring about the extinguishing of beings'
fiery afflictions produced by the three poisons.
If one but hears his name, he then attains irreversibility.
I therefore bow down in reverence to him.

Off in the West, in a realm known as Excellence,
there is a buddha known as Limitless Light.
The light from his body and the brilliance of his wisdom
are boundless in the range of their illumination.

If there be anyone who but hears his name
he will immediately attain irreversibility.
I now bow down in reverence to him,
praying that I may put an end to the limits imposed by *saṃsāra*.

Off in the North, in a realm known as Immovable,
there is a buddha named Emblematic Qualities.
His body is replete with the many signs and minor characteristics
with which he is personally adorned.

He utterly defeats the hordes of Māra, the enemy,
and skillfully teaches both humans and devas.
Those who hear his name attain irreversibility.
I therefore bow down in reverence to him.

Off in the Southeast, in a world known as Lunar Brilliance,
there is a buddha named Sorrowless.
His illumination surpasses that of the sun and moon.
Those who encounter it are thus able to extinguish their afflictions.

正體字	042b09 ‖ 常為眾說法　　除諸內外苦 042b10 ‖ 十方佛稱讚　　是故稽首禮 042b11 ‖ 西南眾相界　　佛號為寶施 042b12 ‖ 常以諸法寶　　廣施於一切 042b13 ‖ 諸天頭面禮　　寶冠在足下 042b14 ‖ 我今以五體　　歸命寶施尊 042b15 ‖ 西北眾音界　　佛號為華德 042b16 ‖ 世界眾寶樹　　演出妙法音 042b17 ‖ 常以七覺華　　莊嚴於眾生 042b18 ‖ 白毫相如月　　我今頭面禮 042b19 ‖ 東北安隱界　　諸寶所合成 042b20 ‖ 佛號[7]三乘行　　無量相嚴身 042b21 ‖ 智慧光無量　　能破無明闇 042b22 ‖ 眾生無憂惱　　是故稽首禮 042b23 ‖ 上方眾月界　　眾寶所莊嚴 042b24 ‖ 大德聲聞眾　　菩薩無有量 042b25 ‖ 諸聖中師子　　號曰廣眾德 042b26 ‖ 諸魔所怖畏　　是故稽首禮 042b27 ‖ 下方廣世界　　佛號為明德 042b28 ‖ 身相妙超絕　　閻浮檀金山	
简体字	常为众说法　　除诸内外苦 十方佛称赞　　是故稽首礼 西南众相界　　佛号为宝施 常以诸法宝　　广施于一切 诸天头面礼　　宝冠在足下 我今以五体　　归命宝施尊 西北众音界　　佛号为华德 世界众宝树　　演出妙法音 常以七觉华　　庄严于众生 白毫相如月　　我今头面礼 东北安隐界　　诸宝所合成 佛号三乘行　　无量相严身 智慧光无量　　能破无明闇 众生无忧恼　　是故稽首礼 上方众月界　　众宝所庄严 大德声闻众　　菩萨无有量 诸圣中师子　　号曰广众德 诸魔所怖畏　　是故稽首礼 下方广世界　　佛号为明德 身相妙超绝　　阎浮檀金山	

Chapter 9 — On the Easy Practice

He always explains the Dharma for the sake of the multitude,
thus ridding them of all inward and outward sufferings.
The buddhas of the ten directions praise him.
I therefore bow down in reverence to him.

Off in the Southwest, in a realm known as Multitude of Signs,
there is a buddha named Giver of Jewels.
He always uses all manner of Dharma jewels
to engage in extensive universal giving.

All the devas bow down in reverence to him
so that their jeweled crowns are brought low at his feet.
I now, bowing in reverence with all five extremities,
take refuge in the Bhagavat, Giver of Jewels.

Off in the Northwest, in a realm known as Multitude of Sounds,
there is a buddha named Floral Qualities.
That world is graced with an abundance of jeweled trees
that send forth sounds expounding the sublime Dharma.

He always uses the flowers of the seven limbs of enlightenment
to bestow adornments on those beings.
His mid-brow white hair tuft mark is like the moon.
I now bow down in reverence to him.

Off in the Northeast, in a world known as Peaceful and Secure,
one that is composed of all manner of jewels,
there is a buddha named Three Vehicles Practices
whose body is adorned with the measureless marks.

The light from his wisdom is measureless.
It is able to dispel the darkness of ignorance
and cause beings to become free of worry and afflictions.
I therefore bow down in reverence to him.

Off toward the Zenith, in a world known as Many Moons,
adorned with the many types of jewels,
attended by a congregation of greatly virtuous *śrāvaka* disciples
and bodhisattvas who are incalculable in number,

there is a lion among the Āryas
named Vast Multitude of Qualities.
He is feared by all the *māras*.
I therefore bow down in reverence to him.

Off toward the Nadir, there is world known as Expansive
in which there is a buddha named Brilliant Qualities.
His physical marks are far more marvelous
even than a mountain of *jambūnada* gold.

正體字	042b29 ‖　　常以智慧日　　開諸善根華 042c01 ‖　　寶土甚廣大　　我遙稽首禮 042c02 ‖　　過去無數劫　　有佛號海德 042c03 ‖　　是諸現在佛　　皆從彼發願 042c04 ‖　　壽命無有量　　光明照無極 042c05 ‖　　國土甚清淨　　聞名定作佛 042c06 ‖　　今現在十方　　具足成十力 042c07 ‖　　是故稽首禮　　人天中最尊 042c08 ‖ 問曰。但聞是十佛名號執持在心。便得不 042c09 ‖ 退阿耨多羅三藐三菩提。為更有餘佛餘 042c10 ‖ 菩薩名得至阿惟越致耶。答曰。 042c11 ‖ 　　[8]阿彌陀等佛　　及諸大菩薩 042c12 ‖ 　　稱名一心念　　亦得不退轉 042c13 ‖ 更有阿彌陀等諸佛。亦應恭敬禮拜稱其名 042c14 ‖ 號。今當具說。無量壽佛。世自在王佛。師子 042c15 ‖ [9]意佛。法意佛。梵相佛。世相佛。世妙佛。慈悲 042c16 ‖ 佛。世王佛。人王佛。月德佛。寶德佛。相德佛。 042c17 ‖ 大相佛。[10]珠蓋佛。師子[11]鬘佛。破無明佛。智華 042c18 ‖ 佛。多摩羅跋栴檀香佛。持大功德佛。	
简体字	常以智慧日　　开诸善根华 　　宝土甚广大　　我遥稽首礼 　　过去无数劫　　有佛号海德 　　是诸现在佛　　皆从彼发愿 　　寿命无有量　　光明照无极 　　国土甚清净　　闻名定作佛 　　今现在十方　　具足成十力 　　是故稽首礼　　人天中最尊 问曰。但闻是十佛名号执持在心。便得不退阿耨多罗三藐三菩提。为更有余佛余菩萨名得至阿惟越致耶。答曰。 　　阿弥陀等佛　　及诸大菩萨 　　称名一心念　　亦得不退转 更有阿弥陀等诸佛。亦应恭敬礼拜称其名号。今当具说。无量寿佛。世自在王佛。师子意佛。法意佛。梵相佛。世相佛。世妙佛。慈悲佛。世王佛。人王佛。月德佛。宝德佛。相德佛。大相佛。珠盖佛。师子鬘佛。破无明佛。智华佛。多摩罗跋栴檀香佛。持大功德佛。	

Chapter 9 — On the Easy Practice

> He always uses the sun of his wisdom
> to open the blossoms of beings' roots of goodness.
> His land of jewels is extremely vast.
> From afar, I bow down in reverence to him.
>
> In the past, countless kalpas ago,
> there was a buddha named Oceanic Meritorious Qualities.
> These buddhas of the present era
> all made their vows under him.
>
> His life span was incalculably long
> and the reach of his light's illumination was endless.
> His country was extremely pure.
> Those hearing his name became definitely bound for buddhahood.
>
> These [buddhas] who now abide in the ten directions
> are completely equipped with the ten powers.
> I therefore bow down in reverence to them,
> these most venerable ones among all humans and devas.

2. Q: CAN ONE INSTEAD CALL ON OTHER BUDDHAS AND BODHISATTVAS?

Question: Is it the case that one may only be able to reach irreversibility with respect to *anuttarasamyaksaṃbodhi* through hearing these ten buddhas' names and bearing them in mind? Or is it the case that there are yet other buddhas' and other bodhisattvas' names through which one may succeed in reaching the station of the *avaivartika*?

3. A: YES, THERE IS AMITĀBHA AS WELL AS OTHER SUCH BUDDHAS

Response:

> There is Amitābha and also other such buddhas
> as well as the great bodhisattvas.
> If one invokes their names and single-mindedly bears them in mind,
> one will also thereby attain irreversibility.

In addition, there is Amitābha as well as other buddhas to whom one should also respectfully bow down in reverence and utter their names. I shall now set forth their names in full:

Limitless Life Buddha, King of Sovereign Mastery in the World Buddha, Lion Mind Buddha, Dharma Mind Buddha, Brahman Signs Buddha, World Signs Buddha, Sublimity of the World Buddha, Kindness and Compassion Buddha, World King Buddha, King Among Men Buddha, Moon-like Virtues Buddha, Precious Virtues Buddha, Qualities of the Marks Buddha, Great Marks Buddha, Jeweled Canopy Buddha, Lion Mane Buddha, Destroyer of Ignorance Buddha, Flower of Wisdom Buddha, Tamālapattra Candana Fragrance Buddha, and Upholder of Great Meritorious Qualities Buddha.

正體字	雨七寶 042c19 ‖ 佛。超勇佛。離瞋恨佛。大莊嚴佛。無相佛。寶 042c20 ‖ 藏佛。德頂佛。多伽羅香佛。栴檀香佛。蓮華香 042c21 ‖ 佛。莊嚴道路佛。龍蓋佛。雨華佛。散華佛。華 042c22 ‖ 光明佛。日音聲佛。蔽日月佛。琉璃藏佛。梵音 042c23 ‖ 佛。淨明佛。金藏佛。須彌頂佛。山王佛。音聲 042c24 ‖ 自在佛。淨眼佛。月明佛。如須彌山佛。日月 042c25 ‖ 佛。得眾佛。華[12]生佛。梵音說佛。世主佛。師子 042c26 ‖ 行佛。妙法意師子吼佛。珠寶蓋珊瑚色佛。破 042c27 ‖ 癡愛闇佛。水月佛。眾華佛。開智慧佛。持雜寶 042c28 ‖ 佛。菩提佛。華超出佛。真琉璃明佛。蔽日明 042c29 ‖ 佛。持大功德佛。得正慧佛。勇健佛。離諂曲 043a01 ‖ 佛。除惡根栽佛。大香佛。道[1]映佛。水光佛。海 043a02 ‖ 雲慧遊佛。德頂華佛。華莊嚴佛。日音聲佛。月 043a03 ‖ 勝佛。琉璃佛。梵聲佛。光明佛。金藏佛。山頂 043a04 ‖ 佛。山王佛。音王佛。龍勝佛。無染佛。淨面佛。 043a05 ‖ 月面佛。如須彌佛。栴檀香佛。威勢佛。燃燈 043a06 ‖ 佛。難勝佛。寶德佛。喜音佛。光明佛。龍勝佛。 043a07 ‖ 離垢明佛。師子佛。王王佛。力勝佛。華[2]齒佛。 043a08 ‖ 無畏明佛。香頂佛。普賢佛。普華佛。寶相佛。
简体字	雨七宝佛。超勇佛。离嗔恨佛。大庄严佛。无相佛。宝藏佛。德顶佛。多伽罗香佛。栴檀香佛。莲华香佛。庄严道路佛。龙盖佛。雨华佛。散华佛。华光明佛。日音声佛。蔽日月佛。琉璃藏佛。梵音佛。净明佛。金藏佛。须弥顶佛。山王佛。音声自在佛。净眼佛。月明佛。如须弥山佛。日月佛。得众佛。华生佛。梵音说佛。世主佛。师子行佛。妙法意师子吼佛。珠宝盖珊瑚色佛。破痴爱闇佛。水月佛。众华佛。开智慧佛。持杂宝佛。菩提佛。华超出佛。真琉璃明佛。蔽日明佛。持大功德佛。得正慧佛。勇健佛。离谄曲佛。除恶根栽佛。大香佛。道映佛。水光佛。海云慧游佛。德顶华佛。华庄严佛。日音声佛。月胜佛。琉璃佛。梵声佛。光明佛。金藏佛。山顶佛。山王佛。音王佛。龙胜佛。无染佛。净面佛。月面佛。如须弥佛。栴檀香佛。威势佛。燃灯佛。难胜佛。宝德佛。喜音佛。光明佛。龙胜佛。离垢明佛。师子佛。王王佛。力胜佛。华齿佛。无畏明佛。香顶佛。普贤佛。普华佛。宝相佛。

Chapter 9 — On the Easy Practice

There are also: Rain of the Seven Precious Things Buddha, Excellent Bravery Buddha, Enmity Transcendence Buddha, Great Adornment Buddha, Signlessness Buddha, Jewel Treasury Buddha, Summit of Virtue Buddha, Tagara Fragrance Buddha, Candana Incense Buddha, Lotus Fragrance Buddha, Adorned Path Buddha, Dragon Canopy Buddha, Rain of Flowers Buddha, Scatterer of Flowers Buddha, Floral Radiance Buddha, Solar Voice Buddha, Eclipsing the Sun and Moon Buddha, Lapis Lazuli Treasury Buddha, Brahman Sound Buddha, and Pure Radiance Buddha.

There are also: Treasury of Gold Buddha, Sumeru Summit Buddha, King of the Mountains Buddha, Masterful Voice Buddha, Pure Eyes Buddha, Lunar Radiance Buddha, Mount Sumeru Likeness Buddha, Sun and Moon Buddha, Acquirer of Multitudes Buddha, Flower-born Buddha, Proclaimer of the Brahman Sounds Buddha, Lord of the Worlds Buddha, Lion-like Practice Buddha, Sublime Dharma Mind Lion's Roar Buddha, Pearl Canopy Coral Appearance Buddha, Dispeller of the Darkness of Delusion and Desire Buddha, Water Moon Buddha, Multitude of Flowers Buddha, Opener of Wisdom Buddha, and Retainer of Various Jewels Buddha.

There are also: Bodhi Buddha, Flower Transcendence Buddha, Radiance of True Lapis Lazuli Buddha, Outshining Sunlight Buddha, Retainer of Great Qualities Buddha, Realizer of Right Wisdom Buddha, Heroic Strength Buddha, Beyond Flattery and Deception Buddha, Dispensing with Planting Roots of Evil Buddha, Great Fragrance Buddha, Path Splendor Buddha, Water Light Buddha, Roamer in Oceanic Clouds of Wisdom Buddha, Virtue Summit Flower Buddha, Floral Adornment Buddha, Solar Voice Buddha, Lunar Supremacy Buddha, Lapis Lazuli Buddha, Brahmā-like Voice Buddha, and Light Buddha.[145]

There are also: Treasury of Gold Buddha, Mountain Summit Buddha, Mountain King Buddha, Sound King Buddha, Dragon Vigor Buddha, Stainless Buddha, Pure Countenance Buddha, Lunar Countenance Buddha, Sumeru Semblance Buddha, Candana Fragrance Buddha, Awesome Strength Buddha, Blazing Lamp Buddha, Difficult to Overcome Buddha, Precious Virtue Buddha, Joyous Sound Buddha, Radiance Buddha,[146] Dragon Supremacy Buddha, Defilement Transcendence Light Buddha, Lion Buddha, and King Among Kings Buddha.

And there are also Supremacy of Powers Buddha, Floral Garden Buddha,[147] Fearless Brilliance Buddha, Fragrant Summit Buddha, Universally Worthy Buddha, Universal Flower Buddha, and Precious Signs Buddha.

正體字

043a09 ‖ 是諸佛世尊現在十方清淨世界。皆稱名憶
043a10 ‖ 念。阿彌陀佛本願如是。若人念我稱名自
043a11 ‖ 歸。即入必定得阿耨多羅三藐三菩提。是
043a12 ‖ 故常應憶念以偈稱讚。
043a13 ‖ 　　無量光明慧　　身如真金山
043a14 ‖ 　　我今身口意　　合掌稽首禮
043a15 ‖ 　　金色妙光明　　普流諸世界
043a16 ‖ 　　隨物[3]增其色　　是故稽首禮
043a17 ‖ 　　若人命終時　　得生彼國者
043a18 ‖ 　　即具無量德　　是故我歸命
043a19 ‖ 　　人能念是佛　　無量力[4]威德
043a20 ‖ 　　即時入必定　　是故我常念
043a21 ‖ 　　彼國人命終　　設應受諸苦
043a22 ‖ 　　不墮惡地獄　　是故歸命禮
043a23 ‖ 　　若人生彼國　　終不墮三趣
043a24 ‖ 　　及與阿修羅　　我今歸命禮
043a25 ‖ 　　人天身相同　　猶如金山頂
043a26 ‖ 　　諸勝所歸處　　是故頭面禮
043a27 ‖ 　　其有生彼國　　具天眼耳通
043a28 ‖ 　　十方普無礙　　稽首聖中尊

简体字

是诸佛世尊现在十方清净世界。皆称名忆念。阿弥陀佛本愿如是。若人念我称名自归。即入必定得阿耨多罗三藐三菩提。是故常应忆念以偈称赞。
　　无量光明慧　　身如真金山
　　我今身口意　　合掌稽首礼
　　金色妙光明　　普流诸世界
　　随物增其色　　是故稽首礼
　　若人命终时　　得生彼国者
　　即具无量德　　是故我归命
　　人能念是佛　　无量力威德
　　即时入必定　　是故我常念
　　彼国人命终　　设应受诸苦
　　不墮恶地狱　　是故归命礼
　　若人生彼国　　终不墮三趣
　　及与阿修罗　　我今归命礼
　　人天身相同　　犹如金山顶
　　诸胜所归处　　是故头面礼
　　其有生彼国　　具天眼耳通
　　十方普无碍　　稽首圣中尊

Chapter 9 — On the Easy Practice

These buddhas, *bhagavats*, abide now in pure worlds throughout the ten directions. One should invoke the names of all of them and bear them in mind.

    a. Amitābha's Original Vows and a Praise Verse

The original vows of Amitābha are of this sort: "If any person bears me in mind, invokes my name, and takes refuge in me, he will immediately enter the stage of certainty with respect to attaining *anuttarasamyaksaṃbodhi*."

One should therefore always remain mindful of him. I set forth his praises here with a verse:

He possesses boundless illumination and wisdom
and his body is like a mountain of gold.
Paying homage to him with body, speech, and mind, I now
place my palms together and bow down in reverence to him.

His marvelous golden-colored light
everywhere streams into all worlds,
increasing in its brilliance in response to each being.
I therefore bow down in reverence to him.

If, when life's end comes, a person
succeeds in being reborn in that land,
he immediately acquires countless meritorious qualities.
I do therefore take refuge in him.

Whoever is able to bear in mind this buddha
possessed of measureless powers and awe-inspiring qualities
will immediately enter the stage of certainty.
I do therefore always bear him in mind.

That land is such that if, at the end of one's life,
one should otherwise undergo all manner of suffering,
even so, one will not then fall into those terrible hells.
Therefore, taking refuge in him, I now bow down in reverence.

If a person gains rebirth in his land,
he will never again fall into the three wretched destinies
or into the realms of the *asuras*.
Taking refuge in him, I now bow down in reverence.

Though his body is similar to that of humans and devas,
it resembles the summit of a mountain of gold.
This is the place to which all supreme [qualities] return.
I therefore bow down in reverence to him.

Those who have been reborn in his land
gain the powers of the heavenly eye and ear
that reach unimpededly throughout the ten directions.
I bow down in reverence to the one honored among the Āryas.

正體字	043a29 ‖ 其國諸眾生 神變及心通
	043b01 ‖ 亦具宿命智 是故歸命禮
	043b02 ‖ 生彼國土者 無我無我所
	043b03 ‖ 不生彼此心 是故稽首禮
	043b04 ‖ 超出三界獄 目如蓮華葉
	043b05 ‖ 聲聞眾無量 是故稽首禮
	043b06 ‖ 彼國諸眾生 其性皆柔和
	043b07 ‖ 自然行十善 稽首眾聖[5]王
	043b08 ‖ 從善生淨明 無量無邊數
	043b09 ‖ 二足中第一 是故我歸命
	043b10 ‖ 若人願作佛 心念阿彌陀
	043b11 ‖ 應時為現身 是故我歸命
	043b12 ‖ 彼佛本願力 十方諸菩薩
	043b13 ‖ 來供養聽法 是故我稽首
	043b14 ‖ 彼土諸菩薩 具足諸相好
	043b15 ‖ 以自莊嚴身 我今歸命禮
	043b16 ‖ 彼諸大菩薩 日日於三時
	043b17 ‖ 供養十方佛 是故稽首禮
	043b18 ‖ 若人種善根 疑則華不開
	043b19 ‖ 信心清淨者 華開則見佛
简体字	其国诸众生 神变及心通
	亦具宿命智 是故归命礼
	生彼国土者 无我无我所
	不生彼此心 是故稽首礼
	超出三界狱 目如莲华叶
	声闻众无量 是故稽首礼
	彼国诸众生 其性皆柔和
	自然行十善 稽首众圣王
	从善生净明 无量无边数
	二足中第一 是故我归命
	若人愿作佛 心念阿弥陀
	应时为现身 是故我归命
	彼佛本愿力 十方诸菩萨
	来供养听法 是故我稽首
	彼土诸菩萨 具足诸相好
	以自庄严身 我今归命礼
	彼诸大菩萨 日日于三时
	供养十方佛 是故稽首礼
	若人种善根 疑则华不开
	信心清净者 华开则见佛

All the beings in his land
perform supernatural transformations, know others' thoughts,
and are endowed with the knowledge of past lives as well.
Therefore, taking refuge in him, I bow down in reverence.

Those who are reborn in his land
have no conception of either "I" or "mine."
They do not have thoughts conceiving of "others" or "self."
I therefore bow down in reverence to him.

He has stepped beyond the prison of the three realms.
His eyes are like the petals of a lotus.
The assembly of *śrāvaka* disciples there is measurelessly vast.
I therefore bow down in reverence to him.

All the beings in his land
are in nature gentle and harmonious
and they naturally practice the ten good deeds.
I bow down in reverence to this king of the many *āryas*.

It is from such goodness that his pure light is produced
that, in the number of its rays, is measureless and boundless.
He is foremost among those who stand on two feet.
I do therefore take refuge in him.

If a person vows to become a buddha
and then bears in mind Amitābha,
when the time is right, he will appear for his sake.
I do therefore take refuge in him.

Through the power of that buddha's vows
the bodhisattvas of the ten directions
come to make offerings and listen to the Dharma.
I therefore bow down in reverence to him.

All the bodhisattvas in his land
are endowed with all the major marks and secondary characteristics
by which they thereby adorn their own bodies.
Taking refuge in him, I now bow down in reverence.

Three times every day,
all those great bodhisattvas
make offerings to the buddhas of the ten directions.
I therefore bow down in reverence.

If a person who has planted roots of goodness
retains doubts, then the flower will not open.
If one's mind of faith is pure,
the flower will open and one will then see the Buddha.

正體字	043b20 ‖	十方現在佛	以種種因緣
	043b21 ‖	歎彼佛功德	我今歸命禮
	043b22 ‖	其土[6]甚嚴飾	殊彼[7]諸天宮
	043b23 ‖	功德甚深厚	是故禮佛足
	043b24 ‖	佛足千輻輪	柔軟蓮華色
	043b25 ‖	見者皆歡喜	頭面禮佛足
	043b26 ‖	眉間白毫光	猶如清淨月
	043b27 ‖	增益面光色	頭面禮佛足
	043b28 ‖	本求佛道時	行諸奇妙事
	043b29 ‖	如諸經所說	頭面稽首禮
	043c01 ‖	彼佛所言說	破除諸罪根
	043c02 ‖	美言多所益	我今稽首禮
	043c03 ‖	以此美言說	救諸著樂病
	043c04 ‖	已度今猶度	是故稽首禮
	043c05 ‖	人天中最尊	諸天頭面禮
	043c06 ‖	七寶冠摩[8]足	是故我歸命
	043c07 ‖	一切賢聖眾	及諸人天眾
	043c08 ‖	咸皆共歸命	是故我亦禮
	043c09 ‖	乘彼八道船	能度難度海
	043c10 ‖	自度亦度彼	我禮自在者
简体字		十方现在佛	以种种因缘
		叹彼佛功德	我今归命礼
		其土甚严饰	殊彼诸天宫
		功德甚深厚	是故礼佛足
		佛足千辐轮	柔软莲华色
		见者皆欢喜	头面礼佛足
		眉间白毫光	犹如清净月
		增益面光色	头面礼佛足
		本求佛道时	行诸奇妙事
		如诸经所说	头面稽首礼
		彼佛所言说	破除诸罪根
		美言多所益	我今稽首礼
		以此美言说	救诸着乐病
		已度今犹度	是故稽首礼
		人天中最尊	诸天头面礼
		七宝冠摩足	是故我归命
		一切贤圣众	及诸人天众
		咸皆共归命	是故我亦礼
		乘彼八道船	能度难度海
		自度亦度彼	我礼自在者

Chapter 9 — On the Easy Practice

For many different reasons,
the buddhas of the present throughout the ten directions
praise the qualities of that buddha.
Taking refuge in him, I now bow down in reverence.

His land is especially majestic in its adornment,
surpassing in its excellence the palaces of all the devas.
Its qualities are especially profound and abundant.
I therefore bow down in reverence at the feet of the Buddha.

The Buddha's feet carry the sign of the thousand-spoked wheel.
They are soft and, in appearance, resemble the blossoms of a lotus.
Those who see them are all filled with delight
and bow down their heads in reverence at the feet of the Buddha.

The light from the white hair tuft between his brows
appears like a pristinely shining moon,
enhancing the radiance displayed by his countenance.
I bow down in reverence at the feet of the Buddha.

When he originally sought out the path to buddhahood,
he performed all manner of distinctive and marvelous works.
These are just as described in the sutras.
I bow down in reverence to him.

That which is proclaimed by that buddha
eliminates the roots of karmic offenses.
His eloquent discourse brings benefit to many.
I now bow down in reverence to him.

By resorting to such eloquent discourse,
he rescues beings from all maladies arising by clinging to pleasures.
He has already liberated such beings and now liberates yet more.
I therefore bow down in reverence to him.

The devas bow down in reverence
to he who is the most honored of all humans and devas.
Their seven-jeweled crowns are brought low and touch his feet.
I do therefore take refuge in him.

The Sangha of all the Worthies and the Āryas
as well as the multitudes of humans and devas
all join in taking refuge in him.
Therefore I too bow down in reverence to him.

One who boards his ship of the eightfold path,
will be able to cross beyond that sea so difficult to cross,
delivering himself to liberation while liberating others as well.
I bow in reverence to he who has achieved sovereign mastery in this.

正體字		
043c11 ‖	諸佛無量劫	讚揚其功德
043c12 ‖	猶尚不能盡	歸命清淨人
043c13 ‖	我今亦如是	稱讚無量德
043c14 ‖	以是福因緣	願佛常念我
043c15 ‖	我於今先世	福德若大小
043c16 ‖	願我於佛所	心常得清淨
043c17 ‖	以此福因緣	所獲上妙德
043c18 ‖	願諸眾生類	皆亦悉當得

043c19 ‖ 又亦應念毘婆尸佛。尸棄佛。毘首婆[9]伏佛。
043c20 ‖ 拘樓珊提佛。迦那迦牟尼佛。迦葉佛。釋迦牟
043c21 ‖ 尼佛。及未來世彌勒佛。皆應憶念禮拜以 043c22 ‖ 偈稱讚。

043c23 ‖	毘婆尸世尊	無憂道樹下
043c24 ‖	成就一切智	微妙諸功德
043c25 ‖	正觀於世間	其心得解脫
043c26 ‖	我今以五體	歸命無上尊
043c27 ‖	尸棄佛世尊	在於邠[10]他利
043c28 ‖	道場樹下坐	成就於菩提
043c29 ‖	身色無有比	如然紫金山
044a01 ‖	我今自歸命	三界無上尊
044a02 ‖	毘首婆世尊	坐娑羅樹下
044a03 ‖	自然得通達	一切妙智慧

简体字

诸佛无量劫　　赞扬其功德
犹尚不能尽　　归命清净人
我今亦如是　　称赞无量德
以是福因缘　　愿佛常念我
我于今先世　　福德若大小
愿我于佛所　　心常得清净
以此福因缘　　所获上妙德
愿诸众生类　　皆亦悉当得

又亦应念毗婆尸佛。尸弃佛。毗首婆伏佛。拘楼珊提佛。迦那迦牟尼佛。迦葉佛。释迦牟尼佛。及未来世弥勒佛。皆应忆念礼拜以偈称赞。

毗婆尸世尊　　无忧道树下
成就一切智　　微妙诸功德
正观于世间　　其心得解脱
我今以五体　　归命无上尊
尸弃佛世尊　　在于邠他利
道场树下坐　　成就于菩提
身色无有比　　如然紫金山
我今自归命　　三界无上尊
毗首婆世尊　　坐娑罗树下
自然得通达　　一切妙智慧

Chapter 9 — On the Easy Practice

If, for countless kalpas, the Buddhas
proclaimed their praises of his meritorious qualities,
they would still be unable to come to the end of them.
I take refuge in he who has become such a purified person.

In this same manner, I now proclaim
the praises of his boundless qualities.
I pray that, due to the causes and conditions of this merit,
the Buddha may therefore always bear me in mind.

By whatever merit I have created in the present or previous lives,
whether it be but little or much,
I pray that my mind will become forever purified
in the very presence of the Buddha.

As for the supremely marvelous qualities that may be acquired
through the causes and conditions of such merit as this,
I pray that all of the many varieties of beings
shall all become able to acquire them as well.

4. ALSO, THE SEVEN BUDDHAS OF THE PAST AS WELL AS MAITREYA

One should also bear in mind Vipaśyin Buddha, Śikhin Buddha, Viśvabhū Buddha, Krakucchanda Buddha, Kanakamuni Buddha, Kāśyapa Buddha, and Śākyamuni Buddha, as well as Maitreya, the future Buddha. One should bear them all in mind and bow down in reverence to them. I set forth their praises here in verse:

The Bhagavat Vipaśyin
abides beneath an *aśoka* bodhi tree,[148]
having perfected all-knowledge
and all of the subtle and marvelous meritorious qualities.

Having rightly contemplated the world,
his mind has succeeded in gaining liberation.
I now, with all five extremities, bow down in reverence,
taking refuge in that unsurpassable Honored One.

The Bhagavat, Śikhin Buddha,
sat in the *bodhimaṇḍa*
beneath a *puṇḍarīka* bodhi tree
where he then achieved the complete realization of bodhi.[149]

His physical appearance is incomparable.
It resembles a mountain of flaming purple gold.
I now take refuge in the Honored One
who is unsurpassed by anyone in the three realms of existence.

Viśvabhū Bhagavat
sits beneath the *śāla* tree
where he naturally acquired the penetrating comprehension
of all forms of sublime wisdom.

044a04 ‖	於諸人天中	第一無有[1]比
044a05 ‖	是故我歸命	一切最勝尊
044a06 ‖	迦求村大佛	得阿耨多羅
044a07 ‖	三藐三菩提	尸利沙樹下
044a08 ‖	成就大智慧	永脫於生死
044a09 ‖	我今歸命禮	第一無比尊
044a10 ‖	迦那含牟尼	大聖無上尊
044a11 ‖	優曇鉢樹下	成就得佛道
044a12 ‖	通達一切法	無量無有邊
044a13 ‖	是故我歸命	第一無上尊
044a14 ‖	迦葉佛世尊	眼如雙蓮華
044a15 ‖	[2]弱拘樓陀樹	於下成佛道
044a16 ‖	三界無所畏	行步如象王
044a17 ‖	我今自歸命	稽首無極尊
044a18 ‖	釋迦牟尼佛	阿輸陀樹下
044a19 ‖	降伏魔怨敵	成就無上道
044a20 ‖	面貌如滿月	清淨無瑕塵
044a21 ‖	我今稽首禮	勇猛第一尊
044a22 ‖	當來彌勒佛	那伽樹下坐
044a23 ‖	成就[3]廣大心	自然得佛道

正體字

于诸人天中	第一无有比
是故我归命	一切最胜尊
迦求村大佛	得阿耨多罗
三藐三菩提	尸利沙树下
成就大智慧	永脱于生死
我今归命礼	第一无比尊
迦那含牟尼	大圣无上尊
优昙钵树下	成就得佛道
通达一切法	无量无有边
是故我归命	第一无上尊
迦葉佛世尊	眼如双莲华
弱拘楼陀树	于下成佛道
三界无所畏	行步如象王
我今自归命	稽首无极尊
释迦牟尼佛	阿输陀树下
降伏魔怨敌	成就无上道
面貌如满月	清净无瑕尘
我今稽首礼	勇猛第一尊
当来弥勒佛	那伽树下坐
成就广大心	自然得佛道

简体字

Chapter 9 — On the Easy Practice

Among all humans and devas,
he is the foremost and without peer.
I do therefore take refuge in the Honored One
who is the most supreme among them all.

Krakucchanda Buddha
succeeded in attaining
anuttarasamyaksaṃbodhi
beneath the *śirīṣa* tree.[150]

He perfected the great wisdom,
and became forever liberated from *saṃsāra*.
I now take refuge and bow in reverence
to that supreme and incomparable Honored One.

Kanakamuni,
the great Ārya and unsurpassable Honored One,
attained the perfect realization of buddhahood
beneath the *udumbara* tree

and reached the penetrating comprehension
of all the measurelessly and boundlessly many dharmas.
I do therefore take refuge in him,
that foremost and unsurpassable Honored One.

Kāśyapa Buddha, the Bhagavat,
with eyes like a pair of lotus blossoms,
achieved the perfect realization of buddhahood
beneath the *nyagrodha* tree.

Throughout the three realms, there is nothing he fears.
His gait is like that of the king of the elephants.
I now take refuge in him, bowing down in reverence
to that insuperable Honored One.

Śākyamuni Buddha,
beneath the *aśvattha* tree,[151]
conquered Māra, the enemy,
and perfected the unsurpassed enlightenment.

His countenance is like the full moon,
pure and free of any blemish.
I now bow down in reverence
To that heroically brave and supreme Honored One.

Maitreya, the buddha of the future,
sitting beneath the *nāga* tree,
shall attain the perfect realization of the vast resolve
and then naturally realize buddhahood.

正體字

```
044a24 ||    功德甚堅牢    莫能有勝者
044a25 ||    是故我自歸    無比妙法王
044a26 || 復有德勝佛。普明佛。勝敵佛。王相佛。相王
044a27 || 佛。無量功德明自在王佛。藥王無[4]閡佛。寶
044a28 || 遊行佛。寶華佛。安住佛。山王佛。亦應憶念
044a29 || 恭敬禮拜以偈稱讚。
044b01 ||    無勝世界中    有佛號德勝
044b02 ||    我今稽首禮    及法寶僧寶
044b03 ||    隨意喜世界    有佛號普明
044b04 ||    我今自歸命    及法寶僧寶
044b05 ||    普賢世界中    有佛號勝敵
044b06 ||    我今歸命禮    及法寶僧寶
044b07 ||    善淨集世界    佛號王幢相
044b08 ||    我今稽首禮    及法寶僧寶
044b09 ||    離垢集世界    無量功德明
044b10 ||    自在於十方    是故稽首禮
044b11 ||    不誑世界中    無礙藥王佛
044b12 ||    我今頭面禮    及法寶僧寶
044b13 || [5]今集世界中    佛號寶遊行
044b14 ||    我今頭面禮    及法寶僧寶
```

简体字

功德甚坚牢　　莫能有胜者
是故我自归　　无比妙法王
复有德胜佛。普明佛。胜敌佛。王相佛。相王佛。无量功德明自在王佛。药王无阂佛。宝游行佛。宝华佛。安住佛。山王佛。亦应忆念恭敬礼拜以偈称赞。
　　无胜世界中　　有佛号德胜
　　我今稽首礼　　及法宝僧宝
　　随意喜世界　　有佛号普明
　　我今自归命　　及法宝僧宝
　　普贤世界中　　有佛号胜敌
　　我今归命礼　　及法宝僧宝
　　善净集世界　　佛号王幢相
　　我今稽首礼　　及法宝僧宝
　　离垢集世界　　无量功德明
　　自在于十方　　是故稽首礼
　　不诳世界中　　无碍药王佛
　　我今头面礼　　及法宝僧宝
　　今集世界中　　佛号宝游行
　　我今头面礼　　及法宝僧宝

His meritorious qualities are so extremely solid and durable
that no one is able to surpass them.
I do therefore take refuge in him,
that incomparable king of the sublime Dharma.

5. ALSO, BY CALLING ON TEN OTHER BUDDHAS

Additionally, there are: Supreme in Meritorious Qualities Buddha, Universal Illumination Buddha, Victorious over Adversaries Buddha, Marks of the Sovereign[152] Buddha, King of the Marks Buddha,[153] King of Measureless Qualities' Brilliance and Sovereign Mastery Buddha, Unimpeded Medicine King Buddha, Jeweled Traveler Buddha, Precious Flower Buddha, Peacefully Abiding Buddha,[154] and Mountain King Buddha. One should remain mindful of them as well, respectfully bowing in reverence to them. I set forth their praises here in verse:

In the world known as Invincible,
there is a buddha named Supreme in Meritorious Qualities.
I now bow down in reverence to him
as well as to his Dharma Jewel and his Sangha Jewel.

In a world known as Joy in Whatever One Wishes,
there is a buddha named Universal Illumination.
I now take refuge in him
as well as in his Dharma Jewel and his Sangha Jewel.

In the world known as Universal Excellence,
there is a buddha named Victorious over Adversaries.
I now take refuge in him and bow down in reverence to him
as well as to his Dharma Jewel and his Sangha Jewel.

In the world known as Accumulation of Goodness and Purity,
there is a buddha named Marks of the Sovereign's Banner.
I now bow down in reverence to him
as well as to his Dharma Jewel and his Sangha Jewel.

In the world known as Accumulation of Stainlessness,
there is a buddha named Measureless Qualities' Brilliance
whose sovereign mastery extends throughout the ten directions.
I therefore bow down in reverence to him.

In the world known as Undeceptive,
there is a buddha named Unimpeded Medicine King.
I now bow down in reverence to him
as well as to his Dharma Jewel and his Sangha Jewel.

In the world known as Present Accumulation,
there is a buddha named Jeweled Traveler.
I now bow down in reverence to him
as well as to his Dharma Jewel and his Sangha Jewel.

正體字

044b15 ‖	美音界寶花　　安立山王佛
044b16 ‖	我今頭面禮　　及法寶僧寶
044b17 ‖	今是諸如來　　住在東方界
044b18 ‖	我以恭敬心　　稱揚歸命禮
044b19 ‖	唯願諸如來　　深加以慈愍
044b20 ‖	現身在我前　　皆令[6]目得見
044b21 ‖	復次過去未來現在諸佛。盡應總[7]念恭敬禮
044b22 ‖	拜以偈稱讚。
044b23 ‖	過去世諸佛　　降伏眾魔怨
044b24 ‖	以大智慧力　　廣利於眾生
044b25 ‖	彼時諸眾生　　盡心皆供養
044b26 ‖	恭敬而稱揚　　是故頭面禮
044b27 ‖	現在十方界　　不可計諸佛
044b28 ‖	其數過恒沙　　無量無有邊
044b29 ‖	慈愍諸眾生　　常轉妙法輪
044c01 ‖	是故我恭敬　　歸命稽首禮
044c02 ‖	未來世諸佛　　身色如金山
044c03 ‖	光明無有量　　眾相自莊嚴
044c04 ‖	出世度眾生　　當入於涅槃
044c05 ‖	如是諸世尊　　我今頭面禮

简体字

美音界宝花　　安立山王佛
我今头面礼　　及法宝僧宝
今是诸如来　　住在东方界
我以恭敬心　　称扬归命礼
唯愿诸如来　　深加以慈愍
现身在我前　　皆令目得见
复次过去未来现在诸佛。尽应总念恭敬礼拜以偈称赞。
过去世诸佛　　降伏众魔怨
以大智慧力　　广利于众生
彼时诸众生　　尽心皆供养
恭敬而称扬　　是故头面礼
现在十方界　　不可计诸佛
其数过恒沙　　无量无有边
慈愍诸众生　　常转妙法轮
是故我恭敬　　归命稽首礼
未来世诸佛　　身色如金山
光明无有量　　众相自庄严
出世度众生　　当入于涅槃
如是诸世尊　　我今头面礼

In the Beautiful Sound World, there is Precious Flower Buddha.
[So too,] Peacefully Established and Mountain King Buddhas.
I now bow down in reverence to them
as well as to the Dharma Jewel and the Sangha Jewel.

All of these *tathāgatas* now abide
off in the regions to the East.
With a respectful mind, I spread their praises and,
taking refuge in them, bow down in reverence to them.

I only pray that the Tathāgatas
will bestow their deep kindness and sympathy
and thus manifest their bodies before me
so that I might be allowed to personally[155] see them all.

6. ALSO, BY CALLING ON ALL BUDDHAS OF THE THREE TIMES

Additionally, one should exhaustively and comprehensively bear in mind and respectfully bow in reverence to all buddhas of the past, the future, and the present. I set forth their praises here in verse:

All buddhas of the past
conquered the many *māras*, their adversaries
and, using the power of great wisdom,
provided vast benefit to beings.

The beings who existed in those eras
were entirely devoted to making offerings to them all,
showed them reverence, and proclaimed their praises.
I therefore bow down in reverence to them.

The incalculably many buddhas of the present
throughout the worlds of the ten directions
are so measurelessly and boundlessly many
as to surpass the number of sands in the Ganges River.

Out of kindness and pity for beings,
they always turn the wheel of the sublime Dharma.
I do therefore accord them respect,
take refuge in them, and bow down my head to them in reverence.

The buddhas of the future
shall appear with bodies resembling mountains of gold
that emanate measureless illumination
and display the self-adornment of their many characteristic signs.

They shall appear in the world and liberate beings,
after which they shall then enter nirvāṇa.
To all such *bhagavats* as these,
I do now bow down in reverence.

正體字	044c06 ‖ 復應憶念諸大菩薩。善意菩薩。善眼菩薩。聞 044c07 ‖ 月菩薩。尸毘王菩薩。一切勝菩薩。知大地菩 044c08 ‖ 薩。大藥菩薩。鳩舍菩薩。阿離念彌菩薩。頂生 044c09 ‖ 王菩薩。喜見菩薩。欝多羅菩薩。[8]薩和檀菩薩。 044c10 ‖ 長壽王菩薩。羼提菩薩。韋藍菩薩。睒菩薩。月 044c11 ‖ 蓋菩薩。明首菩薩。法首菩薩。[9]成利菩薩。彌 044c12 ‖ 勒菩薩。復有金剛藏菩薩。金剛首菩薩。無垢 044c13 ‖ 藏菩薩。無垢稱菩薩。除疑菩薩。無垢德菩薩。 044c14 ‖ 網明菩薩。無量明菩薩。大明菩薩。無盡意菩 044c15 ‖ 薩。意王菩薩。無邊意菩薩。日音菩薩。月音菩 044c16 ‖ 薩。美音菩薩。美音聲菩薩。大音聲菩薩。堅精 044c17 ‖ 進菩薩。常堅菩薩。堅發菩薩。[10]莊嚴王菩薩。 044c18 ‖ 常悲菩薩。常不輕菩薩。法上菩薩。法意菩薩。 044c19 ‖ 法喜菩薩。法首菩薩。法積菩薩。發精進菩薩。 044c20 ‖ 智慧菩薩。淨威德菩薩。那羅延菩薩。善思惟 044c21 ‖ 菩薩。法思惟菩薩。跋陀婆羅菩薩。法益菩薩。 044c22 ‖ 高德菩薩。師子遊行菩薩。喜根菩薩。上寶月 044c23 ‖ 菩薩。不虛德菩薩。龍德菩薩。文殊師利菩薩。 044c24 ‖ 妙音菩薩。雲音菩薩。勝意菩薩。照明菩薩。勇 044c25 ‖ 眾菩薩。勝眾菩薩。威儀菩薩。師子意菩薩。上 044c26 ‖ 意菩薩。益意菩薩。增[11]意菩薩。寶明菩薩。慧 044c27 ‖ 頂菩薩。樂說頂菩薩。有德菩薩。觀世自在王 044c28 ‖ 菩薩。陀羅尼自在王菩薩。
简体字	复应忆念诸大菩萨。善意菩萨。善眼菩萨。闻月菩萨。尸毗王菩萨。一切胜菩萨。知大地菩萨。大药菩萨。鸠舍菩萨。阿离念弥菩萨。顶生王菩萨。喜见菩萨。郁多罗菩萨。萨和檀菩萨。长寿王菩萨。羼提菩萨。韦蓝菩萨。睒菩萨。月盖菩萨。明首菩萨。法首菩萨。成利菩萨。弥勒菩萨。复有金刚藏菩萨。金刚首菩萨。无垢藏菩萨。无垢称菩萨。除疑菩萨。无垢德菩萨。网明菩萨。无量明菩萨。大明菩萨。无尽意菩萨。意王菩萨。无边意菩萨。日音菩萨。月音菩萨。美音菩萨。美音声菩萨。大音声菩萨。坚精进菩萨。常坚菩萨。坚发菩萨。庄严王菩萨。常悲菩萨。常不轻菩萨。法上菩萨。法意菩萨。法喜菩萨。法首菩萨。法积菩萨。发精进菩萨。智慧菩萨。净威德菩萨。那罗延菩萨。善思惟菩萨。法思惟菩萨。跋陀婆罗菩萨。法益菩萨。高德菩萨。师子游行菩萨。喜根菩萨。上宝月菩萨。不虚德菩萨。龙德菩萨。文殊师利菩萨。妙音菩萨。云音菩萨。胜意菩萨。照明菩萨。勇众菩萨。胜众菩萨。威仪菩萨。师子意菩萨。上意菩萨。益意菩萨。增意菩萨。宝明菩萨。慧顶菩萨。乐说顶菩萨。有德菩萨。观世自在王菩萨。陀罗尼自在王菩萨。

Chapter 9 — On the Easy Practice

7. ALSO, BY CALLING ON THE GREAT BODHISATTVAS

Additionally, one should bear in mind the great bodhisattvas, namely: Good Intentions Bodhisattva, Good Eyes Bodhisattva, Moon Hearer Bodhisattva, King Śibi Bodhisattva, Universally Supreme Bodhisattva, Knower of the Great Earth Bodhisattva, Great Medicine Bodhisattva, Kapotagṛha Bodhisattva, Arenemin Bodhisattva, Summit Born King Bodhisattva, Delightful View Bodhisattva, Uttara Bodhisattva, Sarvadāna Bodhisattva, Long Life King Bodhisattva, Kṣānti Bodhisattva, Velāma Bodhisattva, Flashing Light Bodhisattva, Moon Covering Bodhisattva, Brilliant Leader Bodhisattva, Dharma Leader Bodhisattva, Perfecting Benefit Bodhisattva, and Maitreya Bodhisattva.

In addition, there are: Vajragarbha Bodhisattva, Vajra Leader Bodhisattva, Treasury of Non-defilement Bodhisattva, Vimalakīrti Bodhisattva, Dispeller of Doubts Bodhisattva, Undefiled Virtue Bodhisattva, Net-like Brilliance Bodhisattva, Immeasurable Brilliance Bodhisattva, Great Brilliance Bodhisattva, Akṣayamati Bodhisattva, Mind King Bodhisattva, Boundless Mind Bodhisattva, Sun Sound Bodhisattva, Moon Sound Bodhisattva, Beautiful Sound Bodhisattva, Beautiful Voice Bodhisattva, Great Voice Bodhisattva, Solid Vigor Bodhisattva, Ever Solid Bodhisattva, and Solidly Generated Bodhisattva.

There are also: Adornment King Bodhisattva, Ever Compassionate Bodhisattva, Never slighting Bodhisattva, Dharma Superior Bodhisattva, Dharma Mind Bodhisattva, Dharma Joy Bodhisattva, Dharma Leader Bodhisattva, Dharma Accumulation Bodhisattva, Generator of Vigor Bodhisattva, Wisdom Bodhisattva, Pure Awesome Virtue Bodhisattva, Nārāyaṇa Bodhisattva, Good Meditation Bodhisattva, Dharma Meditation Bodhisattva, Bhadrapāla Bodhisattva, Dharma Benefit Bodhisattva, Lofty Virtue Bodhisattva, Lion Traveler Bodhisattva, Joyous Faculties Bodhisattva, and Supreme Jewel Moon Bodhisattva.

There are also: Virtue Free of Falseness Bodhisattva, Dragon Virtue Bodhisattva, Mañjuśrī Bodhisattva, Wonderful Sound Bodhisattva, Cloud Sound Bodhisattva, Supreme Mind Bodhisattva, Illuminating Brilliance Bodhisattva, Brave Assembly Bodhisattva, Supreme Assembly Bodhisattva, Awesome Deportment Bodhisattva, Lion Mind Bodhisattva, Superior Mind Bodhisattva, Beneficial Intentions Bodhisattva, Augmented Mind Bodhisattva, Precious Brilliance Bodhisattva, Wisdom Summit Bodhisattva, Peak of Eloquence Bodhisattva, Possessed of Virtue Bodhisattva, Avalokiteśvara King Bodhisattva, and Dhāraṇī Mastery King Bodhisattva.

<table>
<tr><td rowspan="17">正體字</td><td></td><td>大自在王菩薩。無</td></tr>
<tr><td>044c29 ||</td><td>憂德菩薩。不虛見菩薩。離惡道菩薩。一切勇健</td></tr>
<tr><td>045a01 ||</td><td>菩薩。破闇菩薩。功德寶菩薩。花威德菩薩。金</td></tr>
<tr><td>045a02 ||</td><td>瓔珞明德菩薩。離諸陰蓋菩薩。心無閡菩薩。</td></tr>
<tr><td>045a03 ||</td><td>一切行淨菩薩。等見菩薩。不等見菩薩。三昧</td></tr>
<tr><td>045a04 ||</td><td>遊戲菩薩。法自在菩薩。法相菩薩。明莊嚴菩</td></tr>
<tr><td>045a05 ||</td><td>薩。大莊嚴菩薩。寶頂菩薩。寶印手菩薩。常舉</td></tr>
<tr><td>045a06 ||</td><td>手菩薩。常下手菩薩。常慘菩薩。常喜菩薩。喜</td></tr>
<tr><td>045a07 ||</td><td>王菩薩。得辯才音聲菩薩。虛空雷音菩薩。持</td></tr>
<tr><td>045a08 ||</td><td>寶炬菩薩。勇施菩薩。帝網菩薩。馬光菩薩。空</td></tr>
<tr><td>045a09 ||</td><td>無閡菩薩。寶勝菩薩。天王菩薩。破魔菩薩。電</td></tr>
<tr><td>045a10 ||</td><td>德菩薩。自在菩薩。頂相菩薩。出過菩薩。師子</td></tr>
<tr><td>045a11 ||</td><td>吼菩薩。雲蔭菩薩。能勝菩薩。山相[1]幢王菩</td></tr>
<tr><td>045a12 ||</td><td>薩。香象菩薩。大香象菩薩。白香象菩薩。常精</td></tr>
<tr><td>045a13 ||</td><td>進菩薩。不休息菩薩。妙生菩薩。華莊嚴菩薩。</td></tr>
<tr><td>045a14 ||</td><td>觀世音菩薩。得大勢菩薩。水王菩薩。山王菩</td></tr>
<tr><td>045a15 ||</td><td>薩。帝網菩薩。寶施菩薩。破魔菩薩。莊嚴國土</td></tr>
<tr><td>045a16 ||</td><td>菩薩。金髻菩薩。珠髻菩薩。如是等諸大菩</td></tr>
<tr><td>045a17 ||</td><td>薩。皆應憶念恭敬禮拜求阿惟越致[2]地。[3]</td></tr>
</table>

<table>
<tr><td>简体字</td><td>大自在王菩萨。无忧德菩萨。不虚见菩萨。离恶道菩萨。一切勇健菩萨。破闇菩萨。功德宝菩萨。花威德菩萨。金璎珞明德菩萨。离诸阴盖菩萨。心无阂菩萨。一切行净菩萨。等见菩萨。不等见菩萨。三昧游戏菩萨。法自在菩萨。法相菩萨。明庄严菩萨。大庄严菩萨。宝顶菩萨。宝印手菩萨。常举手菩萨。常下手菩萨。常惨菩萨。常喜菩萨。喜王菩萨。得辩才音声菩萨。虚空雷音菩萨。持宝炬菩萨。勇施菩萨。帝网菩萨。马光菩萨。空无阂菩萨。宝胜菩萨。天王菩萨。破魔菩萨。电德菩萨。自在菩萨。顶相菩萨。出过菩萨。师子吼菩萨。云荫菩萨。能胜菩萨。山相幢王菩萨。香象菩萨。大香象菩萨。白香象菩萨。常精进菩萨。不休息菩萨。妙生菩萨。华庄严菩萨。观世音菩萨。得大势菩萨。水王菩萨。山王菩萨。帝网菩萨。宝施菩萨。破魔菩萨。庄严国土菩萨。金髻菩萨。珠髻菩萨。如是等诸大菩萨。皆应忆念恭敬礼拜求阿惟越致地。</td></tr>
</table>

There are also: Great Sovereign Mastery King Bodhisattva, Sorrowless Virtue Bodhisattva, Not Seen in Vain Bodhisattva, Beyond the Wretched Destinies Bodhisattva, Universally Brave and Strong Bodhisattva, Dispeller of Darkness Bodhisattva, Merit Jewel Bodhisattva, Floral Awesome Virtue Bodhisattva, Gold Necklace Brilliant Virtue Bodhisattva, Beyond the Aggregates and Hindrances Bodhisattva, Unimpeded Mind Bodhisattva, Pure in All Actions Bodhisattva, Equal Vision Bodhisattva, Unequaled Vision Bodhisattva, Wandering Joyfully in Samādhi Bodhisattva, Sovereign Mastery in Dharma Bodhisattva, Dharma Marks Bodhisattva, Brilliant Adornment Bodhisattva, Great Adornment Bodhisattva, and Jeweled Summit Bodhisattva.

There are also: Jeweled Mudrā Hand Bodhisattva, Ever Raised Hand Bodhisattva, Ever Lowered Hand Bodhisattva, Ever Piteous Bodhisattva, Ever Joyful Bodhisattva, Joy King Bodhisattva, Possessed of Eloquent Voice Bodhisattva, Sound of Thunder in Space Bodhisattva, Upholder of the Jeweled Torch Bodhisattva, Valiant Giving Bodhisattva, Imperial Net Bodhisattva, Horse Light Bodhisattva, Empty and Unimpeded Bodhisattva, Jeweled Supremacy Bodhisattva, Celestial King Bodhisattva, Demon Crusher Bodhisattva, Lightning Virtue Bodhisattva, Sovereign Mastery Bodhisattva, Summit Sign Bodhisattva, and Beyond Transgressions Bodhisattva.

And there are also: Lion's Roar Bodhisattva, Cloud Shade Bodhisattva, Able to Conquer Bodhisattva, Mountainous Marks Banner Bodhisattva, Fragrant Elephant Bodhisattva, Great Fragrant Elephant Bodhisattva, White Fragrant Elephant Bodhisattva, Ever Vigorous Bodhisattva, Never Resting Bodhisattva, Sublime Birth Bodhisattva, Floral Adornment Bodhisattva, Avalokiteśvara Bodhisattva, Mahāsthāmaprāpta Bodhisattva, Water King Bodhisattva, Mountain King Bodhisattva, Indra's Net Bodhisattva, Jewel Giving Bodhisattva, Crusher of Demons Bodhisattva, Adorner of Lands Bodhisattva, Golden Topknot Bodhisattva, and Pearl Topknot Bodhisattva.

One should bear in mind all such bodhisattvas and bow down to them in reverence as one seeks to attain the ground of the *avaivartika*.

The End of Chapter Nine

正體字

045a18 ||　　　[4]除業品第十
045a19 || 問曰。但憶念阿彌陀等諸佛及念餘菩薩
045a20 || 得阿惟越致。更有餘方便耶。答曰。求阿惟
045a21 || 越致地者。非但憶念稱名禮敬而已。復應
045a22 || 於諸佛所懺悔勸請隨喜迴向。問曰。是事何
045a23 || 謂。答曰。
045a24 ||　　十方無量佛　　所知無不盡
045a25 ||　　我今悉於前　　發露諸黑惡
045a26 ||　　三三合九種　　從三煩惱起
045a27 ||　　今身若先身　　是罪盡懺悔
045a28 ||　　於三惡道中　　若應受業報
045a29 ||　　願於今身償　　不入惡道受
045b01 || 十方諸佛者。現在一切諸佛。命根成就未入
045b02 || 涅槃。十方名四方四維上下。

简体字

十住毗婆沙论卷第五
除业品第十

问曰。但忆念阿弥陀等诸佛及念余菩萨得阿惟越致。更有余方便耶。答曰。求阿惟越致地者。非但忆念称名礼敬而已。复应于诸佛所忏悔劝请随喜回向。问曰。是事何谓。答曰。

　　十方无量佛　　所知无不尽
　　我今悉于前　　发露诸黑恶
　　三三合九种　　从三烦恼起
　　今身若先身　　是罪尽忏悔
　　于三恶道中　　若应受业报
　　愿于今身偿　　不入恶道受

十方诸佛者。现在一切诸佛。命根成就未入涅槃。十方名四方四维上下。

CHAPTER 10
Getting Rid of Karma

X. CHAPTER 10: GETTING RID OF BAD KARMA
   A. Q: IS BUDDHA MINDFULNESS ALL ONE MUST DO TO BECOME IRREVERSIBLE?

Question: Is it the case that, in order to become an *avaivartika*, one need only bear in mind Amitābha and those other buddhas while also bearing in mind the others, the bodhisattvas [mentioned above]? Or are there other additional skillful means [that must be used]?

   B. A: ONE SHOULD ALSO REPENT, ENTREAT, REJOICE & DEDICATE MERIT

Response: For one who seeks to become an *avaivartika*, it is not the case that one must only remain mindful of them, utter their names, and make reverential obeisance to them, and that is all there is to it. In addition, one should, in the presence of the buddhas, perform repentances, entreat them, rejoice [in their meritorious deeds], and dedicate one's own merit.

     1. HOW DOES ONE PERFORM THESE ENDEAVORS?

Question: How does one go about carrying out these endeavors?

     2. "REPENTANCE" IS PERFORMED AS FOLLOWS:

Response:

> There is nothing not exhaustively known by
> the countless buddhas of the ten directions,
> Now, in the presence of them all,
> I reveal all of my black and evil deeds.

> Three times three, nine kinds in all,[156]
> all of them have arisen from the three types of afflictions.
> Whether committed in the present body or in prior births,
> I repent of all of these karmic offenses.

> If I should otherwise be bound to undergo karmic retribution
> in the three wretched destinies,
> I pray that [my offenses] may instead be repaid in this very body
> so that I will not enter the wretched destinies to undergo retribution.

"The buddhas of the ten directions" refers to all of the buddhas of the present whose life faculty has become completely perfected but who have still not yet entered nirvāṇa. "Ten directions" refers to the four directions, the four midpoints, the zenith, and the nadir. "Buddhas"

正體字

　　　　佛名所應知
045b03 ‖ 事悉知無餘。發露者。於諸佛所發露一切
045b04 ‖ 罪無所覆藏。後不復作如堤防水。黑惡
045b05 ‖ 者。無智慧明故多犯眾惡若不善法若隱沒
045b06 ‖ 無記。三三種者。身口意生惡現報生報後報。
045b07 ‖ 自作教他作隨喜作。從三種煩惱起三種
045b08 ‖ 煩惱。謂欲界繫色界繫無色界繫。若助貪欲
045b09 ‖ 煩惱。若助瞋恚煩惱。若助愚癡煩惱。若上
045b10 ‖ 煩惱若中煩惱若下煩惱。今身先身盡懺悔
045b11 ‖ 者。今世先世所作眾惡盡悔無餘。地獄者。
045b12 ‖ 八種熱地獄。十種寒冰地獄。畜生者。若地生
045b13 ‖ 若水生若無足若二足若多足。餓鬼者。食唾
045b14 ‖ 食吐[5]食蕩滌汁。食膿血屎尿等。若我[6]行
045b15 ‖ 業應於此三惡道受者。願令是罪此身現
045b16 ‖ 受。若後身受莫於地獄餓鬼畜生中受。
045b17 ‖ 復次佛自說懺悔法。若菩薩欲懺悔罪。應
045b18 ‖ 作是言。

简体字

　　佛名所应知事悉知无余。发露者。于诸佛所发露一切罪无所覆藏。后不复作如堤防水。黑恶者。无智慧明故多犯众恶若不善法若隐没无记。三三种者。身口意生恶现报生报后报。自作教他作随喜作。从三种烦恼起三种烦恼。谓欲界系色界系无色界系。若助贪欲烦恼。若助瞋恚烦恼。若助愚痴烦恼。若上烦恼若中烦恼若下烦恼。今身先身尽忏悔者。今世先世所作众恶尽悔无余。地狱者。八种热地狱。十种寒冰地狱。畜生者。若地生若水生若无足若二足若多足。饿鬼者。食唾食吐食荡涤汁。食脓血屎尿等。若我行业应于此三恶道受者。愿令是罪此身现受。若后身受莫于地狱饿鬼畜生中受。

　　复次佛自说忏悔法。若菩萨欲忏悔罪。应作是言。

Chapter 10 — *Getting Rid of Karma*

refers to those who, with regard to all things that should be known, know them all without exception.

"Reveal" means that, in the presence of all buddhas, one reveals all of one's karmic offenses, leaving none hidden, [while also resolving] to not commit them ever again. [In so doing, one's resolve becomes] like a dike that holds back the waters.

As for "black and evil deeds," because one has not had the bright light of wisdom, one has often committed many types of evil deeds, in some cases practicing unwholesome dharmas, and in some cases involving oneself in obscured morally indeterminate dharmas.[157]

"Three times three, nine kinds in all" refers to creation of evil karma on the part of body, mouth, and mind that brings about negative retribution in the present life, negative retribution in the next rebirth, and negative retribution in subsequent lives. [This retribution may arise through] directly committing the deed oneself, instructing others to commit it, or by rejoicing that others have committed it.

As for "all arisen from three types of afflictions," the "three types of afflictions" refers to [those actions] connected to the desire realm, the form realm, or the formless realm, whether promoting the affliction of desire, the affliction of hatred, or the affliction of delusion, and whether involving a supreme degree of affliction, a middling-degree of affliction, or a lesser-degree of affliction.

As for "whether it be that committed in the present body or in prior births, I repent of all of these karmic offenses," this means that one repents of all of the many kinds of evil deeds committed in this present life and former lives, repenting of them all without exception.

[With regard to "the three wretched destinies,"] there are the hells, namely the eight hot hells and the ten cold-and-ice hells. There are the animals, including those that are earth-born, water-born, legless, two-legged, or many-legged. And there are the hungry ghosts, in particular those who feed upon spittle, vomit, rinsings, pus-and-blood, excrement and urine, and other such things.

[The intent here is to state]: "If my karma is such that I should undergo retribution in these three wretched destinies, I pray that I will instead be allowed to undergo that retribution in this very body. If it is to be undergone in a subsequent rebirth's body, may I not be compelled to undergo it in the hells, among hungry ghosts, or in the animal realm."

Also, the Buddha himself explained the dharma to be used in repentance, indicating that, if a bodhisattva wishes to repent of karmic offenses, he should utter his repentance as follows:

正體字	我於今現在十方世界中諸佛得 045b19 ‖ 阿耨多羅三藐三菩提。轉法輪雨法雨。擊 045b20 ‖ 法鼓吹法[7]蠡建法幢。以法布施滿足眾 045b21 ‖ 生。多所利益多所安隱。憐愍世間饒益 045b22 ‖ 天人。我今以身口意。頭面禮現在諸佛足。 045b23 ‖ 諸佛知者見者世間眼世間燈。我於無始生 045b24 ‖ 死已來所起罪業。為貪欲瞋恚愚癡所逼 045b25 ‖ 故。或不識佛不識法不識僧。或不識罪 045b26 ‖ 福。或身口意多作眾[8]罪。或以惡心出佛身 045b27 ‖ 血。或毀滅正法。[9]破壞眾僧。殺真人阿羅 045b28 ‖ 漢。或自行十不善道。或教他令行。或復隨 045b29 ‖ 喜。若於眾生有不愛語。若以斗[10]秤欺誑 045c01 ‖ 侵人。以諸邪行惱亂眾生。或不孝父母。 045c02 ‖ 或盜塔物及四方僧物。佛所說經戒或有毀 045c03 ‖ 破。違逆和[11]尚阿闍梨。若人發聲聞乘辟 045c04 ‖ 支佛乘。
简体字	我于今现在十方世界中诸佛得阿耨多罗三藐三菩提。转法轮雨法雨。击法鼓吹法蠡建法幢。以法布施满足众生。多所利益多所安隐。怜愍世间饶益天人。我今以身口意。头面礼现在诸佛足。诸佛知者见者世间眼世间灯。我于无始生死已来所起罪业。为贪欲瞋恚愚痴所逼故。或不识佛不识法不识僧。或不识罪福。或身口意多作众罪。或以恶心出佛身血。或毁灭正法。破坏众僧。杀真人阿罗汉。或自行十不善道。或教他令行。或复随喜。若于众生有不爱语。若以斗秤欺诳侵人。以诸邪行恼乱众生。或不孝父母。或盗塔物及四方僧物。佛所说经戒或有毁破。违逆和尚阿闍梨。若人发声闻乘辟支佛乘。

Chapter 10 — *Getting Rid of Karma*

Facing the Buddhas of the present time throughout the worlds of the ten directions, namely those who have realized *anuttarasamyaksaṃbodhi*, turned the Dharma wheel, rained down the Dharma rain, sounded the Dharma drum, blown the Dharma conch, planted the Dharma banner, and who have, through the giving of Dharma, fulfilled the needs of beings, benefited the many, brought peace and security to the many, taken pity on the world, and abundantly benefited devas and humans—I now, with body, mouth, and mind, make full reverential prostrations at the feet of the buddhas of the present, the buddhas who know, who see, who are the eyes of the world, and who are the lamps for the world.

[I hereby reveal] all of the karmic offenses I have created throughout the course of beginningless births and deaths due to being driven along by greed, hatred, and delusion, including:

> Sometimes failing to recognize the Buddhas, failing to recognize the Dharma, or failing to recognize the Sangha;
>
> Sometimes failing to distinguish between offense-generating karma and meritorious karma;
>
> Sometimes abundantly creating the many sorts of karmic offenses through actions of body, speech, and mind;
>
> Sometimes, with evil intentions, drawing the blood of a buddha;
>
> Sometimes contributing to the destruction of right Dharma;
>
> Sometimes bringing about the destruction of the Sangha;
>
> Sometimes murdering arhats;
>
> Sometimes engaging in the ten courses of bad karmic action;
>
> Sometimes instructing others to engage in them;
>
> Sometimes subjecting others to speech that displeases them;
>
> Sometimes cheating and deceiving others with altered weights and measures;
>
> Sometimes afflicting beings with immoral behavior;
>
> Sometimes failing in filial piety toward parents;
>
> Sometimes stealing belongings from stupas;
>
> Sometimes stealing possessions from the Sangha of the four directions;
>
> Sometimes destroying or transgressing against [the teachings of] sutras or moral-precept codes originally set forth by the Buddha;
>
> And sometimes disobeying monastic preceptors or monastic Dharma teachers.[158]
>
> Sometimes, when people have set their resolve on realization of the Śrāvaka Disciple Vehicle or the Pratyekabuddha Vehicle,

正體字

```
            發大乘者。惡言毀辱輕賤嫌恨慳
045c05 ||   嫉覆心故。於諸[12]佛所或起惡口。或說是
045c06 ||   法非法。說非法是法。今以是罪於現在
045c07 ||   諸佛知者見者證者所。盡皆發露不敢覆藏。
045c08 ||   從今已後不敢復作。若我有罪應墮地獄
045c09 ||   畜生餓鬼阿修羅中。不值三尊生在諸難。
045c10 ||   願以此罪今世現受。如過去諸菩薩求佛
045c11 ||   道者。懺悔惡業罪。我亦如是發露懺悔不
045c12 ||   敢覆藏後不復作。若今諸菩薩求佛道者。
045c13 ||   懺悔惡業罪。我亦如是發露懺悔不敢覆
045c14 ||   藏後不復作。如未來諸菩薩求佛道者。懺
045c15 ||   悔惡業罪。我亦如是發露懺悔不敢覆藏後
045c16 ||   不復作。
045c17 ||   如過去未來現在諸菩薩求佛道者。懺悔
045c18 ||   惡業罪。已懺悔今懺悔當懺悔。我亦如是懺
045c19 ||   悔惡業罪不敢覆藏後不復作。
045c20 || 問曰。汝已說懺悔法。云何為勸請。答曰。
045c21 ||     十方一切佛       現在成道者
```

简体字

发大乘者。恶言毁辱轻贱嫌恨悭嫉覆心故。于诸佛所或起恶口。或说是法非法。说非法是法。今以是罪于现在诸佛知者见者证者所。尽皆发露不敢覆藏。从今已后不敢复作。若我有罪应堕地狱畜生饿鬼阿修罗中。不值三尊生在诸难。愿以此罪今世现受。如过去诸菩萨求佛道者。忏悔恶业罪。我亦如是发露忏悔不敢覆藏后不复作。若今诸菩萨求佛道者。忏悔恶业罪。我亦如是发露忏悔不敢覆藏后不复作。如未来诸菩萨求佛道者。忏悔恶业罪。我亦如是发露忏悔不敢覆藏后不复作。

如过去未来现在诸菩萨求佛道者。忏悔恶业罪。已忏悔今忏悔当忏悔。我亦如是忏悔恶业罪不敢覆藏后不复作。

问曰。汝已说忏悔法。云何为劝请。答曰。
　　十方一切佛　　现在成道者

or have set their resolve on realization of the Great Vehicle, due to having a mind covered over by hatred or jealousy, I have used evil speech to vilify and slight them.

And sometimes, in the presence of buddhas, I have uttered abusive speech, have claimed right Dharma to be non-Dharma, and have claimed non-Dharma to be right Dharma.

Now, in the presence of the buddhas of the present, those who know, who see, and who have become realized, I entirely reveal all of these karmic offenses, not daring to conceal any of them, and I vow, from this point on, that I shall not dare to commit them again.

If I have committed karmic offenses through which I should fall into the hells, into the animal realm, into the hungry-ghost realm, or into the *asura* realm,[159] or if I ought not encounter the three objects of reverence,[160] but rather should be reborn in the midst of the [eight] difficulties,[161] I pray that I may [instead be allowed to] undergo retribution for these karmic offenses in this present life.

Just as all the bodhisattvas of the past who sought realization of buddhahood did themselves repent of offenses created through bad karma, in the very same manner, I too reveal all of my offenses, repent of them, do not dare to conceal any of them, and vow not to commit them again.

Just as all the bodhisattvas of the present who seek realization of buddhahood do repent of offenses created through bad karma, in the very same manner, I too reveal all of my offenses, repent of them, do not dare to conceal any of them, and vow not to commit them again.

Just as all of the bodhisattvas of the future who shall seek realization of buddhahood shall repent of offenses created through bad karma, in the very same manner, I too reveal all of my offenses, repent of them, do not dare to conceal any of them, and vow not to commit them again.

Just as all of the past, future, and present bodhisattvas seeking realization of buddhahood did repent, do repent, and shall repent of offenses created through bad karma, in the very same manner, I too repent of offenses created through bad karma, do not dare to conceal any of them, and vow not to commit them again.

3. Q: How Does One Go about "Entreating"?

Question: Having already explained the method for repentance, how does one go about "entreating"?

4. A: "Entreating" Is Performed as Follows:

Response:
Whenever any of the buddhas of the ten directions now attain buddhahood,

正體字

045c22 ‖	我請轉法輪　　安樂諸眾生
045c23 ‖	十方一切佛　　若欲捨壽命
045c24 ‖	我今頭面禮　　勸請令久住
045c25 ‖	轉法輪者。說四聖諦義三轉十二相是苦諦
045c26 ‖	是苦集是苦滅是至苦滅道。是名一轉四相。
045c27 ‖	是苦諦應知。是苦集應斷。是苦滅應證。是
045c28 ‖	至苦滅道應修。是名第二轉四相。是苦諦知
045c29 ‖	已。是苦集斷已。是苦滅證已。是至苦滅道修
046a01 ‖	已。是名第三轉四相。四相者。四諦中生眼
046a02 ‖	智明覺。有[1]人言聲聞乘辟支佛乘大乘。是
046a03 ‖	名法輪解[2]說。是三乘義名為轉法輪。安
046a04 ‖	樂諸眾生者。五欲樂不名為安樂。為今世
046a05 ‖	後世。得清淨安[3]樂入於三乘。是名安樂。
046a06 ‖	是人勸請諸佛轉法輪。令諸眾生受涅槃
046a07 ‖	樂。若未得涅槃令受世間樂。是故說安
046a08 ‖	樂。

简体字

　　我请转法轮　　安乐诸众生
　　十方一切佛　　若欲舍寿命
　　我今头面礼　　劝请令久住

　　转法轮者。说四圣谛义三转十二相是苦谛是苦集是苦灭是至苦灭道。是名一转四相。是苦谛应知。是苦集应断。是苦灭应证。是至苦灭道应修。是名第二转四相。是苦谛知已。是苦集断已。是苦灭证已。是至苦灭道修已。是名第三转四相。四相者。四谛中生眼智明觉。有人言声闻乘辟支佛乘大乘。是名法轮解说。是三乘义名为转法轮。安乐诸众生者。五欲乐不名为安乐。为今世后世。得清净安乐入于三乘。是名安乐。是人劝请诸佛转法轮。令诸众生受涅槃乐。若未得涅槃令受世间乐。是故说安乐。

> I request them to turn the wheel of Dharma
> and bring peace and happiness to all beings.
>
> Whenever any of the buddhas of the ten directions
> are about to relinquish their life spans,
> I now make full reverential prostrations to them,
> and entreat them to remain for a long time.

As for "turning the wheel of Dharma," this refers to the proclamation of the four truths of the Āryas in three turnings, thereby revealing their twelve aspects:

> This is the truth of the existence of suffering. This is the origination of suffering. This is the extinguishing of suffering. This is the path leading to the extinguishing of suffering. This is what is meant by the four aspects of the first turning.
>
> This truth of the existence of suffering should be known. This origination of suffering should be cut off. This extinguishing of suffering should be realized. This path leading to the extinguishing of suffering should be cultivated. This is what is meant by the four aspects of the second turning.
>
> This truth of the existence of suffering has been known. This origination of suffering has been cut off. This extinguishing of suffering has been realized. This path leading to the extinguishing of suffering has been cultivated. This is what is meant by the four aspects of the third turning.

As for the four aspects, within the four truths, they correspond to the development of the eyes, the knowledges, the clear knowledges, and the awakenings.[162]

There are those who explain that the Śrāvaka Disciple Vehicle, the Pratyekabuddha Vehicle, and the Great Vehicle are what constitute "the Dharma wheel" and that it is the explanation of the meaning of the Three Vehicles that constitutes the "the turning of the Dharma wheel."

As for "bringing peace and happiness to all beings," the pleasures associated with the five objects of desire do not constitute peace and happiness. Rather, it is entry into the Three Vehicles for the sake of achieving pure peace and happiness in the present and future lifetimes—this is what is meant by peace and happiness.

This person entreats the Buddhas to turn the wheel of Dharma to cause all beings to receive the bliss of nirvāṇa and, so long as they have not yet gained entry into nirvāṇa, to cause them to receive the types of happiness available in the world. It is for this reason that "peace and happiness" are mentioned here.

正體字

046a09 ‖ 壽者。受業報因緣故。命根相續得住。如
046a09 ‖ 變化所作隨心業而住。心業止則滅。勸請
046a10 ‖ 名至誠求願。諸佛觀諸眾生巨細無異。是
046a11 ‖ 故求請望得從願。莫捨壽命住無量阿僧
046a12 ‖ 祇劫度脫眾生。
046a13 ‖ 復次佛自說勸請法。菩薩應作是言。我禮
046a14 ‖ 現在十方諸佛。始得阿耨多羅三藐三菩提
046a15 ‖ 未轉法輪我今求請。願轉法輪擊法鼓
046a16 ‖ 吹法[*]蠡建法幢。設大法祠然大法炬。以
046a17 ‖ 是法施滿足眾生。多所利益多所安樂。
046a18 ‖ 憐愍世間饒益天人。是故我今勸請。是名
046a19 ‖ 勸請。諸佛轉法輪久住者。亦應言現在十方
046a20 ‖ 諸佛。[4]是諸佛欲捨壽命我請久住。多所
046a21 ‖ 利益多所安樂。憐愍世間饒益天人。問
046a22 ‖ 曰。汝已說懺悔勸請。云何名為隨喜。答曰。
046a23 ‖   所有布施福   持戒修禪行

简体字

　　寿者。受业报因缘故。命根相续得住。如变化所作随心业而住。心业止则灭。劝请名至诚求愿。诸佛观诸众生巨细无异。是故求请望得从愿。莫舍寿命住无量阿僧祇劫度脱众生。
　　复次佛自说劝请法。菩萨应作是言。我礼现在十方诸佛。始得阿耨多罗三藐三菩提未转法轮我今求请。愿转法轮击法鼓吹法蠡建法幢。设大法祠然大法炬。以是法施满足众生。多所利益多所安乐。怜愍世间饶益天人。是故我今劝请。是名劝请。诸佛转法轮久住者。亦应言现在十方诸佛。是诸佛欲舍寿命我请久住。多所利益多所安乐。怜愍世间饶益天人。问曰。汝已说忏悔劝请。云何名为随喜。答曰。
　　　所有布施福　　持戒修禅行

Chapter 10 — Getting Rid of Karma

As for this matter of a "life span," it is due to the causes and conditions involved in undergoing karmic retribution that the continuity of one's life faculty is sustained. It is comparable to an apparition created through a magical conjuration that continues to be sustained in correspondence with [the magician's] mental actions. When those mental actions cease, [that conjuration] is then extinguished.[163]

"Entreat" refers to the most ultimately sincere prayerful beseeching. The Buddhas regard all beings [equally], great and small, without treating them differently. Therefore one sets forth this earnest request, hoping that they will accede to one's wishes and refrain from relinquishing their life spans and instead remain in the world for *asaṃkhyeyas* of kalpas in order to liberate beings.

Then again, the Buddha himself described the method to be used in entreating the Buddhas, indicating that the bodhisattva should speak as follows: "I bow down in reverence to all buddhas of the present throughout the ten directions." Then, at that time when they have just realized *anuttarasamyaksaṃbodhi* but have not yet begun to turn the wheel of Dharma, [he is to say]:

> I now beseech you, praying that you will turn the wheel of Dharma, sound the Dharma drum, blow the Dharma conch, plant the Dharma banner, establish the great Dharma rituals, and ignite the great Dharma torch, using these means of Dharma giving to fulfill the needs of beings so that there will be many who are benefited and many who are made happy. Have pity on the world and bestow abundant benefit on devas and humans. It is for these reasons that I now present this entreaty.

This is what is meant by "entreating." As for entreating the buddhas who have turned the wheel of Dharma to then "remain for a long time," in that case as well, one should address all buddhas of the present throughout the ten directions at just that time when those buddhas are about to relinquish their life spans, saying, "I beseech you to remain for a long time so that there will be many who are benefited and many who are made happy. Have pity on the world and bestow abundant benefit on devas and humans."

5. Q: What is meant by "Rejoicing"?

Question: Having already explained "repentance" and "entreating," what is meant by "rejoicing"?

6. A: "Rejoicing" Is Performed as Follows:

Response:
> All of the merit produced by giving,
> observance of moral precepts, and *dhyāna* practice—

正體字

```
046a24 ||    從身口意生    去來今所有
046a25 ||    習行三乘人    具足三乘者
046a26 ||    一切凡夫福    皆隨而歡喜
046a27 || 布施福者。從捨慳法生。持戒福者。能伏身
046a28 || 口業生。禪行者諸禪定是。從身口生者。因
046a29 || 身口布施持戒迎來送去等。因意生者禪定
046b01 || 慈悲等。去來今所有者。一切眾生三世福德。
046b02 || 行三乘者。求聲聞乘辟支佛乘大乘。具足
046b03 || 三乘者。成就阿羅漢乘辟支佛乘佛乘。一切
046b04 || 者皆盡無餘。凡夫者未得四諦者是。福德
046b05 || 者有二種業。善及不隱沒無記業是。隨喜者。
046b06 || 他人作福心生歡喜稱以為善。
046b07 || 問曰。汝以說懺悔勸請隨喜。云何為迴向。
```

简体字

　　　　从身口意生　　去来今所有
　　　　习行三乘人　　具足三乘者
　　　　一切凡夫福　　皆随而欢喜

布施福者。从舍悭法生。持戒福者。能伏身口业生。禅行者诸禅定是。从身口生者。因身口布施持戒迎来送去等。因意生者禅定慈悲等。去来今所有者。一切众生三世福德。行三乘者。求声闻乘辟支佛乘大乘。具足三乘者。成就阿罗汉乘辟支佛乘佛乘。一切者皆尽无余。凡夫者未得四谛者是。福德者有二种业。善及不隐没无记业是。随喜者。他人作福心生欢喜称以为善。

　　问曰。汝以说忏悔劝请随喜。云何为回向。

all of it arising through body, speech, and mind,
all of it created throughout the past, the future, and the present,

all of it created by those who cultivate the Three Vehicles,
by those who have fulfilled the practice of any of the Three Vehicles,
and all of the merit created by common people—
I rejoice in accordance with all of it.

As for "the merit produced by giving," it is created through relinquishing the dharma of miserliness.

As for "the merit arising from observance of moral precepts," this is created through being able to subdue the body and speech.

"*Dhyāna* practice" refers to developing all of the *dhyāna* concentrations.

As for "that arising through body and speech," this refers to acts arising because of the body or speech such as giving, observance of the moral precepts, welcoming others when they come, escorting them off when they leave,[164] and other such actions.

As for "that arising through the mind," this refers to the *dhyāna* concentration states[165] as well as to kindness, compassion, and so forth.[166]

As for "all of it created in the past, the future, or the present," this is referring to all merit produced by all beings throughout the three periods of time.

As for "those who cultivate the Three Vehicles," this refers to those who aspire to success in the Śrāvaka Disciple Vehicle, the Pratyekabuddha Vehicle, and the Great Vehicle.

As for "those who have fulfilled the practice of any of the Three Vehicles," this refers to those who have perfected the cultivation of either the Arhat Vehicle, the Pratyekabuddha Vehicle, or the Buddha Vehicle.

"All" means every single instance, exhaustively, excluding none.

"Common people" refers to those who have not yet realized the four truths.

With respect to "merit," there may be two types of actions which may be involved here, namely good actions or unobscured morally indeterminate actions.[167]

"Rejoicing in accordance with it" refers to circumstances where, when others engage in meritorious actions, one's mind is filled with delight and one praises that deed as good.

7. Q: What Is Meant by "Dedication"?

Question: Since you have already explained "repentance," "entreating," and "rejoicing," what is meant by "dedication"?

正體字

046b08 ‖ 答曰。
046b09 ‖ 　我所有福德　　一切皆和合
046b10 ‖ 　為諸眾生故　　正迴向佛道
046b11 ‖ 我者己身。所有福德者。若從身生。若從口
046b12 ‖ 生。若從意生。若因布施生。若因持戒生。
046b13 ‖ 若因修禪生。若因隨喜生。若因勸請生。
046b14 ‖ 如是等及餘所有善。皆名所有福德。一切
046b15 ‖ [5]皆和合者。心念諸福德合集稱[6]量知其廣
046b16 ‖ 大。諸眾生者三界眾生。正者如諸佛迴向。
046b17 ‖ 如真實迴向。[7]迴向菩提。[8]迴向菩提者。
046b18 ‖ 迴諸福德向阿耨多羅三藐三菩提。又隨喜
046b19 ‖ 迴向。此二事佛亦自說。有菩薩摩訶薩。欲
046b20 ‖ 隨喜迴向應念諸佛。斷三界相續道滅諸
046b21 ‖ 戲論。乾煩惱淤泥。滅諸刺棘除諸重擔逮
046b22 ‖ 得己利。正智解脫心得自在盡諸有結。無
046b23 ‖ 量無邊不可思議阿僧祇十方世界。[9]一一世
046b24 ‖ 界中。亦無量無邊不可思議阿僧祇諸佛出
046b25 ‖ 已滅度。從初發心乃至

简体字

答曰。
　我所有福德　　一切皆和合
　为诸众生故　　正回向佛道
　我者己身。所有福德者。若从身生。若从口生。若从意生。若因布施生。若因持戒生。若因修禅生。若因随喜生。若因劝请生。如是等及余所有善。皆名所有福德。一切皆和合者。心念诸福德合集称量知其广大。诸众生者三界众生。正者如诸佛回向。如真实回向。回向菩提。回向菩提者。回诸福德向阿耨多罗三藐三菩提。又随喜回向。此二事佛亦自说。有菩萨摩诃萨。欲随喜回向应念诸佛。断三界相续道灭诸戏论。干烦恼淤泥。灭诸刺棘除诸重担逮得己利。正智解脱心得自在尽诸有结。无量无边不可思议阿僧祇十方世界。一一世界中。亦无量无边不可思议阿僧祇诸佛出已灭度。从初发心乃至

8. A: DEDICATION IS PERFORMED AS FOLLOWS:

Response:
> May all of the merit that I have acquired
> be gathered together,
> and then, for the sake of all beings,
> may it be rightly dedicated to attaining buddhahood.

"I" refers to oneself. "All of the merit," whether produced through physical actions, produced through verbal actions, produced through mental actions, produced through giving, through upholding the moral precepts, through cultivation of *dhyāna* meditation, through rejoicing, or through entreating—all such goodness as this as well as any other goodness—all of these are what constitute "all of the merit."

As for "may it all be gathered together," this refers to a reflection whereby one envisions all of the merit being gathered together and assessed in a manner whereby one becomes aware of its expansiveness.

"All beings" refers to all beings throughout the three realms of existence.

"Rightly" refers to performing this dedication of merit in a manner corresponding to the way it is done by all buddhas. It is that dedication that aligns itself with reality. It is dedication directed toward bodhi. This "dedication directed toward bodhi" involves dedicating all merit toward the realization of *anuttarasamyaksaṃbodhi*.

Again, these two matters of "rejoicing" and "dedication" were explained by the Buddha himself who spoke of them as follows:

> Where there is a bodhisattva *mahāsattva* who wishes to engage in rejoicing and in dedication, he should bring to mind all of the roots of goodness and merit of all buddhas, those who have cut off continuous abiding in the three realms of existence, who have extinguished all conceptual elaborations, who have dried up the mud of the afflictions, who have destroyed their piercing thorns, who have thrown off the heavy burden, who have accomplished their own benefit, who have obtained right knowledge and liberation, whose minds have achieved sovereign mastery, and who have put an end to the fetters of existence.
>
> So too, he should bring to mind all of the measurelessly, boundlessly, and inconceivably many *asaṃkhyeyas* of buddhas in each and every one of the measurelessly, boundlessly, and inconceivably many *asaṃkhyeyas* of worlds throughout the ten directions while also bringing to mind all the roots of goodness and merit of all of these buddhas from the time they come forth [into the world] to the time they enter nirvāṇa, from the time they first brought forth their resolve to

正體字	得佛入無餘涅槃。 046b26 ‖ 至遺法未盡於其中間是諸佛所有善根福 046b27 ‖ 德。應六波羅蜜及所[10]受辟支佛記所有善 046b28 ‖ 根。又聲聞人善根。若布施持戒修禪。及學無 046b29 ‖ 學無漏善根。及諸[11]佛戒品定品慧品[12]解脫 046c01 ‖ 知見品。大慈大悲等無量功德。及諸佛有所 046c02 ‖ 說法。於此法中有人信解受學得此法利。 046c03 ‖ 是諸人等所有善根。於此法中及凡夫所種 046c04 ‖ 善根及諸天龍夜叉乾闥婆阿修羅迦樓羅緊 046c05 ‖ 那羅摩[13]睺羅伽。得聞法已生諸善心。乃 046c06 ‖ 至畜生聞法生諸善心。及諸佛欲入涅槃 046c07 ‖ 時。眾生所種善根。是諸善根福德一切和合 046c08 ‖ 稱量使無遺餘。以最上最妙最勝無上無 046c09 ‖ 等無等等隨喜。隨喜已。以是隨喜所生福 046c10 ‖ 德。迴向阿耨多羅三藐三菩提。未來現在諸 046c11 ‖ 佛亦如是。
简体字	得佛入无余涅槃。至遗法未尽于其中间是诸佛所有善根福德。应六波罗蜜及所受辟支佛记所有善根。又声闻人善根。若布施持戒修禅。及学无学无漏善根。及诸佛戒品定品慧品解脱知见品。大慈大悲等无量功德。及诸佛有所说法。于此法中有人信解受学得此法利。是诸人等所有善根。于此法中及凡夫所种善根及诸天龙夜叉乾闼婆阿修罗迦楼罗紧那罗摩睺罗伽。得闻法已生诸善心。乃至畜生闻法生诸善心。及诸佛欲入涅槃时。众生所种善根。是诸善根福德一切和合称量使无遗余。以最上最妙最胜无上无等无等等随喜。随喜已。以是随喜所生福德。回向阿耨多罗三藐三菩提。未来现在诸佛亦如是。

Chapter 10 — Getting Rid of Karma

realize buddhahood to the time they actually realize buddhahood on to that time when they enter the nirvāṇa without residue, and on to all of the remaining time before the Dharma they bequeath finally comes to an end.

He should bring to mind the roots of goodness associated with [bodhisattvas' practice of] the six *pāramitās* as well as the roots of goodness of those who have received the prediction that they are bound to become *pratyekabuddhas*.

He should also bring to mind the roots of goodness of the *śrāvaka* disciples, whether they are the product of giving, of upholding moral precepts, or of cultivation of *dhyāna* meditation, including in this the uncontaminated roots of goodness those in training and those beyond training.[168]

He should also [bring to mind the roots of goodness] associated with all buddhas' measureless meritorious qualities related to moral precept observance, meditative absorptions, wisdom, liberations, knowledge and vision of liberation, great kindness, and great compassion, including as well that related to all buddhas' proclamation of Dharma, for there are those people who have consequently brought forth faith and understanding in these dharmas, who have then undertaken training in them, and who have then acquired the benefit of these dharmas. Hence he should bring to mind all the roots of goodness planted by these people in relation to these dharmas.

He should also include all the roots of goodness of all common people as well those of all the devas, dragons, *yakṣas*, *gandharvas*, *asuras*, *garuḍas*, *kinnaras*, and *mahoragas* who, on being able to hear the proclamation of Dharma, then brought forth thoughts of goodness. He should also include here even [those roots of goodness planted] by animals who heard the Dharma and then brought forth thoughts of goodness. And he should also include here the roots of goodness planted by beings [who gathered together] when the Buddhas were about to enter nirvāṇa.

All of these roots of goodness and all of this merit are brought together and assessed, excluding none, and are, then and there, made the object of the most superior rejoicing, of the most sublime rejoicing, of the most excellent rejoicing, of unsurpassable rejoicing, of incomparable rejoicing, and of rejoicing that is equal to the unequaled.

Having rejoiced in all of this, one then takes all of the merit arising from this rejoicing and dedicates it to the realization of *anuttarasamyaksaṃbodhi*. In precisely the same manner, one does this with respect to the merit associated with all buddhas of the future and all buddhas of the present.

正體字	是三世諸佛福德及因諸佛所生 046c12 ‖ 福德心皆隨喜。迴向阿耨多羅三藐三菩提。 046c13 ‖ 是故偈說。 046c14 ‖ 　罪應如是懺　　勸請隨喜福 046c15 ‖ 　迴向無上道　　皆亦應如是 046c16 ‖ 　如諸佛所[14]說　我悔罪勸請 046c17 ‖ 　隨喜及迴向　　皆亦復如是 046c18 ‖ 無始世界來。有無量遮佛道罪。應於十方 046c19 ‖ 諸佛前懺悔。勸請諸佛隨喜迴向[15]亦應如 046c20 ‖ 是。如佛所知所見所許懺悔。我亦如是懺 046c21 ‖ 悔勸請諸佛。隨喜迴向亦復如是。若如是 046c22 ‖ 懺悔勸請隨喜迴向。是名正迴向。問曰。云何 046c23 ‖ 名為諸佛所知所見所許懺悔勸請隨喜迴 046c24 ‖ 向。答曰。懺悔勸請如先說。隨喜迴向。如大 046c25 ‖ 品經中。須菩提白佛言。世尊。所說菩薩於 046c26 ‖ 過去未來現在一切諸佛及諸弟子一切眾生 046c27 ‖ 所有福德善根盡和合稱量。以最上隨喜。世 046c28 ‖ 尊。云何名為最上隨喜。
简体字	是三世诸佛福德及因诸佛所生福德心皆随喜。回向阿耨多罗三藐三菩提。是故偈说。 　罪应如是忏　　劝请随喜福 　回向无上道　　皆亦应如是 　如诸佛所说　　我悔罪劝请 　随喜及回向　　皆亦复如是 无始世界来。有无量遮佛道罪。应于十方诸佛前忏悔。劝请诸佛随喜回向亦应如是。如佛所知所见所许忏悔。我亦如是忏悔劝请诸佛。随喜回向亦复如是。若如是忏悔劝请随喜回向。是名正回向。问曰。云何名为诸佛所知所见所许忏悔劝请随喜回向。答曰。忏悔劝请如先说。随喜回向。如大品经中。须菩提白佛言。世尊。所说菩萨于过去未来现在一切诸佛及诸弟子一切众生所有福德善根尽和合称量。以最上随喜。世尊。云何名为最上随喜。

Chapter 10 — *Getting Rid of Karma*

> One's mind rejoices in all merit created by all these buddhas of the three periods of time, rejoicing as well in all merit produced by others due to the influence of all these buddhas. One then dedicates the merit [produced by this rejoicing] to the realization of *anuttarasamyaksaṃbodhi*.
>
> Therefore we have a verse here that states:
>
> One should repent of karmic offenses in this manner.
> As for entreating, rejoicing in merit, and
> dedicating merit to the unsurpassable path,
> all of these should be carried out in this manner as well.
>
> Just as taught by the Buddhas,
> I repent of karmic offenses, entreat,
> rejoice, and also dedicate merit,
> all in this very same manner.

Throughout the course of the beginningless time in which one has dwelt in the world, one has committed an immeasurable number of karmic offenses that obstruct one's path to buddhahood. One should repent of these offenses in the presence of all buddhas of the ten directions and, in this same way, one should also present entreaties to all buddhas, rejoice in others' merit, and dedicate one's merit accordingly, [reflecting], "Just such repentance as does accord with what is known, seen, and permitted by the Buddhas—it is in accordance with this that I repent of my own karmic offenses." One's entreaties to all buddhas and one's dedications of merit should also be performed in this way. If one repents, entreats, rejoices, and then dedicates one's merit in this manner, this is what is meant by "right dedication."

9. Q: WHICH WAYS OF PERFORMING THESE ACCORDS WITH THE BUDDHAS?

Question: Just what is meant by "repentance, entreating, rejoicing, and dedicating merit that accord with what is known, seen, and permitted by the Buddhas"?

10. A: WHICHEVER WAYS ACCORD WITH THIS PASSAGE FROM SCRIPTURE

Response: "Repentance" and "entreating" are as previously explained. As for "rejoicing in merit" and "dedicating merit," they should accord with the following statements in the large edition of the *[Great Perfection of Wisdom] Sutra*:[169]

> Subhūti addressed the Buddha, saying, "O Bhagavat, as for the aforementioned 'supreme rejoicing' brought forth by the bodhisattva after comprehensively considering and assessing all the merit and roots of goodness of all past, future, and present buddhas, of all their disciples, and of all other beings—O Bhagavat, precisely what is meant by this 'supreme rejoicing'?"

正體字

```
         佛告須菩提。若菩
046c29 ‖ 薩於過去未來現在諸法。不取不念不見
047a01 ‖ 不得不分別而能如是思惟。是諸法皆從
047a02 ‖ 憶想分別眾緣和合有一切法實不生無
047a03 ‖ 所從來。是中乃至無有一法已生今生當
047a04 ‖ 生。亦無已滅今滅當滅。諸法相如是。我順
047a05 ‖ 諸法相隨喜。隨喜已亦隨諸法實相迴向
047a06 ‖ 阿耨多羅三藐三菩提。是名最上隨喜迴向。
047a07 ‖ 復次須菩提。求佛道善男子善女人。不欲
047a08 ‖ 謗佛者。應以善根如是迴向。應作是念。
047a09 ‖ 如諸佛心佛智佛眼。知見是善根福德本末
047a10 ‖ 體相從何而有。我亦如是隨諸佛知見隨
047a11 ‖ 喜。如諸佛所許我亦如是以善根迴向。若
047a12 ‖ 菩薩如是迴向。則不謗諸佛亦無過咎。深
047a13 ‖ 心信解如實迴向。是名大迴向具足迴向。復
047a14 ‖ 次須菩提。善男子善女人以諸善根福德應
047a15 ‖ 如是迴向。如諸賢聖。戒品定品慧品解脫品
047a16 ‖ 解脫知見品。
```

简体字

佛告须菩提。若菩萨于过去未来现在诸法。不取不念不见不得不分别而能如是思惟。是诸法皆从忆想分别众缘和合有一切法实不生无所从来。是中乃至无有一法已生今生当生。亦无已灭今灭当灭。诸法相如是。我顺诸法相随喜。随喜已亦随诸法实相回向阿耨多罗三藐三菩提。是名最上随喜回向。

复次须菩提。求佛道善男子善女人。不欲谤佛者。应以善根如是回向。应作是念。如诸佛心佛智佛眼。知见是善根福德本末体相从何而有。我亦如是随诸佛知见随喜。如诸佛所许我亦如是以善根回向。若菩萨如是回向。则不谤诸佛亦无过咎。深心信解如实回向。是名大回向具足回向。复次须菩提。善男子善女人以诸善根福德应如是回向。如诸贤圣。戒品定品慧品解脱品解脱知见品。

Chapter 10 — *Getting Rid of Karma*

The Buddha then told Subhūti, "It is when, with respect to all dharmas of the past, the future, and the present, a bodhisattva does not seize on them, does not retain them in mind, does not perceive them, does not apprehend them, and does not make discriminations about them, even as he is still able to reflect in this way:

> All of these dharmas are supposed to exist merely due to perceptions and mental discriminations regarding the coming together of many conditions. In reality, none of these dharmas is ever produced nor do any of them have any place from which they come forth. There is not even a single dharma among them that has ever been produced, is now being produced, or ever will be produced. Nor are there any of them that have ever been destroyed, are now being destroyed, or ever will be destroyed. The character of all dharmas is precisely of this sort.
>
> It is in accordance with the character of dharmas that I rejoice and, having rejoiced, it is then also in accordance with the true character of all dharmas that I dedicate all merit to *anuttarasamyaksaṃbodhi*.

"It is precisely this that constitutes the most supreme rejoicing and dedication.

"Furthermore, Subhūti, a son or daughter of good family striving to follow the path to buddhahood who wishes to refrain from slandering the Buddha should dedicate their roots of goodness in this way and they should think as follows:

> Just as, using the buddha mind, the buddha wisdom, and the buddha eye, all buddhas know and see from root to branch and in terms of substance and signs on which bases this merit and these roots of goodness exist—so too do I also accord with all buddhas' knowledge and vision as I rejoice. And just as all buddhas have permitted it, so too do I also dedicate these roots of goodness.

"If a bodhisattva dedicates merit in this manner, then he will thereby refrain from slandering the buddhas. Thus he will remain free of fault by acting in this way. Dedicating merit with deep-seated aspirations and resolute faith, doing so in a manner that accords with reality—this is what is meant by 'great dedication' and 'perfectly complete dedication.'

"Furthermore, Subhūti, a son or daughter of good family should dedicate roots of goodness and merit in the following manner: This dedication should be done in a way that conforms to the moral precept observance, meditative absorptions, wisdom, liberation, and knowledge and vision of liberation possessed by worthies and *āryas*.

正體字	不繫欲界不繫色界不繫 047a17 ‖ 無色界。不在過去不在未來不在現在。 047a18 ‖ 以不繫三界故。是迴向亦如是不繫。所 047a19 ‖ 迴向處亦不繫。若菩薩能如是得心信解 047a20 ‖ 如實。是名不失迴向無毒迴向法性迴向。若 047a21 ‖ 菩薩於此迴向取相貪著是名邪迴向。是故 047a22 ‖ 諸菩薩摩訶薩。應如諸佛所知法相。以是 047a23 ‖ 法相迴向。能至阿耨多羅三藐三菩提。是 047a24 ‖ 名正迴向。[1] 047a25 ‖ 十住毘婆沙論卷第五
简体字	不系欲界不系色界不系无色界。不在过去不在未来不在现在。以不系三界故。是回向亦如是不系。所回向处亦不系。若菩萨能如是得心信解如实。是名不失回向无毒回向法性回向。若菩萨于此回向取相贪着是名邪回向。是故诸菩萨摩诃萨。应如诸佛所知法相。以是法相回向。能至阿耨多罗三藐三菩提。是名正回向。

Those dedications are not anchored in the desire realm, are not anchored in the form realm, are not anchored in the formless realm, and are not situated in the past, the future, or the present. Just as those qualities are not anchored anywhere within the three realms, just so should this dedication of merit not be anchored there, either. Nor should the bases for the dedication of merit be anchored in any such way, either.

"If a bodhisattva is able in this way to gain aspirations and resolute faith that accord with reality, this is what is meant by dedication that is free of error, dedication that is free of the poisons, and dedication that accords with the nature of dharmas.

"If, however, in performing dedications of merit, a bodhisattva were to seize on any signs or were to have any fond attachment to them, this would constitute wrong dedication.

"Therefore, all bodhisattvas and *mahāsattvas* should understand the character of dharmas as it is known by buddhas. When one dedicates merit in a manner that accords with the character of dharmas, one becomes able to reach *anuttarasamyaksaṃbodhi*. This is what is meant by 'right dedication.'"

The End of Chapter Ten

正體字

047b02 ‖ 十住毘婆沙論卷第六
047b03 ‖
047b04 ‖ 　　聖者龍樹造
047b05 ‖ 　　後秦龜茲國三藏鳩摩羅什譯
047b06 ‖ 　　[2]分別功德品第十一
047b07 ‖ 問曰。懺悔勸請隨喜迴向。應云何作[3]於晝
047b08 ‖ 夜中幾時行。答曰。
047b09 ‖ 　　以右膝著地　　偏袒於右肩
047b10 ‖ 　　合掌恭敬心　　晝夜各三時
047b11 ‖ 以恭敬相故。右膝著地偏袒右肩合掌。是
047b12 ‖ 事應初夜一時禮一切佛。懺悔勸請隨喜迴
047b13 ‖ 向。中夜後夜皆亦如是。於日初分日中分日
047b14 ‖ 後分亦如是。一日一夜合為六時。一心念
047b15 ‖ 諸佛如現在前。問曰。作是行已得何果
047b16 ‖ 報。答曰。
047b17 ‖ 　　若於一時行　　福德有形者
047b18 ‖ 　　恒河沙世界　　乃自不容受
047b19 ‖ 若於一時中。行此事者。所得福德若有形　047b20 ‖[4]者。

简体字

分別功德品第十一
　　问曰。忏悔劝请随喜回向。应云何作于昼夜中几时行。答曰。
　　　以右膝着地　　偏袒于右肩
　　　合掌恭敬心　　昼夜各三时
　　以恭敬相故。右膝着地偏袒右肩合掌。是事应初夜一时礼一切佛。忏悔劝请随喜回向。中夜后夜皆亦如是。于日初分日中分日后分亦如是。一日一夜合为六时。一心念诸佛如现在前。问曰。作是行已得何果报。答曰。
　　　若于一时行　　福德有形者
　　　恒河沙世界　　乃自不容受
　　若于一时中。行此事者。所得福德若有形者。

Chapter 11
Distinctions with Regard to Merit

XI. Chapter 11: Distinctions with Regard to Merit
   A. Q: How Should One Repent, Entreat, Rejoice, and Dedicate Merit?

Question: In what way should one carry out repentance, entreating, rejoicing, and dedication? How many times during the course of the day and night should one perform these actions?

   B. A: With Reverence and Pressed Palms, Three Times Each Day & Night

Response:
> With the right knee touching the ground
> and with the right shoulder bared,
> place the palms together and, with reverential mind,
> do these three times each day and night.

Because these actions are emblematic of reverential behavior, one touches the right knee to the ground, bares the right shoulder, and presses one's palms together. This observance should be carried out at the beginning of the night as one simultaneously pays reverence to all buddhas, repents, entreats, rejoices, and dedicates merit. One does so yet again in this same way in the middle of the night and again at the end of the night.

   One proceeds in this same way at the beginning of the day, again in the middle of the day, and again at the end of the day, doing so altogether six times in the day and night, doing so while single-mindedly bringing to mind all buddhas, envisioning them as if they were manifesting right before one's very eyes.

   C. Q: What Karmic Result Ensues from Doing This?

Question: What karmic result ensues from acting in this way?

   D. A: If One Did This but Once, the Merit Would Be Incalculably Great

Response:
> If one were to practice this but a single time
> and the associated merit were to have physical form,
> not even world systems as numerous as the Ganges' sands
> would be capable of holding it all.

If one were to carry out this procedure even once and if the resulting merit was given physical form, that merit would be so immense that it

正體字		恒河沙等無量無邊不可思議三千大千
	047b21 ‖	世界所不容受。如三[5]支經除罪業品中說。
	047b22 ‖	佛告舍利弗。若善男子善女人。以滿恒河沙
	047b23 ‖	等三千大千世界七寶布施諸佛。若復有人
	047b24 ‖	勸請諸佛轉法輪此福為勝。又[6]佛於般若
	047b25 ‖	波羅蜜隨喜迴向品中說。善哉善哉須菩提。
	047b26 ‖	汝能[7]作佛事。與諸菩薩說迴向法。若菩
	047b27 ‖	薩作是念。如諸佛知見是善根福德本末
	047b28 ‖	體相。何因緣故有。我亦如是隨佛所知所
	047b29 ‖	見迴向。是人得福多。譬如恒河沙等三千
	047c01 ‖	大千世界中眾生皆成就十善道。菩薩迴向
	047c02 ‖	福德最上最妙最勝無比無等無等等。須菩
	047c03 ‖	提。置是恒河沙等三千大千世界眾生。成就
	047c04 ‖	十善道。若恒河沙等三千大千世界眾生皆
	047c05 ‖	得四禪。其福比此。亦復最上最妙最勝。四
	047c06 ‖	無量心四無色定五神通。得須陀洹果斯陀
	047c07 ‖	含果阿那含果

简体字	恒河沙等无量无边不可思议三千大千世界所不容受。如三支经除罪业品中说。佛告舍利弗。若善男子善女人。以满恒河沙等三千大千世界七宝布施诸佛。若复有人劝请诸佛转法轮此福为胜。又佛于般若波罗蜜随喜回向品中说。善哉善哉须菩提。汝能作佛事。与诸菩萨说回向法。若菩萨作是念。如诸佛知见是善根福德本末体相。何因缘故有。我亦如是随佛所知所见回向。是人得福多。譬如恒河沙等三千大千世界中众生皆成就十善道。菩萨回向福德最上最妙最胜无比无等无等等。须菩提。置是恒河沙等三千大千世界众生。成就十善道。若恒河沙等三千大千世界众生皆得四禅。其福比此。亦复最上最妙最胜。四无量心四无色定五神通。得须陀洹果斯陀含果阿那含果

Chapter 11 — *Distinctions with Regard to Merit*

could not be contained even in a measureless, boundless, and inconceivable number of great trichiliocosms equal the number of sands in the Ganges River. This is as described in the "Getting Rid of Karmic Offenses" chapter of *The Three Branches Sutra*:[170]

> The Buddha told Śāriputra, "Even if a son or daughter of good family made an offering to the Buddhas of a quantity of the seven precious things sufficient to fill up the worlds of great trichiliocosms equal in number to the sands of the Ganges, that merit would still be superseded by the amount of merit created by some other person who entreated the Buddhas to turn the wheel of Dharma."

Moreover, in the "Rejoicing and Dedication" chapter of *The [Mahā] prajñāpāramitā [Sūtra]*, the Buddha said:[171]

> It is good indeed, good indeed, Subhūti, that you are able to carry on the work of the Buddha by explaining to the bodhisattvas this dharma of dedicating [merit]. Suppose a bodhisattva were to engage in the following reflection:
>
>> Just as all buddhas know and see from root to branch and in terms of substance and signs which causes and conditions serve as the bases for the existence of this merit and these roots of goodness, so too, as I engage in this dedication [of merit], I also accord with what the buddhas know and see.
>
> This person [who carries out dedications in this manner] thereby acquires an immense amount of merit. By way of analogy, even if beings as numerous as those in the worlds of great trichiliocosms as numerous as the Ganges' sands were all to achieve perfect adherence to the ten courses of good karmic action, still, the merit gained by that bodhisattva [mentioned above] would be, in its magnitude, the most superior, the most sublime, and the most excellent. It would be matchless, unequaled, and equal to the unequaled.
>
> But, Subhūti, set aside this example of all beings in the worlds of great trichiliocosms as numerous as the Ganges' sands achieving perfect adherence to the ten courses of good karmic action. Even if beings as numerous as those in the worlds of great trichiliocosms as numerous as the Ganges' sands were all to acquire the four *dhyānas*, when compared to the merit arising from all of this, his merit would still be the most superior, the most sublime, and the most excellent.
>
> So too would this also be the case with regard to the merit that those beings would gain if they acquired the four immeasurable minds, if they acquired the four formless-realm absorptions, if they acquired the five spiritual superknowledges, or if they realized the fruit of the path of the stream enterer, the fruit of the path of the *sakṛdāgāmin*, the fruit of the path of the *anāgāmin*, the fruit of the path

正體字	阿羅漢果辟支佛道亦如是。 047c08 ‖ 如法迴向福德最上最妙最勝。須菩提。置此 047c09 ‖ 恒河沙等三千大千世界眾生皆作辟支佛。 047c10 ‖ 若有恒河沙等三千大千世界眾生。皆發阿 047c11 ‖ 耨多羅三藐三菩提心。復有恒河沙等三千 047c12 ‖ 大千世界眾生。其一菩薩以取相心。供養 047c13 ‖ 是諸眾生衣服飲食臥具醫藥。於恒河沙等 047c14 ‖ 劫。以一切樂具供養恭敬尊重讚歎。一一菩 047c15 ‖ 薩皆亦如是。須菩提。於意云何。是諸菩薩 047c16 ‖ 以此因緣。得福多不。甚多世尊。如是福德 047c17 ‖ 算數譬喻所不能及。若是福德有形。恒河 047c18 ‖ 沙等世界所不能受。佛告須菩提。善哉善 047c19 ‖ 哉須菩提。是菩薩為般若波羅蜜守護。以 047c20 ‖ 善根隨法性迴向所得福德。先諸菩薩取相 047c21 ‖ 布施福德。百分不及一。千分萬分百千萬億 047c22 ‖ 分。乃至算數譬喻所不能及。何以故。先諸 047c23 ‖ 菩薩取相分別布施。皆是有量有數。
简体字	阿罗汉果辟支佛道亦如是。如法回向福德最上最妙最胜。须菩提。置此恒河沙等三千大千世界众生皆作辟支佛。若有恒河沙等三千大千世界众生。皆发阿耨多罗三藐三菩提心。复有恒河沙等三千大千世界众生。其一菩萨以取相心。供养是诸众生衣服饮食卧具医药。于恒河沙等劫。以一切乐具供养恭敬尊重赞叹。一一菩萨皆亦如是。须菩提。于意云何。是诸菩萨以此因缘。得福多不。甚多世尊。如是福德算数譬喻所不能及。若是福德有形。恒河沙等世界所不能受。佛告须菩提。善哉善哉须菩提。是菩萨为般若波罗蜜守护。以善根随法性回向所得福德。先诸菩萨取相布施福德。百分不及一。千分万分百千万亿分。乃至算数譬喻所不能及。何以故。先诸菩萨取相分别布施。皆是有量有数。

of the arhat, or if they achieved the realization of the *pratyekabuddha*'s path. In those cases as well, comparatively speaking, the merit derived from dedications of merit made in accordance with the Dharma would be the most superior, the most sublime, and the most excellent.

But, Subhūti, set aside this example of all the beings in the worlds of great trichiliocosms as numerous as the Ganges' sands achieving [all of these accomplishments up to and including] the realization of the *pratyekabuddha*'s path.

Suppose instead that, on the one hand, there were a number of beings in the worlds of great trichiliocosms as numerous as the Ganges' sands who all brought forth the resolve to attain *anuttarasamyaksaṃbodhi* while, on the other hand, there were a number of beings equivalent to those in the worlds of great trichiliocosms as numerous as the Ganges' sands. If one of those bodhisattvas [who had brought forth the resolve], relying on a mind that still seizes upon signs, were to make offerings to all those beings of clothing, food and drink, bedding, and medicines, doing so for kalpas as numerous as the Ganges' sands, using every sort of happiness enhancing gift while making offerings to them, paying reverence to them, and also praising them. Supposing that each and every one of those bodhisattvas all acted in this very same manner, what do you think, Subhūti? Would all of these bodhisattvas gain a great deal of merit because of this, or not?

[Subhūti replied:]

O Bhagavat, they would gain an extremely great amount. Such an amount of merit as this would be beyond the reach of any calculation or analogy. If such a quantity of merit were to be given physical form, it could not be contained even within worlds as numerous as the Ganges' sands.

The Buddha told Subhūti:

Good indeed, good indeed, Subhūti. [Even so], the merit of this bodhisattva guarded and protected by the *prajñāpāramitā* who performs the dedication of roots of goodness in a manner conforming to the nature of dharmas—that merit is such that the merit gained by all of those aforementioned bodhisattvas whose giving involved seizing on signs could not equal even a hundredth of it, a thousandth of it, one ten-thousandth of it, or even one billionth of a *koṭi*'s part of it. This comparison would even be beyond the reach of calculation or analogy. And why is that? It is because the giving practiced by those aforementioned bodhisattvas involved mental discriminations seizing on signs. [Because of this], their merit remains confined entirely within the sphere of what is measurable and calculable.

正體字	又般若 047c24 ‖ 波羅蜜迴向品中說。佛告淨居天子。置此恒 047c25 ‖ 河沙等三千大千世界眾生皆發阿耨多羅三 047c26 ‖ 藐三菩提心。餘恒河沙等三千大千世界眾 047c27 ‖ 生。一一菩薩以取相心供養是諸眾生衣服 047c28 ‖ 飲食臥具醫藥資生之物。隨意供養於恒河 047c29 ‖ 沙等劫。諸天子。若是恒河沙等三千大千世 048a01 ‖ 界眾生發阿耨多羅三藐三菩提心。餘恒河 048a02 ‖ 沙等三千大千世界中眾生皆亦發阿耨多 048a03 ‖ 羅三藐三菩提心。其一菩薩供養是諸菩薩 048a04 ‖ 衣服飲食臥具醫藥資生之物於恒河沙等 048a05 ‖ 劫。是布施取相分別。如是諸菩薩各於恒河 048a06 ‖ 沙等劫。供養是諸菩薩衣服飲食臥具醫藥 048a07 ‖ 資生之物。隨意供養恭敬尊重讚歎。皆是取 048a08 ‖ 相布施。若菩薩為般若波羅蜜所護。過去未 048a09 ‖ 來現在諸佛戒品定品慧品解脫品解脫知見 048a10 ‖ 品。及聲聞五品。及諸凡[1]夫人於中種善根。 048a11 ‖ 已種今種當種。盡和合稱量
简体字	又般若波罗蜜回向品中说。佛告净居天子。置此恒河沙等三千大千世界众生皆发阿耨多罗三藐三菩提心。余恒河沙等三千大千世界众生。一一菩萨以取相心供养是诸众生衣服饮食卧具医药资生之物。随意供养于恒河沙等劫。诸天子。若是恒河沙等三千大千世界众生发阿耨多罗三藐三菩提心。余恒河沙等三千大千世界中众生皆亦发阿耨多罗三藐三菩提心。其一菩萨供养是诸菩萨衣服饮食卧具医药资生之物于恒河沙等劫。是布施取相分别。如是诸菩萨各于恒河沙等劫。供养是诸菩萨衣服饮食卧具医药资生之物。随意供养恭敬尊重赞叹。皆是取相布施。若菩萨为般若波罗蜜所护。过去未来现在诸佛戒品定品慧品解脱品解脱知见品。及声闻五品。及诸凡夫人于中种善根。已种今种当种。尽和合称量

Chapter 11 — *Distinctions with Regard to Merit*

Also, the "Dedication" of the *[Mahā]prajñāpāramitā [Sūtra]* records that, in speaking to the devas of the Pure Abodes Heavens, the Buddha said the following:

> Let us set aside this case of there being on the one hand beings as numerous as those in the worlds of great trichiliocosms as numerous as the Ganges' sands who had brought forth the resolve to attain *anuttarasamyaksaṃbodhi* while on the other hand there is another group of beings as numerous as those in the worlds of great trichiliocosms as numerous as the Ganges' sands and then each and every one of these bodhisattvas [in the former group] made offerings to all these beings [in the latter group], giving clothing, food and drink, bedding, medicines, and other means of sustenance, freely making such offerings for a number of kalpas as numerous as the Ganges' sands, but doing all of this giving with minds attached to signs.
>
> Devas, [consider instead a case where, on the one hand, there are] all these beings in the worlds of great trichiliocosms as numerous as the Ganges' sands who had brought forth the resolve to attain *anuttarasamyaksaṃbodhi* while on the other hand there was yet another group of beings in the worlds of great trichiliocosms as numerous as Ganges' sands who had also brought forth the resolve to attain *anuttarasamyaksaṃbodhi*.
>
> If one of that latter group of bodhisattvas made offerings to every one of that former group of bodhisattvas, making offerings of clothing, food and drink, bedding, medicines, and means of sustenance, doing so for kalpas as numerous as the Ganges' sands, but doing so with mental discriminations seizing on signs even as, in addition, in this same manner, every one of all of the rest of those bodhisattvas [in this latter group] made offerings to all those bodhisattvas [in the former group], giving clothing, food and drink, bedding, medicines, and means of sustenance, freely making such offerings for kalpas as numerous as the Ganges' sands while also paying reverence to them and uttering their praises, but with all of this giving also involving seizing on signs.
>
> [Now consider yet another case, as follows:] If a bodhisattva guarded and protected by the *prajñāpāramitā* were to consider the roots of goodness of all buddhas of the past, future, and present, including that associated with their qualities of moral precept observance, meditative absorption, wisdom, liberation, and knowledge and vision of liberation, [and the roots of goodness] associated with these same five qualities as acquired by the *śrāvaka* disciples, and also [the roots of goodness of] common people—if he were to consider all these roots of goodness planted in the past, present, and future, considering them all together, and assessing them all without

正體字

```
              使無遺餘。最
048a12 ||  上最妙最勝無等無等等不可思議隨喜福
048a13 ||  德。迴向阿耨多羅三藐三菩提。作是念。我
048a14 ||  是福德能至佛道。是福德於先取相福德百
048a15 ||  分不及一。千[2]分萬分億分乃至算數譬喻
048a16 ||  所不能及。何以故。是諸菩薩取相分別布
048a17 ||  施故。復有恒河沙等三千大千世界眾生。皆
048a18 ||  發阿耨多羅三藐三菩提心。身行善業口
048a19 ||  行善業意行善業。復有恒河沙等三千大
048a20 ||  千世界眾生。皆發阿耨多羅三藐三菩提心。
048a21 ||  若人於恒河沙等劫惡口罵詈皆能忍受。於
048a22 ||  恒河沙等劫。身心精進除諸懈怠。攝心禪定
048a23 ||  無諸亂想。而皆取相不如菩薩如法性迴
048a24 ||  向其福為勝。是故如汝先說。作如是事得
048a25 ||  何等利者。得如是大福德聚。是故若人欲
048a26 ||  得如是無量無邊不可思議福德聚者。應
048a27 ||  行是懺悔勸請隨喜迴向。不惜身命利養
048a28 ||  名聞。於晝夜中常應勤行。
```

简体字

使无遗余。最上最妙最胜无等无等等不可思议随喜福德。回向阿耨多罗三藐三菩提。作是念。我是福德能至佛道。是福德于先取相福德百分不及一。千分万分亿分乃至算数譬喻所不能及。何以故。是诸菩萨取相分别布施故。复有恒河沙等三千大千世界众生。皆发阿耨多罗三藐三菩提心。身行善业口行善业意行善业。复有恒河沙等三千大千世界众生。皆发阿耨多罗三藐三菩提心。若人于恒河沙等劫恶口骂詈皆能忍受。于恒河沙等劫。身心精进除诸懈怠。摄心禅定无诸乱想。而皆取相不如菩萨如法性回向其福为胜。是故如汝先说。作如是事得何等利者。得如是大福德聚。是故若人欲得如是无量无边不可思议福德聚者。应行是忏悔劝请随喜回向。不惜身命利养名闻。于昼夜中常应勤行。

excluding any—if with respect to all that merit he were to then perform the most supreme, the most sublime, the most excellent rejoicing, unequaled rejoicing, rejoicing that is equal to the unequaled and inconceivable—and if he were then to dedicate the merit arising from that rejoicing to *anuttarasamyaksaṃbodhi*, reflecting, "May this merit of mine enable the realization of buddhahood,"—if one were to compare the former merit involving seizing on signs with this latter stock of merit, it could not equal even a hundredth part, a thousandth part, a ten-thousandth part, or even the smallest fraction of a *koṭi*'s part. The comparison is such that it would be beyond the reach of calculation or analogy. Why is this so? This is because the giving done by that former group of bodhisattvas involved mental discriminations seizing on signs.

Furthermore, suppose that on the one hand there was a group of beings as numerous as those in all worlds in great trichiliocosms as numerous as the Ganges' sands who had brought forth the resolve to attain *anuttarasamyaksaṃbodhi* and who practiced good physical karma, good verbal karma, and good mental karma, while [on the other hand] there was yet another group of beings as numerous as those in all the worlds in great trichiliocosms as numerous as the Ganges' sands who had also brought forth the resolve to attain *anuttarasamyaksaṃbodhi*, [doing so with such solidity of resolve that], even if they were scolded, reviled, and cursed for kalpas as numerous as the Ganges' sands, they would still be able to endure this for kalpas as numerous as the Ganges' sands even as they continued with physical and mental vigor to rid themselves of every form of indolence and focus their minds in *dhyāna* concentration free of scattered thoughts, but doing so while still seizing on signs. The merit of those [described in both these latter cases], would still not compare with that of the single bodhisattva who carried out his dedication of merit in a manner conforming to the nature of dharmas, for his merit would be superior.

Therefore, regarding your earlier question as to what benefit results from these practices [involving repentance, entreating, rejoicing, and dedication], one gains a mass of merit of such magnitude as this. Therefore, if someone wishes to gain such an immeasurable, boundless, and inconceivable mass of merit, he should practice this repentance, entreating, rejoicing, and dedication, not sparing even his own body and life and not caring about receiving offerings or enjoying fame, but rather always diligently devoting himself to these practices both by day and by night.

正體字	問曰。汝但說勸 048a29 ‖ 請隨喜迴向中福德。何故不說懺悔中福德 048b01 ‖ 耶。答曰。於諸福德中。懺悔福德最大。除業 048b02 ‖ 障罪故。得善行菩薩道行勸請隨喜迴向 048b03 ‖ 與空無相無願和合無異。復次懺悔。如如 048b04 ‖ 意珠隨願皆得。如佛說。若人欲於婆羅門 048b05 ‖ 大姓中生。剎利大姓中生。居士大家中生。 048b06 ‖ 應如是懺悔罪業無所覆藏後不更作。若 048b07 ‖ 有人欲生四天王天上忉利天上夜摩天上 048b08 ‖ 兜率陀天上化樂天上他化自在天上。亦應 048b09 ‖ 如是懺悔罪業無所覆藏後不更作。若人 048b10 ‖ 欲生梵世乃至非想非非想處。是人亦應 048b11 ‖ 如是懺悔罪業無所覆藏後不更作。若人 048b12 ‖ 欲得須陀洹果斯陀含果阿那含果阿羅漢 048b13 ‖ 果。亦應如是懺悔罪業。若人欲得三明六 048b14 ‖ 神通聲聞道中自在力盡聲聞功德彼岸。亦 048b15 ‖ 應如是懺悔罪業。若人欲得辟支佛道。亦 048b16 ‖ 應如是懺悔罪業。若人欲得一切智慧不 048b17 ‖ 可思議智慧無礙智慧無上智慧。
简体字	问曰。汝但说劝请随喜回向中福德。何故不说忏悔中福德耶。答曰。于诸福德中。忏悔福德最大。除业障罪故。得善行菩萨道行劝请随喜回向与空无相无愿和合无异。复次忏悔。如如意珠随愿皆得。如佛说。若人欲于婆罗门大姓中生。刹利大姓中生。居士大家中生。应如是忏悔罪业无所覆藏后不更作。若有人欲生四天王天上切利天上夜摩天上兜率陀天上化乐天上他化自在天上。亦应如是忏悔罪业无所覆藏后不更作。若人欲生梵世乃至非想非非想处。是人亦应如是忏悔罪业无所覆藏后不更作。若人欲得须陀洹果斯陀含果阿那含果阿罗汉果。亦应如是忏悔罪业。若人欲得三明六神通声闻道中自在力尽声闻功德彼岸。亦应如是忏悔罪业。若人欲得辟支佛道。亦应如是忏悔罪业。若人欲得一切智慧不可思议智慧无碍智慧无上智慧。

E. Q: Why Have You Not Discussed the Merit Arising from Repentance?

Question: You have still only described the merit derived from entreating, rejoicing, and dedication of merit. Why have you not discussed the merit involved in repentance?

F. A: The Merit Arising from Repentance Is the Greatest

Response: Among all of these sources of merit, the merit associated with repentance is the greatest. Because one is thereby able to get rid of the offenses constituting one's karmic obstacles, one therefore becomes able to skillfully practice the bodhisattva path and practice entreating, rejoicing, and dedication of merit, doing so in a manner that is conjoined with and no different from the realization of emptiness, signlessness, and wishlessness.

Additionally, repentance is comparable to some wish-fulfilling jewel through which one is able to obtain whatever one wishes. As the Buddha said:

> If someone wishes to be reborn within a great brahman-caste family, within a great *kṣatriyan*-caste family, or within a great *vaiśya*-caste clan, he should repent of his karmic offenses, concealing none of them, and vowing not to repeat them.
>
> If someone wishes to be reborn in the Heaven of the Four Heavenly Kings, in the Trāyastriṃśa Heaven, in the Yāma Heaven, in the Tuṣita Heaven, in the Nirmāṇarati Heaven, or in the Paramirmita Vaśavartin Heaven, in those cases as well, he should carry out the repentance of karmic offenses, concealing none of them, and vowing not to repeat them.
>
> If someone wishes to be reborn in the Brahma Heaven or anywhere on up to the station of neither perception nor non-perception, this person too should repent of karmic offenses in this very same way, concealing none of them, and vowing not to repeat them.
>
> If someone wishes to gain the fruit of the stream enterer, the fruit of the *sakṛdāgāmin*, the fruit of the *anāgāmin*, or the fruit of arhatship, he too should carry out this repentance of karmic offenses.
>
> If someone wishes to gain the three clear knowledges,[172] the six types of psychic power, or the powers of sovereign mastery associated with the *śrāvaka* disciple path, or if he wishes to reach the far shore of perfection in the meritorious qualities associated with the *śrāvaka* disciple path, in these cases too, he should carry out repentance of karmic offenses in this manner.
>
> If someone wishes to become a *pratyekabuddha*, in this case too, he should carry out repentance of karmic offenses in this manner.
>
> If someone wishes to gain the wisdom of omniscience, inconceivable wisdom, unimpeded wisdom, or unsurpassable wisdom, in

正體字	亦應如是 048b18 ‖ 懺悔罪業無所覆藏後不更作。是故當知 048b19 ‖ 懺悔有大果報。問曰。汝言懺悔除業障罪。 048b20 ‖ 餘經中說。佛告阿難故作業必當受報。又 048b21 ‖ 阿毘曇中說。諸業因緣不空。果報不失 048b22 ‖ 不滅。又經說眾生皆屬業。皆從業有依止 048b23 ‖ 於業。眾生隨業各自受報。若現報若生報若 048b24 ‖ 後報。又業報經中閻羅王為眾生說言。咄眾 048b25 ‖ 生。汝此罪非父母作天作沙門婆羅門作。汝 048b26 ‖ 自作自應受報。又賢聖偈中說。 048b27 ‖ 　實法如金剛　　業力將無勝 048b28 ‖ 　今我已得道　　而受惡業報 048b29 ‖ 又佛自說。 048c01 ‖ 　大海諸[3]名山　　丘陵樹林木 048c02 ‖ 　地水火風等　　日月諸星宿 048c03 ‖ 　若至劫燒時　　皆盡無有餘 048c04 ‖ 　業於無量劫　　常在而不失 048c05 ‖ 　汝遇具相者　　一切智人師
简体字	亦应如是忏悔罪业无所覆藏后不更作。是故当知忏悔有大果报。问曰。汝言忏悔除业障罪。余经中说。佛告阿难故作业必当受报。又阿毗昙中说。诸业因缘不空。果报不失不灭。又经说众生皆属业。皆从业有依止于业。众生随业各自受报。若现报若生报若后报。又业报经中阎罗王为众生说言。咄众生。汝此罪非父母作天作沙门婆罗门作。汝自作自应受报。又贤圣偈中说。 　实法如金刚　　业力将无胜 　今我已得道　　而受恶业报 又佛自说。 　大海诸名山　　丘陵树林木 　地水火风等　　日月诸星宿 　若至劫烧时　　皆尽无有余 　业于无量劫　　常在而不失 　汝遇具相者　　一切智人师

these cases too, he should carry out repentance of karmic offenses in this manner, concealing none of them, and vowing not to repeat them.

Therefore, one should realize that repentance has great karmic effects.

G. Q: How Can You Say That Repentance Gets Rid of Karmic Offenses?

Question: You claim that repentance allows one to eliminate the karmic offenses that create karmic obstacles. However, another sutra states: "The Buddha told Ānanda, 'If one intentionally commits a karmic act, one is certainly bound to undergo its retribution.'"

Additionally, the Abhidharma states, "The causes and conditions involved in karmic acts are not empty. Their retributions are neither lost nor extinguished."

Furthermore, it states in the sutras that beings all belong to their karma, that they all exist on the basis of their karma, that they depend upon and abide within their karma, that beings follow their karma, and that everyone individually undergoes their own corresponding karmic retribution, whether that be present-life retribution, retribution undergone in the next life, or retribution undergone in subsequent lives.[173]

Also, in *The Karmic Retribution Sutra*, King Yāma says to beings, "Tut! You beings! These karmic offenses of yours were not created by your parents, by devas, by *śramaṇas*, or by brahmans. You created them yourselves and so you should undergo retribution for them yourselves."

Furthermore, in "The Verse of the Worthies and Āryas," it says:

The true Dharma is like vajra.
The general of karmic power remains unconquerable.
Even though I have now already attained buddhahood,
I would still be bound to undergo retribution for bad karma.

Additionally, the Buddha said:

The great seas and the famous mountains,
the hills, the trees, the forests,
the earth, the water, fire, wind, and such,
as well as the sun, the moon, the stars and constellations—

Once they reach the time of the kalpa's burning,
all without exception will come to an end.
Karma, however, even for countless kalpas,
always abides and never is lost.

You have encountered the one replete with all the marks,
the omniscient one, the teacher of men.

| 048c06 ‖ 　　先所造罪業　　已償其果報
| 048c07 ‖ 　　今雖得值佛　　垢盡證聖果
| 048c08 ‖ 　　以餘因緣故　　木刺猶在身
| 048c09 ‖ 是故不應言懺悔除[4]業罪。答曰。我不言
| 048c10 ‖ 懺悔則罪業滅盡無有[5]報果。我言懺悔罪
| 048c11 ‖ 則輕薄於少時受。是故懺悔。偈中說。若應
| 048c12 ‖ 墮三惡道願人身中受。又如來智印經中
| 048c13 ‖ 說。佛告彌勒。諸菩薩深心愛樂阿耨多羅三
| 048c14 ‖ 藐三菩提者。有罪應在惡道受報是罪輕
| 048c15 ‖ 微。後世受惡形。或多疾病無有威德生
| 048c16 ‖ 下賤家貧窮家邪見家邪業自活家。生違意
| 048c17 ‖ 處多憂愁處。國土破壞聚落破壞。居家破壞
| 048c18 ‖ 所愛破壞。不遇善知識常不聞法不得
| 048c19 ‖ 利養。若得麁弊常不自供。

　　先所造罪业　　已偿其果报
　　今虽得值佛　　垢尽证圣果
　　以余因缘故　　木刺犹在身

是故不应言忏悔除业罪。答曰。我不言忏悔则罪业灭尽无有报果。我言忏悔罪则轻薄于少时受。是故忏悔。偈中说。若应堕三恶道愿人身中受。又如来智印经中说。佛告弥勒。诸菩萨深心爱乐阿耨多罗三藐三菩提者。有罪应在恶道受报是罪轻微。后世受恶形。或多疾病无有威德生下贱家贫穷家邪见家邪业自活家。生违意处多忧愁处。国土破坏聚落破坏。居家破坏所爱破坏。不遇善知识常不闻法不得利养。若得粗弊常不自供。

As for the karmic offenses committed in the past,
his resulting retributions have already been repaid.

Now, although you have succeeded in meeting the Buddha,
in ending the defilements, and in attaining the fruits of the Ārya,
because of residual causes and conditions,
slivers of wood are still able to penetrate the body.

Therefore one should not claim that repentance gets rid of karmic offenses.

H. A: Although Not Eliminated Entirely, They Are Greatly Reduced

Response: I did not claim that if one repents, then offense karma is entirely extinguished so that there is no resulting karmic retribution. I said that if one repents of one's karmic offenses, then [their retribution] may be lightened and undergone in a short period of time. Therefore, a verse on repentance says, "If I should fall into the three wretched destinies, I pray that I might instead undergo [the retribution] in a human body."

Additionally, in *The Sutra on the Wisdom Seal of the Tathāgata*, it states that the Buddha informed Maitreya, saying:

> Bodhisattvas who, with deep-seated aspirations, delight in [the prospect of attaining] *anuttarasamyaksaṃbodhi* may still have karmic offenses whereby they should otherwise undergo retribution in the wretched destinies. When these karmic offenses have become lighter, they may then be bound in later lifetimes:
>
> To receive an ugly physical form;
> To be much afflicted by sickness;
> To have no awe-inspiring personal presence;
> To be born into a lower-class family, into a poor family, into a family in which wrong views are dominant, or into a family supporting itself with a deviant livelihood;
> To be born into a place contrary to their wishes or a place beset with many worries;
> To be born into a country that becomes destroyed, a village that becomes destroyed, a family compound that becomes destroyed, or a circumstance where whatever they love becomes destroyed;
> To be unable to encounter a good spiritual guide;
> To never be able to hear the Dharma;
> To be unable to receive any means of support, or, if they acquire it, it is coarse, inferior, and always inadequate for self-sustenance;

正體字

能令下賤之所
048c20 ‖ 信敬於諸大人不得信敬。修集諸福時。
048c21 ‖ 多有障礙不得成就。諸根闇鈍習禪意亂。
048c22 ‖ 不得無漏覺意功德。不知經法隨宜所趣
048c23 ‖ 乃至惡夢償惡道報。又佛說人有小罪。今世
048c24 ‖ 可受報。是罪轉多便墮地獄。云何是人今
048c25 ‖ 世小罪轉多而墮地獄。有人不修身不修
048c26 ‖ 戒不修心不修慧無有大意。是人小罪便
048c27 ‖ 墮地獄。云何是人有罪今世應受報。罪不
048c28 ‖ 增長不入地獄。有人修身修戒修心修
048c29 ‖ 慧。有大志意心無拘[6]閡。如是人有罪不
049a01 ‖ 復增長今世現受。譬如人以小器盛水。著
049a02 ‖ 一升鹽則不可飲。若復有人。以一升鹽
049a03 ‖ 投於大[1]池尚不覺鹽味。何[2]況叵飲。何以
049a04 ‖ 故。

简体字

能令下贱之所信敬于诸大人不得信敬。修集诸福时。多有障碍不得成就。诸根闇钝习禅意乱。不得无漏觉意功德。不知经法随宜所趣乃至恶梦偿恶道报。又佛说人有小罪。今世可受报。是罪转多便墮地狱。云何是人今世小罪转多而墮地狱。有人不修身不修戒不修心不修慧无有大意。是人小罪便墮地狱。云何是人有罪今世应受报。罪不增长不入地狱。有人修身修戒修心修慧。有大志意心无拘阂。如是人有罪不复增长今世现受。譬如人以小器盛水。着一升盐则不可饮。若复有人。以一升盐投于大池尚不觉盐味。何况叵饮。何以故。

To have the ability to inspire the faith and respect of those who are of inferior or base character, but to never be able to inspire the faith and respect of great men;

To have it happen that, whenever they cultivate the accumulation of merit, they encounter a multitude of hindrances and end up being unsuccessful in the attempt;

To have all of their faculties be dim and dull;

To have it be that, whenever they practice *dhyāna*, their mind is subject to confusion;

To be unable to gain the qualities of an awakened mind free of contaminants;

To be unable to understand the correct import of the Dharma of the sutras;

And so forth, including even experiencing nightmares, thereby undergoing [in these various ways] the retribution [that would otherwise entail descent into] the wretched destinies.[174]

Additionally, the Buddha stated:[175]

If a person has a minor karmic offense, he may be able to undergo the retribution in this present life, but if that karmic offense increases in its magnitude, he will be bound to fall into the hells.

What is meant by this statement that a small karmic offense in the present life might increase in magnitude to the point that one is then bound to fall into the hells? It could be that someone fails to cultivate [the actions of] the body, fails to cultivate observance of the moral precepts, fails to cultivate qualities of mind, fails to cultivate wisdom, and also remains bereft of great intentions. This is a person who, if he commits even a minor karmic offense, may become bound to fall into the hells.

What is meant by the statement that this person with a karmic offense entailing retribution in the present life may avoid falling into the hells provided that his karmic offenses do not increase in magnitude? This refers to someone of this sort who cultivates [the actions of] the body, cultivates observance of the moral precepts, cultivates qualities of mind, cultivates wisdom, and also possesses great intentions unconstrained by hindrances. If someone of this sort has karmic offenses, but they do not increase in their magnitude, their retribution will occur in the present life.

Suppose for example that someone mixed a pint of salt into a small container of water. He would then find it to be undrinkable. But if another person casts a pint of salt into a large pond, he would not find its water the least bit salty, how much the less would he find it undrinkable. What is the reason for this? It is because the volume

正體字

水多鹽少故。罪亦如是。偈說。
049a05 ‖ 升鹽投大海　　其味無有異
049a06 ‖ 若投小器水　　鹹苦不可飲
049a07 ‖ 如人大積福　　而有少罪惡
049a08 ‖ 不墮於惡道　　餘緣而輕受
049a09 ‖ 又人薄福德　　而有少罪惡
049a10 ‖ 心志狹小故　　罪令墮惡道
049a11 ‖ 若人火勢弱　　食少難消食
049a12 ‖ 此人雖不死　　其身受大苦
049a13 ‖ 若人身勢強　　食少難消食
049a14 ‖ 此人終不死　　但受輕微苦
049a15 ‖ 善福慧[3]火弱　　而有少惡罪
049a16 ‖ 是罪無救者　　能令墮地獄
049a17 ‖ [4]有大福德者　　雖有罪惡事
049a18 ‖ 不令墮地獄　　現身而輕受
049a19 ‖ 譬如鴦崛魔　　多殺於人眾
049a20 ‖ 又欲害母佛　　得阿羅漢道
049a21 ‖ 今世輕受又如阿闍世害得道父王。以佛及
049a22 ‖ 文殊師利因緣故重罪輕受。

简体字

水多盐少故。罪亦如是。偈说。
　　升盐投大海　　其味无有异
　　若投小器水　　碱苦不可饮
　　如人大积福　　而有少罪恶
　　不堕于恶道　　余缘而轻受
　　又人薄福德　　而有少罪恶
　　心志狭小故　　罪令堕恶道
　　若人火势弱　　食少难消食
　　此人虽不死　　其身受大苦
　　若人身势强　　食少难消食
　　此人终不死　　但受轻微苦
　　善福慧火弱　　而有少恶罪
　　是罪无救者　　能令堕地狱
　　有大福德者　　虽有罪恶事
　　不令堕地狱　　现身而轻受
　　譬如鸯崛魔　　多杀于人众
　　又欲害母佛　　得阿罗汉道
　　今世轻受又如阿阇世害得道父王。以佛及文殊师利因缘故重罪轻受。

Chapter 11 — *Distinctions with Regard to Merit*

of water is great while that of the salt is but little. So too it is with karmic offenses.

Accordingly, we have the following verses:

When a pint of salt is thrown into an immense pond,
its flavor remains no different,
However, if one instead mixes it into a small container of water,
the harshness of the salt makes the water undrinkable.

This is analogous to there being a person with a great stock of merit
who has but few karmic offenses
and who is not bound to fall into the wretched destinies,
but rather undergoes mild retribution under other conditions

while there is another person with only a scant amount of merit
who has committed but few karmic offenses that,
because his mental resolve is but narrow and small,
is caused by those karmic offenses to fall into the wretched destinies.

If someone's physical vitality (lit. "fire") is weak in its strength,
when he eats but a little of something difficult to digest,
although this person doesn't die,
his body undergoes much suffering.

If someone's physical vitality is strong,
when he eats but a little of something difficult to digest,
such a person never dies from it
and undergoes only a minor amount of suffering.

If the vitality of one's goodness, merit, and wisdom is weak,
and he has committed but few bad karmic offenses,
there is nothing to save him from these karmic offenses,
and hence they are able to cause his descent into the hells.

In the case of someone possessed of great merit,
even though he may have done bad things involving karmic offenses,
they may not compel him to fall into the hells,
for he may instead undergo only mild present-life retribution.

Take for example the case of Aṅgulimāla.
Although he murdered many people
and also wished to harm his mother and the Buddha,
he still attained the path of arhatship.

The principle of undergoing only mild retribution in this present life is also illustrated by Ajātaśatru who killed his father, the King, a man who had already attained enlightenment. Through causes and conditions having to do with the Buddha and Mañjuśrī, this grave karmic offense resulted in only relatively mild retribution.

正體字		
		又如人毒蛇生
	049a23 ‖	時雨血。後漸長大意欲殺人眼看即死。若
	049a24 ‖	以氣噓亦死。是故時人號為氣噓。是人命
	049a25 ‖	終時。舍利弗往至其所。心中瞋恚眼看不死
	049a26 ‖	噓亦不死。舍利弗身色方更光顯。心即清淨
	049a27 ‖	上下七觀。以是因緣命終之後七反生天上
	049a28 ‖	七反生人中。於後人壽四萬歲時。當得辟
	049a29 ‖	支佛道。身黃金色。時人謂是金聚來。欲斫
	049b01 ‖	取即命終涅槃。又如阿輸伽王。以兵伏閻
	049b02 ‖	浮提。殺萬八千宮人。先世施佛土故。[5]起
	049b03 ‖	八萬塔。常於大阿羅漢所聽受經法。後得
	049b04 ‖	須陀洹道。即人身輕償。如是等罪多行福
	049b05 ‖	德志意曠大。集諸功德故不墮惡道。是故
	049b06 ‖	汝先難若懺悔罪業。則滅盡無有果報者
	049b07 ‖	是語不然。復次若言罪不可滅者。毘尼中
	049b08 ‖	佛說懺悔除罪則不可信。是事

简体字
又如人毒蛇生时雨血。后渐长大意欲杀人眼看即死。若以气嘘亦死。是故时人号为气嘘。是人命终时。舍利弗往至其所。心中瞋恚眼看不死嘘亦不死。舍利弗身色方更光显。心即清净上下七观。以是因缘命终之后七反生天上七反生人中。于后人寿四万岁时。当得辟支佛道。身黄金色。时人谓是金聚来。欲斫取即命终涅槃。又如阿输伽王。以兵伏阎浮提。杀万八千宫人。先世施佛土故。起八万塔。常于大阿罗汉所听受经法。后得须陀洹道。即人身轻偿。如是等罪多行福德志意旷大。集诸功德故不堕恶道。是故汝先难若忏悔罪业。则灭尽无有果报者是语不然。复次若言罪不可灭者。毗尼中佛说忏悔除罪则不可信。是事

[This principle is also illustrated by] the case of "Poisonous Snake Man." When he was born, it rained blood. Afterward, as he grew up, if he wished to kill some person, he only needed to glare at him, whereupon they would immediately fall dead. If he so much as blew his breath on someone, then too, they would fall dead. Because of this, the people of the time called him "Breath Blower."

When this man's life was about to come to an end, Śāriputra went to his abode, whereupon he became angry and glared at Śāriputra. Even so, this did not cause Śāriputra to fall dead. He then blew his breath onto Śāriputra, but that did not cause him to fall dead, either. Rather, the radiance of Śāriputra's body simply shone ever brighter.

When this happened, his mind immediately became pure and he gazed at Śāriputra, scanning him up and down seven times. Based on these causes and conditions, after he died, he was born seven times up in the heavens and seven times back in the human realm and became bound to become a *pratyekabuddha* at that time when the human life span extends to forty thousand years. Then his body will become the color of gold, whereupon the people of that time will mistake him for a mass of gold and will attempt to hack away chunks of it. His life will then immediately come to an end and he will enter nirvāṇa.

This is also illustrated by the case of King Aśoka who, having used his troops to subdue the continent of Jambudvīpa, was responsible for killing eighteen thousand palace courtiers [in those conquered domains]. However, because, as a child in a previous life, he had gifted the Buddha with a lump of clay, he was later moved to erect eighty thousand stupas, always listened to and accepted the Dharma taught to him by great arhats, and later attained the enlightenment of the stream enterer. This is yet another instance of being able to undergo mild retribution while still abiding in a human body.

In instances where one undergoes [retribution for] karmic offenses in this way, it is when one has practiced many meritorious deeds while also being possessed of a vast and immense resolve. Then, because one has accumulated all manner of merit, he does not fall into the wretched destinies.

Therefore, as for the challenge that you presented earlier [with regard to the teaching that], if one repents of karmic offenses, they will then be completely extinguished so that there is no resulting karmic retribution—[that challenge] is erroneous. Furthermore, if one claims that karmic offenses cannot be extinguished at all, then one would be unable to believe the Buddha's statement in the Vinaya that, if one repents, one may thereby get rid of one's offenses. This matter is not as

正體字

不然。是故
049b09 ‖ 業障罪應懺悔。

简体字

不然。是故业障罪应忏悔。

you have claimed. Therefore, one should indeed repent of the karmic offenses that create karmic obstacles.

The End of Chapter Eleven

正體字

049b10 ‖　　　分別布施品第十二
049b11 ‖ 菩薩能行如是懺悔勸請隨喜迴向。
049b12 ‖　福德力轉增　　心亦益柔軟
049b13 ‖　即信佛功德　　及菩薩大行
049b14 ‖ 是菩薩以懺悔勸請隨喜迴向故。福力轉增
049b15 ‖ 心調柔軟。於諸佛無量功德清淨第一凡夫
049b16 ‖ 所不信而能信受。及諸大菩薩清淨大行。希
049b17 ‖ 有難事亦能信受。復次。
049b18 ‖　苦惱諸眾生　　無是深淨法
049b19 ‖　於此生愍傷　　而發深悲心
049b20 ‖ [6]菩薩信諸佛菩薩無量甚深清淨第一功德
049b21 ‖ 已愍傷諸眾生。無此功德但以諸邪見受
049b22 ‖ 種種苦惱故。深生悲心。
049b23 ‖　念是諸眾生　　沒在苦惱泥
049b24 ‖　我當救拔之　　令在安隱處

简体字

分别布施品第十二

菩萨能行如是忏悔劝请随喜回向。
　福德力转增　　心亦益柔软
　即信佛功德　　及菩萨大行

是菩萨以忏悔劝请随喜回向故。福力转增心调柔软。于诸佛无量功德清净第一凡夫所不信而能信受。及诸大菩萨清净大行。希有难事亦能信受。复次。

　苦恼诸众生　　无是深净法
　于此生愍伤　　而发深悲心

菩萨信诸佛菩萨无量甚深清净第一功德已愍伤诸众生。无此功德但以诸邪见受种种苦恼故。深生悲心。

　念是诸众生　　没在苦恼泥
　我当救拔之　　令在安隐处

Chapter 12
Distinctions with Regard to Giving

XII. Chapter 12: Distinctions with Regard to Giving
  A. With More Merit & Mental Pliancy, the Bodhisattva Develops Faith

As for the bodhisattva who is able in this manner to carry out repentance, entreating, rejoicing, and dedication:

> As the power of his merit increases,
> and his mind also becomes more pliant,
> he then develops faith in the Buddhas' meritorious qualities
> and in the great conduct of the bodhisattvas.

Because of his repentance, entreating, rejoicing, and dedication, the power of this bodhisattva's merit increases and his mind becomes well-trained and possessed of pliancy. Thus he becomes able to have faith in and accept what the common person has no faith in, namely the Buddhas' measureless and supremely pure meritorious qualities. He is also able to place faith in and accept the rare and difficult endeavors accomplished by the great bodhisattvas' as they carry out their pure and great practices.

Now, again, a verse:

  B. The Bodhisattva's Sympathy for Beings Leads to Compassion for Them

> Beings who are all afflicted with suffering
> do not possess this profound and pure Dharma.
> He feels pity and sadness for them
> and so brings forth a mind of deep compassion for them.

Having developed faith in the measureless, extremely profound, and supremely pure meritorious qualities of the buddhas and bodhisattvas, the bodhisattva feels pity and sadness for all beings who have none of these meritorious qualities. Because they hold every sort of wrong view, they only experience the many different types of suffering. Consequently, he brings forth a mind of deep compassion for them.

  C. The Bodhisattva Is Then Motivated to Rescue Beings from Suffering

> He is mindful of all these beings
> that are mired in the mud of suffering, and thinks,
> "I should rescue them by extricating them from this,
> thereby causing them to abide in a state of peace and security."

正體字

049b25 ‖ 是菩薩得悲心已作是念。是諸眾生常為
049b26 ‖ 貪恚癡所病。以身心受諸苦惱。我當拔濟
049b27 ‖ 使離身心苦惱深[7]塹。畢竟無生老病死患。
049b28 ‖ 得住安隱涅槃樂處。是故於此苦惱眾生
049b29 ‖ 生深悲心。以悲心故為求隨意使得安
049c01 ‖ 樂。則名慈心。
049c02 ‖ 　若菩薩如是　　深隨慈悲心
049c03 ‖ 　斷所有貪惜　　為施勤精進
049c04 ‖ 菩薩是求佛道。度苦惱眾生。念者隨名隨
049c05 ‖ 順慈悲不隨餘心。深慈名遍。諸眾生念徹
049c06 ‖ 骨髓。所有名一切內外。所有金銀珍寶國城
049c07 ‖ 妻子等。貪名欲得無厭惜名。愛著不欲與
049c08 ‖ 他斷名。離此[8]三惡如是則開檀波羅蜜
049c09 ‖ 門。是故常應一心勤行無令放逸。何以故。
049c10 ‖ 菩薩作是念。我今隨所能作利益眾生。發
049c11 ‖ 堅固施心。
049c12 ‖ 　所有一切物　　有命若無命

简体字

是菩萨得悲心已作是念。是诸众生常为贪恚痴所病。以身心受诸苦恼。我当拔济使离身心苦恼深堑。毕竟无生老病死患。得住安隐涅槃乐处。是故于此苦恼众生生深悲心。以悲心故为求随意使得安乐。则名慈心。

　若菩萨如是　　深随慈悲心
　断所有贪惜　　为施勤精进

菩萨是求佛道。度苦恼众生。念者随名随顺慈悲不随余心。深慈名遍。诸众生念彻骨髓。所有名一切内外。所有金银珍宝国城妻子等。贪名欲得无厌惜名。爱着不欲与他断名。离此三恶如是则开檀波罗蜜门。是故常应一心勤行无令放逸。何以故。菩萨作是念。我今随所能作利益众生。发坚固施心。

　所有一切物　　有命若无命

Having brought forth the mind of compassion, this bodhisattva thinks, "All of these beings are always afflicted by greed, hatred, and delusion and because of that they undergo all manner of physical and mental suffering. I shall rescue them by extricating them from that, thereby causing them to leave behind the deep mud of physical and mental suffering. Then they will finally become free of the misfortunes of birth, aging, sickness, and death and become able to abide in the peace and security of nirvāṇa's bliss."

He therefore brings forth a deeply compassionate mind for these suffering beings. If, because of this mind of compassion, he seeks for their sakes to bring about whatever they wish for, thereby causing them to find happiness, this is what is known as the mind of loving kindness.

D. Due to Kindness & Compassion, He Devotes Himself to Giving

When, in this manner, the bodhisattva
deeply accords with the mind of kindness and compassion,
he cuts off all covetous cherishing
and devotes himself to giving with diligence and vigor.

It is in this manner that the bodhisattva seeks to realize buddhahood and to liberate beings afflicted by sufferings. As for the "accordance" [engaged in by this individual] who is mindful in this way, this refers to his accordance with kindness and compassion and to his refraining from according with any other states of mind. "Deep kindness" refers to that which extends universally to all beings and involves a degree of mindfulness of them that penetrates to the very marrow of his bones.

"All" refers to every inward and outward thing, to all gold, silver, precious jewels, the state, its cities, his wife and children, and so forth. "Covetousness" refers to the insatiable desire to obtain something. "Cherishing" refers to affectionate attachment on account of which one does not wish to give up something to someone else. "Cut off" refers to abandoning these two bad influences.[176]

If one accords with this, then one thereby throws open the gates of *dāna pāramitā* (the perfection of giving). Therefore, one should always engage in its single-minded and diligent practice, not allowing any room for negligence. And how does one go about accomplishing this? The bodhisattva thinks to himself, "I will now strive to benefit beings however I am able." And so it is that he brings forth a solid resolve to practice giving.

1. The Bodhisattva Is Willing to Give Everything to Beings

As for all of those things he possesses,
whether living or not living,

<table>
<tr><td rowspan="17">正體字</td><td>049c13 ||</td><td colspan="2">轉輪天王位　　無求而不與</td></tr>
<tr><td>049c14 ||</td><td colspan="2">乃至於男女　　族姓好妻妾</td></tr>
<tr><td>049c15 ||</td><td colspan="2">年少甚端嚴　　巧便能事人</td></tr>
<tr><td>049c16 ||</td><td colspan="2">恭順心柔和　　愛念情甚至</td></tr>
<tr><td>049c17 ||</td><td colspan="2">惜之過壽命　　求者皆能與</td></tr>
<tr><td>049c18 ||</td><td colspan="2">乃至身血肉　　骨髓及手足</td></tr>
<tr><td>049c19 ||</td><td colspan="2">頭目耳鼻等　　及身皆能與</td></tr>
<tr><td>049c20 ||</td><td colspan="2">是菩薩定心布施。凡所[9]有外物。若有命若無</td></tr>
<tr><td>049c21 ||</td><td colspan="2">命。無有乞而不與。無命物者金銀珍寶。乃</td></tr>
<tr><td>049c22 ||</td><td colspan="2">至轉輪聖王位天王位。有命物者男女貴[10]族</td></tr>
<tr><td>049c23 ||</td><td colspan="2">好家年少妻妾。端嚴柔和恭敬善順。愛惜之</td></tr>
<tr><td>049c24 ||</td><td colspan="2">至過於身命而能施人。如一切施菩薩所有</td></tr>
<tr><td>049c25 ||</td><td colspan="2">外物及妻子等皆能施與。是菩薩乃至自身肉</td></tr>
<tr><td>049c26 ||</td><td colspan="2">血頭目手足耳鼻。割肉出骨破骨出髓。如</td></tr>
<tr><td>049c27 ||</td><td colspan="2">薩陀波崙。或舉身施與。一切所愛無過身</td></tr>
<tr><td>049c28 ||</td><td colspan="2">者。亦能施與如薩和檀。如菩薩為[11]兔以身</td></tr>
<tr><td>049c29 ||</td><td colspan="2">施與仙人。如尸毘王以身代鴿。</td></tr>
<tr><td rowspan="8">简体字</td><td colspan="3">转轮天王位　　无求而不与</td></tr>
<tr><td colspan="3">乃至于男女　　族姓好妻妾</td></tr>
<tr><td colspan="3">年少甚端严　　巧便能事人</td></tr>
<tr><td colspan="3">恭顺心柔和　　爱念情甚至</td></tr>
<tr><td colspan="3">惜之过寿命　　求者皆能与</td></tr>
<tr><td colspan="3">乃至身血肉　　骨髓及手足</td></tr>
<tr><td colspan="3">头目耳鼻等　　及身皆能与</td></tr>
<tr><td colspan="3">是菩萨定心布施。凡所有外物。若有命若无命。无有乞而不与。无命物者金银珍宝。乃至转轮圣王位天王位。有命物者男女贵族好家年少妻妾。端严柔和恭敬善顺。爱惜之至过于身命而能施人。如一切施菩萨所有外物及妻子等皆能施与。是菩萨乃至自身肉血头目手足耳鼻。割肉出骨破骨出髓。如萨陀波仑。或举身施与。一切所爱无过身者。亦能施与如萨和檀。如菩萨为兔以身施与仙人。如尸毗王以身代鸽。</td></tr>
</table>

Chapter 12 — *Distinctions with Regard to Giving*

including even the throne of a wheel-turning or heavenly king,
there are no instances of their being requested but not given.

This is still the case even with sons and daughters
as well as the clan's wives and consorts of which he is fond,
these who in their youthfulness have extremely fine appearances
and are skillful in their ability to render service to others,

Whose respectful and acquiescent minds are pliant and congenial,
whom he lovingly bears in mind with utmost depth of feeling,
cherishing them even more than his own life—
If someone seeks to have them, he is able to give them all.

This is so even with the flesh and blood of his own body,
his own marrow, his hands and feet,
his head, eyes, ears, nose, and so forth.
He is even able to sacrifice his entire body.

This bodhisattva fixes his mind on giving. As regards whatever outward things he owns, whether sentient or insentient, there is never any case where someone seeks to have them and yet he fails to make a gift of them.

"Not living things" refers to all such things as gold, silver, and precious jewels even up to and including the position of a wheel-turning king or the position of a king among the devas.

"Living things" refers to sons or daughters or to the youthful wives and consorts of the nobility and the best of the clans. Though they are of fine appearance, gentle and agreeable, respectful, and thoroughly acquiescent and even though he feels the most extremely affectionate cherishing for them, greater even than what he feels for his own life, he is still able to give them away to others.

In doing so, he is like "Comprehensive Giving Bodhisattva"[177] who was able to give away all outward possessions including his wife and children. This bodhisattva was able to give even the flesh and blood from his own body, his head, his eyes, his hands and feet, his ears, and his nose, and he was also able to cut into his own flesh, expose the bones, break the bones, and extract his own marrow.

In this, he is also like Sadāprarudita Bodhisattva who would even give his entire body. One cherishes nothing more than one's own body and yet he, too, was able to give like Sarvadāna.

In this, he is also like the bodhisattva who, when he was a rabbit, gave his body as a gift to a rishi.[178]

And, in doing so, he is also like King Śibi who gave up his body to substitute for [and save the life of] a pigeon.

正體字

050a01 ‖ 問曰。是菩
050a01 ‖ 薩為分別知布施及布施果報故。[1]能以難
050a02 ‖ 事施。為但以慈悲心所發故施。答曰。
050a03 ‖ 　如是布施者　　則得如是報
050a04 ‖ 　內以支節等　　并及諸外物
050a05 ‖ 內物名頭目手足等。外物名妻子金銀寶物
050a06 ‖ 等。是菩薩如實知施。是得是報各各分別。
050a07 ‖ 又信諸經所說。或以天眼得知。問曰。汝先
050a08 ‖ 說知以身支節布施及外物布施所得果
050a09 ‖ 報。今可說所得果報。答曰。寶頂經中無盡
050a10 ‖ 意菩薩第三十品檀波羅蜜義中說。菩薩立
050a11 ‖ 願須食者施食。令我得五事報。一者得壽
050a12 ‖ 命。二者得[2]膽。三者得樂。四者得力。五者得
050a13 ‖ 色。須漿與漿者。先於人中得香美飲。後
050a14 ‖ 得除諸煩惱渴愛。須乘與乘則得隨意樂
050a15 ‖ 報。成就四如意足。後得三乘道。

简体字

问曰。是菩萨为分别知布施及布施果报故。能以难事施。为但以慈悲心所发故施。答曰。
　如是布施者　　则得如是报
　内以支节等　　并及诸外物
内物名头目手足等。外物名妻子金银宝物等。是菩萨如实知施。是得是报各各分别。又信诸经所说。或以天眼得知。问曰。汝先说知以身支节布施及外物布施所得果报。今可说所得果报。答曰。宝顶经中无尽意菩萨第三十品檀波罗蜜义中说。菩萨立愿须食者施食。令我得五事报。一者得寿命。二者得胆。三者得乐。四者得力。五者得色。须浆与浆者。先于人中得香美饮。后得除诸烦恼渴爱。须乘与乘则得随意乐报。成就四如意足。后得三乘道。

Chapter 12 — *Distinctions with Regard to Giving*

2. Q: Is His Giving Done for Merit or Due to Kindness and Compassion?

Question: Is this bodhisattva able to perform such difficult acts of giving because of his discriminating knowledge of the value of different types of giving and their corresponding karmic rewards, or does he instead give simply because of the mind of kindness and compassion that he has brought forth?

3. A: He Knows, Has Faith, May Have the Heavenly Eye & So Gives All

Response:
> If one practices giving of this sort,
> then one will gain karmic results of this very same sort.
> Inwardly, one gives up his limbs and such
> while also giving away even all of one's outward possessions.

"Inward possessions" refers to one's own head, eyes, hands, feet, and so forth. "Outward possessions" refers to one's wife, children, gold, silver, jeweled objects, and so forth. This bodhisattva understands giving in accordance with reality in a manner whereby, making distinctions with regard to each case, he realizes, "When this is achieved, then this will be the corresponding karmic result."

In addition, he has faith in what is taught in the sutras and may also be able to use the heavenly eye to know such matters.

a. Q: As You Said He Knows Them, Please Explain These Karmic Results

Question: You just said that he knows the karmic results obtained by giving his body or limbs or by giving away his outward possessions. Could you now speak of the karmic results that may be obtained from this?

b. A: Akṣayamati Bodhisattva's Explanation Is As Follows:

Response: In Chapter Thirty of the *Precious Summit Sutra*, "On the Meaning of Dāna Pāramitā,"[179] Akṣayamati Bodhisattva states that the bodhisattva makes the following aspirational vows:

> May giving food to the hungry result in my receiving five things as karmic results: First, long life; second, courage; third, happiness; fourth, strength; and fifth, physical beauty;
> May providing drinks to those needing something to drink first result in being able when abiding in the human realm to have fragrant and delicious beverages, and then, afterward, being able to dispel the thirst-like cravings associated with the afflictions;
> May giving vehicles to those needing vehicles result in gaining happiness through whatever one wishes, in perfecting the four bases of psychic power, and later on, in attaining success in the paths of the Three Vehicles;

|正體字|

050a16 ‖ 須衣與衣則得慚愧衣報。須燈明與燈明。則得佛眼
050a17 ‖ 光明。須伎樂與伎樂。則得具足天耳。須
050a18 ‖ 末香塗香與末香塗香。則得身無臭穢。須
050a19 ‖ 汁與汁則得味味相報。須房舍與房舍。則
050a20 ‖ 得與一切眾生作歸依救護。施資生之具
050a21 ‖ 者。則得助菩提功德。施醫藥者則得無
050a22 ‖ [3]老病死常樂安隱。施奴婢者。則得自在隨
050a23 ‖ 意具足智慧。施金銀珊瑚[4]車璩馬腦者。則
050a24 ‖ 得具足三十二相。施種種雜物莊嚴[5]具。則
050a25 ‖ 得八十隨形好。施象馬車者。則得具足大
050a26 ‖ 乘。施園林者則得具足禪定樂。施男女
050a27 ‖ 者。得所[6]愛阿耨多羅三藐三菩提。施倉穀
050a28 ‖ 寶藏者。則得具足法藏。施以一國土一閻
050a29 ‖ 浮提四天下王位者。則得道場自在法王。
050b01 ‖ 施諸戲樂具者。則得法樂。以足施者。則得
050b02 ‖ 法足能到道場。以手施者。則得寶手。能施
050b03 ‖ 一切

|简体字|

须衣与衣则得惭愧衣报。须灯明与灯明。则得佛眼光明。须伎乐与伎乐。则得具足天耳。须末香涂香与末香涂香。则得身无臭秽。须汁与汁则得味味相报。须房舍与房舍。则得与一切众生作归依救护。施资生之具者。则得助菩提功德。施医药者则得无老病死常乐安隐。施奴婢者。则得自在随意具足智慧。施金银珊瑚车磲马脑者。则得具足三十二相。施种种杂物庄严具。则得八十随形好。施象马车者。则得具足大乘。施园林者则得具足禅定乐。施男女者。得所爱阿耨多罗三藐三菩提。施仓谷宝藏者。则得具足法藏。施以一国土一阎浮提四天下王位者。则得道场自在法王。施诸戏乐具者。则得法乐。以足施者。则得法足能到道场。以手施者。则得宝手。能施一切

May providing clothing to those in need of clothes bring about the karmic result of then being able to wear the robes of a sense of shame and a dread of blame;

May giving lamplight to those in need of lamplight result in gaining the light of the buddha eye;

May giving music to those wishing for music result in complete acquisition of the heavenly ear;

May giving powdered incenses and perfumes to those needing powdered incense and perfumes result in gaining a body free of unpleasant odors;

May giving juices to those needing juices result in obtaining flavorful tastes;

May providing homes to those in need of homes result in becoming a place of refuge and a source of rescue and protection for all beings;

May providing life-sustaining things to beings result in acquiring the meritorious qualities assisting the attainment of bodhi;

May the giving of medical treatment and medicines result in becoming free of aging, sickness, and death, and in always being able to abide in happiness and security;

May the providing of servants result in perfect wisdom that is masterfully and freely implemented;

May giving gold, silver, coral, mother-of-pearl, and carnelian result in complete acquisition of all thirty-two marks;

May giving all manner of adornments result in gaining the eighty secondary characteristics;

May giving elephants, horses, and carriages result in complete acquisition of the Great Vehicle;

May giving gardens and groves result in complete acquisition of the bliss of *dhyāna* meditation;

May providing male and female [servants] for others result in gaining the *anuttarasamyaksaṃbodhi* that one so cherishes;

May giving granaries and treasuries result in gaining the complete treasury of Dharma;

May bestowing royal dominion over a country, over a Jambudvīpa continent or over the four continents result in becoming a Dharma king exercising sovereign mastery in the *bodhimaṇḍa*;

May the giving all manner of happiness enhancing amusements result in acquiring Dharma bliss;

May giving away one's feet result in gaining the feet of Dharma with which one is able to arrive at the *bodhimaṇḍa*;

May giving away one's hands result in gaining the jewel-bestowing hands with which one is able to give everything;

正體字

050b04 ‖ 以耳鼻施者。則得具足身體。以眼施
050b04 ‖ 者。則得具足無閡法眼。以頭施者。則得三
050b05 ‖ 界特尊一切智慧。以血肉施者。令諸眾生
050b06 ‖ 得堅固行。以髓施者得金剛身無能壞者。
050b07 ‖ 如是開施門果報。餘施果報亦應知。以臥
050b08 ‖ 具施者。得三乘安隱解脫。[7]床以坐處施者。
050b09 ‖ 則得菩提樹下道場不可壞處。以妻施者。為
050b10 ‖ 得法喜娛樂故。以道施者。為生死失道眾
050b11 ‖ 生得入正道故。以筏施者為得度欲流有
050b12 ‖ 流見流無明流故。以骨施者。為得戒堅定
050b13 ‖ [8]堅解脫堅解脫知見堅眾生堅故。以眷屬
050b14 ‖ 施者。為得成就無量無邊阿僧祇福德天
050b15 ‖ 人眷屬同心清淨不可沮壞故。以善哉施
050b16 ‖ 者。為得說法時天龍夜叉乾闥婆沙門婆羅
050b17 ‖ 門歡喜稱讚故。以經卷施者。為得九部經
050b18 ‖ [9]久住無量時故。以法施者。為得通達一
050b19 ‖ 切法故。

简体字

以耳鼻施者。则得具足身体。以眼施者。则得具足无阂法眼。以头施者。则得三界特尊一切智慧。以血肉施者。令诸众生得坚固行。以髓施者得金刚身无能坏者。如是开施门果报。余施果报亦应知。以卧具施者。得三乘安隐解脱。床以坐处施者。则得菩提树下道场不可坏处。以妻施者。为得法喜娱乐故。以道施者。为生死失道众生得入正道故。以筏施者为得度欲流有流见流无明流故。以骨施者。为得戒坚定坚解脱坚解脱知见坚众生坚故。以眷属施者。为得成就无量无边阿僧祇福德天人眷属同心清净不可沮坏故。以善哉施者。为得说法时天龙夜叉乾闼婆沙门婆罗门欢喜称赞故。以经卷施者。为得九部经久住无量时故。以法施者。为得通达一切法故。

May giving away one's ears and nose result in gaining the perfect physical body;

May giving away one's eyes result in gaining the unimpeded Dharma eye;

May giving up one's head result in gaining the omniscience of he who is especially revered throughout the three realms;

May giving one's flesh and blood result in influencing all beings to achieve solid practice;

May the giving of one's marrow result in gaining the indestructible vajra body.

It is in this manner that karmic rewards ensue from opening the gates to the practice of giving.

c. THE KARMIC RESULTS OF OTHER SORTS OF GIVING

The karmic results derived from other sorts of giving should be readily deducible, as follows:

By giving bedding, one may gain the couch of liberation that comes with the peace and security of the Three Vehicles;

By providing a place for sitting [meditation], one may gain the indestructible abode in the *bodhimaṇḍa* beneath the bodhi tree;

By providing someone with a wife, one may gain the pleasures of Dharma joy;

By providing roads, one may be able to enter the right path for the sake of beings who are lost on the road of *saṃsāra*;

By giving rafts, one becomes able to cross beyond the flood of desire, the flood of existence, the flood of views, and the flood of ignorance;

By giving one's bones, one gains solidity in moral precept observance, solidity in meditative concentration, solidity in wisdom,[180] solidity in liberation, solidity in the knowledge and vision of liberation, and solidity in [dedication to liberating] beings;

By providing others with a following, one becomes able to assemble a retinue consisting of a countless and boundless number of *asaṃkhyeyas* of devas who are endowed with merit and who are all identically possessed of pure minds and inviolable loyalty;

By conferring admiring accolades on others, when one speaks on the Dharma, one elicits the delight and praises of devas, dragons, *yakṣas, gandharvas, śramaṇas,* and brahmans;

By giving volumes of the sutras, one enables the nine categories of canonical texts to remain for an immeasurably long period of time;

By giving the Dharma, one becomes able to gain a penetrating understanding of all dharmas.

正體字	
	集一切功德故。是菩薩如是樂行
050b20 ‖	布施。知布施清淨。知布施果報所得多少。
050b21 ‖	是故。
050b22 ‖	非法財施等　　乃至智呵施
050b23 ‖	無有如是施　　但合空等施
050b24 ‖	非法者。惡行所得財。財名資生之物。取要
050b25 ‖	言之。以惡業得財物施。菩薩[10]知是布施
050b26 ‖	不清淨故。如是等諸餘非法施乃至智所呵
050b27 ‖	施不為此事。菩薩行布施。唯與空智慧等
050b28 ‖	種種功德和合。問曰。所說非法得財施等。及
050b29 ‖	空智慧等和合施。此二施應廣分別。答曰。是
050c01 ‖	二施。無盡意菩薩會品中檀波羅蜜中說。初
050c02 ‖	分別布施功德。所謂　諸菩薩無非法求財施。
050c03 ‖	無熱惱眾生施。無恐畏施。無著故施。無請
050c04 ‖	而不施。

简体字

集一切功德故。是菩萨如是乐行布施。知布施清净。知布施果报所得多少。是故。

　非法财施等　　乃至智呵施
　无有如是施　　但合空等施

　非法者。恶行所得财。财名资生之物。取要言之。以恶业得财物施。菩萨知是布施不清净故。如是等诸余非法施乃至智所呵施不为此事。菩萨行布施。唯与空智慧等种种功德和合。问曰。所说非法得财施等。及空智慧等和合施。此二施应广分别。答曰。是二施。无尽意菩萨会品中檀波罗蜜中说。初分别布施功德。所谓诸菩萨无非法求财施。无热恼众生施。无恐畏施。无著故施。无请而不施。

Because it enables the accumulation of all of the meritorious qualities, this bodhisattva delights in the practice of giving in this manner. He understands how it is that giving is made pure and understands as well the measure of the karmic results that ensue from the practice of giving. Therefore:

> d. He Avoids Wrong Giving and Gives In Accordance with Emptiness
>
> As for giving wealth obtained contrary to Dharma and so forth,
> as well as all those sorts of giving that are censured by the wise,
> he remains free of any such forms of giving, and instead
> gives only in ways that are conjoined with emptiness and such.[181]

Giving that is "contrary to Dharma" involves wealth obtained through bad actions. "Wealth" refers to life-supporting possessions. To sum it up, because the bodhisattva realizes that giving involving wealth obtained through bad actions is not pure, he does not engage in any of these sorts of giving that are contrary to Dharma. He refrains from participating in any of them, including especially such forms of giving as might be censured by the wise. Hence, when the bodhisattva engages in the practice of giving, he only gives in ways that are conjoined with the wisdom that fathoms emptiness and with the other sorts of associated qualities.

> 1) Q: Will You Please Discuss These Two Types of Giving?

Question: As for these two types of giving: that sort of giving which involves wealth obtained contrary to Dharma and that sort of giving which is conjoined with the wisdom that fathoms emptiness, one should present here a broad-ranging discussion elucidating the associated distinctions.

> 2) Akṣayamati Bodhisattva Explains Them as Follows:

Response: These two types of giving are discussed in the treatment of *dāna pāramitā* that is contained within the "Akṣayamati Bodhisattva Assembly" chapter, as below:[182]

> a) The Types of Impure Giving
>
> First, let us consider the distinctions involved in giving-associated merit, specifically as follows:
>
>> Bodhisattvas do not give wealth acquired in a manner that is contrary to Dharma. They do not engage in any giving that has the effect of aggravating other beings. No giving is done out of fearfulness. No giving is done due to some type of attachment. There are no instances where someone makes a request and yet they fail to give. There is no giving that fails

正體字	無不如所許施。無恡好以不好 050c05 ‖ 施。無不深心施。無諂曲施。無假偽施。無損 050c06 ‖ 果施。無邪心施。無癡心施。無雜心施。無 050c07 ‖ 不信解[11]脫施。無疲厭施。無親附施。無以 050c08 ‖ 承望己施。無求福田者施。無輕一切眾 050c09 ‖ 生非福田者施。無持戒毀戒高下心施。無 050c10 ‖ 求名聞施。無自高心施。無卑他施。無懊 050c11 ‖ 惜施。無悔心施。無急喚故施。無惡賤施。無 050c12 ‖ 自然法施。無求果報施。無瞋恚施。無令 050c13 ‖ 人渴乏施。無惱求者施。無輕弄彼施。無 050c14 ‖ 欺誑施。無[12]俾面施。無擲與施。無不一心 050c15 ‖ 施。無不自手施。無不常施。無休息施。無 050c16 ‖ 斷絕施。無競勝施。無輕少物施。無[13]請隨 050c17 ‖ 自恣而以輕物施。無不稱力施。無非福 050c18 ‖ 田施。無於少物劣弱心施。無恃多物憍心　050c19 ‖施。
简体字	无不如所许施。无吝好以不好施。无不深心施。无谄曲施。无假伪施。无损果施。无邪心施。无痴心施。无杂心施。无不信解脱施。无疲厌施。无亲附施。无以承望己施。无求福田者施。无轻一切众生非福田者施。无持戒毁戒高下心施。无求名闻施。无自高心施。无卑他施。无懊惜施。无悔心施。无急唤故施。无恶贱施。无自然法施。无求果报施。无嗔恚施。无令人渴乏施。无恼求者施。无轻弄彼施。无欺诳施。无俾面施。无掷与施。无不一心施。无不自手施。无不常施。无休息施。无断绝施。无竞胜施。无轻少物施。无请随自恣而以轻物施。无不称力施。无非福田施。无于少物劣弱心施。无恃多物憍心施。

to accord with what one has already pledged. There is no giving done wherein, because one is stingy with what is fine, one instead gives an inferior item;

There is no giving not rooted in earnest intentions, no giving intended to curry favor, no giving of anything that is counterfeit, no giving that produces damaging effects, no giving done with perverse intent, no giving done with a deluded mind, no giving done with mixed motivations, no giving involving an absence of resolute conviction,[183] and no giving done out of weariness;

There is no giving involving personal favoritism, no giving with the expectation of self-benefit, no giving seeking to focus [exclusively] on "fields of merit," and no giving that slights other beings as inadequate "fields of merit";[184]

There is no giving with a mind that distinguishes between those who uphold the moral precepts versus those who transgress against the moral precepts or that distinguishes between those who are seen as superior versus those who are seen as inferior;

There is no giving done out of a desire for fame, no giving done with the intent to elevate oneself, no giving done in a way that treats others as inferior, no giving because of intensely painful regret, and no giving that is done out of remorse;

There is no giving done [only as] a response to cries of urgency, no abusive giving, no giving promoting the dharma of spontaneous [acausal] occurrence,[185] no giving done simply to gain the resulting karmic rewards, no giving done out of hatred, and no giving that causes others to be left wanting;

There is no giving involving annoyance toward the supplicant, no giving involving slighting or dallying with the recipient, no deceptive giving, no giving just to save face, no giving done by tossing a donation, no giving not done with focused mind, and no giving of gifts not presented with one's own hands;

There is no failure to always give, no desisting from giving, no halting of giving, no giving as a means of struggling for superiority, no giving of merely insignificant and trivial things, and no giving involving an invitation to take whatever one wishes when one is offering only trivial things;

There is no giving not matching one's powers to give, no giving that considers some to not be fields of merit,[186] no giving of merely trivial things that is accompanied by inferior intentions, no giving accompanied by arrogance because of the

正體字	無邪行施。無樂受生施。無恃色族富 050c20 ‖ 貴施。無求生四王釋梵天上施。無求聲 050c21 ‖ 聞辟支佛乘施。無求國王王子施。無限一 050c22 ‖ 世施。無厭足施。無不迴向薩婆若施。無 050c23 ‖ 不淨施。無非時施。無刀毒施。無惱弄眾生 050c24 ‖ 施。無智者所呵施。如是開示施門餘不淨 050c25 ‖ 施亦應當知。所謂諸菩薩無應棄物施。無 050c26 ‖ 憎惡涅槃施。無豐饒易得物施。無[14]量恩 050c27 ‖ 施。無報恩施。無求反報施。無求守護施。 050c28 ‖ 無求吉施。無慢心施。無家法施。無因得 050c29 ‖ 即施。無不終身施。無垢心施。無遊戲施。 051a01 ‖ 無以善知識故施。無輕施。無遊逸施。無 051a02 ‖ 因失施。無以讚己故施。無以呵罵故施。 051a03 ‖ 無以[1]祝願故施。無以稱希有事故施。無 051a04 ‖ 以明己信故施。無以畏故施。無誑施。無 051a05 ‖ 求眷屬施。無不唱導施。無引眾施。無不 051a06 ‖ 信施。無無因緣施。無隨意施。無現奇特施。
简体字	无邪行施。无乐受生施。无恃色族富贵施。无求生四王释梵天上施。无求声闻辟支佛乘施。无求国王王子施。无限一世施。无厌足施。无不回向萨婆若施。无不净施。无非时施。无刀毒施。无恼弄众生施。无智者所呵施。如是开示施门余不净施亦应当知。所谓诸菩萨无应弃物施。无憎恶涅槃施。无丰饶易得物施。无量恩施。无报恩施。无求反报施。无求守护施。无求吉施。无慢心施。无家法施。无因得即施。无不终身施。无垢心施。无游戏施。无以善知识故施。无轻施。无游逸施。无因失施。无以赞己故施。无以呵骂故施。无以祝愿故施。无以称希有事故施。无以明己信故施。无以畏故施。无诳施。无求眷属施。无不唱导施。无引众施。无不信施。无无因缘施。无随意施。无现奇特施。

Chapter 12 — *Distinctions with Regard to Giving*

abundance of one's gifts, and no giving that involves unprincipled actions;

There is no giving done with the intention of gaining rebirth in pleasurable places, no giving reliant upon the largesse of wealthy and noble clans, no giving done to gain rebirth in the heavens of the Four Heavenly Kings, Śakra, or Brahmā, no giving in pursuit of the Śrāvaka Vehicle or the Pratyekabuddha Vehicle, no giving in quest of becoming a king or a prince, and no giving with only a view to [favorable effects to be gained in] this present lifetime;

There is no self-satisfied [termination of one's] giving, no giving not dedicated to realization of all-knowledge, no impure giving, no giving at the wrong time, no giving of knives or poisons, no giving intended to aggravate or dally with beings, and no giving censured by the wise.

It is in this manner that one opens up and reveals what constitutes the gateway of giving. The other sorts of impure giving are such that one should be able to deduce what they are, as follows:

The bodhisattva does not give cast-off things. There is no giving demonstrating a hatred or abhorrence of nirvāṇa, no giving of easily acquired and abundantly available things, no giving calculated to manipulate kindness, no giving done just to repay kindnesses, and no giving done to elicit some reward in return;

There is no giving to ensure protection, no giving in quest of auspicious occurrences, no giving motivated by pride, no giving only to accord with customs of the clan, no perfunctory giving simply as a response to having received something, no failing to give for one's entire life, and no giving occasioned by defiled thoughts;

There is no giving done for sport, no giving done simply at the behest of a good spiritual guide, no giving done but lightly, no giving done with an unbridled mind, no giving because one has experienced loss, no giving simply as a response to having been praised by someone, no giving done because one has been rebuked, no giving done as a prayer for auspicious developments, no giving in praise of performing miracles, and no giving done to make a show of one's faith;

There is no giving because one has become fearful, no giving done with the intent to deceive, no giving to gain a following, no giving that does not serve to lead others [toward goodness], no giving done to lead others along, no giving done in the absence of faith, no giving that asserts the nonexistence of causes and conditions, no merely frivolous giving, and no giving done to make a display of one's exceptional qualities;

正體字

051a07 ‖ 無自稱讚施。無不隨所求施。無為伏彼
051a08 ‖ 施[2]施。無不愛施。無不任用物施。無不恭
051a09 ‖ 敬施。無下施。無以怪相故施。無抑挫施。
051a10 ‖ 無挾勢得物施。無不清淨心施。無疑心施。
051a11 ‖ 無破求者心施。無禁忌物施。無分別施。
051a12 ‖ 無以酒施。無以兵[3]杖施。無奪彼物施。
051a13 ‖ 無令人生疑心施。無以親近故施。無說
051a14 ‖ 彼過咎施。無隨所愛施。無瞋施。無癡施。
051a15 ‖ 無戲論施。無不為菩提施。問曰。非法求
051a16 ‖ 財施。乃至不為菩提施。菩薩為有為無。若
051a17 ‖ 盡無者則有過咎不求福田。於眾生無差
051a18 ‖ 別心。亦無知恩報恩。亦無家法國法施。若
051a19 ‖ 有者何以皆言無。答曰。是非法得財施。乃
051a20 ‖ 至不為菩提施。菩薩不必盡無。或時有。是
051a21 ‖ 布施。檀波羅蜜所不攝。不能具足檀波羅
051a22 ‖ 蜜故言無。空等功德和合施者。如無盡意
051a23 ‖ 菩薩經檀波羅蜜品中說。

简体字

无自称赞施。无不随所求施。无为伏彼施施。无不爱施。无不任用物施。无不恭敬施。无下施。无以怪相故施。无抑挫施。无挟势得物施。无不清净心施。无疑心施。无破求者心施。无禁忌物施。无分别施。无以酒施。无以兵杖施。无夺彼物施。无令人生疑心施。无以亲近故施。无说彼过咎施。无随所爱施。无瞋施。无痴施。无戏论施。无不为菩提施。问曰。非法求财施。乃至不为菩提施。菩萨为有为无。若尽无者则有过咎不求福田。于众生无差别心。亦无知恩报恩。亦无家法国法施。若有者何以皆言无。答曰。是非法得财施。乃至不为菩提施。菩萨不必尽无。或时有。是布施。檀波罗蜜所不摄。不能具足檀波罗蜜故言无。空等功德和合施者。如无尽意菩萨经檀波罗蜜品中说。

Chapter 12 — *Distinctions with Regard to Giving*

There is no giving to elicit one's own praises, no giving that does not accord with what is sought, no giving done to reduce the significance of someone else's giving, no giving of what does not please, no giving of something that will not be put to use, no giving out of disrespect, no inferior giving, no giving because of the occurrence of strange signs, no giving to restrain or suppress others, no giving of things obtained through intimidation, and no giving done with impure intentions;

There is no giving done with doubting thoughts, no giving intended to mentally crush a supplicant, no giving of forbidden things, no giving done out of discrimination, no giving of alcoholic beverages, no giving of tools of war, no giving of things seized from others, no giving that causes others to have doubts, and no giving done to induce intimacy;

There is no giving that serves to announce the faults of others, no giving in pursuit of something one cherishes, no giving influenced by hatred, no giving influenced by delusion, no giving rooted in fallacious conceptual proliferation,[187] and no giving not done for the sake of bodhi.

i) Q: Is the Bodhisattva Entirely Free of All Such Giving?

Question: [As for the types of giving just listed], from giving of wealth sought in ways contrary to Dharma to giving not done for the sake of bodhi, does the bodhisattva engage in any of them or not? Were he to engage in none of them, then he would be at fault for not seeking out fields of merit, for not making distinctions among beings, for not acknowledging kindnesses, for not repaying kindnesses, for not presenting gifts in accordance with clan customs, or for not giving things in accordance with national customs. If he does in fact engage in such giving, why do you claim here that there are no instances of this?

ii) A: No, but Such Giving Is Not Included in the Perfection of Giving

Response: It is not necessarily the case that the bodhisattva is completely free of all of these sorts of giving from giving of wealth that is acquired in ways contrary to Dharma to giving not done for the sake of bodhi. There may be times when he engages in some of them. However, these sorts of giving are not included within *dāna pāramitā*. It is because they cannot be instrumental in the perfection of *dāna pāramitā* that they are characterized here as being absent.

a) Giving Conjoined with Emptiness, Signlessness, or Wishlessness

Now, as for what is meant by [the above stanza's reference to] "giving conjoined with emptiness and other such meritorious qualities," this is as described in the *Akṣayamati Bodhisattva Sutra*, in the "Dāna Pāramitā" chapter, as follows:[188]

正體字	菩薩布施。與空心 051a24 ‖ 合故不盡。是施無相修故不盡。是施無願守 051a25 ‖ 護故不盡。是施善根所攝故不盡。是施隨 051a26 ‖ 解脫相故不盡。是施能破一切魔故不盡。 051a27 ‖ 是施不[4]雜煩惱故不盡。是施得轉勝利 051a28 ‖ 故不盡。是施決定心故不盡。是施集助菩 051a29 ‖ 提法故不盡。是施正迴向故不盡。是施得 051b01 ‖ 道場解脫果故不盡。是施無邊故不盡。是 051b02 ‖ 施不可盡故不盡。是施不斷故不盡。是施廣 051b03 ‖ 大故不盡。是施不可壞故不盡。是施不可勝 051b04 ‖ 故不盡。是施至一切智慧故不盡。是施斷 051b05 ‖ 非法求財施等垢成就空等諸功德故不 051b06 ‖ 盡。非法求財施等是施垢施。與垢合是不 051b07 ‖ 淨施。與空等功德合是淨。復次是施淨不淨 051b08 ‖ 今當更說。
简体字	菩萨布施。与空心合故不尽。是施无相修故不尽。是施无愿守护故不尽。是施善根所摄故不尽。是施随解脱相故不尽。是施能破一切魔故不尽。是施不杂烦恼故不尽。是施得转胜利故不尽。是施决定心故不尽。是施集助菩提法故不尽。是施正回向故不尽。是施得道场解脱果故不尽。是施无边故不尽。是施不可尽故不尽。是施不断故不尽。是施广大故不尽。是施不可坏故不尽。是施不可胜故不尽。是施至一切智慧故不尽。是施断非法求财施等垢成就空等诸功德故不尽。非法求财施等是施垢施。与垢合是不净施。与空等功德合是净。复次是施净不净今当更说。

Chapter 12 — *Distinctions with Regard to Giving* 401

Because the giving done by the bodhisattva is conjoined with the mind that fathoms emptiness, it is endless;

Because this giving involves the cultivation of signlessness, it is endless;

Because this giving is preserved and protected by the practice of wishlessness, it is endless;

Because this giving is subsumed within roots of goodness, it is endless;

Because this giving accords with the characteristics associated with liberation, it is endless;

Because this giving is able to defeat all *māras*, it is endless;

Because this giving involves no admixture with the afflictions, it is endless;

Because this giving becomes ever more superior in its benefits, it is endless;

Because this giving is done with definite resolve, it is endless;

Because this giving facilitates accumulation of the dharmas constituting the limbs of bodhi, it is endless;

Because this giving is rightly dedicated, it is endless;

Because this giving brings about acquisition of the fruits of the liberation attained in the *bodhimaṇḍa*, it is endless;

Because this giving knows no bounds, it is endless;

Because this giving is inexhaustible, it is endless;

Because this giving is never cut off, it is endless;

Because this giving is vast, it is endless;

Because this giving is indestructible, it is endless;

Because this giving is invincible, it is endless;

Because this giving leads one to all-knowledge, it is endless;

Because this giving cuts off the defilement involved in giving wealth obtained in ways contrary to Dharma and other such forms of giving, and because it leads to the complete development of the realization of emptiness and the other associated meritorious qualities, it is therefore endless.

b) IMPURE GIVING VERSUS PURE GIVING

As for "the giving of wealth obtained in ways contrary to Dharma and other such forms of giving" these types of giving constitute "defiled giving." Whichever types of giving are conjoined with defilement are instances of impure giving whereas whichever types of giving are conjoined with emptiness and the other [associated meritorious qualities]—those are instances of pure giving.

Additionally, this topic of purity versus impurity in the practice of giving is one that now merits further discussion.

正體字

	經說施有四種。有施於施者是
051b09 ‖	淨不於受者淨。有施於受者是淨不於
051b10 ‖	施者淨。有施於施者淨亦於受者淨。有
051b11 ‖	施不於施者淨亦不於受者淨。若施者
051b12 ‖	成就善身口意業受者成就惡身口意業。是
051b13 ‖	名於施者淨不於受者淨。若施者成就惡
051b14 ‖	身口意業受者成就善身口意業。是名於
051b15 ‖	受者淨不於施者淨。若施者成就善身口
051b16 ‖	意業受者亦成就善身口意業。是名於施
051b17 ‖	者淨於受者亦淨。若施者成就不善身口
051b18 ‖	意業受者亦成就不善身口意業。是名不
051b19 ‖	於施者淨亦不於受者淨。貪欲瞋恚愚癡。
051b20 ‖	若斷若不斷。亦應如是分別。復次四種布施
051b21 ‖	中。有淨不淨。一從施者淨。二從受者淨。
051b22 ‖	三共淨是名淨。一不從施者淨。二不從受
051b23 ‖	者淨。三不共淨。是名不淨。

简体字

经说施有四种。有施于施者是净不于受者净。有施于受者是净不于施者净。有施于施者净亦于受者净。有施不于施者净亦不于受者净。若施者成就善身口意业受者成就恶身口意业。是名于施者净不于受者净。若施者成就恶身口意业受者成就善身口意业。是名于受者净不于施者净。若施者成就善身口意业受者亦成就善身口意业。是名于施者净于受者亦净。若施者成就不善身口意业受者亦成就不善身口意业。是名不于施者净亦不于受者净。贪欲瞋恚愚痴。若断若不断。亦应如是分别。复次四种布施中。有净不净。一从施者净。二从受者净。三共净是名净。

Chapter 12 — *Distinctions with Regard to Giving*

i) FOUR TYPES OF GIVING ACCORDING TO THE AGENTS OF ITS PURIFICATION

The sutras state that there are four types of giving, as follows:[189]

There is giving that is purified by the giver and that is not purified by the receiver;

There is giving that is purified by the receiver and that is not purified by the giver;

There is giving that is purified by the giver and that is also purified by the receiver.

There is giving that is not purified by the giver and that is also not purified by the receiver.

Where the giver performs good actions of body, speech, and mind but the receiver has performed bad actions of body, speech, and mind, this is an instance of giving that is purified by the giver and that is not purified by the receiver.

Where the giver performs bad actions of body, speech, and mind and the receiver performs good actions of body, speech, and mind, this is an instance of giving that is purified by the receiver and that is not purified by the giver.

Where the giver performs good actions of body, speech, and mind and the receiver also performs good actions of body, speech, and mind, this is an instance of giving that is purified by the giver and that is also purified by the receiver.

Where the giver performs bad actions of body, speech, and mind and the receiver also performs bad actions of body, speech, and mind, this is an instance of giving that is not purified by the giver and that is also not purified by the receiver.

One should also make distinctions of this sort with regard to whether or not covetousness, hatred, and delusion have been cut off.

(1) THE BASES FOR PRESENCE OR ABSENCE OF PURIFICATION

Additionally, in connection with these four types of giving, there are bases for distinguishing presence or absence of purification:

First, purification may be accomplished by the giver;
Second, purification may be accomplished by the receiver;
Third, purification is accomplished by both of them.

These classifications are determinants of purification. Also:

First, purification is not accomplished by the giver;
Second, purification is not accomplished by the recipient;
Third, they do not both purify [the act of giving].

These classifications are determinants of failure to accomplish purification [of the act of giving].

正體字

```
         是中施者有功
051b24 ‖ 德故從施者施得淨。以受者有功德故
051b25 ‖ 從受[5]者施得淨。以施者受者有功德故
051b26 ‖ 從施者受者施得淨。施者有罪故從施者
051b27 ‖ 施不淨。受者有罪故從受者施不淨。施者
051b28 ‖ [6]受者有罪故從施者受者施不淨。施者功
051b29 ‖ 德受者功德。施者罪受者罪。[7]先已說。問曰。
051c01 ‖ 汝說此四種施中。菩薩[8]應行何施。答曰。
051c02 ‖    四種布施中    行二種淨施
051c03 ‖    不求於名利    及以求果報
051c04 ‖ 是布施有四種三淨三不淨。不淨盡不行。淨
051c05 ‖ 中[9]行二淨。一者施者淨不於受者淨。二者
051c06 ‖ 共淨。於此二[10]淨施中應常精進。何以故。是
051c07 ‖ 菩薩不期果報故。若期果報者。則求受者
051c08 ‖ 清淨。淨名[11]施者受者功德莊嚴其心清淨。
```

简体字

一不从施者净。二不从受者净。三不共净。是名不净。是中施者有功德故从施者施得净。以受者有功德故从受者施得净。以施者受者有功德故从施者受者施得净。施者有罪故从施者施不净。受者有罪故从受者施不净。施者受者有罪故从施者受者施不净。施者功德受者功德。施者罪受者罪。先已说。问曰。汝说此四种施中。菩萨应行何施。答曰。

　　四种布施中　　行二种净施
　　不求于名利　　及以求果报

　　是布施有四种三净三不净。不净尽不行。净中行二净。一者施者净不于受者净。二者共净。于此二净施中应常精进。何以故。是菩萨不期果报故。若期果报者。则求受者清净。净名施者受者功德庄严其心清净。

In these instances, when the giver possesses meritorious qualities, the act of giving derives its qualification as "pure" from the giver. When the receiver possesses meritorious qualities, the act of giving derives its qualification as "pure" from the receiver. When both the giver and the receiver possess meritorious qualities, the act of giving derives its qualification as "pure" from both the giver and the receiver.

When the giver commits karmic offenses, the act of giving derives its qualification as "impure" from the giver. When the receiver commits karmic offenses, the act of giving derives its qualification as "impure" from the receiver. When both the giver and the receiver commit karmic offenses, the act of giving derives its qualification as "impure" from both the giver and the receiver.

As for what constitutes the possession of meritorious qualities on the part of the giver, what constitutes possession of meritorious qualities on the part of the receiver, what constitutes commission of karmic offenses on the part of the giver, and what constitutes the commission of karmic offenses on the part of the receiver, these have already been discussed.

(1) Q: OF THESE FOUR, WHICH SHOULD BE PRACTICED?

Question: Of the approaches to giving that you have described as contained within these four types of giving, which ones should the bodhisattva practice?

(2) A: PRACTICE TWO THAT ARE PURE AND AVOID SELFISH MOTIVES

Response:

Among the four types of giving,
one practices the two types involving pure giving.
In doing so, one does not seek fame or self-benefit
and one also does not seek to obtain any karmic fruits from this.

These types of giving consist of four types of which three contain bases of purity and three contain bases of impurity.[190] He does not practice any type of impure giving and does practice two types of pure giving: First, giving that is purified by the giver but is not purified by the receiver, and, second, giving where the giving is purified by both [the giver and the receiver].

One should always be vigorously devoted to the practice of these two types of pure giving. Why? Because this bodhisattva does not hope for any associated karmic fruits from this. Were one to hope for some sort of karmic fruits [from performing this act], then one would be inclined to seek out a pure receiver.

"Purity" is defined here by the giver and the receiver both being graced by meritorious qualities whereby the minds of each of them are

正體字

051c09 ‖ 不淨名施者有慳惜心。如佛說慳為施垢。
051c10 ‖ 餘煩惱雖為不淨慳最為重。問曰。若菩薩
051c11 ‖ 於施者淨及共[12]淨。應勤行此二施。慳為施
051c12 ‖ 者垢。亦是施大垢。若菩薩未離欲未能斷
051c13 ‖ 慳。云何能行此[13]二淨施。答曰。
051c14 ‖ 　若物能起慳　　則不畜此物
051c15 ‖ 菩薩若於有命無命物知生慳心者則不
051c16 ‖ 畜此物。是故有所施皆無悋惜。問曰。外物
051c17 ‖ 可不畜身當云何。答曰。
051c18 ‖ 　常為利眾生　　解身如藥樹
051c19 ‖ 為利益眾生故。信解身如藥樹。如藥樹
051c20 ‖ 眾生有用根莖枝葉華實等各得差病。隨
051c21 ‖ 意而取無有遮護。菩薩亦如是。為利眾
051c22 ‖ 生故能自捨身。作是念。若眾生取

简体字

不净名施者有悭惜心。如佛说悭为施垢。余烦恼虽为不净悭最为重。问曰。若菩萨于施者净及共净。应勤行此二施。悭为施者垢。亦是施大垢。若菩萨未离欲未能断悭。云何能行此二净施。答曰。

　若物能起悭　　则不畜此物

　菩萨若于有命无命物知生悭心者则不畜此物。是故有所施皆无吝惜。问曰。外物可不畜身当云何。答曰。

　常为利众生　　解身如药树

　为利益众生故。信解身如药树。如药树众生有用根茎枝叶华实等各得差病。随意而取无有遮护。菩萨亦如是。为利众生故能自舍身。作是念。若众生取

pure. "Impurity" is defined by the presence in the giver of a miserliness. This accords with the Buddha's declaration that, in the practice of giving, miserliness constitutes a defilement. Although the other afflictions also constitute bases of impurity, here it is miserliness that constitutes the most serious [form of defilement].

(2) Q: How Can One Possessed of Desires Practice Pure Giving?

Question: If the bodhisattva should engage in diligent practice of these two types of giving, that wherein the giving is purified by the giver [but not by the receiver] and that wherein the giving is purified by both the giver and the receiver, since miserliness constitutes a defilement on the part of the giver and a major defilement of the act of giving, if the bodhisattva has not yet transcended desire and hence cannot yet cut off miserliness, how then could he succeed in practicing these two types of pure giving?

(3) A: Do Not Accumulate Things That Engender Miserliness

Response:
> If some possession is capable of causing the arising of miserliness,
> then one should refrain from accumulating such things.

If a bodhisattva realizes that some possession, whether living or not, causes the arising of miserly thoughts, then he should not accumulate such things. As a consequence [of refraining from accumulating such things], whenever he gives something, he will always be free of miserliness.

(a) Q: How Can One Accomplish This with One's Own Body?

Question: Outward possessions are such that one might refrain from accumulating them. But how does one accomplish this in relation to one's own body?

(b) A: Consider One's Body to Be Like a Medicine Tree

Response:
> In order to always be of benefit to beings,
> understand the body as like a medicinal tree.

In order to provide benefit to beings, one should possess a firm belief that one's body is like a medicinal tree that beings may use as medicine, taking roots, trunk, branches, leaves, blossoms, fruit, and so forth, each to cure a particular disease. In such a case, they may take whatever they wish without [the tree] preventing them from doing so in order to protect itself.

The bodhisattva is just like this. In order to be of benefit to beings, he is able to relinquish his body, thinking in this way: "If beings take

正體字

我頭目手足肢節脊腹髀膊耳鼻齒舌血肉骨髓
等。隨其所須皆能與之。或舉身盡施。如是
降伏其心修集善根。為方便所護。行檀波
羅蜜。

　　總相別相施　　皆悉能迴向
是菩薩能以二種淨施能知二種迴向。一
為總相。二為別相。總相迴向者。有所施皆
迴向阿耨多羅三藐三菩提。別相施者。如布
施果報中說。復次總相迴向者。為安樂利
益一切眾生。別相迴向者。無信眾生令得信
故。破戒者得持戒故。少聞者得多聞故。懈
怠者得精進故。散亂心者得禪定故。愚癡
眾生得智慧故。慳者得捨心故。如是等種
種別相。復次總相迴向者。以六波羅蜜。迴
向阿耨多羅三藐三菩提。別相迴向者。施外
物時願諸眾生得大最樂。支節布施時願
諸眾生具足佛身。問曰。布施有幾種迴向幾
種不迴向。

简体字

我头目手足肢节脊腹髀膊耳鼻齿舌血肉骨髓等。随其所须皆能与之。或举身尽施。如是降伏其心修集善根。为方便所护。行檀波罗蜜。

十住毗婆沙论卷第六
分别布施品第十二之余）

　　总相别相施　　皆悉能回向

是菩萨能以二种净施能知二种回向。一为总相。二为别相。总相回向者。有所施皆回向阿耨多罗三藐三菩提。别相施者。如布施果报中说。复次总相回向者。为安乐利益一切众生。别相回向者。无信众生令得信故。破戒者得持戒故。少闻者得多闻故。懈怠者得精进故。散乱心者得禅定故。愚痴众生得智慧故。悭者得舍心故。如是等种种别相。复次总相回向者。以六波罗蜜。回向阿耨多罗三藐三菩提。别相回向者。施外物时愿诸众生得大最乐。支节布施时愿诸众生具足佛身。问曰。布施有几种回向几种不回向。

Chapter 12 — *Distinctions with Regard to Giving*   409

whatever they need of my head, eyes, hands, feet, limbs, spine, abdomen, arms, ears, nose, teeth, tongue, blood, flesh, bones, marrow, and so forth, I shall be able to give them up, perhaps even giving them my entire body."

It is in this manner that one subdues one's mind as one cultivates and accumulates roots of goodness and remains protected by the adoption of skillful means in one's practice of *dāna pāramitā* (the perfection of giving).

E. THE BODHISATTVA'S DEDICATION OF THE MERIT ARISING FROM HIS GIVING

In ways that are general in character and specific in character,
one is always able to dedicate all acts of giving that one performs.

This bodhisattva is able to understand and pursue two sorts of dedication in relation to the two types of pure giving. The first is that which is of a general character and the second is that which is of a specific character.

As for dedications that are of a general character, one dedicates the merit from all of one's giving to *anuttarasamyaksaṃbodhi*. As for dedication of a specific character, this is as described in the above treatment of the karmic fruits resulting from acts of giving.

Then again, in the case of dedication of a general character, it is done for the sake of bringing peace, happiness, and benefit to all beings. As for dedication of a specific character, it is done for the sake of influencing beings without faith to gain faith, for the sake of influencing those who have broken the precepts to succeed in upholding the precepts, for the sake of influencing those of but little learning to develop extensive learning, for the sake of influencing those who are indolent to become vigorous in their efforts, for the sake of influencing those whose minds are scattered to gain *dhyāna* concentration, for the sake of influencing deluded beings to gain wisdom, and for the sake of influencing the miserly to develop minds inclined toward generosity.[191] And so it is that there are many different sorts of specifically-directed dedications.

Additionally, with regard to dedication of a general character, one dedicates the merit associated with the six *pāramitās* to *anuttarasamyaksaṃbodhi*, whereas, with regard to dedication of a specific character, when one gives outward things, one prays that all beings will gain the most supreme happiness. When giving one's limbs, one prays that all beings will gain the perfect body of a buddha.

1. Q: HOW MANY TYPES OF RIGHT AND WRONG DEDICATION ARE THERE?

Question: In the practice of giving, how many kinds of dedication are there? And how many kinds of dedication does one not practice?

正體字

答曰。一為淨[1]四迴向[2]三種不迴
向。[3]一菩薩布施為清淨四事故迴向。三種
不迴向。不為得王故迴向。不為得欲樂
故迴向。不為得聲聞辟支佛地故迴向。不
為得王故迴向者。遮王則并遮一切貴人
力勢自在者。不為得欲樂迴向者。除上貴
人餘受富樂五欲自娛者。不為得聲聞辟
支佛迴向者。遮因小乘入無餘涅槃。令
得安住大乘。久後乃[4]入無餘涅槃。為四
淨迴向者。菩薩所施為清淨佛土故迴向。
為清淨[5]菩薩故迴向。為清淨教化眾生故
迴向。為淨薩婆若故迴向。菩薩應如是方
便迴向無令布施損減使得勢力。問曰。以
何法令布施損減。以何法令布施增益。

简体字

答曰。一为净四回向三种不回向。一菩萨布施为清净四事故回
向。三种不回向。不为得王故回向。不为得欲乐故回向。不为得
声闻辟支佛地故回向。不为得王故回向者。遮王则并遮一切贵人
力势自在者。不为得欲乐回向者。除上贵人余受富乐五欲自娱
者。不为得声闻辟支佛回向者。遮因小乘入无余涅槃。令得安住
大乘。久后乃入无余涅槃。为四净回向者。菩萨所施为清净佛土
故回向。为清净菩萨故回向。为清净教化众生故回向。为净萨婆
若故回向。菩萨应如是方便回向无令布施损减使得势力。问曰。
以何法令布施损减。以何法令布施增益。

2. There Are 4 Pure Objectives of Dedication and 3 Not Practiced

Response: The first category, those done for the sake of pure objectives, consist of four types of dedication. There are three types of dedication that one does not practice. The bodhisattva's giving may be dedicated to four types of pure objectives.

a. The Three Types of Dedication One Does Not Practice

The three objectives toward which one does not dedicate merit are as follows:

One does not dedicate merit for the sake of becoming a king.
One does not dedicate merit for the sake of sensual pleasures.
And one does not dedicate merit for the sake of gaining any of the grounds of a *śrāvaka* disciple or a *pratyekabuddha*.

Now, as for "not dedicating merit for the sake of becoming a king," this restriction of the objective of becoming a king is also intended to restrict dedications done to acquire the power and sovereign freedom of the nobility.

As for "not dedicating merit for the sake of acquiring sensual pleasures," this refers, aside from the above-mentioned nobility, to all others who partake of wealth's enjoyments and indulge themselves in the pleasures of the five types of desire.

As for "not dedicating merit for the sake of gaining any of the grounds of a *śrāvaka* disciple or a *pratyekabuddha*," this restricts entry into the Small Vehicle's nirvāṇa without residue but it does enable one to become securely established in the Great Vehicle in which, after a long time, one eventually enters the nirvāṇa without residue.

b. The Four Types of Dedication Done for the Sake of Pure Objectives

Now, as for the four types of dedication done for the sake of pure objectives, the merit from a bodhisattva's giving:

Is dedicated for the sake of purifying buddha lands;
Is dedicated for the sake of purifying one's realization of bodhi;[192]
Is dedicated for the sake of purifying one's teaching of beings;
And is dedicated for the sake of purifying one's realization of all-knowledge.[193]

The bodhisattva should adopt skillful means such as these in making dedications so as to not diminish the effectiveness of his giving and so as to cause it to become powerful.

1) Q: Which Dharmas Diminish Its Benefit and Which Increase It?

Question: Through which dharmas does one diminish the effectiveness of one's giving and through which dharmas does one cause the benefits of one's giving to increase?

正體字

　　　　答 052a25 ‖曰。
052a26 ‖　　若施不迴向　　亦無有方便
052a27 ‖　　求生於下處　　親近惡知識
052a28 ‖　　如是布施者　　是則為損減
052a29 ‖ 若布施不迴向阿耨多羅三藐三菩提。隨逐
052b01 ‖ 世間樂故。求生下處無有方便。能出布
052b02 ‖ 施禪定果報自在所生。親近障閡大乘知
052b03 ‖ 識。以是四法則布施損減。
052b04 ‖　　離四施得增　　又應三心施
052b05 ‖　　菩薩順佛語　　亦不求果報
052b06 ‖ 離此四法布施則得增益。一迴向阿耨多
052b07 ‖ 羅三藐三菩提。二有方便迴向。三求法王
052b08 ‖ 處。四親近善知識。又應以三法心而行布
052b09 ‖ 施。一者憐愍一切眾生故以菩提心行施。
052b10 ‖ 二者不遠佛法而行布施。三者不求果報
052b11 ‖ 而行布施。

简体字

　　　　答曰。
　　若施不回向　　亦无有方便
　　求生于下处　　亲近恶知识
　　如是布施者　　是则为损减

若布施不回向阿耨多罗三藐三菩提。随逐世间乐故。求生下处无有方便。能出布施禅定果报自在所生。亲近障阂大乘知识。以是四法则布施损减。

　　离四施得增　　又应三心施
　　菩萨顺佛语　　亦不求果报

离此四法布施则得增益。一回向阿耨多罗三藐三菩提。二有方便回向。三求法王处。四亲近善知识。又应以三法心而行布施。一者怜愍一切众生故以菩提心行施。二者不远佛法而行布施。三者不求果报而行布施。

Chapter 12 — *Distinctions with Regard to Giving* 413

b) A: There Are Four Causes of Diminishment, as Follows:

Response:

> If one gives but fails to dedicate the merit,
> if one has no skillful means,
> if one seeks rebirth in an inferior station of existence,
> or if one draws close to bad friends—
>
> If one's giving takes place under such conditions,
> then its effectiveness will thereby be diminished.

[This means]:

> If one gives, but fails to dedicate the merit to *anuttarasamyaksaṃbodhi*—
> If, because one is pursuing worldly happiness, one seeks rebirth in an inferior station of existence—
> If one has no skillful means by which one can freely bring forth the karmic fruits of giving and *dhyāna* concentration—
> Or if one draws near to [bad] friends who obstruct one's progress in the Great Vehicle—

Then, because of [any of] these four dharmas, [the effectiveness of] one's giving will be diminished.

c) For Increase, Stop These Four and Adopt Three Types of Thought

> If one abandons these four, the power of one's giving will increase.
> Also, one should adopt three types of thought as one gives.
> In this, the bodhisattva accords with the words of the Buddha
> while also not seeking to gain any karmic rewards [from giving].

If one abandons the above four dharmas, then the effectiveness of one's giving will be able to increase. [One does so as follows]:

> First, one dedicates one's merit to *anuttarasamyaksaṃbodhi*;
> Second, one adopts appropriate skillful means in carrying out dedications of merit;
> Third, one seeks to reach the station of a Dharma king;
> Fourth, one draws near to good spiritual guides.

Also, in one's practice of giving, one should use three types of Dharma-based thought, as follows:

> First, because one feels pity for all beings, one bases one's giving on the resolve to attain bodhi;
> Second, in one's practice of giving, one does not depart from the Dharma of the Buddha;
> Third, in one's practice of giving, one does not seek any karmic rewards.

正體字

復次。
052b12 ‖　　[6]為得三法故　　而行於布施
052b13 ‖　　為欲求二法　　應當行布施
052b14 ‖ 菩薩為得三法故行布施。一者佛法。二者
052b15 ‖ 說法。三者令諸眾生住無上樂。又欲求二
052b16 ‖ 法行布施者。一者大富。二者具足檀波羅
052b17 ‖ 蜜。何以故。若菩薩大富。則離貧苦不取他
052b18 ‖ 財不求息利。無有債主不憂償債。多財
052b19 ‖ 富足能自衣食。有能惠施利益親族及善知
052b20 ‖ 識。眷屬安樂其家豐饒。常如節會心常歡悅
052b21 ‖ 能大施與。眷屬不輕人所敬仰。言皆信受眾
052b22 ‖ 所依附人來師仰入眾無畏。常好洗浴名
052b23 ‖ 香塗身。著好新衣具足莊嚴。見諸好色
052b24 ‖ 聽好音聲聞諸妙香。常食最上美味。細觸

简体字

复次。
　　为得三法故　　而行于布施
　　为欲求二法　　应当行布施
菩萨为得三法故行布施。一者佛法。二者说法。三者令诸众生住无上乐。又欲求二法行布施者。一者大富。二者具足檀波罗蜜。何以故。若菩萨大富。则离贫苦不取他财不求息利。无有债主不忧偿债。多财富足能自衣食。有能惠施利益亲族及善知识。眷属安乐其家丰饶。常如节会心常欢悦能大施与。眷属不轻人所敬仰。言皆信受众所依附人来师仰入众无畏。常好洗浴名香涂身。着好新衣具足庄严。见诸好色听好音声闻诸妙香。常食最上美味。细触

Chapter 12 — *Distinctions with Regard to Giving*

F. ONE GIVES FOR THE SAKE OF CAUSING 3 DHARMAS AND SEEKING 2 DHARMAS

Moreover:

> It is for the sake of bringing about three dharmas
> that one engages in the practice of giving
> and it is also for the sake of seeking two dharmas
> that one should engage in the practice giving.

It is for the sake of bringing about three dharmas that the bodhisattva engages in the practice of giving:

First, to acquire the Dharma of a Buddha;
Second, to bring about the proclamation of the Dharma;
Third, to cause all beings to abide in unsurpassable happiness.

Additionally, it is because one wishes to seek two dharmas that one practices giving: First, to acquire great wealth, and second, to perfect the practice of *dāna pāramitā*. Why? If the bodhisattva is endowed with great wealth, then:

He will leave behind the suffering of poverty;
He will not take others' wealth;
He will not seek to earn interest;
He will have nobody to whom he is indebted;
And he will have no worries about the repayment of debts.

When one possesses much wealth and one's assets are adequate, then:

One is able to see to one's own clothing and food while also being able to give out of kindness, thereby benefiting one's relatives, one's clan, and one's good spiritual guides;

One's retinue will be happy, one's household will prosper for their minds will always be as delighted as if they were always participating in a celebratory gathering;

One will be able to practice great giving, one's retinue will not slight him, and people will look up to him with respect;

Everyone will be inclined to believe and accept one's words;

One will be relied upon by the many;

When others come, one will be looked up to as a mentor;

On entering an assembly, one will have nothing to fear;

One will always delight in bathing, smoothing famous fragrances onto the body, wearing fine new clothes, and being adorned by a full array of ornaments;

One will become able to behold fine physical forms, to hear agreeable sounds, to smell marvelous fragrances, to always eat the most supremely exquisite flavors, [and to experience] subtle tactile sensations;

正體字	052b25 ‖ 怨賊難壞。善知識歡喜。是於人身得善果 052b26 ‖ 報。人所欽慕常稱吉善。忘其醜惡。雖生 052b27 ‖ 下賤有大人相。雖無巧言成巧言者。雖 052b28 ‖ 不多聞成多聞者。雖少智慧成智慧者。 052b29 ‖ 若先端正倍復殊勝。若先大家倍復尊貴。若 052c01 ‖ 先巧言倍復巧言。若先多聞倍復多聞。若先 052c02 ‖ 智慧倍復有智。所可坐臥貴價寶床㡉㡢安 052c03 ‖ 隱侍衛具足。眾寶為舍極意遊戲。其身貴重 052c04 ‖ 須諸經書應意即得。勢位隨意親近王易。 052c05 ‖ 諸貴[7]人所念。諸醫自往常有親信消息所 052c06 ‖ 宜。有疾輕微若病易差。遠離今世後世怖 052c07 ‖ 畏。
简体字	怨贼难坏。善知识欢喜。是于人身得善果报。人所钦慕常称吉善。忘其丑恶。虽生下贱有大人相。虽无巧言成巧言者。虽不多闻成多闻者。虽少智慧成智慧者。若先端正倍复殊胜。若先大家倍复尊贵。若先巧言倍复巧言。若先多闻倍复多闻。若先智慧倍复有智。所可坐卧贵价宝床㡉㡢安隐侍卫具足。众宝为舍极意游戏。其身贵重须诸经书应意即得。势位随意亲近王易。诸贵人所念。诸医自往常有亲信消息所宜。有疾轻微若病易差。远离今世后世怖畏。

One will become indomitable by adversaries and will become well-liked by good spiritual friends.

These are instances of karmic rewards for goodness as experienced in the human body. Moreover:

One will become respected and admired, one will always be praised as wonderfully good, and others will forget one's disgraceful lapses;

Although one may be been born into a lower-class household, one will have the marks of a great man;

Although one might have no skill in speech, one will become a skillful speaker;

Although one might not be learned, one will acquire extensive learning;

Although one might be deficient in wisdom, one will become a wise person;

If one is already a person of fine appearance, one will develop a doubly outstanding appearance;

If one was formerly from a great clan, one will rise to a doubly revered social station;

If one is already a skillful speaker, one will become a doubly skillful speaker;

If one was already learned, one will become doubly learned;

If one was already wise, one will become doubly wise;

Wherever one sits or lies down, it will be on a precious bejeweled couch;

Whether asleep or awake, one will be peaceful and secure and surrounded by an abundance of attendants;

One's house will be made from the many sorts of jewels and one will be completely free to roam about at will;

One will be regarded as a personage worthy of the highest esteem;

If one has need of any scriptures or books, one will readily obtain whichever ones he seeks;

One's power and position will ensure that one has easy access to the king and one will be borne in mind by all of the nobility;

Physicians will voluntarily come and one will always have those who are close and trustworthy, attending as appropriate to the vicissitudes [of one's health];

If one catches some disease, it will be only minor and mild;

Whatever one's disease, it will be easily cured;

One will leave far behind any fears with respect to either present or later lives;

正體字	
	畢竟永離不活怖畏常有救護。多有人
052c08 ‖	眾諸親近者自謂多福。為同意者深自欣
052c09 ‖	慶。有少施恩得大酬報。若加小惡得大殃
052c10 ‖	禍。族姓女人少年端正具足莊嚴。自求給
052c11 ‖	侍諸有諧利悉來歸己。若作惡事事[8]輒
052c12 ‖	輕微。少有施作即獲大利。多善知識怨憎
052c13 ‖	轉少。蛇虺毒藥放逸惡人如是等事不得妄
052c14 ‖	近。諸愛敬事皆悉歸趣。若獲利時眾人代喜。
052c15 ‖	若有衰惱人皆憂戚。眾共示導競以善[9]吉。
052c16 ‖	令遠非法安住善法。所施業大見莫不歡。
052c17 ‖	若與同心則以為足。不期世間富貴榮利。
052c18 ‖	假使居位人思匡助除其衰惱。見他富貴
052c19 ‖	無所悕尚。

简体字

毕竟永离不活怖畏常有救护。多有人众诸亲近者自谓多福。为同意者深自欣庆。有少施恩得大酬报。若加小恶得大殃祸。族姓女人少年端正具足庄严。自求给侍诸有谐利悉来归己。若作恶事事辄轻微。少有施作即获大利。多善知识怨憎转少。蛇虺毒药放逸恶人如是等事不得妄近。诸爱敬事皆悉归趣。若获利时众人代喜。若有衰恼人皆忧戚。众共示导竞以善吉。令远非法安住善法。所施业大见莫不欢。若与同心则以为足。不期世间富贵荣利。假使居位人思匡助除其衰恼。见他富贵无所悕尚。

Chapter 12 — *Distinctions with Regard to Giving* 419

One will ultimately forever abandon any fear of one's life not continuing on and one will always be rescued and protected;

There will be many people close to one who will feel immensely blessed with good fortune;

One will be sincerely and joyously celebrated by those of like mind;

Whenever anyone extends even a small kindness to one, that person will be repaid magnanimously and whenever anyone afflicts one with even a minor evil deed, that person will encounter a major personal disaster;

Young women from one's own clan who are possessed of fine appearance and complete adornments will voluntarily seek to serve as retainers;

Whoever is seeking to reach agreements will take refuge in one [as a source of resolution];

If one falls into some bad action, that action will usually be only minor;

If one expends even a small effort [in some endeavor], one will immediately receive great benefit as a result;

One will have an abundance of good spiritual friends whereas those who dislike one will grow ever fewer;

One will not be susceptible to accidental encounters with venomous snakes, poison, negligence, evil people, or other such occurrences;

All of one's kindly and respectful actions will tend to be returned in kind;

Whenever one experiences some kind of good fortune, everyone will join in sympathetic rejoicing;

If one experiences some sort of anguishing misfortune, everyone will join in sympathetic commiseration;

Everyone will join in assisting one's guidance, vying to provide one with whatever is good and auspicious while influencing one to avoid whatever is contrary to Dharma and to abide securely in good dharmas;

The works that one accomplishes will be grand and none who witness them will fail to be delighted by them;

If one is able to abide together with those of identical aims, one will find satisfaction in that and will not aspire for worldly wealth, noble birth, acclamation, or benefit;

If one comes to abide in a position of power, people will devote their thoughts to assisting one and doing away with anything that might cause anguishing misfortune;

On observing the wealth and high social stature of others, one entertains no aspirations to assume them for himself;

正體字

```
         人詠其德不揚其過。[10]雖小人
052c20 || 名得大人號無不足色。視他顏貌不作
052c21 || 矯異。若作婆羅門。於天寺中大獲果報。
052c22 || [11]讀諸經書得其實利得而能施。若是剎利
052c23 || 所習成就。善射音聲善能貫練。治世典籍
052c24 || 能得果報若是[12]毘舍播[13]殖如意。若是商
052c25 || [14]估能獲其利。若是首陀羅所作事業多得
052c26 || 如意。問曰。汝先說菩薩不以求果報心
052c27 || 施。又復不為豪貴故施。而今說求大富故
052c28 || 布施。是語得無自相違[15]背。答曰。不相違
052c29 || 也。若自為身求富受樂。是故說不應求
053a01 || 富。今說求富但為利益眾生。是故說為
053a02 || 欲大施故求富。不為身已求富受樂。
053a03 || 是則果中說因。若菩薩不得[1]大富雖信
053a04 || 樂布施無財可與。是故汝不應作難。復次
053a05 || 斷二法故應行布施。何等為二。一者慳。
```

简体字

人咏其德不扬其过。虽小人名得大人号无不足色。视他颜貌不作矫异。若作婆罗门。于天寺中大获果报。读诸经书得其实利得而能施。若是刹利所习成就。善射音声善能贯练。治世典籍能得果报若是毗舍播殖如意。若是商估能获其利。若是首陀罗所作事业多得如意。问曰。汝先说菩萨不以求果报心施。又复不为豪贵故施。而今说求大富故布施。是语得无自相违背。答曰。不相违也。若自为身求富受乐。是故说不应求富。今说求富但为利益众生。是故说为欲大施故求富。不为身已求富受乐。是则果中说因。若菩萨不得大富虽信乐布施无财可与。是故汝不应作难。复次断二法故应行布施。何等为二。一者悭。

The people sing the praises of one's virtues but do not propagate reports of one's errors;

Although one might be from a family of inferior social stature, one will acquire the reputation of a great personage;

One never displays a disapproving expression and, whenever one observes someone else's appearance, one does not adopt a pretentious demeanor;

If one becomes a brahman,[194] one will garner great karmic rewards from his works within the temples of the deities. When studying the scriptures, one gains their genuine benefits and, having gained them, one is able to bestow them on others;

If one becomes a *kṣatriya*,[195] one succeeds in his endeavors, is renowned for his skill in archery, is consummate in one's abilities, and is well able to gain the results taught in the classics on ruling the world;

If one becomes a *vaiśya*,[196] one is well able to grow whichever crops one wishes;

If one becomes a merchant, one is well able to gain the profit one seeks;

If one becomes a *śūdra*,[197] whatever work one does becomes abundantly successful in a way that matches one's wishes.

1. Q: You Said One Doesn't Seek Rewards. Isn't This Contradictory?

Question: Earlier, you claimed that the bodhisattva does not have the motivation to seek karmic rewards from his practice of giving, and, beyond that, that he is not motivated by a desire for wealth and high social status. Now, however, you state that one gives in quest of great wealth. How are these statements not contradictory?

2. A: No, Because This Wealth Is Gained & Used Only to Benefit Beings

Response: They are not contradictory. It is with reference to cases where one seeks to acquire wealth and enjoyment of pleasures for oneself that it was said that one should not seek for wealth. Now, however, we speak of seeking wealth solely to benefit beings. It is for that reason that it was stated that one seeks wealth out of an aspiration to engage in great giving. This is not a case of seeking wealth and pleasures for oneself. Hence we discuss here the causal factors within such karmic results.

If a bodhisattva fails to come by great wealth, then, even though he has a resolute belief in giving, he still has no wealth that he can use in giving. Therefore you should not raise such a challenge.

G. One Also Gives to Cut Off Two Dharmas and Gain Two Dharmas

Additionally, it is for the sake of cutting off two types of dharmas that one should practice giving. What are those two? The first is miserliness

正體字

```
              二
053a06 ‖ 者貪。此二法最為施垢。又得二法故行布
053a07 ‖ 施。所謂盡智無生智。又增益三種慧。一者自
053a08 ‖ 利慧。二者本慧。三者多聞慧。有人言。增長
053a09 ‖ 二法故應行施。一善二慧。略說菩薩應行
053a10 ‖ 四種施攝一切善法。一者等心施。二者無對
053a11 ‖ 施。三者迴向菩提施。四者具足善寂滅心施。
053a12 ‖ 菩薩如是具[2]足檀波羅蜜故勤行財施。[3]
053a13 ‖ 十住毘婆沙論[第卷>卷第]六
```

简体字

二者贪。此二法最为施垢。又得二法故行布施。所谓尽智无生智。又增益三种慧。一者自利慧。二者本慧。三者多闻慧。有人言。增长二法故应行施。一善二慧。略说菩萨应行四种施摄一切善法。一者等心施。二者无对施。三者回向菩提施。四者具足善寂灭心施。菩萨如是具足檀波罗蜜故勤行财施。

and the second is covetousness. These two dharmas are the most extreme sorts of defilement that may sully one's practice of giving.

Then again, it is for the sake of gaining two types of dharmas that one practices giving, namely the knowledge of cessation and also the knowledge of non-production.

H. One Also Gives to Increase Three Types of Wisdom

Also, [giving is done] in order to increase three types of wisdom:

First, the wisdom that serves to achieve self-benefit;[198]
Second, fundamental wisdom;
Third, the wisdom arising from extensive learning.

I. Others Say That Giving Is Practiced to Increase Two Dharmas

There are yet others who say that one should give in order to bring about the increase of two dharmas: First, goodness. Second, wisdom.

J. In Summary, the Bodhisattva Should Practice Four Kinds of Giving

To present a general summation here, the bodhisattva should engage in four kinds of giving in order to subsume within his practice all of the different types of good dharmas, as follows:

First, giving that originates in a mind that perceives everyone as equal;
Second, giving that transcends opposites;
Third, giving that is dedicated to attaining bodhi;
Fourth, giving characterized by the presence of a thoroughly quiescent mind.

It is in order to completely perfect *dāna pāramitā* in this manner that the bodhisattva diligently practices the giving of material wealth.

The End of Chapter Twelve

正體字

053a16 ‖ 十住毘婆沙論卷第七 053a17 ‖
053a18 ‖　　聖者龍樹造
053a19 ‖　　後秦龜茲國三藏鳩摩羅什譯
053a20 ‖　　[4]分別法施品第十三
053a21 ‖ 菩薩於財施應如是修學又應修學法施
053a22 ‖ 如說。
053a23 ‖　　眾施法施最　　智者應修行
053a24 ‖ 一切布施中第一最上最妙。所謂法施。是施
053a25 ‖ 智者所應行。問曰。何故但言智者應行法
053a26 ‖ 施。答曰。不智者若行法施即說[5]異論。說
053a27 ‖ [*]異論故自失利亦失他利。問曰。何謂[*]異
053a28 ‖ 論。答曰。佛欲滅度時告阿難。從今日後
053a29 ‖ 依修多羅莫依人。阿難云何名依修多羅
053b01 ‖ 不依人。有比丘來作是言。我現從佛聞現
053b02 ‖ 從佛受。是法是善是佛所教。是比丘語莫
053b03 ‖ 受莫捨。審諦聽已應以經律撿其所說。若
053b04 ‖ 不入修多羅不入毘尼。又復違逆諸法相
053b05 ‖ 義。

简体字

分别法施品第十三

菩萨于财施应如是修学又应修学法施如说。

　　众施法施最　　智者应修行

一切布施中第一最上最妙。所谓法施。是施智者所应行。问曰。何故但言智者应行法施。答曰。不智者若行法施即说异论。说异论故自失利亦失他利。问曰。何谓异论。答曰。佛欲灭度时告阿难。从今日后依修多罗莫依人。阿难云何名依修多罗不依人。有比丘来作是言。我现从佛闻现从佛受。是法是善是佛所教。是比丘语莫受莫舍。审谛听已应以经律捡其所说。若不入修多罗不入毗尼。又复违逆诸法相义。

Chapter 13
Distinctions with Regard to the Giving of Dharma

XIII. Chapter 13: Distinctions with Regard to the Giving of Dharma
   A. Dharma Giving Is Supreme and the Wise Should Practice It

The bodhisattva should cultivate the giving of material wealth in the above-discussed manner and should also cultivate the giving of Dharma, doing so in accordance with this statement:

> Of the many sorts of giving, the giving of Dharma is supreme.
> Thus the wise should cultivate its practice.

Of all of the kinds of giving, the foremost, the most superior, and the most sublime is the giving of Dharma. This is the type of giving that the wise should practice.

   B. Q: Why Do You Say Only the Wise Should Practice Dharma Giving?

Question: Why do you say that [only] the wise should engage in the practice of giving Dharma?

   C. A: Erroneous Interpretations Do Not Benefit Anyone

Response: If those who are not wise pursue the giving of Dharma, they will set forth erroneous interpretations. By setting forth erroneous interpretations they will fail to benefit themselves and will also fail to benefit others.

     1. Q: What Do You Mean by "Erroneous Interpretations"?

Question: What is meant here by "erroneous[199] interpretations"?

     2. A: Wrong Ideas of Spurious Origin (Four Cases from Scripture)

Response: When the Buddha was on the verge of entering nirvāṇa, he told Ānanda:

> From this day forward, one should rely upon the sutras. Do not rely on persons. Ānanda, what is meant by relying on the sutras and not relying on persons?[200]
>
> If a bhikshu comes and speaks thus: "In his presence, I have heard this from the Buddha, and in his presence, I have received this from the Buddha. It is Dharma, it is good, and it is as taught by the Buddha," neither accept nor reject the words of this bhikshu, but rather, having listened carefully, one should search for what has been said in the sutras and in the moral code.
>
> If it is not included in the sutras, is not included in the Vinaya, and it also contradicts the true character of dharmas,[201] one should

正體字

053b06 應報是比丘言。是法或非佛所說。或長
053b06 老謬受。何以故。是法不入修多羅不入毘
053b07 尼。又復違逆諸法相義。是則非法非善非
053b08 佛所教。如是知已即應除却。復有比丘來
053b09 作是言。彼住處有大眾。有明經上座善說
053b10 戒律。我現從彼聞。現從彼受。是法是善是
053b11 佛所教。是比丘語莫受莫捨。審諦聽已應
053b12 以經律撿其所說。若不入修多羅不入
053b13 毘尼。又復違逆諸法相義。應報是比丘言。
053b14 長老彼比丘僧法相善相。或作非法非善說。
053b15 或長老謬受。何以故。是法不入修多羅不
053b16 入毘尼。又復違逆諸法相義。是則非法非
053b17 善非佛所教。如是知已即應除却。復有比
053b18 丘來作是言。彼住[6]處多諸比丘。持修多
053b19 羅持毘尼持摩多羅迦。我現從彼聞現從
053b20 彼受。是法是善是佛所教。是比丘語莫受
053b21 莫捨。審諦聽已應以經律撿其所說。若不
053b22 入修多羅不入毘尼。

简体字

应报是比丘言。是法或非佛所说。或长老谬受。何以故。是法不入修多罗不入毗尼。又复违逆诸法相义。是则非法非善非佛所教。如是知已即应除却。复有比丘来作是言。彼住处有大众。有明经上座善说戒律。我现从彼闻。现从彼受。是法是善是佛所教。是比丘语莫受莫舍。审谛听已应以经律捡其所说。若不入修多罗不入毗尼。又复违逆诸法相义。应报是比丘言。长老彼比丘僧法相善相。或作非法非善说。或长老谬受。何以故。是法不入修多罗不入毗尼。又复违逆诸法相义。是则非法非善非佛所教。如是知已即应除却。复有比丘来作是言。彼住处多诸比丘。持修多罗持毗尼持摩多罗迦。我现从彼闻现从彼受。是法是善是佛所教。是比丘语莫受莫舍。审谛听已应以经律捡其所说。若不入修多罗不入毗尼。又复违逆诸法相义。应报是比丘言。长老彼比丘僧法相善相。或作非法非善说。或长老谬受。何以故。是法不入修多罗不入毗尼。

reply to this bhikshu, saying, "Perhaps this dharma is one that was not spoken by the Buddha. Perhaps the Venerable One has mistakenly accepted it as such. Why? This dharma is not included in the sutras and is not included in the Vinaya, either. What's more, it contradicts the true character of dharmas. Therefore this is non-Dharma, not good, and not taught by the Buddha." Having realized this, one should then immediately reject this.

Now suppose some other bhikshu comes and speaks thus: "There is a large sangha in which I reside wherein there is a senior monk, one who understands the sutras and who is skillful in explaining the moral code. In his presence, I have heard this from him, and in his presence, I have received this from him. It is Dharma, it is good, and it is as taught by the Buddha."

Again, neither accept nor reject the words of this bhikshu, but rather, having listened carefully, one should search for what he has said in the sutras and in the moral code. If it is not included in the sutras, is not included in the Vinaya, and it also contradicts the true character of dharmas, one should reply to this bhikshu, saying, "Venerable One, that sangha of bhikshus—regarding their understanding of the character of dharmas and the character of what constitutes goodness—perhaps they have spoken of these things in a manner that is contrary to Dharma and contrary to goodness. Perhaps the Venerable One has mistakenly accepted it. Why? This dharma is not included in the sutras and is not included in the Vinaya, either. What's more, it contradicts the true character of dharmas. Therefore this is non-Dharma, not good, and not spoken by the Buddha." Having realized this, one should then immediately reject this.

Suppose yet another bhikshu comes and speaks thus: "There are many bhikshus where I abide who preserve the sutras, preserve the Vinaya, and preserve the *mātṛkās*."[202] In their presence, I have heard this from them, and in their presence, I have accepted this from them. It is Dharma, it is good, and it is as taught by the Buddha."

Neither accept nor reject the words of this bhikshu, but rather, having listened carefully, one should search in the sutras and in the moral code for what he has said. If it is not included in the sutras, is not included in the Vinaya, and it also contradicts the true character of dharmas, one should reply to this bhikshu, saying, "Venerable One, that sangha of bhikshus—regarding their understanding of the character of dharmas and the character of what constitutes goodness—perhaps they have spoken of these things in a manner that is contrary to Dharma and contrary to goodness. Perhaps the Venerable One has mistakenly accepted it. Why? This dharma is not included in the sutras and is not included in the Vinaya, either. What's more,

正體字

又復違逆諸法相
053b23 ‖ 義。應報是比丘言。長老彼比丘僧法相[7]善
053b24 ‖ 相。或作非法非善說。或長老謬受。何以故。
053b25 ‖ 是法不入修多羅不入毘尼。又復違逆諸
053b26 ‖ 法相義。是則非法非善非佛所教。如是知
053b27 ‖ 已即應除却。復有比丘來作是言。彼住處
053b28 ‖ 中有長老比丘。多知多識人所尊重。我現從
053b29 ‖ 彼聞現從彼受。是法是善是佛所教。是比
053c01 ‖ 丘語莫受莫捨。審諦聽已應以經律撿其
053c02 ‖ 所說。若不入修多羅不入毘尼。又復違逆
053c03 ‖ 諸法相義。應報是比丘言。長老彼諸比丘
053c04 ‖ 法相善相。或作非法非善說。或長老謬受。何
053c05 ‖ 以故。是法不入修多羅不入毘尼。又復違
053c06 ‖ 逆諸法相義。是則非法非善非佛所教。如
053c07 ‖ 是知已即應除却。是四名[*]異論。是故言智
053c08 ‖ 者不依[*]異論而行清白法施。問曰。云何知
053c09 ‖ 諸施中法施第一。答曰。經說有二施[8]財法
053c10 ‖ 施。二施之中法施為上。復次。
053c11 ‖ 　　決定王經中　　讚說法功德
053c12 ‖ 　　及說法儀式　　應常修習行
053c13 ‖ 若菩薩欲以法施眾生者。應如決定王大
053c14 ‖ 乘經中稱讚法師功德

简体字

又复违逆诸法相义。是则非法非善非佛所教。如是知已即应除却。复有比丘来作是言。彼住处中有长老比丘。多知多识人所尊重。我现从彼闻现从彼受。是法是善是佛所教。是比丘语莫受莫舍。审谛听已应以经律捡其所说。若不入修多罗不入毗尼。又复违逆诸法相义。应报是比丘言。长老彼诸比丘法相善相。或作非法非善说。或长老谬受。何以故。是法不入修多罗不入毗尼。又复违逆诸法相义。是则非法非善非佛所教。如是知已即应除却。是四名异论。是故言智者不依异论而行清白法施。问曰。云何知诸施中法施第一。答曰。经说有二施财法施。二施之中法施为上。复次。
　　决定王经中　　赞说法功德
　　及说法仪式　　应常修习行
若菩萨欲以法施众生者。应如决定王大乘经中称赞法师功德

it contradicts the true character of dharmas. Therefore this is non-Dharma, not good, and not taught by the Buddha." Having realized this, one should then immediately reject this.

Suppose yet another bhikshu comes and speaks thus: "There is a senior bhikshu where I abide, one who understands much, one who is aware of much, and one whom people revere. In his presence, I have heard this from him, and in his presence, I have received this from him. It is Dharma, it is good, and it is as taught by the Buddha."

Neither accept nor reject the words of this bhikshu, but rather, having listened carefully, one should search for what he has said in the sutras and in the moral code. If it is not included in the sutras, is not included in the Vinaya, and it also contradicts the true character of dharmas, one should reply to this bhikshu, saying, "Venerable One, that sangha of bhikshus—regarding their understanding of the character of dharmas and the character of what constitutes goodness—perhaps they have spoken of these things in a manner that is contrary to Dharma and contrary to goodness. Perhaps the Venerable One has mistakenly accepted it. Why? This dharma is not included in the sutras and is not included in the Vinaya, either. What's more, it contradicts the true character of dharmas. Therefore this is non-Dharma, not good, and not taught by the Buddha." Having realized this, one should then immediately reject this.

These four cases illustrate what is meant here by "erroneous interpretations." It is therefore said that the wise do not rely upon erroneous interpretations, but rather practice pristinely pure Dharma giving.

D. Q: How Does One Know That Dharma Giving Is Supreme?

Question: How is it that one knows the giving of Dharma is the foremost among all forms of giving?

E. A: The Sutras Say So

Response: The sutras state that there are two types of giving, the giving of material wealth and the giving of Dharma, and that, among those two types of giving, it is the giving of Dharma that is superior.

F. A Sutra Explains Propriety in Speaking Dharma as Follows:

Furthermore:

> In *The Sutra of the Resolute King*,[203]
> there are praises of Dharma giving's merit
> and explanations of propriety in the speaking of Dharma.
> One should always cultivate and practice in accordance with these.

If the bodhisattva wishes to bestow Dharma on beings, he should follow and cultivate in accordance with the passages in *The Sutra of the Resolute King* that praise the meritorious qualities possessed by a

正體字	及說法儀式隨順修 053c15 ‖ 學。謂說法者應行四法。何等為四。一者廣 053c16 ‖ 博多學能持一切言辭章句。二者決定善知 053c17 ‖ 世間出世間諸法生滅相。三者得禪定[9]慧。 053c18 ‖ 於諸經法隨順無諍。四者不增不損如所 053c19 ‖ 說行。說法者處師子座復有四法。何等為 053c20 ‖ 四。一者欲昇高座。先應恭敬禮拜大眾 053c21 ‖ 然後昇座。二者眾有女人應觀不淨。三者 053c22 ‖ 威儀視瞻有大人相。敷演法音顏色和悅人 053c23 ‖ 皆信受。不說外道經書心無怯畏。四者於 053c24 ‖ 惡言問難當行忍辱。處師子座復有四法。 053c25 ‖ 何等為四。一者於諸眾生生饒益想。二者 053c26 ‖ 於諸眾生不生我想。三者於諸文字不 053c27 ‖ 生法想。
简体字	及说法仪式随顺修学。谓说法者应行四法。何等为四。一者广博多学能持一切言辞章句。二者决定善知世间出世间诸法生灭相。三者得禅定慧。于诸经法随顺无诤。四者不增不损如所说行。说法者处师子座复有四法。何等为四。一者欲升高座。先应恭敬礼拜大众然后升座。二者众有女人应观不净。三者威仪视瞻有大人相。敷演法音颜色和悦人皆信受。不说外道经书心无怯畏。四者于恶言问难当行忍辱。处师子座复有四法。何等为四。一者于诸众生生饶益想。二者于诸众生不生我想。三者于诸文字不生法想。

Chapter 13 — *Distinctions with Regard to the Giving of Dharma* 431

teacher of Dharma and that set forth the correct ceremonial procedures involved in speaking Dharma. It stipulates the following:

1. FOUR QUALITIES OF A QUALIFIED DHARMA SPEAKER

The speaker of Dharma should incorporate four dharmas in his practice. What are those four?

First, he is to be one possessed of vast and extensive learning while also being well able to bear in mind [the meaning of] all the phrases and passages [of the scripture at hand];

Second, he is to be resolutely and skillfully cognizant of the marks of production and extinction as they manifest in all worldly and world-transcending dharmas;

Third, having acquired the wisdom arising from *dhyāna* concentration, he accords with the Dharma set forth in the sutras while also remaining free of any contentiousness;

Fourth, neither adding anything to nor taking anything away [from the Dharma set forth in the sutras], he practices in accordance with what is proclaimed therein.

2. FOUR CORRECT BEHAVIORS WHEN ASCENDING THE HIGH SEAT TO TEACH

There are four additional dharmas that are to be observed when the speaker of Dharma occupies the lion throne. What are those four?

First, when about to ascend to the high seat, one should first respectfully pay reverence to the great assembly in attendance and then afterward ascend to that seat;

Second, in audiences including women, one should contemplate impurity [of the body];

Third, in one's deportment and bearing, one maintains the appearance of a great man. As one spreads forth the sound of Dharma, one's countenance appears harmonious and pleased, inspiring all in attendance to accept [one's words] with faith. One does not teach non-Buddhist scriptures and one's mind remains fearless;

Fourth, in the face of harsh words and challenging questions, one should practice patience.

3. FOUR MORE CORRECT BEHAVIORS FOR WHEN ONE SITS ON THE HIGH SEAT

There are four additional dharmas pertaining to sitting in the high seat. What are those four?

First, one brings forth the motivation to be of abundant benefit to beings;

Second, one does not conceive of the idea of a self in connection with any being;

Third, one does not conceive of the words as synonymous with the dharmas [that they describe];

	四者願諸眾生從我聞法者於阿
053c28 ‖	耨多羅三藐三菩提而不退轉。處師子座復
053c29 ‖	有四法。何等為四。一者善能安住陀羅尼
054a01 ‖	門。深信樂法。二者善得般舟三昧。勤行精進
054a02 ‖	持戒清淨。三者不樂一切生處。不貪利養。
054a03 ‖	不求果報。四者於三解脫心無有疑。又能
054a04 ‖	善起諸深三昧具足威儀。憶念堅固有念
054a05 ‖	安慧。不調戲不輕躁。不無羞不癡亂。言
054a06 ‖	無錯謬守護諸根不貪美味。善攝手足
054a07 ‖	所念不忘。樂行頭陀分別世間出世間法。
054a08 ‖	心無疑悔言辭章句不可窮盡。為諸聽者
054a09 ‖	求安隱利不求他過。有如是法應處師
054a10 ‖	子座。

四者愿诸众生从我闻法者于阿耨多罗三藐三菩提而不退转。处师子座复有四法。何等为四。一者善能安住陀罗尼门。深信乐法。二者善得般舟三昧。勤行精进持戒清净。三者不乐一切生处。不贪利养。不求果报。四者于三解脱心无有疑。又能善起诸深三昧具足威仪。忆念坚固有念安慧。不调戏不轻躁。不无羞不痴乱。言无错谬守护诸根不贪美味。善摄手足所念不忘。乐行头陀分别世间出世间法。心无疑悔言辞章句不可穷尽。为诸听者求安隐利不求他过。有如是法应处师子座。

Chapter 13 — Distinctions with Regard to the Giving of Dharma

Fourth, one vows, "May any being who hears me speak on Dharma thereby gain irreversibility in the path to *anuttarasamyaksaṃbodhi*."

4. ANOTHER FOUR CORRECT BEHAVIORS WHEN SITTING ON THE HIGH SEAT

There are another four dharmas pertaining to sitting in the high seat. What are these four?

First, one is well able to abide securely within the gateway of *dhāraṇī* practice[204] and in resolute faith in the Dharma;

Second, one is skilled in realization of the *pratyutpanna* samādhi, diligent in the practice of vigor, and pure in observance of the moral precepts;

Third, one sees no happiness inhering in any place of rebirth, does not covet offerings, and does not seek to obtain any sort of karmic reward;

Fourth, one's mind is free of any doubt regarding the three gates to liberation.

5. EIGHTEEN MORE QUALIFICATIONS FOR ONE WHO SITS ON THE HIGH SEAT

Additionally:

One is well able to bring forth deep samādhis;

One is completely adherent to the awesome deportment;

One has a strong memory;

One's thoughts are imbued with stable wisdom;

One refrains from joking and teasing;

One refrains from acting with a frivolous demeanor;

One refrains from shamelessness;

One refrains from falling into delusion and confusion;

One's discourse remains free of error;

One's sense faculties remain well-guarded;

One does not covet fine flavors;

One is careful to maintain proper deportment with one's arms and legs;

One does not forget what one has chosen to bear in mind;

One enjoys practicing the *dhūta* austerities;[205]

One is well able to make distinctions regarding worldly and world-transcending dharmas;

One's mind is free of doubts and regrets;

One's discourse is inexhaustible in its phrasing and in its command of scriptural passages;

And one seeks to promote the security and benefit of the audience and also refrains from finding fault with them.

If one is in possession of dharmas of this sort, then one should occupy the lion throne.

正體字

	復有四法。一不自輕身。二不輕聽
054a11 ‖	者。三不輕所說。四不[1]為利養。佛告阿難。
054a12 ‖	說法者應說何法。阿難。所可說法不可示
054a13 ‖	不可說無相無為。世尊。法若爾者云何可說。
054a14 ‖	阿難。是法甚深。如來以四相方便而為演
054a15 ‖	說。一以音聲。二以名字。三以語言。四以義
054a16 ‖	理。又以四因緣而為說法。一者為度應度
054a17 ‖	眾生。二者但說色受想行識名字。三者以種
054a18 ‖	種文辭章句利益眾生。四者雖說名字而
054a19 ‖	亦不得。譬如鉢油清淨無垢。於中觀者自
054a20 ‖	見面相。阿難。汝若見若聞智慧男子若持戒
054a21 ‖	女人若聖弟子能作是說我於鉢油見實
054a22 ‖	人不。世尊我不聞不見智慧男子持戒女人
054a23 ‖	若聖弟子能作是言我於鉢油見真實人。
054a24 ‖	何以故。智者先知鉢油非有何況有人。但
054a25 ‖	以假名說言[2]鉢油而見人相。

简体字

复有四法。一不自轻身。二不轻听者。三不轻所说。四不为利养。佛告阿难。说法者应说何法。阿难。所可说法不可示不可说无相无为。世尊。法若尔者云何可说。阿难。是法甚深。如来以四相方便而为演说。一以音声。二以名字。三以语言。四以义理。又以四因缘而为说法。一者为度应度众生。二者但说色受想行识名字。三者以种种文辞章句利益众生。四者虽说名字而亦不得。譬如钵油清净无垢。于中观者自见面相。阿难。汝若见若闻智慧男子若持戒女人若圣弟子能作是说我于钵油见实人不。世尊我不闻不见智慧男子持戒女人若圣弟子能作是言我于钵油见真实人。何以故。智者先知钵油非有何况有人。但以假名说言钵油而见人相。

Chapter 13 — *Distinctions with Regard to the Giving of Dharma*

6. Four More Dharmas To Be Observed When Sitting on the High Seat

There are yet four more dharmas in this connection:

First, one does not slight oneself;
Second, one does not slight audience members;
Third, one does not slight the topic that is being discussed;
Fourth, one does not [teach Dharma] for the sake of obtaining offerings or support.

G. A Scriptural Citation Regarding the Buddha's Teaching of Dharma

[Nāgārjuna introduces another passage from scripture]:

The Buddha spoke to Ānanda, saying, "On which dharmas should the speaker of Dharma speak? Ānanda, whichever dharma one may discuss—it cannot be demonstrated, it cannot be described, it is signless, and it is unconditioned."

"O Bhagavat, if this is the case, how can they be discussed?"

"Ānanda, this Dharma is extremely profound. When the Tathāgata expounds [on Dharma], he uses an expedient device that involves four factors:

First, the sound of his voice;
Second, names;
Third, verbal discourse;
Fourth, principles.

Additionally, there are four causal circumstances associated with his speaking about the Dharma for others:

First, it is done for the sake of liberating beings who are amenable to being liberated;
Second, in doing so, he only deals in designations associated with forms, feelings, perceptions, formative factors, and consciousnesses;
Third, he uses all sorts of phrases and sentences to benefit beings;
Fourth, although, in speaking, he uses such names, [their referents] still cannot be apprehended.

This is just as when there is a basin of clean, unsullied oil in which an observer can see an image of his own face. Ānanda, have you ever seen or heard of any wise man, virtuous woman, or disciple of an *ārya* who was able to claim, 'I have seen a real person right there in a basin of oil'?"

"O Bhagavat, I have neither heard nor seen any wise man, virtuous woman, or disciple of an *ārya* who has claimed, 'I have seen a real person in a basin of oil.' Why is that so? One who is wise would know ahead of time that even the basin of oil was not [intrinsically] existent. How much the less might he claim the existence of a person there. It is solely by resort to artificial naming that one may claim the existence of a basin of oil in which one sees a person's image."

正體字	阿難。如來亦 054a26 ‖ 復如是。但以名字假有所說。阿難。如來以 054a27 ‖ 四因緣而為說法。眾生聞者心得安樂。種 054a28 ‖ 涅槃因。如來說法音聲遍滿十方世界。眾生 054a29 ‖ 聞者心得歡喜。離諸惡趣生兜術天。如來 054b01 ‖ 聲中無男無女。男不取女相女不取男相。 054b02 ‖ 如來音者不惱眾生不壞諸法。但為示現 054b03 ‖ 音聲之性。說法者應習行是事。應隨所行 054b04 ‖ 而為法施。施者受者所得果報。後當廣說。
简体字	阿难。如来亦复如是。但以名字假有所说。阿难。如来以四因缘而为说法。众生闻者心得安乐。种涅槃因。如来说法音声遍满十方世界。众生闻者心得欢喜。离诸恶趣生兜术天。如来声中无男无女。男不取女相女不取男相。如来音者不恼众生不坏诸法。但为示现音声之性。说法者应习行是事。应随所行而为法施。施者受者所得果报。后当广说。

"Ānanda, the Tathāgata is just the same in this respect. It is only through reliance upon names that there is an artificial existence of anything of which he speaks.

Ānanda, there are four causes and conditions involved in the Tathāgata's speaking about the Dharma for others:

> When beings hear this, their minds experience peace and happiness and they plant the causes for attaining nirvāṇa.
>
> The sound of the Tathāgata's proclamation of Dharma pervades the worlds of the ten directions. When beings hear this, their minds are delighted, they abandon the wretched destinies, and they gain rebirth in the Tuṣita Heaven.
>
> In the sounds of the Tathāgata's voice, there is nothing that is either masculine or feminine. Men do not seize on any feminine aspects and women do not seize on any masculine aspects.
>
> The sound of the Tathāgata's voice does not cause distress to beings nor does it interfere with [the correct representation of] any dharma. It is resorted to solely in order to make manifest the nature of the sounds."

H. CONCLUSION: IN DHARMA GIVING, ONE SHOULD PRACTICE ACCORDINGLY

The speaker of Dharma should practice in accord with these ideas [discussed above] and should perform the giving of Dharma in compliance with these practices. As for the karmic results that accrue to the giver and the receiver, these should be extensively discussed later on.

The End of Chapter Thirteen

正體字	054b05 ‖ 　　歸命相品第十四 054b06 ‖ 上已解說財施法施。今更分別。 054b07 ‖ 　白衣在家者　　應多行財施 054b08 ‖ 　餘諸善行法　　今當復解說 054b09 ‖ 是二施中。在家之人當行財施。出家之人當 054b10 ‖ 行法施。何以故。在家法施不及出家。以 054b11 ‖ 聽受法者於在家人信心淺薄故。又在家 054b12 ‖ 之人多有財物。出家之人於諸經法讀誦通 054b13 ‖ [3]達為人解說在眾無畏。非在家[4]人之所 054b14 ‖ 能及。又使聽者起恭敬心不及出家。又若 054b15 ‖ 欲說法降伏人心不及出家。如說。 054b16 ‖ 　先自修行法　　然後教餘人 054b17 ‖ 　乃可作是言　　汝隨我所行 054b18 ‖ 是事出家者所宜。非在家者所行。又說。
简体字	归命相品第十四 　上已解说财施法施。今更分别。 　白衣在家者　　应多行财施 　余诸善行法　　今当复解说 　是二施中。在家之人当行财施。出家之人当行法施。何以故。在家法施不及出家。以听受法者于在家人信心浅薄故。又在家之人多有财物。出家之人于诸经法读诵通达为人解说在众无畏。非在家人之所能及。又使听者起恭敬心不及出家。又若欲说法降伏人心不及出家。如说。 　先自修行法　　然后教余人 　乃可作是言　　汝随我所行 　是事出家者所宜。非在家者所行。又说。

CHAPTER 14
The Characteristics of the Refuges

XIV. CHAPTER 14: THE CHARACTERISTICS OF THE [THREE] REFUGES
  A. DISTINCTIONS REGARDING MATERIAL GIVING VERSUS DHARMA GIVING

The giving of material wealth and the giving of Dharma were already explained above. Now, we shall make further distinctions in this regard:

> The "white-robed ones," the householders,[206]
> should extensively practice the giving of material wealth.
> The dharmas associated with the rest of the good practices
> shall now be explained as well.

   1. LAITY EXCEL AT MATERIAL GIVING & MONASTICS EXCEL AT DHARMA GIVING

Of these two types of giving, the householder should practice the giving of material wealth. Those who have left the home life should practice the giving of Dharma. Why is this? It is because, in the giving of Dharma, the layperson is unable to match those who have left the home life. This is because those who listen to and accept the Dharma have only shallow and scant faith in a householder's [ability to teach Dharma].

   2. MONASTICS ARE BETTER TRAINED TO PRACTICE DHARMA GIVING

Moreover, whereas the householders possess greater resources of material wealth, it is the monastics who have studied, recited, and deeply understood the dharmas of the sutras to the point that, in the midst of assemblies, they are fearless in explaining them for others. The householders are unable to match them in this. Additionally, they do not match the monastics' ability to inspire a reverential frame of mind in the listener. Also, in instances where one might wish, through expounding the Dharma, to overcome [doubts in] the minds of others, [the householders] are unable to match the monastics. This is as described [in this verse]:

> If one first cultivates the Dharma oneself
> and then later engages in the teaching of others.
> Then and only then can one utter these words:
> "You should accord with what I myself practice."

This is an endeavor that is fitting for those who have left the home life. It is not something that the householder carries out in practice. It is also said that:

正體字

054b19 ‖ 　身自行不善　　安能令彼善
054b20 ‖ 　自不得寂滅　　何能令人寂
054b21 ‖ 　是故身自善　　能令彼行善
054b22 ‖ 　自身得寂滅　　能令人得寂
054b23 ‖ 善法寂滅。是出家者之所應行。又出家之人
054b24 ‖ 於聽法者恭敬心勝。又出家之人若行財
054b25 ‖ 施則妨餘善。又妨行遠離阿練若處空閑
054b26 ‖ 林澤。出家之人若樂財施悉妨修行。如是
054b27 ‖ 等事。若行財施必至聚落與白衣從事多
054b28 ‖ 有言說。若不從事無由得財。若出入聚
054b29 ‖ 落見聞聲色。諸根難攝發起三毒。又於持
054c01 ‖ 戒忍辱精進禪定智慧心薄。又與白衣從
054c02 ‖ 事。利養垢染發起愛恚慳嫉煩惱。[5]惟心思
054c03 ‖ 惟力。而自抑制心志。弱者或不自制。或乃
054c04 ‖ 致死。或得死等諸惱苦患貪著五欲捨戒

简体字

　身自行不善　　安能令彼善
　自不得寂灭　　何能令人寂
　是故身自善　　能令彼行善
　自身得寂灭　　能令人得寂

善法寂灭。是出家者之所应行。又出家之人于听法者恭敬心胜。又出家之人若行财施则妨余善。又妨行远离阿练若处空闲林泽。出家之人若乐财施悉妨修行。如是等事。若行财施必至聚落与白衣从事多有言说。若不从事无由得财。若出入聚落见闻声色。诸根难摄发起三毒。又于持戒忍辱精进禅定智慧心薄。又与白衣从事。利养垢染发起爱恚悭嫉烦恼。惟心思惟力。而自抑制心志。弱者或不自制。或乃致死。或得死等诸恼苦患贪着五欲舍戒

If one personally practices what is not good,
how can one influence others to engage in goodness?
If one personally fails to attain quiescence,
how can one cause others to attain quiescence?

Hence, if one personally practices goodness,
one can influence others to practice goodness.
If one personally attains quiescence,
one can cause others to attain quiescence.

Good dharmas and quiescence are matters that should be practiced by those who have left the home life. Also, monastics have a superior ability to inspire reverence in those who listen to the Dharma.

3. THE HAZARDS TO MONASTICS OF DEVOTION TO MATERIAL GIVING

Furthermore, if those who have left the home life practice the giving of material wealth, then this prevents their own development of the other forms of goodness. They are also thus prevented from practicing renunciation in a forest hermitage where they dwell off in a wilderness forest or marshland. If those who have left the home life take pleasure in the giving of material wealth, that will completely interfere with their pursuit of such cultivation.

It is the nature of these sorts of endeavors that, if one practices the giving of material wealth, one must certainly go into the villages and involve oneself in the endeavors of the layperson. In such instances, there will be much talk.[207]

If one does not take up such work, then there will be no means by which one can obtain such material wealth. If one is involved in coming and going from the villages, then one will be exposed to seeing and hearing the sights and sounds therein. Thus one's sense faculties will become difficult to restrain and one will become prone to give rise to the three poisons.[208]

Moreover, one's mind will become only shallowly engaged in the practice of moral virtue, patience, vigor, *dhyāna* absorption, and wisdom.[209]

Also, when one takes up the endeavors of the laity, defilements arise in relation to offerings and support that entail the production of afflictions such as craving, anger, miserliness, and jealousy. It is solely by resort to the power of contemplative practice that one is able to restrain such mental inclinations. [Absent the power of such contemplative practice], those who are weak may fail to restrain themselves and may then go so far as to encounter death itself or a painful calamity comparable to death.

"Death" refers here to becoming so covetously attached to the objects of the five types of desire that one relinquishes the moral

正體字

054c05 ‖ 還俗故名為死。或能反戒多起重罪。是名
054c06 ‖ 死等諸惱苦患。以是因緣故。於出家者稱
054c07 ‖ 歎法施。於在家者稱歎財施。如是廣說在
054c08 ‖ 家菩薩所行財施。餘諸善行今當說之。發
054c09 ‖ 心菩薩先應歸依佛歸依法歸依僧。從
054c10 ‖ [6]三歸[7]所得功德。皆應迴向阿耨多羅三
054c11 ‖ 藐三菩提。復次。
054c12 ‖ 　歸依佛法僧　　菩薩所應知
054c13 ‖ 菩薩應當如實善解歸依佛歸依法歸依
054c14 ‖ 僧。問曰。云何名為歸依佛。答曰。
054c15 ‖ 　不捨菩提心　　不壞所受法
054c16 ‖ 　不[8]捨大悲心　　不貪樂餘乘
054c17 ‖ 　如是則名為　　如實歸依佛
054c18 ‖ 菩提心者。發心求佛不休不息不捨是心。
054c19 ‖ 不壞所受法者。[9]謂菩薩各[10]受所樂善法
054c20 ‖ 戒行。是行應行

简体字

还俗故名为死。或能反戒多起重罪。是名死等诸恼苦患。以是因缘故。于出家者称叹法施。于在家者称叹财施。如是广说在家菩萨所行财施。余诸善行今当说之。发心菩萨先应归依佛归依法归依僧。从三归所得功德。皆应回向阿耨多罗三藐三菩提。复次。

　归依佛法僧　　菩萨所应知

菩萨应当如实善解归依佛归依法归依僧。问曰。云何名为归依佛。答曰。

　不舍菩提心　　不坏所受法
　不舍大悲心　　不贪乐余乘
　如是则名为　　如实归依佛

菩提心者。发心求佛不休不息不舍是心。不坏所受法者。谓菩萨各受所乐善法戒行。是行应行

precepts and returns to the lay life. Or one may find one is even able to allow oneself to transgress the moral precepts and incur numerous grave offenses. This is what is meant by "encountering a painful calamity comparable to death."[210]

It is for these reasons that one praises the giving of Dharma as the province of those who have left the home life while praising the giving of material wealth as the province of the householder. This being so, there are extensive discussions of the householder bodhisattva's practice of giving material wealth.

B. TAKING REFUGE IN THE THREE JEWELS

The other sorts of good conduct should now be discussed. The bodhisattva who has brought forth the resolve [to attain buddhahood] should first take refuge in the Buddha, take refuge in the Dharma, and take refuge in the Sangha. The merit that is gained from taking the Three Refuges should then all be dedicated to the realization of *anuttarasamyaksaṃbodhi*. Additionally:

> Taking refuge in the Buddha, the Dharma, and the Sangha
> is a matter that the bodhisattva should comprehend.

The bodhisattva should understand well and in accordance with reality this matter of taking refuge in the Buddha, taking refuge in the Dharma, and taking refuge in the Sangha.

1. Q: WHAT IS MEANT BY TAKING REFUGE IN THE BUDDHA?

Question: What is meant by taking refuge in the Buddha?

2. A: THE PRIMARY ASPECTS OF TAKING REFUGE IN THE BUDDHA

Response:

> Do not relinquish the resolve to attain bodhi,
> do not damage the Dharma that one has received,
> do not abandon the mind of great compassion,
> and do not covet other vehicles [to liberation].
>
> If one acts in this fashion, then this is what is meant by
> taking refuge in the Buddha in accordance with reality.

"The resolve to attain bodhi" refers to bringing forth the determination to seek buddhahood without ever desisting from it, without ever letting it cease, and without ever relinquishing this determination.

As for "do not damage the Dharma that one has received," this refers to the fact that the bodhisattvas have each taken on the practice of the moral precepts as components of the dharmas of goodness that they delight in. Consequently, there are circumstances where one particular practice should be taken up whereas yet another practice

正體字

是不應作。若應諸波羅蜜。
054c21 ‖ 若應四功德處。如是等種種善法。為利益
054c22 ‖ 眾生故。受持修行不令毀缺。大悲心者欲
054c23 ‖ 度苦惱眾生為求佛道乃至夢中亦不離
054c24 ‖ 大悲。不貪餘乘者。深信樂佛道故。不貪
054c25 ‖ 聲聞辟支佛乘。有是法故。當知如實歸
054c26 ‖ 依佛。問曰。云何名為歸依法。答曰。
054c27 ‖ 　親近說法者　　一心聽受法
054c28 ‖ 　念持而演說　　名為歸依法
054c29 ‖ 說法者於佛深法解說敷演。開示善惡斷
055a01 ‖ 諸疑惑。常數親近往至其所。供養恭敬一心
055a02 ‖ 聽受。以憶念力執持不忘。思惟籌量隨順
055a03 ‖ 義趣。然後為人如知演說。以是法施功德。
055a04 ‖ 迴向佛道。是名歸依法。問曰。云何名為歸
055a05 ‖ 依僧。

简体字

是不应作。若应诸波罗蜜。若应四功德处。如是等种种善法。为利益众生故。受持修行不令毁缺。大悲心者欲度苦恼众生为求佛道乃至梦中亦不离大悲。不贪余乘者。深信乐佛道故。不贪声闻辟支佛乘。有是法故。当知如实归依佛。问曰。云何名为归依法。答曰。

　亲近说法者　　一心听受法
　念持而演说　　名为归依法

说法者于佛深法解说敷演。开示善恶断诸疑惑。常数亲近往至其所。供养恭敬一心听受。以忆念力执持不忘。思惟筹量随顺义趣。然后为人如知演说。以是法施功德。回向佛道。是名归依法。问曰。云何名为归依僧。

should be avoided. Thus, if a particular practice corresponds to any of the *pāramitās*, to any of the four bases of meritorious qualities,[211] or to any of the many other different sorts of good dharmas such as these, for the sake of benefiting beings, one accepts and upholds it, cultivates it, and does not allow it to deteriorate or to become deficient.

As for "the mind of great compassion," one wishes to liberate beings who are afflicted by suffering. In order to pursue the attainment of buddhahood, even in a dream, one never abandons the great compassion.

As for "do not covet other vehicles [to liberation]," because one possesses a deep resolute faith in the path to buddhahood, one does seek to take up the vehicles of *śrāvaka* disciples or *pratyekabuddhas*.

One should realize that it is through the possession of dharmas such as these that one "takes refuge in the Buddha in accordance with reality."

3. Q: What Is Meant by Taking Refuge in the Dharma?

Question: What is meant by taking refuge in the Dharma?

4. A: The Primary Aspects of Taking Refuge in the Dharma

Response:
> Draw near to those who speak the Dharma.
> Single-mindedly listen to and accept the Dharma.
> Be mindful of it, uphold it, and then expound upon it.
> This is what is meant by taking refuge in the Dharma.

"Those who speak the Dharma" refers to those who explain, set forth, and proclaim the profound Dharma of the Buddha, offering instruction as to what is good and what is evil while also cutting away all one's doubts. One always repeatedly draws near to them, going forth to wherever they may dwell, making offerings and displaying reverential respect as one single-mindedly listens to and accepts [the Dharma]. One uses the power of memory to retain it and does not forget it. One reflects upon it, assesses it, and accords with its import.

Afterward, one expounds upon it for others, doing so in a manner that accords with the way one has been led to understand it. Then one dedicates the merit arising from this gift of Dharma to the attainment of buddhahood. This is what is meant by "taking refuge in the Dharma."

5. Q: What Is Meant by Taking Refuge in the Sangha?

Question: What is meant by taking refuge in the Sangha?

正體字

答曰。 055a06 ‖　　若諸聲聞人　　未入法位者
055a07 ‖　令發無上心　　使得佛十力
055a08 ‖　先以財施攝　　後乃以法施
055a09 ‖　深信[1]四果僧　　不分別貴眾
055a10 ‖　求聲聞功德　　而不證解脫
055a11 ‖　[2]是名歸依僧　　又應念三事
055a12 ‖ 聲聞人者成聲聞乘。未入法位者。於聲聞
055a13 ‖ 道未得必定。能令此人發佛道心而得十
055a14 ‖ 力。若入法位者終不可令發無上心。設或
055a15 ‖ 發心亦不成就。如般若波羅蜜中尊者須菩
055a16 ‖ 提所說。已入正法位。不能發無上心。何
055a17 ‖ 以故。是人於生死已作障隔。不復往來
055a18 ‖ 生死。發無上心先以財施。攝者。以衣服
055a19 ‖ 飲食臥具醫藥所須之物攝。出家者以衣服
055a20 ‖ 飲食臥具醫藥雜香塗香攝。在家者以攝因
055a21 ‖ 緣生親愛心。所言信受然後法施。令發無
055a22 ‖ 上道心果。

简体字

答曰。
　　若诸声闻人　　未入法位者
　　令发无上心　　使得佛十力
　　先以财施摄　　后乃以法施
　　深信四果僧　　不分别贵众
　　求声闻功德　　而不证解脱
　　是名归依僧　　又应念三事

声闻人者成声闻乘。未入法位者。于声闻道未得必定。能令此人发佛道心而得十力。若入法位者终不可令发无上心。设或发心亦不成就。如般若波罗蜜中尊者须菩提所说。已入正法位。不能发无上心。何以故。是人于生死已作障隔。不复往来生死。发无上心先以财施。摄者。以衣服饮食卧具医药所须之物摄。出家者以衣服饮食卧具医药杂香涂香摄。在家者以摄因缘生亲爱心。所言信受然后法施。令发无上道心果。

6. A: The Primary Aspects of Taking Refuge in the Sangha
Response:
> In the case of *śrāvaka* disciple practitioners
> who have not yet entered the Dharma position,[212]
> induce them to bring forth the unsurpassable resolve
> by which they are caused to acquire the ten powers of a buddha.
>
> One first uses the giving of material resources to attract them
> and afterward resorts to the giving of Dharma.
> One maintains deep faith in the Sangha that attains four fruitions[213]
> and does not discriminate among members of that noble community.
>
> One may strive to gain the *śrāvaka* disciples' meritorious qualities
> while still not opting for realization of their liberation.
> This is the meaning of taking refuge in the Sangha.
> Moreover, one should maintain mindfulness of three matters.[214]

"*Śrāvaka* disciple practitioners" refers to those who achieve success in the Śrāvaka Disciple Vehicle. "Who have not yet entered the Dharma position" refers to those who have not yet reached the stage of absolute irreversibility on the *śrāvaka* disciple path. One may still influence such persons to bring forth the resolve to attain buddhahood so that they will then be able to acquire the ten powers.

In the case of those who have already entered the Dharma position, one can never influence them to bring forth the unsurpassable resolve. Even supposing that some of these were to be caused to bring forth such an aspiration, they would still not succeed [in bringing it to realization].

This is as stated by the venerable Subhūti in the *[Mahā]prajñāpāramitā [Sūtra]* where he said, "Those who have already entered the "right Dharma position" are unable to bring forth the unsurpassable resolve. Why is this the case? Such persons have already created an obstacle to further transmigration in *saṃsāra*."[215] Thus they will never again come and go within *saṃsāra*.

[To induce those who have not yet entered the Dharma position] to bring forth the unsurpassable resolve, one first uses the giving of material resources. "To attract them," refers to bestowing the requisites of robes, food and drink, bedding, and medicine to attract them.

In the case of those who have left the home life, one attracts them by giving them robes, food-and-drink, bedding, medicines, and various incenses including unguent incenses. As for householders, one uses means of attraction that cause them to feel a sense of close friendship through which they tend to trust and accept one's words. Afterward, one engages in Dharma giving that causes them to gain the fruits of bringing forth the unsurpassable resolve.

正體字	僧者四向四果。眾者於佛法中。 055a23 ‖ 受出家[3]者相。具持諸戒未有果向不分 055a24 ‖ 別。如是僧以離恩愛奴故名為貴僧。信樂 055a25 ‖ 空無相無願。而不分別戲論。依止是僧名 055a26 ‖ 為歸依僧。求聲聞功德而不證解脫者。 055a27 ‖ 知是僧持戒具足禪定具足智慧具足解 055a28 ‖ 脫具足解脫知見具足三明六通心得自 055a29 ‖ 在有大威德。捨世間樂出魔境界。利譽 055b01 ‖ 稱樂不以為喜。衰毀譏苦不以為憂。常 055b02 ‖ 行六捨得八解脫隨佛所教。有行道者 055b03 ‖ 有解脫者行一道者。破二種煩惱。善知三 055b04 ‖ 界。善通四諦善除五蓋。安住六和敬法。具 055b05 ‖ 足七不退法八大人覺。
简体字	僧者四向四果。众者于佛法中。受出家者相。具持诸戒未有果向不分别。如是僧以离恩爱奴故名为贵僧。信乐空无相无愿。而不分别戏论。依止是僧名为归依僧。求声闻功德而不证解脱者。知是僧持戒具足禅定具足智慧具足解脱具足解脱知见具足三明六通心得自在有大威德。舍世间乐出魔境界。利誉称乐不以为喜。衰毁讥苦不以为忧。常行六舍得八解脱随佛所教。有行道者有解脱者行一道者。破二种烦恼。善知三界。善通四谛善除五盖。安住六和敬法。具足七不退法八大人觉。

"Sangha" refers to those who have gained the four preliminary stages as well as those who have actually attained the four corresponding fruits [of the path].

"Community" refers to those who have taken on the characteristic features of the monastic in accordance with the Buddha's Dharma. They completely uphold the moral precepts, yet may not have attained the fruits [of the path] or the corresponding preliminary stages. One does not make discriminating distinctions among members of the Sangha such as these.

It is because they have abandoned the bondage of sensual desire that they are known as "noble" members of the Sangha. They maintain resolute belief in emptiness, signlessness, and wishlessness while still not indulging in conceptual elaboration rooted in the making of discriminating distinctions. When one relies on members of the Sangha of this sort, this is what is meant by "taking refuge in the Sangha."

As for "One may strive to gain the meritorious qualities of the *śrāvaka* disciples while still not opting for realization of their liberation," one knows that these members of the Sangha are accomplished in the upholding of the moral precepts, that they are accomplished in the *dhyāna* absorptions, that they are accomplished in wisdom, that they are accomplished in liberation, that they are accomplished in the knowledge and vision of liberation, that they possess the three clear knowledges and six superknowledges, that their minds have gained sovereign mastery, that they possess great awe-inspiring qualities, and that that they have forsaken the pleasures of the world and have escaped Māra's realms.[216]

One knows that they do not experience joy due to attaining profit, fine reputation, praise, or pleasure and that they do not experience distress due to loss, disrepute, derision, or pain.[217] One knows that they always practice six kinds of equanimity[218] and knows that they have gained the eight liberations in accordance with the Buddha's instructions.

One knows that there are those who practice the path, that there are those who have achieved liberation, that there are those who practice the singular path, that they have demolished the two kinds of afflictions,[219] that they well understand the three realms of existence, that they have a well-developed penetrating understanding of the four truths, that they have thoroughly done away with the five hindrances,[220] that they have come to peacefully abide in the six dharmas of harmony and respect, that they have become accomplished in seven dharmas of non-retreat,[221] that they possess the eight realizations of great men,

	捨離九結得聲聞十
055b06 ‖	種力。成就如是諸功德[4]者。名為佛弟子
055b07 ‖	眾求如是功德。不求其解脫。何以故。深
055b08 ‖	心信樂佛無礙[5]解故。是名歸依僧。復次若
055b09 ‖	聞章句文字法。即得念實相法。名為歸命
055b10 ‖	法。若見聲聞僧即念發菩提心諸菩薩眾
055b11 ‖	是名歸依僧。見佛形像即念真佛是[6]故
055b12 ‖	歸依佛。問曰。云何名為念真佛。答曰。如無
055b13 ‖	盡意菩薩經中說念佛三昧義。念真佛者。
055b14 ‖	不以色。不以相。不以生。不以[7]性。不以
055b15 ‖	家。不以過去未來現在。不以五陰十二入
055b16 ‖	十八界。不以見聞覺知。不以心意識。不
055b17 ‖	以戲論行。不以生滅住。不以取捨。不以
055b18 ‖	憶念分別。不以法相。不以自相。不以一
055b19 ‖	相。不以異相。

正體字

舍离九结得声闻十种力。成就如是诸功德者。名为佛弟子众求如是功德。不求其解脱。何以故。深心信乐佛无碍解故。是名归依僧。复次若闻章句文字法。即得念实相法。名为归命法。若见声闻僧即念发菩提心诸菩萨众是名归依僧。见佛形像即念真佛是故归依佛。问曰。云何名为念真佛。答曰。如无尽意菩萨经中说念佛三昧义。念真佛者。不以色。不以相。不以生。不以性。不以家。不以过去未来现在。不以五阴十二入十八界。不以见闻觉知。不以心意识。不以戏论行。不以生灭住。不以取舍。不以忆念分别。不以法相。不以自相。不以一相。不以异相。

简体字

that they have abandoned the nine types of fetters, and that they have gained the ten powers of the *śrāvaka* disciples.

It is those who have perfected meritorious qualities such as these who are referred to as the Buddha's *śrāvaka* disciple sangha. One may strive to acquire meritorious qualities such as these even as one still does not seek to attain their type of liberation. Why? This is because one maintains deep-seated aspirations and resolute belief[222] in the unimpeded liberation of the Buddha.

This [preceding discussion explains] what is meant by "taking refuge in the Sangha."

Then again, if on hearing the passages, sentences and words of the Dharma, one immediately brings to mind the dharma of the true character [of dharmas],[223] this is what is meant by "taking refuge in the Dharma."

If upon seeing a member of the *śrāvaka*-disciple sangha, one immediately brings to mind the community of all bodhisattvas who have brought forth the resolve to attain bodhi, this is what is meant by "taking refuge in the Sangha."

If on viewing an image of the Buddha, one immediately becomes mindful of the true Buddha, this is what is meant by "taking refuge in the Buddha."[224]

7. THE MEANING OF MINDFULNESS OF THE BUDDHA, DHARMA, AND SANGHA
   a. THE MEANING OF MINDFULNESS OF THE BUDDHA
   1) Q: WHAT IS MEANT BY "MINDFULNESS OF THE TRUE BUDDHA"?

Question: What is meant by "mindfulness of the true Buddha"?

2) A: "MINDFULNESS OF THE TRUE BUDDHA" AS SET FORTH IN A SUTRA

Response: This corresponds to the discussion of the meaning of the mindfulness-of-the-Buddha samādhi as found in the *Akṣayamati Bodhisattva Sutra* wherein it states:[225]

> As for "mindfulness of the true Buddha," it is not based on physical form, is not based on characteristic signs, is not based on birth, is not based on caste,[226] is not based on clan, is not based on the past, future, or present, and is not based on the five aggregates, twelve sense bases, or eighteen sense realms.
>
> It is not based on seeing, hearing, sensing, or cognizing,[227] is not based on the mind or mind consciousness, is not based in practice associated with conceptual elaboration, is not based on production, extinction, or abiding, is not based on either grasping or relinquishing, is not based on bearing in mind discriminating distinctions, is not based on dharma characteristics, is not based on individual characteristics, is not based on a unitary characteristic, and is not based on differentiating characteristics.

正體字

055b20 ‖	不以心緣數。不以內外。不以取相覺觀。不以入出。不以形色相貌。
055b21 ‖	不以所行威儀。不以持戒禪定智慧解脫
055b22 ‖	解脫知見。不以十力四無所畏諸[8]佛法。如
055b23 ‖	實念佛者。無量不可思議。無行無知無我
055b24 ‖	我所。無憶無念。不分別五陰十二入十八
055b25 ‖	界。無形無礙無發無住無非住。不住色
055b26 ‖	不住受想行識。不住眼色不住眼識。不
055b27 ‖	住耳聲不住耳識。不住鼻香不住鼻識。
055b28 ‖	不住舌味不住舌識。不住身觸。不住身
055b29 ‖	識。不住意法不住意識。不住一切諸緣。
055c01 ‖	不起一切諸相。不生一切動念憶想分別
055c02 ‖	等。不生見聞覺知。隨行一切正解脫相。心
055c03 ‖	不相續滅諸分別。破諸愛恚壞諸因相。
055c04 ‖	除斷先際後際中際。究暢明了無有彼此。
055c05 ‖	無動故無喜。不受味故無樂。本相寂滅故
055c06 ‖	無熱。

简体字

不以心缘数。不以内外。不以取相觉观。不以入出。不以形色相貌。不以所行威仪。不以持戒禅定智慧解脱解脱知见。不以十力四无所畏诸佛法。如实念佛者。无量不可思议。无行无知无我我所。无忆无念。不分别五阴十二入十八界。无形无碍无发无住无非住。不住色不住受想行识。不住眼色不住眼识。不住耳声不住耳识。不住鼻香不住鼻识。不住舌味不住舌识。不住身触。不住身识。不住意法不住意识。不住一切诸缘。不起一切诸相。不生一切动念忆想分别等。不生见闻觉知。随行一切正解脱相。心不相续灭诸分别。破诸爱恚坏诸因相。除断先际后际中际。究畅明了无有彼此。无动故无喜。不受味故无乐。本相寂灭故无热。

Chapter 14 — The Characteristics of the Refuges

It is not based on the mental factors associated with the mind's cognition of objective phenomena,[228] is not based on what is either inward or outward, is not based on any seizing on characteristics by either primary ideation (*vitarka*), or mental discursion (*vicāra*), is not based on either what is taken in or what is produced, is not based on physical appearances, is not based on any aspects of deportment that one might cultivate, is not based on moral precepts, *dhyāna* absorption, wisdom, liberation, or the knowledge and vision of liberation, and is not based on the ten powers, four fearlessnesses, or any other dharmas of the Buddha.

As for "mindfulness of the Buddha that accords with reality," it is immeasurable, is inconceivable, has no practice, has no knowing, has no self or anything belonging to a self, has no recollection, and has nothing it bears in mind. It does not engage in discriminations regarding the five aggregates, twelve sense bases, or eighteen sense realms. It has no shape, is unobstructed, and has no initiation, no abiding, and no non-abiding. It does not abide in forms, and does not abide in feelings, perceptions, formative factors, or consciousness.

It does not abide in the eye or visual forms and does not abide in eye consciousness. It does not abide in the ear or sounds and does not abide in ear consciousness. It does not abide in the nose or fragrances and does not abide in olfactory consciousness. It does not abide in the tongue or flavors and does not abide in gustatory consciousness. It does not abide in the body or touchables and does not abide in tactile consciousness. It does not abide in the mind faculty or dharmas and does not abide in mind consciousness.

It does not abide in any objective conditions. It does not give rise to any characteristic signs. It does not involve the production of any movement of mind, of any recollective thought, of any discriminations, or of any other such phenomena. Nor does it involve the production of any seeing, hearing, sensing, or cognition.

It accords in its practice with all the characteristic features of right liberation. It does not involve any continuity of thought but does involve the cessation of all mental discriminations. It demolishes all forms of affection and anger.

It confutes (lit. "ruins") all normative characteristics of causality. It does away with [conceptions of what is temporally] past, future, or intermediate. It perceives with utter clarity the nonexistence of any [duality of] object and subject.

Because it is motionless, it is free of [any attraction to] joyfulness. Because it declines to indulge the delectable, it is free of [any attraction to] bliss.[229]

Because its fundamental character is that of quiescence, it remains free of the heat [of mental agitation].

正體字	心無所營故解脫。相無色故無身。不受故無受。無想故無結。無行故無為。無知故無識。無取故[9]無行。不捨故非不行。無處故無住。空故無來。不生故無去。一切憶念心心數法及餘諸法。不貪不著不取不受不然不滅。先來不生無有生相。攝在法性過眼色虛空道。如是相名為真念佛。又念法者。佛法是善說。得今世報無有定時。可得觀察善。將至道智者。內知初中後善言善義善淳善無雜具足清淨。能斷貪欲能斷瞋恚能斷愚癡。能除慢心能除諸見能除疑悔。能除憍貴能除諸渴。破所歸趣斷相續道。盡愛離欲寂滅涅槃。
简体字	心无所营故解脱。相无色故无身。不受故无受。无想故无结。无行故无为。无知故无识。无取故无行。不舍故非不行。无处故无住。空故无来。不生故无去。一切忆念心心数法及余诸法。不贪不着不取不受不然不灭。先来不生无有生相。摄在法性过眼色虚空道。如是相名为真念佛。又念法者。佛法是善说。得今世报无有定时。可得观察善。将至道智者。内知初中后善言善义善淳善无杂具足清净。能断贪欲能断瞋恚能断愚痴。能除慢心能除诸见能除疑悔。能除憍贵能除诸渴。破所归趣断相续道。尽爱离欲寂灭涅槃。

Line markers (正體字 column): 055c07, 055c08, 055c09, 055c10, 055c11, 055c12, 055c13, 055c14, 055c15, 055c16, 055c17, 055c18

Because the mind has no endeavors in which it is involved, it is liberated.

Because appearances are devoid of any existent form, there is no body. Because one does not indulge them, there are no feelings. Because there are no perceptions, there are no fetters. Because there are no actions, there is nothing that one does. Because there is no knowing, there is no consciousness.[230]

Because there is no grasping, there is no engagement in actions. Because there is no relinquishing, it is not the case that one does not act.

Because there is no dwelling [in any dharma], there is no abiding. Because it is empty [of inherent existence], there is no coming. Because there is no arising, there is no departing.

Because one does not covet, does not become attached to, does not seize upon, does not indulge, does not "ignite," and does not extinguish any recollective thought, any mental dharmas or any other sort of dharmas, from the very beginning on forward to the present, there has never been any production [of dharmas] nor have there ever been any marks of their production. They are all entirely subsumed within the nature of dharmas that extends beyond the path [defined by the duality of] the eye, visual forms, and [their intervening] empty space.

Characteristics such as these define what is meant by "true mindfulness of the Buddha."

b. The Meaning of "Mindfulness of the Dharma"

Also, as for mindfulness of the Dharma, the Dharma of the Buddha is well spoken. One gains results from it in this very life. [Its benefits] are not limited to some fixed time. This is amenable to one's own contemplation and investigation. It is excellent in its ability to lead one to attainment of the path. It is such that the wise can inwardly realize. It is good in the beginning, good in the middle, and good in the end. Its words are good. Its meaning is good. It is completely pure in its goodness and free of any admixture [with anything not good]. It is perfect in its purity.

It is able to cut off covetousness, able to cut of hatred, able to cut off delusion, able to do away with prideful thoughts, able to do away with all [erroneous] views, able to do away with doubt and regret, able to do away with arrogance, and able to do away with all craving.

It breaks [one's attachment to] whatever one is inclined to take refuge in. It cuts short the path of continuance [in *saṃsāra*]. It puts an end to craving, leads to the abandonment of sensual desires, and leads to quiescence and nirvāṇa.

正體字

055c19 ‖ 如是相名為念法。以空無相無願。不生不滅畢竟寂滅無比無
055c20 ‖ 示。如念佛義中說。又念法有三種。從佛法
055c21 ‖ 是善說。至具足清淨名為道。能斷貪欲至
055c22 ‖ 寂滅涅槃。名為涅槃。空等至無比無示名
055c23 ‖ 為法體。又念僧者如先說僧功德。念是三
055c24 ‖ 寶得決定心。以如是念求於佛道而行
055c25 ‖ 布施。是名歸依佛。為守護法而行布施。
055c26 ‖ 是名歸依法。以是布施起迴向心。成佛
055c27 ‖ 道時攝菩薩聲聞僧。是名歸依僧。

简体字

如是相名为念法。以空无相无愿。不生不灭毕竟寂灭无比无示。如念佛义中说。又念法有三种。从佛法是善说。至具足清净名为道。能断贪欲至寂灭涅槃。名为涅槃。空等至无比无示名为法体。又念僧者如先说僧功德。念是三宝得决定心。以如是念求于佛道而行布施。是名归依佛。为守护法而行布施。是名归依法。以是布施起回向心。成佛道时摄菩萨声闻僧。是名归依僧。

Characteristics such as these illustrate what is meant by "mindfulness of the Dharma." [It is characterized] by emptiness, signlessness, and wishlessness. It is unproduced and undestroyed, ultimately quiescent, incomparable, and devoid of any [phenomenal] manifestation. These ideas are just as set forth in the discussion of the meaning of "mindfulness of the Buddha."[231]

Additionally, "mindfulness of the Dharma" is of three types. The descriptions from "the Dharma of the Buddha is well spoken" to "it is completely pure in its goodness" are all references to the path. From "it is able to cut off covetousness" to "it leads to quiescence and nirvāṇa" are all references to nirvāṇa. From "emptiness" and so forth on up to "incomparable, and devoid of any [phenomenal] manifestation," is all a reference to the very essence of the Dharma.

    c. The Meaning of Mindfulness of the Sangha

Also, regarding "mindfulness of the Sangha," this is as explained earlier in the discussion of the meritorious qualities of the Sangha.

    C. A Concluding Statement on the Three Refuges

In one's mindfulness of these Three Jewels, one develops a definite resolve. When one uses such mindfulness as one strives to attain buddhahood and then takes up the practice of giving, this is what is meant by "taking refuge in the Buddha."

When one endeavors to preserve and protect the Dharma and thus takes up the practice of giving, this is what is meant by "taking refuge in the Dharma."

When, based on this practice of giving, one dedicates the merit, resolving that, once one has realized buddhahood, one will bring together a sangha community consisting of both bodhisattvas and śrāvaka disciples, this is what is meant by "taking refuge in the Sangha."

The End of Chapter Fourteen

正體字	055c28 ‖　　　五戒品第十五 055c29 ‖ 如是在家菩薩。能修善人業。遠離惡人業。 056a01 ‖ 如說。 056a02 ‖　　修起善人業　　如法集財用 056a03 ‖　　堪則為重任　　不堪則不受 056a04 ‖ 善人業者。略說善人業。自住善利亦能利 056a05 ‖ 人。惡人業者。自陷衰惱令人衰惱。如法 056a06 ‖ 集財用者。不殺不盜不誑欺人。以力集財 056a07 ‖ 如法用之供養三寶濟恤老病等。堪受能 056a08 ‖ 行者則為重任。不堪行者則不受。若菩薩 056a09 ‖ 於今世事及後世事。若自利若利他如先 056a10 ‖ 所說必能成立。若知不堪行者此則不受 056a11 ‖ 復次。
简体字	五戒品第十五 　　如是在家菩萨。能修善人业。远离恶人业。如说。 　　修起善人业　　如法集财用 　　堪则为重任　　不堪则不受 　　善人业者。略说善人业。自住善利亦能利人。恶人业者。自陷衰恼令人衰恼。如法集财用者。不杀不盗不诳欺人。以力集财如法用之供养三宝济恤老病等。堪受能行者则为重任。不堪行者则不受。若菩萨于今世事及后世事。若自利若利他如先所说必能成立。若知不堪行者此则不受复次。

Chapter 15
The Five Moral Precepts

XV. Chapter 15: The Five Moral Precepts
  A. The Lay Bodhisattva Cultivates Goodness and Avoids Bad Actions

It is in this [above-discussed] manner that the lay bodhisattva becomes able to cultivate the karmic deeds of a good person while leaving far behind the karmic deeds of a bad person. In this connection, there is a verse:

> One cultivates and brings forth the karmic deeds of a good person,
> Accumulating wealth for one's use in a way consistent with Dharma.
> Whatever one is capable of, one takes that on as a grave duty.
> That of which one is not capable—one refrains from taking it on.[232]

As for "the karmic deeds of a good person," to sum it up, the karmic deeds of a good person involve abiding in what is good and beneficial for oneself while also being able to facilitate the benefit of others.

As for "the karmic deeds of a bad person" these bring about descent into decline and anguish for oneself while also bringing about decline and anguish in others.

"Accumulating wealth for one's own use in a way consistent with Dharma" refers to not killing, not stealing, and neither deceiving nor cheating others. One devotes one's energies to accumulating wealth and then puts it to use in a way that accords with the Dharma by making offerings to the Three Jewels, by rescuing those fallen into misfortune, by aiding the old and the sick, and by carrying out other such deeds.

Whatever one can take on and can adhere to in practice—one regards that as a grave responsibility. As for what one would be unable to adhere to in practice, one does not take that on.

As for the works of the bodhisattva, whether it be those of this life or those of future lives, whether it be those concerned with self-benefit or those concerned with benefiting others, these are as discussed earlier and they are endeavors that definitely must be brought to a state of successful completion. If there are endeavors that one realizes one cannot yet carry out in practice, then one does not take these on.

  B. One Relinquishes Self Benefit, Benefits Others & Repays Kindness

Furthermore:

正體字

056a12 ‖ 　　世法無憂喜　　能捨於自利
056a13 ‖ 　　常勤行他利　　深知恩倍報
056a14 ‖ 世間法者。利衰毀譽稱譏苦樂。於此法中心
056a15 ‖ 無憂喜。捨自利勤行他利者。菩薩乃至未
056a16 ‖ 曾知識。無因[1]緣者所[2]行善行捨置自利助
056a17 ‖ 成彼善。問曰。捨自利勤行他利此事不然。
056a18 ‖ 如佛說。雖大利人不應自捨己利如說
056a19 ‖ 捨一人以成一家。捨一家[3]成一聚落。捨
056a20 ‖ 一聚落成一國土。捨一國土以成己身。捨
056a21 ‖ 己身以為正法。
056a22 ‖ 　　先自成己利　　然後乃利人
056a23 ‖ 　　捨己利利人　　後則生憂悔
056a24 ‖ 　　捨自利利人　　自謂為智慧
056a25 ‖ 　　此於世間中　　最為第一癡
056a26 ‖ 答曰。於世間中為他求利猶稱為善以為
056a27 ‖ 堅心。況菩薩所行出過世間。若利他者即
056a28 ‖ 是自利。如說。
056a29 ‖ 　　菩薩於他事　　心意不劣弱

简体字

　　世法无忧喜　　能舍于自利
　　常勤行他利　　深知恩倍报
　世间法者。利衰毁誉称讥苦乐。于此法中心无忧喜。舍自利勤行他利者。菩萨乃至未曾知识。无因缘者所行善行舍置自利助成彼善。问曰。舍自利勤行他利此事不然。如佛说。虽大利人不应自舍己利如说舍一人以成一家。舍一家成一聚落。舍一聚落成一国土。舍一国土以成己身。舍己身以为正法。
　　先自成己利　　然后乃利人
　　舍己利利人　　后则生忧悔
　　舍自利利人　　自谓为智慧
　　此于世间中　　最为第一痴
　答曰。于世间中为他求利犹称为善以为坚心。况菩萨所行出过世间。若利他者即是自利。如说。
　　菩萨于他事　　心意不劣弱

One neither sorrows nor rejoices over worldly dharmas.
One is able to relinquish one's own benefit,
while always acting diligently for the benefit of others.
Being deeply grateful for others' kindnesses, one repays them doubly.

"Worldly dharmas" refers to profit and loss, ill repute and esteem, praise and blame, and pain and pleasure. One's mind remains free of any tendency to become either dejected or joyful in response to any of these dharmas.

In "relinquishing one's own benefit," and "acting diligently for the benefit of others," the bodhisattva sets aside self-benefit to devote the good works he does to facilitating what is good for others, doing so even for those he has not yet befriended and even for those with whom he has no causal affinities.

C. Q: Relinquishing Self-Benefit to Benefit Others Is Wrong

Question: As for [your recommending] "relinquishing self-benefit in order to work diligently for the benefit of others," this is wrong. As stated by the Buddha, "Although one might accomplish greatly beneficial works for others, one should not relinquish attention to one's own self-benefit."

This idea is reminiscent of the saying that: "One may have to sacrifice a person for the success of a clan, may have to sacrifice a single clan for the success of a village, may have to sacrifice a village for the success of a country, may have to sacrifice a country for the success of oneself, or may have to sacrifice oneself for the sake of right Dharma."

One first accomplishes self-benefit
and then, afterward, benefits others.
If one sacrifices self-benefit to benefit others,
later on, one will experience sorrow and regret.

If one relinquishes self-benefit to benefit others
while thinking to oneself that this constitutes wisdom,
this is something that in the context of the world
amounts to the foremost sort of stupidity.

D. A: No. This Is Good Even in Worldly Terms & Also Benefits Oneself

Response: Even from the worldly standpoint, seeking to bring about good for the benefit of others is regarded as good and as the mark of solid resolve. How much the more so is this true of the bodhisattva whose practice transcends worldly concerns. If one benefits others, that is just benefiting oneself. This is as described here:

Regarding matters pertaining to others, the bodhisattva
is neither inferior nor weak in the quality of his determination.

正體字

056b01 ‖　　發菩提心者　　他利即自利
056b02 ‖ 此義初品中已廣說。是故汝語不然。深知恩
056b03 ‖ 倍報者。若人於菩薩所作好事應當厚報。
056b04 ‖ 又深知其恩。此是善人相。復次。
056b05 ‖　　貧者施以財　　畏者施無畏
056b06 ‖　　如是等功德　　乃至於堅牢
056b07 ‖ 施貧以財者。有人先世不種福德。今無方
056b08 ‖ 便資生儉少。如是之人隨力給恤。施無畏
056b09 ‖ 者。於種種諸怖畏。若怨賊怖畏飢餓怖畏水
056b10 ‖ 火寒熱等。菩薩於此眾怖畏中教喻諸人。
056b11 ‖ 安隱歡悅[4]令無怖畏。如是功德最堅牢。最
056b12 ‖ 在後者於諸憂者為除其憂。於無力者而
056b13 ‖ 行忍辱。離慢大慢等。於諸所尊深加恭敬。
056b14 ‖ 於多聞者常行親近。於智慧者諮問善惡。
056b15 ‖ 自於所行常行正見。於諸眾生不諂不曲
056b16 ‖ 不作假愛。求善無厭多聞無量。諸所施作
056b17 ‖ 堅心成就。常與善人而共從事。於惡人中
056b18 ‖ 生大悲心。

简体字

　　发菩提心者　　他利即自利

此义初品中已广说。是故汝语不然。深知恩倍报者。若人于菩萨所作好事应当厚报。又深知其恩。此是善人相。复次。

　　贫者施以财　　畏者施无畏
　　如是等功德　　乃至于坚牢

施贫以财者。有人先世不种福德。今无方便资生俭少。如是之人随力给恤。施无畏者。于种种诸怖畏。若怨贼怖畏饥饿怖畏水火寒热等。菩萨于此众怖畏中教喻诸人。安隐欢悦令无怖畏。如是功德最坚牢。最在后者于诸忧者为除其忧。于无力者而行忍辱。离慢大慢等。于诸所尊深加恭敬。于多闻者常行亲近。于智慧者咨问善恶。自于所行常行正见。于诸众生不谄不曲不作假爱。求善无厌多闻无量。诸所施作坚心成就。常与善人而共从事。于恶人中生大悲心。

> For whoever has brought forth the resolve to attain bodhi,
> benefit of others is just benefit of oneself.

The meaning of this has already been extensively discussed in the first chapter. Therefore, your statements on this matter are wrong.

As for "being deeply grateful for others' kindnesses, one repays them doubly," whenever others do good things for the bodhisattva, he should repay them liberally and also be deeply grateful for their kindnesses. This is the mark of a good person. Additionally:

> One gives wealth to the poor
> and bestows fearlessness on the fearful.
> One engages in meritorious deeds of these sorts
> until they become solidly and durably established.

As for "giving wealth to the poor," there are those who, in previous lives, did not plant the causes of merit. Hence they now do not have the means to provide for their scarcity of life-sustaining necessities. As befits one's capacities, one gives aid to such people.

As for "bestowing fearlessness on the fearful," in all sorts of cases where beings are frightened, whether that be due to fear of enemies, fear of hunger, fear of floods, fire, cold, heat, or some other cause of fear—in the midst of these many fears, the bodhisattva instructs and guides these people, sees to their security and happiness, and thereby causes them to become free of fear.

Meritorious qualities such as these [are caused to become] the most solid and enduring. Finally:

> For those beset with sorrow, one strives to rid them of their sorrows.
> Regarding those lacking in strength, one practices patience and abandons arrogance, great arrogance, and so forth.[233]
> One acts with deep reverence toward those who are venerable.
> One always draws close to those who are learned and consults with the wise on matters of good and evil.
> One always maintains right views with respect to one's own practice.
> In one's relations with beings, one does not flatter them, deceive them, or make false declarations of affection.
> One is insatiable in quest of goodness and one pursues the acquisition of immeasurably vast learning.
> All of one's endeavors are accomplished with solid resolve.
> One always carries on one's endeavors in the company of good people.
> One maintains a mind of great compassion toward those who are evil.

正體字

	於善知識非善知識。皆作堅固
056b19 ‖	善知識[5]想。等心眾生不悋要法。如所聞者
056b20 ‖	為人演說。諸所聞法得其趣味。於諸五欲
056b21 ‖	戲樂事中生無常想。於妻子所生地獄想。
056b22 ‖	於資生物所生疲苦想。於產業事生憂惱
056b23 ‖	想。於諸所求破善根想。於居家中生牢獄
056b24 ‖	想。親族知識生獄卒想。日夜思量得何利
056b25 ‖	想。於不牢身得牢身想。於不堅財生堅財
056b26 ‖	想。復次。
056b27 ‖	在家法五戒　　心應[6]堅牢住
056b28 ‖	在家菩薩以三自歸行上諸功德應堅住
056b29 ‖	五戒。五戒是總在家之法。應離殺心慈愍
056c01 ‖	眾生。

简体字

于善知识非善知识。皆作坚固善知识想。等心众生不吝要法。如所闻者为人演说。诸所闻法得其趣味。于诸五欲戏乐事中生无常想。于妻子所生地狱想。于资生物所生疲苦想。于产业事生忧恼想。于诸所求破善根想。于居家中生牢狱想。亲族知识生狱卒想。日夜思量得何利想。于不牢身得牢身想。于不坚财生坚财想。复次。

　在家法五戒　　心应坚牢住

在家菩萨以三自归行上诸功德应坚住五戒。五戒是总在家之法。应离杀心慈愍众生。

Regarding both those who are good spiritual friends and those who are not good spiritual friends, one establishes a solid conception of them all as being one's good spiritual friends.

One maintains a mind of equal regard toward beings and refrains from stinginess in the dispensation of essential Dharma [teachings].

One expounds [the Dharma] for others in a manner consistent with what one has heard.

One realizes the import and flavor of all the Dharma teachings that one has heard.

Regarding the entertaining and pleasurable matters associated with the five types of desire, one contemplates them all as merely transitory.

One contemplates having a spouse (lit. "a wife") and children as comparable to abiding in the hells.

One contemplates the things required to sustain one's life as a source of weariness and suffering.

One contemplates matters having to do with carrying on a business as freighted with worry and distress.

One contemplates whatever one might seek to obtain as tending to destroy one's roots of goodness.

One contemplates abiding in the life of a householder as comparable to living in a prison.

One contemplates relatives, clan, and friends as comparable to jailers.

One contemplates one's persistent day-and-night thinking by inquiring, "What benefit is gained by this?"

One contemplates this non-enduring body as the basis for acquiring the body that does endure.[234]

One contemplates wealth that is not durable as capable of bringing forth the wealth that does endure.[235]

E. ONE SHOULD STEADFASTLY OBSERVE THE FIVE MORAL PRECEPTS

Additionally:

One's mind should steadfastly abide in observance of
the five moral precepts of the layperson's Dharma.

The lay bodhisattva who relies on the Three Refuges as he practices the above meritorious qualities should steadfastly abide in the five moral precepts. The five moral precepts constitute the comprehensively encompassing standard for the layperson's Dharma.

One should abandon all thoughts of killing and maintain compassionate pity for beings.

正體字		知自止足不貪他物。乃至一草非與
	056c02 ‖	不取。離於邪婬厭惡房內。防遠外色目
	056c03 ‖	不邪視。常觀惡露生厭離想。了知五欲究
	056c04 ‖	竟皆苦。若念妻欲亦應除捨。常觀不淨心
	056c05 ‖	懷怖畏。結使所逼離欲不著。常知世間為
	056c06 ‖	苦無我應發是願。我於何時心中當得不
	056c07 ‖	生欲想。況復身行遠離妄語。樂行實語不
	056c08 ‖	欺於人。心口相應有念安慧如見聞覺知
	056c09 ‖	而為人說。以法自處乃至失命言不詭異。
	056c10 ‖	酒是放逸眾惡之[7]門。常應遠離不過於口。
	056c11 ‖	不狂亂不迷醉。不輕躁不驚怖。不無羞
	056c12 ‖	不戲調。常能一心籌量好醜。是菩薩或時樂
	056c13 ‖	捨一切而作是念。須食與食須飲與飲。若
	056c14 ‖	以酒施應生是念。今是行檀波羅蜜時隨
	056c15 ‖	所須與。後當方便教使離酒得念智慧
	056c16 ‖	令不放逸。
简体字		知自止足不贪他物。乃至一草非与不取。离于邪淫厌恶房内。防远外色目不邪视。常观恶露生厌离想。了知五欲究竟皆苦。若念妻欲亦应除舍。常观不净心怀怖畏。结使所逼离欲不着。常知世间为苦无我应发是愿。我于何时心中当得不生欲想。况复身行远离妄语。乐行实语不欺于人。心口相应有念安慧如见闻觉知而为人说。以法自处乃至失命言不诡异。酒是放逸众恶之门。常应远离不过于口。不狂乱不迷醉。不轻躁不惊怖。不无羞不戏调。常能一心筹量好丑。是菩萨或时乐舍一切而作是念。须食与食须饮与饮。若以酒施应生是念。今是行檀波罗蜜时随所须与。后当方便教使离酒得念智慧令不放逸。

Chapter 15 — The Five Moral Precepts

One should know when enough is enough and not covet the possessions of others even to the point where one will not even take a blade of grass that has not been given.

One abandons sexual misconduct and become weary of and averse to the affairs of one's private chambers. One guards against and distances oneself from any outside sensual involvements and so does not gaze at others inappropriately. One is ever mindful of the body as something productive of repulsive outflows and thereby brings forth thoughts of renunciation while also fully realizing that the five types of desire all ultimately conduce to suffering.

If desire for one's wife comes to mind, one should dispel and relinquish it. One should always contemplate the body's unloveliness[236] and nurture a fear of becoming someone driven along by the fetters. Hence one should abandon desire and not be attached to its objects. Always remaining aware of the world as suffering and nonself, one should bring forth this prayerful aspiration: "Oh when will I finally succeed in no longer giving rise to thoughts of desire?" How much the less would one actually engage in such physical actions.

One abandons false speech, takes pleasure in speaking truthfully, and refrains from deceiving others. One's speech reflects what is known by the mind and one's thoughts are a reflection of serene wisdom. What one says to others accords with what one sees, hears, senses, and knows. One naturally abides in a way so determined by the Dharma that, even at the cost of one's life, one would not speak in ways that mislead others.

Alcohol is the gateway to neglectfulness and a multitude of bad actions. One should always stay far from it and never let it pass one's lips. One will thereby refrain from acting crazy and deranged, will not become inebriated and confused, will not become agitated, will not become seized by fears, will not act shamelessly, and will not engage in inappropriate sorts of joking. Rather, one will always be able to single-mindedly distinguish between what is good and what is disgraceful.

Now, there may be times when this bodhisattva delights in giving everything and thus is moved to think, "To those who want food, I shall provide food, and for those who seek drink, I shall provide drink." If, as a consequence, one does provide alcohol, in doing so, one should reflect: "Now, this is an occasion in the practice of *dāna pāramitā* when one gives whatever is sought. Later, I will use skillful expedients to teach and coax them into abandoning alcohol altogether and into developing the mindfulness and wisdom that shall cause them to refrain from any such negligence."

正體字

```
             何以故。檀波羅蜜法悉滿人願。
056c17 ||   在家菩薩以酒施者是則無罪。以是五戒福
056c18 ||   德迴向阿耨多羅三藐三菩提。護持五戒
056c19 ||   如護重寶如自護[8]身命。問曰。是菩薩但
056c20 ||   應護持五戒。不護持諸餘善業耶。答曰。
056c21 ||       菩薩應堅住      總相五戒中
056c22 ||       餘身口意業      悉亦復應行
056c23 ||   在家五戒已說其義。受此五戒應堅牢住。
056c24 ||   及餘三種善業亦應修行。復次在家菩薩所
056c25 ||   應行法。
056c26 ||       隨應利眾生      說法而教化
056c27 ||   是菩薩於諸眾生。隨有所乏皆能施與。若
056c28 ||   在國土城郭聚落林間樹下。是中眾生隨所
056c29 ||   利益說法教化。所謂不信者為說信法。不恭
057a01 ||   敬者為說禮節。為少聞者說多聞法。為慳
057a02 ||   貪者說布施法。為瞋恚者說和忍法。為懈
057a03 ||   怠者說精進法。為亂意者。說正念處。為愚
057a04 ||   癡者解說智慧。復次。
```

简体字

何以故。檀波罗蜜法悉满人愿。在家菩萨以酒施者是则无罪。以是五戒福德回向阿耨多罗三藐三菩提。护持五戒如护重宝如自护身命。问曰。是菩萨但应护持五戒。不护持诸余善业耶。答曰。

　　菩萨应坚住　　总相五戒中
　　余身口意业　　悉亦复应行

在家五戒已说其义。受此五戒应坚牢住。及余三种善业亦应修行。复次在家菩萨所应行法。

　　随应利众生　　说法而教化

是菩萨于诸众生。随有所乏皆能施与。若在国土城郭聚落林间树下。是中众生随所利益说法教化。所谓不信者为说信法。不恭敬者为说礼节。为少闻者说多闻法。为悭贪者说布施法。为嗔恚者说和忍法。为懈怠者说精进法。为乱意者。说正念处。为愚痴者解说智慧。复次。

Now, how can this be? It is because the essence of *dāna pāramitā* lies in fulfilling the wishes of others. Hence, in circumstances of this sort, the lay bodhisattva's provision of alcoholic beverages does not constitute a karmic offense.[237]

One dedicates the merit from upholding the five moral precepts to one's future realization of *anuttarasamyaksaṃbodhi*. One guards and upholds the five precepts in the same manner that one would guard precious jewels and in the same manner that one protects one's own body and life.

1. Q: DOES THIS BODHISATTVA ONLY OBSERVE THESE PRECEPTS?

Question: Does this bodhisattva only observe these five moral precepts while not upholding any of the other sorts of good actions?

2. A: UPHOLD THE 5 PRECEPTS & ALSO PRACTICE THE OTHER GOOD ACTIONS

Response:

The bodhisattva should steadfastly abide
in these five general moral precepts.
The other [wholesome] actions of body, speech, and mind
should all also be practiced as well.

We have already discussed the meaning of the layperson's five precepts. Having taken on these five moral precepts, one should steadfastly abide in their observance and, in addition, should cultivate the rest of the three types of good karmic deeds. Additionally, as for those dharmas that the lay bodhisattva should practice, [there are the following practices]:

a. HE SHOULD EXPLAIN DHARMA FOR BEINGS & PROCEED TO TEACH THEM

As befits those beings whom one should benefit,
one explains the Dharma and thus teaches and transforms them.

This bodhisattva is able to give to all beings in ways appropriately addressing any deficiencies they may have. No matter what country one lives in and no matter whether one is in a city, in a village, in the forest, or beneath some tree, one explains Dharma and teaches the beings there in accordance with whatever might benefit them. As it is said, one explains dharmas conducive to faith for those bereft of faith, explains propriety in etiquette for those who are disrespectful, explains dharmas conducive to extensive learning for those deficient in learning, explains the dharma of giving for those who are miserly, explains the dharma of harmoniousness and patience for those who are full of hatred, explains the dharma of vigor for those who are indolent, explains the stations of right mindfulness for those of chaotic mind, and speaks in a way conducive to wisdom for those who are foolish or deluded. In addition:

正體字

057a05 ‖ 　　隨諸所乏者　　皆亦應給足
057a06 ‖ 諸眾生有所乏少皆應給足。有人雖富猶
057a07 ‖ 有不足。乃至國王亦應有所[1]乏[2]少。是故
057a08 ‖ 先雖說貧窮者施財。今更說隨所乏少而
057a09 ‖ 給足之。復次。
057a10 ‖ 　　諸有惡眾生　　種種加惱事
057a11 ‖ 　　諂曲懷憍逸　　惡罵輕欺詆
057a12 ‖ 　　背恩無返復　　癡弊難開化
057a13 ‖ 　　菩薩心愍傷　　勇猛加精進
057a14 ‖ 諸惡眾生以種種惡事侵嬈菩薩。菩薩於
057a15 ‖ 此心無懈厭不應作是念。如是惡人誰能
057a16 ‖ 調伏誰能教化誰能勸[3]勉。令度生死究竟
057a17 ‖ 涅槃。誰能與此往來生死。誰能與此和合同
057a18 ‖ 事。諸惡無理誰能忍之。我意止息不復共
057a19 ‖ 事。我悉捨遠不復共事。亦復不能與之和
057a20 ‖ 合。

简体字

　　随诸所乏者　　皆亦应给足
诸众生有所乏少皆应给足。有人虽富犹有不足。乃至国王亦应有所乏少。是故先虽说贫穷者施财。今更说随所乏少而给足之。复次。
　　诸有恶众生　　种种加恼事
　　谄曲怀憍逸　　恶骂轻欺诋
　　背恩无返复　　痴弊难开化
　　菩萨心愍伤　　勇猛加精进
诸恶众生以种种恶事侵娆菩萨。菩萨于此心无懈厌不应作是念。如是恶人谁能调伏谁能教化谁能劝勉。令度生死究竟涅槃。谁能与此往来生死。谁能与此和合同事。诸恶无理谁能忍之。我意止息不复共事。我悉舍远不复共事。亦复不能与之和合。

b. ONE SHOULD PROVIDE BEINGS WITH WHATEVER THEY ARE DEFICIENT IN

In accordance with whatever one finds to be deficient,
one should supply all such things in sufficient measure.

All beings have that in which they are deficient. One should provide all such things in sufficient measure. There are those people who, although wealthy, still have ways in which they are deficient. This may even be true of kings, for they too should have those things in which they are deficient. Hence, even though it was previously explained that one bestows wealth on the poor, it is now further stated that one provides in sufficient measure whatever beings are deficient in. Additionally:

c. THE BODHISATTVA TEACHES ALL SORTS OF EVIL BEINGS

There are all sorts of evil beings
who, in various ways, bring about troublesome circumstances
through flattery, deviousness, or unbridled arrogance,
through cursing, slighting, cheating, or deceiving,

or by turning their backs on kindnesses, leaving them unrequited.
Though the stupid and the base are difficult to instruct and transform,
because the bodhisattva's mind feels pity and sadness for them,
he valiantly redoubles his vigor [in teaching them].

d. WHEN EVIL BEINGS DISTURB HIM, HE MUST NOT THINK IN THESE WAYS:

Evil beings use many different sorts of evil behavior to attack and disturb the bodhisattva. Even in the midst of this, the bodhisattva's resolve does not withdraw in disgust. He should not think in these ways:

Who would be able to train such evil people as these?

Who would be able to instruct them?

Who would be able to exhort them, causing them to be liberated from *saṃsāra* so that they might reach nirvāṇa?

Who would be able to go and come in *saṃsāra* in the company of such beings?

Who would be able to work together harmoniously with them?

As for all these evil deeds and such unprincipled behavior, who would be able to endure it?

My resolve is exhausted. I cannot engage in joint endeavors with them anymore.

I am going to leave them all far behind and never again participate in joint endeavors with them.

What's more, I am unable to even remain together with them at all.

正體字

057a21 ‖ 是惡中之惡無有返復。何用此等而共
057a21 ‖ 從事。菩薩知見眾生惡[4]罪難除。應還作
057a22 ‖ 是念。是等惡人非少。精進能得令住如所
057a23 ‖ 樂法。為是等故我當加心勉力勤行億倍
057a24 ‖ 精進後得大力乃能化。此惡中之惡。難悟
057a25 ‖ 眾生如大醫王。以小因緣便能療治眾生
057a26 ‖ 重病。菩薩如是除煩惱病。令住隨意所樂
057a27 ‖ 功德。我於重罪大惡眾生。倍應憐愍起深
057a28 ‖ 大悲。如彼良醫多有慈心療治眾病。其病
057a29 ‖ 重者深生憐愍勤作方便為求良藥。菩薩
057b01 ‖ 如是於諸眾生煩惱病者悉應憐愍。於惡
057b02 ‖ 中之惡煩惱重者深生[5]憐愍。勤[6]作方便
057b03 ‖ 加心療治。何以故。
057b04 ‖ 　菩薩隨所住　　不開化眾生
057b05 ‖ 　令墮三惡道　　深致諸佛責
057b06 ‖ 菩薩隨所住國土城邑聚落山間樹下。力能
057b07 ‖ 饒益教化眾生。而懈厭

简体字

是恶中之恶无有返复。何用此等而共从事。菩萨知见众生恶罪难除。应还作是念。是等恶人非少。精进能得令住如所乐法。为是等故我当加心勉力勤行亿倍精进后得大力乃能化。此恶中之恶。难悟众生如大医王。以小因缘便能疗治众生重病。菩萨如是除烦恼病。令住随意所乐功德。我于重罪大恶众生。倍应怜愍起深大悲。如彼良医多有慈心疗治众病。其病重者深生怜愍勤作方便为求良药。菩萨如是于诸众生烦恼病者悉应怜愍。于恶中之恶烦恼重者深生怜愍。勤作方便加心疗治。何以故。

　菩萨随所住　　不开化众生
　令堕三恶道　　深致诸佛责

菩萨随所住国土城邑聚落山间树下。力能饶益教化众生。而懈厌

> These people, the most evil among the evil—there is no way I can have any interactions with them.
> What is the use of any further involvement with people such as these?

   e. HE SHOULD REDOUBLE HIS RESOLVE & ACT LIKE A GREAT PHYSICIAN

The bodhisattva knows and sees that it is difficult to rid beings of their evil karmic offenses. He should instead reflect in this manner:

> These sorts of evil people are not few. It is through the application of vigor that they may be influenced to abide in dharmas such as they will delight in. For their sakes, I should intensify my resolve and exert myself to the utmost in diligent practice. I should redouble my practice in a million-fold application of vigor so that, later on, I will acquire great powers by which I will then be able to transform through teaching these most evil among evil beings who are so very difficult to awaken. I should be like the great king of physicians who, by resorting to some small circumstantial method, can cure beings' severe illnesses.

It is in this way that the bodhisattva does away with the disease of the afflictions and is then allowed to abide in whichever meritorious qualities he wishes. [He reflects]:

> I should feel doubly strong pity for these extremely evil beings who are burdened by grave karmic offenses and so I should bring forth profoundly great compassion for them, doing so like that especially fine physician who is abundantly endowed with kindheartedness as he cures the many sorts of illnesses. For those who are seriously ill, he brings forth deep pity and then diligently invents skillful means by which he can seek out an especially fine medicine for them.

It is in this manner that the bodhisattva should feel pity for all beings beset by the disease of the afflictions. Thus, even for the most evil among the evil and those beset with the most serious afflictions, he still feels profound pity. Hence he is diligent in creating means through which, by intensifying his resolve, he is able to cure them. And why?:

   f. FAILING IN THIS, HE WOULD BE WORTHY OF THE BUDDHAS' CENSURE

No matter where the bodhisattva abides,
if he fails to initiate the transformative teaching of beings,
thus allowing them to fall into the three wretched destinies,
he is deeply deserving of the censure of the Buddhas.

And so it is that the bodhisattva, no matter in what country he abides, and no matter whether he is in the city, a village, in the mountains, or beneath some tree—wherever he has the power through which to be able to benefit and teach beings—if he instead withdraws from them

正體字

嫌恨貪著世樂。不
057b08 ‖ 能開化令墮惡道。是菩薩即為十方現在
057b09 ‖ 諸佛。深所呵責甚可慚恥。云何以小因緣
057b10 ‖ 而捨大事。是故菩薩不欲諸佛所呵責
057b11 ‖ [7]者。於種種諂曲重惡眾生。心不應沒隨力
057b12 ‖ 饒益。應以諸方便勤心開化。譬如猛將將
057b13 ‖ 兵多所傷損王則深責以諸兵眾。無所知
057b14 ‖ [8]故王不責之。[9]

简体字

嫌恨贪着世乐。不能开化令堕恶道。是菩萨即为十方现在诸佛。深所呵责甚可惭耻。云何以小因缘而舍大事。是故菩萨不欲诸佛所呵责者。于种种谄曲重恶众生。心不应没随力饶益。应以诸方便勤心开化。譬如猛将将兵多所伤损王则深责以诸兵众。无所知故王不责之。

in disgust, resents their covetous attachment to the pleasures of the world, and thus becomes unable to initiate their transformative teaching, he thereby allows them to fall into the wretched destinies. This bodhisattva thereby becomes deeply deserving of the censure of all buddhas now abiding throughout the ten directions before whom he ought to feel deeply ashamed and embarrassed, [knowing that they would demand to know], "Oh, how could you let such petty reasons cause you to abandon such a great endeavor?"

Therefore, if the bodhisattva does not wish to become someone deserving of the rebuke and censure of the Buddhas, even when faced with all sorts of deceitful and extremely evil beings, he should not let his resolve sink away. Rather he should benefit them in whatever way suits his power to help them. He should use all manner of expedient means and diligent resolve to begin their transformative teaching.

In this respect, he is like a brave military general. If the general's troops encounter catastrophic losses, he is the one who will then be severely reprimanded by the king. Since the soldiers themselves had no way of knowing [how to avoid this defeat], the king would not reprimand them.

The End of Chapter Fifteen

正體字

057b15 ‖	[10]知家過患品第十六
057b16 ‖	菩薩如是學。應知家過惡。何以故。若知過
057b17 ‖	惡或捨家入道。又化餘人令知家過出
057b18 ‖	家入道。問曰。家過云何。答曰。如經中說。佛
057b19 ‖	告郁迦羅。家是破諸善根。家是深棘刺林
057b20 ‖	難得自出。家是壞清白法。家是諸惡覺觀住
057b21 ‖	處。家是弊惡不調凡夫住處。家是一切不善
057b22 ‖	所行住處。家是惡人所聚會處。家是貪欲瞋
057b23 ‖	恚愚癡住處。家是一切苦惱住處。家是消盡
057b24 ‖	先世諸善根處。凡夫住此家中不應作而
057b25 ‖	作不應說而說。不應行而行。在此中住。
057b26 ‖	輕慢父母及諸師長。不敬諸尊福田沙門婆
057b27 ‖	羅門家是貪愛憂悲苦惱眾[11]患因緣。家是
057b28 ‖	惡口罵詈苦切刀[12]杖繫縛[13]考掠割截之所住
057b29 ‖	處。

简体字

十住毗婆沙论卷第七
知家过患品第十六

　　菩萨如是学。应知家过恶。何以故。若知过恶或舍家入道。又化余人令知家过出家入道。问曰。家过云何。答曰。如经中说。佛告郁迦罗。家是破诸善根。家是深棘刺林难得自出。家是坏清白法。家是诸恶觉观住处。家是弊恶不调凡夫住处。家是一切不善所行住处。家是恶人所聚会处。家是贪欲嗔恚愚痴住处。家是一切苦恼住处。家是消尽先世诸善根处。凡夫住此家中不应作而作不应说而说。不应行而行。在此中住。轻慢父母及诸师长。不敬诸尊福田沙门婆罗门家是贪爱忧悲苦恼众患因缘。家是恶口骂詈苦切刀杖系缚考掠割截之所住处。

Chapter 16
On Realizing the Faults of the Householder's Life

XVI. Chapter 16: On Realizing the Faults of the Householder's Life
   A. The Bodhisattva Should Know the Faults of the Householder's Life

As the bodhisattva trains in this manner, he should realize the serious faults of the householder's life. Why? If he realizes those serious faults, he might then abandon the householder's life and enter the path. Moreover, he might then be able to instruct others, make them aware of the faults of the household life, and thereby inspire them to leave the home life and enter the path.

   B. Q: What Are the Faults of the Householder's Life?

Question: What are the faults of the householder's life?

   C. A: They Are Well Described in This Passage from a Sutra

Response: As stated in a sutra, the Buddha informed Ugradatta:[238]

> The home life destroys all roots of goodness. The household is a deep forest of thorns from which it is difficult to escape. The household is a circumstance that destroys the dharmas of purity. The household is the dwelling place of all manner of bad ideation and discursion.[239] The household is the dwelling place of the foolish common person[240] unrestrained in corrupt and evil actions. The household is the place in which one dwells when carrying out every sort of unwholesome endeavor. The household is the gathering place of bad people. The household is the dwelling place of greed, hatred, and delusion. The household is the dwelling place of all forms of suffering. The household is the place where one entirely uses up all the roots of goodness established in previous lives.
>
> When the foolish common person abides in this household, he does what should not be done, says what should not be said, and practices what should not be practiced. When he dwells herein, he slights his parents as well as his teachers and elders. He does not respect the venerable fields of merit, the *śramaṇas*, or the brahmans.
>
> The life of the householder involves causes and conditions conducing to craving, sorrow, grief, suffering, afflictions, and the many sorts of tribulations. The home life is the circumstance in which one encounters the sufferings of harsh speech and scolding, wherein one becomes vulnerable to blades and cudgels, to being bound up and imprisoned, to being beaten, or to being subjected to [punitive]

正體字	057c01 ‖ 未種善根不種已種能壞。能令凡夫在 057c01 ‖ 此貪欲因緣而墮惡道。瞋恚因緣愚癡因緣 057c02 ‖ 而墮惡道怖畏因緣而墮惡道。家是不持 057c03 ‖ 戒品。捨離定品。不觀慧品。不得解脫品。 057c04 ‖ 不生解脫知見品。於此家中生。父母愛兄 057c05 ‖ 弟妻子眷屬車馬。增長貪求無有厭足。家 057c06 ‖ 是難滿如海吞流。家是無足如火焚薪。家 057c07 ‖ 是無[14]息覺觀相續如空中風。家是後有惡 057c08 ‖ 如美食有毒。家是苦性如怨詐親。家是障 057c09 ‖ 礙能妨聖道。家是鬪亂種種因緣共相違諍。 057c10 ‖ 家是多瞋呵責好醜。家是無常雖久失壞。
简体字	未种善根不种已种能坏。能令凡夫在此贪欲因缘而堕恶道。瞋恚因缘愚痴因缘而堕恶道怖畏因缘而堕恶道。家是不持戒品。舍离定品。不观慧品。不得解脱品。不生解脱知见品。于此家中生。父母爱兄弟妻子眷属车马。增长贪求无有厌足。家是难满如海吞流。家是无足如火焚薪。家是无息觉观相续如空中风。家是后有恶如美食有毒。家是苦性如怨诈亲。家是障碍能妨圣道。家是斗乱种种因缘共相违诤。家是多嗔呵责好丑。家是无常虽久失坏。

Chapter 16 — On Realizing the Faults of the Householder's Life

amputations.[241] One fails to plant whichever roots of goodness one has not yet planted and those roots of goodness one has already planted become vulnerable to destruction.

[The householder's life] is able to cause the common person involved in these desire-related causal circumstances to fall into the wretched destinies. Causal circumstances related to hatred or delusion may also precipitate descent into the wretched destinies. [So, too], causal circumstances related to fearfulness may result in one's falling into the wretched destinies.[242]

The householder's life is a circumstance in which one does not maintain the aggregate (skandha) of the moral precepts, abandons the aggregate of meditative absorption, does not contemplate the aggregate of wisdom, does not acquire the aggregate of the liberations, and does not bring forth the aggregate of the knowledge and vision of liberation.

One is born into this householder's life, a circumstance in which parents lovingly dote on their sons, and in which one indulges affection for one's wife and children, for one's retinue, and even for one's carriages and horses. This situation encourages the proliferation of desires to the point where they become insatiable.

[The desires associated with] the householder's life are as difficult to fulfill as the ocean is as it swallows up every tributary that flows into it.

[The desires associated with] the household are as insatiable as a fire in its burning up of firewood.

The life of the householder involves ceaseless ideation and mental discursiveness that are just as continuous as the winds that blow through empty space.

The life of the householder conduces to misfortune in one's future existences just as surely as does delectable food laced with poison [surely leads to one's death].

The life of the householder, by its very nature, is linked to suffering and, in that, it is comparable to having enemies posing as close relations.

Being a householder is an obstruction, for it is able to block one's access to the path of the Āryas.

The householder's life is beset with discord arising from disputation and many different causes and conditions involving mutual opposition and conflict.

The householder's life involves much hatred associated with scolding and much censure over what is desirable versus what is detestable.

The household is impermanent. Even though it may have endured for a long time, it is bound for destruction.

正體字	家 057c11 ‖ 是眾苦求衣食等方便守護。家是[15]多疑處猶 057c12 ‖ 如怨賊。家是無我顛倒貪著假名為有。家是 057c13 ‖ [16]技人雖以種種文飾莊嚴現為貴人。須臾 057c14 ‖ 不久莊嚴還作貧賤。家是變異會必離散。家 057c15 ‖ 如幻假借和合無有實事。家如夢一切富 057c16 ‖ 貴久則還失。家如朝露須臾滅失。家如蜜 057c17 ‖ 渧其味甚少。家如棘[17]叢受五欲味惡刺傷 057c18 ‖ 人。家是[18]鍼[口*(隹/乃)]虫。不善覺觀常唼食人。家污 057c19 ‖ 淨命多行欺誑。家是憂愁心多濁亂。家是眾 057c20 ‖ 共王賊水火[19]惡親所壞。家是多病多諸錯 057c21 ‖ 謬如是長者在家菩薩。應當如是善知家 057c22 ‖ 過。復次。
简体字	家是众苦求衣食等方便守护。家是多疑处犹如怨贼。家是无我颠倒贪着假名为有。家是技人虽以种种文饰庄严现为贵人。须臾不久庄严还作贫贱。家是变异会必离散。家如幻假借和合无有实事。家如梦一切富贵久则还失。家如朝露须臾灭失。家如蜜渧其味甚少。家如棘丛受五欲味恶刺伤人。家是针嘴虫。不善觉观常唼食人。家污净命多行欺诳。家是忧愁心多浊乱。家是众共王贼水火恶亲所坏。家是多病多诸错谬如是长者在家菩萨。应当如是善知家过。复次。

Chapter 16 — On Realizing the Faults of the Householder's Life

The household is beset by many forms of suffering as one strives to acquire clothing, food, and so forth and then does whatever is necessary to preserve and protect them.

The householder's life is a circumstance involving much mutual doubting, just as when abiding in close proximity to thieves.

One's household is not intrinsically "mine." It is solely through inverted views and covetous attachment that, by resort to conventional designations, one claims "it exists."

The circumstance of the householder is like that of an actor who, although he may use all different sorts of makeup and costumes to present the appearance of a member of the aristocracy, before long, in but an instant, all of those adornments disappear and he resumes his role as someone who is poor and of inferior social status.[243]

The household is ever-changing. Once its components have come together, they are bound to fall apart and disperse.

A household is like a magical conjuration. It depends upon the mere aggregation of components and thus is devoid of any reality.

The household is like a dream. After a while, all of one's wealth and high social status are bound to be lost.

The household is like the morning dew. After a short while, it disappears entirely.

[The happiness derived from] the householder's life is like a mere drop of honey. Its flavor is extremely weak.

The household is like a thicket of thorns. As a person enjoys the taste of the objects of the five types of desire, poisonous piercings inflict injuries.

The household is analogous to a needle-beaked insect. Unwholesome ideation and discursive thought always gnaw at and consume the people within it.

Life as a householder sullies the purity of one's life. One becomes predisposed by it to engage in much cheating and deception.

The life of a householder is plagued by anxiety and worries. Thus one's mind is often muddled and confused.

The house becomes the common property of many others and it is vulnerable to destruction by [agents of] the king, thieves, floods, fires, and evil relatives.

The householder's life is freighted with many defects. It involves the commission of numerous erroneous actions. This being the case, an elder who is a lay bodhisattvas should well realize the faults of the householder's life.

D. Also Practice Giving, Uphold Precepts, and Contemplate Almsmen

Next we have:

正體字	057c23 ‖　　菩薩應當知　　在家之過惡 057c24 ‖　　親近於布施　　持戒善好喜 057c25 ‖　　若見諸乞人　　應生五三想 057c26 ‖ 在家菩薩應如是知家過患。當行布施持 057c27 ‖ 戒善好。布施名捨貪心。持戒名身口業清 057c28 ‖ 淨。善名善攝諸根。好喜名同[20]心歡樂。五三 057c29 ‖ 想名見乞兒應生五三想。初三者善知識 058a01 ‖ 想轉身大富想。[1]裨助菩提想。又有三想。折 058a02 ‖ 伏慳貪想。捨一切想。貪求一切智慧想。又 058a03 ‖ 有三想。隨如來教想。不求果報想。降伏 058a04 ‖ 魔想。又有三想。見來求者生眷屬想。不 058a05 ‖ 捨攝法想。捨邪受想。又有三想。離欲想。 058a06 ‖ 修慈想。無癡想。
简体字	菩萨应当知　　在家之过恶 　　亲近于布施　　持戒善好喜 　　若见诸乞人　　应生五三想 　　在家菩萨应如是知家过患。当行布施持戒善好。布施名舍贪心。持戒名身口业清净。善名善摄诸根。好喜名同心欢乐。五三想名见乞儿应生五三想。初三者善知识想转身大富想。裨助菩提想。又有三想。折伏悭贪想。舍一切想。贪求一切智慧想。又有三想。随如来教想。不求果报想。降伏魔想。又有三想。见来求者生眷属想。不舍摄法想。舍邪受想。又有三想。离欲想。修慈想。无痴想。

Chapter 16 — On Realizing the Faults of the Householder's Life 483

> The bodhisattva should know
> the serious faults of the householder's life.
> He should draw close to the practice of giving
> and skillfulness in observing moral precepts, delighting in these.
>
> Whenever one sees any almsman,
> he should bring forth five threefold contemplations.

The lay bodhisattva should know in this way the tribulations of the householder's life. He should adopt in practice the excellence of giving and observance of moral precepts. "Giving" refers here to relinquishing the covetous mind. "Observing moral precepts" refers to purity of physical and verbal actions. "Skillfulness" refers to skillful restraint of the sense faculties. "Delighting in these" refers to like-mindedness and exultant happiness [in the adoption of these practices].

1. FIVE THREEFOLD CONTEMPLATIONS WHENEVER SEEING AN ALMSMAN

"Five threefold contemplations" refers to five different threefold contemplations one should take up whenever encountering an almsman.
The first of the threefold contemplations is as follows:

> Contemplating [the almsman] as a good spiritual guide.[244]
> Contemplating [the acquisition of] great wealth in future lives.[245]
> Contemplating [one's giving] as assisting the realization of bodhi.[246]

There is yet another threefold contemplation, as follows:

> Contemplating the conquering of miserliness.
> Contemplating the relinquishing of everything.
> Contemplating striving for the acquisition of all-knowledge.[247]

There is yet another threefold contemplation, as follows:

> Contemplating in accordance with the teachings of the Tathāgata.
> Contemplating refraining from seeking any karmic result.[248]
> Contemplating the defeat of Māra.[249]

There is yet another threefold contemplation, as follows:

> Contemplating those who come for alms as one's own retinue.[250]
> Contemplating the importance of not abandoning the dharmas comprising "the means of attraction."[251]
> Contemplating the relinquishing of what has been wrongfully acquired.

There is yet another threefold contemplation, as follows:

> Contemplating dispassion.[252]
> Contemplating the cultivation of kindness.
> Contemplating non-delusion.

正體字

今當解第五三想。菩薩因
來求者。令三毒折薄捨所施物生離欲想。
於求者與樂因緣故。瞋恨心薄名修慈想。
是布施迴向無上道則癡心薄。是名不癡
想。餘想義應如是知。復次。

　　菩薩因求者　　具六波羅蜜
　　以是因緣故　　見求應大喜

六波羅蜜者。布施持戒忍辱精進禪定智慧。
以因求者能得具足。以是利故。菩薩遙見
求者心大歡喜作是念。行福田自然而至。
我因此人得具足六波羅蜜。所以者何。若
於所施物心不貪惜。是名檀波羅蜜。為阿
耨多羅三藐三菩提施與。是名尸羅波羅蜜。
若不瞋乞者是名羼提波羅蜜。當行施時
不慮空匱心不退沒。是名毘梨耶波羅蜜。

简体字

今当解第五三想。菩萨因来求者。令三毒折薄舍所施物生离欲想。于求者与乐因缘故。嗔恨心薄名修慈想。是布施回向无上道则痴心薄。是名不痴想。余想义应如是知。复次。

　　菩萨因求者　　具六波罗蜜
　　以是因缘故　　见求应大喜

六波罗蜜者。布施持戒忍辱精进禅定智慧。以因求者能得具足。以是利故。菩萨遥见求者心大欢喜作是念。行福田自然而至。我因此人得具足六波罗蜜。所以者何。若于所施物心不贪惜。是名檀波罗蜜。为阿耨多罗三藐三菩提施与。是名尸罗波罗蜜。若不嗔乞者是名羼提波罗蜜。当行施时不虑空匮心不退没。是名毗梨耶波罗蜜。

Chapter 16 — On Realizing the Faults of the Householder's Life

We should now explain this fifth of these five threefold contemplations:

Because an almsman has come, a bodhisattva may be able to diminish the three poisons. Through relinquishing some possession as a gift one may thereby bringing forth the contemplation of dispassion.[253]

Through providing causes and conditions for the happiness of the supplicant, one's thoughts of hatred become but scant. This is cultivation of the contemplation of kindness.

If the [merit from] this act of giving is dedicated to success in the unsurpassable path, this diminishes one's deluded mind states. This is the contemplation of non-delusion.

One should understand the meaning of the other contemplations in accordance with the above explanations.

2. IT IS DUE TO ALMSMEN THAT ONE IS ABLE TO PERFECT THE SIX PĀRAMITĀS

Furthermore:

> It is because of the almsman
> that the bodhisattva perfects the six *pāramitās*.
> For this reason, one should feel great joy
> on seeing someone who has come to seek alms.

The six *pāramitās* consist of giving, moral virtue, patience, vigor, *dhyāna* concentration, and wisdom. It is because of the almsman that one becomes able to bring them to a state of completion. It is because he gains such benefit that, whenever a bodhisattva sees from afar that a supplicant is coming, his mind is filled with great delight and he thinks, "A walking field of merit has arrived here of his own accord. It is because of just such people as these that I shall be able to perfect the six *pāramitās*." Now, how might this be so? [Consider the following]:

> When one's mind feels no miserly cherishing for the object one gives, this is *dāna pāramitā*, [the perfection of giving].
>
> When one gives for the sake of attaining *anuttarasamyaksaṃbodhi*, [the utmost, right, and perfect enlightenment], this is an instance of practicing *śīla pāramitā*, [the perfection of moral virtue].[254]
>
> When one is able to refrain from feeling hatred toward the mendicant, this is an instance of practicing *kṣānti pāramitā*, [the perfection of patience].
>
> When, as one is carrying out the act of giving, one refrains from reflecting on one's own resulting material scarcity while also not retreating from one's resolve, this is an instance of practicing *vīrya pāramitā*, [the perfection of vigor].[255]

正體字

058a21 ‖ 若與乞者若自與時心定不悔。是名禪波
058a22 ‖ 羅蜜。以不得一切法而行布施不求果
058a23 ‖ 報。如賢聖無所著。以是布施迴向阿耨多
058a24 ‖ 羅三藐三菩提。是名般若波羅蜜。復次。
058a25 ‖ 　所施物果報　　種種皆能知
058a26 ‖ 　慳惜在家者　　亦知種種過
058a27 ‖ [2]所施物所獲功德利物。慳惜在家所有過
058a28 ‖ 惡菩薩於此皆悉了知。問曰。若施得何功
058a29 ‖ 德。若惜在家有何過咎。答曰。菩薩以真智
058b01 ‖ 慧如是知。施與已是我物。在家者非我物。
058b02 ‖ 物施已則堅牢。在家者不堅牢。物施已[3]後
058b03 ‖ 世樂。在家少時樂。物施已不憂守護。在家
058b04 ‖ 者有守護。[4]苦物施已愛心薄。在家者增長
058b05 ‖ 愛。

简体字

若与乞者若自与时心定不悔。是名禅波罗蜜。以不得一切法而行布施不求果报。如贤圣无所著。以是布施回向阿耨多罗三藐三菩提。是名般若波罗蜜。复次。

　所施物果报　　种种皆能知
　悭惜在家者　　亦知种种过

所施物所获功德利物。悭惜在家所有过恶菩萨于此皆悉了知。问曰。若施得何功德。若惜在家有何过咎。答曰。菩萨以真智慧如是知。施与已是我物。在家者非我物。物施已则坚牢。在家者不坚牢。物施已后世乐。在家少时乐。物施已不忧守护。在家者有守护。苦物施已爱心薄。在家者增长爱。

If, in giving to an almsman, at that very time when one is presenting the gift, one's mind remains fixed [in its resolve] and does not entertain any regretfulness, this is an instance of practicing *dhyāna pāramitā*, [the perfection of meditative concentration].

By not apprehending [any inherent existence in] any dharma as one carries out an act of giving, by not seeking any karmic reward from it, and by remaining free of any attachment in this, thereby doing so after the manner of a worthy or an *ārya*,[256] when one then dedicates that act of giving to *anuttarasamyaksaṃbodhi*, one's giving then becomes an instance of practicing *prajñā pāramitā*, [the perfection of wisdom].

3. ONE KNOWS THE BENEFITS OF GIVING AND THE FAULTS OF MISERLINESS

Furthermore:

As for the karmic results ensuing from giving the gift,
he is able to know all of its various forms.
He also knows the various faults associated with
keeping it at home due to miserliness.

As for the merit acquired from the giving of the gift that has been given as well as all the serious faults associated with keeping the gift due to miserliness, the bodhisattva completely comprehends all of these matters.

a. Q: WHAT ARE THE MERITS OF GIVING AND FAULTS OF KEEPING THE GIFT?

Question: If one gives it, what sort of merit is gained by that? And if one instead keeps it at home, what fault or blame is there in that?

b. A: USING TRUE WISDOM, THE BODHISATTVA UNDERSTANDS AS FOLLOWS:

Response: The bodhisattva uses true wisdom to understand this matter in the following manner, [reflecting]:

After this gift has been given away, it is still mine [in terms of its ongoing karmic rewards]. However, if it is instead kept at home, it is not [rightfully] mine.

Once the gift has been given, it endures.[257] However, if it is instead kept at home, it will not endure.[258]

After the gift has been given, future-life happiness will follow from that. However, if it is instead kept at home, it will provide happiness only for a brief period of time.

Once the gift has been given away, there is no longer any need to be anxious about preserving and guarding it. However, if it is instead kept at home, one will continue to feel protective concern for it.

If one has already given away the gift, one's thoughts of affection for it become scant. However, if it is instead kept at home, one increases one's affection for it.

正體字

物施已無我所。在家者是我所。物施已
058b06 ‖ 無所屬。在家者有所屬。物施已無所畏。
058b07 ‖ 在家者多所畏。物施已助菩提道。在家者
058b08 ‖ 助魔道。物施已無有盡。在家則有盡。物施
058b09 ‖ 已從得樂。在家從得苦。[5]施已捨煩惱。在
058b10 ‖ 家增煩惱。施已得大富樂。在家不得大富
058b11 ‖ 樂。施已大人業。在家小人業。施已諸佛所
058b12 ‖ [6]歎。在家愚癡所讚。復次。
058b13 ‖ 　　於妻子眷屬　　及與善知識
058b14 ‖ 　　財施及畜生　　應生幻化想
058b15 ‖ 　　一切諸行業　　是則為幻師
058b16 ‖ 在家菩薩。於妻子等應生幻化想。如幻化
058b17 ‖ 事但誑人[7]目。行業是幻主。

简体字

物施已无我所。在家者是我所。物施已无所属。在家者有所属。物施已无所畏。在家者多所畏。物施已助菩提道。在家者助魔道。物施已无有尽。在家则有尽。物施已从得乐。在家从得苦。施已舍烦恼。在家增烦恼。施已得大富乐。在家不得大富乐。施已大人业。在家小人业。施已诸佛所叹。在家愚痴所赞。复次。

　　于妻子眷属　　及与善知识
　　财施及畜生　　应生幻化想
　　一切诸行业　　是则为幻师

在家菩萨。于妻子等应生幻化想。如幻化事但诳人目。行业是幻主。

Once the gift has been given, one becomes free of [any thought of it as] "mine." However, if it is instead kept at home, it is [still thought of as] "mine."

Once the gift has been given, there is no [conception of] anyone to whom it belongs. However, if it is instead kept at home, there is [the conception of] someone to whom it belongs.

Once the gift has been given, one is free of concerns about it. However, if it is instead kept at home, one entertains many fears about it.

Once the gift has been given, it assists progress on the path to bodhi. However, if it is instead kept at home, it assists progress on the path of Māra.

Once the gift has been given, [the benefit from having given it] is endless. However, if it is instead kept at home, it remains finite [in its capacity to provide benefit].

Once the gift has been given, one continues to experience happiness from it. However, if it is instead kept at home, one continues to experience suffering [from one's concerns about it].

Having given the gift, one relinquishes afflictions. However, if it is instead kept at home, it increases one's afflictions.

Having given the gift, one gains great wealth and happiness. However, if it is instead kept at home, one does not gain great wealth and happiness.

Having given the gift, one has done the deed of a great man. However, if it is instead kept at home, one has done the deed of a petty man.

Having given the gift, one is praised by the Buddhas. However, if it is instead kept at home, one is praised only by fools.

4. CONTEMPLATE RELATIVES AND POSSESSIONS AS LIKE MERE ILLUSIONS

Furthermore:

> Regarding one's wife, children, and retinue
> as well as one's good spiritual friends,
> one's giving of wealth, and one's animals, too—
> one should contemplate them all as mere illusory conjurations.
>
> It is one's karma consisting of all of one's actions
> that serves as their conjuring magician.

Regarding his wife, children, and so forth, the householder bodhisattva should contemplate them as mere illusory conjurations. They are just like phenomena manifesting as illusory conjurations that merely deceive a person's eyes. It is the karma of one's actions that serves as their conjurer.

正體字

妻子等事不久
058b18 ‖ 則滅。如經說。佛告諸比丘。諸行如幻化誑
058b19 ‖ 惑愚人無有實事。當知因業故有業盡則
058b20 ‖ 滅。是故如幻作是念。
058b21 ‖ 　我非彼所有　　彼非我所有
058b22 ‖ 　彼我皆屬業　　隨業因緣有
058b23 ‖ 　如是正思惟　　不應起惡業
058b24 ‖ 父母妻子親[8]里知識奴婢僮[9]客等。不能為
058b25 ‖ 我作救作歸作趣。非我非我所。五陰十二
058b26 ‖ 入十八界。尚非我非我所。何況父母妻子
058b27 ‖ 等。我亦不能為彼作救作歸作趣。我亦屬
058b28 ‖ 業隨業所受。彼亦屬業隨業所受。好惡果
058b29 ‖ 報如是三種籌量。一有義趣。二見經說。三
058c01 ‖ 見現事。不應為父母妻子等起身口意毫
058c02 ‖ 釐惡業。

简体字

妻子等事不久则灭。如经说。佛告诸比丘。诸行如幻化诳惑愚人无有实事。当知因业故有业尽则灭。是故如幻作是念。
　我非彼所有　　彼非我所有
　彼我皆属业　　随业因缘有
　如是正思惟　　不应起恶业

父母妻子亲里知识奴婢僮客等。不能为我作救作归作趣。非我非我所。五阴十二入十八界。尚非我非我所。何况父母妻子等。我亦不能为彼作救作归作趣。我亦属业随业所受。彼亦属业随业所受。好恶果报如是三种筹量。一有义趣。二见经说。三见现事。不应为父母妻子等起身口意毫厘恶业。

As for phenomena such as one's wife, sons, and so forth, they will all disappear before long. This is as explained in the sutras where the Buddha told the bhikshus, "All of one's actions are like an illusory conjuration that deceives and deludes foolish people for there are no genuinely-existent phenomena present there at all."

One should realize that it is because of karma that these phenomena exist. Once that karma has finally become exhausted, then they all disappear. Hence they are all like illusory conjurations. Thus one should reflect on them as follows:

5. ONE SHOULD REFLECT ON THEM ALL AS THE RESULTS OF KARMA

I am not a possession of theirs,
nor are they possessions of mine.
Those things and myself all belong to karma
and exist in accordance with karmic causes and conditions.

If one carries on right contemplation in this manner,
one should not create any bad karma.

[The bodhisattva reflects in the following manner]:

My father, mother, wife, children, relatives, fellow villagers, friends, slaves, maidservants, servant boys, guests, and such—none of them are able to save me, to be a refuge for me, or to serve as my ultimate resort. They are neither my self nor a possession of my self.

Not even the five aggregates, twelve sense bases, or eighteen sense fields constitute either a self or anything that is owned by a self. How much the less could this be so in the case of my parents, my wife, my children, or those other individuals?

Neither am I capable of serving as a savior for them, of serving as a refuge for them, or of serving as an ultimate resort for them. I too belong to my own karma and am thereby bound to accord with my karma in what I experience. They too belong to their own karma and are thereby bound to accord with their karma in what they experience.

In this connection, regarding this matter of experiencing good and bad karmic retributions, there are three bases for evaluating and assessing [this idea]:

First, it has meaningful significance.
Second, we see this in the sutras' explanations.
Third, we see this in presently manifest circumstances.

[This being the case], one should not perform even the slightest bad physical, verbal, or mental karmic deed [even when it is done] for the sake of one's parents, wife, or children.

正體字

復次。
058c03 ‖ 　　菩薩於妻所　　應生三三想
058c04 ‖ 　　亦復有三三　　又復有三三
058c05 ‖ 在家菩薩應生[10]三想。所謂三者。妻是無常
058c06 ‖ 想失想壞想。又有三想。是戲笑伴非後世
058c07 ‖ 伴。是共食伴非受業果報伴。是樂時伴非苦
058c08 ‖ 時伴。又有三想。是不淨想臭穢想可厭想。又
058c09 ‖ 有三想。是怨家想惱害想相違想。又有三
058c10 ‖ 想。羅剎想毘舍闍鬼想醜陋想。又有三想。入
058c11 ‖ 地獄想入畜生想入餓鬼想。又有三想。重擔
058c12 ‖ 想減想屬畏想。又有三想。非我想無[11]定屬
058c13 ‖ 想假借想。又有三想。因起身惡業想起口
058c14 ‖ 惡業想起意惡業想。又有三想。欲覺處想
058c15 ‖ 瞋覺處想惱覺處想。又有三想。枷杻[12]相鎖
058c16 ‖ 械[*]相縛繫[*]相。

简体字

复次。
　　菩萨于妻所　　应生三三想
　　亦复有三三　　又复有三三
　在家菩萨应生三想。所谓三者。妻是无常想失想坏想。又有三想。是戏笑伴非后世伴。是共食伴非受业果报伴。是乐时伴非苦时伴。又有三想。是不净想臭秽想可厌想。又有三想。是怨家想恼害想相违想。又有三想。罗刹想毗舍阇鬼想丑陋想。又有三想。入地狱想入畜生想入饿鬼想。又有三想。重担想减想属畏想。又有三想。非我想无定属想假借想。又有三想。因起身恶业想起口恶业想起意恶业想。又有三想。欲觉处想嗔觉处想恼觉处想。又有三想。枷杻相锁械相缚系相。

Chapter 16 — On Realizing the Faults of the Householder's Life

6. USE THE FOLLOWING THREEFOLD CONTEMPLATIONS OF ONE'S SPOUSE

Furthermore:

Regarding a spouse,[259] the bodhisattva
should bring forth three threefold contemplations
in addition to which there are another three that are threefold,
after which there are yet more sets of three that are threefold as well.[260]

The lay bodhisattva should take up the threefold contemplations, as below:[261]

The first three are as follows: One's spouse is impermanent, bound to be lost, and bound for destruction.

There are three more contemplations: One's spouse is a companion for enjoyment and laughter now, but not a companion in future lives, a companion with whom to share meals, but not a companion in the undergoing of karmic retributions, and is a companion in times of happiness, but not a companion in [future] times of suffering.

There are three more contemplations: One's spouse is an object for the contemplation of the body as unlovely,[262] as malodorous and filled with filth, and as loathsome.

There are three more contemplations: One's spouse is to be contemplated as an adversary, as a source of injurious anguish, and as one who stands in mutual opposition [to one's aims].

There are three more contemplations: One's spouse is to be contemplated as a *rākṣasa*, a *piśācī*, and as physically ugly.

There are three more contemplations: One's spouse is to be contemplated as a cause for falling into the hells, as a cause for falling into the animal realm, and as a cause for falling into the realm of hungry ghosts.

There are three more contemplations: One's spouse is to be contemplated as a heavy burden, as a cause of decline, and as fearsome.

There are three more contemplations: One's spouse is to be contemplated as not-self, as of no certain loyalty, and as merely borrowed.

There are three more contemplations: One's spouse is to be contemplated as the cause for generating bad physical karma, as the cause for generating bad verbal karma, and as the cause for generating bad mental karma.

There are three more contemplations: One's spouse is to be contemplated as the basis for thoughts of lust, as the basis for thoughts of hatred, and as the basis for thoughts of annoyance.

There are three more contemplations:[263] One's spouse is to be contemplated as manacles, as chains, and as a cangue.

正體字	復有三[*]相。遮持戒[*]相。遮 058c17 ‖ 禪定[*]相。遮智慧[*]相。復有三[*]相坑[*]相羅 058c18 ‖ 網[*]相圍合[*]相。復有三[*]相。災害[*]相疾病 058c19 ‖ [*]相衰惱[*]相。復有三[*]相。罪[*]相黑[13]耳[*]相災 058c20 ‖ 雹[*]相。復有三相。病[*]相老[*]相死[*]相。復有三 058c21 ‖ [*]相。魔[*]相魔處[*]相[14]畏[*]相。復有三[*]相。憂愁 058c22 ‖ [*]相懊惱[*]相啼哭[*]相。復有三[*]相。大豺狼 058c23 ‖ [*]相大摩竭魚[*]相大貓狸[*]相。復有三[*]相。黑 058c24 ‖ 毒蛇[*]相鱓魚[*]相奪勢力[*]相。復有三[*]相。無 058c25 ‖ 救[*]相無歸[*]相無[15]舍[*]相。復有三[*]相。失[*]相 058c26 ‖ 退[*]相疲極[*]相。復有三[*]相賊[*]相獄卒[*]相 058c27 ‖ 地獄卒[*]相。復有三[*]相。留[*]相縛[*]相結[*]相。 058c28 ‖ 復有三[*]相。泥[*]相流[*]相[16][漂*寸][*]相。復有三 058c29 ‖[*]相。械[*]相鎖[*]相[17][米*离]粘[*]相。復有三[*]相。猛 059a01 ‖ 火聚[*]相刀輪[*]相草炬[*]相。
简体字	复有三相。遮持戒相。遮禅定相。遮智慧相。复有三相坑相罗网相围合相。复有三相。灾害相疾病相衰恼相。复有三相。罪相黑耳相灾雹相。复有三相。病相老相死相。复有三相。魔相魔处相畏相。复有三相。忧愁相懊恼相啼哭相。复有三相。大豺狼相大摩竭鱼相大猫狸相。复有三相。黑毒蛇相鱓鱼相夺势力相。复有三相。无救相无归相无舍相。复有三相。失相退相疲极相。复有三相贼相狱卒相地狱卒相。复有三相。留相缚相结相。复有三相。泥相流相[漂*寸]相。复有三相。械相锁相[米*离]粘相。复有三相。猛火聚相刀轮相草炬相。

Chapter 16 — On Realizing the Faults of the Householder's Life

There are three more contemplations: One's spouse is to be contemplated as an obstacle to maintaining the moral precepts, as an obstacle to *dhyāna* concentration, and as an obstacle to wisdom.

There are three more contemplations: One's spouse is to be contemplated as a deep pit, as a net-trap, and as a corral-trap.

There are three more contemplations: One's spouse is to be contemplated as a natural disaster, as a plague, and as causing the anguish of decline.

There are three more contemplations: One's spouse is to be contemplated as associated with karmic offenses, as a black-eared kite,[264] and as a disastrous hailstorm.

There are three more contemplations: One's spouse is to be contemplated as symbolic of illness, as symbolic of aging, and as symbolic of death.

There are three more contemplations: One's spouse is to be contemplated as Māra, as the abode of Māra, and as fearsome.

There are three more contemplations: One's spouse is to be contemplated as emblematic of worry, as emblematic of anguish, and as emblematic of weeping.

There are three more contemplations: One's spouse is to be contemplated as a large jackal or wolf, as the *makara* sea monster, and as a huge leopard.

There are three more contemplations: One's spouse is to be contemplated as a black venomous serpent, as the Sakhalin sturgeon,[265] and as the force of violent pillaging.

There are three more contemplations: One's spouse is to be contemplated as not a savior, as not a refuge, and as not a shelter.

There are three more contemplations: One's spouse is to be contemplated as associated with failure, as associated with retreat, and as associated with physical exhaustion.

There are three more contemplations: One's spouse is to be contemplated as a thief, as a jailer, and as one of the minions in hell.

There are three more contemplations: One's spouse is to be contemplated as detention, as bondage, and as a fetter.

There are three more contemplations: One's spouse is to be contemplated as like mire, as like a flood, and as like being adrift.

There are three more contemplations: One's spouse is to be contemplated as fetters, as a lock, and as glue.

There are three more contemplations: One's spouse is to be contemplated as a fierce conflagration, as a spinning wheel of knives, and as a flaming torch.

正體字

```
         復有三[*]相。無利
059a02 ‖ [*]相刺棘[*]相惡毒[*]相。復有三[*]相。[1]陵上[*]相
059a03 ‖ 覆映[*]相貪著[*]相。復有三[*]相。恨[*]相鞭杖
059a04 ‖ [*]相刀矟[*]相。復有三[*]相。忿恚[*]相諍訟[*]相
059a05 ‖ [2]打棒相。復有三[*]相。怨憎會[*]相離愛[*]相鬪
059a06 ‖ [*]相。取要言之。是[3]以一切臭惡不淨[*]相。一
059a07 ‖ 切衰濁[*]相。是一切不善根[*]相。是故在家菩
059a08 ‖ 薩。於妻子見如是[*]相。應生厭離心出家
059a09 ‖ 修善為善。若不能出家。不應於[4]妻起諸
059a10 ‖ 惡業。復次。
059a11 ‖    若於子偏愛    即以智力捨
059a12 ‖    因子行平等    普慈諸眾生
059a13 ‖ 在家菩薩。若自知於子愛心偏多。即以智
059a14 ‖ 力思惟捨離。智力者應如是念。菩薩平等
059a15 ‖ 心。乃有阿耨多羅三藐三菩提。高下心者則
059a16 ‖ 無菩提。是阿耨多羅三藐三菩提。
```

简体字

复有三相。无利相刺棘相恶毒相。复有三相。陵上相覆映相贪着相。复有三相。恨相鞭杖相刀矟相。复有三相。忿恚相诤讼相打棒相。复有三相。怨憎会相离爱相闹相。取要言之。是以一切臭恶不净相。一切衰浊相。是一切不善根相。是故在家菩萨。于妻子见如是相。应生厌离心出家修善为善。若不能出家。不应于妻起诸恶业。复次。

　　若于子偏爱　　即以智力舍
　　因子行平等　　普慈诸众生

在家菩萨。若自知于子爱心偏多。即以智力思惟舍离。智力者应如是念。菩萨平等心。乃有阿耨多罗三藐三菩提。高下心者则无菩提。是阿耨多罗三藐三菩提。

Chapter 16 — *On Realizing the Faults of the Householder's Life*

> There are three more contemplations: One's spouse is to be contemplated as of no benefit, as a thicket of thorns, and as noxious poison.
>
> There are three more contemplations: One's spouse is to be contemplated as on a burial mound, as obscuring radiance, and as symbolic of desirous attachment.
>
> There are three more contemplations: One's spouse is to be contemplated as symbolic of resentment, as symbolic of whips and cudgels, and as symbolic of swords and lances.
>
> There are three more contemplations: One's spouse is to be contemplated as symbolic of rage, as symbolic of disputatiousness, and as symbolic of being beaten with a cudgel.
>
> There are three more contemplations: One's spouse is to be contemplated as symbolic of proximity to what one detests, as symbolic of separation from what one loves, and as symbolic of quarrelsomeness.
>
> To sum up what is essential: One's spouse is to be contemplated as symbolic of every sort of malodorousness, repulsiveness, and impurity, as symbolic of every sort of ruin and corruption, and as symbolic of all sorts of bad karmic roots.

Therefore, having visualized such contemplations of one's spouse and children, the lay bodhisattva should bring forth feelings of renunciation, leave behind the householder's life, cultivate goodness, and do good deeds. If one is unable to leave behind the householder's life,[266] one should at least refrain from creating any sort of bad karma in one's relationship with one's spouse.

7. Use Wisdom to Reduce Bias Toward One's Own Children

Additionally:

> If one cherishes a preferential affection for one's children,
> one should then use the power of wisdom to relinquish it, and,
> based on [such feeling for] one's children, practice equal regard for all
> by which one then extends universal kindness to all beings.

If the lay bodhisattva realizes that he cherishes an especially great partiality toward his own children, he should then use the power of wisdom to reflect upon it and relinquish it. One who is possessed of the power of wisdom should reflect in this manner:

> It is only once the bodhisattva develops a mind of equal regard for all that he then attains *anuttarasamyaksaṃbodhi*. If one's mind discriminates between those who are regarded as superior and those who are regarded as inferior, then he will have no attainment of bodhi. This *anuttarasamyaksaṃbodhi* is acquired through [realization of] the

正體字

　　　　從一相無
059a17 ‖ 相得。不從別異相得。我今求阿耨多羅三
059a18 ‖ 藐三菩提。若於子所愛心偏多即有高下不
059a19 ‖ 名平等。即是別相非是一相。若如是者去
059a20 ‖ 阿耨多羅三藐三菩提。則為甚遠。是故我不
059a21 ‖ 應於子偏生愛心。爾時於子應生三[*]相。
059a22 ‖ 一於我為賊佛說等慈破令不等。愛心偏
059a23 ‖ 多故。二為賊害因是子故。破諸善根遮
059a24 ‖ 正智命。三我因是子逆道中行不行順道。
059a25 ‖ 即時因子於諸眾生等行慈心應作是念。
059a26 ‖ 子從餘處來我亦從餘處來。子至異處我
059a27 ‖ 去異處。我不知彼去處。彼不知我去處。
059a28 ‖ 彼不知我來處。我不知彼來處。是子非我
059a29 ‖ 所有。何為無故橫生愛縛。如說。
059b01 ‖ 　彼我不相知　　所來所去處
059b02 ‖ 　彼我云何親　　而生我所心

简体字

从一相无相得。不从别异相得。我今求阿耨多罗三藐三菩提。若于子所爱心偏多即有高下不名平等。即是别相非是一相。若如是者去阿耨多罗三藐三菩提。则为甚远。是故我不应于子偏生爱心。尔时于子应生三相。一于我为贼佛说等慈破令不等。爱心偏多故。二为贼害因是子故。破诸善根遮正智命。三我因是子逆道中行不行顺道。即时因子于诸众生等行慈心应作是念。子从余处来我亦从余处来。子至异处我去异处。我不知彼去处。彼不知我去处。彼不知我来处。我不知彼来处。是子非我所有。何为无故横生爱缚。如说。
　彼我不相知　　所来所去处
　彼我云何亲　　而生我所心

one characteristic, that of signlessness. It is not attained through discriminating on the basis of different characteristics.

Now, I am seeking the realization of *anuttarasamyaksaṃbodhi*. If the mind of affection that I maintain toward my own children is preferentially greater than for others, then this is an instance of retaining discriminations as to who is regarded as superior and who is regarded as inferior. This does not qualify as "equal regard for all." It is just a case of making discriminations based on different characteristics and it is not a case of perceiving a singular unitary character.

If I allow this to happen, then I will remain very far from *anuttarasamyaksaṃbodhi*. Therefore I should not bring forth a mind of preferentially greater affection for my own children.

8. TAKE UP THIS THREEFOLD CONTEMPLATION OF ONE'S CHILDREN

One should then take up a threefold contemplation regarding one's own children:

First, "They are for me like thieves, for, although the Buddha has taught that one is to feel equal kindness for all, because of my preferentially greater affection for them, this has been destroyed, resulting in my failure to maintain equal regard for everyone."

Second, "They bring about the harm inflicted by thieves, for it is because of these children that roots of goodness have been destroyed and a life of great wisdom has been obstructed."

Third, "It is because of these children that I have gone against the middle-way practice of the path and do not practice in accordance with the path."

9. USE THE FOLLOWING THOUGHTS TO DEVELOP EQUAL REGARD FOR ALL

Then, due to [having contemplated] one's children, one immediately takes up the practice of being equally kind toward all beings. One should then reflect in this manner:

"My children have come from some other place and I too have come from some other place. My children will go off to some different location and I too shall depart to some different location. I do not know where they shall go and they do not know where I shall go. They do not know where I have come from and I do not know where they have come from. These children are not my possessions. Why for no reason do I just suddenly develop these bonds of affection?" This is as described here:

They and I do not know of each other
from where we have come or where we shall go.
In what respect then are they and I such "close relatives"
that we conceive of each other as "mine"?

正體字

059b03 ‖ 復次無始生死中。一切眾生曾為我子。我亦
059b04 ‖ 曾為彼子。有為法中無有決定此是我子彼
059b05 ‖ 是他子。何以故。眾生於六道中轉輪互為
059b06 ‖ 父子。如說。
059b07 ‖ 　無明蔽慧眼　　數數生死中
059b08 ‖ 　往來多所作　　更互為父子
059b09 ‖ 　貪著世間樂　　不知有勝事
059b10 ‖ 　怨數為知識　　知識數為怨
059b11 ‖ 是故我方便莫生憎愛心。何以故。若有善
059b12 ‖ 知識。常種種求利益。若有怨賊。常種種生
059b13 ‖ 無益[*]相。有此憎愛心則不得通達諸法平
059b14 ‖ 等想。心高下者死後生邪處。正行者生正行
059b15 ‖ 處。是故我不應行邪行。於眾生行平等。
059b16 ‖ 當得平等薩婆若。
059b17 ‖ 十住毘婆沙論卷第七[5]

简体字

复次无始生死中。一切众生曾为我子。我亦曾为彼子。有为法中无有决定此是我子彼是他子。何以故。众生于六道中转轮互为父子。如说。
　无明蔽慧眼　　数数生死中
　往来多所作　　更互为父子
　贪着世间乐　　不知有胜事
　怨数为知识　　知识数为怨
是故我方便莫生憎爱心。何以故。若有善知识。常种种求利益。若有怨贼。常种种生无益相。有此憎爱心则不得通达诸法平等想。心高下者死后生邪处。正行者生正行处。是故我不应行邪行。于众生行平等。当得平等萨婆若。

Additionally, [one should reflect]: "Throughout the course of *saṃsāra's* beginningless cycle of births and deaths, all beings have previously been my children. I too have been their child. In this sphere of conditioned dharmas, there is no fixed relationship whereby this one is my child or that one is someone else's child. Why? While traveling through the six destinies of rebirth, beings take turns in serving as either the father or the child of the other." This is as described here:

> Ignorance covers over the eye of wisdom.
> Time and time again, during the course of our births and deaths,
> we have gone and come, each having much that we have done,
> as each has taken turns in serving for the other as father or child.
>
> One becomes attached through desire for the pleasures of the world,
> remaining oblivious to the existence of the supreme endeavor.
> Time and time again, adversaries become each other's friends,
> and, time and time again, friends become each other's adversaries.

[One continues to reflect, as follows]:

> Therefore I should adopt expedient means that compel me to refrain from feeling thoughts of either hatred or love. Why? If one has those one considers to be "good friends," then one will always seek in many different ways to benefit them, whereas, if one has those one considers to be "adversaries," one will always bring forth many different sorts of thoughts that cause one to refrain from benefitting them. Hence, if one retains these thoughts of hatred or love, then one will remain unable to gain a penetrating understanding of the uniform equality of all dharmas.
>
> After death, those whose minds discriminate between those who are superior and those who are inferior are bound to be reborn in a place where wrong [practice] is prevalent, whereas, those who adhere to right practice are bound to be reborn in a place where right practice is prevalent.
>
> Therefore, I should refrain from cultivating wrong practices. If one practices uniformly equal regard toward other beings, then one will be bound in the future to attain all-knowledge[267] where the uniform equality [of all things is realized].

The End of Chapter Sixteen

正體字

| 059b20 ‖ 十住毘婆沙論卷第八 059b21 ‖
| 059b22 ‖ 　　聖者龍樹造
| 059b23 ‖ 　　後秦龜茲國三藏鳩摩羅什譯
| 059b24 ‖ 　　[6]入寺品第十七
| 059b25 ‖ 如是在家菩薩。不應於諸事中[7]生貪著
| 059b26 ‖ 心我我所心。何以故。隨所貪著難捨之物
| 059b27 ‖ 法應施與。若能施與則除此過。菩薩如是
| 059b28 ‖ 無有貪著慳惜之心可以處家。問曰。在家
| 059b29 ‖ 菩薩。或有貪惜愛著之物有來求者。此應
| 059c01 ‖ 云何。答曰。
| 059c02 ‖ 　　於所貪著物　　有來求索者
| 059c03 ‖ 　　當自勸喻心　　即施勿慳惜
| 059c04 ‖ 菩薩所貪惜物。若有乞人急從求索。汝以
| 059c05 ‖ 此物施與我者速得成佛。菩薩即時應自
| 059c06 ‖ 勸喻而施與之。如是思惟。若我今者不捨
| 059c07 ‖ 此物。此物必當遠離於我。設至死時不隨
| 059c08 ‖ 我去。此物則是遠離之相。今為阿耨多羅三
| 059c09 ‖ 藐三菩提。具足檀波羅蜜故施與。

简体字

入寺品第十七

　　如是在家菩萨。不应于诸事中生贪着心我我所心。何以故。随所贪着难舍之物法应施与。若能施与则除此过。菩萨如是无有贪着悭惜之心可以处家。问曰。在家菩萨。或有贪惜爱着之物有来求者。此应云何。答曰。

　　　　于所贪着物　　有来求索者
　　　　当自劝喻心　　即施勿悭惜

　　菩萨所贪惜物。若有乞人急从求索。汝以此物施与我者速得成佛。菩萨即时应自劝喻而施与之。如是思惟。若我今者不舍此物。此物必当远离于我。设至死时不随我去。此物则是远离之相。今为阿耨多罗三藐三菩提。具足檀波罗蜜故施与。

Chapter 17
On Entering the Temple

XVII. Chapter 17: On Entering the Temple
   A. One Should Be Able to Relinquish Whatever One Is Attached to

In this way, the lay bodhisattva should refrain from generating thoughts of attachment, thoughts imputing the existence of a self, or thoughts imputing the existence of anything belonging to a self. Why is this so? As for whatever has become such an object of affectionate attachment that one finds it difficult to relinquish, to accord with the Dharma, one should relinquish it. If one can give it away, then this is the means for getting rid of this fault. Bodhisattvas who are able by this means to remain free of thoughts of attachment or miserliness are capable of abiding as householders.

   B. Q: If One Is Attached to Something, What if Someone Asks for It?

Question: It might happen that the lay bodhisattva has things for which he feels a miserly cherishing and to which he is affectionately attached. When someone comes wishing to receive them as a gift, what should he do?

   C. A: Exhort Oneself to Abandon Miserliness and Relinquish It

Response:
> Regarding those things to which one is attached,
> whenever someone comes seeking to obtain them,
> one should exhort and persuade his mind
> to simply relinquish them, for he must not indulge miserliness.

As for possessions toward which a bodhisattva feels a covetous cherishing, if a beggar were to come urgently seeking to obtain it from him, saying, "If you give this thing to me, you will quickly attain buddhahood," the bodhisattva should immediately exhort and persuade himself to go ahead and give it to him, reflecting as follows:

> If I fail to relinquish this possession just now, this thing is certainly bound in due course to depart far from me anyway. Once I am at the point of death, this thing will not accompany me when I go. If this is so, then this possession is characterized by the inevitability of its departure.
>
> Now, for the sake of *anuttarasamyaksaṃbodhi* and for the sake of perfecting *dāna pāramitā* (the perfection of giving), I shall give it

正體字

```
           後至死
059c10 ‖ 時心無有悔。經說。不悔心死必生善處。是
059c11 ‖ 得大利云何不捨。如是自勸猶貪惜者應
059c12 ‖ 辭謝乞者言。
059c13 ‖    我今是新學     善根未成就
059c14 ‖    心未得自在     願後當相與
059c15 ‖ 應辭謝乞者言。勿生瞋恨。我新發意善根
059c16 ‖ 未具。於菩薩行法未得勢力。是以未能
059c17 ‖ 捨於此物。後得勢力善根成就。心得堅固
059c18 ‖ 當以相與。復次。
059c19 ‖    若眾不和合     斷於經法事
059c20 ‖    菩薩應隨力     方便令不絕
059c21 ‖ 眾僧或以事緣諍競乖散法事有廢。在家菩
059c22 ‖ 薩應勤心方便彼此之間心無所偏。若以
059c23 ‖ 財物若以言說禮敬求請令還和合。或以
059c24 ‖ 乏少衣食因緣。或邪見者橫作障礙。或說
059c25 ‖ 法者欲求利養。或聽法者心不恭敬。在家
059c26 ‖ 菩薩於此事中隨宜方便。若以財物若以
059c27 ‖ 言說
```

简体字

后至死时心无有悔。经说。不悔心死必生善处。是得大利云何不舍。如是自劝犹贪惜者应辞谢乞者言。

　　我今是新学　　善根未成就
　　心未得自在　　愿后当相与

应辞谢乞者言。勿生嗔恨。我新发意善根未具。于菩萨行法未得势力。是以未能舍于此物。后得势力善根成就。心得坚固当以相与。复次。

　　若众不和合　　断于经法事
　　菩萨应随力　　方便令不绝

众僧或以事缘诤竞乖散法事有废。在家菩萨应勤心方便彼此之间心无所偏。若以财物若以言说礼敬求请令还和合。或以乏少衣食因缘。或邪见者横作障碍。或说法者欲求利养。或听法者心不恭敬。在家菩萨于此事中随宜方便。若以财物若以言说

Chapter 17 — On Entering the Temple

away. Later, when I am on the verge of death, my mind will be free of regrets. The sutras state that if one dies with a mind free of regrets, one will be reborn in a good place. This amounts to a great benefit. How then could I fail to relinquish this?

D. IF ONE IS STILL UNABLE TO RELINQUISH IT, ONE MAY POLITELY DECLINE

If, even after having exhorted oneself in this manner, one still retains a miserly cherishing for the possession, then, politely declining, he should speak to the beggar, saying:

> I am now still only new in my training.
> Hence my roots of goodness are not yet well established.
> Thus my mind has not yet achieved sovereign mastery in this.
> I hope that, later on, I will be able to give to you.

One should politely decline the beggar's entreaty, saying, "Do not become angry with me. I have only recently brought forth the resolve and my roots of goodness are not yet fully developed. Thus I have not yet gained adequate strength in the methods of the bodhisattva's practice. As a consequence I am not yet able to relinquish this possession. Later, once I have gained strength in this and my roots of goodness have become completely developed, my resolve will then be solid enough that I will be able to give it to you."

E. IF A DIVIDED SANGHA STOPS FUNCTIONING, ONE SHOULD TRY TO MEDIATE

Additionally:

> If it happens that the community, failing to abide in harmony,
> is about to suspend the Dharma activities prescribed in the sutras,
> the bodhisattva should do whatever lies within his powers
> to implement skillful means that will prevent their termination.

It could happen that, due to the circumstances associated with some matter, the monastic community becomes involved in disputes so severe that it splits into factions, thus causing its Dharma activities to be abandoned. In such a case, the lay bodhisattva should apply diligent thought to implementing some skillful method to restore the relationship between the factions, doing so with a mind free of partisan favoritism. One may use gifts of valuables, [mediating] discussion, or reverential entreaty to somehow cause the factions to become reunited.

The situation could have been caused by deficiencies in clothing or food, by someone with wrong views obstinately creating obstacles, by the speaker of Dharma seeking donations or support, or by the audience failing to be respectful. In such circumstances, the lay bodhisattva should use whichever skillful means are appropriate, perhaps doing so by contributing valuables, or perhaps doing so by speaking

正體字

059c28 ‖ 　　下意求請使法事不廢。法事不廢者。
059c28 ‖ 是為然佛法燈供養十方三世諸佛。復次。
059c29 ‖ 　　齋日受八戒　　親近淨戒者
060a01 ‖ 　　以戒善因緣　　深心行愛敬
060a02 ‖ 齋日者。月八日十四日十五日二十三日二
060a03 ‖ 十九日三十日。及遮三忌。三忌者。十五日
060a04 ‖ 為一忌。從冬至後四十五日。此諸惡日多
060a05 ‖ 有鬼神侵剋縱暴。世人為守護日故過中
060a06 ‖ 不食。佛因教令受一日戒。既得福德。諸天
060a07 ‖ 來下觀察世間見之歡喜則便護念。在家菩
060a08 ‖ 薩於諸小事猶尚增益。何況先有此齋而
060a09 ‖ 不隨順。是故應行一日齋法。既得自利亦
060a10 ‖ 能利人。問曰。齋法云何。答曰。應作是言。

简体字

下意求请使法事不废。法事不废者。是为然佛法灯供养十方三世诸佛。复次。

　　斋日受八戒　　亲近净戒者
　　以戒善因缘　　深心行爱敬

斋日者。月八日十四日十五日二十三日二十九日三十日。及遮三忌。三忌者。十五日为一忌。从冬至后四十五日。此诸恶日多有鬼神侵克纵暴。世人为守护日故过中不食。佛因教令受一日戒。既得福德。诸天来下观察世间见之欢喜则便护念。在家菩萨于诸小事犹尚增益。何况先有此斋而不随顺。是故应行一日斋法。既得自利亦能利人。问曰。斋法云何。答曰。应作是言。

to those involved with a humbled mind and sincere entreaties, thus somehow preventing their abandonment of Dharma activities.

If the abandoning of Dharma activities is prevented, this amounts to lighting the lamp of the Buddha's Dharma and making an offering to all buddhas of the ten directions and the three periods of time.

F. ON ABSTINENCE DAYS, THE LAY BODHISATTVA TAKES THE EIGHT PRECEPTS

Additionally:
> On the abstinence days, take the eight moral precepts
> and draw near to those pure in the moral precepts.
> Because of the good causes and conditions created by the precepts,
> be deeply sincere in observing them with fond regard and reverence.

As for the abstinence days, they are the eighth, the fourteenth, the fifteenth, the twenty-third, the twenty-ninth, and the thirtieth days of the lunar month. One additionally observes the three days of personal restraint. To determine these three days of personal restraint, one counts forward fifteen days for each day of restriction, starting with the winter solstice, [doing this three times] until one comes to the forty-fifth day thereafter.

On each of these inauspicious days, there are many more ghosts and spirits going about inflicting wanton violence. Because common people of the world observed these as days to be on their guard [against improper behavior], they made a practice of not eating after midday on such occasions. The Buddha took this circumstance as a basis for teaching them the practice of "the single-day precept observance," since they could thereby create merit and make the devas happy when they descended [from the heavens] to monitor the quality of people's behavior in the world. As a consequence, the devas would be inspired to be protectively mindful of those who observe this practice.

The lay bodhisattva would take even the most minor matters as bases for increasing beneficial actions. How much the more so then would he be sure to avoid failing to accord with these previously ordained days of abstinence? Therefore one should take up the practice of the single-day abstinence dharma. If one does so, one not only garners self-benefit by doing this but also thereby becomes able to benefit others.

1. Q: HOW SHOULD ONE PRACTICE THIS ABSTINENCE DHARMA?

Question: How is it that this abstinence dharma is to be observed?

2. A: SOLEMN VOW TO UPHOLD THE EIGHT PRECEPTS AS FOLLOWS:

Response: One should utter the following words:[268]

正體字	060a11 ‖ 如諸聖人常離殺生。棄捨刀[1]杖常無瞋 060a12 ‖ 恚。有慚愧心慈悲眾生。我某甲今一日一 060a13 ‖ 夜遠離殺生。棄捨刀[2]杖無有瞋恚。有慚 060a14 ‖ 愧心慈悲眾生。以如是法隨學聖人。如 060a15 ‖ 諸聖人常離不與取。身行清淨受而知足。 060a16 ‖ 我今一日一夜遠離劫盜不與取。求受清淨 060a17 ‖ 自活。以如是法隨學聖人。如諸聖人常 060a18 ‖ 斷婬[3]泆遠離世樂。我今一日一夜除斷婬 060a19 ‖ [*]泆遠離世樂淨修梵行。以如是法隨學 060a20 ‖ 聖人。如諸聖人。常離妄語。真實語正直 060a21 ‖ 語。我今一日一夜遠離妄語。真實語正直語。 060a22 ‖ 以如是法隨學聖人。如諸聖人常遠離 060a23 ‖ 酒。酒是放逸處。我今一日一夜遠離於酒。 060a24 ‖ 以如是法隨學聖人。如諸聖人常遠離歌 060a25 ‖ 舞作樂花香瓔珞嚴身之具。我今一日一夜 060a26 ‖ 遠離歌舞作樂華香瓔珞嚴身之具。以如 060a27 ‖ 是法隨學聖人。如諸聖人常遠離高廣大 060a28 ‖ 床處在小榻草蓐為座。我今一日一夜。遠 060a29 ‖ 離高廣大床。處在小榻。草蓐為座。以如是 060b01 ‖ 法隨學聖人。如諸聖人常過中不食。遠 060b02 ‖ 離非時行非時食。我今一日一夜過中不食 060b03 ‖ 遠離非時行非時食。以如是法隨學聖人。
简体字	如诸圣人常离杀生。弃舍刀杖常无嗔恚。有惭愧心慈悲众生。我某甲今一日一夜远离杀生。弃舍刀杖无有嗔恚。有惭愧心慈悲众生。以如是法随学圣人。如诸圣人常离不与取。身行清净受而知足。我今一日一夜远离劫盗不与取。求受清净自活。以如是法随学圣人。如诸圣人常断淫泆远离世乐。我今一日一夜除断淫泆远离世乐净修梵行。以如是法随学圣人。如诸圣人。常离妄语。真实语正直语。我今一日一夜远离妄语。真实语正直语。以如是法随学圣人。如诸圣人常远离酒。酒是放逸处。我今一日一夜远离于酒。以如是法随学圣人。如诸圣人常远离歌舞作乐花香璎珞严身之具。我今一日一夜远离歌舞作乐华香璎珞严身之具。以如是法随学圣人。如诸圣人常远离高广大床处在小榻草蓐为座。我今一日一夜。远离高广大床。处在小榻。草蓐为座。以如是法随学圣人。如诸圣人常过中不食。远离非时行非时食。我今一日一夜过中不食远离非时行非时食。以如是法随学圣人。

Chapter 17 — On Entering the Temple

Just as all the Āryas have forever abandoned killing, have cast aside the knife and cudgel, are always free of hatred, are possessed of a sense of shame and dread of blame, and treat beings with kindness and compassion, I, so-and-so, for one day and one night, shall also abandon killing, shall cast aside the knife and cudgel, shall remain free of hatred, shall be possessed of a sense of shame and dread of blame, and shall also treat beings with kindness and compassion, adopting this dharma in emulation of the Āryas.

Just as the Āryas have forever abandoned taking anything not given, are pure in their physical actions, and are content with whatever they receive, I now, for one day and one night, shall also abandon theft and taking what is not given, and shall pursue pure livelihood, adopting this dharma in emulation of the Āryas.

Just as the Āryas have forever cut off sexual indulgence and have abandoned such worldly pleasures, I now, for one day and one night, shall also cut off sexual indulgence, shall abandon such worldly pleasures, and shall purely cultivate celibate *brahmacarya*, adopting this dharma in emulation of the Āryas.

Just as the Āryas have forever abandoned false speech and always practice true speech and speech that is right and direct, I now, for one day and one night, shall also abandon false speech and shall also practice true speech and speech that is right and direct, adopting this dharma in emulation of the Āryas.

Just as the Āryas have forever abandoned the consumption of intoxicants,[269] this because intoxicants are the basis for falling into neglectfulness, I now, for one day and one night, shall also abandon intoxicants, adopting this dharma in emulation of the Āryas.

Just as the Āryas have forever abandoned singing, dancing, making music, wearing flowers, perfumes, necklaces, and other bodily adornments, I now, for one day and one night, shall also abandon singing, dancing, making music, wearing flowers, perfumes, necklaces, and other bodily adornments, adopting this dharma in emulation of the Āryas.

Just as the Āryas have forever abandoned the use of large high-and-wide beds, preferring instead small beds and sitting cushions made of straw, I now, for one day and one night, shall also abandon large high-and-wide beds, preferring a small bed and sitting cushions made of straw, adopting this dharma in emulation of the Āryas.

And just as the Āryas have forever abandoned meals after midday and have abandoned actions and eating done at the wrong times, I now, for one day and one night, shall also abstain from eating after midday, abandoning actions and eating done at the wrong time, adopting this dharma in emulation of the Āryas.

正體字

060b04 ‖ 如說。
060b05 ‖ 　殺盜[4]淫妄語　　飲酒及華香
060b06 ‖ 　瓔珞歌舞等　　　高床過中食
060b07 ‖ 　聖人所捨離　　　我今亦如是
060b08 ‖ 　以此福因緣　　　一切共成佛
060b09 ‖ 親近持淨戒比丘者。在家菩薩應親近諸
060b10 ‖ 比丘盡能護持清淨禁戒成就功德防遠
060b11 ‖ 眾惡者。以戒善因緣者。又應親近持戒比
060b12 ‖ 丘身口業淨心行直善無眾惡者。深心愛敬
060b13 ‖ 者於上直心善行持戒比丘成就諸功德者。
060b14 ‖ 應生最上恭敬深心愛樂。問曰。在家菩薩
060b15 ‖ 若於持戒比丘成就功德生愛敬心者。應
060b16 ‖ 於破戒比丘生輕恚心耶。答曰。
060b17 ‖ 　若見破戒者　　　不應起輕恚
060b18 ‖ 在家菩薩若見破戒雜行比丘威儀不具所
060b19 ‖ 行穢濁覆藏瑕疵無有梵行自稱梵行。

简体字

如说。
　杀盗淫妄语　　饮酒及华香
　璎珞歌舞等　　高床过中食
　圣人所舍离　　我今亦如是
　以此福因缘　　一切共成佛
亲近持净戒比丘者。在家菩萨应亲近诸比丘尽能护持清净禁戒成就功德防远众恶者。以戒善因缘者。又应亲近持戒比丘身口业净心行直善无众恶者。深心爱敬者于上直心善行持戒比丘成就诸功德者。应生最上恭敬深心爱乐。问曰。在家菩萨若于持戒比丘成就功德生爱敬心者。应于破戒比丘生轻恚心耶。答曰。
　若见破戒者　　　不应起轻恚
在家菩萨若见破戒杂行比丘威仪不具所行秽浊覆藏瑕疵无有梵行自称梵行。

Chapter 17 — *On Entering the Temple*

This is as described in the following lines:
> Killing, stealing, sexual indulgence, and lying,
> consuming intoxicants and also wearing flowers and perfumes,
> wearing necklaces, singing, dancing, and so forth,
> also high beds and eating after midday—
> These are behaviors that the Āryas have abandoned.
> Hence I too now act accordingly,
> dedicating these causes and conditions for the creation of merit
> to everyone's joint success in the attainment of buddhahood.

As for "drawing near to bhikshus pure in observing the moral precepts," the lay bodhisattva should draw near to those bhikshus who are completely able to guard and uphold the precepts of moral purity, who have thoroughly developed the meritorious qualities, and who defend against and distance themselves from the many sorts of evil.

As for "because of the good causes and conditions created by the precepts," in addition, one should draw near to bhikshus who observe the moral precepts, whose physical and verbal actions are pure, and whose mental actions are direct, good, and free of the many sorts of evil.

As for being "deeply sincere in treating them with fond regard and reverence," with respect to the above-referenced bhikshus whose minds are direct, whose actions are imbued with goodness, who uphold the moral precepts, and who have thoroughly developed the meritorious qualities, one should extend supreme reverence toward them that is accompanied by deeply sincere thoughts of fond regard.

3. Q: Should One Treat Bad Monks with Disdain and Anger?

Question: If the lay bodhisattva is to bring forth a fond and reverential attitude toward the bhikshus who uphold the moral precepts and who have thoroughly developed the meritorious qualities, should he then adopt a disdainful or angry attitude toward bhikshus who break the moral precepts?

4. A: Do Not Adopt a Disdainful or Angry Attitude toward Them

Response:
> If one encounters someone who breaks the moral precepts,
> one should not adopt a disdainful or angry attitude toward them.

Supposing that a lay bodhisattva were to encounter a bhikshu who breaks the precepts and engages in corrupt practices, whose deportment is defective, whose cultivation is defiled, who conceals his own faults, and who, while failing to observe celibate *brahmacarya*, nonetheless claims to observe celibate *brahmacarya*, even then, one should not

正體字

	於
060b20 ‖	此比丘不應輕慢有瞋恚心。問曰。若不瞋
060b21 ‖	恨應生何心。答曰。
060b22 ‖	應生憐愍心　　訶責諸煩惱
060b23 ‖	在家菩薩若見破戒比丘不應生瞋恨輕
060b24 ‖	慢應生憐愍利益之心。作是念。咄哉此人
060b25 ‖	遇佛妙法。得離地獄畜生餓鬼色無色界邊
060b26 ‖	地生處。諸根具足不聾啞不頑鈍。值佛妙
060b27 ‖	法別識好醜。心存正見解知義理。人身難
060b28 ‖	得如大海中有一眼[5]鼈頭入板孔。生在
060b29 ‖	人中倍難於此。既聞佛法能滅諸惡度諸
060c01 ‖	苦惱得至正智。捨諸資生所有多少。永割
060c02 ‖	親族無所顧戀。若生凡庶或在種姓。信
060c03 ‖	佛語故能捨出家。常聞破戒之罪。所謂自
060c04 ‖	賤其身智所訶責。惡名流布常懷疑悔。死
060c05 ‖	墮

简体字

于此比丘不应轻慢有嗔恚心。问曰。若不嗔恨应生何心。答曰。

　应生怜愍心　　诃责诸烦恼

在家菩萨若见破戒比丘不应生嗔恨轻慢应生怜愍利益之心。作是念。咄哉此人遇佛妙法。得离地狱畜生饿鬼色无色界边地生处。诸根具足不聋哑不顽钝。值佛妙法别识好丑。心存正见解知义理。人身难得如大海中有一眼鳖头入板孔。生在人中倍难于此。既闻佛法能灭诸恶度诸苦恼得至正智。舍诸资生所有多少。永割亲族无所顾恋。若生凡庶或在种姓。信佛语故能舍出家。常闻破戒之罪。所谓自贱其身智所诃责。恶名流布常怀疑悔。死堕

behave toward this bhikshu with slighting disdainfulness or angry thoughts.

> 5. Q: If Hatred Is Wrong, What Attitude Is Most Appropriate?

Question: If one is to refrain from feeling hatred toward him, then just what sort of attitude should one adopt?

> 6. A: Feel Pity for Him and Condemn His Afflictions Instead

Response:
> One should bring forth thoughts of pity toward him,
> making it the afflictions themselves that one condemns.

If a lay bodhisattva encounters a precept-breaking bhikshu, he should not feel hatred or adopt a slighting and disdainful attitude toward him. Rather he should feel pity for him and think of ways to benefit him, reflecting:

> How terrible! This man has been able to encounter the sublime Dharma of the Buddha. He has succeeded in leaving behind the destinies of hell-dwellers, animals, hungry ghosts, form and formless-realm devas, and those reborn in borderlands [distant from Dharma]. Being complete in his faculties and hence neither deaf, dumb, or dim-witted, he has encountered the sublime Dharma of the Buddha through which one may distinguish what is good from what is disgraceful and through which one's mind may still retain right views and understand what is meaningfully principled.
>
> This human body is so difficult to come by. It is just as in the case of the one-eyed tortoise out on the great sea who, emerging from the depths, happens by chance to poke his head up through a knothole in a floating plank. Even when compared to the rarity of this, the opportunity to gain a human rebirth is doubly difficult to acquire.
>
> Having heard the Dharma of the Buddha through which one can extinguish all forms of evil, become liberated from all suffering and afflictions, and succeed in reaching right wisdom, one relinquishes all of one's life-supporting possessions however extensive they may be and then severs forever one's relations with one's relatives and clan, having no one for whom one retains any further sentimental attachment. Regardless of whether one is from the common classes or from an elevated caste, because one has faith in the Buddha's words, one is able to leave behind the home life.
>
> One constantly hears of the moral transgressions associated with breaking the moral precepts, of the associated self-loathing, of becoming someone rebuked and censured by the wise, of coming to have a bad reputation that circulates widely, and of being constantly beset by doubts and regrets. Then, at death, one is bound to

正體字	惡道得聞此事而猶破戒。行十善道 060c06 ‖ 乃得人身。而不能如法善用以自利益。咄 060c07 ‖ 哉三毒其力甚惡。常[6]陵眾生難得捨離。諸 060c08 ‖ 佛種種呵罵煩惱惡賊惡行如實有理。如 060c09 ‖ 是思惟不應輕賤破戒之人。又作是念。若 060c10 ‖ 我不能都離瞋恚輕慢心者。應自思惟。佛 060c11 ‖ 法無量猶如大海。或有開通而我不知。如 060c12 ‖ 大乘決定王經中。佛告阿難。或有比丘。根 060c13 ‖ 鈍闇塞心不明了。不達諸法相。常念有想 060c14 ‖ 無想法中而取有想。生男女想生罪礙 060c15 ‖ 想生垢想[7]生淨想。生如是想者。名為 060c16 ‖ 鈍根。心不明了則為有罪。阿難。若人一切 060c17 ‖ 法中不能善解名為不了。一切諸法從初 060c18 ‖ 以來。本體性相常不可得。是人不知如是 060c19 ‖ 之事。生是諸想則與外道無有差別。
简体字	恶道得闻此事而犹破戒。行十善道乃得人身。而不能如法善用以自利益。咄哉三毒其力甚恶。常陵众生难得舍离。诸佛种种呵骂烦恼恶贼恶行如实有理。如是思惟不应轻贱破戒之人。又作是念。若我不能都离嗔恚轻慢心者。应自思惟。佛法无量犹如大海。或有开通而我不知。如大乘决定王经中。佛告阿难。或有比丘。根钝闇塞心不明了。不达诸法相。常念有想无想法中而取有想。生男女想生罪碍想生垢想生净想。生如是想者。名为钝根。心不明了则为有罪。阿难。若人一切法中不能善解名为不了。一切诸法从初以来。本体性相常不可得。是人不知如是之事。生是诸想则与外道无有差别。

Chapter 17 — *On Entering the Temple*

plummet into the wretched destinies. Even having heard of these circumstances, one nonetheless still persists in breaking the moral precepts.

It is through practice of the ten courses of good karmic action that one then gains a human rebirth. Even so, one remains unable to put them to skillful use in accordance with Dharma so as to secure his own self-benefit.

What a shame! The power of the three poisons is so extremely terrible that they constantly assail beings and remain difficult to successfully abandon.

In all sorts of ways, the Buddhas rebuke the evil actions caused by the evil bandits of the afflictions.

If, in accordance with reality and in a principled fashion, one contemplates the matter in this way, [one realizes] one should not slight and disdain those people who have broken the moral precepts. One also reflects as follows:

If I am not completely able to abandon thoughts of anger and condescending disdain, I should consider that, given that the Dharma of the Buddha is as vast as a great sea, it could be that there are exceptional circumstances of which I am unaware.

This accords with the passage in the Mahāyāna's *Sutra of the Resolute King* wherein it is recorded that the Buddha told Ānanda:[270]

It could be that there are bhikshus of dull faculties who are obstructed by their mental dimness, whose minds are not completely clear, and who do not possess a penetrating comprehension of the true character of dharmas. They may forever be bearing in mind dharmas associated with the perception of existence or with the perception of nonexistence whereupon they then seize on perceptions of existence whereby they produce perceptions of male versus female, produce perceptions of obstacles associated with transgressions, produce perceptions of defilement, or produce perceptions of purity.

The production of these sorts of perceptions is a function of dull faculties. If someone's mind is not completely clear, then he is bound to commit transgressions. Ānanda, if, within the sphere of all dharmas, someone remains unable to well understand their character, then this is a case of failing to completely comprehend them.

From the very beginning on forward to the present, there has never been any fundamental substance, nature, or characteristic of any dharma that could be apprehended. This sort of person fails to realize such things. When one produces perceptions such as these, then he becomes indistinguishable from the followers of non-Buddhist traditions.

正體字	阿 060c20 ‖ 難。我所說法皆有開通明了清淨。此中無 060c21 ‖ 罪亦無罪者。阿難。罪名疑悔愚癡闇冥。罪 060c22 ‖ 者名生眾生想我想命想人想。皆因身見 060c23 ‖ 名為罪者。於我法中無如此人。若我法中 060c24 ‖ 定實有我眾生命人身見等者。不言我法 060c25 ‖ 有開非是不開。我法從本已來常清淨明 060c26 ‖ 了。復次阿難。若決定有罪有[8]受罪者則身 060c27 ‖ 即是神即墮常見則無佛道。若身異於神 060c28 ‖ 即墮斷見亦無佛道。如是六十二見皆可 060c29 ‖ 是菩提但是事不然。是故阿難。我於大眾 061a01 ‖ 中師子吼說而無所畏言。我法有開非不 061a02 ‖ 有開。從本[1]已來常清淨明了。阿難。若罪定 061a03 ‖ 有。則畢竟無涅槃。我則不言我法有開。阿 061a04 ‖ 難。我法實從本[*]已來清淨明了。
简体字	阿难。我所说法皆有开通明了清净。此中无罪亦无罪者。阿难。罪名疑悔愚痴闇冥。罪者名生众生想我想命想人想。皆因身见名为罪者。于我法中无如此人。若我法中定实有我众生命人身见等者。不言我法有开非是不开。我法从本已来常清净明了。复次阿难。若决定有罪有受罪者则身即是神即堕常见则无佛道。若身异于神即堕断见亦无佛道。如是六十二见皆可是菩提但是事不然。是故阿难。我于大众中师子吼说而无所畏言。我法有开非不有开。从本已来常清净明了。阿难。若罪定有。则毕竟无涅槃。我则不言我法有开。阿难。我法实从本已来清净明了。

Chapter 17 — On Entering the Temple 517

Ānanda, within all the dharmas I have explained, there are exceptional circumstances that are consistent with complete clarity and purity. In these circumstances, there is no such thing as a "transgression" or a "transgressor."

Ānanda, the commission of transgressions is characterized by the existence of doubts and regrets, by stupidity, and by benightedness. The commission of transgressions involves the production of perceptions of the existence of a being, perceptions of the existence of a self, perceptions of the existence of a living entity, or perceptions of the existence of a person. In all cases, it is because of the fallacious view that a "self" exists in association with the body that one speaks of some "transgressor." But, within my Dharma, no such "person" exists at all.

If it were the case that, within my Dharma, there was some fixed and genuinely-existent self, being, living entity, person, body-associated self, or other such thing, I would not declare that, within my Dharma, there are exceptional circumstances and it is not the case that there are no such exceptional circumstances. From the beginning on through to the present, my Dharma has always been pure and completely clear.

Furthermore, Ānanda, if it were definitely the case that transgressions existed and that there was some being who takes on those transgressions, then it would be the case that the body is identical with some "soul." But [positing any such view] would amount to falling into the eternalist fallacy by the dictates of which no path to buddhahood could even exist.

Then again, if the body were distinct from some "soul," then [positing any such view] would amount to falling into an annihilationist view. In that case too, no path to buddhahood could exist. In much the same manner, all of the sixty-two false views might be posited as consistent with bodhi, but these cases are all wrong.

Therefore, Ānanda, in the midst of the Great Assembly, I roar the lion's roar and, possessed of the fearlessnesses, declare that within my Dharma, there are exceptional circumstances and it is not the case that there are no such exceptional circumstances. From its very origin on through to the present, it has always been pure and completely clear.

Ānanda, if moral transgressions had any sort of definite existence, then there could never be any nirvāṇa. If that were so, then I would not state that, within of my Dharma, there may be exceptional circumstances.

Ānanda, in truth, my Dharma has been pure and completely radiant from its very inception on forward to the present. Consequently

正體字	是故我弟 061a05 ‖ 子降心安隱無有疑悔。無諸罪惡清淨行 061a06 ‖ 道。菩薩應如是思惟不應瞋恚破戒者。又 061a07 ‖ 作是念。是戒必定得住阿耨多羅三藐三菩 061a08 ‖ 提。何以故。曾聞必定菩薩有起罪者。如過 061a09 ‖ 去十萬劫。有菩薩誹謗漏盡阿羅漢。名為 061a10 ‖ 阿羅漢。又聞必定菩薩於此劫前三十一劫。 061a11 ‖ 以[2]矛刺須陀洹。又此賢劫中。聞有菩薩 061a12 ‖ 誹謗[3]劬樓孫佛言何有禿人而當得道。 061a13 ‖ 如是等眾生難可得知。是故我於此事何 061a14 ‖ 用知為。得失好惡彼自作自受何[4]豫於我。 061a15 ‖ 我今若欲實知彼事。或自傷害籌量眾生。 061a16 ‖ 佛所不許。如經中說。佛告阿難。若人籌量 061a17 ‖ 於他即自傷身。唯我可得籌量。眾生與我 061a18 ‖ 等者亦應籌量。如說。 061a19 ‖ 　有瓶蓋亦空　　無蓋亦復空 061a20 ‖ 　有瓶蓋亦滿　　無蓋亦復滿
简体字	是故我弟子降心安隐无有疑悔。无诸罪恶清净行道。菩萨应如是思惟不应嗔恚破戒者。又作是念。是戒必定得住阿耨多罗三藐三菩提。何以故。曾闻必定菩萨有起罪者。如过去十万劫。有菩萨诽谤漏尽阿罗汉。名为阿罗汉。又闻必定菩萨于此劫前三十一劫。以矛刺须陀洹。又此贤劫中。闻有菩萨诽谤劬楼孙佛言何有秃人而当得道。如是等众生难可得知。是故我于此事何用知为。得失好恶彼自作自受何豫于我。我今若欲实知彼事。或自伤害筹量众生。佛所不许。如经中说。佛告阿难。若人筹量于他即自伤身。唯我可得筹量。众生与我等者亦应筹量。如说。 　有瓶盖亦空　　无盖亦复空 　有瓶盖亦满　　无盖亦复满

Chapter 17 — On Entering the Temple

my disciples are able to subdue their minds so that they are stable and free of doubts and regrets. They become free of the evil of moral transgressions and become pure in their practice of the path.

Having reflected in this manner, the bodhisattva should refrain from maintaining a hostile attitude toward those who break the moral precepts. He should also reason in this manner:

> Those who have taken on these precepts will definitely succeed in coming to abide in *anuttarasamyaksaṃbodhi*. How is this so? I have heard that even bodhisattvas who have reached the right and definite position (*samyaktva niyāma*) still have had occasions on which they have committed moral transgressions. Take for instance that case from one hundred thousand kalpas ago when a bodhisattva slandered an arhat who had already extinguished all contaminants, saying of him that he was an arhat in name only.
>
> I have also heard of that bodhisattva thirty-one kalpas prior to the present one who, although he had already reached the right and definite position, nonetheless stabbed a stream enterer with a spear. Additionally, I have heard of that case during this current Auspicious Kalpa where a bodhisattva slandered Krakucchanda Buddha,[271] saying to him, "How could one of you bald pates ever succeed in attaining buddhahood?"
>
> It would be hard to understand [the actual circumstances of] beings such as these. Hence, what would be the use in my knowing in this situation what constitutes gain versus loss or right versus wrong? They will each individually undergo the consequences of what they have each individually done. How is that any of my business? If I wish to pursue actual knowledge of their circumstances, it could result in injury to myself through my making judgments regarding other beings. This is the sort of thing that the Buddha himself would not permit.

This accords with the testimony of the sutras wherein it states, "The Buddha told Ānanda, 'If a person makes judgmental assessments regarding others, he will thereby bring injury on himself. It is I alone who can make such assessments. [Only] beings who are my equal may also make such assessments.'"[272] This is as described in the following lines:[273]

> A covered pitcher may still be empty
> while an uncovered pitcher may be empty as well.
> Other covered pitchers may themselves be full
> as, so too, may uncovered pitchers be full.

正體字	061a21 ‖ 當知諸世間　有此四種人 061a22 ‖ 威儀及功德　有無亦如是 061a23 ‖ 若非一切智　何能籌量人 061a24 ‖ 寧以見威儀　而便知其德 061a25 ‖ 正智有善心　名為賢人相 061a26 ‖ 但見外威儀　何由知其內 061a27 ‖ 內有功德慧　外現無[5]威儀 061a28 ‖ 遊行無知者　如以灰覆火 061a29 ‖ 若以外量內　而生輕賤心 061b01 ‖ 敗身及善根　命終墮惡道 061b02 ‖ 外詐現威儀　遊行似賢聖 061b03 ‖ 但有口言說　如雷而無雨 061b04 ‖ 諸心所行處　錯謬難得知 061b05 ‖ 是故諸眾生　不可妄度量 061b06 ‖ 唯有一切智　悉知諸心心 061b07 ‖ 微[6]密所行處　是故量眾生 061b08 ‖ 佛言與我等　乃能量眾生 061b09 ‖ 若佛如是說　誰能籌量人 061b10 ‖ 若見外威儀　稱量其內德 061b11 ‖ 自敗其善根　如水自崩岸
简体字	当知诸世间　有此四种人 威仪及功德　有无亦如是 若非一切智　何能筹量人 宁以见威仪　而便知其德 正智有善心　名为贤人相 但见外威仪　何由知其内 内有功德慧　外现无威仪 游行无知者　如以灰覆火 若以外量内　而生轻贱心 败身及善根　命终堕恶道 外诈现威仪　游行似贤圣 但有口言说　如雷而无雨 诸心所行处　错谬难得知 是故诸众生　不可妄度量 唯有一切智　悉知诸心心 微密所行处　是故量众生 佛言与我等　乃能量众生 若佛如是说　谁能筹量人 若见外威仪　称量其内德 自败其善根　如水自崩岸

Chapter 17 — On Entering the Temple

One should realize that, throughout the world,
there are these four different types of people.
Matters of awesome deportment and possession of merit,
whether existent or not, are very much the same as this.

If one is not possessed of all-knowledge,
how could one make judgments about others?
How could one merely observe another's deportment
and yet then know the level of their virtue?

It is right wisdom and the possession of a wholesome mind
that define the characteristic qualities of a worthy person.
By merely observing someone's outward deportment,
how could one know what lies within?

There are those who, inwardly, possess merit and wisdom,
even as, outwardly, they reveal no awesome deportment.
As they wander about, there is no one who recognizes them.
In this, they are like hot coals hidden by ashes.

If one assesses inward qualities on the basis of externals
and hence develops an attitude of slighting condescension,
one brings ruin on oneself as well as on one's own roots of goodness
so that, at the end of one's life, one falls into the wretched destinies.

Those displaying outward pretenses of awesome deportment
and parading about as if they were worthies or *āryas*
even as they only possess impressive rhetoric
are like the sounds of thunder that fail to bring rain.

As for the places to which someone else's mind proceeds,
one may be mistaken about them, for they are hard to know.
Therefore one must not make false assessments
with regard to any being.

It is only someone possessed of all-knowledge
who can fully know their minds' mind states
and the subtle and secret places to which they may proceed.
Hence, with regard to judging other beings,

the Buddha said, "It is only those who are my equals
who can pass judgment on other beings."
If the Buddha himself spoke in this manner,
who then could have the ability to pass judgment on others?

If one merely observes someone's outward deportment
and thereby presumes to assess his inner virtue,
one will ruin one's own roots of goodness
just as a flooding river may collapse its own banks.

正體字

061b12 ‖　　若於此錯謬　　則起大業障
061b13 ‖　　是故於此人　　不應起輕賤
061b14 ‖ 是故在家菩薩不應於破戒人起輕慢瞋
061b15 ‖ 恚。又持戒破戒白衣之人不與同住。何由得
061b16 ‖ 知。我若欲於此事分別明了者則起罪障。
061b17 ‖ 罪障因緣故於千萬劫受諸苦分。如無行
061b18 ‖ 經中說。又大乘經中。佛告郁伽羅長者。如
061b19 ‖ 是在家菩薩應於破戒比丘生憐愍心。是
061b20 ‖ 人垢行惡行不善。何以故。是人[7]披如來善
061b21 ‖ 寂滅聖主法衣。自不善軟不能調伏諸根
061b22 ‖ 行敗壞行。又佛經中說。不輕未學。此非人
061b23 ‖ 罪是煩惱罪。此人以是煩惱起不善事。又
061b24 ‖ 佛法有開。是人或能自除過罪。正念因緣得
061b25 ‖ 入法位。若入必定在於阿耨多羅三藐三
061b26 ‖ 菩提。又如佛言。唯有智慧可破煩惱。又復
061b27 ‖ 說言。不應妄稱量人。若稱量者則為自傷。
061b28 ‖ 唯佛智慧乃能明了。

简体字

　　若于此错谬　　则起大业障
　　是故于此人　　不应起轻贱

　　是故在家菩萨不应于破戒人起轻慢瞋恚。又持戒破戒白衣之人不与同住。何由得知。我若欲于此事分别明了者则起罪障。罪障因缘故于千万劫受诸苦分。如无行经中说。又大乘经中。佛告郁伽罗长者。如是在家菩萨应于破戒比丘生怜愍心。是人垢行恶行不善。何以故。是人披如来善寂灭圣主法衣。自不善软不能调伏诸根行败坏行。又佛经中说。不轻未学。此非人罪是烦恼罪。此人以是烦恼起不善事。又佛法有开。是人或能自除过罪。正念因缘得入法位。若入必定在于阿耨多罗三藐三菩提。又如佛言。唯有智慧可破烦恼。又复说言。不应妄称量人。若称量者则为自伤。唯佛智慧乃能明了。

Chapter 17 — On Entering the Temple

If one is mistaken about such things,
one creates immense karmic obstacles.
Therefore, with regard to these people,
one should not bring forth an attitude of slighting disdain.

Therefore the lay bodhisattva should refrain from adopting an attitude of slighting arrogance or anger toward those who may have broken the moral precepts. What's more, regarding this matter of upholding the moral precepts or breaking the moral precepts, a layperson does not dwell together with these people. What basis then might he have for acquiring knowledge of such matters?

[One should reflect], "If I strive to make such clear distinctions with regard to these matters, then I am bound to create the obstacle of transgressions and, because of such karmic obstacles, I shall be bound to undergo every sort of suffering for thousands of myriads of kalpas." This is as stated in *Sutra on the Inaction of Dharmas*.[274]

Additionally, in a Mahāyāna sutra,[275] the Buddha told Ugra, the Elder, "Thus the lay bodhisattva should feel pity for any bhikshu who has broken the precepts, [reflecting as follows]: 'This man's defilement is such that he engages in what is evil and engages in what is unwholesome. Why? This man has donned the Dharma robes of the Tathāgata, the well-extinguished lord of the Āryas, yet he has not made his mind pliant and has not been able to subdue his sense faculties. Hence he engages in such self-destructive conduct.'"

Moreover, one of the Buddha's sutras states, "One does not slight those who have not yet become accomplished in learning. These are not a person's moral transgressions so much as they are transgressions committed at the behest of the afflictions themselves. It is because of these afflictions that this person has engaged in such unwholesome behavior."

Also, within the Buddha's Dharma, there are exceptional circumstances. This person may actually be able to rid himself of these moral transgressions. Then, with right mindfulness as the cause and condition, he may be able to enter the Dharma position. If he does indeed gain entry to the right and definite position, then he will eventually abide in *anuttarasamyaksaṃbodhi*.

Then again, as stated by the Buddha himself, "It is only through the possession of wisdom that one can then defeat the afflictions." He additionally stated, "One should not make false assessments of others. If one makes such assessments, he thereby wreaks injury on himself. It is only one in possession of the wisdom of a buddha who is able to completely understand these matters." [Hence one should reflect],

正體字

```
                如此事者非我所知。
061b29 ‖ 即於破戒人中不生瞋恚輕慢之心。復次。
061c01 ‖    菩薩若入寺    應行諸威儀
061c02 ‖    恭敬而禮拜    供養諸比丘
061c03 ‖ 是在家菩薩若入佛寺。初欲入時於寺門
061c04 ‖ 外五體投地。應作是念。此是善人住處。是
061c05 ‖ 空行者住處。無[8]想行者住處。無願行者住
061c06 ‖ 處。此是行慈悲喜捨者住處。此是正行正念
061c07 ‖ 者住處。若見諸比丘威儀具足視瞻安詳攝
061c08 ‖ 持衣鉢坐臥行止寤寐[9]飲食言說寂默容儀
061c09 ‖ 進止皆可觀察。若見比丘修行四念聖所行
061c10 ‖ 處持戒清淨誦讀經法精思坐禪。見已恭肅
061c11 ‖ 敬心禮拜親近問訊。應作是念。
061c12 ‖    若我恒沙劫    常於天[10]祠中
061c13 ‖    大施不休廢    不如一出家
061c14 ‖ 是菩薩爾時應作是念[11]我如法求財。於恒
061c15 ‖ 河沙等劫常行大施。是諸施福猶尚不如
061c16 ‖ 發心出家。
```

简体字

如此事者非我所知。即于破戒人中不生嗔恚轻慢之心。复次。

　　菩萨若入寺　　应行诸威仪
　　恭敬而礼拜　　供养诸比丘

是在家菩萨若入佛寺。初欲入时于寺门外五体投地。应作是念。此是善人住处。是空行者住处。无想行者住处。无愿行者住处。此是行慈悲喜舍者住处。此是正行正念者住处。若见诸比丘威仪具足视瞻安详摄持衣钵坐卧行止寤寐饮食言说寂默容仪进止皆可观察。若见比丘修行四念圣所行处持戒清净诵读经法精思坐禅。见已恭肃敬心礼拜亲近问讯。应作是念。

　　若我恒沙劫　　常于天祠中
　　大施不休废　　不如一出家

是菩萨尔时应作是念我如法求财。于恒河沙等劫常行大施。是诸施福犹尚不如发心出家。

"Matters of this sort are not such as I can know." One should then refrain from adopting an angry and condescending attitude toward those who may have broken the precepts.
Moreover:

G. ON ENTERING A TEMPLE, ONE SHOULD BE RESPECTFUL AND MAKE OFFERINGS

When a bodhisattva enters a temple,
he should observe all the protocols of deportment,
should act respectfully and bow down in reverence,
and should make an offering to the bhikshus.

When this lay bodhisattva is about to enter a Buddhist temple, right before entering, he should bow down outside the temple door in a five-point prostration and should then reflect, "This is the dwelling place of good people. It is the dwelling place of those who practice emptiness, the dwelling place of those who practice signlessness,[276] the dwelling place of those who practice wishlessness, the dwelling place of those who practice kindness, compassion, sympathetic joy, and equanimity,[277] and it is the dwelling place of those who practice in right conduct and right mindfulness."

If one encounters bhikshus perfect in deportment, serene in gaze, and restrained in wearing the robe and holding the bowl, bhikshus who bear observation in the way they sit, lie down, walk, stand, awaken, retire, drink, eat, speak, and remain silent, bhikshus who also bear observation in the appearance of their countenance and in their going forth and coming to a halt—if one encounters bhikshus who cultivate the four stations of mindfulness practiced by the Āryas, who uphold the moral precepts purely, who recite and study the Dharma of the sutras, and who are refined in their contemplations and devoted to sitting in *dhyāna* meditation—having observed them, with respectful solemnity and reverential mind, one should bow down in reverence to them. Then, drawing nearer, one should greet them and reflect thus:

H. ONE SHOULD REFLECT ON THE MERIT OF BECOMING A MONASTIC

Even were I for kalpas in number as a Ganges' sands
to always perform great acts of giving at the shrines of the devas
and never cease or neglect this practice,
that would still not compare to becoming a monk but a single time.

This bodhisattva should then reflect:

If, in pursuing wealth in accordance with the Dharma, I were to always perform great acts of giving for a number of kalpas equal to the sands in the Ganges, all the merit derived from that giving would still not even equal that from merely generating the resolve to leave

正體字	何況有實。何以故。在家則有無 061c17 ‖ 量過惡。出家能成無量功德。在家則[12]潰鬧。 061c18 ‖ 出家則閑靜。在家則屬垢。出家則無屬。在 061c19 ‖ 家是惡行處。出家是善行處。在家則染諸塵 061c20 ‖ 垢。出家則離諸塵垢。在家則沒五欲泥。出 061c21 ‖ 家則出五欲泥。在家難得淨命。出家易得 061c22 ‖ 淨命。在家則多怨賊。出家則無怨賊。在家 061c23 ‖ 則多惱礙。出家則無惱礙。在家是憂處。出 061c24 ‖ 家是喜處。在家是惡道門。出家是利益門。在 061c25 ‖ 家是繫縛。出家是解脫。在家則雜畏。出家則 061c26 ‖ 無畏。在家有鞭杖。出家無鞭杖。在家有刀 061c27 ‖ 稍。出家無刀稍。在家有悔熱。出家無悔熱。 061c28 ‖ 在家多求故苦。出家無求故樂。在家則戲調。 061c29 ‖ 出家則寂滅。
简体字	何况有实。何以故。在家则有无量过恶。出家能成无量功德。在家则溃闹。出家则闲静。在家则属垢。出家则无属。在家是恶行处。出家是善行处。在家则染诸尘垢。出家则离诸尘垢。在家则没五欲泥。出家则出五欲泥。在家难得净命。出家易得净命。在家则多怨贼。出家则无怨贼。在家则多恼碍。出家则无恼碍。在家是忧处。出家是喜处。在家是恶道门。出家是利益门。在家是系缚。出家是解脱。在家则杂畏。出家则无畏。在家有鞭杖。出家无鞭杖。在家有刀槊。出家无刀槊。在家有悔热。出家无悔热。在家多求故苦。出家无求故乐。在家则戏调。出家则寂灭。

Chapter 17 — On Entering the Temple

behind the householder's life, how much the less could it equal the merit of actually doing so?

How could this be so? [This is so because]:

I. NINETY-NINE REFLECTIONS ON THE ADVANTAGES OF MONASTIC LIFE

The householder's life is possessed of countless serious faults whereas a monastic can perfect countless meritorious qualities.

The householder's life is overrun with confusion and disturbance whereas the monastic's life is carefree and serene.

The householder's life belongs to the sphere of defilement whereas the monastic's life has nothing to which it belongs.

The household is the place for committing bad actions whereas the monastic life is the place for good actions.

If one pursues the householder's life, then one becomes stained by all manner of defilement whereas the monastic abandons every sort of defilement.

The householder becomes mired in the mud of the five types of desire whereas the monastic abandons the five types of desire.

For the householder, it is difficult to pursue a pure livelihood whereas it is easy for a monastic to pursue right livelihood.

The householder is subject to the incursions of many adversaries whereas the monastic is free of incursions by adversaries.

The householder is encumbered by many troublesome obstructions whereas the monastic remains free of troublesome obstructions.

The household is the place beset by sorrows whereas the monastic life is the place of joyfulness.

The household is the gateway to the wretched destinies whereas the monastic life is the gateway to benefit.

The household life is one of bondage whereas the monastic's life is one of liberation.

The householder is subject to various forms of fear whereas the monastic is free of fear.

The householder possesses whips and cudgels whereas the monastic has no whips or cudgels.

The householder owns a sword and spear whereas the monastic has no swords or spears.

The householder is subject to the heat of regretfulness whereas the monastic is free of the heat of regretfulness.

Because the householder seeks many things, he is subject to sufferings whereas the monastic is happy because he seeks nothing.

The householder tends toward frivolous agitation whereas the monastic is bound for tranquility.

正體字	在家是可愍。出家無可愍。在 062a01 ‖ 家則愁悴。出家無愁悴。在家則卑下。出家則 062a02 ‖ 高顯。在家則熾然。出家則寂滅。在家則為 062a03 ‖ 他。出家則自為。在家少勢力。出家多勢力。 062a04 ‖ 在家隨順垢門。出家隨順淨門。在家增刺 062a05 ‖ 棘。出家破刺棘。在家成就小法。出家成就 062a06 ‖ 大法。在家作不善。出家則修善。在家則有 062a07 ‖ 悔。出家則無悔。在家增淚乳血海。出家竭 062a08 ‖ 淚乳血海。在家則為諸佛辟支佛聲聞所呵 062a09 ‖ 賤。出家則為諸佛辟支佛聲聞所稱歎。在 062a10 ‖ 家則不知足。出家則知足。在家則魔喜。出 062a11 ‖ 家則魔憂。在家後有衰。出家後無衰。在家 062a12 ‖ 則易破。出家則難破。在家是奴僕。出家則 062a13 ‖ 為主。在家永在生死。出家究竟涅槃。在家 062a14 ‖ 則墮坑。出家則出坑。在家則黑闇。出家則 062a15 ‖ 明顯。
简体字	在家是可愍。出家无可愍。在家则愁悴。出家无愁悴。在家则卑下。出家则高显。在家则炽然。出家则寂灭。在家则为他。出家则自为。在家少势力。出家多势力。在家随顺垢门。出家随顺净门。在家增刺棘。出家破刺棘。在家成就小法。出家成就大法。在家作不善。出家则修善。在家则有悔。出家则无悔。在家增泪乳血海。出家竭泪乳血海。在家则为诸佛辟支佛声闻所呵贱。出家则为诸佛辟支佛声闻所称叹。在家则不知足。出家则知足。在家则魔喜。出家则魔忧。在家后有衰。出家后无衰。在家则易破。出家则难破。在家是奴仆。出家则为主。在家永在生死。出家究竟涅槃。在家则堕坑。出家则出坑。在家则黑闇。出家则明显。

The householder is worthy of pity whereas the monastic has nothing for which he could be pitied.

The householder is subject to worry and sorrow whereas the monastic is free of worry and sorrow.

The householder is of lowly social station whereas the monastic is one who is lofty and prominent.

The householder is burning up with a raging fire whereas the monastic extinguishes it.

The householder's life is lived for others whereas the monastic is able to act in his own self-interest.

The householder has but little power whereas the monastic has abundant power.

The householder enters the gateway of defilement whereas the monastic enters the gateway to purity.

The householder grows an ever larger thicket of thorns whereas the monastic crushes the thicket of thorns.

The householder achieves success in lesser dharmas whereas the monastic achieves success in the great Dharma.

The householder engages in what is unwholesome whereas the monastic cultivates what is good.

The householder is bound to have regrets whereas the monastic is bound to become free of regrets.

The householder fills up an ocean of tears, milk, and blood whereas the monastic dries up the ocean of tears, milk, and blood.[278]

The household life is censured and considered base by buddhas, *pratyekabuddhas*, and *śrāvaka* disciples whereas the monastic life is praised by buddhas, *pratyekabuddhas*, and *śrāvaka* disciples.

The householder tends to be discontented whereas the monastic tends to be easily contented.

The householder causes Māra to be delighted whereas the monastic causes Māra to feel sorrowful.

The householder is bound for later ruination whereas the monastic is bound to become free of ruination.

The householder is one who is easy to defeat whereas the monastic is one who is difficult to defeat.

The householder is like a slave whereas the monastic is like a lord.

The householder is bound to remain forever in *saṃsāra* whereas the monastic will ultimately reach nirvāṇa.

The householder has fallen into a pit whereas the monastic has escaped from a pit.

The householder abides in darkness whereas the monastic emerges into bright light.

正體字

	在家不能降伏諸根。出家則能降伏
062a16 ‖	諸根。在家則傲誕。出家則謙遜。在家則鄙陋。
062a17 ‖	出家則尊貴。在家有所由。出家無所由。在
062a18 ‖	家則多務。出家則小務。在家則[1]果小。出家
062a19 ‖	則果大。在家則諂曲。出家則質直。在家則多
062a20 ‖	憂。出家則多喜。在家如箭在身。出家如身
062a21 ‖	離箭。在家則有病。出家則病愈。在家行惡
062a22 ‖	法故速老。出家行善法故少壯。在家放逸
062a23 ‖	為死。出家有智慧命。在家則欺誑。出家則
062a24 ‖	真實。在家則多求。出家則少求。在家則飲雜
062a25 ‖	毒漿。出家則飲甘露漿。在家多侵害。出家
062a26 ‖	無侵害。在家則衰耗。出家無衰耗。在家如
062a27 ‖	毒樹果。出家如甘露果。在家則怨憎和合。出
062a28 ‖	家則離怨憎會苦。

简体字

在家不能降伏诸根。出家则能降伏诸根。在家则傲诞。出家则谦逊。在家则鄙陋。出家则尊贵。在家有所由。出家无所由。在家则多务。出家则小务。在家则果小。出家则果大。在家则谄曲。出家则质直。在家则多忧。出家则多喜。在家如箭在身。出家如身离箭。在家则有病。出家则病愈。在家行恶法故速老。出家行善法故少壮。在家放逸为死。出家有智慧命。在家则欺诳。出家则真实。在家则多求。出家则少求。在家则饮杂毒浆。出家则饮甘露浆。在家多侵害。出家无侵害。在家则衰耗。出家无衰耗。在家如毒树果。出家如甘露果。在家则怨憎和合。出家则离怨憎会苦。

The householder remains unable to subdue his own sense faculties whereas the monastic is able to subdue his sense faculties.

The householder tends toward haughtiness and grandiosity whereas the monastic abides in humility and modesty.

The householder's life tends toward what is coarse and inferior whereas the monastic's life is one of venerable nobility.

The householder has origins from which he comes whereas the monastic has no origins from which he comes.[279]

The householder has many duties whereas the monastic has but few duties.

The householder attains only minor karmic fruits whereas the monastic is bound to attain great karmic fruits.

The householder tends to fall into flattery and deviousness whereas the monastic cultivates a straightforward character.

The householder has an abundance of sorrows whereas the monastic has an abundance of joy.

The householder's life is like being shot with an arrow whereas the monastic's life is like [being able to] extricate that arrow.

The household life is like being afflicted with a sickness whereas the monastic life is like becoming cured of that sickness.

Because the householder practices dharmas associated with evil, he ages swiftly whereas, because the monastic practices good dharmas, he tends to be youthful and strong.

The householder courses in neglectfulness synonymous with death whereas the monastic possesses the life of wisdom.

The householder tends to indulge in deception whereas the monastic behaves in a manner that is genuine.

The householder has many things for which he seeks whereas the monastic seeks but few things.

The householder sips a broth mixed with poisons whereas the monastic drinks the elixir of immortality.[280]

The householder suffers harm from numerous external encroachments whereas the monastic is free of any such harms brought about by external encroachments.[281]

The householder is bound for a ruinous decline whereas the monastic has no such ruinous decline.

The householder's life is like fruit from a poisonous tree whereas the monastic's life is like fruits suffused with sweet-dew nectar.

The householder is bound to remain associated with whatever he detests whereas the monastic abandons the suffering of association with whatever he detests.

正體字		在家則愛別離苦。出家則
	062a29 ‖	親愛和合。在家則癡重。出家則癡輕。在家
	062b01 ‖	則失淨行。出家則得淨行。在家則破深心。
	062b02 ‖	出家則成深心。在家則無救。出家則有救。
	062b03 ‖	在家則孤窮。出家不孤窮。在家則無舍。出
	062b04 ‖	家則有舍。在家則無歸。出家則有歸。在家
	062b05 ‖	則多瞋。出家則多慈。在家則重擔。出家則
	062b06 ‖	捨擔。在家則事務無盡。出家則無有事務。
	062b07 ‖	在家則罪會。出家則福會。在家則苦惱。出家
	062b08 ‖	則無苦惱。在家則有熱。出家則無熱。在家
	062b09 ‖	則有諍。出家則無諍。在家則染著。出家無
	062b10 ‖	染著。在家有我慢。出家無我慢。在家貴財
	062b11 ‖	物。出家貴功德。在家有災害。出家滅災害。
	062b12 ‖	在家則減失。出家則增益。
简体字		在家则爱别离苦。出家则亲爱和合。在家则痴重。出家则痴轻。在家则失净行。出家则得净行。在家则破深心。出家则成深心。在家则无救。出家则有救。在家则孤穷。出家不孤穷。在家则无舍。出家则有舍。在家则无归。出家则有归。在家则多嗔。出家则多慈。在家则重担。出家则舍担。在家则事务无尽。出家则无有事务。在家则罪会。出家则福会。在家则苦恼。出家则无苦恼。在家则有热。出家则无热。在家则有诤。出家则无诤。在家则染着。出家无染着。在家有我慢。出家无我慢。在家贵财物。出家贵功德。在家有灾害。出家灭灾害。在家则减失。出家则增益。

Chapter 17 — On Entering the Temple

The householder is beset with the suffering of separation from what he loves whereas the monastic remains in close proximity to what he loves.

The householder is burdened with heavy delusions whereas the delusions of the monastic are only slight.

The householder fails to carry on with a life of pure conduct whereas the monastic lives a life of pure conduct.

The householder's life destroys one's resolute intentions whereas the monastic succeeds in his resolute intentions.

The householder is beyond rescue whereas the monastic has acquired the means to be rescued.

The householder is bound for solitude and poverty whereas the monastic does not fall into solitude and poverty.

The householder has no shelter whereas the monastic does indeed have shelter.

The householder has no place of refuge whereas the monastic does indeed have a place of refuge.

The householder abides in the midst of much hatred whereas the monastic is possessed of an abundance of kindness.

The householder carries a heavy burden whereas the monastic has relinquished that burden.

The householder is beset with endless responsibilities whereas the monastic has none of those responsibilities.

The householder's life is characterized by encounters with karmic transgressions whereas the monastic's life is characterized by encounters with fortuitous karma.

The householder is subject to distressing afflictions whereas the monastic becomes free of distressing afflictions.

The householder's life is one beset by heat whereas the monastic life has no such heat.[282]

The householder's life involves disputation whereas the monastic is free from disputation.

The householder is involved in defiling attachments whereas the monastic is free of defiling attachments.

The householder tends toward arrogance whereas the monastic becomes free of arrogance.

The householder esteems wealth whereas the monastic esteems meritorious qualities.

The householder is subject to disastrous harm whereas the monastic puts an end to disastrous harm.

The householder is subject to decrease and loss whereas the monastic enjoys increasing advantage.

正體字

在家則易得。出家
062b13 ‖ 則難遇。千萬劫中時乃一得。在家則易行。
062b14 ‖ 出家則難行。在家則順流。出家則逆流。在
062b15 ‖ 家則漂流。出家則乘栰。在家則為煩惱所
062b16 ‖ [2][漂＊寸]。出家則有橋[3]樑自度。在家是此岸。出
062b17 ‖ 家是彼岸。在家則纏縛。出家離纏縛。在家
062b18 ‖ 懷結恨。出家離結恨。在家隨官法。出家隨
062b19 ‖ 佛法。在家有事故。出家無事故。在家有苦
062b20 ‖ 果。出家有樂果。在家則輕躁。出家則威重。
062b21 ‖ 在家伴易得。出家伴難得。在家以婦為伴。
062b22 ‖ 出家堅心為伴。在家則入圍。出家則解圍。
062b23 ‖ 在家則以侵惱他為貴。出家則以利益他
062b24 ‖ 為貴。在家則貴財施。出家則貴法施。在家
062b25 ‖ 則持魔幢。出家則持佛[4]幢。在家[5]有歸處。
062b26 ‖ 出家壞諸歸處。在家增長身。出家則離身。

简体字

在家则易得。出家则难遇。千万劫中时乃一得。在家则易行。出家则难行。在家则顺流。出家则逆流。在家则漂流。出家则乘筏。在家则为烦恼所[漂＊寸]。出家则有桥梁自度。在家是此岸。出家是彼岸。在家则缠缚。出家离缠缚。在家怀结恨。出家离结恨。在家随官法。出家随佛法。在家有事故。出家无事故。在家有苦果。出家有乐果。在家则轻躁。出家则威重。在家伴易得。出家伴难得。在家以妇为伴。出家坚心为伴。在家则入围。出家则解围。在家则以侵恼他为贵。出家则以利益他为贵。在家则贵财施。出家则贵法施。在家则持魔幢。出家则持佛幢。在家有归处。出家坏诸归处。在家增长身。出家则离身。

Chapter 17 — On Entering the Temple

The householder's life is easily come by whereas the monastic's life is one which is so rarely encountered that one may take it on but once in thousands of myriads of kalpas.

The householder's life is easy to practice in whereas the monastic's life involves difficult practices.

The household simply goes along with the current whereas the monastic moves against the current.

The householder's life is one of drifting in a flood whereas the monastic's is one of riding on a raft.

The householder floats along on a torrent of afflictions whereas the monastic has a bridge by which he passes beyond them.

The householder's life takes place on the near shore whereas the monastic's life is concerned with reaching the far shore.

The householder's life is one of being tied up in bondage whereas the monastic's life is one of separation from bondage.

The householder harbors enmity whereas the monastic relinquishes enmity.

The householder is bound to follow the laws of officialdom whereas the monastic follows the law of the Buddha.

The householder's life is characterized by mishaps whereas the monastic's life is one that has become free of mishaps.

The household life has suffering as its karmic fruits whereas the monastic life has happiness as its karmic fruits.

The householder tends to develop an agitated demeanor whereas the monastic possesses awe-inspiring dignity.

Householder companions are easily come by whereas monastic companions are only rarely found.

The householder takes a wife as his companion whereas the monastic takes a solid resolve as his companion.

The householder is entrapped in a corral whereas the monastic escapes from the corral.

The householder tends to esteem inflicting troubles on others whereas the monastic esteems benefiting others.

The householder tends to esteem the giving of wealth whereas the monastic esteems the giving of Dharma.

The householder holds up the banner of Māra whereas the monastic holds up the banner of the Buddha.

The householder has some place he goes back to whereas the monastic demolishes all places of refuge.

The householder is concerned with the growth of his body whereas the monastic is one who abandons the body.

正體字

062b27 ‖ 在家入深榛。出家出深榛。復次。
062b28 ‖ 　又於出家者　　心應深貪慕
062b29 ‖ 是在家菩薩。如是思惟出家功德。於出家
062c01 ‖ 者心應貪慕。我何時當得出家得有如是
062c02 ‖ 功德。我何時當得出家次第具行沙門法。
062c03 ‖ 則說戒布薩安居自恣次第而坐。我何時當
062c04 ‖ 得聖人所著戒定慧解脫解脫知見熏修法
062c05 ‖ 衣。何時當得持聖人相。何時當得閑林靜
062c06 ‖ 住。何時當得持鉢乞食得與不得。若多若
062c07 ‖ 少若美若惡若冷若熱次第而受趣以支身
062c08 ‖ 如塗瘡膏車。何時當得於世八法心無
062c09 ‖ 憂喜。何時當得關閉六情如繫狗鹿魚蛇
062c10 ‖ 猴鳥。狗樂聚落鹿樂[6]山澤。魚樂池沼蛇
062c11 ‖ 好穴處。猴樂深林鳥依虛空。眼耳鼻舌身
062c12 ‖ 意常樂色聲香味觸法。非是凡夫淺智弱志
062c13 ‖ 所能降伏。唯有智慧堅心正念。

简体字

在家入深榛。出家出深榛。复次。
　又于出家者　　心应深贪慕
　　是在家菩萨。如是思惟出家功德。于出家者心应贪慕。我何时当得出家得有如是功德。我何时当得出家次第具行沙门法。则说戒布萨安居自恣次第而坐。我何时当得圣人所著戒定慧解脱解脱知见熏修法衣。何时当得持圣人相。何时当得闲林静住。何时当得持钵乞食得与不得。若多若少若美若恶若冷若热次第而受趣以支身如涂疮膏车。何时当得于世八法心无忧喜。何时当得关闭六情如繫狗鹿鱼蛇猴鸟。狗乐聚落鹿乐山泽。鱼乐池沼蛇好穴处。猴乐深林鸟依虚空。眼耳鼻舌身意常乐色声香味触法。非是凡夫浅智弱志所能降伏。唯有智慧坚心正念。

Chapter 17 — On Entering the Temple

The householder plunges into the deep undergrowth whereas the monastic escapes the deep undergrowth.

Additionally:

J. ONE SHOULD DEVELOP A DEEP YEARNING TO BECOME A MONASTIC

Moreover, in regard to becoming a monastic,
one's mind should feel a deep yearning admiration.

As this lay bodhisattva thus ponders the meritorious aspects of becoming a monastic, he should feel a yearning admiration for it, wondering:

Oh, when will I myself finally be able to leave behind the home life and acquire such meritorious qualities?

Oh, when will I myself be able to leave behind the home life and carry out in correct sequence the dharmas of the śramaṇa wherein, one participates in the poṣada recitation of the moral precepts, joins in the rains retreat, and freely sits in the order of seniority

Oh, when will I be able to don the Dharma robes of the Āryas who are imbued with their cultivation of the moral precepts, meditative concentration, wisdom, liberation, and the knowledge and vision of liberation?

Oh, when will I be able to maintain the deportment of the Āryas?

Oh, when will I be able to abide peacefully, meditating in a quiet forest?

Oh, when will I be able to carry the alms bowl and go out on the alms round, either being given something or not being given anything, either being given much or only a little, either being given delectable food or bad food, either being given cold food or hot food, thus proceeding in sequential order along the alms round, thereby coming by what is needed merely to sustain the body, accepting alms merely as one might apply ointment on an ulceration or as one might apply grease to the axle of a cart?

Oh, when will I become free of distress and joyfulness over the eight worldly dharmas?

Oh, when will I be able to restrain the six sense faculties in the same manner as one might confine some dog, deer, fish, snake, monkey, or bird? Just as a dog enjoys a village, a deer enjoys mountains and marshes, a fish enjoys ponds, a snake is fond of his den, a monkey enjoys a jungle, and a bird enjoys flying in the air, the eye, ear, nose, tongue, body, and mind always enjoy forms, sounds, smells, tastes, touchables, and dharmas as objects of mind.[283] The sense faculties are not things that common people of shallow wisdom and weak resolve are able to subdue. It is only one possessed of wisdom, solid resolve, and right mindfulness who is able to

正體字

```
       乃能摧伏
062c14 ‖ 六情寇賊不令為患自在無畏。何時當得
062c15 ‖ 樂欲坐禪誦讀經法樂斷煩惱樂修善法
062c16 ‖ 樂著弊衣。趣足障體。念昔在俗多行放逸。
062c17 ‖ 今得自利又利他故。當勤精進。何時當得
062c18 ‖ 隨順菩薩所行道法。何時當得亦為世間
062c19 ‖ 作無上福田。何時當得離恩愛奴。何時當
062c20 ‖ 得脫是家獄。如說。
062c21 ‖    禮敬諸塔寺    因佛生三心
062c22 ‖ 是在家菩薩既已慕尚出家。若入塔寺敬
062c23 ‖ 禮佛時。應生三心。何等為三。我當何時
062c24 ‖ 得於天龍夜叉乾闥婆阿修羅迦樓[7]羅摩睺
062c25 ‖ 羅伽人非人中受諸供養。何時當得神力
062c26 ‖ 舍利流布世間利益眾生。我今深心行大
062c27 ‖ 精進。當得阿耨多羅三藐三菩提。我作佛
062c28 ‖ 已入無餘涅槃。復次。
062c29 ‖    詣諸比丘時    隨所行奉事
063a01 ‖    默然順所誨    濟[1]乏無所惜
063a02 ‖ 是在家菩薩敬禮塔已。求造諸比丘說法
063a03 ‖ 者。
```

简体字

乃能摧伏六情寇贼不令为患自在无畏。何时当得乐欲坐禅诵读经法乐断烦恼乐修善法乐着弊衣。趣足障体。念昔在俗多行放逸。今得自利又利他故。当勤精进。何时当得随顺菩萨所行道法。何时当得亦为世间作无上福田。何时当得离恩爱奴。何时当得脱是家狱。如说。

　　礼敬诸塔寺　　因佛生三心

　　是在家菩萨既已慕尚出家。若入塔寺敬礼佛时。应生三心。何等为三。我当何时得于天龙夜叉乾闼婆阿修罗迦楼罗摩睺罗伽人非人中受诸供养。何时当得神力舍利流布世间利益众生。我今深心行大精进。当得阿耨多罗三藐三菩提。我作佛已入无余涅槃。复次。

　　诣诸比丘时　　随所行奉事
　　默然顺所诲　　济乏无所惜

　　是在家菩萨敬礼塔已。求造诸比丘说法者。

Chapter 17 — On Entering the Temple

> control the rebels of the six senses so that they are prevented from doing harm to one's sovereign mastery and fearlessness.
> Oh, when will I be able to delight in *dhyāna* meditation, delight in recitation and study of the sutras' dharmas, delight in cutting off afflictions, delight in cultivating good dharmas, and delight in donning rag robes, going forth with the body well covered, recalling then that, formerly, when I was a layperson, I was for the most part neglectful, but, now, in order to bring about self-benefit and the benefit of others, I should be diligently vigorous?
> Oh, when will I be able to follow the dharmas of the path practiced by bodhisattvas?
> Oh, when will I too become one who can serve as an unsurpassable field of merit for those in the world?
> Oh, when will I be able to quit being a slave of familial affection?
> And when will I be able to be freed from this prison of the household?

This is as stated here:

> K. THREE ASPIRATIONAL THOUGHT WHEN BOWING AT A STUPA OR TEMPLE
> Whenever one bows down in reverence at any stupa or temple, inspired by the Buddha, one should bring forth three thoughts.

Having already been inspired to feel a yearning to go forth into homelessness, whenever this lay bodhisattva enters the grounds of a stupa or temple and bows down in reverence, he should bring forth three thoughts. And what are these three? They are as follows:

> Oh, when will I become one worthy to receive the offerings of devas, dragons, *yakṣas*, *gandharvas*, *asuras*, *kinnaras*, *mahoragas*, humans, and nonhumans?
> Oh, when will I be able to produce the *śarīra* relics imbued with spiritual powers that, distributed throughout the world, bestow benefit on beings?
> I now bring forth the deep resolve to practice the great vigor by which I shall attain *anuttarasamyaksaṃbodhi*. Then, after serving as one of the buddhas, I shall enter the nirvāṇa without residue.

Additionally:

> L. ON MEETING ANY MONK, SERVE, FOLLOW INSTRUCTIONS, AND ASSIST
> Whenever meeting any of the bhikshus,
> offer to serve in a manner appropriate to whatever he is doing,
> quietly obey all instructions he might offer,
> and be unstinting in providing any requisites he needs.

After this lay bodhisattva bows down in reverence at any stupa site, he seeks to visit the bhikshus, including those who teach Dharma, those

正體字
所持律者。讀修多羅者。讀摩多羅迦
063a04 ‖ 者。讀菩薩藏者。作阿練若者。著納衣者。乞
063a05 ‖ 食者。一食者。常坐者。過中不飲漿者。但三
063a06 ‖ 衣者。著褐衣者。隨敷坐者。在樹下者。在
063a07 ‖ 塚間者。在空地者。少欲者。知足者。遠離者。
063a08 ‖ 坐禪者。勸化者。應各隨諸比丘所行奉事。
063a09 ‖ 若至讀阿毘曇者所。隨其所說諸法性相
063a10 ‖ 相應不相應等請問所疑。問已習學。若遇
063a11 ‖ 持律者。應當請問起罪因緣罪之輕重滅罪
063a12 ‖ 之法及阿[2]波陀那事。問已修學[3]行。若遇讀
063a13 ‖ 修多羅者。應當請問諸阿含諸部中義習
063a14 ‖ 學多聞。若遇讀摩多羅迦應利眾經憂陀那
063a15 ‖ [4]波羅延法句者。應當學習如是等經。若
063a16 ‖ 遇讀菩薩藏者。應當請問六波羅蜜及方
063a17 ‖ 便事問已修學。若遇阿練若。應學其遠離
063a18 ‖ 法。若遇坐禪者。應學其坐禪法。餘諸比丘
063a19 ‖ 亦應如是隨其所行請問[5]修學

简体字

所持律者。读修多罗者。读摩多罗迦者。读菩萨藏者。作阿练若者。着纳衣者。乞食者。一食者。常坐者。过中不饮浆者。但三衣者。着褐衣者。随敷坐者。在树下者。在冢间者。在空地者。少欲者。知足者。远离者。坐禅者。劝化者。应各随诸比丘所行奉事。若至读阿毗昙者所。随其所说诸法性相相应不相应等请问所疑。问已习学。若遇持律者。应当请问起罪因缘罪之轻重灭罪之法及阿波陀那事。问已修学行。若遇读修多罗者。应当请问诸阿含诸部中义习学多闻。若遇读摩多罗迦应利众经忧陀那波罗延法句者。应当学习如是等经。若遇读菩萨藏者。应当请问六波罗蜜及方便事问已修学。若遇阿练若。应学其远离法。若遇坐禅者。应学其坐禅法。余诸比丘亦应如是随其所行请问修学

Chapter 17 — On Entering the Temple 541

who uphold the moral-precept codes, those who study sutras, those who study *mātṛkās*, those who study the bodhisattva canon, those who dwell in a forest hermitage, those who wear robes made of cast-off rags, those who obtain their sustenance from the alms round, those who eat but once each day, those who only sit and never lie down, those who do not drink broths after midday, those who possess only the three-part robe,[284] those who wear only robes sewn from coarse cloth, those who take their rest wherever they stop to sit, those who dwell only at the base of a tree, those who dwell in charnel fields, those who dwell only out on open grounds, those who have but little that they wish for, those who are easily satisfied, those who dwell in seclusion, those who sit in *dhyāna* meditation, and those who exhort and instruct others.

One should offer up one's service to each bhikshu in a manner appropriate to whichever practice he focuses upon. For instance:

If one goes to the dwelling place of a bhikshu who studies *abhidharma*, then, in accordance with those dharmas and their nature and characteristics, whether they be dharmas associated with the mind or whether they be unassociated compositional-factor dharmas, one should inquire into any related points about which one has doubts. Having inquired, one should then proceed to study them.

If one meets an expert on the moral-precept codes, one should inquire about the causes and conditions involved in the commission of moral transgressions, about the relative severity of moral transgressions, about the means for extinguishing moral transgressions, and about the *avadāna* stories.[285] Having inquired about these matters, one should then study and practice accordingly.

If one meets someone specializing in study of sutras, one should inquire into the meanings contained within the *Āgama Sutra* collections, practice accordingly, and become learned himself.

If one meets someone specializing in study of *mātṛkās* associated with the *Sutra on Benefiting the Many*, the *Udānas*, the *Assalāyano*, and the *Dharmapada*, one should then study such sutras.

If one meets someone specializing in the bodhisattva canon, one should inquire about the six *pāramitās* and also the matter of using expedients and then, having thus inquired, one should study and practice accordingly.

If one meets someone abiding in a forest hermitage, one should study those dharmas related to practice in seclusion.

If one meets someone practicing *dhyāna* meditation, one should study his *dhyāna* meditation methods.

As for the other types of bhikshus, on meeting them, one should inquire into whatever they have chosen to practice and then study and

正體字	
	無所違
063a20	逆。攝護口者詣諸比丘應善攝口安[6]詳默
063a21	然。觀時觀土隨事思惟心不錯亂少於語
063a22	言。又於說法者所。諸比丘等隨所乏少。若
063a23	衣若鉢若尼師壇。資生之物隨力而施無所
063a24	[7]匱惜。所以者何。菩薩尚應施諸惡人。何況
063a25	比丘有功德者。乃至身肉猶當不惜。況復
063a26	外物。助道因緣。復次。
063a27	若行布施時　　莫生他煩惱
063a28	行布施時若與一人。一人不得便生恚惱。
063a29	應善籌量而行布施。勿使他人生於恚惱。
063b01	何以故。
063b02	將護凡夫心　　應勝阿羅漢
063b03	是在家菩薩。施諸比丘衣服飲食醫藥臥具
063b04	供養迎送敬禮親近。將護凡夫心。應勝將
063b05	護阿羅漢。何以故。諸阿羅漢於利衰毀譽稱
063b06	譏苦樂心無有異。凡夫有愛恚慳嫉故能

简体字	
	无所违逆。摄护口者诣诸比丘应善摄口安详默然。观时观土随事思惟心不错乱少于语言。又于说法者所。诸比丘等随所乏少。若衣若钵若尼师坛。资生之物随力而施无所匮惜。所以者何。菩萨尚应施诸恶人。何况比丘有功德者。乃至身肉犹当不惜。况复外物。助道因缘。复次。
	若行布施时　　莫生他烦恼
	行布施时若与一人。一人不得便生恚恼。应善筹量而行布施。勿使他人生于恚恼。何以故。
	将护凡夫心　　应胜阿罗汉
	是在家菩萨。施诸比丘衣服饮食医药卧具供养迎送敬礼亲近。将护凡夫心。应胜将护阿罗汉。何以故。诸阿罗汉于利衰毁誉称讥苦乐心无有异。凡夫有爱恚悭嫉故能

practice accordingly, doing so without disobeying any instructions they provide.

As for the matter of guarding one's speech, when meeting bhikshus, one should thoroughly restrain oneself from talking, remaining serenely silent. Giving due regard to issues of time and place and considering the circumstance at hand, one should ensure that one's mind does not stray into confusion and that one speaks but few words.

Additionally, as regards the place in which the speaker of Dharma resides, in accordance with whatever those bhikshus and others there have grown short of, according to one's own capacity to do so, one should supply them with such things, whether they be robes, bowls, sitting cloths,[286] or other life-supporting requisites, not being stinting in one's generosity in providing any of them.[287]

Why should one do this? A bodhisattva should provide even for people who are bad, how much the more so should one provide for bhikshus, those who are possessed of meritorious qualities. In assisting them, one should not even be sparing of one's own flesh, how much the more readily then should one provide them with the outward possessions that serve as causes and conditions supporting their progress on the path.

Additionally:

M. Avoid Causing Afflictions in Those Not Receiving One's Gifts

When one engages in giving,
do not instigate afflictions in others.

When one carries out an act of giving, if one gives to but a single person, it might well be that another person, not having received anything, becomes angry. This is a matter that one should skillfully assess in one's practice of giving. Do not influence others to become afflicted with anger. Why must one take care in this?

The careful consideration one accords those with common minds
should surpass even that which one reserves for arhats.

When this lay bodhisattva provides clothing, drink and food, medicines, and bedding for bhikshus, making offerings to them, welcoming them and escorting them off, bowing in reverence, and drawing personally close to them, he should be even more solicitous about the needs of those still possessed of a common person's mind than he would be in his deferential treatment of an arhat.

And why should this be so? Arhats do not differ in their mental response to gain and loss, ill repute and esteem, praise and blame, or pain and pleasure. But because a common person is subject to feelings of craving, hatred, miserliness, and jealousy, he is able in these

063b07 ‖ 起罪業。以是罪業墮在地獄畜生餓鬼。是
063b08 ‖ 故應深將護凡夫。菩薩事者。皆為利益一
063b09 ‖ 切眾生布施。非為自樂不為自得後世果
063b10 ‖ 報。非如市易。復次。
063b11 ‖ 　因以財施故　　可以法施攝
063b12 ‖ 　隨所欲利益　　教發無上心
063b13 ‖ 是在家菩薩為自利故隨所利益。比丘若以
063b14 ‖ 衣施。若以鉢施。如是等種種餘財物施。如
063b15 ‖ 是比丘未入法位未得道果。應勸令發
063b16 ‖ 阿耨多羅三藐三菩提願。何以故。因財施攝
063b17 ‖ 故得以法施攝。或於所施檀越有愛敬心
063b18 ‖ 信受其語。復次。
063b19 ‖ 　為欲護持法　　捨命而不惜
063b20 ‖ 　療治病比丘　　乃至以身施
063b21 ‖ 是在家菩薩為欲護持法故。乃至自捨身
063b22 ‖ 命。勤行精進摧破[8]六十二種外道及諸魔民
063b23 ‖ 憎嫉佛法者。佛弟子中或有邪行詭異佛
063b24 ‖ 法。如是之人如法摧破。名為護持法。

起罪业。以是罪业堕在地狱畜生饿鬼。是故应深将护凡夫。菩萨事者。皆为利益一切众生布施。非为自乐不为自得后世果报。非如市易。复次。

　因以财施故　　可以法施摄
　随所欲利益　　教发无上心

是在家菩萨为自利故随所利益。比丘若以衣施。若以钵施。如是等种种余财物施。如是比丘未入法位未得道果。应劝令发阿耨多罗三藐三菩提愿。何以故。因财施摄故得以法施摄。或于所施檀越有爱敬心信受其语。复次。

　为欲护持法　　舍命而不惜
　疗治病比丘　　乃至以身施

是在家菩萨为欲护持法故。乃至自舍身命。勤行精进摧破六十二种外道及诸魔民憎嫉佛法者。佛弟子中或有邪行诡异佛法。如是之人如法摧破。名为护持法。

Chapter 17 — On Entering the Temple

circumstances to commit transgressions because of which he may fall into the hell realms, the animal realms, or the hungry-ghost realms.

Consequently one should be extremely careful to be protective of those with a common person's mentality. Thus, when a bodhisattva offers his services, he does so in a manner intended to benefit all beings. His giving is not done merely for the sake of his own happiness, is not done for the sake of acquiring karmic rewards for himself in future lives, and is not done merely as if it were some business transaction.

Additionally:

N. GIVING AS AN OPPORTUNITY TO ENCOURAGE HIGHEST BODHI RESOLVE

Due to having given some sort of material wealth,
one may then be able to draw forth others through Dharma giving.
In accordance with whatsoever is desired, one bestows benefit,
and then instructs others in bringing forth the unsurpassable resolve.

Even as one pursues one's own benefit, whether it be through the giving of robes, through the giving of bowls, or through the many other various sorts of giving of material wealth, if bhikshus such as these have not yet entered the [right and definite] Dharma position and have not yet attained the fruits of that path, this lay bodhisattva should encourage the bhikshus he benefits to bring forth the vow to attain *anuttarasamyaksaṃbodhi*. Why? Having drawn them forth through the giving of wealth, he may then be able to draw them forth through the giving of Dharma. It may well be that, due to their fondness and respect for the benefactor who has made gifts to them, they will be inclined to believe and accept what he says to them.

Additionally:

O. DO WHATEVER IS NECESSARY TO PRESERVE AND PROTECT THE DHARMA

For the sake of protecting and preserving the Dharma,
one should remain unstinting even if it means sacrificing one's life.
One should strive to cure bhikshus who have fallen ill
even to the point where one makes a gift of one's own body.

Even to the point of sacrificing his own life in order to preserve and protect the Dharma, this lay bodhisattva should be diligently vigorous in overcoming those who detest the Dharma of the Buddha, whether they be from among the sixty-two types of non-Buddhist traditions or whether they be from among the retinues of Māra.

Among the disciples of the Buddha, there may be those who deviate in their practice through spurious distortion of the Buddha's Dharma. [The influence of] such people should be overcome in a manner consistent with Dharma. This constitutes the protecting and preservation

正體字

```
          又應
063b25 ‖ 於諸多聞說法者。加信敬心四事供養。亦
063b26 ‖ 名護持法。若自讀誦解說書寫修多羅毘
063b27 ‖ 尼阿毘曇摩多羅迦菩薩藏者。亦教他人讀
063b28 ‖ 誦解說書寫。以是因緣法得久住利益一
063b29 ‖ 切。在家出家稱揚歎說法久住利。若法疾滅
063c01 ‖ 說有過惡。又念如來久遠已來。行菩薩道
063c02 ‖ 行諸難行乃得是法。以是因緣於諸在家
063c03 ‖ 出家。勤心精進示教利喜。若令得道。若令
063c04 ‖ 入阿惟越致。略說護法因緣。令得一切安
063c05 ‖ 樂之具。亦復自能如說修行。皆名護持法。
063c06 ‖ 復次是在家菩薩法。若有病比丘應須療治。
063c07 ‖ 是菩薩乃至捨身為治其病而不愛惜是
063c08 ‖ 最為要。出家之人應於在家求此要事。所
063c09 ‖ 謂身自瞻視疾病供給醫藥。復次。
063c10 ‖    決定心布施    施已而無悔
063c11 ‖ 是菩薩若為護持正法。若為瞻視病人。應
063c12 ‖ 時供施心無有悔。是名清淨施。
```

简体字

又应于诸多闻说法者。加信敬心四事供养。亦名护持法。若自读诵解说书写修多罗毗尼阿毗昙摩多罗迦菩萨藏者。亦教他人读诵解说书写。以是因缘法得久住利益一切。在家出家称扬叹说法久住利。若法疾灭说有过恶。又念如来久远已来。行菩萨道行诸难行乃得是法。以是因缘于诸在家出家。勤心精进示教利喜。若令得道。若令入阿惟越致。略说护法因缘。令得一切安乐之具。亦复自能如说修行。皆名护持法。复次是在家菩萨法。若有病比丘应须疗治。是菩萨乃至舍身为治其病而不爱惜是最为要。出家之人应于在家求此要事。所谓身自瞻视疾病供给医药。复次。

  决定心布施　　施已而无悔

是菩萨若为护持正法。若为瞻视病人。应时供施心无有悔。是名清净施。

of the Dharma. Furthermore, with increased thoughts of faith and respect, one should make offerings of the four requisites to those who are learned speakers of the Dharma. This too constitutes the protection and preservation of the Dharma.

If one studies, recites, explains, or transcribes sutras, *vinaya* texts, *abhidharma* texts, *mātṛkās*, or canonical bodhisattva texts while also instructing others in their study, recitation, explanation, and transcription, due to these causes and conditions, the Dharma will remain for a long time, providing benefit to everyone.

To laypeople and monastics alike, one should extol and speak in praise of the benefits of the Dharma's enduring for a long time while also describing the extreme evil bound to ensue in the event of the Dharma's rapid demise. One should also bear in mind that the Tathāgata, from the distant past on forward to the present, practiced the bodhisattva path, carried out all kinds of difficult practices, and only then succeeded in acquiring this Dharma.

For these reasons, with diligent resolve, one should be vigorous in using it to show, instruct, benefit, and delight both laypeople and monastics, thereby perhaps instigating them to become enlightened or perhaps instigating them to reach the station of the *avaivartika*.[288]

To summarize the causes and conditions subsumed in the protection of the Dharma, they amount to enabling others' acquisition of the means for universal peace and happiness while also enabling one's own cultivation of [the Dharma] in accordance with the manner in which it was proclaimed. All of these ideas define what is meant by protecting and preserving the Dharma.

Additionally, it is the Dharma of the lay bodhisattva to see to it that any sick bhikshu gets medical treatment. This bodhisattva should be willing even to sacrifice his own life to cure that illness, not being the least bit stinting in his efforts. This is a matter of the greatest importance. The monastics should seek this essential service from the laity, instigating them to personally look after whoever is sick, supplying them with medical care and medicines.

Additionally:

P. When Giving, Have No Regrets or Selfish Motives & Dedicate Merit

One gives with a resolute mind
and, having given the gift, one remains free of any regrets.

Whether this bodhisattva is doing some deed for the sake of protecting and preserving right Dharma, or whether he is personally looking after someone fallen ill, responding in a manner appropriate to the circumstance, he bestows offerings with a mind free of any regrets. It is this that qualifies as pure giving.

正體字

若不求果
報。不分別是應受是不應受。但以憐愍
利益心與。是名清淨施。如說。

　　若人悲心施　　是名清淨施
　　不言是福田　　不言非福田
　　若人行布施　　無所為故與
　　若人為果報　　是名為出息
　　是故說施已　　心無有悔恨
　　乃至微小福　　皆向無上道

以是布施因緣所得福德。皆應迴向阿耨
多羅三藐三菩提。不求今世後世利樂及小
乘果。但為眾生求阿耨多羅三藐三菩提。
如我先說在家菩薩餘行當說者今已說竟。
皆於大乘經中處處抄集。隨順經法菩薩
住是行中。疾得阿耨多羅三藐三菩提。第二
地中多說出家菩薩所行。在家出家菩薩共
行今當復說。[9]

简体字

若不求果报。不分别是应受是不应受。但以怜愍利益心与。是名清净施。如说。

　　若人悲心施　　是名清净施
　　不言是福田　　不言非福田
　　若人行布施　　无所为故与
　　若人为果报　　是名为出息
　　是故说施已　　心无有悔恨
　　乃至微小福　　皆向无上道

以是布施因缘所得福德。皆应回向阿耨多罗三藐三菩提。不求今世后世利乐及小乘果。但为众生求阿耨多罗三藐三菩提。如我先说在家菩萨余行当说者今已说竟。皆于大乘经中处处抄集。随顺经法菩萨住是行中。疾得阿耨多罗三藐三菩提。第二地中多说出家菩萨所行。在家出家菩萨共行今当复说。

If one gives without seeking for any resulting karmic rewards, if one gives without distinguishing, "This one should be able to be a recipient whereas that one should not be a recipient," and if one gives only with thoughts of pity and the motivation to be beneficial in one's actions, these are the factors that define pure giving. This is as described below:

> If one gives with a compassionate mind,
> this is what qualifies as giving that is pure.
> He does not say of this one, "He is a field of merit,"
> and does not say of that one, "He is not a field of merit."
>
> If someone is to take up the practice of giving,
> he remains free of any selfish motivation as a basis for giving.
> If one does this for the sake of acquiring some karmic reward,
> then this just amounts to seeking to earn interest.
>
> Therefore, having pledged to give,
> one proceeds with a mind free of regret or resentment.
> Even the most minor amount of merit thus derived
> is all dedicated to realization of the unsurpassable path.

All of the merit produced by the causes and conditions of giving should be entirely dedicated to *anuttarasamyaksaṃbodhi*. One should not seek to derive from it any benefit or bliss in present or future lifetimes and should not seek to thereby gain the fruits of the Small Vehicle. It is solely for the sake of beings that one seeks the realization of *anuttarasamyaksaṃbodhi*.

As for my earlier statement that discussion of the additional lay bodhisattva practices would follow—that explanation has now been concluded. These practices were all selected from their various locations throughout the Great Vehicle sutras. In order to accord with the Dharma taught in the sutras, the bodhisattva abides in these very practices and thereby swiftly attains *anuttarasamyaksaṃbodhi*. The treatment of the second bodhisattva ground shall be mostly devoted to the practices of the monastic bodhisattva. Now, however, we shall proceed to a discussion of the jointly shared practices taken up by both lay and monastic bodhisattvas.

The End of Chapter Seventeen

正體字

063c29 ‖　　　[10]共行品第十八
064a01 ‖ 問曰。汝言當說在家出家菩薩共行法今
064a02 ‖ 可說之。答曰。忍辱法施法忍思惟不曲法。
064a03 ‖ 尊重法不障法。供養法信解修空。不貪
064a04 ‖ 嫉隨所說行。燈明施伎樂施乘施正願攝
064a05 ‖ 法思量利安眾生。等心於一切。此是在家
064a06 ‖ 出家共行要法。是故偈說。
064a07 ‖ 　行忍身端嚴　　法施知宿命
064a08 ‖ 　法忍得總持　　思惟獲智慧
064a09 ‖ 　於諸法不曲　　常得正憶念

简体字

十住毗婆沙论卷第八
共行品第十八

　　问曰。汝言当说在家出家菩萨共行法今可说之。答曰。忍辱法施法忍思惟不曲法。尊重法不障法。供养法信解修空。不贪嫉随所说行。灯明施伎乐施乘施正愿摄法思量利安众生。等心于一切。此是在家出家共行要法。是故偈说。

　　行忍身端严　　法施知宿命
　　法忍得总持　　思惟获智慧
　　于诸法不曲　　常得正忆念

Chapter 18
The Jointly Shared Practices

XVIII. CHAPTER 18: THE JOINTLY SHARED PRACTICES
  A. Q: WOULD YOU PLEASE DISCUSS THE JOINTLY SHARED PRACTICES?

Question: You stated earlier that you would discuss the practices jointly shared by both lay and monastic bodhisattvas. You could now begin that discussion.

  B. A: THE JOINTLY SHARED PRACTICES ARE AS FOLLOWS: (LIST)

Response: They are:
Patience;
Dharma giving;
Dharmas patience;[289]
Contemplation;
Not distorting the Dharma;
Maintaining reverential esteem for the Dharma;
Refraining from presenting any obstacle to Dharma;
Making offerings in support of the Dharma;
Resolute faith;[290]
Cultivation of emptiness;
Not being covetous or envious;
Acting in accordance with one's own words;
Giving lamp light;
Giving musical performances;
Giving means of transport;
Right vows;
Thought imbued with the means of attraction;
Benefiting and comforting beings;
Maintaining a mind of equal regard toward everyone.

These are the essential dharmas jointly practiced by both lay peo-ple and monastics. Hence there is this verse which says:

  1. PATIENCE, DHARMA GIVING, DHARMAS PATIENCE, AND CONTEMPLATION:

Practicing patience results in a well-formed, handsome body.
The giving of Dharma results in knowledge of previous lifetimes.
By dharmas patience, one acquires the *dhāraṇīs*.[291]
Contemplation results in the procuring of wisdom.
By never distorting any dharma
one always acquires right recollective mindfulness.

正體字

064a10 ‖ 行忍得端嚴者。能忍惡言罵詈呪誓繫縛
064a11 ‖ 刀杖[1]考掠榜笞。心不動異悉能堪受。如是
064a12 ‖ 忍辱所獲果報。生於人天常得端正。後成
064a13 ‖ 佛時相好無比。法施知宿命者。行法施者
064a14 ‖ 能知過去無量劫事。法施名為種種分別。聲
064a15 ‖ 聞乘辟支佛乘佛乘解說義理。法施果報雖
064a16 ‖ 有三十五。要者知宿命。說法因緣斷人所
064a17 ‖ 疑。是故得知宿命。法忍得總持者。法名
064a18 ‖ 應空無相無願應六波羅蜜菩薩諸地。一切
064a19 ‖ 菩薩所行之法。曉了明解心能忍持。名為法
064a20 ‖ 忍。行是忍者則得總持。總持名為如所聞
064a21 ‖ 經如所讀誦其中義趣乃至百千萬劫終
064a22 ‖ 不忘失。

简体字

　　行忍得端严者。能忍恶言骂詈咒誓系缚刀杖考掠榜笞。心不动异悉能堪受。如是忍辱所获果报。生于人天常得端正。后成佛时相好无比。法施知宿命者。行法施者能知过去无量劫事。法施名为种种分别。声闻乘辟支佛乘佛乘解说义理。法施果报虽有三十五。要者知宿命。说法因缘断人所疑。是故得知宿命。法忍得总持者。法名应空无相无愿应六波罗蜜菩萨诸地。一切菩萨所行之法。晓了明解心能忍持。名为法忍。行是忍者则得总持。总持名为如所闻经如所读诵其中义趣乃至百千万劫终不忘失。

Chapter 18 — The Jointly Shared Practices

a. PATIENCE

As for "practicing patience results in a well-formed, handsome body," this means that, if one is able to endure harsh speech, curses, hate-filled oaths, being bound and tied, being assailed with knives and staves, being tortured, and being beaten and whipped, being able to endure all of this without any quavering or variation in one's state of mind—the karmic result procured through such patience is that, whether one is reborn among humans or devas, one always obtains a well-formed body. Then, later on, when one becomes a buddha, one's major marks and minor characteristics are incomparable in their perfection.

b. DHARMA GIVING

As for "the giving of Dharma results in knowledge of previous lifetimes," this means that those who practice the giving of Dharma become able to know the events that have occurred throughout the course of countless past kalpas. The giving of Dharma refers to explaining all of the many different distinctions present in the teachings of the Śrāvaka Disciple Vehicle, the Pratyekabuddha Vehicle, and the Buddha Vehicle, providing explanations of the associated meanings and principles. Although there are thirty-five different karmic rewards resulting from the giving of Dharma, the most essential among them is the gaining of the knowledge of past lifetimes. The causes and conditions associated with the speaking of Dharma bring about the severance of doubts held by others. Consequently the corresponding karmic result is that one comes to know previous lifetimes.

c. DHARMAS PATIENCE

As for "by dharmas patience, one acquires the *dhāraṇīs*," "dharmas" refers here to those dharmas that are associated with emptiness, signlessness, and wishlessness, with the six *pāramitās*, with the grounds through which the bodhisattva progresses, and with the dharmas practiced by all bodhisattvas. One so thoroughly comprehends and clearly understands them that one's mind becomes able to acquiesce in them and uphold them in practice. This is what is meant by "dharmas patience."

If one practices this patience, then one gains the means for "comprehensive retention" (*dhāraṇīs*) as a result. "Comprehensive retention" refers to the ability to never forget the significance of any of the scriptures one has ever heard or recited even after hundreds of thousands of myriads of kalpas.

正體字

064a23 ‖ 思惟得智慧者。思惟名為籌量善
064a23 ‖ 法分別義趣。是故能得今世後世利益。不
064a24 ‖ 曲心得正念者。不曲名為質直無諂。修行
064a25 ‖ 此法則於一切法中得堅固念。復次。
064a26 ‖ 　重法法則堅　　不障得守護
064a27 ‖ 　供養法值佛　　信解捨諸難
064a28 ‖ 重法[2]法則堅者。若人尊重恭敬於法法則
064a29 ‖ 堅固。堅法名為所受持習學之法自然牢堅
064b01 ‖ 不可動轉。後成佛時多有菩薩聲聞弟子。
064b02 ‖ 住是堅固法無能障其所受法者。又堅名
064b03 ‖ 為法得久住。不障得守護者。若人說法及
064b04 ‖ 人聽法。不橫與作障礙之事。後成佛時。諸
064b05 ‖ 天世人共守護法。未得佛道常能護持諸
064b06 ‖ 佛正法。諸佛滅後守護遺法。乃能至於後佛
064b07 ‖ 出世。

简体字

思惟得智慧者。思惟名为筹量善法分别义趣。是故能得今世后世利益。不曲心得正念者。不曲名为质直无谄。修行此法则于一切法中得坚固念。复次。
　重法法则坚　　不障得守护
　供养法值佛　　信解舍诸难
重法法则坚者。若人尊重恭敬于法法则坚固。坚法名为所受持习学之法自然牢坚不可动转。后成佛时多有菩萨声闻弟子。住是坚固法无能障其所受法者。又坚名为法得久住。不障得守护者。若人说法及人听法。不横与作障碍之事。后成佛时。诸天世人共守护法。未得佛道常能护持诸佛正法。诸佛灭后守护遗法。乃能至于后佛出世。

Chapter 18 — *The Jointly Shared Practices*

d. Contemplation

In "contemplation results in the procuring of wisdom," "contemplation" refers to the judicious assessment of good dharmas and the making of right distinctions regarding their significance. As a consequence, one becomes able to attain their benefits in both present and future lifetimes.

e. Not Distorting the Dharma

As for the idea that by "not distorting [the Dharma]," one's mind acquires "right mindfulness," "refraining from distortion" refers to being straightforward and free of flattery. If one cultivates this dharma, then one gains the ability to maintain solid mindfulness in the midst of all dharmas.

Additionally:

2. Esteem for Dharma, Nonobstruction, Offerings & Resolute Faith

If one esteems the Dharma, the Dharma will be solidly enduring.
If one does not create obstacles, one will be protected.
Through offerings in support of the Dharma, one meets the Buddhas.
Through resolute faith, one sheds all difficulties.

a. Esteem for the Dharma

"If one esteems the Dharma, the Dharma will be solidly enduring" means that if one maintains veneration, esteem, and reverence for the Dharma, then the Dharma will be solidly enduring. "Solidity in the Dharma" refers to the fact that, whatever dharma one accepts and upholds in practice, that will all naturally become so solid and enduring that one can never be shaken or turned back in its practice. Later on, when one becomes a buddha, one will have many bodhisattvas and *śrāvakas* as disciples. Having come to abide in these solidly maintained dharmas, no one will ever be able to obstruct one in the practice of the dharmas one has received. Additionally, "solidity" refers here to the ability of the Dharma to abide for a long time.

"If one does not create obstacles, one will be protected," means that, no matter whether it is with regard to someone's speaking Dharma or someone's being able to hear the Dharma, one refrains from perversely creating obstacles to their being able to do so. As a consequence, later on, when one attains buddhahood, both the devas and the people of the world will jointly serve as protectors of one's Dharma.

If while one has still not yet attained buddhahood one is ever able to protect and preserve the right Dharma of the Buddhas, and if, after the Buddha's passing into nirvāṇa, one strives to protect his Dharma legacy, one will then be able to encounter the next buddha when he appears in the World.

正體字

```
          以是因緣菩薩聲聞。皆應盡心善守
064b08 ‖ 護法。供養法值佛者。供養名為恭敬諸法。
064b09 ‖ 法施法會敬心供養說法之人。施[3]設法座
064b10 ‖ 起立禪坊。莊挍嚴飾講法之處。如是深心
064b11 ‖ 愛樂。供養法因緣故。得值諸佛。以信解
064b12 ‖ 捨諸難者。信名於諸善法深生欲樂。以
064b13 ‖ 是法故得離八難。解者能滅諸罪。能於諸
064b14 ‖ 善法中。以心力故隨意而解。如十一切入
064b15 ‖ 隨意所解。若人多有信解力者。能滅無始
064b16 ‖ 生死已來無量罪惡。如先悔過品中說。復次。
064b17 ‖   修空不放逸    不貪得成利
064b18 ‖   隨說滅煩惱    燈施得天眼
064b19 ‖ 修空不放逸者。修有二種得修行修。
```

简体字

以是因缘菩萨声闻。皆应尽心善守护法。供养法值佛者。供养名为恭敬诸法。法施法会敬心供养说法之人。施设法座起立禅坊。庄挍严饰讲法之处。如是深心爱乐。供养法因缘故。得值诸佛。以信解舍诸难者。信名于诸善法深生欲乐。以是法故得离八难。解者能灭诸罪。能于诸善法中。以心力故随意而解。如十一切入随意所解。若人多有信解力者。能灭无始生死已来无量罪恶。如先悔过品中说。复次。

　　修空不放逸　　不贪得成利
　　随说灭烦恼　　灯施得天眼

　　修空不放逸者。修有二种得修行修。

Chapter 18 — *The Jointly Shared Practices*

For these reasons, bodhisattva and *śrāvaka* disciple practitioners alike should all exert themselves to the utmost in thoroughly preserving and protecting the Dharma.

b. Offerings in Support of the Dharma

In "through offerings in support of the Dharma, one meets the Buddhas," "offerings" refers to demonstrations of reverential respect in all endeavors related to the Dharma. For instance, in a Dharma congregation where there will be the giving of Dharma, with a reverential mind, one makes offerings to those who speak on the Dharma, sets up a Dharma seat for them, establishes places for *dhyāna* meditation, and provides decorative adornments for the place where the lectures on Dharma will take place. Because of such earnest intentions and fondness in making offerings for the sake of Dharma, one will be able to encounter the Buddhas.

c. Resolute Faith

In "through resolute faith, one sheds all difficulties," "faith" refers to the arising of profound zeal and aspiration with respect to all good dharmas. It is because of this dharma that one becomes able to abandon the eight difficulties.

It is through the "resoluteness" [of one's faith] that one becomes able to extinguish all karmic offenses. Thus, through the power of one's resolve, one freely comprehends the import of all good dharmas. This is comparable to when, in cultivating the ten universal bases (*kṛtsnāyatana*), one becomes freely able to comprehend them in accordance with one's wishes.[292]

If one has abundant power of resolute faith, one can then extinguish the measureless karmic evil one has created due to karmic transgressions throughout beginningless time in *saṃsāra*. This accords with the earlier discussion in the chapter on repentance of karmic transgressions.

Additionally:

3. Emptiness, Non-Greed, Congruent Actions & Words, Lamp Light

Through cultivating emptiness one avoids neglectfulness.
By avoiding covetousness, one succeeds in whatever is beneficial.
Through actions faithful to one's words, one extinguishes afflictions.
Through the giving of lamp light, one acquires the heavenly eye.

a. Cultivation of Emptiness

In "through cultivating emptiness, one avoids neglectfulness," "cultivation" is of two types, namely cultivation involving realization and cultivation consisting of practice. Due to the power associated with

正體字	修 064b20 ‖ 空力故。信有為法皆是虛誑亦不[4]住空。諸 064b21 ‖ 法無定。是故常自攝[5]撿心不放逸。不貪得 064b22 ‖ 成利者。貪名於他物中生貪取心。若除 064b23 ‖ 是事所求皆成所願皆滿。隨說滅煩惱者。 064b24 ‖ 隨有所說身即行之則斷煩惱於諸事中 064b25 ‖ 皆如說行。世世已來諸煩惱氣常熏其心則 064b26 ‖ 皆除滅。轉諸煩惱惡氣習性。燈施得天眼 064b27 ‖ 者。若人然燈供養佛聲聞辟支佛及塔像舍 064b28 ‖ 利。以是因緣得天眼報。復次。 064b29 ‖ 　　樂施天耳報　　[6]以正願淨土 064c01 ‖ 　　[7]乘施獲神足　　攝法得具僧 064c02 ‖ 樂施得天耳報者。於大[8]會作諸音樂供 064c03 ‖ 養於佛得天耳報。
简体字	修空力故。信有为法皆是虚诳亦不住空。诸法无定。是故常自摄捡心不放逸。不贪得成利者。贪名于他物中生贪取心。若除是事所求皆成所愿皆满。随说灭烦恼者。随有所说身即行之则断烦恼于诸事中皆如说行。世世已来诸烦恼气常熏其心则皆除灭。转诸烦恼恶气习性。灯施得天眼者。若人然灯供养佛声闻辟支佛及塔像舍利。以是因缘得天眼报。复次。 　　乐施天耳报　　以正愿净土 　　乘施获神足　　摄法得具僧 乐施得天耳报者。于大会作诸音乐供养于佛得天耳报。

cultivating emptiness, one believes that all conditioned dharmas are false and deceptive, yet still does not abide in emptiness. One realizes then that all dharmas are not fixed entities. Consequently, one always naturally focuses and restrains one's mind so that one does not fall into neglectfulness.

b. Not Being Covetous or Envious

In "by avoiding covetousness, one succeeds in whatever is beneficial," "covetousness" refers to bringing forth thoughts desirous of appropriating others' possessions. If one rids oneself of this condition, then whatever one seeks to accomplish will meet with success and whatever one wishes for, those wishes will all be fulfilled.

c. Acting in Accordance with One's Own Words

As for "through actions faithful to one's words, one extinguishes afflictions," if one immediately carries out what one has said one will do, then one will succeed in severing afflictions. If, in all that one does, one always acts in a manner consistent with one's pronouncements, then the karmic propensities associated with the afflictions[293] that have always imbued one's mind in life after life up to the present—these will all be entirely extinguished. One will thereby transform the nature of one's evil habitual karmic propensities associated with the afflictions.

d. Giving Lamp Light

As for "through the giving of lamp light, one acquires the heavenly eye," if one lights lamps as offerings to buddhas, *śrāvaka* disciples, and *pratyekabuddha*s and also makes such offerings wherever there are their stupas, images, or *śarīra* relics, because of these actions, one will acquire the heavenly eye as a karmic result.

Additionally:

4. Music, Means of Transport, Right Vows, the Means of Attraction

Through offerings of music, one gains the heavenly ear as a result.
By giving means of transport, one gains the bases of psychic power.
Through right vows, one reaches a pure land.[294]
Through the means of attraction, one's sangha will be complete.

a. Giving Musical Performances

As for "through offerings of music, one gains the heavenly ear as a result," it is by making offerings of musical performances to the Buddha on the occasion of great Dharma assemblies[295] that one gains the heavenly ear as a karmic result.

正體字

064c04 乘施得神足者。乘名輦
064c04 輿象馬等乘。復有人言。以履屣等施亦得
064c05 神足。以正願淨土者。隨以所願取清淨
064c06 土。若金銀頗梨珊瑚琥珀[9]車璖碼瑙無量眾
064c07 寶清淨國土。攝法得具僧者。若菩薩具足
064c08 行四攝法。得具足僧。以布施愛語利益同
064c09 事。攝取眾生故。後成佛時得清淨具足無
064c10 量菩薩僧及聲聞僧。如阿彌陀佛有二種僧
064c11 清淨具足。願具足者如先十願中說。復次。
064c12 　利益眾生故　　一切所愛敬
064c13 　平等心無二　　得為最勝者
064c14 若菩薩以身口意業有所作。皆為利益安
064c15 樂眾生。是故眾生皆悉敬愛。若菩薩於諸眾
064c16 生怨親中人行平等心。不捨一切眾生。以
064c17 是業報得為最勝。勝名能勝貪欲瞋恚愚
064c18 癡一切煩惱惡法故名為佛。

简体字

乘施得神足者。乘名輦輿象马等乘。复有人言。以履屣等施亦得神足。以正愿净土者。随以所愿取清净土。若金银颇梨珊瑚琥珀车碟码瑙无量众宝清净国土。摄法得具僧者。若菩萨具足行四摄法。得具足僧。以布施爱语利益同事。摄取众生故。后成佛时得清净具足无量菩萨僧及声闻僧。如阿弥陀佛有二种僧清净具足。愿具足者如先十愿中说。复次。

　利益众生故　　一切所爱敬
　平等心无二　　得为最胜者

若菩萨以身口意业有所作。皆为利益安乐众生。是故众生皆悉敬爱。若菩萨于诸众生怨亲中人行平等心。不舍一切众生。以是业报得为最胜。胜名能胜贪欲嗔恚愚痴一切烦恼恶法故名为佛。

b. Giving Means of Transport

In "by giving means of transport, one obtains the bases of psychic power," "means of transport" refers to carriages, sedan chairs, elephants, horses, and the like. There are others who state that one may also gain the bases for psychic power through the giving of shoes, slippers, and such.

c. Right Vows

As for "through right vows, one reaches a pure land," one may take rebirth in a pure land in a manner corresponding to one's vows, thereby becoming able to go to a pure land where everything is made of gold, silver, crystal, coral, amber, mother-of-pearl, carnelian, and countless other precious things.

d. Thought Imbued with the Means of Attraction

"Through the means of attraction, one's sangha will be complete," means that, if a bodhisattva perfects the practice of the four means of attraction, he will acquire a perfectly complete sangha. Thus, by attracting beings through giving, pleasing words, beneficial actions, and joint endeavors, later, when one becomes a buddha, one will have a perfectly pure sangha consisting of countless bodhisattvas and *śrāvaka* disciples just as is the case with Amitābha Buddha who has just such a twofold sangha perfect in its purity. As for [those bodhisattvas'] "perfection in vows," this is as discussed earlier in the treatment of the ten vows.

Additionally, there are these lines:

5. Benefiting and Comforting Beings and Equal Regard for All Beings

Through benefiting beings,
one becomes loved and respected by all.
By preserving a non-dual mind holding all in equal regard,
one is able to become one who is supremely victorious.

Whatever the bodhisattva does in all physical, verbal, and mental actions is for the sake of benefiting beings and causing them to acquire peace and happiness. As a consequence, beings all revere and respect him. If the bodhisattva maintains equal regard for all beings whether they be adversaries, close friends, or those who are neutral in their relationship with him, and if he refuses to forsake any being, the karmic result of this will be that he will become supremely victorious. "Victorious" here refers to the ability to triumph over greed, hatred, delusion, and all of the other afflictions and bad dharmas. One who is able to succeed in this is known as a "buddha."

正體字

```
         問曰。人皆俱
064c19 ‖ 有眼耳鼻[10]舌口等無有異。云何得知是
064c20 ‖ 佛。答曰。佛有三十二大人相。有是相者當
064c21 ‖ 知是佛。在家出家應當分別了知三十二
064c22 ‖ 相。是相以何法得是[11]法。以何業得是相。
064c23 ‖ 是業亦應當知。何以故。欲得功德。當知是
064c24 ‖ 相欲得是相。當知是業。問曰。如此事者於
064c25 ‖ 何得解。答曰。
064c26 ‖   於法相品中     [12]一相三分別
064c27 ‖ 阿毘曇三十二相品中。一一相有三種分別。
064c28 ‖ 悉應當知。問曰。云何為一一相有三種分
064c29 ‖ 別。答曰。一說相體。二說相果。三說得相業。
065a01 ‖ 手足輪相等先已說。
```

简体字

问曰。人皆俱有眼耳鼻舌口等无有异。云何得知是佛。答曰。佛有三十二大人相。有是相者当知是佛。在家出家应当分别了知三十二相。是相以何法得是法。以何业得是相。是业亦应当知。何以故。欲得功德。当知是相欲得是相。当知是业。问曰。如此事者于何得解。答曰。

　　于法相品中　　一相三分别

　　阿毗昙三十二相品中。一一相有三种分别。悉应当知。问曰。云何为一一相有三种分别。答曰。一说相体。二说相果。三说得相业。手足轮相等先已说。

Chapter 18 — *The Jointly Shared Practices*

a. Q: How Can One Differentiate a Buddha from Other People?

Question: People all have eyes, ears, nose, tongue, mouth, and so forth. There are no differences between them in this regard. That being the case, how then might one be able to know which among them is a buddha?

b. A: A Buddha Possesses the Thirty-Two marks

Response: A buddha possesses the thirty-two major physical marks of a great man. One should realize that those possessed of these marks are buddhas. Both laypeople and monastics should be able to distinguish and completely recognize the thirty-two marks, coming to know with respect to this particular physical mark which particular dharma brought about its acquisition and coming to know with respect to this particular dharma which particular sort of action brought about its acquisition. One should also understand these corresponding actions. And why? If one wishes to develop a particular meritorious quality, one should know its corresponding physical mark and if one wishes to acquire a particular physical mark, one should know the corresponding actions by which it is acquired.

1) Q: How Can One Understand Such Matters?

Question: By what means would one be able to understand matters such as these?

2) A: Each of the Thirty-Two marks Has Three Distinctions

Response:
In the chapter on the marks of dharmas,
each one of the marks has three distinctions.

In the Abhidharma's chapter on the thirty-two marks, each and every one of the physical marks has three types of distinctions. One should know all of these.[296]

a) Q: What Is Meant by Each Mark Having Three Distinctions?

Question: What is meant by "each and every one of the marks has three different distinctions"?

b) A: This Refers to Each Mark's Substance, Fruition, and Karma

Response:
The first explains the substance of each mark.
The second explains the karmic effects associated with each mark.
And the third explains the karmic actions producing each mark.

i) A List of the "Substance" of Each of the Thirty-Two Marks

The physical mark consisting of a "wheel" emblem on the hands and on the feet is a matter that has already been discussed. Wheel-turning

正體字	
	轉輪聖王亦有是相。諸
065a02 ‖	菩薩亦有是相。餘人亦有。但不如耳手足
065a03 ‖	輪者。手足掌中有千輻輪。具足明了如印文
065a04 ‖	現。足安住不動名足安立相。[1]網縵軟薄猶
065a05 ‖	如鵝王畫文明了如真金縷故名手足網
065a06 ‖	相。柔軟猶如兜羅樹綿如嬰兒體其色紅
065a07 ‖	赤勝[2]身餘分名為手足柔軟相。手掌足下
065a08 ‖	[3]項上兩腋七處俱滿故名七處滿相。脩指
065a09 ‖	纖傭故名長指相。足跟長廣故名足跟廣
065a10 ‖	相。身長七肘不曲故名身直大相。足上隆起
065a11 ‖	故名足趺高相。毛上向右旋故名毛上旋
065a12 ‖	相。傭[[跳-兆+専]>[跳-兆+専]]漸麁如伊泥鹿[跳-兆+専]故名鹿[[跳-兆+専]>[跳-兆+専]]相。平
065a13 ‖	立兩手摩膝故名長臂相。如寶馬寶象陰
065a14 ‖	不現故名陰藏相。第一金色光明故名金
065a15 ‖	色相。皮軟如成鍊金不受塵垢故名皮
065a16 ‖	薄細密相。一一孔一毛生故名一一毛相。

简体字

转轮圣王亦有是相。诸菩萨亦有是相。余人亦有。但不如耳手足轮者。手足掌中有千辐轮。具足明了如印文现。足安住不动名足安立相。网缦软薄犹如鹅王画文明了如真金缕故名手足网相。柔软犹如兜罗树绵如婴儿体其色红赤胜身余分名为手足柔软相。手掌足下项上两腋七处俱满故名七处满相。修指纤佣故名长指相。足跟长广故名足跟广相。身长七肘不曲故名身直大相。足上隆起故名足趺高相。毛上向右旋故名毛上旋相。佣[跳-兆+専]渐粗如伊泥鹿[跳-兆+専]故名鹿[跳-兆+専]相。平立两手摩膝故名长臂相。如宝马宝象阴不现故名阴藏相。第一金色光明故名金色相。皮软如成炼金不受尘垢故名皮薄细密相。一一孔一毛生故名一一毛相。

kings also have these marks. Bodhisattvas also have these marks. Other people may have this physical mark as well. However, these cases are not the same, that's all.

As for this wheel mark on the hands and the feet, the palms of the hands and the soles of the feet have a mark consisting of a thousand-spoked wheel that is so perfect and utterly clear in its detail that it looks like an inscribed pattern.

[As for that mark whereby the Buddha's] feet are so stable in their stance when standing up that he does not move at all, this is "the mark of securely planted feet."

The mark consisting of proximal [finger and toe] webbing as soft and thin as that of a royal goose marked by lines so utterly clear as to be made from real gold thread—this is "the mark of having webbed fingers and toes."

Softness and tenderness [of hands and feet] like the down of the tala palm[297] or the skin of a baby wherein they are more rosy in hue than the rest of the body—this is "the mark of soft hands and feet."

Fullness in seven places: the palms of both hands; the soles of both feet; the surface of the neck; and the two subaxillary regions—this is what is meant by "the mark of fullness in seven places."

Long fingers that are slender and straight—this is "the mark of long fingers."

Long and broad heels are "the mark of broad heels."

The body being seven cubits in height and in no way crooked—this is "the mark of a large and erect body."

Prominent elevation of the top of the feet—this is "the mark of high arches."

Body hair grown upwards in a clockwise spiral—this is "the mark of upwardly spiraling body hair."

Legs gradually increasing in thickness after the manner of an *aiṇeya* antelope—this is "the mark of antelope-like legs."

The two hands being able to touch the knees even when standing erect—this is "the mark of long arms."

Having the male organ retracted after the manner of the thoroughbred horse or elephant—this is "the mark of genital ensheathment."

Having the most pure sort of golden radiance—this is "the mark of the golden hue."

Having skin that is soft, that appears as if it was made from refined gold, and that cannot be smudged by dirt—this is "the mark of fine skin."

Each and every bodily pore has but a single hair grown from it—this is "the mark of having but a single hair in each pore."

正體字	眉 065a17 ‖ 間白毫光如珂雪故為白毛相。如師子前 065a18 ‖ 身廣厚得所故名師子上身相。肩圓大故 065a19 ‖ 名肩圓大相。腋下平滿故名腋下滿相。舌 065a20 ‖ 根不為風寒熱所壞故善分別諸味餘人 065a21 ‖ 不爾故名知味味相。身縱廣等如尼[4]駒樓 065a22 ‖ 樹故名圓身相。肉髻團圓髮右上旋故名 065a23 ‖ 肉髻相。舌如赤蓮華廣長而薄故名廣長 065a24 ‖ 舌相。聲如梵王迦陵頻伽鳥故名梵音相。 065a25 ‖ 頰圓廣如鏡故名師子頰相。齒白如珂雪 065a26 ‖ 如君[5]坻華故名齒白相。平齊不參差故 065a27 ‖ 名齒齊相。齒密緻不疎故名具足齒相。齒 065a28 ‖ 上下相當故名四十齒相。眼白黑分明淨無 065a29 ‖ 赤脈故名紺青眼相。睫不交亂上下俱眴 065b01 ‖ 不長不短故名為牛王睫相。於諸所尊迎 065b02 ‖ 送恭敬。於塔寺中
简体字	眉间白毫光如珂雪故为白毛相。如师子前身广厚得所故名师子上身相。肩圆大故名肩圆大相。腋下平满故名腋下满相。舌根不为风寒热所坏故善分别诸味余人不尔故名知味味相。身纵广等如尼驹楼树故名圆身相。肉髻团圆发右上旋故名肉髻相。舌如赤莲华广长而薄故名广长舌相。声如梵王迦陵频伽鸟故名梵音相。颊圆广如镜故名师子颊相。齿白如珂雪如君坻华故名齿白相。平齐不参差故名齿齐相。齿密致不疏故名具足齿相。齿上下相当故名四十齿相。眼白黑分明净无赤脉故名绀青眼相。睫不交乱上下俱眴不长不短故名为牛王睫相。于诸所尊迎送恭敬。于塔寺中

Having a white hair mark between the brows that is the color of white agate—this is "the mark of the white hair tuft."[298]

Having an upper body broad and massive like that of a lion—this is "the mark of the lion-like torso."

Having large rounded shoulders—this is "the mark of large round shoulders."

Having the area below the axilla flat and full—this is "the mark of subaxillary fullness."

Because the tongue is invulnerable to injury by wind, cold, or heat, it is able to skillfully distinguish all flavors in a manner unmatched by any other person. This is "the mark of being aware of each and every flavor."

Having a body as thick and wide as the trunk of the *nyagrodha* tree[299]—this is "the mark of a round body."

Having the round *uṣṇīṣa* bulge atop the crown upon which the hair grows in a clockwise spiral—this is "the mark of the fleshy prominence atop the crown."

Having a tongue as red as a red lotus that is broad, long, and thin—this is "the mark of broad and long tongue."

Having a voice like the king of the Brahma Heavens and the *kalaviṅka* bird—this is "the mark of a Brahmā-like voice."

Having a jaw that is round and as broad as a mirror—this is "the mark of the lion-like jaw."

Having teeth that are as white as white agate or the *kunda* jasmine blossom—this is "the mark of white teeth."

Having teeth that are not uneven or skewed—this is "the mark of straight teeth."

Having teeth that are close-set and free of gaps—this is "the mark of perfect teeth."

Having teeth well matched above and below—this is "the mark of forty teeth."

Having bright and clear eyes in which black and white areas are distinctly delineated and there are no reddening surface veins—this is "the mark of blue eyes."

Having eyelashes that are not mismatched above and below, that blink in unison, and that are neither too long nor too short—this is "the mark of eyelashes like the king of bulls."

ii) The 32 Marks' Karmic Actions and Eventual Karmic Effects

Through respectfully welcoming and escorting away those who are venerated and through making sustaining offerings to those who are at stupas and temples, doing so in places where there are Dharma

正體字	大法會處說法處。供給人 065b03 ‖ 使故得手足輪相。有是相故。在家作轉輪 065b04 ‖ 聖王。多得人民。出家學道。多得徒眾。所受 065b05 ‖ 諸法堅持不捨故得安立足相。有是相故 065b06 ‖ 無能傾動。常修四攝法布施愛語利益同 065b07 ‖ 事故得手足網縵相。有是相故速攝人眾。 065b08 ‖ 以諸香甘美濡飲食供施於人及諸所尊 065b09 ‖ 供給所須故得手足柔軟相及七處隆滿 065b10 ‖ 相。有是相故多得香甘美軟飲食。救免應 065b11 ‖ 死及增壽命。又受不殺戒故得纖長指相 065b12 ‖ 足跟滿相身大直相。有是相故壽命長遠。所 065b13 ‖ 受善法增益不失故得足趺高毛上向右 065b14 ‖ 旋相。有是相故得諸功德不退失。能以技 065b15 ‖ 藝及諸經書教授不惜及履屣等施故得 065b16 ‖ 伊[6]尼鹿[[跳-兆+專]>[跳-兆+專]]相。有是相故諸所修學[7]速疾 065b17 ‖ 如意。
简体字	大法会处说法处。供给人使故得手足轮相。有是相故。在家作转轮圣王。多得人民。出家学道。多得徒众。所受诸法坚持不舍故得安立足相。有是相故无能倾动。常修四摄法布施爱语利益同事故得手足网缦相。有是相故速摄人众。以诸香甘美濡饮食供施于人及诸所尊供给所须故得手足柔软相及七处隆满相。有是相故多得香甘美软饮食。救免应死及增寿命。又受不杀戒故得纤长指相足跟满相身大直相。有是相故寿命长远。所受善法增益不失故得足趺高毛上向右旋相。有是相故得诸功德不退失。能以技艺及诸经书教授不惜及履屣等施故得伊尼鹿[跳-兆+專]相。有是相故诸所修学速疾如意。

assemblies, and where Dharma is spoken—it is because of doing these things that one acquires hands and feet that have the wheel mark.

Due to having [planted the karmic causes that result in] this mark, one who is a layperson is destined to become a wheel-turning king who acquires a large population of subjects. If one who has this mark instead leaves the home life and studies the path, he will acquire a retinue consisting of many disciples.

Through continuing to solidly uphold all dharmas one has received without ever forsaking them, one acquires the mark of solidly planted feet. Due to having [planted the karmic causes that result in] this mark, one becomes one who cannot be the least bit moved by anyone at all.

Through always cultivating the four means of attraction, namely giving, pleasing words, beneficial actions, and joint endeavors, one acquires the mark of proximal webbing of fingers and toes. Due to having [planted the karmic causes that result in] this mark, one quickly attracts a community of other people.

Through giving fragrant, sweet, delectable, and soft foods and beverages to others, including giving them to those that are venerated, providing them with everything they need, one comes to possess the mark of soft and tender hands and feet while also obtaining the mark of fullness in seven places. Due to having [planted the karmic causes that result in] these marks, one mostly receives fragrant, sweet, delectable, and soft foods and beverages, is rescued from life-threatening circumstances, and acquires a life span of increased duration.

Also, through taking on the moral precept of abstaining from killing beings, one acquires the mark of slender and long fingers and toes, the mark of fullness of the heels, and the mark of the large and erect body. Due to having [planted the karmic causes that result in] these marks, one's life span is bound to be long-lasting.

Through increased and unfailing development of the good dharmas one has taken on, one acquires the mark of high arches and the mark of having bodily hairs that grow upwardly in a clockwise spiraling fashion. Due to having [planted the karmic causes that result in] these marks, none of the meritorious qualities that one has developed recede or disappear.

Through being able to offer unstinting instruction in special skills and classic texts and through making gifts of shoes, slippers, and such, one acquires the mark of legs that gradually increase in the thickness of their shape in a manner similar to those of the *aiṇeya* [antelope].[300] Due to having [planted the karmic causes that result in] this mark, one rapidly learns whatever one cultivates or studies, doing so in a manner that accords with one's wishes.

正體字

065b18 ‖ 有來求索無所遺惜故得[8]傭長臂
065b18 ‖ 相。有是相故能得勢力能大布施。能善調
065b19 ‖ [9]人不令眾生親里遠離。若有乖離還令
065b20 ‖ 和合故得陰藏相。有是相故多得弟子。
065b21 ‖ 以好淨潔衣服臥具樓閣房舍施故得金色
065b22 ‖ 相及皮膚薄相。有是相故得好淨潔衣服臥
065b23 ‖ 具樓閣房舍。隨所應供養和[10]尚阿闍梨父
065b24 ‖ 母兄弟及所尊重善能衛護故得一一孔一
065b25 ‖ 毛生毛右旋相白[11]毛莊嚴面相。有是相故
065b26 ‖ 無與等者。慚愧語隨順語愛語故得上身
065b27 ‖ 如師子相肩圓大相。有是相故見者樂視無
065b28 ‖ 有厭足。供給疾病醫藥飲食身自看視故
065b29 ‖ 得腋下滿相得味味相。有是相故身少疾
065c01 ‖ 病。布施園林甘果橋梁茂樹池井飲食華香
065c02 ‖ 瓔珞房舍起塔福舍等及共眾施時能出
065c03 ‖ 多物故得身如尼俱樓樹相及肉髻相。

简体字

有来求索无所遗惜故得佣长臂相。有是相故能得势力能大布施。能善调人不令众生亲里远离。若有乖离还令和合故得阴藏相。有是相故多得弟子。以好净洁衣服卧具楼阁房舍施故得金色相及皮肤薄相。有是相故得好净洁衣服卧具楼阁房舍。随所应供养和尚阿阇梨父母兄弟及所尊重善能卫护故得一一孔一毛生毛右旋相白毛庄严面相。有是相故无与等者。惭愧语随顺语爱语故得上身如师子相肩圆大相。有是相故见者乐视无有厌足。供给疾病医药饮食身自看视故得腋下满相得味味相。有是相故身少疾病。布施园林甘果桥梁茂树池井饮食华香瓔珞房舍起塔福舍等及共众施时能出多物故得身如尼俱楼树相及肉髻相。

Chapter 18 — The Jointly Shared Practices

Through unstintingly and completely granting the requests of those who come seeking something, one acquires the mark of long arms. Due to having [planted the karmic causes that result in] this mark, one is able to gain personal power, is able to engage in immensely generous giving, and is able to skillfully establish harmony among others.

Through not allowing estrangement to occur among other beings or among one's relatives, and through being able to cause those who have become estranged to be reunited, one acquires the mark of male genital ensheathment. Due to having [planted the karmic causes that result in] this mark, one acquires many disciples.

Through giving fine and perfectly clean clothing, bedding, halls, and dwellings, one acquires the mark of the golden hue as well as the mark of thin and fine skin. Due to having [planted the karmic causes that result in] these marks, one acquires fine and perfectly clean clothing, bedding, halls, and dwellings.

Through being well able to look after and protect those worthy of one's offerings whether they be monastic preceptors, monastic Dharma teachers,[301] one's parents, one's elder and younger siblings,[302] or those worthy of veneration and esteem, one acquires the mark of a single clockwise spiraling bodily hair in each hair pore and the mark of the mid-brow white hair tuft adorning one's countenance. Due to having [planted the karmic causes that result in] these marks, one becomes someone who has no peer.

Through using speech imbued with a sense of shame and dread of blame, speech that is compliant with the circumstances, and speech that is pleasing, one acquires the mark of having a lion-like torso and the mark of having large and round shoulders. Due to having [planted the karmic causes that result in] these marks, whoever sees one never tires of looking at one.

Through providing medical care, medicines, food, and drink to those who are sick while also personally seeing to their care, one acquires the mark of fullness in the subaxillary region as well as the mark of being able to clearly distinguish each and every flavor. Due to having [planted the karmic causes that result in] these marks, one's body is only seldom assailed by sickness.

Through the giving of parks, groves, sweet fruit, bridges, luxuriantly thriving trees, ponds, wells, food and drink, flowers, incenses, necklaces, and buildings, by building stupas, merit halls,[303] and such, and also through bringing forth many things as gifts at such times as offerings are made to the assembly—through doing these things, one acquires the mark of a body resembling the trunk of the *nyagrodha* tree as well as the mark of having the fleshy *uṣṇīṣa* prominence atop one's

正體字

有
是相故得尊貴自在。長夜修習實語軟語
故得廣長舌相梵音聲相。[12]有是相故得五
功德音聲。五功德音聲者。易解聲。聽者無厭
聲。深遠聲。悅耳聲。不散聲。長夜實語不綺
語故得師子頰相。有是相故言必信受。初
既供養後不輕慢。隨意供給故得齒白相
齒齊相。有是相故得清淨和順同心眷屬。
長夜實語不讒謗故得四十齒相齒密緻
相。有是相故眷屬和同不可沮壞。深心愛
念和顏視眾生無愛恚癡故得紺青眼相
睫如牛王相。有是相故。一切見者無不愛
敬。[13]
十住毘婆沙論卷第八

简体字

有是相故得尊贵自在。长夜修习实语软语故得广长舌相梵音声相。有是相故得五功德音声。五功德音声者。易解声。听者无厌声。深远声。悦耳声。不散声。长夜实语不绮语故得师子颊相。有是相故言必信受。初既供养后不轻慢。随意供给故得齿白相齿齐相。有是相故得清净和顺同心眷属。长夜实语不谗谤故得四十齿相齿密致相。有是相故眷属和同不可沮坏。深心爱念和颜视众生无爱恚痴故得绀青眼相睫如牛王相。有是相故。一切见者无不爱敬。

crown. Due to having [planted the karmic causes that result in] these marks, one is readily honored and regarded with the highest esteem.

Through cultivating the practice of truthful speech and gentle speech during the long night [of previous lifetimes], one acquires the mark of the broad and long tongue as well as the mark of having the Brahmā-like voice. Due to having [planted the karmic causes that result in] these marks, one has the voice replete with five excellent qualities. Those five excellent voice qualities are:

One's voice is easily understood;
A listener can never get enough of listening to this voice;
Its sound is deep and far-reaching;
Its sound is pleasing to the ear of the listener;
And its sound does not easily fade away.

Through practicing truthful speech and non-frivolous speech during the long night [of previous lifetimes], one acquires the mark of the lion-like jaw. Due to having [planted the karmic causes that result in] this mark, one's words are definitely trusted and accepted.

Through never slighting someone after making an offering to them and through being freely generous in making offerings, one acquires the mark of white teeth and the mark of straight teeth. Due to having [planted the karmic causes that result in] this mark, one acquires a pure, harmonious, and like-minded retinue.

Through truthful speech during the long night [of previous lifetimes] and through abstaining from slander, one acquires the mark of forty teeth and the mark of closely set teeth. Due to having [planted the karmic causes that result in] these marks, one acquires a unified retinue that is invulnerable to being impeded or destroyed.

Through having sincere intentions, through thinking fondly of others, through looking upon beings with a harmonious expression free of desire, hatred, or delusion, one acquires the mark of blue eyes as well as the mark of eyelashes like the king of bulls. Due to having [planted the karmic causes that result in] these marks, everyone who sees one is moved to feelings of fondness and respect.

The End of Chapter Eighteen

正體字

065c19 ‖ 十住毘婆沙論卷第九
065c20 ‖
065c21 ‖ 　　聖者龍樹造
065c22 ‖ 　　後秦龜茲國三藏鳩摩羅什譯
065c23 ‖ [14]四法品第十九
065c24 ‖ 如所說得三十二相諸業。菩薩應一心修
065c25 ‖ 習。修如此三十二相業以慧為本。是故。
065c26 ‖ 　　退失慧四法　　菩薩應遠離
065c27 ‖ 　　得慧四種法　　應常修習行
065c28 ‖ 有四法能退失慧。菩薩所應遠離。復有四
065c29 ‖ 得慧法應常修習。何等四法失慧。一不敬
066a01 ‖ 法及說法者。二於要法祕匿悋惜。三樂法者
066a02 ‖ 為作障礙壞其聽心。四懷憍慢自高卑人。
066a03 ‖ 何等四法得慧。一恭敬法及說法者。二如
066a04 ‖ 所聞法及所讀誦為他人說。其心清淨不
066a05 ‖ 求利養。

简体字

四法品第十九

　　如所说得三十二相诸业。菩萨应一心修习。修如此三十二相业以慧为本。是故。
　　　退失慧四法　　菩萨应远离
　　　得慧四种法　　应常修习行
　　有四法能退失慧。菩萨所应远离。复有四得慧法应常修习。何等四法失慧。一不敬法及说法者。二于要法秘匿吝惜。三乐法者为作障碍坏其听心。四怀憍慢自高卑人。何等四法得慧。一恭敬法及说法者。二如所闻法及所读诵为他人说。其心清净不求利养。

Chapter 19
The Fourfold Dharmas

XIX. Chapter 19: The Fourfold Dharmas
  A. One Should Cultivate the Causes for Gaining the 32 Marks

The bodhisattva should single-mindedly cultivate the above-discussed actions by which one acquires the thirty-two marks. Cultivating the actions that lead to acquisition of the thirty-two marks is an endeavor rooted in wisdom. Therefore:

    1. Fourfold Dharmas Causing Either Loss or Gain of Wisdom

The bodhisattva should utterly abandon
the four dharmas leading to lessening and loss of wisdom
He should always cultivate and practice
the four dharmas leading to the acquisition of wisdom.

      a. Four Dharmas Causing Loss of Wisdom

There are four dharmas able to bring about the lessening and loss of wisdom that the bodhisattva should abandon. There are also four dharmas leading to the acquisition of wisdom that one should always cultivate. What are the four dharmas leading to loss of wisdom? They are:

> The first is failing to revere the Dharma or one who speaks the Dharma.
> The second is being secretive and miserly in the teaching of essential dharmas.
> The third is presenting an obstacle to someone fond of Dharma and thereby harming their motivation to listen to the speaking of Dharma.
> The fourth is harboring an arrogant attitude and consequently elevating oneself while looking on others as inferiors.

      b. Four Dharmas Causing Attainment of Wisdom

What are the four dharmas leading to acquisition of wisdom? They are:

> First, one reveres the Dharma as well as those who speak the Dharma.
> Second, one explains Dharma for others as one has heard it and as one has studied and recited it, doing so with a pure mind and without seeking to receive offerings.

正體字

```
              三知從多聞得智慧故。勤求不
066a06 ‖ 息如救頭然。四如所聞法受持不忘。貴
066a07 ‖ 如說行不貴言說。是為四。若人不壞諸
066a08 ‖ 善根者。是人能捨失慧四法。能行得慧四
066a09 ‖ 法。是故求增益智慧者。如偈說。
066a10 ‖     食善根四法    菩薩應遠離
066a11 ‖     增善根四法    菩薩應修習
066a12 ‖ 何等是侵食善根四法。一懷憍慢貪求世事。
066a13 ‖ 二著利養出入諸家。三起憎嫉謗諸菩薩。
066a14 ‖ 四未聞經聞不信受。何等是增長善根四
066a15 ‖ 法。一所未聞經求之無厭。所謂六波羅蜜
066a16 ‖ 菩薩藏。二於眾生除憍慢心謙遜下下。三
066a17 ‖ 如法得財趣足而已。
```

简体字

三知从多闻得智慧故。勤求不息如救头然。四如所闻法受持不忘。贵如说行不贵言说。是为四。若人不坏诸善根者。是人能舍失慧四法。能行得慧四法。是故求增益智慧者。如偈说。

　　食善根四法　　菩萨应远离
　　增善根四法　　菩萨应修习

　　何等是侵食善根四法。一怀憍慢贪求世事。二着利养出入诸家。三起憎嫉谤诸菩萨。四未闻经闻不信受。何等是增长善根四法。一所未闻经求之无厌。所谓六波罗蜜菩萨藏。二于众生除憍慢心谦逊下下。三如法得财趣足而已。

Third, knowing that the realization of wisdom occurs through extensive learning, one diligently and unremittingly applies oneself to one's study, doing so as urgently as if one were putting out a fire in his own turban.

Fourth, one accepts and upholds in practice, in a manner faithful to how it was taught, whatever Dharma one has learned, never forgetting it. In so doing, one esteems actions that are consistent with the words and does not esteem words alone.

These are the four. If one does not damage his roots of goodness, he will be able to abandon the four dharmas leading to loss of wisdom while being able to practice the four dharmas leading to acquiring wisdom. Consequently, one who strives to increase his wisdom acts in accord with the following verse:

2. FOURFOLD DHARMAS CAUSING DECREASE OR INCREASE OF GOOD ROOTS

As for the four dharmas that devour one's roots of goodness,
the bodhisattva should utterly abandon them.
As for the four dharmas that increase one's roots of goodness,
the bodhisattva should cultivate and practice them.

a. FOUR DHARMAS THAT DECREASE ONE'S ROOTS OF GOODNESS

What then are those four dharmas that assail and devour one's roots of goodness? They are:

The first is the harboring of arrogance while coveting worldly matters.

The second is, while being attached to offerings, coming and going from the households.

The third is giving rise to hatred and jealousy through which one slanders bodhisattvas.

The fourth is that, on hearing scriptures one has not previously heard, one refuses to believe or accept them.

b. FOUR DHARMAS THAT INCREASE ONE'S ROOTS OF GOODNESS

What then are the four dharmas conducing to the increase of one's roots of goodness? They are:

First, one strives insatiably to acquire any scriptures that one has not yet heard, in particular those that deal with the six *pāramitās* and those that belong to the bodhisattva canon.

Second, one rids oneself of any arrogance toward other beings, adopting instead an attitude of humility and deferential regard for even to the lowest of the lowly.

Third, whatever wealth one gains is gained only in accordance with Dharma and is sought only to the degree that it satisfies one's

正體字

```
              離諸邪命樂行四聖
066a18 ‖ 種行。四於他罪若實不實無有刺譏不求
066a19 ‖ 人短。若於法中有所不達。心不違逆以
066a20 ‖ 佛為證。佛是一切智其法無量。隨宜而說
066a21 ‖ 非我所知。如是增益善根。四法非諂曲者
066a22 ‖ 所能成就。是故。
066a23 ‖    菩薩應遠離    諂曲相四法
066a24 ‖    應常修習行    直心相四法
066a25 ‖ 在家出家菩薩。應遠離四諂曲法。如曲木
066a26 ‖ 在稠林難可得出。如[1]是世間有佛弟子
066a27 ‖ 雖入佛法不能得出生死深林。何等為
066a28 ‖ 四。一於佛法懷疑不信無有定心。二於
066a29 ‖ 眾生憍慢瞋恨。三於他利心生貪嫉。四毀
066b01 ‖ 謗菩薩惡聲流布。是為四。何等是四直心
066b02 ‖ 相。
```

简体字

离诸邪命乐行四圣种行。四于他罪若实不实无有刺讥不求人短。若于法中有所不达。心不违逆以佛为证。佛是一切智其法无量。随宜而说非我所知。如是增益善根。四法非谄曲者所能成就。是故。

　　菩萨应远离　　谄曲相四法
　　应常修习行　　直心相四法

　　在家出家菩萨。应远离四谄曲法。如曲木在稠林难可得出。如是世间有佛弟子虽入佛法不能得出生死深林。何等为四。一于佛法怀疑不信无有定心。二于众生憍慢瞋恨。三于他利心生贪嫉。四毁谤菩萨恶声流布。是为四。何等是四直心相。

Chapter 19 — The Fourfold Dharmas

needs. Thus one abandons all types of wrong livelihood while delighting in the practice of the four lineage bases of the Āryas.[304]

Fourth, one does not ridicule others' transgressions, whether real or not, and one does not focus on the shortcomings of others. Hence, if there happens to be something within the sphere of Dharma that one has not yet thoroughly understood, one must not harbor a mental opposition to it. Rather one should take the testimony of the Buddha as the basis for certifying its validity. [Thus, one should reflect], "Given that the Buddha is possessed of all-knowledge, his dharmas are countless. He speaks of them in ways that are appropriate to any given circumstance. These are not matters about which I have direct knowledge."

And so it is that one increases one's roots of goodness.

3. Fourfold Dharmas That Increase or Stop Flattery and Deviousness

In addition, there are four dharmas perfectible only by those without flattery or deviousness. Therefore:

> The bodhisattva should utterly abandon
> four dharmas characterized by flattery and deviousness.
> He should always cultivate and practice
> four dharmas characterized by a straightforward mind.

a. Four Dharmas Involving Flattery and Deviousness

Both lay and monastic bodhisattvas should utterly abandon four dharmas involving flattery or deviousness. This is a matter analogous to the difficulty of extricating a crooked tree from a dense forest. In this same manner, there are disciples of the Buddha in the world who, although they have entered the Dharma of the Buddha, they are nonetheless unable to depart from the dense forest of *saṃsāra*. What then are these four dharmas? They are:

> First, one harbors doubts about, does not place faith in, and is unfixed in one's resolve regarding the Buddha's Dharma.
> Second, one maintains an arrogant and hate-filled attitude toward other beings.
> Third, one's mind is beset by covetousness and jealousy when witnessing benefits accruing to others.
> Fourth, the defaming rumors emanating from one's slander of bodhisattvas spread about everywhere.

These are the four.

b. Four Dharmas Characteristic of a Straightforward Mind

What then are the four dharmas characterized by a straightforward mind? They are:

正體字

```
          一者有罪即時發露無所隱藏悔過除
066b03 ‖ 滅行無悔道。二者若以實語失於王位及
066b04 ‖ 諸財寶。猶不妄語口未曾說輕人之言。三
066b05 ‖ 者若人惡口罵詈輕賤譏謗繫閉鞭杖[2]考掠
066b06 ‖ 等罪。但怨前身不咎於他。信業果報心
066b07 ‖ 無患恨。四者安住信功德中。諸佛妙法甚
066b08 ‖ 難信解。心清淨故皆能信受。敗壞菩薩行
066b09 ‖ 四諂曲。調和菩薩有四直行。是故菩薩欲
066b10 ‖ 不行諂曲相。欲行直心如說。
066b11 ‖   應捨離四種    敗壞菩薩法
066b12 ‖   應修習四種    調和菩薩法
066b13 ‖ 云何名為四敗壞菩薩法。一多聞而戲調不
066b14 ‖ 隨法行。二於教化而生戲論。不敬順[3]和
066b15 ‖ 尚阿闍梨。三者不能消人信施。毀壞防制
066b16 ‖ 而受供養。
```

简体字

一者有罪即时发露无所隐藏悔过除灭行无悔道。二者若以实语失于王位及诸财宝。犹不妄语口未曾说轻人之言。三者若人恶口骂詈轻贱讥谤系闭鞭杖考掠等罪。但怨前身不咎于他。信业果报心无患恨。四者安住信功德中。诸佛妙法甚难信解。心清净故皆能信受。败坏菩萨行四谄曲。调和菩萨有四直行。是故菩萨欲不行谄曲相。欲行直心如说。

　　应舍离四种　　败坏菩萨法
　　应修习四种　　调和菩萨法

　　云何名为四败坏菩萨法。一多闻而戏调不随法行。二于教化而生戏论。不敬顺和尚阿阇梨。三者不能消人信施。毁坏防制而受供养。

Chapter 19 — The Fourfold Dharmas

First, if one commits some offense, one immediately reveals it, conceals none of it, extinguishes it through the confession of transgressions, and then proceeds along the path that is free of regrets.

Second, even if, by telling the truth, one would lose the royal throne as well all manner of valuable treasures, one still refuses to utter a falsehood. [What's more], no words disparaging of others ever pass one's lips.

Third, if somebody assails one with harsh speech, curses, ridicule, disparagement, mocking, slanders, bondage, confinement, whipping, beating, torture, or other such offensive behavior, one only blames his own previous-life actions and does not fault others. Because one has faith in karmic retribution, one's mind remains free of anger or resentment.

Fourth, one peacefully abides in the meritorious quality of faith. It is very difficult to maintain resolute faith in the sublime Dharma of the Buddhas. But because one's mind is pure, one is able to maintain faith in it and accept it all.

4. FOURFOLD DHARMAS OF RUINED BODHISATTVAS & THOSE WELL-TRAINED

The bodhisattva fallen into ruin engages in the four sorts of flattery and deviousness. The well-trained bodhisattva has four straightforward practices to which he adheres. Consequently, if the bodhisattva wishes to refrain from engaging in actions characterized by flattery and deviousness and instead wishes to carry forth his practice with a straightforward mind, he should accord with the following lines:

One should abandon four kinds of dharmas
practiced by a bodhisattva fallen into ruin.
One should cultivate four kinds of dharmas
practiced by the well-trained bodhisattva.

a. FOUR DHARMAS PRACTICED BY A BODHISATTVA FALLEN INTO RUIN

What are the four dharmas practiced by a bodhisattva fallen into ruin? They are:

First, even though he may be learned, he nonetheless gives himself over to frivolous joking and thus fails to practice in compliance with the Dharma.

Second, he responds to transformative teaching with frivolous rationalizations and fails to respect or comply with instructions provided by monastic preceptors or monastic Dharma teachers.[305]

Third, he is unable to remain worthy of the offerings bestowed by the faithful. He does away with vigilant restraint of his behavior and yet still continues to accept offerings.

正體字

```
            四者不敬柔善菩薩心懷憍慢
066b17 ‖ 是為四。云何名為四調和菩薩法。一常樂聞
066b18 ‖ 所未聞法。聞已能如所說行。依法依義
066b19 ‖ 依如說行。二隨順義趣不惑言辭調和易
066b20 ‖ 化。於師事中用意施作。三不失戒定清淨
066b21 ‖ 活命。四[4]於調和菩薩生恭敬心隨順情重
066b22 ‖ 破憍慢心求其功德。復次菩薩有四種錯
066b23 ‖ 謬。常於此中求菩薩短。是名敗壞菩薩。若
066b24 ‖ 能親近四種善道。是名調和菩薩。如偈說。
066b25 ‖    菩薩應遠離    四種菩薩謬
066b26 ‖    菩薩應修習    四種菩薩道
066b27 ‖ 何謂菩薩四種錯謬。一於非器眾生說甚
066b28 ‖ 深法。是名錯謬。二樂深大法者。為說小乘。
066b29 ‖ 是名錯謬。
```

简体字

四者不敬柔善菩萨心怀憍慢是为四。云何名为四调和菩萨法。一常乐闻所未闻法。闻已能如所说行。依法依义依如说行。二随顺义趣不惑言辞调和易化。于师事中用意施作。三不失戒定清净活命。四于调和菩萨生恭敬心随顺情重破憍慢心求其功德。复次菩萨有四种错谬。常于此中求菩萨短。是名败坏菩萨。若能亲近四种善道。是名调和菩萨。如偈说。

　　菩萨应远离　　四种菩萨谬
　　菩萨应修习　　四种菩萨道

　　何谓菩萨四种错谬。一于非器众生说甚深法。是名错谬。二乐深大法者。为说小乘。是名错谬。

Fourth, he does not revere bodhisattvas who are gentle and good, but instead maintains an arrogant attitude toward them.

These are the four.

b. Four Dharmas Practiced by the Well-Trained Bodhisattva

What then are the four dharmas practiced by the well-trained bodhisattva? They are:

First, he is always happy to hear Dharma that he has not heard before and, having heard it, he is able to practice in accordance with what is taught. He relies on Dharma, relies on its meaning, and relies on practicing in accord with how it was taught.

Second, he accords with the import [of the teachings], is not misled by words and expressions, and is agreeable and easy to instruct. In matters related to serving as a teacher, he carries on those responsibilities with conscientious purposefulness.

Third, he is unfailing in observance of the moral precepts and in cultivation of meditative concentration while also maintaining a pure livelihood.

Fourth, in his relations with well-trained bodhisattvas, he brings forth respectful thoughts, acts congenially, and treats them with high regard. Thus he does away with any tendencies toward arrogance and focuses on their meritorious qualities.

5. Fourfold Bodhisattva Mistakes versus Good Paths of Conduct

There are also four types of mistakes a bodhisattva may be vulnerable to committing, all the while seeking in these contexts to focus on the shortcomings of other bodhisattvas. These behaviors are the defining features of a bodhisattva fallen into ruin. If, on the other hand, he is able to draw close to four paths of goodness, these serve to define the bodhisattva who is well-trained. This is as described in a verse:

> The bodhisattva should utterly abandon
> four types of bodhisattva mistakes.
> The bodhisattva should cultivate
> four paths of bodhisattva conduct.

a. Four Kinds of Bodhisattva Mistakes

What are the four kinds of bodhisattva mistakes? They are:

First, if one were to teach extremely profound Dharma to beings who are not adequate vessels to receive it, this would be a mistake.

Second, if one were to teach Small Vehicle doctrines to those who delight in profound and magnificent dharmas, this would be a mistake.

正體字

```
         三於正行道者持戒善心。輕慢
066c01 ‖ 不敬。是名錯謬。四於未成就者。未可信而
066c02 ‖ 信。攝破戒惡人以為親善。是名錯謬。何等
066c03 ‖ 為四種菩薩道。一於一切眾生行平等心。
066c04 ‖ 二以善法教化一切。三等為一切眾生說
066c05 ‖ 法。四以正行行於一切眾生。若常行菩薩
066c06 ‖ 四種錯謬。不樂思惟諸法。不勤修習善法。
066c07 ‖ 則是像菩薩。是故。
066c08 ‖    諸菩薩法中       四種像菩薩
066c09 ‖    佛說如是法       一一應遠離
066c10 ‖ 何等為四。一貪重利養不貴於法。二但為
066c11 ‖ 名譽不求功德。三求欲自樂不念眾生。
066c12 ‖ 四貪樂眷屬不樂遠離。是為四問曰像菩
066c13 ‖ 薩法云何可捨。答曰。若菩薩應修菩薩初
066c14 ‖ 行功德。
```

简体字

三于正行道者持戒善心。轻慢不敬。是名错谬。四于未成就者。未可信而信。摄破戒恶人以为亲善。是名错谬。何等为四种菩萨道。一于一切众生行平等心。二以善法教化一切。三等为一切众生说法。四以正行行于一切众生。若常行菩萨四种错谬。不乐思惟诸法。不勤修习善法。则是像菩萨。是故。

　　诸菩萨法中　　四种像菩萨
　　佛说如是法　　一一应远离

何等为四。一贪重利养不贵于法。二但为名誉不求功德。三求欲自乐不念众生。四贪乐眷属不乐远离。是为四问曰像菩萨法云何可舍。答曰。若菩萨应修菩萨初行功德。

Third, if one were to act with condescending arrogance or disrespect toward someone engaged in right practice of the path who, with wholesome mind, observes the moral precepts, this would be a mistake.

Fourth, if with regard to someone who is not yet adequately developed and cannot yet be trusted one were to nonetheless trust him, or if one were to attract a bad person [into the community] who is a breaker of precepts and take him to be a good person worthy of friendship, this would be a mistake.

b. FOUR PATHS OF GOOD BODHISATTVA CONDUCT

What are the four paths of bodhisattva conduct? They are:

First, one treats all beings with a mind of equal regard.
Second, one uses the good Dharma to teach everyone.
Third, one teaches Dharma equally to all beings.
Fourth, one behaves with right conduct toward all beings.

6. FOUR DHARMAS INDICATIVE OF AN IMITATION BODHISATTVA

If one always commits the four kinds of bodhisattva mistakes, fails to delight in judicious reflection on all dharmas, and fails to diligently cultivate good dharmas, then one is an imitation bodhisattva. Therefore:

> Among all of the bodhisattva dharmas,
> there are four that are indicative of imitation bodhisattvas.
> The Buddha said of such dharmas
> that one should utterly abandon each and every one of them.

What then are those four? They are:

First, one covets and esteems offerings and does not regard the Dharma as precious.
Second, one acts solely for the sake of fame and accolades and does not strive to acquire meritorious qualities.
Third, one seeks one's own happiness and is not mindful of other beings.
Fourth, one seeks to attract and delights in having a retinue of followers and does not delight in renunciation.

These are the four.

a. Q: HOW CAN ONE ABANDON IMITATION BODHISATTVA DHARMAS?

Question: How is one able to abandon the dharmas of an imitation bodhisattva?

b. A: CULTIVATE FOUR QUALITIES OF THE INITIAL BODHISATTVA PRACTICES

Response: One who is a bodhisattva should cultivate the meritorious qualities associated with the initial bodhisattva practices. If one does

正體字	
	是則能離像菩薩法。是故菩薩若欲
066c15 ‖	離像菩薩法。如偈說。
066c16 ‖	初行四功德　　精勤令得生
066c17 ‖	生已令增長　　增長已當護
066c18 ‖	何等為四。一者信解空法。亦信業果報。二
066c19 ‖	者樂無我法。而於一切眾生生大悲心。三
066c20 ‖	者心在涅槃而行在生死。四者布施為欲
066c21 ‖	成就眾生。而不求果報。若人欲生菩薩初
066c22 ‖	行四功德。增長守護者。當親近善知識。如
066c23 ‖	偈說。
066c24 ‖	菩薩當親近　　四種善知識
066c25 ‖	亦應當遠離　　四種惡知識
066c26 ‖	菩薩愛樂阿耨多羅三藐三菩提者。應當
066c27 ‖	親近恭敬供養四種善知識。當深遠離四
066c28 ‖	種惡知識。何等為四種善知識。一於來求
066c29 ‖	者生賢友想。以能助成無上道故。

简体字

是则能离像菩萨法。是故菩萨若欲离像菩萨法。如偈说。

　初行四功德　　精勤令得生
　生已令增长　　增长已当护

何等为四。一者信解空法。亦信业果报。二者乐无我法。而于一切众生生大悲心。三者心在涅槃而行在生死。四者布施为欲成就众生。而不求果报。若人欲生菩萨初行四功德。增长守护者。当亲近善知识。如偈说。

　菩萨当亲近　　四种善知识
　亦应当远离　　四种恶知识

菩萨爱乐阿耨多罗三藐三菩提者。应当亲近恭敬供养四种善知识。当深远离四种恶知识。何等为四种善知识。一于来求者生贤友想。以能助成无上道故。

Chapter 19 — *The Fourfold Dharmas*

this, he will then be able to abandon the dharmas of imitation bodhisattvas. Therefore, if a bodhisattva wishes to abandon the dharmas of imitation bodhisattvas, he should act in accordance with the following verse that states:

1) THE FOUR QUALITIES OF THE INITIAL BODHISATTVA PRACTICES

With regard to the four meritorious qualities of the initial practices,
one should be energetically diligent in causing them to arise.
Once they have arisen, cause them to increase.
Having caused them to increase, continue to guard them.

What then are these four? They are:

First, one develops a resolute belief in the dharma of emptiness and yet still believes in karmic retribution.

Second, one delights in the dharma of nonself and yet still brings forth the mind of great compassion for all beings.

Third, one's mind resides in nirvāṇa and yet one's practice abides within *saṃsāra*.

Fourth, one practices giving wishing to facilitate beings' development [in the path] and not because one seeks any karmic reward in return.

2) TO DEVELOP THE QUALITIES, DRAW NEAR TO A GOOD SPIRITUAL GUIDE

If someone wishes to produce, increase, and guard the four meritorious qualities associated with the initial bodhisattva practices, he should draw near to a good spiritual guide.[306] This is as described in this verse:

a) FOURFOLD GOOD AND BAD SPIRITUAL FRIENDS

The bodhisattva should draw near
to four kinds of good spiritual friends
and he should also utterly abandon
four kinds of bad spiritual friends.

The bodhisattva who delights in [the prospect of realizing] *anuttarasamyaksaṃbodhi* should draw near to, pay reverence to, and make offerings to four kinds of good spiritual friends and should remain distant from four kinds of bad spiritual friends.

i) THE FOUR KINDS OF GOOD SPIRITUAL FRIENDS

What then are the four kinds of good spiritual friends? They are:

First, one contemplates anyone who comes seeking something as a worthy friend, for he is thereby able to assist one in realizing the unsurpassable path.

正體字

二於說
067a01 ‖ 法者生善知識想。以能助成多聞智慧故。
067a02 ‖ 三稱讚出家者生善知識想。以能助成一
067a03 ‖ 切善根故。四於諸佛世尊生善知識想。以
067a04 ‖ 能助成一切佛法故。何等為四種惡知識。
067a05 ‖ 一求辟支佛乘心。樂少欲少事。二求聲聞
067a06 ‖ 乘比丘。樂坐禪者。三好讀外道路伽耶經。
067a07 ‖ 莊嚴文頌巧問答者。四所親近者。得世
067a08 ‖ 間利不得法利。是故菩薩應親近四善知
067a09 ‖ 識遠離四惡知識。若菩薩能遠離四惡知
067a10 ‖ 識。親近四善知識者則得四廣大藏。過一
067a11 ‖ 切魔事法。能生無量福德。盡能攝取一切善
067a12 ‖ 法。問曰。何等是菩薩[1]大藏法。何等是能過
067a13 ‖ 一切魔事法。何等是能生無量福德法。何等
067a14 ‖ 是能攝取一切善法。

简体字

二于说法者生善知识想。以能助成多闻智慧故。三称赞出家者生善知识想。以能助成一切善根故。四于诸佛世尊生善知识想。以能助成一切佛法故。何等为四种恶知识。一求辟支佛乘心。乐少欲少事。二求声闻乘比丘。乐坐禅者。三好读外道路伽耶经。庄严文颂巧问答者。四所亲近者。得世间利不得法利。是故菩萨应亲近四善知识远离四恶知识。若菩萨能远离四恶知识。亲近四善知识者则得四广大藏。过一切魔事法。能生无量福德。尽能摄取一切善法。问曰。何等是菩萨大藏法。何等是能过一切魔事法。何等是能生无量福德法。何等是能摄取一切善法。

Chapter 19 — The Fourfold Dharmas

Second, one contemplates anyone who speaks Dharma as a good spiritual guide, for he is able to assist one in achieving the wisdom that arises from extensive learning.

Third, one speaks in praise of monastics, contemplating them as good spiritual guides, for they are able to assist in the growth of all roots of goodness.

Fourth, one contemplates the Buddhas, the Bhagavats, as good spiritual guides, for they are able to assist one in successfully developing all of the dharmas of a buddha.

ii) The Four Kinds of Bad Spiritual Friends

What then are the four types of bad spiritual friends? They are:

First, those who have resolved to seek success in the Pratyekabuddha Vehicle and delight in having but few desires and few tasks to attend to.

Second, bhikshus seeking success in the Śrāvaka Disciple Vehicle who [merely] delight in sitting in *dhyāna* meditation.

Third, those fond of studying the non-Buddhist Lokāyata scriptures,[307] decorous literature, poetry, and polemical sophistry.

Fourth, those who, if one draws close to them, esteem the acquisition of worldly benefits, not the acquisition of benefits associated with the Dharma.

Given the above, the bodhisattva should draw near to the four kinds of good spiritual friends while remaining distant from the four types of bad spiritual friends. If the bodhisattva can remain distant from the four kinds of bad spiritual friends while drawing near to the four kinds of good spiritual friends, then he will acquire four vast treasuries, will go entirely beyond all dharmas associated with the works of Māra, will produce measureless merit, and will exhaustively accumulate all good dharmas.

3) Four Questions on the Good Effects of Good Spiritual Friends

Questions:

What are the dharmas constituting the bodhisattva's vast[308] treasuries?

What is meant by being able to go entirely beyond all dharmas associated with the works of Māra?

What are the dharmas by which one is able to produce measureless merit?

And what all is meant by being able to accumulate all good dharmas?

正體字

答曰。
067a15 ‖ 　　諸菩薩有四　　廣大藏妙法
067a16 ‖ 　　四攝諸善法　　菩提心為先
067a17 ‖ 何等為四。一得值佛。二得聞六波羅蜜。三
067a18 ‖ 於說法者心無瞋[2]閡。四以不放逸心樂
067a19 ‖ 住阿練若處。是為四大藏。能過一切魔者。
067a20 ‖ 有四法。何等四。一不捨菩提心。二於一切
067a21 ‖ 眾生心無瞋礙。三覺知一切諸見。四於諸
067a22 ‖ 菩薩心無憍慢。是為四。得無量福德法。
067a23 ‖ 復有四法。何等為四。一於法施無所悕
067a24 ‖ 求。二於破戒惡人生大悲心。三於教眾生
067a25 ‖ 中發無上菩提。四於下劣眾生而行忍辱。
067a26 ‖ 是為四。攝一切善法者。有四法。何等為四。

简体字

答曰。
　　诸菩萨有四　　广大藏妙法
　　四摄诸善法　　菩提心为先
何等为四。一得值佛。二得闻六波罗蜜。三于说法者心无瞋阂。四以不放逸心乐住阿练若处。是为四大藏。能过一切魔者。有四法。何等四。一不舍菩提心。二于一切众生心无瞋碍。三觉知一切诸见。四于诸菩萨心无憍慢。是为四。得无量福德法。复有四法。何等为四。一于法施无所悕求。二于破戒恶人生大悲心。三于教众生中发无上菩提。四于下劣众生而行忍辱。是为四。摄一切善法者。有四法。何等为四。

Chapter 19 — The Fourfold Dharmas

a) ANSWER #1: THE MEANING OF THE FOUR VAST TREASURIES

Response:
All bodhisattvas are possessed of four
vast treasuries of the sublime Dharma.
Of the four that facilitate accumulation of all good dharmas,
the resolve to attain bodhi is foremost among them.

What then are the four? They are:

First, one is able to meet the Buddha.

Second, one is able to hear [teachings on] the six *pāramitās*.

Third, one's mind remains free of the obstacle of hostility toward teacher of Dharma.

Fourth, because one is not neglectful, one's mind delights in dwelling in a forest hermitage.

These are the four vast treasuries.

b) ANSWER #2: THE MEANING OF GOING BEYOND THE WORKS OF MĀRA

As for "being able to go beyond all [works of] Māra," there are four dharmas in this connection. What are the four? They are:

First, one never abandons one's resolve to attain bodhi.

Second, one's mind remains free of the obstacle of hostility toward any being.

Third, one becomes aware of and knows all views.

Fourth, one's mind remains free of arrogance toward any bodhisattva.

These are the four.

c) ANSWER #3: THE MEANING OF PRODUCING MEASURELESS MERIT

As for the dharmas by which one acquires measureless merit, there are four additional dharmas in this connection. What are the four? They are:

First, in one's giving of Dharma, one has nothing that he hopes for in return.

Second, one brings forth the mind of great compassion for bad people who break the moral precepts.

Third, in teaching other beings, one brings forth [the resolve to attain] the unsurpassable bodhi.

Fourth, in dealing with beings of base character, one practices patience.

These are the four.

d) ANSWER #4: THE MEANING OF ACCUMULATING ALL GOOD DHARMAS

As regards the accumulation of all good dharmas, this refers to four dharmas. And what are those four? They are:

正體字

067a27 ‖ 一於空閑不現矯異常行。二行四攝[3]法不
067a28 ‖ 求恩報。三不惜身命護持正法。四種諸善
067a29 ‖ 根時以菩提心為先。是為四。是一一四法
067b01 ‖ 皆應廣解。於文煩多故不[4]廣。今如佛所
067b02 ‖ 說以偈略解。若菩薩欲得諸菩薩藏。欲過
067b03 ‖ 一切魔事。欲攝一切善法者。皆當遠離。
067b04 ‖ 　　二空繫二縛　　二障二垢法
067b05 ‖ 　　二瘡及二坑　　二燒二病法
067b06 ‖ 若菩薩欲得諸菩薩藏等功德者。應當遠
067b07 ‖ 離是諸二法。何等為二[5]空繫法。一貪著應
067b08 ‖ 路伽耶等經。二嚴飾衣鉢。二縛者。一著諸
067b09 ‖ 見縛。二貪[6]名利縛。二障法者。一親近白
067b10 ‖ 衣。二疏遠善人。

简体字

一于空闲不现矫异常行。二行四摄法不求恩报。三不惜身命护持正法。四种诸善根时以菩提心为先。是为四。是一一四法皆应广解。于文烦多故不广。今如佛所说以偈略解。若菩萨欲得诸菩萨藏。欲过一切魔事。欲摄一切善法者。皆当远离。
　　二空系二缚　　二障二垢法
　　二疮及二坑　　二烧二病法

　　若菩萨欲得诸菩萨藏等功德者。应当远离是诸二法。何等为二空系法。一贪着应路伽耶等经。二严饰衣钵。二缚者。一着诸见缚。二贪名利缚。二障法者。一亲近白衣。二疏远善人。

First, when abiding in the solitary leisure of a recluse, one avoids adopting affected or eccentric practices.

Second, in the practice of the four means of attraction, one does not seek anything in return for one's kindness.

Third, in protecting and preserving right Dharma, one will not be sparing of even one's own body and life.

Fourth, when planting roots of goodness, one takes the resolve to attain bodhi as the foremost priority.

These are the four. Ideally, one should take up an extensive explanation of each and every one of these sets of four dharmas. However, because the text could become tediously complex, we do not present extensive discussions,[309] but now instead use verses to provide concise explanations that accord with what the Buddha has taught.

7. Eight Twofold Dharmas the Bodhisattva Must Completely Abandon

If a bodhisattva wishes to acquire the treasuries of the bodhisattvas, if he wishes to go beyond all the works of Māra, and if he wishes to accumulate all good dharmas, he should completely abandon all of the following things:

The two hollow attachments and the two types of bondage,
the two types of hindrances and the two defiling dharmas,
the two ulcerous sores as well as the two types of abysses,
the two causes of being burned and the two illness dharmas.

If the bodhisattva wishes to gain access to the bodhisattva treasuries and the other sorts of meritorious qualities, then he should utterly abandon all of these twofold dharmas.

a. The Two Hollow Attachments

What is meant by "the two hollow attachments"? The first is that of indulging a covetous attachment to ideas related to the Lokāyata scriptures. The second is adding decorative ornamentation to one's robe and bowl.

b. The Two Types of Bondage

As for "the two types of bondage," the first is the bondage of being attached to views. The second is the bondage of coveting fame and profit.

c. The Two Hindrance Dharmas

Of the "the two hindrance dharmas," the first is that of forming close relationships with members of the laity and the second is that of remaining distant from good people.

正體字

067b11 ‖ 二垢法者。一忍受諸煩惱。二樂諸檀越知識。二瘡法者。一見他人過。
067b12 ‖ 二自藏其過。二坑法者。一毀壞正法。二破
067b13 ‖ 戒受供。二燒法者。一以穢濁心而著袈裟。
067b14 ‖ 二受淨戒者供給。出家之人有二病難治。
067b15 ‖ 一[7]憎上慢人自謂能降伏心。二求大乘者
067b16 ‖ 沮壞其意。若菩薩遠離如是等法。更有疾
067b17 ‖ 得阿耨多羅三藐三菩提法。則能疾得。又得
067b18 ‖ 諸佛辟支佛阿羅漢之所稱歎。問曰。何等法
067b19 ‖ 是疾得阿耨多羅三藐三菩提法。何等是諸
067b20 ‖ 佛辟支佛阿羅漢之所稱歎。答曰。
067b21 ‖ 　能行四諦相　　疾得佛菩提
067b22 ‖ 　[8]又行四法者　　三聖所稱歎

简体字

二垢法者。一忍受诸烦恼。二乐诸檀越知识。二疮法者。一见他人过。二自藏其过。二坑法者。一毁坏正法。二破戒受供。二烧法者。一以秽浊心而着袈裟。二受净戒者供给。出家之人有二病难治。一憎上慢人自谓能降伏心。二求大乘者沮坏其意。若菩萨远离如是等法。更有疾得阿耨多罗三藐三菩提法。则能疾得。又得诸佛辟支佛阿罗汉之所称叹。问曰。何等法是疾得阿耨多罗三藐三菩提法。何等是诸佛辟支佛阿罗汉之所称叹。答曰。
　能行四谛相　　疾得佛菩提
　又行四法者　　三圣所称叹

d. THE TWO DEFILING DHARMAS

As for "the two defiling dharmas," the first is that of simply enduring and accepting one's own afflictions. The second is that of delighting in carrying on friendships with benefactors.[310]

e. THE TWO ULCEROUS SORES

Of "the two ulcerous sores," the first is that of focusing on the transgressions of others. The second is that of concealing one's own transgressions.

f. THE TWO ABYSS-LIKE DHARMAS

As for "the two abyss-like dharmas," the first is that of contributing to the damage and destruction of right Dharma. The second is that of accepting offerings even as one breaks the moral precepts.

g. THE TWO DHARMAS LEADING TO BEING BURNED

Of "the two dharmas leading to being burned," the first is that of continuing to wear the monastic's *kāṣāya* robe even when possessed of a defiled mind. The second is that of [continuing under such circumstances] to accept sustaining offerings from those who are pure in their observance of the precepts.

h. THE TWO TYPES OF ILLNESSES

Monastics may be prone to developing "the two types of illnesses" that are difficult to cure. The first is that of possessing such overweening pride[311] that one thinks he can simply subdue his own mind [without availing himself of a teacher or the appropriate Dharma antidotes]. The second is that of obstructing and destroying the resolve of someone seeking to [cultivate the practices of] the Great Vehicle.

If the bodhisattva is able to completely abandon dharmas such as these, there are additional dharmas by which he may swiftly attain *anuttarasamyaksaṃbodhi*. [If he avails himself of them], he can then swiftly attain it. He may also acquire those that are praised by all buddhas, *pratyekabuddhas*, and arhats.

1) Q: WHICH DHARMAS LEAD TO BODHI & WHICH EARN ĀRYAS' PRAISE?

Question: Which dharmas are those that lead to rapid attainment of *anuttarasamyaksaṃbodhi*? And which of them are praised by all buddhas, *pratyekabuddhas*, and arhats?

2) A: THE FOUR TRUTHS' PRACTICES AND FOUR ADDITIONAL DHARMAS

Response:
> If one is able to practice the characteristic practices of the four truths, one will swiftly attain the bodhi of the Buddha.
> Also, if one practices four additional dharmas, he will be praised by the three classes of *āryas*.

正體字	067b23 ‖ 何等為四諦相。一求一切善法故勤行精 067b24 ‖ 進。二若聽受讀誦經法如所說行。三厭 067b25 ‖ 離三界如殺人處常求[9]免出。四為利益 067b26 ‖ 安樂一切眾生故。自利其心諦名真實不 067b27 ‖ 誑。得阿耨多羅三藐三菩提故名為不虛。 067b28 ‖ 復有四法。為三聖稱歎。何等為四。一乃至 067b29 ‖ 失命不為惡事。二常行法施。三受法常一 067c01 ‖ 其心。四若生染心。即能正觀染心起染因 067c02 ‖ 緣。是染根者何名為染。何者是染於何事 067c03 ‖ 起誰生是染。如是正憶念。知虛妄無實無 067c04 ‖ 有。決定信解諸法空[10]故。無所有法故。如 067c05 ‖ 是正觀染因緣故。不起諸[11]惡業。餘一切煩 067c06 ‖ 惱亦如是觀。菩薩得是大人所稱歎法。離 067c07 ‖ 諸惡
简体字	何等为四谛相。一求一切善法故勤行精进。二若听受读诵经法如所说行。三厌离三界如杀人处常求免出。四为利益安乐一切众生故。自利其心谛名真实不诳。得阿耨多罗三藐三菩提故名为不虚。复有四法。为三圣称叹。何等为四。一乃至失命不为恶事。二常行法施。三受法常一其心。四若生染心。即能正观染心起染因缘。是染根者何名为染。何者是染于何事起谁生是染。如是正忆念。知虚妄无实无有。决定信解诸法空故。无所有法故。如是正观染因缘故。不起诸恶业。余一切烦恼亦如是观。菩萨得是大人所称叹法。离诸恶

Chapter 19 — The Fourfold Dharmas

a) THE FOUR DHARMAS CHARACTERISTIC OF CULTIVATING THE TRUTHS

What are the practices that are characteristic of cultivating the four truths? They are:

First, because one seeks to develop all good dharmas, one is energetically vigorous.

Second, one listens to, accepts, studies, and recites the Dharma of the sutras and then practices in accordance with their teachings.

Third, having renounced the three realms of existence as comparable to a site of human slaughter, one always seeks the means to avoid and transcend them.

Fourth, in order to benefit and bring peace and happiness to all beings, one strives to benefit one's own mind.

The "truth" [of "the four truths"] refers to being genuine and non-deceptive. Because [the four truths] lead to the attainment of *anuttarasamyaksaṃbodhi*, they are not false.

b) THE FOUR DHARMAS PRAISED BY THE THREE CLASSES OF ĀRYAS

Next, there are four dharmas that are praised by the three classes of *āryas*. What are those four? They are:

First, even if abstaining from it will cost one's life, one will not do any bad deed.

Second, one always practices the giving of Dharma.

Third, one remains single-mindedly focused whenever receiving teachings on Dharma.

Fourth, if one produces a defiled thought, one is immediately able to correctly contemplate the defiled thought and the causes and conditions that initiated the defiled thought, [reflecting], "As for these 'roots of defilement,' just what about them is designated as 'defiled'? What is it that becomes 'defiled'? In what circumstances does it arise? And precisely who is it that that generates this defilement?"

As one carries on right reflection in this way, one realizes that these factors are all false, devoid of any genuine substantiality, and devoid of any intrinsic existence of their own. Because one possesses a definite and resolute belief in the emptiness of all dharmas, because no dharmas whatsoever exist intrinsically, and because one carries on such right contemplation of the causes and conditions of defilement, one does not bring forth any sort of evil karmic action. As for all the other afflictions, one also contemplates them in this same manner.

The bodhisattva's acquisition of these dharmas that elicit the praises of the great men is a consequence of his abandoning all bad karmic

正體字	煩惱業故。心則具足捨心者如說。 067c08 ‖ 　具足[12]於捨心　　求世出世利 067c09 ‖ 　求此諸利時　　心無有厭倦 067c10 ‖ 是菩薩具足捨法。欲行法施行財施利益 067c11 ‖ 眾生故。若求世間出世間諸利。未得時心 067c12 ‖ 無疲懈。世間利者。善解世間經書技藝方術 067c13 ‖ 巧便等。出世間利者。[13]諸無漏根力覺道法。 067c14 ‖ 如說。 067c15 ‖ 　如是求二利　　心無有疲懈 067c16 ‖ 　以無疲懈故　　能得諸深法 067c17 ‖ 　因從求經書　　而能得智慧 067c18 ‖ 　具足知世間　　最上第一法 067c19 ‖ 無疲懈者。疲懈名厭惡。所學若無厭惡則 067c20 ‖ 心無疲倦。若無疲倦則求諸經藝醫方技 067c21 ‖ 術禮儀法則皆無疲倦。無疲倦故則得智 067c22 ‖ 慧。具足深知世間宜法。世間法者。方俗所 067c23 ‖ 宜
简体字	烦恼业故。心则具足舍心者如说。 　具足于舍心　　求世出世利 　求此诸利时　　心无有厌倦 是菩萨具足舍法。欲行法施行财施利益众生故。若求世间出世间诸利。未得时心无疲懈。世间利者。善解世间经书技艺方术巧便等。出世间利者。诸无漏根力觉道法。如说。 　如是求二利　　心无有疲懈 　以无疲懈故　　能得诸深法 　因从求经书　　而能得智慧 　具足知世间　　最上第一法 无疲懈者。疲懈名厌恶。所学若无厌恶则心无疲倦。若无疲倦则求诸经艺医方技术礼仪法则皆无疲倦。无疲倦故则得智慧。具足深知世间宜法。世间法者。方俗所宜

actions rooted in the afflictions. His mind then completely develops the relinquishing mind. This is as described below:

> 8. THE BODHISATTVA'S RELINQUISHING MIND & FREEDOM FROM WEARINESS
>
> Having completely developed the relinquishing mind,
> one seeks to bestow both worldly and world-transcending benefit.
> As one seeks to bestow these forms of benefit,
> one's mind remains free of any weariness.

This bodhisattva completely develops the dharma of relinquishing. His desire to practice Dharma giving and to practice the giving of material wealth is due to his motivation to benefit beings. Whether he is striving to bring about worldly benefit or world-transcending benefit, so long as he has not yet succeeded, his mind still remains free of any weariness or any inclination to retreat.

[The bestowal of] "worldly benefit" entails a thorough understanding of the world's classical texts, cultural arts, professional skills, the implementation of clever expedients, and so forth. [The bestowal of "world-transcending benefit" entails [providing instruction in the practice of] the dharmas of the [five] root faculties, [five] powers, [seven] limbs of enlightenment, and [eightfold] path [as practiced by those who have become] free of the contaminants. This is as described here:

> a. THE BODHISATTVA DOESN'T WEARY OF PROVIDING TWO KINDS OF BENEFIT
>
> As one seeks in this manner to bestow the two kinds of benefit,
> one's mind remains free of weariness and neglectfulness.
> Through staying free of weariness and neglectfulness,
> one becomes able to acquire all of the profound dharmas.
> It is due to seeking it from within the classical works
> that one is able to acquire wisdom.
> One thereby develops a perfectly complete knowledge of the world's
> most superior and foremost dharmas.

In "remaining free of weariness and neglectfulness," "weariness and neglectfulness" refer to feelings of loathing. If in one's studies one remains free of loathing, then one's mind will remain free of weariness. If one remains free of weariness, then one will always be free of weariness as one seeks to acquire the dharmas found within the scriptures, the arts, medicine, professional skills, and the codes of propriety. If one remains free of weariness in these pursuits, then one will acquire wisdom and will perfect a deep knowledge of the dharmas appropriate for use in the world.

"Dharmas of the world" refers here to the local customs determining what is appropriate in any given situation for adapting to the

正體字

067c24 ‖ 隨世間心。世間治法皆悉能知。是故能
067c24 ‖ 知上中下眾生。隨宜而引導。善解世間事
067c25 ‖ 深有慚愧心。隨宜引導者。於上中下者各
067c26 ‖ 有所宜。慚愧者。自恥所行名為慚。因他
067c27 ‖ 生恥名為愧。有人以自作而羞見他而愧。
067c28 ‖ 世間法中愧為先用。如經說。二清白法護
067c29 ‖ 持世間。所謂慚愧。如偈說。
068a01 ‖ 　　隨人[1]有愧時　　知法知罪福
068a02 ‖ 　　無愧善人遠　　無惡而不作
068a03 ‖ 問曰。何故慇懃教菩薩善知世間宜法。答
068a04 ‖ 曰。菩薩若知世間法者。則於眾生易相悅
068a05 ‖ 入。化導其心令住大乘。若不知世法。乃
068a06 ‖ 至不能教化一人。是故世間法者。則是教
068a07 ‖ 化眾生方便之道。

简体字

随世间心。世间治法皆悉能知。是故能知上中下众生。随宜而引导。善解世间事深有惭愧心。随宜引导者。于上中下者各有所宜。惭愧者。自耻所行名为惭。因他生耻名为愧。有人以自作而羞见他而愧。世间法中愧为先用。如经说。二清白法护持世间。所谓惭愧。如偈说。

　　随人有愧时　　知法知罪福
　　无愧善人远　　无恶而不作

问曰。何故殷勤教菩萨善知世间宜法。答曰。菩萨若知世间法者。则于众生易相悦入。化导其心令住大乘。若不知世法。乃至不能教化一人。是故世间法者。则是教化众生方便之道。

minds of those in the world. One becomes well able to understand the dharmas necessary to maintain order in the world. One thereby becomes able to understand what is appropriate in addressing beings possessed of superior, middling, and inferior capacities. In guiding them, one accords with whatsoever is appropriate. One becomes skillful in understanding worldly affairs while also maintaining a mind deeply imbued with a sense of shame and a dread of blame.

As for "in guiding them, one accords with whatever is appropriate," this refers to the fact that, in addressing the needs of beings of superior, middling, and inferior capacity, each of them has what is most appropriate for use in instructing them.

As for "a sense of shame and a dread of blame," "shame" refers to a feeling of mortification regarding one's own actions whereas "dread of blame" refers to the potential for feeling mortified by [the critical judgments of] others.

There are those who hold that it is because of one's actions that one feels a sense of shame and that it is because of seeing others that one feels a dread of blame. Within the sphere of worldly dharmas, having a dread of blame is the primary priority. This is as described in a sutra [that says], "There are two dharmas of pristine purity that guard the world, namely a sense of shame and a dread of blame." This is as described in a verse:

Whenever there are people possessed of a dread of blame,
they understand the Dharma, karmic transgressions, and merit.
As for those devoid of a dread of blame, good people avoid them,
for there is no evil that they will not do.

    b. Q: Why Are Bodhisattvas Taught to Understand Worldly Dharmas?

Question: Why do you so assiduously counsel bodhisattvas to develop a good understanding of the dharmas appropriate for use in the world?

    c. A: Knowledge of the World Enables Dharma Teaching Expedients

Response: If the bodhisattva is knowledgeable about the dharmas of the world, it will be easy for him to gain access to beings in a way that is mutually pleasing. He will thereby be able to teach them and guide the development of their minds in a way that causes them to abide in the Great Vehicle.

If one does not understand the dharmas of the world, then he will be incapable of teaching even a single person. Therefore the dharmas of the world serve as an expedient path for teaching beings.

正體字

	菩薩如是知世間法。具
068a08 ‖	足慚愧心。如說。
068a09 ‖	加惡而敬養　　何況利己者
068a10 ‖	有愧有恭敬　　不輕笑善者
068a11 ‖	是菩薩愧心多故。於諸惡人[2]尚能恭敬供
068a12 ‖	養迎送問訊。何況善人能利於我有功德
068a13 ‖	者。有愧恭敬二心故。於諸賢善少知識者
068a14 ‖	而不輕慢。作是念。有功德者自隱於世。
068a15 ‖	如灰覆火。鄙薄世法不應輕賤。若我以小
068a16 ‖	因緣而輕賤者。即便得罪。復次。
068a17 ‖	凡諸有所作　　雖難能究竟
068a18 ‖	則於世間中　　亦是不退相
068a19 ‖	是菩薩凡有所作。若起塔寺若設大會若
068a20 ‖	救罪人。如是等一切世間諸難事中心無廢
068a21 ‖	退。所造未成。要以種種諸方便力身口心
068a22 ‖	力令得成就。不但佛法有不退轉。世間事
068a23 ‖	中亦有不退轉相。

简体字

菩萨如是知世间法。具足惭愧心。如说。

　加恶而敬养　　何况利己者
　有愧有恭敬　　不轻笑善者

是菩萨愧心多故。于诸恶人尚能恭敬供养迎送问讯。何况善人能利于我有功德者。有愧恭敬二心故。于诸贤善少知识者而不轻慢。作是念。有功德者自隐于世。如灰覆火。鄙薄世法不应轻贱。若我以小因缘而轻贱者。即便得罪。复次。

　凡诸有所作　　虽难能究竟
　则于世间中　　亦是不退相

是菩萨凡有所作。若起塔寺若设大会若救罪人。如是等一切世间诸难事中心无废退。所造未成。要以种种诸方便力身口心力令得成就。不但佛法有不退转。世间事中亦有不退转相。

Chapter 19 — *The Fourfold Dharmas*

9. One Must Have a Sense of Shame, Dread of Blame, and Respect

The bodhisattva who understands the dharmas of the world in this way has a mind that is well equipped with a sense of shame and dread of blame. This is as described here:

> When subjected to bad actions, remain respectful and generous.
> How much the more so in dealing with those that benefit oneself.
> One possessed of a dread of blame and an inclination to be respectful
> refrains from slighting or deriding those who are good.

Because this bodhisattva has a well-developed dread of blame, even in dealing with badly-behaved people, he is still able to behave respectfully, bestow offerings, welcome those who arrive, escort those who depart, and extend greetings. How much the more so would this be the case when dealing with good people possessed of meritorious qualities.

Because one is possessed of the two mental attitudes of a dread of blame on the one hand and respectfulness on the other, in dealing with those who are worthy and good but deficient in knowledge, one does not adopt a slighting or arrogant attitude toward them. One reflects: "There are those who are possessed of meritorious qualities, yet conceal their presence in the world just as ashes conceal hot coals. They should not be slighted merely because they feel disdain for such worldly concerns. If I were to slight them for such minor reasons, I would be guilty of a karmic offense."

Additionally:

10. The Bodhisattva Must Never Retreat from Completing His Works

> In whatever endeavor one takes up,
> although it may be difficult, one still completes it.
> This being so, even in endeavors undertaken in the world,
> they are still characterized by never retreating.

No matter what endeavors this bodhisattva takes up, whether that be building a stupa or a temple, arranging for a great Dharma assembly, or rescuing someone who has committed some crime—in all such difficult endeavors in the world, one's mind refuses to desist or retreat from the task. So long as any given endeavor has not yet been completed, it is essential to use the power of all sorts of expedients as well as the power of physical, verbal, and mental persistence to successfully complete the task.

It is not only with respect to endeavors related to the Dharma of the Buddha that one refuses to turn back in retreat, for even in worldly endeavors, one maintains this characteristic of refusing to turn back in retreat.

正體字

068a24 ‖ 　　問曰。以何因緣能成此
　　　　事。答曰。有堪忍力者。則能究竟。如說。
068a25 ‖ 　　　得大堪忍力　　深供養諸佛
068a26 ‖ 　　　隨佛所教化　　皆悉能受持
068a27 ‖ 　　菩薩得堪忍力故。以是力於諸佛供養敬
068a28 ‖ 　　禮。隨宜供奉衣服飲食等。又佛教化。若持戒
068a29 ‖ 　　禪定。若降伏心意。若實觀諸法。於是事中
068b01 ‖ 　　用堪任力。如人得利刀宜應有益中用不
068b02 ‖ 　　於無益中用。如說。
068b03 ‖ 　　　以信悲慈捨　　堪受無疲[3]厭
068b04 ‖ 　　　又能知義趣　　引導眾生心
068b05 ‖ 　　　愧堪受第一　　深供養諸佛
068b06 ‖ 　　　住佛所說中　　正行此十法
068b07 ‖ 　　　[4]能淨治初地　　是則菩薩道
068b08 ‖ 　　若菩薩以信為始後住佛[5]故則能淨治初
068b09 ‖ 　　地。是十法中以信為初。信名於諸佛法因
068b10 ‖ 　　緣中心得決定

簡體字

问曰。以何因缘能成此事。答曰。有堪忍力者。则能究竟。如说。
　　得大堪忍力　　深供养诸佛
　　随佛所教化　　皆悉能受持
菩萨得堪忍力故。以是力于诸佛供养敬礼。随宜供奉衣服饮食等。又佛教化。若持戒禅定。若降伏心意。若实观诸法。于是事中用堪任力。如人得利刀宜应有益中用不于无益中用。如说。
　　以信悲慈舍　　堪受无疲厌
　　又能知义趣　　引导众生心
　　愧堪受第一　　深供养诸佛
　　住佛所说中　　正行此十法
　　能净治初地　　是则菩萨道
若菩萨以信为始后住佛故则能净治初地。是十法中以信为初。信名于诸佛法因缘中心得决定

Chapter 19 — *The Fourfold Dharmas*

a. Q: How Can the Bodhisattva Succeed in Completing His Works?

Question: Based on which causes and conditions is one able to succeed in such endeavors?

b. A: He Has Patience, Makes Offerings, and Follows Teachings

Response: If one is possessed of the power of patient endurance, he will be able to successfully complete his endeavors. This is as described here:

> Having developed this power of great patient endurance,
> one becomes deeply committed to making offerings to the Buddhas.
> Whatever teachings have been taught by the Buddhas,
> one is able to accept and uphold all of them.

Having developed this power of patient endurance, the bodhisattva uses this power to make offerings to the Buddhas, to bow to them in reverence, and to freely offer up, as appropriate, robes, food, drink, and so forth.

Additionally, whatever the Buddha has taught one to do, whether that be upholding the moral precepts, cultivating *dhyāna* concentration, subduing one's own mind, or contemplating all dharmas in accordance with ultimate reality—one uses the power of patient endurance in all of these endeavors.

This is just as when one obtains a sharp knife. He should then use it for beneficial purposes and should not use it for unbeneficial purposes. As it is said:

11. Right Practice of Ten Dharmas Enabling 1st Ground Purification

> It is through faith, compassion, kindness, and relinquishing,
> through the capacity for tireless patient endurance,
> through also being able to understand the significance [of teachings],
> through serving as a guide for the minds of other beings,
>
> through keeping a dread of blame enabling supreme endurance,
> through making momentous offerings to the Buddhas,
> and through abiding in what the Buddha has taught—
> it is through right practice of these ten dharmas
> that one becomes able to purify the first of the grounds.
> These then are what constitute the bodhisattva path.

It is due to the bodhisattva's ability to carry out these practices, beginning with faith and concluding with abiding in the Buddha's teachings, that he is able to purify the first ground.

a. Faith

These ten dharmas all take faith as what is foremost. "Faith" refers to the mind's reaching a definite resolve with respect to the causes and

正體字	又加好樂。何以故。是菩薩 068b11 ‖ 心性清淨故得深根信力。有信力故於眾 068b12 ‖ 生中而生悲心作是念。一切諸佛法以大 068b13 ‖ 悲為本。我今一心好樂佛法。是故於眾生 068b14 ‖ 中應生悲心。此悲漸增則成大悲。得大悲 068b15 ‖ 故於眾生中則生慈心。作是念。我應隨力 068b16 ‖ 利益眾生則成實悲行慈。利眾生時即能 068b17 ‖ 行捨。內外所有皆能施與。作是念。如我是 068b18 ‖ 物。為欲利益安樂眾生則成實慈。又諸眾 068b19 ‖ 生信受我語。為欲行捨求利財物故。堪 068b20 ‖ 受種種諸苦惱事。作是念若有疲厭。則於 068b21 ‖ 世間技藝經書[6]田作工巧諸求財利因緣 068b22 ‖ 則無所獲。是故應於世間技藝經書等無 068b23 ‖ 有疲厭。以堪受故能知義趣。
简体字	又加好乐。何以故。是菩萨心性清净故得深根信力。有信力故于众生中而生悲心作是念。一切诸佛法以大悲为本。我今一心好乐佛法。是故于众生中应生悲心。此悲渐增则成大悲。得大悲故于众生中则生慈心。作是念。我应随力利益众生则成实悲行慈。利众生时即能行舍。内外所有皆能施与。作是念。如我是物。为欲利益安乐众生则成实慈。又诸众生信受我语。为欲行舍求利财物故。堪受种种诸苦恼事。作是念若有疲厌。则于世间技艺经书田作工巧诸求财利因缘则无所获。是故应于世间技艺经书等无有疲厌。以堪受故能知义趣。

conditions of the Dharma of the Buddhas, one that is enhanced by one's delight in it.

How does this come to be the case? It is because this bodhisattva's mind is pure in nature that he is able to develop such a deeply rooted power of faith.

b. COMPASSION

Having acquired this power of faith, he then brings forth the mind of compassion toward beings, reflecting as follows: "The Dharma of all Buddhas takes the great compassion as its very foundation. I now single-mindedly delight in the Dharma of the Buddha. Therefore, when in the midst of beings I should bring forth the mind of compassion."

As this compassion of his gradually increases, it develops into the great compassion.

c. KINDNESS

Having developed the great compassion, one then brings forth thoughts of kindness toward other beings, reflecting as follows: "I should benefit other beings in a manner consistent with my capacity to do so. If I do this, then this would become the practice of kindness based on genuine compassion."

d. RELINQUISHING

When one benefits beings, one is immediately able to practice relinquishing to the degree that one can give away all of his inward or outward possessions, reflecting as follows: "If I dispense with my possessions in this manner, doing so out of a wish to benefit beings and make them happy, this shall become genuine kindness. In addition, these beings will then become well-disposed to trust and accept my words."

e. TIRELESSLY PATIENT ENDURANCE

One then becomes able to endure all manner of distressing situations in order to acquire valuable possessions with which to fulfill one's desire to practice such relinquishing. One then reflects in this manner: "If in doing this I were to become weary, then there would be nothing gained from my pursuit of wealth by involving myself in the means for mastering the world's various skills, arts, classical texts, and agriculture techniques. Therefore I should be tireless in learning the world's skills, arts, classical texts, agricultural techniques, and other such things."

f. THE ABILITY TO UNDERSTAND THE MEANING OF TEACHINGS

Through such a capacity for patient endurance, one is able to understand the meaning and significance [of what one studies], whereupon

正體字		
		作是念。世
	068b24 ‖	間經書以義為味。若人善知經書義味。則
	068b25 ‖	於世[7]間法悉能通了。能通了故則能引導
	068b26 ‖	上中下眾生。作是念。若人無有慚愧則不
	068b27 ‖	能令眾生歡喜。為令[8]歡喜故當行慚愧。
	068b28 ‖	作是念。若無堪受則不成世間出世間利。
	068b29 ‖	有堪受故則能引導一切眾生皆令歡喜
	068c01 ‖	心歡喜故信受我語。以信受故勤行方便
	068c02 ‖	而作唱導。作是念。若眾生供養佛者。則多
	068c03 ‖	所利益。欲令眾生供養佛故。即自一心
	068c04 ‖	供養於佛及形像舍利。眾生信受則便隨效
	068c05 ‖	供養於佛。種人天因緣。住於三乘菩薩。如
	068c06 ‖	是次行十法。則能淨治初地。

简体字: 作是念。世间经书以义为味。若人善知经书义味。则于世间法悉能通了。能通了故则能引导上中下众生。作是念。若人无有惭愧则不能令众生欢喜。为令欢喜故当行惭愧。作是念。若无堪受则不成世间出世间利。有堪受故则能引导一切众生皆令欢喜心欢喜故信受我语。以信受故勤行方便而作唱导。作是念。若众生供养佛者。则多所利益。欲令众生供养佛故。即自一心供养于佛及形像舍利。众生信受则便随效供养于佛。种人天因缘。住于三乘菩萨。如是次行十法。则能净治初地。

one reflects as follows: "The flavor of worldly classics and texts derives from the meaningful ideas contained within them. If one becomes well able to understand the conceptual flavor of such classics, one is thereby able to gain a penetrating comprehension of all worldly dharmas."

    g. SERVING AS GUIDE FOR BEINGS' MINDS

If one becomes able to completely comprehend them, one can then serve as a guide for other beings of superior, middling, and inferior capacities.

    h. A SENSE OF SHAME AND DREAD OF BLAME

One then reflects as follows: "If one has no sense of shame or dread of blame, he will be unable to inspire delight in other beings. In order to cause them to be delighted, I should act with a sense of shame and dread of blame."

One then reflects as follows: "If I have no capacity for patient endurance, then I will not be able to bring about either worldly or world-transcending benefit. It is through the capacity for patient endurance that one can serve as a guide for all beings and cause them all to be delighted. It is because their minds are delighted that they will then trust and accept my words. Because they believe and accept my words, I can diligently implement skillful means by which I can serve as a guide for them."

    i. MAKING OFFERINGS TO THE BUDDHA

One also reflects as follows: "If beings make offerings to the Buddha, then they will gain much benefit from this." Then, wishing to influence beings to make offerings to the Buddha, one immediately adopts this practice oneself by making offerings to the Buddha, his images, and his śarīra relics.

    j. ABIDING IN THE BUDDHA'S TEACHINGS

Because those beings believe and accept whatever one does, they then emulate one's practice of making offerings to the Buddha and thereby establish the causes and conditions for being reborn in the human and celestial realms and for abiding in the Dharma of the Three Vehicles.

It is in this manner that the bodhisattva sequentially develops his practice of these ten dharmas by which he is then able to purify the first bodhisattva ground.

The End of Chapter Nineteen

正體字

068c07 ‖ 　　　念佛品第二十
068c08 ‖ 菩薩於初地。究[9]竟所行處。自以善根力能
068c09 ‖ 見數百佛菩薩。如是[10]降伏其心深愛佛
068c10 ‖ 道。如所聞初地行具足究竟。自以善根福德
068c11 ‖ 力故能見十方現在諸佛皆在目前。問曰。
068c12 ‖ 但以善根福德力故得見諸佛。為更有餘
068c13 ‖ 法耶。答曰。
068c14 ‖ 　佛為跋陀婆　　所說深三昧
068c15 ‖ 　得是三昧寶　　能得見諸佛
068c16 ‖ 跋陀婆羅是在家菩薩。能行頭陀。佛為是菩
068c17 ‖ 薩說般舟[11]三昧經。般舟三昧名見諸佛現
068c18 ‖ 前菩薩。得是大寶三昧。雖未得天眼天耳
068c19 ‖ 而能得見十方諸佛。亦聞諸佛所說經法。
068c20 ‖ 問曰。是三昧者當以何道可得。

简体字

念佛品第二十

　　菩萨于初地。究竟所行处。自以善根力能见数百佛菩萨。如是降伏其心深爱佛道。如所闻初地行具足究竟。自以善根福德力故能见十方现在诸佛皆在目前。问曰。但以善根福德力故得见诸佛。为更有余法耶。答曰。
　　佛为跋陀婆　　所说深三昧
　　得是三昧宝　　能得见诸佛
　　跋陀婆罗是在家菩萨。能行头陀。佛为是菩萨说般舟三昧经。般舟三昧名见诸佛现前菩萨。得是大宝三昧。虽未得天眼天耳而能得见十方诸佛。亦闻诸佛所说经法。问曰。是三昧者当以何道可得。

Chapter 20
Mindfulness of the Buddhas

XX. Chapter 20: Mindfulness of the Buddhas
   A. On Finishing 1st Ground Practices, the Bodhisattva Sees Buddhas

> When the bodhisattva dwelling on the first ground
> has completed what is to be practiced,
> due to the power of his roots of goodness, he will naturally
> be able to see several hundred buddhas.[312]

When, in this [above-discussed] manner, the bodhisattva subdues his own mind, he develops a deep love for the path to buddhahood. He then completely fulfills the first-ground practices in accordance with the way he learned them. Then, due to the power of his roots of goodness and merit, he is naturally able to see the present-era buddhas of the ten directions right before his very eyes.

    1. Q: Is There Any Other Way to Be Able to See the Buddhas?

Question: Is it solely through the power of roots of goodness and merit that one is then able to see buddhas or is there some other method by which one can do so?

    2. A: On Entering the Pratyutpanna Samādhi, One Sees the Buddhas

Response:
> There is a deep samādhi that the Buddha
> explained for the sake of Bhadrapāla.
> If one acquires this samādhi treasure,
> one becomes able to see the Buddhas.

Bhadrapāla was a lay bodhisattva well able to practice the *dhūta* austerities. It was for the sake of this bodhisattva that the Buddha spoke the *Pratyutpanna Samādhi Sūtra*.[313] The *pratyutpanna* samādhi is one in which one sees the Buddhas right before one's very eyes. When the bodhisattva accesses this magnificently precious samādhi, even though he might not yet have gained the heavenly eye and heavenly ear, he is nonetheless able to see the buddhas of the ten directions and he is also able to listen to the Dharma of the sutras being taught by those buddhas.

    3. Q: How Can One Acquire This Samadhi?

Question: What means should one use to acquire this samādhi?

答曰。

正體字

068c21 ||　　當念於諸佛　　處在大眾中
068c22 ||　　三十二相具　　八十好嚴身
068c23 || 行者以是三昧念諸佛三十二相八十種好
068c24 || 莊嚴其身。比丘親近諸天供養。為諸大眾
068c25 || 恭敬圍繞。專心憶念取諸佛相。又念諸佛
068c26 || 是大願者。成就大悲而不斷絕。具足大慈
068c27 || 深安眾生。行於大喜滿一切願。行於捨心
068c28 || 捨離憎愛不捨眾生。行於諦處常不欺
068c29 || 誑。行於捨處淨除慳垢。行於善處其心善
069a01 || 寂。行於慧處得大智慧。具行檀波羅蜜為
069a02 || 法施主。具行尸羅波羅蜜戒行清淨。具行
069a03 || 羼提波羅蜜能忍如地。具行毘梨耶波羅
069a04 || 蜜精進超絕。具行禪波羅蜜滅諸定障。具
069a05 || 行般若波羅蜜破智慧障閡。

简体字

答曰。

　　当念于诸佛　　处在大众中
　　三十二相具　　八十好严身

　行者以是三昧念诸佛三十二相八十种好庄严其身。比丘亲近诸天供养。为诸大众恭敬围绕。专心忆念取诸佛相。又念诸佛是大愿者。成就大悲而不断绝。具足大慈深安众生。行于大喜满一切愿。行于舍心舍离憎爱不舍众生。行于谛处常不欺诳。行于舍处净除悭垢。行于善处其心善寂。行于慧处得大智慧。具行檀波罗蜜为法施主。具行尸罗波罗蜜戒行清净。具行羼提波罗蜜能忍如地。具行毗梨耶波罗蜜精进超绝。具行禅波罗蜜灭诸定障。具行般若波罗蜜破智慧障阂。

Chapter 20 — Mindfulness of the Buddhas

4. A: ENVISION THE BUDDHAS WITH THE 32 MARKS AND 80 CHARACTERISTICS

Response:
One should bring to mind the Buddhas,
envisioning them as residing in a great assembly,
replete with all thirty-two major marks
and eighty secondary characteristics adorning their bodies.

a. RECOLLECTION OF THE BUDDHAS' QUALITIES AND ACCOMPLISHMENTS

In cultivating this samādhi, the practitioner brings to mind the Buddhas with the thirty-two major marks and eighty secondary characteristics gracing their bodies, with bhikshus close by, with devas making offerings, and with a grand and reverential assembly surrounding them. With focused mind, one envisions each of the major marks of those buddhas.

One also recollects the Buddhas as those who are possessed of great vows, recollects their perfection of the great compassion and the fact that it has not been cut off, recollects their perfection of the great kindness through which they bring profound peace to beings, recollects their practice of the great sympathetic joy and their fulfillment of beings' aspirations, and recollects their practice of equanimity through which they have abandoned aversion and craving and do not abandon beings.

One also recollects their practice of the truthfulness basis of meritorious qualities by which they are never deceptive, recollects their practice of the relinquishment basis of meritorious qualities by which they have rid themselves of the miserliness defilement, recollects their practice of the thoroughgoing [quiescence][314] basis of meritorious qualities by which their minds maintain a state of thoroughgoing quiescence, and recollects their practice of the wisdom basis of meritorious qualities through which they have acquired great wisdom.[315]

One recollects too their perfect practice of *dāna pāramitā* by which they have become the lords of Dharma giving, their perfect practice of *śīla pāramitā* by which their observance of the moral precepts is pure, their perfect practice of *kṣānti pāramitā* by which their capacity for patient endurance is analogous to that of the earth, their perfect practice of *vīrya pāramitā* by which their vigor is preeminent, their perfect practice of *dhyāna pāramitā* by which they have destroyed all hindrances to meditative absorption, and their perfect practice of *prajñā pāramitā* by which they have destroyed all obstacles to wisdom.

b. RECOLLECTION OF THE 32 MARKS OF THE BUDDHAS

One recollects too:

正體字	手足輪相能 069a06 ‖ 轉法輪。足安立相安住諸法。手足網縵相 069a07 ‖ 滅諸煩惱。七處滿相諸功德滿。手足柔軟相 069a08 ‖ 說柔和法。纖長指相長夜修集諸善妙法。 069a09 ‖ 足跟廣相眼廣學廣。大直身相說大直道。足 069a10 ‖ 趺高相一切中[1]高毛上旋相能令眾生住上 069a11 ‖ 妙法。伊[2]泥鹿[[跳-兆+專]>[跳-兆+專]]相[[跳-兆+專]>[跳-兆+專]]傭漸麁。臂長過膝相 069a12 ‖ 臂如金[3]關。陰馬藏相有法寶藏。身金色相 069a13 ‖ 有無量色。皮細薄相說細妙法。一一毛相示 069a14 ‖ 一相法。白毫莊嚴面相樂觀佛面無厭。師 069a15 ‖ 子上身相如師子無畏。肩圓大相善分別五 069a16 ‖ 陰。
简体字	手足轮相能转法轮。足安立相安住诸法。手足网缦相灭诸烦恼。七处满相诸功德满。手足柔软相说柔和法。纤长指相长夜修集诸善妙法。足跟广相眼广学广。大直身相说大直道。足趺高相一切中高毛上旋相能令众生住上妙法。伊泥鹿[跳-兆+專]相[跳-兆+專]佣渐粗。臂长过膝相臂如金关。阴马藏相有法宝藏。身金色相有无量色。皮细薄相说细妙法。一一毛相示一相法。白毫庄严面相乐观佛面无厌。师子上身相如师子无畏。肩圆大相善分别五阴。

Chapter 20 — *Mindfulness of the Buddhas*

Their mark of having the wheel insignia on the hands and feet, emblematic of their ability to turn the wheel of Dharma;

Their mark of securely planted feet, emblematic of their standing securely in every dharma;

Their mark of proximal webbing on fingers and toes, emblematic of the extinguishing of all afflictions;

Their mark of seven places of fullness, emblematic of their complete fulfillment of merit;

Their mark of soft and tender hands and feet, emblematic of their harmonious manner of proclaiming the Dharma;

Their mark of slender and long fingers and toes, emblematic of their cultivation and accumulation of every sort of good and sublime dharma during the long night [of previous lifetimes];

Their mark of having broad heels and wide eyes, emblematic of their vast learning;

Their mark of having a large and erect body, emblematic of their proclamation of the great and upright Dharma;

Their mark of having high arches, emblematic of their being lofty in all things;

Their mark of having upwardly spiraling bodily hairs, emblematic of their ability to cause beings to abide in the supreme and sublime dharma;

Their mark of having legs gradually growing in thickness like those of the *aiṇeya* antelope;

Their mark of long arms reaching past the knees, their arms appearing like golden gate bars;[316]

Their mark of the stallion-like retracted male organ, emblematic of their possession of the treasury of Dharma jewels;

Their mark of the golden-hued body emanating light of countless colors;

Their mark of fine and thin skin, emblematic of their proclamation of subtle and sublime Dharma;

Their mark of one hair per hair pore, emblematic of their revealing of the single-mark Dharma;

Their mark of the [mid-brow] white-down tuft adorning the countenance, due to which beings happily and tirelessly gaze at the Buddha's face;

Their mark of a lion-like upper torso, emblematic of the Buddha, like the lion, being one who is fearless;

Their mark of round and large shoulders, emblematic of their ability to make skillful distinctions regarding the nature of the five aggregates;

正體字

069a17 ‖ 腋下滿相滿大善根。得味味相具足寂滅
069a17 ‖ 味。方身相破生死[4]畏。肉髻相頭未嘗低敬。
069a18 ‖ 舌大相色如真珊瑚能自覆面。梵音相身
069a19 ‖ 相至梵天。師子頰車相肩廣相能破外道。齒
069a20 ‖ 齊相行清白[5]禪。齒平等相平等心於一切眾
069a21 ‖ 生。齒密[6]緻相離諸貪著。四十齒相具足四
069a22 ‖ 十不共法。紺青眼相慈心視眾生。牛王睫相
069a23 ‖ 睫長不亂。得希有色樂見無厭。以此三十
069a24 ‖ 二相莊嚴其身。八十種好間錯映發。福德具
069a25 ‖ 足威力殊絕名聞流布。戒香塗身世法所不
069a26 ‖ 動。諸煩惱所不染。

简体字

腋下满相满大善根。得味味相具足寂灭味。方身相破生死畏。肉髻相头未尝低敬。舌大相色如真珊瑚能自覆面。梵音相身相至梵天。师子颊车相肩广相能破外道。齿齐相行清白禅。齿平等相平等心于一切众生。齿密致相离诸贪着。四十齿相具足四十不共法。绀青眼相慈心视众生。牛王睫相睫长不乱。得希有色乐见无厌。以此三十二相庄严其身。八十种好间错映发。福德具足威力殊绝名闻流布。戒香涂身世法所不动。诸烦恼所不染。

Chapter 20 — *Mindfulness of the Buddhas*

Their mark of fullness in the subaxillary region, emblematic of their possession of a full measure of good roots;

Their mark of distinguishing every flavor, emblematic of their having perfectly tasted the flavor of quiescence;

Their mark of having a square-set body, emblematic of having crushed the fear of births and deaths;

Their mark of the fleshy prominence atop the crown, emblematic of their heads never having to be lowered in reverence [to someone superior];

Their mark of the large tongue the color of real coral that is even able to cover the face;

Their mark of the Brahmā-like voice and the physical mark that reaches even to the Brahma Heaven;

Their mark of the lion-like jaw;

Their mark of the broad shoulders, these being emblematic of their ability to demolish [the views held by] non-Buddhist traditions;

Their mark of even teeth, emblematic of their practice of pure *dhyāna* meditation;

Their mark of their teeth being of even height, emblematic of their minds' equal regard for all beings;

Their mark of closely set teeth, emblematic of their abandonment of the desires;

Their mark of having forty teeth, emblematic of their perfection of the forty dharmas exclusive to buddhas;

Their mark of blue eyes, emblematic of their looking on beings with minds imbued with kindness;

Their mark of having eyelashes like those of the royal bull, with the lashes long and in no way disarrayed;

Their obtaining of a rare physical form that beings look on without ever tiring of holding it in their gaze;

Their having bodies adorned with these thirty-two marks;

c. Recollection of Other Qualities of the Buddhas

Their having the eighty minor characteristics like inlaid adornments on their bodies, emanating brilliant radiance;

Their complete fulfillment of merit;

Their transcendently supreme and awesome powers;

Their wide-spread illustrious esteem;

Their bodies' incense-like fragrance produced by purity in observing the moral precepts;

Their invulnerability to being moved by worldly dharmas;

Their ability to remain undefiled by any arising of afflictions;

正體字	惡言所不污。遊戲諸 069a27 ‖ 神通。諸佛如是威力猛盛無敢當者。以慧 069a28 ‖ 說法如師子吼如意自在。以精進力破諸 069a29 ‖ 癡闇。以大光明普照天地。諸問答中最無 069b01 ‖ 有上。一切仰瞻無下觀者。常以慈心觀察 069b02 ‖ 眾生。念如大海。定如須彌。忍辱如地。增長 069b03 ‖ 眾[7]主所種福德如水滋潤。能生眾生諸善 069b04 ‖ 根力如風開發。成就眾生如火熟物。智慧 069b05 ‖ 無邊猶如虛空。普雨大法如大密雲。不染 069b06 ‖ 世法猶如蓮華。[8]破外道[9]師如師子搏鹿。 069b07 ‖ 能舉重擔如大象王。能導大眾如大牛王。 069b08 ‖ 眷屬清淨如轉輪王。世間最上如大梵王。
简体字	恶言所不污。游戏诸神通。诸佛如是威力猛盛无敢当者。以慧说法如师子吼如意自在。以精进力破诸痴闇。以大光明普照天地。诸问答中最无有上。一切仰瞻无下观者。常以慈心观察众生。念如大海。定如须弥。忍辱如地。增长众主所种福德如水滋润。能生众生诸善根力如风开发。成就众生如火熟物。智慧无边犹如虚空。普雨大法如大密云。不染世法犹如莲华。破外道师如师子搏鹿。能举重担如大象王。能导大众如大牛王。眷属清净如转轮王。世间最上如大梵王。

Chapter 20 — *Mindfulness of the Buddhas*

Their ability to remain unsullied by others' verbal abuse;

Their ability to roam and sport through use of their spiritual powers;

The ability of the Buddhas to be so intensely magnificent in the manifestation of their awe-inspiring powers that no one would dare obstruct them;

Their freely exercised sovereign mastery in using wisdom to proclaim the Dharma that is like the roaring of a lion;

Their ability to dispel the darkness of delusion by marshaling the power of vigor;

Their use of magnificent brilliance to everywhere illuminate the heavens and the earth;

Their utter invincibility in debate;

Their being such that everyone looks up to them and no one can look down on them;

Their constancy in regarding all beings with kindness;

Their possession of mindfulness as vast as the great oceans;

Their meditative absorption that is like Mount Sumeru [in its unshakability];

Their possession of patience comparable to the earth's [ability to endure anything];

Their ability to bring about growth in the merit planted by beings that is analogous [to the growth-enhancing capacity of] water's moisture;[317]

Their ability to bring forth roots of goodness in beings that, in its power, is like the rising of the wind;

Their ability to ripen beings that is like fire's ability to cook things;

Their possession of wisdom as boundless as empty space;

Their universal raining down of the great Dharma [rain] that is like [the rain that pours down from] immense dense clouds;

Their ability to remain unstained by worldly dharmas that is like lotus blossoms' [ability to rise from mud and yet remain unsullied by it];

Their ability, like lions pouncing on deer, to decisively refute [the doctrines of] non-Buddhist masters;

Their ability to bear a heavy burden that is like that of the great king of the elephants;

Their ability to lead a great congregation of followers that is like that of the great king of bulls;

Their possession of a retinue of pure followers that is like [the retinue of] a wheel-turning king;

Their utter supremacy in the world that is like that of the lord of the Mahābrahma Heaven;

正體字	可 069b09 ‖ 愛[10]可樂如清天明月。普照能然猶如朗 069b10 ‖ 日。與諸眾生安樂因緣。猶如仁父。憐愍眾 069b11 ‖ 生隨宜將護猶如慈母。所行清淨如天真 069b12 ‖ 金。有大勢力如天帝釋。勤利世間如護世 069b13 ‖ 主。治煩惱病猶如醫王。救諸衰患猶如親 069b14 ‖ 族。積諸功德如大庫藏。其戒無量。其定無 069b15 ‖ 邊。其慧無稱。解脫無等解脫知見無等等。 069b16 ‖ 於一切事最無有比。一切世間最無上故 069b17 ‖ 名第一人。成大法故名為[11]大人。如是菩 069b18 ‖ 薩以大人相念觀諸佛。是諸佛者於無量 069b19 ‖ 無邊百千萬億不可思議不可計劫修習功 069b20 ‖ 德。善能守護身口意業。
简体字	可爱可乐如清天明月。普照能然犹如朗日。与诸众生安乐因缘。犹如仁父。怜愍众生随宜将护犹如慈母。所行清净如天真金。有大势力如天帝释。勤利世间如护世主。治烦恼病犹如医王。救诸衰患犹如亲族。积诸功德如大库藏。其戒无量。其定无边。其慧无称。解脱无等解脱知见无等等。于一切事最无有比。一切世间最无上故名第一人。成大法故名为大人。如是菩萨以大人相念观诸佛。是诸佛者于无量无边百千万亿不可思议不可计劫修习功德。善能守护身口意业。

Their ability to inspire fondness and delight that is like that of a bright moon in the clear night sky;

Their universal illumination that is able to burn as brightly as the brilliantly shining sun;

Their bestowal on beings of the causes and conditions for peace and happiness that is like [the generosity of] a humane father;

Their acting out of pity toward beings, protecting them in whatever way is appropriate, that is like the actions of a lovingly kind mother;

Their purity of conduct that is like [the purity of] the real gold in the heavens;

Their possession of the power of great strength that is like that of Indra in the heavens;

Their diligence in benefiting those in the world that is like that of a world-protecting lord;

Their ability to cure the disease of the afflictions that is like [the curative power of] a king of physicians;

Their ability to rescue one from disastrous circumstances that is like that of close relatives;

Their ability to accumulate a store of meritorious qualities that is like an immense treasury;

Their possession of immeasurably vast moral virtue;

Their possession of boundless meditative absorptions;

Their ineffable wisdom;

Their unequaled liberation;

Their knowledge and vision of liberation that is the equal of the unequaled;

Their incomparability in all things;

Their supremacy over everyone in the world due to which they are recognized as foremost among men;

And their perfection of great dharmas by which they are recognized as great men.

It is in this way that the bodhisattva engages in recollective contemplation of all buddhas in accordance with their possession of the qualities characteristic of the great men. [So, too, he recollects]:

    d. Recollection of More Special Qualities & Abilities of Buddhas

That these buddhas have cultivated these meritorious qualities for a countless, boundless, inconceivable, and incalculable number of hundreds of thousands of myriads of *koṭis* of kalpas during which they have been well able to guard their physical, verbal, and mental karma;

正體字	於過去未來現在無 069b21 ‖ 為不可說五藏法中悉斷諸疑。定答分別答 069b22 ‖ 反問答置答。於四問答無有錯謬。善說根 069b23 ‖ 力覺道念處正勤如意三十七助道法。善能 069b24 ‖ 分別無明諸行識名色六入觸受愛取有生 069b25 ‖ 老死因果。於眼色耳聲鼻香舌味身觸意法 069b26 ‖ 無所繫著。善說九部經法。[12]所謂修多羅 069b27 ‖ [13]岐夜[14]授記伽陀[15]憂陀那尼陀那[16]如是諸 069b28 ‖ 經[17]斐肥[18]儺未曾有經。不為貪欲瞋恚愚癡 069b29 ‖ 憍慢身見邊見邪見見取戒取疑諸使所使。 069c01 ‖ 不為無信無慚愧諂曲戲調放逸懈怠睡眠 069c02 ‖ 瞋恨慳嫉諸惱所侵。知見苦斷集證滅修 069c03 ‖ 道。可去已去。可見已見。所作已辦。盡破怨 069c04 ‖ 賊。具足諸願。是世間尊是世間父是世間 069c05 ‖ [19]主。是善來善去善意善寂善滅善解脫者。 069c06 ‖ 在無量無邊十方恒河沙等世間中住。
简体字	于过去未来现在无为不可说五藏法中悉断诸疑。定答分别答反问答置答。于四问答无有错谬。善说根力觉道念处正勤如意三十七助道法。善能分别无明诸行识名色六入触受爱取有生老死因果。于眼色耳声鼻香舌味身触意法无所系着。善说九部经法。所谓修多罗岐夜授记伽陀忧陀那尼陀那如是诸经斐肥儺未曾有经。不为贪欲嗔恚愚痴憍慢身见边见邪见见取戒取疑诸使所使。不为无信无惭愧谄曲戏调放逸懈怠睡眠嗔恨悭嫉诸恼所侵。知见苦断集证灭修道。可去已去。可见已见。所作已办。尽破怨贼。具足诸愿。是世间尊是世间父是世间主。是善来善去善意善寂善灭善解脱者。在无量无边十方恒河沙等世间中住。

Chapter 20 — *Mindfulness of the Buddhas*

That they are well able to completely sever all doubts with respect to the five categorical repositories of dharmas: past dharmas, future dharmas, present dharmas, unconditioned dharmas, and ineffable dharmas;

That, without falling into any error, they employ the four modes of reply: the definitive reply, the distinguishing reply, the counter-questioning reply, and the reply that sets aside the question;[318]

That they skillfully explain the dharmas of the thirty-seven enlightenment factors, namely: the faculties, the powers, the limbs of enlightenment, the path, the stations of mindfulness, the right efforts, and the foundations of psychic power;[319]

That they are well able to distinguish [each link comprising the chain of] cause-and-effect, namely: ignorance, actions, consciousness, name-and-form, the six sense faculties, contact, feeling, craving, grasping, becoming, birth, and aging-and-death;

That they are free of any attachment to the eye or visual forms, to the ear or sounds, to the nose or fragrances, to the tongue or flavors, to the body or touch, or to the mind or dharmas [as objects of mind];

That they skillfully expound the nine types of passages contained in the Dharma of the sutras, namely: sutras; *geyas*; prophetic teachings or expositions; *gāthās*; *udānas*; *nidānas*; [short] discourses beginning with "Thus [spoke the Buddha]..."; *vaipulyas*; and unprecedented events;

That they are not influenced by any of the negative influences such as: greed, hatred, delusion, arrogance, the view that conceives of the existence of true personhood, extreme views, wrong views, seizing upon views; seizing on rules and regulations, or doubts;

That they are not assailed by such afflictions as absence of faith, absence of a sense of shame, absence of a dread of blame, flattery, deviousness, frivolousness, neglectfulness, indolence, somnolence, animosity, miserliness, or jealousy;

That they have known and seen the truth of suffering, have cut off its origination, have realized cessation, have cultivated the path, have abandoned what is to be abandoned, have seen what is to be seen, have done what is to be done, have utterly destroyed the foes,[320] and have perfectly fulfilled their vows;

That they are venerated in the world, are as fathers to the world, and are lords of the world, are well come, are well gone, are possessed of the well-cultivated mind, are consummately skilled in meditative stillness, are well-realized in the realization of cessation, and are well liberated;

That, as they abide in countless and boundless worlds throughout the ten directions in worlds as numerous as the sands in the

正體字	如現 069c07 ‖ 在前菩薩。又應以八十種好念觀諸佛。甲 069c08 ‖ 色鮮赤行清白法。甲隆而大生在大家。甲色 069c09 ‖ 潤澤深愛眾生。指圓[20]纖長其行深遠。指肉 069c10 ‖ 充滿善根充滿。指漸次而長次第集諸佛法。 069c11 ‖ 脈覆不見不覆身口意[21]念脈。無麁結破 069c12 ‖ 煩惱結。[22]踝平不現不隱藏法。足不邪曲 069c13 ‖ 度[23]墮邪眾。行如師子是人中師子。行如象 069c14 ‖ 王是人象王。行如鵝王。高飛如鴻。行如 069c15 ‖ 牛王人中最尊。行時右旋善說正道。[24]身不 069c16 ‖ 僂曲心常不曲。身堅而直讚堅牢戒。
简体字	如现在前菩萨。又应以八十种好念观诸佛。甲色鲜赤行清白法。甲隆而大生在大家。甲色润泽深爱众生。指圆纤长其行深远。指肉充满善根充满。指渐次而长次第集诸佛法。脉覆不见不覆身口意念脉。无粗结破烦恼结。踝平不现不隐藏法。足不邪曲度堕邪众。行如师子是人中师子。行如象王是人象王。行如鹅王。高飞如鸿。行如牛王人中最尊。行时右旋善说正道。身不偻曲心常不曲。身坚而直赞坚牢戒。

Ganges, [one envisions them] as if they were appearing directly before one's very eyes.

e. CONTEMPLATIVE RECOLLECTION OF THE 80 SECONDARY CHARACTERISTICS

The bodhisattva should also envision in contemplation all of the buddhas as graced with their eighty secondary characteristics,[321] recollecting:

That their nails are copper-colored is emblematic of their practice of pure dharmas;

That their nails are prominent and large is emblematic of birth into the great clan;

That their nails are glossy and smooth is emblematic of a deep affection for beings;

That their fingers are round, tapered, and long is emblematic of the depth and duration of their practice;

That their fingers are fully fleshed is emblematic of fully developed roots of goodness;

That their fingers are tapered and long is emblematic of sequential accumulation of all dharmas of a buddha;

That their veins are hidden and invisible, but they do not hide the lineage of [the quality of their conduct in] body, mouth, and mind;

That there are no thick knots in their veins is emblematic of their having broken up the knots of afflictions;

That their ankle bones are flat and inconspicuous is emblematic of their not hiding away the Dharma;

That their feet are not misaligned in their track is emblematic of their liberation of the multitudes who have fallen into deviant conduct;

That their gait is like that of the lion is emblematic of their being the lions among men;

That their gait is also like that of the king of elephants is emblematic of their being the elephant kings among men;

That their gait is also like the king of geese is emblematic of their flying high, like the wild goose;

That their gait is also like the king of bulls is emblematic of their being the most revered of all men;

That, when walking, they turn around to the right, is emblematic of their skillful proclamation of the right path;

That their posture is not hunched or crooked is emblematic of the fact that their minds are never crooked;

That their bodies stand solid and erect in their posture is emblematic of their praise of solidity and durability in upholding the moral precepts;

正體字	身漸 069c17 ‖ 次大次第說法。普身諸分大而端嚴。善能解 069c18 ‖ 說大妙功德。身相具足具足法者。足步間等 069c19 ‖ 等心眾生。其身淨潔三業清淨。身膚細軟心 069c20 ‖ 性自軟。身離塵垢善見離垢。身不縮沒心 069c21 ‖ 常不沒。身無[25]邊量善根無量。肌肉緊密永 069c22 ‖ 斷後身。支節分明善說十二因緣分別明 069c23 ‖ 了。身色無闇知見無闇。腹圓周滿弟子行具。 069c24 ‖ 腹淨鮮潔善能了知生死過惡。腹不高出 069c25 ‖ 破憍慢[26]山。腹平不現說平等法。臍圓而深 069c26 ‖ 通甚深法。臍畫右旋弟子[27]順教。
简体字	身渐次大次第说法。普身诸分大而端严。善能解说大妙功德。身相具足具足法者。足步间等等心众生。其身净洁三业清净。身肤细软心性自软。身离尘垢善见离垢。身不缩没心常不没。身无边量善根无量。肌肉紧密永断后身。支节分明善说十二因缘分别明了。身色无闇知见无闇。腹圆周满弟子行具。腹净鲜洁善能了知生死过恶。腹不高出破憍慢山。腹平不现说平等法。脐圆而深通甚深法。脐画右旋弟子顺教。

Chapter 20 — *Mindfulness of the Buddhas*

That their bodies gradually grew large is emblematic of their sequential exposition of Dharma;

That all parts of their bodies are large and majestic is emblematic of their ability to skillfully explain the great and sublime meritorious qualities;

That their bodies are perfectly developed is emblematic of their perfection in the Dharma;

That their strides are of equal length is emblematic of their equal-minded regard for all beings;

That their bodies are pristine in their cleanliness is emblematic of the purity of their three types of karma;

That their skin is fine and soft is emblematic of the naturally pliant character of their minds;

That their bodies remain free of all dust and dirt is emblematic of their good views that have abandoned all defilement;

That their bodies do not shrink through wasting [even in old age] is emblematic of their minds' always remaining unsinkable;

That their bodies are boundless and immeasurable is emblematic of the immeasurability of their roots of goodness;

That the flesh of their bodies is taut and finely textured is emblematic of their eternal severance of [karmically-compulsory] later incarnations;

That all of their joints are smooth in their articulations is emblematic of their skillful explication of the twelve causes and conditions and their perfectly clear distinguishing of each of them;

That the hue of their bodies is not dark is emblematic of their knowledge and vision being free of any darkness;

That their waists are full all around is emblematic of their disciples' possession of fully developed conduct;

That their bellies are clear [of blemishes] and of fresh and immaculate appearance is emblematic of their being well able to completely know the serious faults of *saṃsāra*;

That their bellies do not protrude is emblematic of their having crushed the mountain of arrogance;

That their bellies are flat and do not show is emblematic of the fact that their proclamation of Dharma is directed equally toward everyone;

That their umbilici are round and deep is emblematic of their penetrating comprehension of extremely deep dharmas;

That their umbilici have a rightward swirl is emblematic of their disciples' compliance with instruction;

身遍端嚴

069c27 ‖ 弟子遍淨。威儀[28]鮮潔心淨無比。身無點子
069c28 ‖ 無黑印法。手濡勝兜羅綿。受化者身輕如
069c29 ‖ 毛。手畫[29]文深威儀深重。手畫文長觀受法
070a01 ‖ 者長遠後事。手畫潤澤捨親愛潤得大道
070a02 ‖ 果。面貌不長結戒有開。脣赤如頻婆果。見
070a03 ‖ 一切世間。如鏡中像。舌柔而軟先以軟語
070a04 ‖ [1]度脫眾生。舌薄而廣功德純厚。舌赤如[2]深
070a05 ‖ 紅凡夫心難解佛法令解。聲如雷震不畏
070a06 ‖ 雷聲。其聲和柔說柔軟法。四牙圓直說直道
070a07 ‖ 法。四牙俱利度利根者四牙鮮白清白第一。

正體字

身遍端严弟子遍净。威仪鲜洁心净无比。身无点子无黑印法。手濡胜兜罗绵。受化者身轻如毛。手画文深威仪深重。手画文长观受法者长远后事。手画润泽舍亲爱润得大道果。面貌不长结戒有开。唇赤如频婆果。见一切世间。如镜中像。舌柔而软先以软语度脱众生。舌薄而广功德纯厚。舌赤如深红凡夫心难解佛法令解。声如雷震不畏雷声。其声和柔说柔软法。四牙圆直说直道法。四牙俱利度利根者四牙鲜白清白第一。

简体字

Chapter 20 — *Mindfulness of the Buddhas*

That their bodies are in every way graceful in their refinements is emblematic of the thoroughgoing purity of their disciples;

That their awesomeness in deportment is utterly immaculate is emblematic of the incomparable purity of their minds;

That their bodies are free of blemishes is emblematic of their being completely free of any black dharmas;

That the softness of their hands is superior even to that of *tūla*-cotton silk is emblematic of the experience of those receiving their instruction who feel as if their bodies have become as light as a wisp of down;

That the lines on their palms form a deep pattern is emblematic of the profoundly dignified nature of their awesome deportment;

That the lines on their palms are long is emblematic of their contemplative regard for the long-term future of those receiving their Dharma teaching;

That the pattern on their palms is lustrous and smooth is emblematic of their relinquishing of the affection of relatives and of their acquisition of the fruits of the great path;

That their countenances remain free of any long-faced expression is emblematic of the presence of exceptional circumstances in the moral precepts they establish;

That their lips are as red as *bimba* fruit is emblematic of their looking on the entire world as merely like an image reflected in a mirror;

That their tongues are soft and pliant is emblematic of their initial use of gentle speech in liberating beings;

That their tongues are thin and wide is emblematic of the purity and abundance of their meritorious qualities;

That their tongues are crimson red is emblematic of their Dharma's ability to cause common people to understand what they find difficult to understand;

That their voices are like thunder is emblematic of their not fearing the boom of a thunderclap;

That their voices are harmonious and gentle is emblematic of their proclamation of soft and gentle Dharma;

That their four central incisors are rounded [in their visible profile] and straight is emblematic of their proclamation of the Dharma of the straight path;

That their four central incisors are all sharp is emblematic of their liberation of those beings who are possessed of sharp faculties;

That their four central incisors are immaculately white is emblematic of their being foremost in purity;

正體字	070a08 ‖ 四牙齊等住戒平地。牙漸次細漸次說四諦 070a09 ‖ 法。鼻高隆直住智高山。鼻中清淨弟子清白。 070a10 ‖ 眼廣而長智慧廣遠。睫不希疎善擇眾生。 070a11 ‖ 眼白黑[3]鮮淨如青蓮華葉。天人婇女以好 070a12 ‖ 眼敬禮。眉高而長名聞遠流。眉毛潤澤善知 070a13 ‖ 軟法。耳等相似聞法者等。耳根不壞度不壞 070a14 ‖ 心眾生。額平而好善離諸見。額廣無妨廣 070a15 ‖ 破外道。頭分具足善具大願。髮色如黑蜂 070a16 ‖ 轉五欲樂。髮厚而[*]緻結使[4]已盡。美髮柔 070a17 ‖ [5]軟軟利智[6]者能知法味。
简体字	四牙齐等住戒平地。牙渐次细渐次说四谛法。鼻高隆直住智高山。鼻中清净弟子清白。眼广而长智慧广远。睫不希疏善择众生。眼白黑鲜净如青莲华叶。天人婇女以好眼敬礼。眉高而长名闻远流。眉毛润泽善知软法。耳等相似闻法者等。耳根不坏度不坏心众生。额平而好善离诸见。额广无妨广破外道。头分具足善具大愿。发色如黑蜂转五欲乐。发厚而致结使已尽。美发柔软软利智者能知法味。

That their four central incisors are evenly and equally set is emblematic of their standing on the level ground of the moral precepts;

That the profile of their rows of teeth gradually taper to those that are smaller [in height] is emblematic of the graduated sequence in their explanation of the dharma of the four truths;

That they have noses that are high and straight-ridged is emblematic of their standing atop the high mountain of wisdom;

That their nasal apertures are clear and clean is emblematic of the purity of their disciples;

That their eyes are wide and laterally long is emblematic of their wisdom's qualities of being vast and far-reaching;

That their eyelashes are not sparse or in disarray is emblematic of their skill in their differential assessment of beings;

That the whites and pupils of their eyes are as fresh and pristine as the petals of a blue lotus blossom is emblematic of their being such that even devas and heavenly maidens are moved to gaze upon them fondly and bow down in reverence before them;

That their eyebrows are high and long is emblematic of the far-reaching spread of their fame;

That the hair of their eyebrows is smooth and glossy is emblematic of their thoroughgoing knowledge of the dharmas of mental pliancy;

That their ears are equal in their appearance is emblematic of the equality of all who listen to the Dharma;

That their faculty of hearing is undamaged is emblematic of their ability to liberate any being possessed of an undamaged mind;

That their foreheads are flat and of fine appearance is emblematic of their having skillfully abandoned all views;

That their foreheads are unrestricted in their wide breadth is emblematic of their having broadly refuted [the claims of] non-Buddhist traditions;

That their heads are in all respects perfectly developed is emblematic of their having thoroughly perfected [the goals of] their great vows;

That their hair is the color of the black bee is emblematic of their having transformed the pleasures associated with the five types of desire;

That their hair is dense and fine is emblematic of their having already put an end to the fetters;

That their hair, so pleasing in its appearance, is soft in texture is emblematic of their pliant and sharp wisdom's ability to know well the flavor of dharmas;

正體字	
070a18	髮不散亂言常不亂。髮潤而澤常無麁言。髮有美香。以七覺
070a19	意香華隨宜化導。髮中有德字安字喜字。
070a20	手足中亦有德字安字喜字。菩薩如是應
070a21	念諸佛處在大眾[7]講說正法坐師子座。
070a22	其座以琉璃雜寶為脚。以真珊瑚妙赤真
070a23	珠以為[8]枕。金薄[9]幃帳柔軟滑澤種種天衣
070a24	以為敷具。[10]以寶師子赤金為身。[11]虎珀為
070a25	眼。[12]車璩為尾。珊瑚為舌。白金剛為四牙。
070a26	真白銀為髮。毛髮長廣。具足其床在此四
070a27	師子上。大象王牙以為凭机。其承足[*]机眾
070a28	寶所成。為諸天龍夜叉乾闥婆阿修羅迦樓
070a29	羅緊那羅摩睺羅伽之所敬禮。諸佛如是在
070b01	此床上。著竭支泥洹僧。不高不下覆身三
070b02	分。周匝齊整著淺色袈裟。條數分明不高不
070b03	下亦不參差。處[13]八大聖莊嚴眾中人天大
070b04	會。龍金翅鳥俱共聽法心無瞋[14]恨。一切大
070b05	眾深心慚愧敬愛於佛。皆共一心聽佛所說。

简体字

发不散乱言常不乱。发润而泽常无粗言。发有美香。以七觉意香华随宜化导。发中有德字安字喜字。手足中亦有德字安字喜字。菩萨如是应念诸佛处在大众讲说正法坐师子座。其座以琉璃杂宝为脚。以真珊瑚妙赤真珠以为枕。金薄帏帐柔软滑泽种种天衣以为敷具。以宝师子赤金为身。虎珀为眼。车碟为尾。珊瑚为舌。白金刚为四牙。真白银为发。毛发长广。具足其床在此四师子上。大象王牙以为凭机。其承足机众宝所成。为诸天龙夜叉乾闼婆阿修罗迦楼罗紧那罗摩睺罗伽之所敬礼。诸佛如是在此床上。着竭支泥洹僧。不高不下覆身三分。周匝齐整着浅色袈裟。条数分明不高不下亦不参差。处八大圣庄严众中人天大会。龙金翅鸟俱共听法心无嗔恨。一切大众深心惭愧敬爱于佛。皆共一心听佛所说。

That their hair is not in disarray is emblematic of their words never being disordered;

That their hair is smooth and glossy is emblematic of their always being free of any sort of coarse speech;

That their hair has a marvelous fragrance is emblematic of their use of the fragrant blossoms of the seven branches of bodhi to teach and guide beings in whatever way is appropriate.

That their mark of virtue, peace, and joy appears in their hair.

And that their mark of virtue, peace, and joy also appears on the palms of their hands and on the soles of their feet.

f. ENVISIONING THE BUDDHAS IN AN ASSEMBLY, TEACHING, ON THE LION SEAT

1) ENVISIONING THE BUDDHAS AS THEY SIT ON THE LION'S SEAT

It is in this manner that a bodhisattva should envision the Buddhas residing in the midst of a great assembly, speaking on right Dharma, and sitting on the lion seat. The lion seat has feet made from *vaiḍūrya* inset with various jewels, a headrest made from real coral with marvelous red pearls, and a canopy made of hammered gold. It is draped with all sorts of soft, silky, and lustrous heavenly robes and is supported by bejeweled lions whose bodies are made of purple gold. Their eyes are amber and their tails are mother-of-pearl. They have carnelian tongues, four white-diamond tusk-teeth, hair made of real white silver, and long, full manes. That seat rests upon these four lions. They form [the base of] the throne that has armrests made from royal elephant tusks and a footrest made of the many sorts of jewels.

The Buddhas receive there the reverential obeisance of the devas, dragons, *yakṣas*, *gandharvas*, *asuras*, *garuḍas*, *kinnaras*, and *mahoragas*. The Buddhas appear in this way on this throne. They wear the *saṃkakṣikā*[322] and the *nivāsana*,[323] neither too high nor too low, so that they cover the three regions of the body and are neatly arranged and straight all around. They wear a light-colored *saṃghāṭī* robe,[324] with the strips composing it clearly visible, neither too high nor too low, and not misaligned.

2) ENVISIONING THE AUDIENCE AS THE BUDDHAS TEACH DHARMA

They abide in the midst of an audience adorned by the presence of the eight kinds of great *āryas*,[325] surrounded by a great assembly of humans and devas. When in attendance there, the dragons and golden-winged *garuḍa* birds all listen together to the teaching of Dharma, remaining free of any thoughts of mutual hostility.[326]

Everyone in the entire assembly is imbued with a deeply sincere sense of shame and dread of blame as, with reverential affection for the Buddha, they all listen single-mindedly to the discourse of the

正體字

070b06 ‖ 受持思惟如所說行。專心聽受心清淨故能
070b07 ‖ 障諸蓋。一切大眾瞻仰如來無有厭足。衣
070b08 ‖ 毛皆豎泣淚心熱或有大喜。有如是者。則
070b09 ‖ 知其人心得清淨寂默湛然如入禪定。無
070b10 ‖ 愛無恚心無餘緣。有大悲相慈愍眾生。欲
070b11 ‖ 救一切心不諂曲。寂滅清淨分別好醜。有
070b12 ‖ 大志量不沒不縮不高下下。佛悉瞻見處
070b13 ‖ 在如是。大眾說法易解易了樂聞無厭。音
070b14 ‖ 深不散柔軟悅耳從臍而出。咽喉舌根鼻頰
070b15 ‖ 上[15]齗齒脣。氣激變成音句。柔軟悅耳。如大
070b16 ‖ 密雲雷聲隱[16]震。如大海中猛風激浪。如
070b17 ‖ 大梵天音聲引導可度眾生。離眉眼脣可
070b18 ‖ 呵語法。言不闕少又不煩重。所說無疑言
070b19 ‖ 必利益。無有誑語可破語等。離如是過遠
070b20 ‖ 近等聞。四種問難隨意能答。開示四諦令
070b21 ‖ 得

简体字

受持思惟如所说行。专心听受心清净故能障诸盖。一切大众瞻仰如来无有厌足。衣毛皆竖泣泪心热或有大喜。有如是者。则知其人心得清净寂默湛然如入禅定。无爱无恚心无余缘。有大悲相慈愍众生。欲救一切心不谄曲。寂灭清净分别好丑。有大志量不没不缩不高下下。佛悉瞻见处在如是。大众说法易解易了乐闻无厌。音深不散柔软悦耳从脐而出。咽喉舌根鼻颡上齗齿脣。气激变成音句。柔软悦耳。如大密云雷声隐震。如大海中猛风激浪。如大梵天音声引导可度众生。离眉眼脣可呵语法。言不阙少又不烦重。所说无疑言必利益。无有诳语可破语等。离如是过远近等闻。四种问难随意能答。开示四谛令得

Buddha, accept and uphold it, reflect upon it, and practice in accordance with what is taught. Because their minds are focused as they listen and because their thoughts are pure, they are able to block any interference by the hindrances. Everyone in the great assembly gazes insatiably up at the Tathāgata, with all the hairs raised on their bodies, with their eyes filled with tears, with their minds afire with intensity, or with hearts filled with great joy.

Wherever people have become like this, one knows that their minds have become purified. They remain there motionless and silent, serenely still, and as if having entered *dhyāna* absorption. Their minds are free of either love or hatred and remain undistracted by any extraneous matters. They have thoughts of great compassion[327] by which they feel kindness and pity for beings, wishing to rescue them all. Their minds do not descend into flattery or deviousness, but rather have become utterly quiescent and pure as they distinguish what is good from what is bad. They have an immensely strong determination from which they neither fall away or shrink back and they do not regard themselves as superior or others as inferior.

   3) Envisioning the Manner in Which They Teach Dharma

The Buddhas are all observed abiding in such great assemblies, teaching Dharma that is easy to understand and easy to completely fathom. [Their audiences] listen with insatiable delight. Their voices are deep, are not subject to fading [even at a distance], are gentle, and are pleasing to the ear. Originating in the belly, through the interaction of the throat, tongue, nasopharynx, dental palate, teeth, and lips, the air is caused to become sounds and sentences that may be soft and pleasing to the ear, may be as powerfully strong as the earth-quaking thunder emanating from huge, dense rain clouds, may be like those fierce winds off the great ocean that drive up the surf, or may be like the voice of the devas in the Mahābrahma Heaven. With voices such as these, they lead forth and guide those beings that are capable of being liberated.

They have abandoned any modes of expression associated with scolding that may involve contortion of the brow, the countenance, or the lips. Their speech is neither deficient in any way nor unnecessarily long and redundant. There is no doubt in what they proclaim and their words will certainly be beneficial. Their speech is entirely free of any deceptive statements, any statements vulnerable to refutation, or any other such statements. It is entirely free of these faults and it is heard equally well by those far and near.

The Buddhas are freely able to answer the four types of challenging questions. They explain the four truths, thereby causing beings to gain

正體字

070b22 ‖ 四果。建立義端因緣結句。語言法則皆悉
070b22 ‖ 具足。種種所說事義易了。所宣分明[17]不故
070b23 ‖ 隱曲。言不卒疾又不遲緩。始終相稱無能
070b24 ‖ 難者。以如是語敷演說法。初中後善有義
070b25 ‖ 有利唯法具足。能令眾生得今世報。無有
070b26 ‖ 時節可得嘗試能滿所願。深妙智者以內
070b27 ‖ 可知。能滅眾生三毒猛火。能除一切身口
070b28 ‖ 意罪。善能開示戒定慧品。初以名字後令
070b29 ‖ 知義而生歡喜。從喜生樂從樂生定。從
070c01 ‖ 定生如實[18]智。從[19]如實[*]智生厭離。從厭
070c02 ‖ 離滅結使。滅結使故得解脫。如是能令
070c03 ‖ 此法次第。善能開示諦捨滅慧四處。能示眾
070c04 ‖ 生令滿布施持戒忍辱精進禪定智慧波羅
070c05 ‖ 蜜。能令眾生次第得至喜地淨地明地炎地
070c06 ‖ 難勝現前深遠

简体字

四果。建立义端因缘结句。语言法则皆悉具足。种种所说事义易了。所宣分明不故隐曲。言不卒疾又不迟缓。始终相称无能难者。以如是语敷演说法。初中后善有义有利唯法具足。能令众生得今世报。无有时节可得尝试能满所愿。深妙智者以内可知。能灭众生三毒猛火。能除一切身口意罪。善能开示戒定慧品。初以名字后令知义而生欢喜。从喜生乐从乐生定。从定生如实智。从如实智生厌离。从厌离灭结使。灭结使故得解脱。如是能令此法次第。善能开示谛舍灭慧四处。能示众生令满布施持戒忍辱精进禅定智慧波罗蜜。能令众生次第得至喜地净地明地炎地难胜现前深远

the four fruits of the path. They establish points of meaning and make statements supported by reasons. They are completely equipped with all of the methods used in speaking. In the many different sorts of matters that they discuss, their meaning is easy to completely comprehend. Whatever they proclaim is entirely clear and never intentionally cryptic or convoluted. Their speech is neither too fast nor too slow. The beginnings and conclusions of each discourse are mutually compatible and invulnerable to anyone's challenges.

4) Envisioning the Effects of the Buddhas' Teaching of Dharma

With speech such as this, they spread forth and proclaim the Dharma which is good in the beginning, middle, and end, imbued with meaning, beneficial, devoted solely to Dharma, and, in all respects, perfect.[328] It is able to cause beings to gain karmic rewards in in this very lifetime. Their discourse is not meaningful only for a time, is such that one can test it for oneself, and is such that will lead to the fulfillment of one's aspirations. Those possessed of profound and sublime wisdom realize it within themselves. It can extinguish in beings the raging fire set ablaze by the three poisons. It is able to rid one of all karmic offenses committed by body, speech, and mind, and it is also well able to open up and reveal the essence of moral virtue, the meditative absorptions, and wisdom.

It begins with mere naming that in turn provokes realization of meaning that then in its own turn causes one to be filled with joy. From this joy, there then arises bliss, and from this bliss, there then arises meditative concentration. From this meditative concentration, there arises a wise knowing in accordance with reality, and from this wise knowing in accordance with reality, one then develops renunciation. Due to having developed this renunciation, one becomes able to destroy the fetters, and due to having destroyed those fetters, one then gains liberation.

In this very manner, this Dharma is caused to unfold in a sequence whereby:

- It is well able to open forth and reveal the four bases [of meritorious qualities]: truth, relinquishment, quiescence, and wisdom;
- It is able to reveal for beings the means by which they are caused to perfectly fulfill the *pāramitās* of giving, moral virtue, patience, vigor, meditative concentration, and wisdom;
- It is able to cause beings to sequentially enter and proceed through the Ground of Joyfulness, the Ground of Stainlessness, the ground of Shining Light, the Ground of Blazing Brilliance, the Difficult-to-Conquer Ground, the Ground of Direct Presence, the Far-Reaching

正體字

```
           不動善慧法雲。能分別聲聞
070c07 ||  乘辟支佛乘大乘。能令證須陀洹斯陀含阿
070c08 ||  那含阿羅漢果。能令成就人天之中所有富
070c09 ||  樂。是為一切第一利益諸功德藏。如是正心
070c10 ||  憶念諸佛。在閑靜處除却貪欲瞋[20]恚睡眠
070c11 ||  疑悔調戲。一心專念不生障礙失定之心。
070c12 ||  以如是心專念諸佛。若心沒當起若散當
070c13 ||  攝。并見大眾常如現前。未入定時常應
070c14 ||  稱讚相好二事。以偈歎佛令心調習。如此
070c15 ||  偈說。
070c16 ||    世尊諸相好      何業因緣得
070c17 ||    我以相及業      稱讚於大聖
070c18 ||    足相千輻輪      清淨眷屬施
070c19 ||    以是因緣故      賢聖眾圍繞
070c20 ||    足下安立相      受善持不失
070c21 ||    是故魔軍眾      不能得毀壞
```

简体字

不动善慧法云。能分别声闻乘辟支佛乘大乘。能令证须陀洹斯陀含阿那含阿罗汉果。能令成就人天之中所有富乐。是为一切第一利益诸功德藏。如是正心忆念诸佛。在闲静处除却贪欲嗔恚睡眠疑悔调戏。一心专念不生障碍失定之心。以如是心专念诸佛。若心没当起若散当摄。并见大众常如现前。未入定时常应称赞相好二事。以偈叹佛令心调习。如此偈说。

　　世尊诸相好　　何业因缘得
　　我以相及业　　称赞于大圣
　　足相千辐轮　　清净眷属施
　　以是因缘故　　贤圣众围绕
　　足下安立相　　受善持不失
　　是故魔军众　　不能得毁坏

Ground, the Ground of Immovability, the Ground of Excellent Intelligence, and the Ground of the Dharma Cloud;

It is able to make clear distinctions with regard to the Śrāvaka Disciple Vehicle, the Pratyekabuddha Vehicle, and the Great Vehicle;

It is able to provoke realization of the fruits of the path gained by the stream enterer, once returner, non-returner and arhat;[329]

And it is able too to cause complete success in gaining wealth and happiness in the realms of humans and devas.

This is what constitutes the treasury of meritorious qualities that provides all of the foremost forms of benefit.

5) Instruction on This Type of Contemplative Mindfulness

It is in this manner that one uses right thought in the recollective mindfulness of all buddhas. One abides in a peaceful and quiet place, rids oneself of sensual desire, ill will, dullness and drowsiness, doubtfulness, regret and agitation, and single-mindedly carries on focused mindfulness in which one refrains from generating thoughts that obstruct or cause one to lose meditative absorption. One employs this sort of mind in one's focused mindfulness of the Buddhas. If one's mind sinks, one should raise it up again. If one's mind becomes scattered, one should draw it back into a focused state. One then sees the entire great assembly as if it were always right before one's very eyes.

6) The Importance of Praising the Major Marks and Secondary Signs

When one has not yet managed to enter concentrated meditative absorption, one should always praise the two types of phenomena that consist of the Buddha's major marks and secondary characteristics, using verses to celebrate the qualities of the Buddhas and to cause one's mind to become well trained in this.

a) Verses in Praise of the Buddhas' 32 Marks

Accordingly, there are these lines of verse as follows:

Referring to the marks and characteristics of the Bhagavats
and the karmic causes and conditions by which they acquired them,
I shall use these marks and their corresponding karmic actions
to set forth the praises of these great *āryas*:

The thousand-spoked wheel mark on the feet
is associated with a pure retinue and with giving.
It is because of these causes and conditions
that the many worthies and *āryas* surround them.

The mark of the stable stance of the feet
arises from upholding without fail all goodness one has taken on.
It is because of this that the legions of Māra's armies
are unable to succeed in destroying them.

070c22 ‖	手足指網縵	身相紫金色
070c23 ‖	善行攝法故	大眾自然伏
070c24 ‖	手足極柔軟	身相七處滿
070c25 ‖	隨意食施故	多得自然供
070c26 ‖	長指廣腳跟	身[21]傭大直相
070c27 ‖	離殺因緣故	乃至於劫壽
070c28 ‖	毛上向右旋	足趺隆高相
070c29 ‖	常進諸善事	故得不退法
071a01 ‖	伊[1]泥鹿[蹲-酋+(十/田/ㄙ)]相	常樂讀誦經
071a02 ‖	為人說法故	疾得無上道
071a03 ‖	修臂下過膝	一切所有物
071a04 ‖	求者無悋惜	隨意化導人
071a05 ‖	陰藏功德藏	善[和>知]離散故
071a06 ‖	多得人天眾	淨慧眼為子
071a07 ‖	薄皮耀金光	妙衣堂閣施
071a08 ‖	故多得妙衣	清淨房樓觀
071a09 ‖	一孔一毛生	眉間白毫峙
071a10 ‖	常為最上護	故於三界尊
071a11 ‖	身上如師子	兩肩圓而[2]滿
071a12 ‖	常行[3]人愛語	無有違反者

正體字

手足指网缦　　身相紫金色
善行摄法故　　大众自然伏
手足极柔软　　身相七处满
随意食施故　　多得自然供
长指广脚跟　　身佣大直相
离杀因缘故　　乃至于劫寿
毛上向右旋　　足趺隆高相
常进诸善事　　故得不退法
伊泥鹿[跳-兆+專]相　　常乐读诵经
为人说法故　　疾得无上道
修臂下过膝　　一切所有物
求者无吝惜　　随意化导人
阴藏功德藏　　善知离散故
多得人天众　　净慧眼为子
薄皮耀金光　　妙衣堂阁施
故多得妙衣　　清净房楼观
一孔一毛生　　眉间白毫峙
常为最上护　　故于三界尊
身上如师子　　两肩圆而满
常行人爱语　　无有违反者

简体字

Chapter 20 — *Mindfulness of the Buddhas*

Their fingers and toes join with proximal webs
and their bodies have the mark of purple-golden coloration.
Because of their skillful practice of the means of attraction,
the great assembly naturally bows in deferential reverence.

Their hands and feet are extremely soft
and the body has the mark of fullness in the seven places.
It is due to giving food that accords with others' wishes
that they are naturally given many offerings.

They have long fingers, broad heels,
and the body has the mark of being large and upright.
This results from abandoning the causes and conditions of killing
and may lead to a life span lasting even up to a kalpa in length.

The hairs of the body grow in an upward and rightward spiral
and the feet have the mark of high arches.
By always advancing in good endeavors,
they thereby acquired the dharma of irreversibility.

They have the gradually tapering legs of the *aiṇeya* antelope
due to always delighting in study and recitation of scriptures.
It is through speaking the Dharma for others
that they rapidly realized the unsurpassable path.

As for having long arms that reach below the knees,
this is due to never being miserly in giving
anything one possesses to whoever seeks to acquire them.
Thus they can teach and guide others in ways suited to their wishes.

Genital ensheathment reflects a treasury of meritorious qualities
associated with skillfully reconciling those who are estranged.[330]
As a result, they acquire a great congregation of humans and devas
and use the pure wisdom eye to create their sons.[331]

Their thin skin that radiates golden light
is associated with giving marvelous apparel and halls.
As a consequence, they acquire an abundance of fine robes
as well as pristine quarters, buildings, and viewing terraces.

The single hair in each pore
and the white hair tuft between the eyes
are associated with serving as a supreme protector.
Hence they are revered throughout the three realms of existence.

They have an upper body like that of a lion
with the two shoulders rounded and full.
These result from always using speech that is pleasing to others.
As a consequence, there is no one who opposes them.

正體字	071a13 ‖	腋滿知味相	病施醫藥故
	071a14 ‖	人天皆敬愛	身無有疾[4]病
	071a15 ‖	身圓肉髻相	和悅心施福
	071a16 ‖	勸化剛強者	法王中自在
	071a17 ‖	迦陵頻伽音	廣舌聲如梵
	071a18 ‖	所言常軟實	得大聖八音
	071a19 ‖	先加以思慮	後言必有實
	071a20 ‖	故得師子相	見者皆信伏
	071a21 ‖	齒白齊密相	所曾供養者
	071a22 ‖	後常不輕故	眷屬心和同
	071a23 ‖	上下四十齒	密[5]緻不疎漏
	071a24 ‖	無讒不妄語	徒眾不可破
	071a25 ‖	眼黑青白明	睫相如牛王
	071a26 ‖	慈心和視故	觀者無厭足
	071a27 ‖	雖轉輪聖王	典主四天下
	071a28 ‖	有是諸相好	光明不如佛
	071a29 ‖	我所稱歎說	諸相好功德
	071b01 ‖	願令一切人	心淨常安樂
	071b02 ‖	菩薩又應以八十種好念諸佛。如此偈說。		

简体字	腋满知味相	病施医药故
	人天皆敬爱	身无有疾病
	身圆肉髻相	和悦心施福
	劝化刚强者	法王中自在
	迦陵频伽音	广舌声如梵
	所言常软实	得大圣八音
	先加以思虑	后言必有实
	故得师子相	见者皆信伏
	齿白齐密相	所曾供养者
	后常不轻故	眷属心和同
	上下四十齿	密致不疏漏
	无谗不妄语	徒众不可破
	眼黑青白明	睫相如牛王
	慈心和视故	观者无厌足
	虽转轮圣王	典主四天下
	有是诸相好	光明不如佛
	我所称叹说	诸相好功德
	愿令一切人	心净常安乐
	菩萨又应以八十种好念诸佛。如此偈说。	

Chapter 20 — *Mindfulness of the Buddhas*

The marks of subaxillary fullness and cognition of all tastes
stem from providing medical care and medicines for the sick.
As a consequence, devas and men all revere and love them
and their bodies remain ever free of disease.

The roundness of the mid-body and the crown's fleshy *uṣṇīṣa* sign
reflect the merit of giving with a harmonious and delighted mind.
As a consequence of exhorting and teaching even the stubborn,
they reign as sovereignly masterful kings of Dharma.

As for the voice like that of a *kalaviṅka* bird,
the broad tongue, and the voice like a Great Brahma Heaven deva,
they are from the speaking of words that are both gentle and true.
They therefore acquire the Great Ārya's eight voice qualities.[332]

Having first brought contemplative thought to bear
and then afterward spoken words of definite truthfulness,
they acquired the lion-like mark.
Hence all who see them trust them and defer to them.

That their teeth are white, straight, and close-set
is because they have always refrained from slighting
those who have previously given offerings.
Hence the minds of those in their retinue are agreeable and unified.

Above and below, they have a total of forty teeth
that, being close-set, have no gaps.
These result from never slandering and not lying.
Hence their disciples' [loyalty] cannot be destroyed.

The pupils and whites of their eyes are clearly delineated
and they have the mark of eyelashes like those of a royal bull.
These are caused by kindly thought and an amicable view of others.
Consequently all observers look on them with a tireless gaze.

Even though a wheel-turning king
who rules over four continents
possesses these major marks and secondary characteristics,
their radiance still cannot compare with that of a buddha.

I pray that the power of the merit from my setting forth praises
of the major marks and the secondary characteristics
may be able to cause everyone
to have purified minds as well as everlasting peace and happiness.

d) Verses in Praise of the Buddha's Secondary Characteristics

The bodhisattva should also engage in contemplative mindfulness of the buddhas by way of their eighty secondary characteristics. Accordingly, there are these lines of verse, as follows:

正體字	071b03 ‖	諸佛有妙好	八十莊嚴身
	071b04 ‖	汝等應歡喜	一心聽我說
	071b05 ‖	世尊圓纖指	其甲紫紅色
	071b06 ‖	隆高有潤澤	所有無有量
	071b07 ‖	[6]脈平踝不現	雙足無邪曲
	071b08 ‖	行如師子王	威望無等比
	071b09 ‖	行時身右旋	安庠有儀雅
	071b10 ‖	方身分次第	端嚴可愛樂
	071b11 ‖	身堅[7]極柔軟	支節甚分明
	071b12 ‖	行時不逶迤	諸根悉充滿
	071b13 ‖	肌體極密緻	鮮明甚清淨
	071b14 ‖	身形甚端雅	無有可呵處
	071b15 ‖	腹圓不高現	臍深而無孔
	071b16 ‖	其文右向旋	威儀甚清淨
	071b17 ‖	身無有疵點	手足極柔軟
	071b18 ‖	其文深且長	修直有潤色
	071b19 ‖	舌薄面不長	牙白圓[*]纖利
	071b20 ‖	脣色頻婆果	音深若鴻王
	071b21 ‖	鼻隆眼明淨	睫[8]緻而不亂
	071b22 ‖	眉高毛柔軟	端直不邪曲
简体字		诸佛有妙好	八十庄严身
		汝等应欢喜	一心听我说
		世尊圆纤指	其甲紫红色
		隆高有润泽	所有无有量
		脉平踝不现	双足无邪曲
		行如师子王	威望无等比
		行时身右旋	安庠有仪雅
		方身分次第	端严可爱乐
		身坚极柔软	支节甚分明
		行时不逶迤	诸根悉充满
		肌体极密致	鲜明甚清净
		身形甚端雅	无有可呵处
		腹圆不高现	脐深而无孔
		其文右向旋	威仪甚清净
		身无有疵点	手足极柔软
		其文深且长	修直有润色
		舌薄面不长	牙白圆纤利
		唇色频婆果	音深若鸿王
		鼻隆眼明净	睫致而不乱
		眉高毛柔软	端直不邪曲

All buddhas possess the marvelous secondary characteristics,
eighty in number, with which their bodies are adorned.
You should all delight in them
and listen intently as I describe them.

The Bhagavats have round and slender fingers,
nails that are purplish red in hue,
convex in profile, smooth, and glossy,
characteristics of having everything in measureless abundance.

Their veins lie flat, their ankle bones are invisible,
their feet are not skewed in their track,
their gait is like that of the king of lions,
and they are incomparably awe-inspiring to all observers.

When walking, the entire body turns to the right.
They are serene in manner and refined in their deportment.
The parts of their squarely set bodies are orderly in their posture
and their dignified grace inspires fondness and happiness.

Their bodies are firm in tone, but extremely soft.
The articulations of their joints are quite visibly distinct.
When walking, they do not travel in a meandering manner.
All of their sense faculties are fully and perfectly developed.

The flesh on their bodies is extremely taut, finely textured,
freshly radiant, and especially immaculate.
Their physical posture is especially upright, refined,
and devoid of any feature subject to dispraise.

The belly is round, but does not visibly bulge.
The navel, though deep, does not appear to be an orifice.
Its creases manifest as a rightward spiraling swirl.
Their deportment is extremely pure.

The body is free of any blemishes
and the hands and feet are extremely soft.
The lines in the palms are deep and long,
continuous, straight, and lustrous.

The tongue is slender, the face is not too long.
The central incisors are white, rounded, slender, and sharp.
The hue of the lips is like that of the *bimba* fruit.
Their voice is as deep as the king of the wild geese.

The nose is prominent in profile and the eyes are bright and clear.
The eyelashes are close-set and fine, but not in disarray.
The brow is elevated, has eyebrow hair that is soft,
and it is straight and not crooked.

正體字	071b23 ‖　　眉毛齊而整　　善知諸法過 071b24 ‖　　眉毛色潤澤　　善度潤眾生 071b25 ‖　　耳滿長而等　　不壞甚可愛 071b26 ‖　　額廣而齊[9]正　　頭相皆具足 071b27 ‖　　髮[*]緻而不亂　　如黑蜂王色 071b28 ‖　　清淨而香潔　　中有三種相 071b29 ‖ 是名八十種好。以此八十種好間雜莊嚴 071c01 ‖ 三十二相。若人不念三十二相八十種好 071c02 ‖ 讚歎佛身者。是則永失今世後世利樂因 071c03 ‖ 緣。 071c04 ‖ 十住毘婆沙論卷第[10]九
简体字	眉毛齐而整　　善知诸法过 　　眉毛色润泽　　善度润众生 　　耳满长而等　　不坏甚可爱 　　额广而齐正　　头相皆具足 　　发致而不乱　　如黑蜂王色 　　清净而香洁　　中有三种相 　是名八十种好。以此八十种好间杂庄严三十二相。若人不念三十二相八十种好赞叹佛身者。是则永失今世后世利乐因缘。 十住毗婆沙论卷第九

The hair of the brows, being even and straight,
is emblematic of being well aware of the faults in any dharma.
The hair of the brows is smooth and glossy,
a feature emblematic of skillfully liberating and aiding beings.

The ears are full, long, even in shape,
undamaged, and especially pleasing to the eye.
The forehead is broad and straight.
All of the head's features are perfectly formed.

The hair is fine, dense, never in disarray,
the color of the king of the black bees,
clean, pleasantly fragrant, immaculate,
and possessed of three of the marks.

e) SUMMATION ON IMPORTANCE OF SUCH RECOLLECTIVE CONTEMPLATION

This has been the description of the eighty secondary characteristics. Because these eighty secondary characteristics are interspersed with and serve to adorn the thirty-two major marks, if one fails to take up contemplative mindfulness of both the thirty-two marks and the eighty secondary characteristics in one's praises of the Buddha's body, then one may lose forever the causal factors conducing to well-being and happiness in the present and future lives.

The End of Chapter Twenty

Volume One Endnotes

1. This is a reference to the *wojiao shan* (沃焦山), "the boiling and burning mountain" also known as the *wojiao shi* (沃焦石), the "boiling and burning rock," a huge and intensely hot mountain of stone at the bottom of the ocean which, in traditional Indian geography, is responsible for keeping the oceans from overflowing by boiling away the excess water flowing into them from all the great rivers, large and small. This mountain is sometimes held to reside at the bottom of the *wojiao hai* (沃焦海), "the boiling and burning ocean."

2. The four inverted views (*viparyāsa-catuṣka*) consist of imputing permanence to the impermanent, pleasure to what cannot deliver it, self to what is devoid of any inherently existent self, and purity to what does not actually possess that quality.

    Standard objects of such upside-down perception are: thought, or mind states, the six categories of "feeling" manifesting in association with the six sense faculties, dharmas (as components of the falsely imputed "self"), and the body.

    VB, preferring "inversions" to render this term, rightly points out that, per *Aṅguttara nikāya* 4:49, these four *viparyāsa* involve not only views, but rather they infect perceptions and mind as well as view. That said, I still feel comfortable with the now rather common and standard rendering as "four inverted views," not least because, as a practical matter, perception (*saṃjñā*) and mind/thought (*citta*) are nearly always intimately intertwined with and inseparable from views (*dṛṣṭī*), all of which are "inverted" due to delusion.

3. VB recognized these statements about four types of people as similar to statements in the *Aṅguttāra nikāya* (see his *Numerical Discourses of the Buddha*, pp. 476–77).

4. I emend the reading of the text here to correct an apparent graphic-similarity scribal error, preferring on sensibility grounds the *zheng* (拯), "rescue," of the SYMG editions to the *Taisho* edition's *ji* (極), "extremely."

5. The bracketed verse is repeated here to facilitate immediate reference by the reader.

6. Although this could be a reference to the *Mahāprajñāpāramitā Sūtra* wherein such statements do exist, Nāgārjuna might well intend here to cite the *Avataṃsaka Sūtra* (the mother sutra in which this entire ten grounds text is incorporated as "The Ten Grounds Chapter"). We have a number of such statements in the *Avataṃsaka Sūtra* including the famous passage (quoted some 350 times in Sino-Buddhist canonical works): "It is with the very moment of bringing forth the initial

resolve that one thereby achieves the right enlightenment" (初發心時便成正覺), this from Buddhabhadra's circa 400 CE translation (T09; no. 278; 449c).

7. "Vajra path" is an indirect reference to the acquisition of the "vajra-like samādhi" (*vajropama-samādhi*). It is a feature of both Southern and Northern School Buddhist path schemas that refers to the point at which the practitioner destroys the last vestiges of the residual fetters and reaches, for a *śrāvaka*-disciple practitioner, "the stage beyond the need for further training" or, for the bodhisattva path practitioner, the next to last stage of the Mahāyāna path known as "equal enlightenment" (*samasaṃbodhi*). This latter is the stage immediately prior to "sublime enlightenment" wherein the bodhisattva's level of awakening has reached the point that it is virtually the same as that of a fully enlightened buddha.

As a Mahāyāna technical term "vajra path" is in no way any sort of reference to the so-called "Vajrayāna," a very late Hindu-influenced transformation of Buddhism characterized by the tenets and practices of Hindu tantras (Vajrayana texts are all post 6th century in origin, i.e., more than 1000 years post-Śākyamuni).

8. For the most part, I rely here and hereafter on Étienne Lamotte's *Traité de la Grande Vertu De Sagesse de Nāgārjuna* for the parenthetically included Sanskrit equivalents for the Chinese names of the various hells.

9. For Nāgārjuna's very graphic and nearly encyclopedic discussion of each one of the hell realms and hungry ghost realms wherein he explains the causality at the root of each type of suffering therein, see my translation from his *Mahāprajñāpāramitā Upadeśa: Nagarjuna on the Six Perfections*, in particular, within his discussion of the perfection of vigor, Chapter 27: "Specific Aspects of the Perfection of Vigor," p. 513-37 in the original bilingual edition.

10. The inscrutably ambiguous nature of the *Taisho* version of the text's rendering of a number of the instruments of punishment here (鐵鏘[金疾]鍱鐵[矛贊]刀鐵臼) is such that I prefer the alternative reading employed in the Song, Yuan, and Ming editions (槍蒺[卄/梨]刀劍鐵網: "javelins, spikes, short swords, iron nets").

11. "*Bhūta* ghost" is here a conjectural Sanskrit reconstruction of 浮陀鬼. According to MW, one of the many meanings of *bhūta* is: "a spirit (good or evil), the ghost of a deceased person, a demon, imp, goblin."

12. Again, the bracketed verse from the beginning of the chapter is repeated here to facilitate immediate reference by the reader.

13. Nāgārjuna is not implying here that the practitioners of the Śrāvaka Disciple vehicle actually possess all of these eight dharmas of the

bodhisattva. (After all, although they are certainly well-accomplished in the other six, they are not particularly well known for either compassion or skillful means.) Rather, he is primarily pointing out that they are secondary beneficiaries of the bodhisattvas' implementation of these eight dharmas that result in the bodhisattvas' eventual buddhahood and the resulting eternal renewal of Dharma in the world again and again throughout the course of time.

14. This would seem to contradict Nāgārjuna's earlier statement that "all *śrāvaka* disciples and *pratyekabuddhas* come forth in direct reliance upon a buddha." Not so. Even though the *pratyekabuddha* may finally gain his realization when there is no buddha and no Dharma in the world, his ability to gain that realization is entirely rooted in his previous lives' exposure to a buddha's Dharma at such time as there *was* a buddha or his right Dharma still existing in the world. It is at least in part the fruition of the karmic seeds from such earlier learning and practice that finally allows the *pratyekabuddha* at a later time to gain realizations in the absence of a buddha or of any residual Dharma after the end of a buddha's Dharma-ending age.

15. A *vibhāṣā* is an extensively detailed explanatory treatise.

16. VB points out that there is a canonical source for the "four bases" in *Majjhima nikaya* 140, MN III 245-6 for which the Sanskrit correlates of the Pali *saccādhiṭṭhāna, cāgādhiṭṭhāna, upasamādhiṭṭhāna* (= base of peace), and *paññādhiṭṭhāna* would be *satyādhiṣṭhāna, tyāgādhiṣṭhāna, upaśamādhiṣṭhāna,* and *prajñādhiṣṭhāna*. He also notes that there is a Chinese canonical parallel at MĀ 162; T01n0026_p0692a11.

17. I emend the reading of the *Taisho* text here to correct an apparent scribal error, preferring the reading in the SYMG editions (說十地義) to that of *Taisho* (義說十地).

18. The logic of this statement may seem opaque to some. The point here is that, so long as one creates bad karma and does not purify it, one's mind can never be at peace even in conventional terms. As for entering deep states of meditative quiescence such as the *dhyānas*, this would be completely impossible. This is one of the reasons why moral purity is taught as one of the primary prerequisites for meditative accomplishment.

19. VB notes the existence of a slightly variant parallel source in the Pali Canon: AN 3:80 (NDB p. 314). That citation makes it clear that, if Ānanda had somehow died before achieving the arhatship the Buddha predicted of him, his merit would have been so abundant that he would have been reborn in those blissful heavens for such an immensely long time.

20. The first four and a half of these five verses correspond to the KB translation of *The Ten Grounds Sutra* (498b27-c04).
21. The first two of these five verses echo Vajragarbha's preliminary statements in *The Ten Grounds Sutra*, just before embarking on the explanation of the first ground.
22. In this sort of context, *biding* (必定),"stage of certainty," is usually a translation of the Sanskrit *avaivartika, niyata,* or one of their synonyms that refer to the stage of irreversibility from which one can never again fall back in one's progress on the path.
23. I emend the reading of the *Taisho* text to agree with the SYM editions, this by adding the qualifier *shan* (善), "thorough," to *xing* (行), "practice."

    Also, regarding householder practice, N's implication here is that, even though it is extremely difficult to carry on the life of a householder while also accessing the *dhyānas*, householder-level practice should not be disqualified from being referred to as "thorough practice" just because householders are usually unable to develop those meditation states.
24. "Resolute intentions," *shenxin* (深心), here and in most occurrences throughout the text, corresponds to the Sanskrit *āśaya* which has a range of meanings not so easily captured in a single English translation. Hence, in its various occurrences in scriptures and commentaries related to the ten grounds, it may connote "resolute," "deep-seated," or "earnest" "intentions," "aspirations," "dispositions" or "inclinations." In KB and SA, *āśaya* is often translated into Chinese as just *xin* (心) where it would very easily be confused with *citta*. In those instances, depending on the context and especially depending on whether it is referring to bodhisattvas or simply to unenlightened worldly beings, it is probably best rendered into English as "intentions," "aspirations," "dispositions" or "inclinations."
25. I emend the reading of the text here in accordance with the SYMG editions by preferring on sensibility grounds *wei* (未), "not yet," to the *Taisho* edition's *wei* (味), "flavor," the presence of which seems to have been the result of a graphic-similarity scribal error.
26. VB points out that this passage resembles a passage in "The Akṣayamati Chapter" of *"The Great Compilation Sutra"* (*Mahāvaipulya-mahāsaṃnipāta-sūtra*) at T13, no. 0397, p. 187b01.
27. "Forest hermitage" here translates what KJ retained in transliteration as the antecedent term: *araṇya* which is hermitage usually intended for the cultivation of deep meditation and/or various austere (*dhūta*) practices. Since the Sanskrit term does not carry any untranslatable

nuances, from here on I shall for the most part just go ahead and translate it as "forest hermitage."

28. I emend the reading of the text here in accordance with the SYMG editions by preferring on sensibility grounds to eliminate the *gu* (故), "therefore," the inclusion of which seems to have been the result of scribal error.

29. I emend the reading of the text here to correct an apparent scribal error in recording this statement by preferring the zhu fo fa (諸佛法), "all buddhas' Dharma," of the SYMG editions to Taisho's zhu fa (諸法), "all dharmas."

30. Although the Chinese is slightly ambiguous (hence my translation's use of the euphemistic "quiescent cessation"), citing an analogue passage, VB points out that the final couplet is referring to nirvāṇa, noting the following:

"The verse is perhaps alluding to MN I 45: *So vata, cunda, attanā palipapalipanno paraṃ palipapalipannaṃ uddharissatīti netaṃ ṭhānaṃ vijjati. So vata, cunda, attanā apalipapalipanno paraṃ palipapalipannaṃ uddharissatīti ṭhānametaṃ vijjati. So vata, cunda, attanā adanto avinīto aparinibbuto paraṃ damessati vinessati parinibbāpessatīti netaṃ ṭhānaṃ vijjati. So vata, cunda, attanā danto vinīto parinibbuto paraṃ damessati vinessati parinibbāpessatīti ṭhānametaṃ vijjati.* See MLDB 8, part16."

VB's translation there of the most closely relevant part of that passage is: "That one who is himself untamed, undisciplined, [with defilements] unextinguished, should tame another, discipline him, and help extinguish [his defilements] is impossible; that one who is himself tamed, disciplined, [with defilements] extinguished, should tame another, discipline him, and help extinguish [his defilements] is possible."

31. VB points out that this is a reference to *Dhammapada* 158 for which the Acharya Buddharakkhita translation gives: "One should first establish oneself in what is proper; then only should one instruct others. Thus the wise man will not be reproached."

32. VB suggests comparing the version of the ten powers found in *Majjhima nikāya* no. 12 ("The Greater Discourse on the Lion's Roar"). See MLDB, pp. 165-6.

33. Although KJ here uses the *xing* (性) that is usually translated as "nature," the source texts indicate that he is once again translating the Sanskrit *dhātu* which here refers to "realms."

34. This aspect along with the next five emphasize the importance of the six perfections.

35. This aspect along with the next three emphasize the importance of the four immeasurable minds.
36. As suggested by VB, this very likely refers to the twelfth chapter of the *Mahāsaṃnipāta-sūtra*, the "Akṣayamati Chapter" (T13n0397_p0184a16–212c26). In particular, this resembles a passage that begins at 187a26.
37. N refers here to a line from the fourth of his five earlier stanzas on cultivating the first ground:
    > For the sake of gaining the ten powers,
    > one enters the congregation of those at the stage of certainty.
    > Then one is born into the family of the Tathāgatas
    > wherein one is free of any transgressions or faults.
38. VB notes that the Pali version of this passage is found at MLDB 140.26, MN III 245: "For this, bhikkhu, is the supreme noble truth, namely, *nibbāna*, which has an undeceptive nature."
39. The *pratyutpanna* samādhi is a samādhi wherein one becomes able to see the buddhas of the present and listen to them teach the Dharma. The sutra that describes this samādhi and teaches how to acquire it is preserved in the *Taisho* Canon as the *Banzhou Sanmei Jing* (般舟三昧經 / T13.no. 0418.902c23–919c05) of which Paul Harrison has produced a translation for the BDK English Tripitaka. Other Chinese editions and translations of the same text are preserved as *Taisho* text numbers 416, 417, and 419.
40. N alludes here to verse number thirty-four from his *Bodhisaṃbhāra śāstra* (菩提資糧論 / T32n1660_p0528c13–14). See my translation of this treatise, *Nāgārjuna's Guide to the Bodhisattva Path*, page 33:
    > The solid samādhis
    > on the ground of all buddhas' "direct presence"
    > serve for the bodhisattva as his father,
    > whereas the great compassion and patiences serve as his mother.

    (諸佛現前住
    牢固三摩提
    此為菩薩父
    大悲忍為母.)

    N's equating of the *pratyutpanna* samādhi (wherein one sees the buddhas of the present) with a samādhi experienced on the sixth bodhisattva ground associates rather well with the following passage from the discussion of the sixth ground in the KB translation of the Ten Grounds Sutra:
    > "The bodhisattva dwelling on this Ground of Direct Presence succeeds in being able to see many hundreds of buddhas, many thousands of buddhas, and so forth on up to many hundreds of

thousands of myriads of *koṭis* of buddhas, making offerings to them, paying reverence to them, venerating them, praising them, and presenting them with robes, food and drink, bedding, and medicines. He draws close to the Buddhas and listens to the teaching of the Dharma in the presence of the Buddhas. Having heard their teachings on Dharma, he employs the light of reality-concordant wisdom to implement those teachings in practice in a manner accordant with the way they were taught, doing so in a manner that delights all buddhas." (T10n0286_p515c17–21.)

41. N refers again to this earlier verse on cultivating the first ground:

    For the sake of gaining the ten powers,
    one enters the congregation of those at the stage of certainty.
    Then one is born into the family of the Tathāgatas
    wherein one is free of any transgressions or faults.

42. These four bases of meritorious qualities (四功德處: 諦, 捨, 滅, 慧 / truth, relinquishment, cessation, and wisdom) are brought up repeatedly in this treatise and are found as well in N's *Bodhisaṃbhāra Śāstra* and *Ratnāvalī*.

43. I emend the reading of the text here by adopting the variant reading found in the SYMG editions to correct the absence of a single character (出) obviously missing from the *Taisho* text.

44. Throughout this text, I go ahead and translate *"srota-āpanna"* as "stream enterer."

45. "Three wretched destinies" is a reference to rebirth in the realms of hungry ghosts (*pretas*), animals, and hells.

46. The point here is that, since a stream enterer is then bound to enter *nirvāṇa* within seven lifetimes, whereupon he will not be reborn into any of the twenty-eight realms of rebirth (and there are *only* twenty-eight realms of rebirth), he need have no fear that he might somehow stray into some supposed "twenty-ninth" realm of rebirth (because no such place even exists).

47. I emend the reading of the text here in accordance with the SYMG editions by preferring on sensibility grounds *duo* (多), "for the most part," to the *Taisho* edition's *mingwei* (名為), "is known as."

48. "Contaminants" here translates the slightly ambiguous pre-Buddhist Jain term *asrava*, translated into Chinese as "flows" (漏). The allusion is to the defiling influence (read "influents") of either three or four factors, as follows: 1) sensual desire (*kāma*); 2) [craving for] becoming (*bhāva*), i.e., the craving for continued existence; 3) ignorance (*avidyā*), i.e., delusion; 4) views (*dṛṣṭi*) This fourth type is not included in some listings. Often-encountered alternate translations of this term include "taints," "outflows," "influxes," and "fluxes."

49. These forty dharmas (discussed at great length in chapters 21–23) are as follows:
    1) Sovereign mastery of the ability to fly.
    2) [The ability to manifest] countless transformations.
    3) Boundless psychic powers of the sort possessed by *āryas*.
    4) Sovereign mastery of the ability to hear sounds.
    5) Immeasurable power of knowledge to know others' thoughts.
    6) Sovereign mastery in [training and subduing] the mind.
    7) Constant abiding in stable wisdom.
    8) Never forgetting.
    9) Possession of the powers of the vajra samādhi.
    10) Thorough knowing of matters that are unfixed
    11) Thorough knowing of matters pertaining to the formless realm's meditative absorptions.
    12) The completely penetrating knowledge of all matters associated with eternal cessation.
    13) Thorough knowing of the non-form dharmas unassociated with the mind.
    14) The great powers *pāramitā*.
    15) The [four] unimpeded [knowledges] *pāramitā*.
    16) The *pāramitā* of perfectly complete replies and predictions in response to questions.
    17) Invulnerability to harm by anyone.
    18) Their words are never spoken without a purpose.
    19) Their speech is free of errors and mistakes.
    20) Complete implementation of the three turnings [of the Dharma wheel] in speaking Dharma.
    21) They are the great generals among all *āryas*.
    22–25) They are able to remain unguarded in four ways.
    26–29) They possess the four types of fearlessness.
    30–39) They possess the ten powers.
    40) They have achieved unimpeded liberation.
50. I emend the reading of the *Taisho* text here by preferring on sensibility grounds the SYMG editions' *yi* (已), "already," to the *Taisho* edition's *yi* (以), "by means of," "due to," etc."
51. "Musth" refers to a state of increased testosterone in a bull elephant that is characterized by increased willfulness and aggressiveness in doing whatever he wants to do.
52. The first five of these types of fear are brought up at this point in the Ten Grounds Sutra itself. In previewing my translation of that sutra, Bhikkhu Bodhi pointed out that this same fivefold list appears in the Pali (albeit in slightly different order and with mild differences

Endnotes 657

in the interpretation of two of the five points). See his translation of *Numerical Discourses* 9:5, p. 1255.

53. In most cases, "mind-moment" (一念 or 一念頃) translates the Sanskrit *kṣaṇa* or *eka-kṣaṇika*. As for *"kṣaṇa,"* according to PDB: "In Sanskrit, 'instant' or 'moment'; the shortest possible span of time, variously measured as either the ninth part of a thought moment or the 4,500th part of a minute."

54. An *asaṃkhyeya* is an incalculably large Sanskrit number.

55. This is a reference to the seven "treasures" (*sapta ratna*) of a *cakravartin* king. Different from the more common list of "the seven precious things," they are: the wheel treasure, elephant treasure, horse treasure, precious pearl treasure, female treasure, *kulapati* (wealth-accumulation) treasure, and the army-and-ministers lordship treasure.

56. This reconstruction of *"she-ti-luo"* (蛇提羅) as *kṣatriya* is conjectural. It is likely that N is referring to the lesser wheel-turning kings who, unlike the wheel-turning king who is a universal monarch, do not rule over all four continents, but rather over only one, two, or three continents.

57. *Jiaojumo* (憍瞿摩). I cannot find any Sanskrit equivalent for this.

58. The implication in the first foot of the *śloka* is that, if one refrains from erroneously imputing the existence of an inherently-existent self, then the concept of some event called "death" is discovered to be baseless. Similarly, the second foot of the *śloka* indicates that, if one simply refrains from erroneously imputing the existence of some independently-existing concept that one thinks of as "death," then the concept of "some entity that dies" is discovered to be baseless as well.

59. KJ retained the Sanskrit *sarvajña* which I have chosen here to translate.

60. The Taisho text inserts a *ming* (名) here to create the clearly accidentally erroneous duo *mingwen* (多名聞) which means "abundant fame" instead of the "abundant learning" (多聞) referenced in the verse upon which this sentence comments. For obvious reasons, I have aligned my translation here with the clearly intended meaning.

61. N uses the Sanskrit *dānapati*. I prefer to translate it as "benefactor" throughout the following discussion.

62. N uses the Sanskrit *niṣadana*. I prefer to translate it as "sitting mat."

63. VB gives the Pali Canon correlate to this as *Itivuttaka* section 100: "*Tassa me tumhe puttā orasā mukhato jātā dhammajā dhammanimmitā dhammadāyādā, no āmisadāyādā.*"

64. I have been unable to associate this work with any texts extant in the *Taisho* canon.

65. In my translation of the KB *Ten Grounds Sutra*, the complete text of this first vow is as follows:

    I vow that I shall make gifts of every sort of offering to all buddhas without exception, freely making such offerings with pure resolute faith." In making such a great vow as this, his implementation of it is as vast as the Dharma realm and as extensive as empty space as he continues on until the end of future time, exhaustively making offerings of every sort of great gift to all buddhas.

66. In my translation of the KB *Ten Grounds Sutra*, the complete text of this second vow is as follows:

    He also vows that he will uphold and preserve the scriptural Dharma proclaimed by all buddhas, that he will take on the realization of the *anuttarasamyaksaṃbodhi* of all buddhas, that he will always accord with the Dharma taught by all buddhas, and that he will always be able to protect and preserve the Dharma of all buddhas. In making such a great vow as this, his implementation of it is as vast as the Dharma realm and as extensive as empty space as he continues on incessantly until the end of future time, exhaustively protecting and preserving the Dharma of all buddhas in every kalpa.

67. In my translation of the KB *Ten Grounds Sutra*, the complete text of this third vow is as follows:

    He also vows that, in all worlds, with the arrival of all buddhas, when they come down from the Tuṣita Heaven, enter the womb, abide in the womb, are first born, leave behind the home life, and then gain buddhahood, in every case he will entreat them to turn the great wheel of the Dharma, vowing too that, when they manifest entry into the great nirvāṇa, "I will in every case go there, make offerings, and serve as a leader in the compilation of their Dharma," vowing to do these things in order to facilitate [the Dharma wheel's] turning throughout the three periods of time. In making such a great vow as this, his implementation of it is as vast as the Dharma realm and as extensive as empty space as he continues on until the end of future time and throughout all kalpas, incessantly raising up offerings to all buddhas.

68. In my translation of the KB *Ten Grounds Sutra*, the complete text of this fourth vow is as follows:

    He also vows that he will teach all of the practices coursed in by the bodhisattvas, so vast, lofty, and far-reaching, so immeasurable, indestructible, and free of discriminations, those practices that are subsumed within the *pāramitās*, that are purified on the grounds, that generate the dharmas assisting realization of the path, that constitute the path of signs and the path of signlessness, teaching how they may conduce to success and how they may lead to ruination, teaching the path of the grounds coursed in by all bodhisattvas, teaching too the *pāramitās'* foundational practices, teaching these things to others in a manner whereby they are caused to take up their practice and bring forth increased resolve. In making such a great vow as this, his implementation of it is as vast as the Dharma realm and as extensive as empty space as he continues on until the end of future time and throughout all kalpas, incessantly employing the practices coursed in by all bodhisattvas to provide teaching in accord with Dharma for the ripening of beings.

69. In my translation of the KB *Ten Grounds Sutra*, the complete text of this fifth vow is as follows:

> He also vows that he will teach all beings, whether possessed of form or formless, whether possessed of perception, free of perception, or abiding in a state of neither perception nor non-perception, whether egg-born, womb-born, moisture-born, or transformationally born, teaching them all, no matter to which of the stations in the triple world they have become connected, no matter in which of the six destinies of rebirth they have taken birth, no matter in which place they have taken rebirth, thus teaching all who are subsumed in the sphere of name-and-form, proceeding thus for the sake of teaching and ripening all beings, for the sake of influencing them to cut off their coursing through all the destinies of worldly existence, for the sake of influencing them to abide in the Dharma of the Buddha, for the sake of influencing them to accumulate all-knowledge, teaching all of them without exception. In making such a great vow as this, his implementation of it is as vast as the Dharma realm and as extensive as empty space as he continues on until the end of future time and throughout all kalpas, incessantly teaching all beings.

70. *Fawei* (法位), "Dharma position," usually corresponds to "the right and fixed Dharma position" (*samyaktva niyāma*) that in turn involves irreversibility in one's progress on the path to the fruits of the individual-liberation paths of either the *pratyekabuddha* or the arhat. This is usually understood (except in sutras such as the *Lotus Sutra*) to involve the subsequent impossibility of ever entering the universal-liberation path of the bodhisattvas and buddhas.

71. "Reveal, instruct, benefit, and delight" (示教利喜) is an often encountered them in Northern School texts that refers to standard teaching stratagems used to influence beings to enter the universal liberation path of bodhisattvas and buddhas.

72. In my translation of the KB *Ten Grounds Sutra*, the complete text of this sixth vow is as follows:

    He also vows to directly know all of the differentiating aspects of all worlds throughout the ten directions, including all aspects of those worlds that are wide, narrow, extremely towering, of so countlessly many varieties one could never distinguish them all, including those that are immovable, and those that are indescribably coarse, subtle, upright, inverted, formed with their crowns and bases opposing each other, flat, spherical, or cubical, thus being able in this knowing to freely enter the knowledge of all such worlds, knowing them as existing in a manner comparable to appearances in the net-like canopy of Indra wherein things manifest like the phenomena in a conjuration. In making such a great vow as this, his implementation of it is as vast as the Dharma realm and as extensive as empty space as he continues on until the end of future time and throughout all kalpas, incessantly carrying on the direct and complete knowing of all such worlds.

73. This refers to a list of six recommended reflections conducing to clarity of understanding: impermanence, suffering, nonself, impurity of food, unenjoyability of all stations of worldly existence, death (T28.1548.637b).

74. In my translation of the KB *Ten Grounds Sutra*, the complete text of this seventh vow is as follows:

    He also vows to bring about the purification of all buddha lands wherein all buddha lands enter a single buddha land, a single buddha land enters all buddha lands, and each and every buddha land is adorned with measurelessly many radiant phenomena, wherein they all become filled with measurelessly many wise beings who have abandoned all defilements and perfected the path of purification, and wherein he always possesses the power of all buddhas' great superknowledges, accords with the mental dispositions of beings, and thus appears for their sakes. In making such a great vow as this, his implementation of it is as vast as the Dharma realm and as extensive as empty space as he continues on until the end of future time and throughout all kalpas, incessantly purifying lands such as these.

75. The five categories of evil ending with this one are the same ones that were described and thoroughly explained by Nāgārjuna earlier in this text as "five types of wrong livelihood for monastics."

76. These last five categories of evils clearly refer directly to the five hindrances (*nīvaraṇa* or *āvaraṇa*) preventing entry into meditative absorption.

77. I have not been able to find the Sanskrit antecedents for these three Chinese transliterations or the two transliterations that appear a little farther down in this list.
78. VB points out that this is most likely a reference to the Digambara Jains.
79. VB points out that this is most likely a reference to the Śvetāmbara Jains.
80. VB points out that Maskarī Gośālīputra was the "founder of the Ājivikas, See DN 2.20. He held that everything was determined by fate."
81. VB suggests that this is Sañjaya Vairāṭīputra, a.k.a. Saṃjayin Vairāṭīputra (Pali: Sañjaya Belaṭṭhiputta), a skeptical ascetic teacher, a contemporary of the Buddha. See DN 2.32
82. Per VB: "Probably Pakudha Kaccāyana. See DN 2.26. He taught a kind of atomism."
83. Per VB: "Perhaps Ajita Kesakambali, who taught a moral nihilism. See DN 2.23."
84. Per VB: "On the above [various theorists on nirvāṇa], see the five types of "final nirvāṇa in this very life" mentioned in the *Brahmajāla Sutta*, DN 1.3.19."
85. One should understand that this does not refer to the *dhūta* austerities so extensively discussed and praised by N in the 32nd chapter of this treatise, but rather only to the non-beneficial ascetic practices (lying down on a bed of nails, etc.) adopted by non-Buddhist traditions.
86. This is probably a reference to the ten "entangling thickets" (*gahana*) of which the first is indeed "afflictions." They are routinely translated as "difficulties" in KJ and KB translations. They are listed in the translation of the *Ten Grounds Sutra* (T10.286.524c10–12) in the discussion of the ninth *bhūmi* as follows:
    The entangling difficulties associated with the afflictions;
    The entangling difficulties associated with karmic actions;
    The entangling difficulties associated with the faculties;
    The entangling difficulties associated with resolute dispositions;
    The entangling difficulties associated with sense realms;
    The entangling difficulties associated with the mind's deep-seated intentions;
    The entangling difficulties associated with latent tendencies;
    The entangling difficulties associated with births;
    The entangling difficulties associated with residual karmic propensities;

And the entangling difficulties associated with the differences in the three categories of beings.

87. Probably *adbhuta* (Pali: *abbhuta*), "wondrous, supernatural, etc." for which the standard Chinese rendering is: "rarely encountered" (希有).

88. Per VB: "We have here five terms that are characteristic of the Buddha's teaching which we encounter again and again in the *Nikāyas* (particularly the *Saṃyutta Nikāya*, where they are applied to all the doctrinal items: the five aggregates (in Ch. 22), the six or twelve sense bases (Ch. 35), feelings (Ch. 36), the elements (Ch. 14), etc. The five are: *samudaya, atthaṅgama, assāda, ādīnava, nissaraṇa,* 'arising, passing away, enjoyment, danger, and escape.'

    "See e.g. SN 22: 73–74, 107–109, 129–34, and many other suttas.

    "For example SN 22:74 says, 'The unlearned worldling does not correctly understand the arising (through 'escape') regarding form … consciousness. The learned noble disciple correctly understands the arising (through 'escape') regarding form … consciousness.'

    "On the five-term template, see SN 14:38; 17:26; 22:108; 23:6; 36:28. The threefold "enjoyment" template is also common—see 14:37; 17:25; 22:107; 23:5; 36:27; 48:6, 29, 34."

89. [With reference to the Pali tradition], VB notes: "Here we have *vimokṣa* as eight stages of samādhi."

90. The Pali meditation tradition refers to these as *kasiṇas*.

91. The earlier line (33a22) upon which this comments referred instead to *ligen* (利根) "sharp faculties."

92. I emend the *Taisho* reading here by accepting the variant "moths" (蛾) found in four other editions. Without this emendation, "ants" (蟻) would be duplicated in this list.

93. VB suggests that this most likely corresponds to *saṃhita*.

94. In my translation of the KB Ten Grounds Sutra, the complete text of this eighth vow is as follows:

    He also vows that he will be of like mind with and pursue the same studies as all other bodhisattvas, joining together with them in the accumulation of every sort of goodness, remaining free of enmity or jealousy toward them, developing identical states of mental awareness as theirs, holding thoughts of equal regard toward them, maintaining harmonious relations with them, never becoming mutually estranged from them, being able as well to manifest buddha bodies according to what suits the needs of others, being able in one's own mind to completely understand and know the domains, spiritual powers, and powers of cognition of all buddhas, always being able to freely employ spiritual superknowledges to roam at will to all lands, manifesting the appearance of one's body in the assemblies of all buddhas, being able as well to everywhere take up births into all stations of rebirth, being possessed of all such inconceivably great wisdom, and perfecting the practices of the bodhisattvas. In making such a great vow as this, his implementation of it is as vast as the Dharma realm and as extensive as empty space as he continues on until the end of future time and throughout all kalpas, incessantly carrying forth the practice of just such a great path of wisdom.

95. In my translation of the KB Ten Grounds Sutra, the complete text of this ninth vow is as follows:

He also vows that he will take up the irreversible turning of the wheel of Dharma, that he will course in the bodhisattva path, that, of all of his physical, verbal, and mental actions, none will be such as are done in vain, that any being who merely sees him will thereby immediately become bound for definite success in the Buddha's Dharma, that, "Any being who so much as hears my voice will thereby immediately become bound for success in the path of genuine wisdom," that, "Any being who merely lays eyes on me will immediately be filled with joyous delight and abandon afflictions," that, in this, he will become like the great king of medicine trees, and that, in order to develop such resolve as this, he will course in the bodhisattva path. In making such a great vow as this, his implementation of it is as vast as the Dharma realm and as extensive as empty space as he continues on until the end of future time and throughout all kalpas, incessantly coursing along in the path of irreversibility, ensuring that none of his actions will have been done in vain.

96. In my translation of the KB Ten Grounds Sutra, the complete text of this tenth vow is as follows:

He also vows that he will gain the realization of *anuttarasamyaksaṃbodhi* in all worlds, that even in those places manifesting within the tip of a single hair, he will manifest entry into the womb, leaving behind the home life, sitting in the *bodhimaṇḍa*, gaining buddhahood, turning the wheel of Dharma, bringing about the liberation of beings, and manifesting the appearance of entering the great nirvāṇa, that he will manifest the great spiritual and cognitive powers of the *tathāgatas*, that he will adapt to the circumstances of all individual beings and that, according to what is appropriate for their liberation, he will, even in every successive mind-moment, manifest realization of the buddha path, facilitate the liberation of beings, and bring about the extinguishing of their suffering and afflictions, that he will gain the cognition that realizes all dharmas are characterized by identity with nirvāṇa, that, employing a single voice, he will be able to cause all beings to become established in joyfulness, that, even though he manifests entry into the great nirvāṇa, he will nonetheless never cut off his coursing in the bodhisattva practices, that he will reveal to beings the grounds of great knowledge, that he will cause them to realize all dharmas are in every case false and deceptive, accomplishing these endeavors by resort to great wisdom, great superknowledges, and freely manifested spiritual transformations. In making such a great vow as this, his implementation of it is as vast as the Dharma realm and as extensive as empty space as he continues on until the end of future time and throughout all kalpas, incessantly persisting in accomplishing the works associated with the path to buddhahood, in seeking great wisdom, and in acquiring the great spiritual powers and other such realizations.

97. We know from comparisons with Sanskrit editions that, in some of the translations attributed to Kumārajīva (such as the *Daśabhumika Sutra*), *xing* (性) (usually translated into English as "nature" from the Sanskrit antecedent *bhāva*) instead often translates the Sanskrit antecedent *dhātu* which most often corresponds to the English word "realm." This section of text appears to be one of those passages. Hence my repeated translation here of *xing* (性) as "realm" and not as "nature."

98. "Range of actions" here translates *xingchu* (行處), a standard translation for the Sanskrit *gocara* which, per MW, means "pasture ground for cattle, range, field for action, abode, dwelling place, district, etc."

99. To correct an obvious scribal error involving the dropping of a crucial character from this phrase already occurring twice in this section, I emend the reading of the *Taisho* text by accepting the SYMG editions' retention of *fo* (佛), "buddhas."

100. Since it only requires one of these seven reasons for generating the resolve to actually do so, one might wonder why N mentions: "it may find its origin in [one of] three reasons or else in [one of] four reasons." I suspect he is referring to two different lists of reasons prevalent in different teaching traditions.

101. VB notes: "I think this is alluding to the seven good dharmas. See *Majjhima Nikāya* 53 (also *Anguttara Nikāya* 7:67): śraddhā, hrī, avatapta [apatrāpya], bāhuśrutya, vīrya, smṛti, and prajñā." (Faith, sense of shame, dread of blame, abundant learning, vigor, mindfulness, wisdom.)

102. VB proposes that this may refer to "eleven benefits of lovingkindness" enumerated in the *Aṅguttara Nikāya*'s treatment of "The Elevens," this based on his observation that Chinese translators

sometimes use this *gongde* (功德), usually "meritorious qualities," to translate *ānusaṃsā*, "benefits."

103. "Seventeen physical dharmas" is a provisional translation for *"shen shi qi"* (身十七). The text is opaque and a digital search of the entire *Taisho* canon failed to turn up any plausible analogues for this list.

104. VB notes that there are five faculties here that are distributed among these four listed types.

105. Comparison with the Sanskrit of the occurrences of this *xinle* (信樂) compound in the KB translation of the Ten Grounds Sutra confirm that this is an alternate Kumārajiva translation for *adhimukti* which is more commonly rendered into Kumārajiva translations as *xinjie* (信解), lit. "faithful comprehension." This refers to a strong mental inclination toward a (usually) wholesome mental object, hence the need to translate it in some contexts as "resolute belief," "resolute comprehension," etc.

106. I emend the reading of the *Taisho* text here, preferring the *chang* (常), "always," of the SYMG editions to *Taisho*'s *dang* (當), "should," this to correct an apparent graphic-similarity scribal error.

107. As Nāgārjuna makes clear elsewhere (*Bodhisaṃbhāra Śāstra* [菩提資糧論 – T32, no. 1660]), for one who aspires to continue all the way along the bodhisattva path to ultimate realization of buddhahood, it is essential that they first genuinely and solidly generate the resolve to gain the utmost, right, and perfect enlightenment, doing so *prior* to entering this "stage of certainty" or "right and fixed position" (*samyaktva niyāma*), lest they otherwise fall irreversibly into the path to arhatship.

Nāgārjuna's rationale for warning bodhisattva path practitioners about this possibility is that, absent prior genuine generation of highest-bodhi resolve, the diligent cultivator of good dharmas who gains such a realization will become irreversible on the path to arhatship, this effective with his realization of the unproduced-dharmas patience. As a consequence, he entirely eliminates the possibility of his own future buddhahood.

In that treatise, Nāgārjuna even goes so far as to equate this prospect with a tragedy far worse than falling into the hells, this because the hells, unlike arhatship, do not eliminate the possibility of future buddhahood. For my complete English translation of Nāgārjuna's *Bodhisaṃbhāra Śāstra*, and its early Indian Commentary, see *Nāgārjuna's Guide to the Bodhisattva Path* and *The Bodhisaṃbhāra Treatise Commentary*, both published by Kalavinka Press.

108. The "stage of certainty" or "right and fixed position" referenced here is that of the bodhisattva who has by this point become invulnerable to being turned away from the path to buddhahood.
109. Bhikkhu notes: "Velāma is the subject of AN 9.20."
110. "*Weishouduoluo*" (韋首多羅), the Chinese transliteration of this bodhisattva's name, is found only in this once in the entire Taisho canon. VB suggests that the Pali reconstruction might be "Vessantara," the name of the marvelously generous bodhisattva celebrated in a *jātaka* tale of one of the Buddha's previous lives. He also suggests that a Sanskrit equivalent might be the "Viśvantara" that I have chosen to use here.
111. These five Sanskrit terms refer to increasingly serious levels of transgression against the monastic moral code ranging from relatively minor offenses (*duṣkṛta*) to offenses involving a meeting of the Sangha with a probationary period (*saṃghāvaśeṣa*) or permanent expulsion from the monastic community (*pārājika*).
112. Because the Chinese of this statement is terse and vague, my translation here is somewhat tentative.
113. This appears to be subcommentary on this earlier statement regarding the abandonment of dharmas conducing to loss of the bodhi resolve: "By 'abandonment,' it is meant that one entirely extinguishes those dharmas that are bad and thus prevents them from entering one's mind."
114. A *pārājika* offense entails expulsion from the monastic sangha. A *saṃgha-vaśeṣa* offense entails a meeting of the local monastic sangha to determine the penalty and how to achieve purification of the transgression.
115. An instance of "at the time of certification" would be, for instance, during the semimonthly recitation of monastic precepts, when one is asked with respect to precepts just recited, "Are you pure in this?"
116. "Two Vehicles" refers to the two non-Mahāyāna individual-liberation paths, those of the arhats and the *pratyekabuddhas*.
117. The *Taisho* annotations state that the SYMG editions all format these twenty characters as a quatrain. As it is obvious that the immediately following text comments on them as if they did indeed constitute a verse, I have emended the English formatting accordingly.
118. In accordance with the SYMG editions, I emend the *Taisho* text here by substituting *sui* (雖), "although," for *shui* (誰), "who," this to correct an obvious graphic-similarity scribal error.

119. Again, those four originally mentioned in the above verse are: unawareness of the work of *māras*; weakness of the resolve to attain bodhi; karmic obstacles; and Dharma obstacles.
120. I translate here as "monastic preceptor" and "monastic Dharma teacher" what the KJ text retains in transliteration as *"upādhyāya"* and *"ācārya"* respectively.
121. When KJ refers to "the true character of dharmas" (諸法實相), he is typically translating the Sanskrit term *"dharmatā."*
122. This is clearly a reference to the eight worldly dharmas. In this connection VB offers the following citation: "See AN 8:5–6; IV 156 foll."
123. This seems to be a situation where some monk or nun wants to divert to themselves the material support of families that currently support other monastics. VB suggests, "This is what is called in Pali *kulamacchariya*, 'miserliness regarding families.'" He offers the following citation: AN 5:254–255.
124. "Five objects of desire" refers not only to the five types of "sensual" desire (forms, sounds, smells, tastes, touchables), but also to wealth, sex, fame, food, and leisure.
125. VB notes that the following verses reflect ideas found in Nāgārjuna's *Mūlamadhyamaka-kārikā*, in particular chapters 18, 10, and 6.
126. These four lines comprise the Buddhist tetralemma used to point to the futility of capturing the nature of ultimate reality in logical formulations.
127. In other words, ash has been traditionally used in making bleaching agents. So too with words: They may be used to remove the stain of wrong views from the mind, but they cannot ever entirely embody the truth reached through right views. Thus they are always bound to be freighted to a degree with the "stains" of dual concepts that are then bound to sully the direct perception of the truth of the emptiness of all phenomena.
128. This same verse is repeated later in the treatise in Chapter 33, at 118b05–26. There are eight variant characters as noted below.
129. The Chapter 33 version of this verse has "and is identical with whatever is an existent dharma" instead of "and is identical with whatever is possessed of signs" (即為是有法 instead of 即為是有相).
130. The Chapter 33 version of this verse has "Were one to relinquish all strategizing and attachments" instead of "Were one to relinquish all covetousness" (若捨諸計著 instead of 若捨諸貪著).
131. The Chapter 33 version of this verse has "such seizing on this sign of having relinquished attachments" instead of "such seizing on this

sign of having relinquished covetousness" (取是捨著相 instead of 取是捨貪相).

132. The Chapter 33 version of this verse has "It is the abandonment of grasping and whatever thing is grasped—" instead of "There is someone who grasps and something that is grasped" (離取取何事 instead of 誰取取何事).

133. The Chapter 33 version of this verse has "whether as conjoined or separate, they are all entirely nonexistent" instead of "whether as conjoined or separate, they all do not exist" (共離俱無有 instead of 共離俱不有).

134. The Chapter 33 version of this verse has "It is precisely because it is synonymous with signlessness" instead of "It is precisely because it is signless" (即名為無相 instead of 即為是無相).

135. These first two verse lines are referring to the four alternative propositions of the tetralemma, as in: 1) It exists; 2) It does not exist; 3) It both exists and does not exist; and 4) It neither exists nor does not exist.

136. The Chapter 33 version of this verse has a fairly nonconsequential variant for one of the characters in this line (先來非寂滅 instead of 先亦非寂滅).

137. VB notes the following here: "This is the first alternative among the four ways of construing a self. See SN 22:47."

138. The usual Sanskrit antecedent for this "traceless vajra-wielding dharma protectors" is *guhyapāda vajra*.

139. These *ślokas* correspond to *ślokas* 24–28 of Nāgārjuna's *Bodhisambhāra Śāstra*. In my English translation of that entire text with its Indian commentary, they read as follows:

> So long as he has not generated great compassion or the patiences,
> even though he may have gained an irreversibility,
> the bodhisattva is still subject to a form of "dying"
> which occurs through allowing negligence to arise.

> The grounds of the *śrāvaka* disciples or the *pratyekabuddha*s,
> if entered, become for him the same as dying
> because he would thereby sever the bodhisattva's
> roots of understanding and awareness.

> Even at the prospect of falling into the hell-realms,
> the bodhisattva would not be struck with fright.
> The grounds of the *śrāvaka* disciples and the *pratyekabuddha*s, however,
> *do* provoke a great terror in him.

> It is not the case that falling into the hell realms

would bring about an ultimate obstacle to his bodhi.
The grounds of the *śrāvaka* disciples and the *pratyekabuddha*s, however,
do create just such an ultimate obstacle.

Just as is said of he who loves long life,
that he becomes fearful at the prospect of his own beheading,
so too, the grounds of the *śrāvaka* disciples and *pratyekabuddha*s
should bring about a fearfulness of just this sort.

140. The first two quatrains correspond to the *Bodhisaṃbhāra Śāstra*'s *śloka* numbers 22 and 23 which read as follows:

In the bodhisattva's striving for bodhi,
so long as he has not yet gained irreversibility,
he acts as urgently as the person whose turban has caught fire.
Thus one should take up just such intensely diligent practice.

Thus it is that those bodhisattvas,
when striving for the realization of bodhi,
should not rest in their practice of vigor,
for they have shouldered such a heavy burden.

141. These last two quatrains correspond to the *Bodhisaṃbhāra Śāstra*'s *śloka* numbers 91 and 92 which read as follows:

Even if one were to take up the vehicle of the *śrāvaka* disciples
or the vehicle of the *pratyekabuddha*s,
and hence practiced solely for one's own self benefit,
still, one would not relinquish the enduring practice of vigor.

How much the less could it be that a great man,
one committed to liberate himself and liberate others,
might somehow not generate
a measure of vigor a thousand *koṭis* times greater?

142. I emend here the verse-abbreviated "Three Practices Buddha" reading to "Three *Vehicles* Practices Buddha" to accord with the explanatory text which follows at 42a02–06.

143. See *The Sutra on the Youth Precious Moon's Questions on Dharma* (大乘寶月童子問法經 / T14n0437_p108c01–110a07). The names vary, but the ideas are the same, i.e., sincere mindfulness of ten buddhas in the ten directions can bring irreversibility with respect to one's future attainment of buddhahood.

144. "*Candana*" usually refers to sandalwood, but as noted in MW, it may also be used as a term to refer to anything that is the most excellent of its kind. MW: "mn. sandal (*Sirium myrtifolium*), either the tree, wood, or the unctuous preparation of the wood held in high estimation as perfumes; hence; a term for anything which is the most excellent of its kind."

145. The Chinese translation for this eightieth buddha's name, *guangming fo* (光明佛), "Light Buddha," is duplicated in the name of the ninety-sixth buddha (see next paragraph). Since we do not know the Sanskrit antecedents for these two buddhas' names, I have distinguished them here with slightly variant English translations ("Light Buddha," "Radiance Buddha").

146. The Chinese translation for this ninety-sixth buddha's name, *guangming fo* (光明佛), "Radiance Buddha," is duplicated in the name of the eightieth buddha (see previous paragraph). Since we do not know the Sanskrit antecedents for these two buddhas' names, I have distinguished them here with slightly variant English translations ("Light Buddha," "Radiance Buddha").

147. On sensibility grounds, I adopt here the SYMG editions' variant, *hua yuan fo* (華園佛), "Floral Garden Buddha," to correct what seems to be a graphic-similarity scribal error in the *Taisho* edition, *hua chi fo* (華齒佛), "Floral Teeth Buddha."

148. I reconstruct *"aśoka,"* lit. "sorrowless" as the name of this bodhi tree as it is a tree that grows throughout India (*Saraca asoca*) and is in fact said to also be the same kind of tree under which the historical Buddha's mother gave birth to him.

149. VB provides the following citation: "See DN II 4: *Sikhī, bhikkhave, bhagavā arahaṃ sammāsambuddho puṇḍarīkassa mūle abhisambuddho.*"

150. The *śirīṣa* tree is identified by MW as *acacia sirissa*.

151. An *"aśvattha"* tree is an ancient name for what is more commonly known in Buddhist texts as the "bodhi" tree (*ficus religiosa*).

152. In the verses below (at 44b07), this Buddha's name is enhanced with an additional character to "Marks of the Sovereign's Canopy" (王幢相).

153. I suspect that there should only be ten buddhas in this list and that this buddha's name may appear here only as a result of an accidental scribal redundancy, this for two reasons:
    a) The Chinese name is identical to that of the previously listed buddha except that the characters are in reverse order (*wangxiang* [王相] versus *xiangwang* [相王]); and
    b) Although the other ten buddhas' names are mentioned in the following praise verses, this buddha's name is not mentioned there at all.

154. This buddha's name is only slightly different in the verses that follow, occurring there (at 44b15) as "Peacefully Established" (安立).

155. I emend the reading of the reading here by preferring the *zi* (自), "personally," of the SYMG editions to the *mu* (目), "eyes" of the *Taisho* text, this to correct an apparent graphic-similarity scribal error.

156. "Three times three, nine kinds in all" appears to refer to the nine varieties of bad karma produced through physical, verbal, and mental actions under the influence of the three kinds of afflictions or poisons (greed, hatred, and delusion).

157. One of two types of "morally indeterminate" or "neutral dharmas," *yin mo wu ji* (隱沒無記) or *you fu wu ji* (有覆無記), "obscured morally indeterminate [dharmas]," (*nivṛta-avyākṛta-dharma*) are those that are karmically neutral, but which involve a mind that is accompanied by subtle hindrances that impede liberation. "Subtle hindrances" refers for example to having the view that assumes the existence of a "self," to having the tendency to think, "I am," to engaging in self-cherishing thoughts, words, and deeds, and to being forever under the influence of ignorance.

158. I translate here as "monastic preceptor" and "monastic Dharma teacher" what the KJ text retains in transliteration as *"upādhyāya"* and *"ācārya"* respectively.

159. Rebirth as an *asura* is one of the six rebirth destinies within cyclic existence. *Asuras* are typically described as "titans" or "demigods" whose most emblematic characteristic aside from a deficiency of merit is a fondness for fighting, especially with the desire-realm devas, in particular with the devas of the Trāyastriṃśa Heaven ("The Heaven of the Thirty-three"). The term is also used more loosely to describe beings within other realms of cyclic existence whose dominant character traits are marked by an analogous fondness for hatred, disputation, and combat.

160. The "three objects of reverence" are variously interpreted. In descending order of intended likelihood here, they are: the Three Jewels (Buddha, Dharma, Sangha); those who have attained the three fruitions of valid Buddhist paths (the buddhas, the *pratyekabuddhas*, and the arhats); in Pure Land contexts, Amitābha Buddha, Avalokiteśvara Bodhisattva, and Mahāsthāmaprāpta Bodhisattva; and, especially in *Avataṃsaka Sūtra* contexts, Śākyamuni Buddha, Mañjuśrī Bodhisattva, and Samantabhadra Bodhisattva.

161. By "the difficulties" (諸難), N most likely means to refer specifically to "the eight difficulties.". They refer to rebirth: in the hell realm; in the hungry ghost realm; in the animal realm; in the long life heavens (where there is no motivation to cultivate the path); on the Northern Continent of *Uttarakuru* (where, again, there is no context there for cultivating the path); in a body with impaired faculties (as when

deaf, dumb, or blind); in a circumstance where one's mentality is exclusively focused on worldly knowledge and eloquence in debating secular issues irrelevant to the path of liberation; or in a place where the Buddha Dharma is no longer extant in that world.

Referring to the above, VB offers further perspectives here:

> "The eight in the Pali Canon are at AN 8:29: (1–4) are the same; (5) rebirth in the outlying provinces among the uncouth foreigners (maybe Uttarakuru is one example, but there must be many other 'outlying provinces,' including most of Eurasia, Africa and the Americas); (6) one holds wrong view and has a distorted perspective: 'There is nothing given, nothing sacrificed, nothing offered …' in other words, a view that denies karma and results; (7) 'one is unwise, stupid, obtuse, unable to understand the meaning of what has been well stated and badly stated' (probably = 'rebirth with impaired faculties'); (8) 'a Tathāgata has not arisen in the world … and the Dhamma leading to peace, nibbāna, and enlightenment is not taught.'"

162. The Sanskrit for these: *cakṣu, jñāna, vidyā*, and *āloka*.

163. N is referring here specifically to the life span of a buddha who, certainly more readily than an unenlightened person, he is able to either extend or shorten his life span at will. Another example of this phenomenon is described in Vasubandhu's *Abhidharmakośa-bhāṣya* in which it is noted that an arhat may either extend or shorten his life span through a corresponding diminishment or enhancement of his stock of karmic merit.

164. In most traditional Dharma community contexts, this would refer to welcoming and seeing off eminent Dharma teachers, preceptors, visiting monks or nuns, etc.

165. Although "*dhyāna* concentration states" usually refers primarily to the four *dhyānas* associated with the form realm, it also refers to the four *dhyāna* concentration states associated with the formless realm, namely: infinite space, infinite consciousness, nothing whatsoever, and neither perception nor non-perception.

166. By "kindness, compassion, and so forth," N is very likely referring to the four immeasurable minds (*apramāṇa-citta*) consisting of kindness, compassion, sympathetic joy, and equanimity.

167. "Unobscured morally indeterminate (*anivṛta-avyākṛta*)" actions are those that are karmically neutral and involve a mind that is free of subtle hindrances that impede liberation. As mentioned in an earlier note, "subtle hindrances" refers for example to having the view that assumes the existence of a "self," to having a the tendency to think, "I am," to engaging in self-cherishing thoughts, words, and deeds, and

Endnotes 673

to being forever under the influence of ignorance. In this case, there are none of these hindrances that might impede liberation.

168. "Those in training and those beyond training" (*śaikṣa-aśaikṣa*) is a reference to the eight stages of realization culminating in arhatship, the eighth and final stage in the Śrāvaka Vehicle's individual-liberation path.

169. For similar passages in the KJ translation of the *Great Perfection of Wisdom Sutra*, see the "Rejoicing" chapter (chapter 39 in fascicle 11) of 摩訶般若波羅蜜經 that begins at T08n0223_p0297b18.

170. I could not locate this title in the *Taisho* edition of the Buddhist canon.

171. A very long and very similar corresponding passage, beginning with precisely this statement of praise can be found in Kumārajīva's translation of this chapter of the *Mahāprajñāpāramitā Sūtra in 25,000 lines*, beginning at T08, no. 223, p. 300b26.

172. The three clear knowledges (*tri-vidya*) are the heavenly eye, the cognition of past lives of oneself and others, and the extinguishing of the contaminants.

173. For a complete explanation of these three types of retribution, see Harivarman's *Satyasiddhi Śāstra*, Chapter 104, "The Three Types of Karmic Retribution" (T32; no. 1646; p. 297b–c.).

174. This sutra is extant in the Taisho canon and the cited passage is easily identifiable (T15; no. 633; p. 472c06–14).

175. VB recognized this passage as a quote from *A Lump of Salt* in the *Anguttara Nikāya*, 3:100 (NDB pp.331 foll.) for which the *Taisho* canon parallel is found in the *Madhyama Āgama* at T01n0026, beginning at page 433a12.

176. To correct an apparent graphic-similarity scribal error, I emend the reading of the *Taisho* text here by preferring the SYMG editions' *er* (二), "two," to the *Taisho* edition's *san* (三), "three."

177. The Sanskrit name for this "Comprehensive Giving Bodhisattva" (一切施菩薩) is Sarvadāna. Its Chinese transliteration (薩和檀) is used directly below in the paragraph related to Sadāprarudita.

178. This is a reference to Jātaka tale number 316 as recorded in the Pali tradition. It describes a previous life of the Buddha when he was a rabbit who sacrificed his life as a meal for a hungry rishi.

179. VB traced this passage to the "Akṣayamati" Chapter in the *Taisho* canon's 413 CE Chinese translation by Dharmakṣema of the *Mahāsaṃnipāta Sūtra* (大方等大集經卷第二十七 –無盡意菩薩品第十二之一 T13n0397_p0189a18 foll.), noting that this text's version of the

passage seems somewhat more elaborate than the passage as found in the T397 Chinese translation.

180. I emend the reading of the text by following two alternate editions (YM) in including *huijian* (慧堅) "solidity in wisdom" which completes this traditional fivefold list of five categories of mastery.

181. As will become clear in due course, "emptiness and such" refers primarily to emptiness, signlessness, and wishlessness (the three gates to liberation) and secondarily to a whole host of other qualities associated with the bodhisattva path.

182. Per VB, see *Mahāsaṃnipāta Sūtra* (大方等大集經,卷第二十七, 無盡意菩薩品第十二之一 [T13n0397_p0189b20 foll.]).

183. I emend the reading of the text here to correct a fairly obvious scribal error by preferring on sensibility grounds the SYMG editions' *xinjie* (信解), "resolute conviction, firm belief, etc.," to *Taisho's xinjietuo* (信解脫), "liberation of faith."

184. "Field of merit" is a characterization typically but not exclusively reserved for more advanced or spiritually pure practitioners of the path such as senior monastics. In fact, anyone truly in need is often also regarded as "a field of merit." The idea behind the metaphoric designation is that, if one gives such people a gift, the karmic reward to the benefactor in terms of merit thereby accrued will be abundant in a way that is analogous to the results one might expect from the planting of good seeds in especially fertile soil.

185. Per VB, this is probably a reference to non-Buddhist teachings such as those promoted by Maskarī-gośālī-putra and Ajita-keśakambala who denied the existence of karmic cause-and-effect in human affairs.

186. Lit., "no giving where the recipient is not a field of merit." This is a reference to instances of discriminating against some potential recipients because they are considered to be insufficiently virtuous or to be of only inferior monastic rank ("mere novices," etc.).

187. "Fallacious conceptual proliferation" translates *xilun* (戲論), lit. "frivolous discourse," a Chinese translation of the Sanskrit *prapañca*, a term with numerous connotations that usually refers primarily to conceptual proliferation that imputes a self where none exists and spins out all sorts of other egotistical ideation with no basis in ultimate reality.

188. For the corresponding Chinese translation, VB notes that the passage begins at T13n0397_p0189c12.

189. VB notes: "On the following, see *Majjhima Nikāya* 142 (at the end). The *Madhyama Āgama* parallel is found at T01n0026_p0722b28. See also: T01n0084_p0904a23."

190. Lest this statement seem somewhat confusing, these four types each contain two entities, namely a giver and a receiver. Three of them have at least one entity that serves as a basis for purity and three of them have at least one entity that serves as a basis for impurity.

191. As VB points out, in these contexts, this *she* (捨) which otherwise most directly connotes "relinquishing" usually translates the Sanskrit *tyāga* which is also often used in Indian Buddhist texts to connote "generosity," hence my use of that translation here. In support of this translation, VB points to a Pali texts classical definition at AN 4:61: "*Katamā ca, gahapati, cāgasampadā? Idha, gahapati, ariyasāvako vigatamala-maccherena cetasā agāraetasā agārasāvako vigatamalaion.*"

192. I emend the reading of the text here to correct an apparent scribal error by preferring on sensibility grounds the SYMG editions' *puti* (菩提), "bodhi," to the *Taisho* edition's *pusa* (菩薩), "bodhisattva."

193. KJ retains the transliteration (*sarvajña*). I prefer to go ahead and translate it (as "all-knowledge").

194. The brahman caste corresponds to the priestly class.

195. The *kṣatriya* caste corresponds to the military class.

196. The *vaiśya* caste corresponds to the agricultural and merchant classes.

197. The *śūdra* caste, in traditional Indian culture, is considered a low class. Of course, the Buddha emphatically repudiated the caste system, stating that all castes flow with equality into the Dharma of the Buddha just as all waters, when they flow into the ocean, immediately become of but a single flavor.

198. "Self-benefit" here is one of the two types of benefit to which the bodhisattva is dedicated, namely the self-benefit that brings about one's own complete awakening and the other-benefit that facilitates the complete awakening of all other beings.

199. The "erroneous" of "erroneous interpretations" here translates the Chinese *yi* (異), literally "aberrant," "divergent," or "deviating."

200. VB offers this note: "The following is in the *Dīgha Nikāya* 16.4.7 foll. (Long Discourses of the Buddha, pp. 255–56). Also in *Aṅguttara Nikāya* 4:180. A Chinese parallel is at T01n0001_p0017c01."

201. Here and hereafter, I translate *zhu fa xiang yi* (諸法相義) as "the true character of dharmas. Although it might more literally translate as "the meaning of the character of dharmas," or as "the character and meaning of dharmas," it would seem to more probably correspond to the Sanskrit *dharmatā* which, in other KJ texts is rendered into Chinese as *zhu fa shi xiang* (諸法實相). This seems especially likely when one notes that Hirakawa (p. 190) gives *dharmatā* as the Sanskrit antecedent for "諸法實相義."

202. *Mātṛkās* were systematic "matrices" (same etymological root) and/or lists of the technical terms, topics, and other doctrinal details contained in the sutras. They served as memorization aids in the preservation of the sutras and the teachings contained within them, this during the time after the Buddha's nirvāṇa and before the sutras and the abhidharma literature based upon them were first systematically committed to writing on palm leaves or other transcription media.

203. Although the title of such a scripture is indeed referenced in numerous places in the Chinese Buddhist canon, I could not find this textual passage anywhere in the canon as an extant scriptural translation. Of course this does not rule out the possible presence of a slightly variant Chinese translation of these ideas in either in this so-named scripture or somewhere else in the canon.

204. *Dhāraṇīs* usually take the form of mantras serving to retain Dharma as dominant in one's karmic continuum from lifetime to lifetime and to also retain very precise memory of all teachings one has learned from lifetime to lifetime. They are also commonly used to protect the practitioner of the path from negative influences arising both from without and from within his own mind. They are also regularly used to bestow benefit on other beings and to enhance one's capabilities on the bodhisattva path in numerous additional ways. Nāgārjuna writes at great length on this topic in his exegesis on the 25,000-line *Great Perfection of Wisdom Sutra*.

205. Although the *dhūtas are* austerities, here they refer not to austerities in general, but rather specifically to the twelve *dhūtaguṇa* austerities.

206. *Baiyi* (白衣), "white-robed ones," is a Sino-Buddhist translation of the Sanskrit *avadāta-vasana*, a term specifically referring to members of the Buddhist laity.

207. The apparent implication here is not only that a monastic will find his mind distracted by conversation with villagers, but also that his unconventional activities will become the subject of disapproving rumors that degrade the laity's respect for all members of the monastic sangha.

208. "Three poisons" is an alternate designation for the three primary psycho-spiritual afflictions of greed, hatred, and delusion.

209. N refers here to the rest of the six perfections aside from the practice of giving.

210. VB notes: "Nāgārjuna probably has in mind a passage that occurs in Pāli Saṃyutta Nikāya 20:10, and elsewhere: 'Here some bhikkhu dresses in the morning and, taking bowl and robe, enters a village or town for alms with body, speech, and mind unguarded, without

setting up mindfulness, unrestrained in his sense faculties. He sees women there lightly clad or lightly attired and lust invades his mind. With his mind invaded by lust, he meets death or deadly suffering. For this, bhikkhus, is death in the Noble One's Discipline: that one gives up the training and returns to the lower life. This is deadly suffering: that one commits a certain defiled offence of a kind that allows for rehabilitation.' ...Giving up the training is "death in the Noble One's discipline, the equivalent of dying." Breaking a grave precept approaches death but does not cross the line."

211. The four bases of meritorious qualities (truth, relinquishment, quiescence, and wisdom) were introduced by N in Chapter One (at 22b28–9). Their importance as defining qualities of both buddhas and bodhisattvas was emphasized repeatedly in Chapter Two.

212. N's use of "Dharma position" or "right Dharma position" (*samyaktva niyāma*) refers in this context to a stage on the *śrāvaka* disciple's path that is synonymous with attainment of the path of seeing, a stage from which one cannot readily switch over to cultivation of the bodhisattva path to buddhahood. See Leo Pruden's translation of *Abhidharma Kośa Bhāṣyam* (321, 944, 1055–6n, 1243).

In the Mahāyāna context, this "right Dharma position" connotes a stage of progress on the bodhisattva path wherein one directly perceives the emptiness of dharmas, yet nonetheless continues on with kindness and compassion in the universal-liberation path to buddhahood and remains invulnerable to retreating to the *śrāvaka* disciple's path to the attainment of individual liberation.

213. "Four fruitions" here is a reference to the four fruits of the *śrāvaka* disciples' path beginning with stream entry and ending with arhatship.

214. "Three matters" refers to mindfulness of the Buddha, mindfulness of the Dharma, and mindfulness of the Sangha in a manner accordant with the ensuing chapter-concluding discussion.

215. This statement is found in N's *Exegesis on the Mahāprajñāpāramitā Sūtra* (T25n1509.442c05–07) as well as in the *Mahāprajñāpāramitā Sūtra* itself (T08n0223.p273b29–c02).

216. VB Notes: "This must be *māraviṣaya* or *māradheyya*, the realm/domain of Māra, a metaphor for *saṃsāra*."

217. This is a reference to the "eight winds" or "eight worldly dharmas" (*aṣṭalokadharma*) that consist of four pairs of affective mind states strongly influencing the life priorities of beings trapped in cyclic existence: gain (*lābha*) and loss (*alābha*), fame (*yaśas*) and disgrace (*ayaśas*), praise (*praśaṃsā*) and blame (*nindā*), and pleasure (*sukha*) and pain (*duḥkha*).

218. Per the *Mahā-saṃgīti-sūtra* (佛說大集法門經) translated into Chinese by Dānapāla in 1005, these "six kinds of equanimity" (六捨) refer to equanimity or indifference at each of the six sense gates of eye, ear, nose, tongue, body, and mind with regard to the objects of those six sense faculties: visual forms, sounds, smells, tastes, touchables, and dharmas as objects of mind (T01n0012_p0231c15–18).

219. "Two kinds of afflictions" commonly refers to latent afflictions and manifest afflictions.

220. "The five hindrances" is a reference to desire, ill will, lethargy-and-sleepiness, excitedness-and-regretfulness, and afflicted doubtfulness. These five hindrances must be overcome in order to successfully enter deep states of meditation.

221. These are explained by the Buddha in the Ekottara Āgama Sūtra (T02.125.738b18–c17). In summary, these refer to avoidance of being taken advantage of by māras, i.e., "demons" (this is reiterated in all seven) by not retreating from these seven practices:

   1) Dwelling together in a single place with mutual respect involving mutual assistance between juniors and seniors while persisting in the cultivation of good dharmas;
   2) Accordance with the teachings within a harmonious and united Sangha;
   3) Non-attachment to worldly responsibilities or reputation;
   4) Avoidance of the recitation of miscellaneous (non-Buddhist) texts while forever goading on one's resolve;
   5) Non-indulgence of drowsiness and persistence in wakefulness;
   6) Avoidance of the study or propagation of "calculations" (probably referring to astronomically-based predictions and various sorts of divination, etc.);
   7) Bringing forth the reflection that there is nothing in the entire world that is worthy of delight, practicing *dhyāna* meditation, and persevering in accordance with the teachings.

222. Assuming that KJ is using the same Sanskrit-to-Chinese correspondences that we find in the KB translation of the *Daśabhūmika Sūtra*, what I translate here as "deep-seated aspirations and resolute belief" (*shenxin xinle* [深心信樂]) would correspond to *āśaya* and *adhimukti*.

223. "True character of dharmas" (usually *zhu fa shi xiang* - 諸法實相) is KJ's usual rendering for what Hirakawa notes (p. 1090) may be *tattvasya-lakṣaṇam, dharmatā, dharma-svabhāva*, etc. As such it is a reference to the true nature of dharmas as they really are. Hence it is a synonym for true suchness (*tathatā*).

224. I emend the reading of the *Taisho* text here by preferring on sensibility grounds the SYMG editions' *ming* (名), "is what is meant by," to the *Taisho* edition's *gu* (故), "therefore."
225. This extended sutra passage has direct correspondences to a section of a four-fascicle scripture that is included in the *Mahāvaipulya-mahāsamnipata-sūtra* (大方等大集經) otherwise known as the *Akṣayamati-nirdeśa* (無盡意菩薩品). That passage is in the *Taisho* canon at T13.397.186b–c.
226. On sensibility grounds, I emend the reading of the *Taisho* text's *xing* (性), "nature," here by preferring the SYMG editions' graphically similar *xing* (姓), "caste."
227. This *"jian wen jue zhi"* (見聞覺知) that I translate here as "seeing, hearing, sensing, or cognizing" corresponds to the Sanskrit *"dṛṣṭaṃ, śrutaṃ, mataṃ, vijñānam"* which collectively refer to the knowing of their respective objects by the six sense faculties of eye, ear, nose, tongue, body, and mind. In this tetrad, the cognitive functions of three of the senses (the olfactory, gustatory, and tactile sensing that are accomplished by the nose, tongue, and body) are collapsed under the single term "sensing" whereas the other three senses' functions are individually specified as "seeing" (the eye sense faculty), "hearing" (the ear sense faculty), and "cognizing" (the mind faculty).
228. The *Taisho* analogue text has *"jing jie gong de"* (境界功德), "qualities of the state of mind" (T13.397.0186b20).
229. "Joy" and "bliss" are two factors on a continuum of subtlety (joy being more coarse, bliss being more sublime) that arise and fall away in progressing through the four *dhyāna*s. "Declining to indulge the delectable" refers to remaining unattached to delectably pleasurable meditation states (*āsvādana-samādhi*) encountered in one's meditation practice that would otherwise pose a danger to progress in meditation.
230. Lest the reader find this passage somewhat opaque, this paragraph is primarily referring to transcendence of the five aggregates.
231. N. may be referring here either to the immediately preceding "mindfulness of the true Buddha" discussion or else to his later six-chapter (20–25) discussion of "mindfulness of the buddha" and its associated *pratyutpanna* samādhi.
232. As inferred by the following discussion, this may be a reference to the layperson's option of starting out in the cultivation of moral purity by only formally obligating himself to observe whichever moral precepts he can confidently uphold. Hence it is not uncommon for a layperson to start by taking just the three precepts proscribing

killing, stealing, and lying and then only later on formally taking the other two of the five precepts which prohibit sexual misconduct and the consumption of intoxicants.

233. This is probably a reference to the seven (or eight) kinds of arrogance variously listed in the canon.

234. "The body that does endure" is probably intended to refer to the Dharma body shared by all buddhas.

235. This refers to the recognition that, wisely used, the wealth of this life may bring about a circumstance of being wealthy in the Dharma. This is accomplished through using such wealth to do good deeds, support the Dharma, and otherwise generate merit that brings forth success in encountering right Dharma, the good spiritual guide, and conditions for cultivating the path to buddhahood in life after life.

236. The Chinese is more literally "impurity of the body," however, the Indian Buddhist tradition refers to it more specifically as "contemplation of the unloveliness of the body (aśubha-bhāvanā or aśubhā-saṃjñā)." This practice involves such contemplations as the contemplation of the 32 (or 36) parts of the body, the contemplation of the nine stages of decomposition of a corpse, and the contemplation of the white-boned skeleton.

237. This statement is probably intended to apply to socially obligatory serving of alcoholic beverages in circumstances such as the hosting of a large wedding reception where many of the people in attendance will surely be drinking anyway. In this connection, however, it is perhaps useful to recall the major bodhisattva precept forbidding any purveyance of intoxicants. It is stated therein that something so apparently minor as passing a glass of wine to someone may result in being born for five hundred lifetimes with no hands. Also, if it is not already obvious, Nāgārjuna would not condone a precepted layperson's personal consumption of alcohol, even when attending the sorts of events alluded to here.

238. Many of the statements contained in this scriptural passage correlate quite closely with those recorded in the very short fourth chapter of the single-fascicle *Sutra on the Questions of Ugradatta* (郁迦羅越問菩薩行經 / T12.n0323.p23a–30b). This edition of the *Ugraparipṛcchā Sūtra*, one of three translations made into Chinese, was translated by Dharmarakṣa sometime in the late 3rd or early 4th century.

239. "Ideation and discursion" translates the standard Chinese rendering of *vitarka* and *vicāra* (覺觀).

240. "Foolish common person," translates the standard Chinese rendering of *pṛthagjana* (凡夫). Although obviously not very flattering, this

English translation by Edward Conze is unfortunately very accurate. It basically refers to anyone who has not yet attained one of the fruits of the path by which one would become an *ārya*. The rest of us are always running mental and spiritual software deeply encoded with ignorance which produces delusion which in turn generates every permutation of greed, hatred, and stupidity. Hence the "foolishness" to which the term alludes.

241. The text reflects conditions in ancient India dominated by tribal customs. Occurrences such as those listed here might have easily followed from offending tribal authorities, the rich, the powerful, organized crime, ad hoc groups of bandits, local Taliban-like zealots, or invading armies.

242. VB points out that these four causal influences of desire, hatred, delusion, and fear (*chanda, doṣa, moha,* and *bhaya*) are called "the four wrong courses" (*agati*) and cites AN 4:17–19 as a specific Pali canon reference.

243. Unlike today, during ancient times actors and entertainers did not necessarily possess a particularly high social status.

244. The almsman provides the opportunity to practice giving and by his presence influences one to engage in giving, a necessary practice for advancement on the path because it generates merit while also diminishing miserliness.

245. Giving to an almsman generates karmic merit which in turn brings about material abundance in the future lives of the benefactor.

246. This act of giving assists realization of bodhi for both the benefactor and the recipient. For the former, it contributes to an essential stock of merit without which one cannot make meaningful progress on the path. For the latter, it provides the physical sustenance without which the almsman could not continue cultivating the path.

247. All-knowledge is a quality exclusive to the Buddhas. When giving to an almsman cultivating the path that culminates in attaining this utmost, right, and perfect enlightenment, one's contemplation of this goal could then serve as an inspiration to one's own pursuit of this very same state of ultimately supreme liberation.

248. Although giving to an almsman is certainly productive of a rewarding karmic result, to give for the sake of a rewarding karmic result is just another form of covetousness. It does not accord with the path and it also massively diminishes the quality of the positive karmic result that this act of giving might otherwise bring about.

249. Māra, the Sixth Desire Heaven *devaputras*, demonic ghosts, and, figuratively speaking, the demon of one's own miserliness—all of these

types of "demons" may manipulate the mind state of the bodhisattva cultivator, thereby discouraging him from generating merit through the practice of giving. By resisting these, one overcomes the forces of Māra.

250. It is said to be karmically quite usual for the beneficiaries of such generosity to eventually become disciples or members of one's own familial or spiritual clan in this and/or future lives. Additionally, the almsman may indeed have been a previous-life clan member or Dharma-family relation.

251. The bodhisattva employs the four means of attraction (giving, pleasing words, beneficial actions, and joint endeavors) as essential skillful means to be used in drawing beings forth into pursuing the path to liberation.

252. "Dispassion" translates a standard Chinese rendering of *virāga* (離欲).

253. "Dispassion" (*virāga*) is most likely intended here in the sense of "indifference" or "detachment" with regard to one's own possessions.

254. Dedicating the merit arising from giving to the eventual attainment *anuttarasamyaksaṃbodhi* greatly elevates one's dedication to moral purity because focusing one's resolve exclusively on attaining buddhahood necessarily entails strict adherence ever-after to the highest level of moral virtue. If one fails to dedicate one's merit to the attainment of buddhahood, that merit will otherwise naturally just go merely to greater personal abundance in subsequent rebirths.

255. This manner of giving is consistent with the perfection of vigor because the benefactor has moved right along with the act, maintaining zeal, resolve, and a degree of determination that remains invulnerable to any tendency to retreat from this virtuous act.

256. "Worthy" (*bhadra*) and *ārya* are technical terms with specific meanings in Mahāyāna doctrine. Basically, a "worthy" has advanced well beyond the spiritually untutored mind of the foolish common person, but he is still vulnerable to being impeded in his progress to spiritual liberation. An *ārya*, on the other hand, has already reached one of the stages of realization through which progression to spiritual liberation is guaranteed.

257. "It endures" reflects the realization that the gift, once given, will continue to generate merit for the benefactor even after it is no longer in his possession.

258. "It will not endure" reflects the realization that this possession, like all other phenomena, is impermanent.

259. The text actually specifies "wife" here, but I deliberately instead translate with the rather more neutral term, "spouse." Nāgārjuna certainly would have used such a word if he had thought a woman might ever read this text which was, after all, written for a readership consisting entirely of men. This work was written at a time when only men were able to read. Thus it was never envisioned that women or prospective nuns might actually read the text (as opposed to having it orally taught in a lecture format more precisely tailored to the contemplations best suited to a woman reflecting on the suboptimal aspects and potential spiritual liabilities inherent in marriage). Obviously, in order to derive the intended salutary effect of reading this (and other similar) commentaries, a woman reading this text should simply "flip" any references specifying "women" or "wives" as objects of critical contemplation to "men" or "husbands."

260. There is a total of ninety-nine negative spousal contemplations here consisting of thirty-three sets of three, all of them intended to provoke the lay practitioner already weary of the tedium of married life to consider abandoning the householder's life in favor of monastic life, a path that is described step-by-step in the ensuing chapters of this treatise.

261. VB points out that the triple contemplations that follow are taken from the *Ugraparipṛcchā Sūtra*. See Jan Nattier's translation of this scripture, *A Few Good Men*, pp. 247–55.

262. "Contemplation of the body as unlovely" generally translates the Sanskrit *aśubha-bhāvanā* or *aśubhā-saṃjñā*.

263. Starting here and continuing for the rest of these spousal contemplations, the *Taisho* text has *xiang* (相) as a more-or-less standard short-form abbreviation for *xiang* (想) whilst the other four editions (SYMG) all have *xiang* (想) throughout.

264. The black-eared kite (*Milvus lineatus*) is a medium sized Asian raptor.

265. *Acipenser mikadoi*.

266. Responsible spiritual teachers will generally forbid married disciples from precipitously abandoning a marriage when the family is financially dependent on one's ongoing presence. They will usually instead counsel joint lay bodhisattva practice that includes the cultivation of patience, the planting of merit, the development of wisdom, and continued kindness and compassion in the context of the ongoing marriage until, by mutual agreement, the husband and wife together decide that more efficient progression along the bodhisattva path is best pursued in a monastic context.

Serious married lay practitioners may explore the option of celibacy by mutual agreement, beginning by formally taking on the eight precepts that include celibacy, observing those precepts for a day and a night on six days of each lunar month, usually, the eighth, fourteenth, fifteenth, twenty-third, twenty-ninth, and thirtieth of the lunar month.

267. Again, as in many other places in this text, rather than retain the Sanskrit term, I go ahead and translate KJ's *"sarvajña"* as "all-knowledge."

268. VB notes the parallels from *Āgama* and *Nikāya* sources: SA 861–863, EA 24.6, T 88, T 89, T 87, MA 202, AN 3.37–38, AN 3:70, AN 8.43 and points out that the full text of the eight precepts is found in AN 3:70 and 8:43.

269. "Consumption of intoxicants" here is literally "alcoholic beverages," but it also refers to any substance that, once consumed, skews normal clear consciousness. Hence the various forms and methods of ingesting mind-altering *cannabis* products (marijuana, hashish, etc.), opiates, amphetamines, psychedelics, and other such mind-altering substances would be included as well. Coffee and tea, although they can interfere with meditation, are not proscribed.

270. This scripture has apparently been lost as a search of the canon does not turn up any remotely similar texts with such a name.

271. Krakucchanda Buddha was the fourth of the seven buddhas of antiquity mentioned in the Nikāyas and Āgamas.

272. VB notes that this statement's corresponding Pali canon passage is found at AN 6:44. Hence, on page 913 of NDB, we find: "Therefore, Ānanda, do not be judgmental regarding people. Do not pass judgment on people. Those who pass judgment on people harm themselves. I alone, or one like me, may pass judgment on people."

273. VB notes that the following passage's corresponding Pali canon passage is found at AN 4:103 and NDB pp. 484–5.

274. 諸法無行經 / *Sarva-dharma-apravṛtti-nirdeśa-sūtra* (T15; no. 650; 750–761). See also other translations (T15; nos. 651, 652).

275. Perhaps *The Inquiry of Ugra*, (*Ugraparipṛcchā*).

276. To correct an obvious graphic-similarity scribal error, I emend the reading of the *Taisho* text here by preferring the SYMG editions' *xiang* (相), "sign," to the *Taisho* edition's *xiang* (想), "thought." These three successive phrases are clearly intended to refer specifically to practitioners of the three gates to liberation (emptiness, signlessness, and wishlessness) of which this phrase refers to the second of those three gates.

277. "Kindness, compassion, sympathetic joy, and equanimity" is a direct reference to the four immeasurable minds (*apramāṇa-citta*).

278. VB notes corresponding Pali text passages: SN 15:3, 4, and 13.
279. This statement is slightly ambiguous, but most likely refers to the Indian layperson's caste origins and associated social stature which are entirely transcended and dispensed with once one becomes a monastic in the Buddha's Sangha.
280. "Elixir of immortality," lit. "sweet dew" (*ganlu* [甘露]) corresponds to the Sanskrit "*amṛta*," which, as with the western analogue term, "ambrosia," means "the undying" and refers to the nectar or food of the gods which confers immortality. "Poisons" likely refers to the three poisons: greed, hatred, and delusion along with their numerous subsidiary afflictions.
281. Although this statement is somewhat ambiguous, it likely refers to the layperson's relatively greater vulnerability to having his interests encroached upon and harmed by the power of the king, the power of thieves, the power of *māras*, or the power of the afflictions.
282. This is probably intended to refer to the "heat" of anger and lust.
283. VB notes the corresponding Pali text passage: SN 35:247; CDB pp. 1255–57.
284. The "three-part robe" consists of a sarong, an upper robe, and a *sanghāti* robe.
285. "*Avadāna* stories" are stories of the previous lives of a buddha.
286. The Chinese text preserves a transliteration of the Sanskrit word for "sitting cloth" (*niṣīdana*). I have preferred to go ahead and translate it.
287. To correct an apparent graphic-similarity scribal error, I emend the reading of the *Taisho* text here by preferring the SYMG editions' *yi* (遺), "omitted, left out, held back, or neglected," to the *Taisho* edition's *gui* (匱).
288. "The station of the *avaivartika*" corresponds to irreversibility on the bodhisattva path to buddhahood.
289. "Patience" here is to be construed in the sense of "acquiescence."
290. The Chinese term that I translate here as "resolute faith" (信解) is perhaps the most standard Sino-Buddhist translation of the Sanskrit *adhimukti*.
291. I insert the Sanskrit term "*dhāraṇī*" here in place of its sometimes slightly opaque Chinese translation as "comprehensive retention [formulae]." This Chinese translation (總持) as well as the Sanskrit term itself both refer to one of the most important types of *dhāraṇīs*, those which aid the remembrance of particular Dharma teachings even for many lifetimes. There are other types of *dhāraṇīs* such as those that consist of untranslated Sanskrit syllables which serve as

powerful mantra-like "mystic formulae." N discusses this topic at length in his Mppu.

292. These "universal bases" (*kṛtsnāyatana*) are ten visualization devices traditionally used as one of a number of basic techniques in early Buddhist meditation practice that were aimed at developing and strengthening deep meditative concentration. These are synonymous with the ten types of *kasiṇa* familiar to students of Southern Tradition Buddhism's meditation practice aimed at acquisition of the four *dhyāna* (*jhāna*) concentration states associated with the form realm.

These *kasiṇas* may be discs representing earth, water, fire, air, blue, yellow, red, white, space, consciousness (or as an alternative to "consciousness": "bright light"), or empty space. Through correctly developed meditation on any one of these discs, one is able to produce a precise image of the given *kasiṇa* that then abides in the mind's eye or may be called forth to the mind's eye at will and independently of the original meditation object. Then one becomes able in response to one's own volition to freely develop any representational image that one wishes that incorporates the original elements, colors, etc. upon which the meditation was originally focused.

These representational images are then no longer limited to an exact replica of that original meditation object. For example, one is then able to transform one element into another and produce certain supernormal effects as a result. Hence the analogy here to developing the practice through "resolve" "in accordance with one's wishes."

293. "Karmic propensities" (here: *qi* [氣] and *qixing* [氣性], more usually *xiqi* [習氣], lit. "habit energies") would usually correspond to the Sanskrit "*vāsanā*" which refers to the habitual tendencies created in the mind through repetition of similar volitions and actions that produce the likelihood one will quite readily stumble into repeating the same affliction-associated karmic errors.

294. Emendation: To correct an apparent scribal error, I'm reversing the order of the second and third lines of this four-line *śloka* to accord with the obviously correct order revealed in N's subsequent discussion and in the Ming edition of the text.

295. I emend the reading of the *Taisho* text here by preferring on sensibility grounds the SYMG editions' *dafahui* (大法會), "great Dharma assemblies," to the *Taisho* edition's *dahui* (大會), "great assemblies."

296. It is not clear to which *abhidharma* text Nāgārjuna is referring here.

297. The "tala palm" (*Borassus flabellifer*) is native to the Indian subcontinent and Southeast Asia.

298. "White hair tuft" = *ūrṇākeśa*.

299. "The *nyagrodha* tree" (*Ficus benghalensis*) is the Indian banyan tree.
300. According to MW, "*aiṇeya*" refers to the Indian black antelope. I suspect the intended species may be the Indian blackbuck (*Antilope cervicapra*).
301. I translate here as "monastic preceptor" and "monastic Dharma teacher" what the KJ text retains in transliteration as "*upādhyāya*" and "*ācārya*" respectively.
302. Although in later period literature *xiongdi* (兄弟) refers exclusively to elder and younger brothers, ancient texts used it to refer to elder and younger sisters as well.
303. In India, "merit halls" (*puṇya-śālā*) were a type of "hostel" for the lodging, sustenance, and medical care of travelers and the poor. These were usually donated by the kings and the wealthy.
304. The four lineage bases of the Āryas (*catur-āryavaṃśa*) are: delighting in mere sufficiency in clothing, delighting in mere sufficiency of food and drink, delighting in mere sufficiency of bedding, and delighting in the severance [of evil] and the cultivation [of goodness].
305. I translate here as "monastic preceptor" and "monastic Dharma teacher" what the KJ text retains in transliteration as "*upādhyāya*" and "*ācārya*" respectively.
306. In this translation, "good spiritual friend" and "good spiritual guide" are alternative renderings for the same Chinese terms (善知識) and Sanskrit (*kalyāṇa-mitra*). "Good spiritual friend" is used to refer to those who are companions on the spiritual path who support one's adherence to the teachings. "Good spiritual guide" is used to refer to spiritual friends who also serve as mentors upon whom one relies for spiritual guidance as one cultivates the path.
307. The Lokāyata school of ancient Indian philosophy is a materialist doctrine the founding of which is often attributed to Bṛhaspati who is thought to have lived around 1000 BCE.
308. Given the readings in the immediately preceding passage and in the verse which follows below, for consistency's sake, I emend the *Taisho* reading of *da zang* (大藏), "great treasuries," here in favor of the SYMG reading of *guangda zang* (廣大藏), "vast treasuries."
309. I emend the reading of the *Taisho* text here by preferring on sensibility grounds the SYM editions' *guang shuo* (廣說), "extensive explanation," to the *Taisho* edition's *guang* (廣), "extensive."
310. I translate here as "benefactors" what the KJ text retains in transliteration as "*dānapati*."

311. To correct an apparent graphic-similarity scribal error, I emend the reading of the *Taisho* text here by preferring the SYMG editions' *zengshang man* (增上慢), "overweening pride," to the *Taisho* edition's untranslatable *zengshang man* (憎上慢).
312. Although the arrangement of the *Taisho* text does not make this clear, it is obvious that these first four five-character phrases form a quatrain upon which the following paragraph comments. Hence I have formatted the text accordingly.
313. This most likely refers to "The Pratyutpanna Samādhi Sūtra" preserved in the *Taisho* Canon as the *Banzhou Sanmei Jing* (般舟三昧經 / T13.no. 0418.902c23–919c05). Paul Harrison has produced a translation of this text for the BDK English Tripitaka.
314. I emend the reading of the text here (but still keep the emendation in brackets since there are no supporting variants in any of the other editions), this to correct an obvious scribal error wherein the name of the third of these "four bases of meritorious qualities" is missing from this sentence. The missing "basis" here is *mie* (滅), "quiescence" (*upaśamādhiṣṭhāna*).
315. These four bases of meritorious qualities (四功德處: 諦, 捨, 滅, 慧; *satyādhiṣṭhāna, tyāgādhiṣṭhāna, upaśamādhiṣṭhāna, prajñādhiṣṭhāna*; truth, relinquishment [generosity], quiescence, and wisdom) are brought up repeatedly in this and other Nāgārjunian treatises, sometimes in slightly varying order and sometimes, as in the present case, with the Chinese translation using slightly variant terminological choices for one of the four list components.
316. "Arms appearing like golden gate bars" is a rather obscure simile that I have never encountered. The SYMG editions have *chan* (鋋) which would be the equally obscure "like golden spears."
317. To correct an apparent graphic-similarity scribal error, I emend the reading of the *Taisho* text here by preferring the SYMG editions' *sheng* (生), "growth," to the *Taisho* edition's *zhu* (主), "ruler."
318. The "reply that sets aside the question" is one of polite refusal to provide an answer, not because the answer is not known, but because the question involves a false premise making the query absurd on the face of it, because providing the answer would only promote endless frivolous and fruitless speculation on the part of the questioner (as with the fourteen imponderables), or because providing an answer would in no way serve the goal of spiritual liberation.
319. More specifically, the component lists comprising the thirty-seven wings of enlightenment are: the five faculties, the five powers, the seven limbs of bodhi, the eightfold path, the four stations of

Endnotes 689

mindfulness, the four right efforts, and the four foundations of psychic power.

320. "Foes" refers here to the three poisons, i.e., the afflictions. An arhat has completely destroyed them. VB points out that this pronouncement references the word play in the word *"arahant"* where it is explained that they are those who are enemy (*ari*) destroyers (*hanta*).

321. Perhaps due to corruption of the manuscript at some point in its long history, the following list contains only 74 of the 80 secondary characteristics.

322. The *saṃkakṣikā* is the monastic's robe that is worn over the left shoulder and under the right arm.

323. The *nivāsana* is the monastic's skirt-like inner robe.

324. The *saṃghāṭī* is the monastic's outer robe.

325. "Eight kinds of *āryas*" usually refers to those eminences who reside at the four candidate stages and the four realization stages on the Śrāvaka Vehicle path. The first is candidate for stream entry and the eighth is the fully realized arhat.

326. *Garuḍa* birds prey on young dragons, hence the mention that, at least when attending Dharma teachings by buddhas, they manage to remain uncharacteristically free of any mutual hostility.

327. Although the *Taisho* text has *xiang* (相), "appearance," here it is as an often-encountered and more-or-less standard short-form abbreviation for *xiang* (想), "thought."

328. VB notes that this is a stock description of the Buddha's teaching of the Dharma as found in the *suttas* of the Nikāyas, as for example: "*ādikalyāṇaṃ majjhe kalyāṇaṃ pariyosāne kalyāṇaṃ sātthaṃ sabyañjanaṃ*, etc.," and "*sandiṭṭhiko akālika ehipassiko opanayako paccattaṃ veditabbo viññūhi*."

329. KJ transliterated rather than translated these fruits of the path (*srotaāpanna, sakṛdāgāmin, anāgamin*) that, with the exception of "arhat," I have elected to translate.

330. The emendation proposed by the 2009 edition of CBETA ([和>知]) involving a supposed graphic-similarity scribal error is itself erroneous and irrelevant. This verse simply restates an idea clearly articulated late in Chapter 18: "Through not allowing estrangement to occur among other beings or among one's relatives, and through being able to cause those who have become estranged to be reunited, one acquires the mark of male genital ensheathment. Due to having [planted the karmic causes that result in] this mark, one acquires many disciples." See 65b18-20: 能善調人不令眾生親里遠離。若有乖離還令和合故得陰藏相。有是相故多得弟子。

331. "Genital ensheathment" of course also associates with transcendence of sensual desire and, as an incidental implication, that there may therefore be no biological sons via which the patrilineal lineage might continue on.

Here, the metaphoric interpretation points out that it is the pure wisdom eye (pure by virtue of an absence of attachments) that leads to the continuance of the lineage of the Buddhas, this because it is a buddha's wise teachings flowing from his possession of the wisdom eye that beget "the sons of the Buddha," i.e., the bodhisattvas who will themselves become the buddhas of the future who carry on his Dharma lineage.

332. These are eight voice qualities possessed only by the Buddhas: 1) Extremely fine; 2) Gentle; 3) Appropriate; 4) Possessed of venerable wisdom; 5) Non-feminine; 6) Unmistaken; 7) Deep and far-reaching; and 8) Inexhaustible. These are discussed at length in Section 59 of "A Sequential Explanation of the Initial Gateway into the Dharma Realm" (法界次第初門 / T46n1925_p0697a15–b20) composed by the famous meditation master and immensely prolific Tiantai hermeneutic school exegete Zhiyi (沙門釋智顗, a.k.a. 陳隋國師智者大師).

www.ingramcontent.com/pod-product-compliance
Lightning Source LLC
Chambersburg PA
CBHW031609160426
43196CB00006B/70